MW01274147

THE ENCYCLOPEDIC DICTIONARY OF

AMERICAN GOVERNMENT

FOURTH EDITION

THE
ENCYCLOPEDIC
DICTIONARY
OF

AMERICAN
GOVERNMENT
FOURTH EDITION

Alex Wellek, *Quinnipiac College,* served as Editorial Adviser for *The Encyclopedic Dictionary of American Government, Fourth Edition*. He reviewed entries for currentness and accuracy, provided updated information where it was necessary, and wrote new or revised entries for this edition.

The Dushkin Publishing Group, Inc.

Credits and Acknowledgments

Cover: created by Meredith Scheld—DPG; p. 2 Peace Corps; p. 13 Library of Congress; p. 27 Library of Congress; p. 30 The White House; p. 37 Architect of the Capitol; p. 38 The White House; p. 42 Library of Congress; p. 50 Library of Congress; p. 66 National Archives; p. 81 John F. Kennedy Library; p. 82 Library of Congress; United Nations; p. 83 National Archives; p. 85 Department of Defense; p. 87 Library of Congress; p. 92 U.S. Senate; p. 94 Drug Enforcement Agency; p. 98 The White House; p. 118 House of Representatives; p. 119 The White House; p. 131 Federal Reserve Board; p. 139 Federal Bureau of Investigation, United States Department of Justice; p. 140 U.S. Capitol Historical Society; p. 142 Library of Congress; p. 144 Library of Congress; p. 150 Museum of New Mexico; p. 152 National Archives; p. 155 Department of the Interior; Internal Revenue Service; p. 159 Library of Congress; p. 161 The White House; p. 165 Pamela Carley Petersen; p. 169 The White House; p. 173 Department of Labor; p. 177 Library of Congress; p. 184 National Archives; p. 186 Library of Congress; p. 187 Library of Congress; p. 194 Library of Congress; p. 197 Library of Congress; p. 203 Library of Congress; p. 207 NASA; p. 208 National Bureau of Standards; p. 210 National Gallery of Art; p. 213 National Portrait Gallery; p. 219 United Nations; p. 229 Department of Defense; p. 243 Library of Congress; p. 245 Library of Congress; p. 246 Library of Congress; p. 247 Library of Congress; p. 248 Library of Congress; p. 263 The White House; p. 265 The White House; p. 271 United Nations; p. 272 Library of Congress; p. 273 Library of Congress; p. 306 Harry S. Truman Library; p. 309 AFL-CIO; p. 310 United Nations; p. 313 U.S. Army; p. 325 National Gallery; p. 326 National Gallery; p. 334 Library of Congress.

Library of Congress Catalog Card Number: 90-81964

Manufactured in the United States of America

Fourth Edition, First Printing

ISBN: 0-87967-883-6

Preface

In order to understand a discipline—its development, accomplishments, contributions, and problems, one must have an understanding of the language of that discipline. The social sciences in general, and political science in particular, use language with specific meaning to the practitioners of that discipline. The publication of this revised and updated edition of the *Encyclopedic Dictionary of American Government* is an undertaking designed to provide easy access to a substantial representation of the language, institutions, and practices unique to the study of American government.

AUTHORITY

Each of the more than 1500 entries and articles in the *Encyclopedic Dictionary of American Government* was prepared by an authority working in his or her area of specialization. The longer articles bear the signature of the author. The shorter, unsigned entries were prepared by the same authorities who authored the longer articles.

This revised edition is the result of the efforts of a large number of experts over a long period of time. In some instances we have retained articles that were prepared by contributors to previous editions. These entries have been reviewed for accuracy and currentness by the Editorial Adviser for this volume, and revision or updating has been done as required. Within each area of specialization, our advisers had responsibility for additions, deletions, or revisions of material from previous editions. The Editorial Adviser had the role of coordinator and reviewer. These advisers and contributors were: Charles R. Adrian, William G. Andrews, Ellis L. Armstrong, Earl M. Baker, Sergio Barzanti, Lewis M. Branscomb, Adam C. Breckenridge, Michael Burlingame, Mark W. Clark, Ronald Fiscus, Theodore B. Fleming, Jr., David F. Forte, Martin Gruberg, Walter W. Haines, Philip J. Hannon, H.J. Humphrey, Donald E. Johnson, Jan Karski, Allen F. Kifer, Algin B. King, E.T. Klassen, Marvin Koenigsberg, Rod Kreger, Erwin L. Levine, Allan B. Mandelstamm, David R. Mosena, John R. Matthews, Jr., William D. Nordhaus, James Officer, C. Herman Pritchett, Samuel Raphalides, Leonard G. Schifrin, Paul B. Sheatsley, Frank E. Smith, Robert F. Smith, Eli M. Spark, Murray S. Stedman, Jr., Paul P. Van Riper, Dale Vinyard, William Walton, and George M. White.

Preparing an encyclopedic dictionary of this nature presents a problem of what to leave out as much as what to include. Difficult decisions had to be made, especially in the areas of biographies, acts of Congress, and Supreme Court decisions. The advisers were involved in a process of assembling an enormous body of information, while at the same time, paring it down to the essentials. We have sought to create a reference tool of greatest use to the nonprofessional reader, and this goal guided our decisions concerning presentation of the information. Readers who find that there is no entry for their favorite Civil War hero, for example, can be sure that the omission was the result of careful consideration of the available space. Many of our contributors and advisers have made important contributions to the professional literature, but for this volume, they were asked to approach the material from the viewpoint of the needs of the nonprofessional.

It is not within the scope of a reference tool such as this to provide exhaustive information on particular subject matter. Rather, the goal of the *Encyclopedic Dictionary of American Government* is to answer specific questions quickly and easily and to demonstrate the nature of the interrelationships among the elements of American government.

For maximum utility, the short-entry, alphabetical form was adopted. Where it is appropriate, simple definitions have been provided for specific terms, with cross-references for background information and further in-depth discussion. The major products and processes of American government, including political parties, presidential elections, Supreme Court decisions, and other areas, are given comprehensive treatment in lengthier articles. Several unique features have been provided to make these major subject areas easily accessible.

ORGANIZATION

This encyclopedic dictionary was constructed topically to ensure complete coverage and then arranged alphabetically for ease of access. This organization has allowed us to include a number of guidance features as an integral part of the volume.

Cross-References are of three kinds. *See* references, which appear as individual entries in the alphabetical sequence, take the place of an additional index and send you directly to the location of the information you want. *See also* references at the end of an article direct you to supplementary information. Some entries contain a "defining cross-reference" which gives a simple definition and refers the reader to another article for more complete information.

Illustrations are used functionally in the encyclopedic dictionary. Maps, diagrams, organization charts, tables, cartoons, and photographs are included as integral parts of the articles in which they appear.

Topic Guides point out specific relationships between individual articles in the book and lead in a meaningful sequence from one article to another. These topic guides appear on the following pages:

Subject Directories follow this introduction. For selected major subject areas, we have provided an alphabetical directory of the articles pertaining to that subject. These areas are:

Biographical Entries
Supreme Court Decisions
Presidents
Acts of Congress

In addition to these Subject Directories, we have provided a listing of the *Acronyms for U.S. Government Agencies*. This will greatly increase the ease of understanding the entries on these government agencies.

GUIDELINES FOR USING THIS
ENCYCLOPEDIC DICTIONARY

The structure of this encyclopedic dictionary is designed to provide the information and background necessary to understand the institutions, people, decisions, trends, and movements that have defined the American system of government. With this in mind, many narrow or specific entries have been treated under the broader headings of which they are a part. If an individual or event does not have an entry, that subject may be discussed in one of the many major articles contained in this encyclopedic dictionary. If, for example, a reader were to look for the details of the sit-in demonstrations that took place during the 1960s, he or she would find that that subject is discussed in the major article on Civil Rights. This would be the case as well for some specific individuals, less significant court cases, or other events that contributed to a broader aspect of American government.

Government agencies are listed by full name with common acronyms in parenthesis. A reader who knows an agency only by its acronym can find the complete name listed on page X.

We believe that this encyclopedic dictionary is a unique and indispensable resource for the study of American government. It will be updated and revised as necessary so that it will remain a source of current information. We welcome suggestions or comments that will assist us in continuing to make this encyclopedic dictionary as valuable as possible.

Biographies

Below are listed the biographical entries contained in the encyclopedic dictionary.

Acronyms

Government agencies, departments, and other groups are often better known by their acronyms than by their formal names. Articles in the encyclopedic dictionary are entered under the full name. Listed below are the acronyms used in the encyclopedic dictionary for which there are articles under the formal name.

ACLU American Civil Liberties Union, 10
ADA Americans for Democratic Action, 12
AFL-CIO American Federation of Labor and Congress of Industrial Organizations, 11
AID Agency for International Development, 5
AMTRAK National Railroad Passenger Corporation, 148
BLS Labor Statistics, Bureau of, 176
CCC Commodity Credit Corporation, 55
CEA Council of Economic Advisers, 80
CIA Central Intelligence Agency, 40
CORE Congress of Racial Equality, 60
CU Consumers Union of the United States, 76
DEA Drug Enforcement Agency, 94
DIA Defense Intelligence Agency, 86
DOD Defense, United States Department of, 85
EPA Environmental Protection Agency, 103
FAA Federal Aviation Administration, 112
FAO Food and Agriculture Organization of the United States, 118
FBI Federal Bureau of Investigation, 112
FCC Federal Communications Commission, 113
FDA Food and Drug Administration, 119
FDIC Federal Deposit Insurance Corporation, 113
FEMA Federal Emergency Management Agency, 113
FHA Federal Housing Administration, 114
FMCS Federal Mediation and Conciliation Service, 115
FNMA Federal National Mortgage Association, 115
FRA Federal Railroad Administration, 115
FTC Federal Trade Commission, 116
GAO General Accounting Office, 124
GATT General Agreement on Tariffs and Trade, 125
GNP Gross National Product, 131
GSA General Services Administration, 125
HUD Housing and Urban Development, United States Department of, 141
ICC Interstate Commerce Commission, 157
ILO International Labor Organization, 157

IMF International Monetary Fund, 157
INF Intermediate-Range Nuclear Forces, 154
IRS Internal Revenue Service, 155
JCS Joint Chiefs of Staff, 162
NAACP National Association for the Advancement of Colored People, 207
NAS National Academy of Science, 206
NASA National Aeronautics and Space Administration, 207
NATO North Atlantic Treaty Organization, 221
NBS National Bureau of Standards, 208
NLRB National Labor Relations Board, 211
NRC Nuclear Regulatory Commission, 221
NSA National Security Agency, 214
NSC National Security Council, 214
NOW National Organization for Women, 212
OAS Organization of American States, 224
OECD Organization for Economic Cooperation and Development, 224
OMB Office of Management and Budget, 195
ONDCP Office of National Drug Control Policy, 222
PAC Political Action Committee, 232
PR Proportional Representation, 261
RTC Resolution Trust Corporation, 269
REA Rural Electrification Administration, 274
SALT Strategic Arms Limitations Talks, 293
SBA Small Business Administration, 283
SCLC Southern Christian Leadership Conference, 287
SDI Strategic Defense Initiative, 293
SDS Students for a Democratic Society, 294
SEATO Southeast Asia Treaty Organization, 287
SEC Securities and Exchange Commission, 276
SNCC Student Nonviolent Coordinating Committee, 294
SSS Selective Service System, 276
TVA Tennessee Valley Authority, 302
UNRRA United Nations Relief and Rehabilitation Administration, 312
VISTA Volunteers in Service to America, 319
WHO World Health Organization, 336

Supreme Court Decisions

The decisions of the United States Supreme Court listed below have articles in the encyclopedic dictionary.

Topic Guides

The topic guides contained in the encyclopedic dictionary are as follows:

Presidents

Below are listed the entries for the presidents that are contained in the encyclopedic dictionary:

Acts of Congress

Below are listed those acts of Congress for which there are entries in the encyclopedic dictionary:

ABINGTON SCHOOL DISTRICT v. SCHEMPP, 374 U.S. 203 (1963) and its companion case *Murray v. Curlett* question the validity of laws requiring morning religious exercises in public schools. Schempp and his family, members of the Unitarian faith, sought to force the Abington School District of Pennsylvania to stop conducting readings from the Bible and recitations of the Lord's Prayer during the opening exercises of each school day, because they objected to some of the doctrines set forth by the literal reading of the Bible.

The Murrays were professed atheists who objected to a rule in the Baltimore, Maryland schools which provided for the reading, without comment, of a chapter from the Bible and/or the use of the Lord's Prayer. The Court held these practices unconstitutional and stated that in both cases the state's required religious exercises to be in direct violation of the Court's interpretation of the First and Fourteenth Amendments which require state and federal governments to maintain strict neutrality, neither aiding nor opposing religion.

ABRAMS v. UNITED STATES, 250 U.S. 626 (1919), involves the publication of two leaflets by a group of so-called Bolshevists who were urging strikes in ammunition plants to prevent American military interference with the Russian Revolution. The five defendants were convicted of conspiracy to violate the Federal Espionage Act of 1917. At issue was the meaning and scope of the First Amendment guarantees of freedom of speech and a free press. The Court sustained the conviction on the grounds that the defendants had intended to "urge, incite, and advocate" curtailment of production necessary to the war, but Mr. Justice Holmes and Mr. Justice Brandeis dissented, saying that although the United States may constitutionally seek to prevent speeches and publications that are clearly intended to produce imminent danger to the country, it cannot forbid all efforts to change the mind of the country.

See also Schenck v. United States.

ABSCAM, an expression coined from "Arab scam," which was used to refer to a 1980 FBI undercover investigation into political corruption involving several members of the U.S. Congress and a number of state and local political figures. Undercover agents posing as wealthy Arab businessmen offered bribes to several members of Congress in exchange for political favors. The resulting interchange was secretly videotaped and was used to secure the conviction of one senator and six members of the House of Representatives. Of the seven who were convicted, one was expelled from the House of Representatives, three resigned to avoid expulsion, and three were defeated in their bids for reelection prior to their convictions in court. —*Mary L. Carns*

See also Ethics in Government Act.

ABSENTEE VOTING, practice, permitted by most states, of allowing individuals who are not able to be present at the polls during an election, to vote by absentee ballot. The individual is permitted to obtain a ballot, mark it, and submit it before leaving the area. He may also mail it after he leaves. The ballot is then counted either before, during, or after the counting of regular ballots, depending on state law. In California in 1960, the presidential election was so close that the outcome had to await the counting of absentee ballots, by California law counted only after regular ballots. Because of the agonizing delay, the California law was changed, and absentee ballots are now counted earlier.

ABSOLUTISM, Can the rainforests of the earth be saved? What is the climatic impact of their wholesale destruction? The article by Ellen Hosmer deals with the potential problems in the rainforest areas of the world. One United Nations study estimates that the tropical rainforests may be gone by the first decade of the next century unless land-clearing practices are curtailed.

Can the rainforests of the earth be saved? What is the climatic impact of their wholesale destruction? The article by Ellen Hosmer deals with the potential problems in the rainforest areas of the world. One United Nations study estimates that the tropical rainforests may be gone by the first decade of the next century unless land-clearing practices are curtailed.

Can the rainforests of the earth be saved? What is the climatic impact of their wholesale destruction? The article by Ellen Hosmer deals with the potential problems in the rainforest areas of the world. One United Nations study estimates that the tropical rainforests may be gone by the first decade of the next century unless land-clearing practices are curtailed.

ACCUSATORIAL PROCEDURE, the presumption in Anglo-Saxon theories of law that a person is "innocent until proven guilty." U.S. law, operating under this principle, places the legal burden on the government to prove guilt "beyond a reasonable doubt" and not on the defendant to prove innocence. Although there have been violations of this principle, emphasis in accusatorial systems is placed on legal safeguards that protect the rights of the accused. —*Mary L. Carns*

See also Inquisitorial Procedure.

ACCUSED PERSONS, RIGHTS OF, as stated in the Sixth Amendment: the right to a speedy and public trial by impartial jury in the state where the crime was committed; the right to be informed of the nature and cause of the accusation; the right to confront witnesses in court (cross-examination); the right to subpoena witnesses in favor of the accused; and the right to counsel. Although the Sixth Amendment originally restricted only the federal courts, Supreme Court decisions have construed the due-process clause of the Fourteenth Amendment to apply most of these restrictions to the state courts also.

History. The Sixth Amendment evolved from the early American colonists' grievance against George III that the benefit of trial by jury was withheld from many of them. The Supreme Court has clarified most of the provisions of the amendment. In 1968, for instance, the Court ruled that the states must provide a jury trial in criminal cases. Although this right is provided by the Sixth Amendment, it does not include the constitutional right for trial without jury. A defendant may waive his right to jury trial in favor of being tried by a judge, but the government and the judge must consent to the waiver.

The demand for a speedy and public trial stemmed from the Old World's secret inquisitions and long questioning. Thus far, no fixed time limit has been set for a speedy trial, and some accused persons may wait more than a year before being brought to trial. The due-process clause requires public trials in the state courts and establishes the right to subpoena witnesses to appear and testify, even if they are unwilling.

The requirement that the trial should be held where the crime was committed was included because the American colonists had to be transported to England for trial. So far, the Supreme Court has not decided whether or not the Fourteenth Amendment can dictate the place of trial to the states.

The right to counsel is another requirement that stemmed from the colonists' experience under the common law of Old England, under which the accused had to rely on the judge for counsel. In 1963 this right to counsel was also applied to the states. Decisions in 1964 and 1966 stated that if a person is too poor to hire counsel, it must be provided for him and that the right to counsel extends to the time before the trial.

See also Betts vs. Brady; Due Process of Law; Escobedo v. Illinois; Gideon v. Wainwright; Mapp v. Ohio; Miranda v. Arizona.

ACTION, independent federal agency established in 1971 to coordinate various voluntary service programs within the federal government. Among these programs are Volunteers in Service to America (VISTA), working to aid impoverished communities, and the Peace Corps, whose members assist development in over 60 foreign nations.

ACTION also administers the Foster Grandparents Program, the Retired Senior Volunteers Program (RSVP), the Senior Companion Program, and the National Center for Service Learning. The central ACTION office in Washington, D.C., directs domestic and overseas operations.

ACT OF CONGRESS, a bill or resolution passed into law by both the House of Representatives and the Senate. The term can also be used to refer to a bill that has passed in only one house, but is more commonly applied to a bill that has passed both houses of Congress.

ACTION: Peace Corps volunteer in Togo.

Both houses are equal in legislative power; bills must be passed in identical form by each house before they can be submitted to the president for his signature. All public laws are published annually in the *Statutes at Large*; all statutes still in force are compiled in the *United States Code*.

See also Bill; Private Bill; Public Bill; Veto.

ADA. *See* Americans for Democratic Action.

ADAMS, JOHN (1735-1826), second President of the United States (1797-1801), early advocate of independence from Great Britain, revolutionary essayist, defender of civil liberties, diplomat, legislator, administrator during the formative years of the republic. He was born in Braintree (now Quincy), Mass., of an established colonial family. After four years at Harvard College and an unrewarding interval of teaching he decided on a career at law, gaining admission to the

John Adams, second President of the United States, who also served as the country's first vice president.

President. In the presidential election of 1796 Adams defeated Jefferson, the Republican candidate, by three electoral votes. Succeeding Washington, in 1797 Adams became the second chief executive. During his administration the capital was moved to Washington, D.C. Opposed on many issues by Vice President Jefferson and the Republicans and by Hamilton, Adams sought to stabilize the government and reconcile differences. He succeeded in preserving American neutrality in Europe and negotiated a treaty with France in 1800. When the Alien and Sedition Acts were passed in 1798 Adams supported them, a position that he later regretted taking. This unpopular legislation, providing punishment for critics of government, contributed to the decline of the Federalist party and to the election of Jefferson and the Republicans in 1800. Adams' most notable appointment was that of John Marshall as Secretary of State and later Chief Justice of the Supreme Court.

In 1801 Adams retired to Quincy, where he remained active in public affairs and continued his extensive correspondence and erudite philosophical writings. His son, John Quincy Adams, became sixth president of the United States. John Adams and Thomas Jefferson, who had renewed their friendship, died on the same day, July 4, 1826, the 50th anniversary of the Declaration of Independence.

Adams' principled aversion to partisan politics as well as the intemperance with which he often faced his critics hampered him in the practical exercise of his responsibilities. He devoted his life to building the foundations of the new state in accordance with his concepts of parliamentary democracy and balanced authority.

ADAMS, JOHN QUINCY (1767-1848), 6th President of the United States (1825-1829), born in Braintree (now Quincy), Mass. The son of President John Adams, he was minister to the Netherlands and Prussia and was elected Senator from Massachusetts in 1803. As minister to Russia, he took part in negotiations for the Treaty of Ghent ending the War of 1812, and as Secretary of State (1817-1825), he was the guiding force behind the Monroe Doctrine in 1823. Elected by the Democratic-Republican party, he accomplished little as president due to bitter opposition in Congress; he later served in the House of Representatives (1831-1848).

See also Presidential Elections.

ADAMS, SAMUEL (1722-1803), governor of Massachusetts, agitator of the colonies against British and Tory oppression. Samuel Adams, second cousin of President John Adams, was born in Boston. An able student, he graduated from Harvard in 1740 and obtained his master's degree in 1743. He was married twice, first to Elizabeth Checkley, who died leaving two children, and later to Elizabeth Wells. Although he had studied law and was persuaded for a time to enter business, he realized that his interests lay in colonial politics.

bar in 1758. In 1764 he married Abigail Smith, one of the first supporters of women's suffrage. A principled advocate of justice and human rights, he defended in court the British soldiers responsible for the Boston Massacre, yet he was so incensed by the inequities of the Stamp Act that he supported the Boston Tea Party and soon became actively involved in the patriotic movement. The Massachusetts radicals sent him as a delegate to the First Continental Congress, where he was instrumental in obtaining Washington's appointment as colonial military commander and in activating the American navy. Although Jefferson is rightly credited with the language of the Declaration of Independence, many of its revolutionary principles were formulated by Adams, who led the struggle for adoption of the document by Congress. For nine years Adams served as diplomatic representative in Europe, in 1785 becoming the first American ambassador to Great Britain.

In 1789 he was elected the first vice president of the United States and was re-elected in 1792. Although he regarded this position as a "most insignificant office," he served energetically, shaping Senate policy and procedure and casting deciding votes to strengthen the authority of the federal government and the executive branch.

Influenced by John Locke's *On Civil Government,* with its espousal of the "natural right" of man to be self-governing and free of taxation without representation, Adams attacked the hated Stamp Act of 1765. When the citizens of Boston rioted against this tyrannical measure, Adams, elected by them to the Massachusetts House of Representatives, advocated open defiance of the act and helped to force its repeal. When Parliament passed the Townshend Acts of 1767, imposing import duties on tea and other commodities, Adams organized the Circular Letter, urging other colonial assemblies to join in resistance. When British troops occupied the port, leading up to the Boston Massacre of 1770, Adams demanded that Governor Hutchinson evacuate the soldiers. Through agitational articles in the press Adams moved the population toward further confrontation with British authority, preparing the way for the armed struggles to come. In 1772 he initiated the Committees of Correspondence to move the colonies to unite against the threat to their liberties. It was Adams, presiding over a militant town meeting, who gave the signal for the Boston Tea Party. When the British retaliated with the Intolerable Acts of 1774, closing the port of Boston and again occupying the city, Adams physically barred the Tory governor from dissolving the Assembly until it had elected representatives to the Continental Congress. Adams, one of the delegates, served as a member from 1774 to 1781.

He was a signer of the Declaration of Independence, a member of the Massachusetts Constitutional Convention and of the convention that ratified the federal Constitution. In 1789 Adams was elected lieutenant governor of Massachusetts. When Governor John Hancock died Adams succeeded him, serving from 1793 to 1797. Samuel Adams died in Boston in 1803.

Although he performed solid legislative chores in the framing of the constitutions of both his state and his nation, he is primarily remembered for his prerevolutionary role as publicist and political activist. He personified the radical spirit of his times.

ADAMSON ACT (1916), the first federal legislation to set an eight-hour working day. The act covers most employees of carriers involved in foreign and interstate commerce. Whereas earlier federal legislation regulating railroad workers had repeatedly been overturned, the Supreme Court reluctantly approved the act to avoid a strike of the four major railroad unions.

ADDERLY v. FLORIDA, 385 U.S. 39 (1966), concerns a public protest against state and local policies of segregation, including segregation in the local jail. In this first sit-in case, the Court upheld the conviction of demonstrators who had marched onto jail grounds to protest the arrest of protestors the previous day. The defendants maintained that they had a constitutional right to stay on the property, because the area chosen for the peaceful demonstration was reasonable and appropriate. The state contended that, like a private property owner, it had the power to preserve the property under its control for the use to which it is lawfully dedicated. The Court, in upholding the conviction, held that the defendants were not constitutionally free to ignore Florida's trespass law and to carry their battle into the streets, and that the Constitution does not forbid a state to control the use of its own property for its own lawful, nondiscriminatory purposes.

See also Edwards v. South Carolina.

ADJOURNMENT terminates proceedings; applied to the end of a legislative day, a break of one or more days or the end of a session. Since the rules of each chamber provide that certain matters must be taken up at the beginning of a day, the Senate may ocasionally recess, rather than adjourn, in order to resume proceedings without undue delay. The House generally adjourns. Neither chamber may adjourn for more than three days without the other chamber's consent. In such cases the chambers adjourn to a specific date. At the end of a session they adjourn *sine die* (without setting a new date), thus ending the session.

ADKINS v. CHILDREN'S HOSPITAL, 261 U.S. 525 (1923), concerns the constitutionality of a congressional statute which established a minimum wage for women employed in the District of Columbia. The Children's Hospital employed a large number of women with whom it had agreed on rates of wages. In some cases the wages were less than the minimum wage ordered by the Wage Board of the District. A suit was filed to restrain the board from enforcing its order on the ground that it violated the due process clause of the Fifth Amendment. The court, in a five to three decision which was overruled in 1936, held that there is no connection between the wages women receive and their health, and that the exercise of police power to destroy the freedom of contract of employers and their women employees violates one of the individual liberties protected by the Fifth Amendment.

ADMINISTRATIVE COURT, one of a system of courts in civil-law countries with jurisdictions over disputes to which the government or an official is a party. Ordinary courts in those countries have no jurisdiction over such disputes.

ADMINISTRATIVE LAW, that part of law that concerns the establishment and practices of administrative agencies—including government boards and commissions—and that governs rules, regulations, and orders of administrative agencies. Administrative law also deals with the rights of individuals in their relationships with public officials.   —*Mary L. Carns*

ADMIRALTY LAW, or maritime law, deals with ships and the sea, including events and transactions, both civil and criminal, occurring at sea or involving the sea. Although now administered by national courts and affected by municipal law, the legal principles of admiralty law, being a composite of customs of the sea and maritime nations, antedate even Roman law and transcend national borders.

ADVERSARY SYSTEM, the assumption that justice is best served when the two parties in a legal dispute are seen as adversaries, on opposite sides of the law. In adversarial proceedings, the judge functions as an independent and neutral arbiter, while each "side" attempts to present the best case. The adversarial system is closely related to the accusatory procedure in criminal law, in which the defendant is presumed to be "innocent until proven guilty."   —*Mary L. Carns*

ADVICE AND CONSENT, legislative check on the treaty-making and appointment powers of the President of the United States, provided for by Section II of the Constitution. The provision is part of the system of checks and balances. Although the Senate deliberates on presidential appointments and treaties with foreign governments, these debates are usually a mere formality. A notable exception was the refusal of the Senate to ratify membership in Woodrow Wilson's League of Nations in 1919.

See also Confirmation.

ADVISORY OPINION, a legal opinion given before legal proceedings have been instituted. It is often an official legal opinion given in response to a request for information and may involve interpretation of a statute or advice concerning the constitutionality of a proposed action.

Federal judges will not render advisory opinions because the jurisdiction established in the U.S. Constitution is limited to "cases and controversies." Judges of some state courts give advisory opinions, and it is a frequent function of certain legal officers such as state attorneys-general. Advisory opinions usually are not legally binding, but do carry legal weight.   —*Mary L. Carns*

See also Cases and Controversies.

AFFIRMATIVE ACTION, a term used to describe programs that combat discrimination. It calls for measures to counter attitudes and processes that tend to subordinate, exclude, or segregate by race and sex. Affirmative action programs are mandated by both state and federal laws and apply both to government and the private sector. Recipients of government funds and those with a history of discriminatory practices are expected to make positive efforts to recruit, employ, train, and promote qualified minority members. Where minority members have not been employed in proportion to their presence in the available work force, there is an obligation to undertake measures to secure a better balance.

Critics claim that affirmative action can degenerate into reverse discrimination, denying equal protection of the law to all citizens and creating a new class of victims. Proponents feel that affirmative action rectifies previous discrimination.

A new Supreme Court majority, appointed during the Reagan years, began to modify the range of permissible affirmative action programs.

See also City of Richmond v. J.A. Croson Company; Reverse Discrimination.

AFROYIM v. RUSK, 387 U.S. 253 (1967), concerns Beys Afroyim, a naturalized American citizen living in Israel, who was denied renewal of his passport on the grounds that he had voted in Israeli elections. Afroyim brought suit in federal District Court but lost there and on appeal. The lower courts cited a 1958 Supreme Court decision upholding sections of the Nationality Act of 1940 that provided for loss of citizenship for any American who voted in a foreign political election. In finding for Afroyim the court ruled that the Fourteenth Amendment protected citizens against attempts by Congress to define the conditions of citizenship. The 5 to 4 decision was delivered by Justice Black. He concluded that citizenship was a right and retained unless voluntarily relinquished.

See also Trop v. Dulles.

AGENCY FOR INTERNATIONAL DEVELOPMENT (AID), established as an agency of the Department of State in 1961, and transferred to the International Development Corporation in 1979, carries out United States overseas programs of economic and technical assistance to less developed countries to bring them to the level of self-sufficiency. The agency provides technical advisers, particularly in agriculture, education, population control, and health. In addition to technical assistance, AID helps obtain and finance goods and services requried for specific development projects on more favorable terms than private banks would offer. Development loans, generally limited to countries that have begun their growth process, are provided by AID in cooperation with the World Bank.

See also International Bank for Reconstruction and Development.

AGING, ADMINISTRATION ON (AOA), federal agency, part of the Office of Human Development Service of the Department of Health and Human Services. It is the primary agency with responsibility for administration of the Older Americans Act of 1965. AOA advises other agencies about the needs of older people in an attempt to develop programs that meet their needs.

See also Health and Human Services, Department of.

AGNEW, SPIRO (THEODORE) (1918-   ), 39th Vice President of the United States, born in Baltimore, the son of a Greek immigrant. He attended Johns Hopkins University and received his law degree from the University of Baltimore in 1947.

Agnew became active in Republican politics in the late 1950s and in 1966 was elected governor of Maryland. He was elected vice president on the Republican ticket headed by Richard M. Nixon in 1968 and 1972. In 1973 Agnew was forced to resign after a Justice Department investigating committee uncovered evidence of corruption during Agnew's governorship. He was also charged with federal income tax evasion, for which he was fined and put on probation. He was disbarred in 1974.

AGRICULTURAL ADJUSTMENT ADMINISTRATION (AAA). *See* New Deal Legislation.

AGRICULTURAL EXTENSION SERVICE. *See* Extension Service.

AGRICULTURE, UNITED STATES DEPARTMENT OF (USDA). The history of the USDA, established in 1889, is illuminated by the fact that the farm population of America has dropped drastically since 1910. After reaching a peak of influence and progressivism in the first half of the twentieth century, USDA came under increasing attack. President Nixon proposed disbanding the department at one point, but he was soundly discouraged by the same system that has given rural states power in Congress far out of proportion to their size and economic strength. The department came under even sharper criticism for claiming to protect family farms at the same time that it administers crop surplus subsidies that strongly favor the big grower. USDA played a very positive role in bolstering farm productivity (the so-called green revolution) and helping build a very efficient and profitable agricultural industry in the United States.

The department is made up of many self-perpetuating offices: Economics, Statistics, and Cooperatives Service; World Food and Agricultural Outlook and Situation Board; Food and Nutrition Service; Food Safety and Quality Service; Agricultural Marketing Service; Animal and Plant Health Inspection Service; Federal Grain Inspection Service; Agricultural Stabilization and Conservation Service; Commodity Credit Corporation; Federal Crop Insurance Corporation; Foreign Agricultural Service; Office of International Cooperation and Development; Farmer's Home Administration; Rural Electrification Administration; Rural Telephone Bank; Forest Service; Office of Environmental Quality; Soil Conservation Service; Science and Education Administration. A number of the new agencies that have flourished in Washington since 1950 have offered serious competition to USDA and provided a new focus where it lagged behind.

AGUILAR v. TEXAS, 378 U.S. 108 (1964), concerns the use of unconstitutionally seized evidence as a basis for a conviction. Two Hudson police officers obtained a search warrant on hearsay information that heroin, marijuana, barbiturates, and other narcotics were being kept by Aguilar at his premises for the purpose of sale and for use contrary to the law. The Texas court's conviction of Aguilar for illegal possession of heroin was based on police findings during the search. The Court, in reversing the conviction, held that the mere suspicion that the petitioner possessed narcotics was not enough to obtain a search warrant by valid means, and that affiants must inform the magistrate of some underlying evidence from which to conclude that the narcotics were where the informant claimed they were.

AID TO DEPENDENT CHILDREN. *See* Social Security.

AIR FORCE, DEPARTMENT OF THE. *See* Defense, United States Department of.

AIR QUALITY ACTS. In 1967 the first (also known as the National Emissions Standards Act) of several increasingly strict pollution regulations ordered that special procedures be inaugurated by the Secretary of HEW by 1971 to govern the emission of hazardous substances into the air. Referring mainly to auto pollution, the law advised the secretary to set compliance dates according to timetables favorable to industry. The act provided for an ongoing federal advisory committee to maintain evaluation of research on air pollution.

Under the 1971 act the Environmental Protection Agency set specific air quality standards, as ordered by the Clean Air Amendments (1970). Though enforcement is spelled out under the 1970 law, resistance from industry and local government weakened the thrust of the regulations. No sooner were standards promulgated than auto makers, for example, protested they could not possibly comply within the specified period.

See also Clean Air Amendments; Council on Environmental Quality.

ALBERTSON v. SUBVERSIVE ACTIVITIES CONTROL BOARD (SACB), 382 U.S. 70 (1965), concerns an individual's right to self-protection against compulsory self-incrimination. The Communist Party of the United States of America failed to register and supply a list of party members to the SACB as required by statute. Each member of the party was also required to register and file a registration statement. The petitioners, ordered by the board to register, challenged the validity of the order as a violation of their Fifth Amendment privilege against self-incrimination. The Court, in reversing the order, held that the risks of incrimination in registering were obvious. Such an admission of membership might be used to prosecute the registrants under clauses in federal criminal statutes.

See also Communist Party v. Subversive Activities Control Board.

ALDERMAN, an elected member of a municipal legislative body. Aldermen are more commonly called councilmen. The term originated in Anglo-Saxon England, where the alderman represented the crown and was responsible for interpreting the common law. In colonial America city councils consisted of aldermen, who were generally elected by the people and common councilers. By the end of the nineteenth century this bicameral municipal legislature was being replaced by councils of councilmen.

ALEXANDER v. HOLMES COUNTY BOARD OF EDUCATION, 396 U.S. 19 (1969), concerns the length of time permitted to effect an admittedly difficult transition from a segregated school system to the integrated schools required by *Brown v. Board of Education of Topeka* (1954). *Brown*(1955), had required integration "with all the deliberate speed," but the State of Mississippi had been procrastinating for fourteen years. The United States Supreme Court by this time had lost patience and here ordered the United States Court of Appeals for the Fifth Circuit to "decree and order, effective immediately, declaring that each of the [33 Mississippi] school districts here involved may no longer operate a dual school system based on race or color, and directing that they begin immediately to operate as unitary school systems. . . ."

See also Brown v. Board of Education of Topeka.

ALIEN, noncitizen, resident or transient, who owes allegiance to a foreign government. Aliens are subject to the laws of the country of residence. In the United States, resident aliens can be drafted and own property, but they are subject to certain obligations, having for instance, to register every year. Aliens have no voting rights. The problems posed by the presence of millions of illegal aliens was addressed by the Immigration Reform and Control Act of 1986. The law provides for conditional amnesty, employer sanctions, and other terms designed to regulate the influx and residence of aliens.

See also Immigration Reform and Control Act of 1986.

ALIEN AND SEDITION ACTS, four acts, passage of which was secured in 1798 by the Federalist party. War against France being considered imminent, these measures were designed to safeguard the United States and, in fact, to hurt the pro-French Republican party.

They were: (1) the Naturalization Act, extending to fourteen years the period of residence prior to obtaining citizenship; (2) the Alien Act, giving to the President the power to deport aliens he considered dangerous; (3) the Alien Enemy Act, enabling the president to expel enemy subjects in wartime; and (4) the Sedition Act, providng for fines or imprisonment for anyone who slandered the government, the Congress or the president. The first three acts were never enforced, but they created much uneasiness among aliens and frightened many of them away from the United States. The fourth was used to indict and convict a small number of critics of the president.

The reaction caused by these acts contributed to the defeat of President John Adams and the election of the Jeffersonian Republicans in 1800.

ALIEN REGISTRATION ACT (1940) *or* **SMITH ACT.** Originally a measure to keep track of aliens during wartime, the law requires aliens above fourteen years old and parents of alien minors to register with the Justice Department, be fingerprinted, and carry a registration card at all times. The diplomatic corps and state guests are, however, exempt. More important, the statute carries the first major sedition clauses in federal law since 1798.

As consolidated in 1948 the law states: "Whoever knowingly or willfully advocates, abets, advises or teaches the duty, necessity, desirability, or propriety of overthrowing . . ." federal or state governments is ineligible for government employment and subject to a fine of up to $20,000 and/or 20 years in prison. Further, it is a crime to undermine or conspire to undermine the loyalty and morale of the United States armed forces.

The Supreme Court upheld (1951) the prosecutions of American Communist party leaders under provisions of the Smith Act. However, in subsequent rulings (1957, 1969), the court severely restricted the application of the Smith Act.

See also Dennis v. United States, Internal Security Act of 1950, Scales v. United States.

ALLIANCE FOR PROGRESS (Span., Alianza para Progreso), economic assistance program for Latin America. The program, proposed by President John Kennedy in 1961, was joined by twenty member states of the Organization of American States for a period of ten years and an investment of $100 billion. The major part of the financial burden was to be borne by the Latin American states. United States aid to the plan was to be administered by the Agency for International Development.

Delegates met in Punta del Este, Uruguay, in August 1961 and ratified the charter, agreeing that major goals were free schooling, literacy for 50 million Latin Americans, elimination of malaria, land and tax reform, public housing programs, and providing good drinking water for more than half of the Latin America population. After a promising start, the program bogged down as political differences divided the participants. The election of Richard Nixon as president brought an effective end to the alliance, as he believed the Latin American states must assume responsibility for their economic development.

AMBASSADOR. *See* Foreign Service.

AMENDMENT, CONGRESSIONAL, an action that the Senate or House may take to modify or remove language of an act or bill. In this process a bill may be subjected to such extreme revision that it becomes completely different. Instead of trying to kill bills outright, legislators often add amendments that make the bills ineffectual or entirely unacceptable to the majority. New legislation is required to amend a bill once it has passed into law.

See also Legislation and Legislative Processes.

AMENDMENT, CONSTITUTIONAL, a change in the wording of or an addition to the United States Constitution according to an explicit procedure outlined in the Constitution itself (Article V).

History. The Articles of Confederation, which governed the nation from 1781 to 1789, required the assent of all thirteen states to pass amendments. The framers of the 1787 Constitution realized it would be impossible to obtain unanimous approval. Thus they decided that the new Constitution would only need the ratification of three-quarters of the states. They also included a complicated procedure in the Constitution that would make future amendment difficult.

Procedure. To amend the Constitution, two-thirds of both houses of Congress must recommend to the states the exact wording of the proposed amendment. The amendment must then be approved by three-fourths of the states. Article V gives Congress the power to decide whether state legislatures must approve the amendment or whether special state conventions must do so. Congress also has the right to set a specific time period for ratification; otherwise the amendment becomes void. The president has no veto power in the amendment process. As an alternate procedure, two-thirds of the state legislatures may petition Congress to call a national convention to propose amendments, but this has never been done. However, if this procedure were followed, the rest of the ratification process would be the same as outlined above, except when Congress specifies a different process by special legislation.

Summary of Amendments. The first ten amendments (The Bill of Rights) were ratified by the states with the Constitution in 1791; Amendment XI (1795) forbade a citizen of one state to sue the government of another state; Amendment XII (1804) established separate ballots for the president and vice president in the electoral college; Amendments XIII (1865), XIV (1868), and XV (1870) were known as the Civil War amendments

---

CONSTITUTIONAL AMENDMENTS: TOPIC GUIDE

The first ten amendments (the Bill of Rights) were ratified by the states with the Constitution in 1791; **Amendment XI** (1795) forbade a citizen of one state to sue the government of another state; **Amendment XII** (1804) established separate ballots for the president and vice president in the electoral college; **Amendments XIII** (1861), **XIV** (1868), and **XV** (1870) were known as the Civil War amendments and declared people of all races constitutionally equal before national and state laws; **Amendment XVI** (1913) gave Congress the right to enact individual income tax legislation; **Amendment XVII** (1913) changed the selection process of United States senators from election by state legislatures to a direct election by the people of the states; **Amendment XVIII** (1919) enabled Congress to establish the prohibition of liquor traffic in the United States. **Amendment XIX** (1920) gave women the right to vote; **Amendment XX** (1933) changed the inauguration dates for the president and vice president and established annual congressional sessions beginning each January; **Amendment XXI** (1933) repealed Amendment XVIII (it has been the only Amendment ratified by state conventions, not state legislatures); **Amendment XXII** (1951) prohibited any person from serving as president for more than two elected terms; **Amendment XXIII** (1961) gave the people of the District of Columbia the right to vote for presidential electors; **Amendment XXIV** (1964) prohibited the use of a poll tax to prevent anyone from voting for a federal office; **Amendment XXV** (1967) established a procedure to fill the vice-presidency in the event of a vacancy and also stated that the vice president should become acting president in the event that the president could not carry out his duties; **Amendment XXVI** (1971) lowered the voting age in all the states to eighteen.

---

and declared people of all races constitutionally equal before national and state laws; Amendment XVI (1913) gave Congress the right to enact individual income tax legislation; Amendment XVII (1913) changed the selection process of United States senators from election by state legislatures to a direct election by the people of the states; Amendment XVIII (1919) enabled Congress to establish the prohibition of liquor traffic in the United States. Amendment XIX (1920) gave women the right to vote; Amendment XX (1933) changed the inauguration dates for the president and vice president and established annual congressional sessions beginning each January; Amendment XXI (1933) repealed Amendment XVIII (it has been the only amendment ratified by state conventions, not state legislatures); Amendment XXII (1951) prohibited any person from serving as president for more than two elected terms;

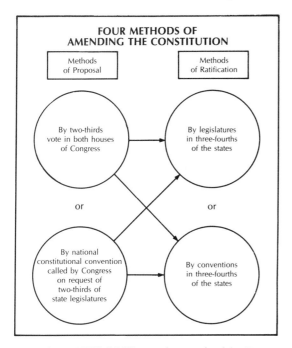

**FOUR METHODS OF
AMENDING THE CONSTITUTION**

Methods
of Proposal

Methods
of Ratification

By two-thirds
vote in both houses
of Congress

By legislatures
in three-fourths
of the states

or

or

By national
constitutional convention
called by Congress
on request of
two-thirds of
state legislatures

By conventions
in three-fourths
of the states

Amendment XXIII (1961) gave the people of the District of Columbia the right to vote for presidential electors; Amendment XXIV (1964) prohibited the use of a poll tax to prevent anyone from voting for a federal office; Amendment XXV (1967) established a procedure to fill the vice-presidency in the event of a vacancy and also stated that the vice president should become acting president in the event that the president could not carry out his duties; Amendment XXVI (1971) lowered the voting age in all the states to eighteen.

—*Erwin L. Levine*

See also Bill of Rights; Constitution of the United States; Equal Rights Amendment.

AMENDMENTS TO THE CONSTITUTION. As early as the struggle over the ratification of the Constitution (1787-1788), critics faulted it for not including protections for the individual citizens. Advocates of the document, such as James Madison and Alexander Hamilton, first argued that, inasmuch as the central government was restricted to those functions enumerated in the text, it could not trespass on individual rights, which were guaranteed in the state constitutions. When this answer did not mollify critics, they contended that the Constitution did indeed (in Article I, Sections 9 and 10; Article III; and Article IV) guarantee rights. However, those who were cautious, if not suspicious, regarding the new central government were hesitant to endorse the new arrangement until assured by proponents that the Constitution's defects would be remedied as soon as the new Congress convened.

Madison, who was beaten in Virginia for a Senate seat by objectors to the Constitution as adopted, was responsible for convincing his House colleagues to proceed with proposing a Bill of Rights. Initially, twelve amendments were forwarded to the states. The proposals for enlarging the House of Representatives and to prevent members of the House from raising their own pay were rejected; ten amendments were ratified.

A suit brought against the state of Georgia in the U.S. Supreme Court by the executors of a British creditor (*Chisholm v. Georgia;* 1793) paved the way for a flood of other such suits and violated the doctrine of "sovereign community," e.g. that a state could never be sued without its consent. It provoked an outburst of indignation and a successful effort to amend the Constitution to prevent this sort of action. The Eleventh Amendment was declared effective in January 1798.

When Republican-Democratic electors who were in the majority in 1800 cast the same number of undifferentiated votes for Thomas Jefferson and Aaron Burr, another crisis occurred. The tie threw the choice of president into the House of Representatives, which was controlled by the Federalists. Eventually, Jefferson was chosen. His supporters succeeded in getting the Twelfth Amendment, providing for separate balloting for president and vice president by the Electoral College, ratified quickly so it would be in effect in time for the election of 1804.

The next three amendments were the nation's effort to resolve the problems brought about by slavery, although their language and implications go much further. The Thirteenth (1865), which abolished slavery, was the only one to be proposed before Abraham Lincoln's death. The Fourteenth (1868) was designed to override discriminatory legislation by southern states. The Fifteenth (1870) forbade suffrage discrimination on racial grounds.

Although a Civil War income tax had been upheld by the Supreme Court, in 1895 the Court held such a levy unconstitutional *(Pollack v. Farmer's Loan and Trust Company)* because it was a direct tax and was not apportioned according to population or representation in Congress as demanded in the Constitution. The Sixteenth Amendment (1913) overturned the impact of this decision and gave Congress the right to pass such a tax.

Popular election of the senators, the Seventeenth Amendment, was universalized in 1913. (Several states had already adopted this reform.) Bribery and corruption of state legislators as well as frequent deadlocks and distractions combined with the growing strength of the democratic spirit to bring about this change over the opposition of party bosses and conservative forces.

The Eighteenth Amendment (1919), prohibiting alcohol consumption, was hurried through Congress and the states in a surge of wartime patriotism, nativism, and idealism over a poorly organized opposition. The "noble experiment" encountered problems of enforcement. These, coupled with the hope that the liquor trade could help the nation surmount the post-1929 economic

Depression, led to repeal of Prohibition in the Twenty-first Amendment (1933).

Liquor interests had opposed women's suffrage, because it was felt that the women's vote would lead to prohibition. It was, therefore, more than coincidental that woman suffrage came about shortly after the prohibition amendment. The Nineteenth Amendment, culminating a 70-year effort, was ratified in August 1920, in time for women to vote in the presidential election.

Senator George Norris of Nebraska deserves credit for his perennial and ultimately successful sponsorship of the Twentieth Amendment (1933), the so-called "Lame Duck" Amendment, which shortened the period between election and the swearing in of congressmen, the president, and the vice president. Herbert Hoover, defeated by Franklin D. Roosevelt in 1932, was the last president to serve until March 4.

The Republican Eighteenth Congress, after Franklin Roosevelt had been elected for four presidential terms, submitted the Twenty-second Amendment to limit to two terms the tenure of the president. Ratified in 1951, it exempted the incumbent President Harry S Truman. Truman's successor, Republican Dwight D. Eisenhower, was the first restricted by the amendment's provisions. Since Lyndon Johnson had served less than two years of John Kennedy's term, he could, under the amendment's provisions, have served two complete terms of his own.

Amendment Twenty-three, ratified in 1961, gave residents of the District of Columbia electoral votes in the presidential selection. Twenty years later, another amendment, proposing to give the District's citizens voting representation in both houses of Congress, was submitted to the states but was given scant chance of success.

The Twenty-fourth Amendment, ratified in 1964, ended the use of poll taxes as barriers to voting in federal elections. Once this became the law of the land states found it awkward to monitor two sets of eligible voter lists and two sets of ballots. Thus, poll taxes were dropped as prerequisites for voting for state offices.

For many years there was concern about presidential disability. The Twenty-fifth Amendment, adopted in 1967, provided a means for dealing with issues of presidential incompetence. The amendment's first implementations, however, came about through vacancies in the office of vice president, first when Spiro T. Agnew resigned that office during Richard M. Nixon's administration and, second, when Nixon himself resigned from the presidency.

The Twenty-sixth Amendment, which lowered the voting age to 18 in all elections, was submitted to the states in March 1971, three months after the Supreme Court had held unconstitutional the Voting Rights Act Amendment of 1970, which had authorized 18-year-olds to vote in state elections. Three months later, the ratification process was completed.

The proposed Twenty-seventh Amendment, the Equal Rights Amendment (ERA), prohibiting discrimination based on sex by any government, was submitted to the states in March 1972. Although about half of the necessary number of states ratified the proposal in the first three months after submission, the drive for adoption slowed. In October 1978, Congress extended the period for ratification (originally 1979) until June 30, 1982. The time lapsed with the ERA still three states short of ratification. It was resubmitted to Congress in July 1982.
    —*Martin Gruberg*

See also Bill of Rights; Constitution of the United States; Equal Rights Amendment.

AMERICAN AGRICULTURAL MOVEMENT (AAM), an organization of family farmers and ranchers that tries to influence government agricultural policy. The organization was founded in September 1977 in order to bring about legislation that would support a fair rate of return on their farm products. During the first few months, a period when the price of farm products was very low, the organization grew very rapidly. By December 1977, there were 1100 local chapters and 40 state organizations. AAM used an initially effective caravan of tractors, a tractorcade, to demonstrate their concern for farm prices.

AMERICAN ASSOCIATION OF RETIRED PERSONS (AARP), an interest group composed of retired or employed individuals over 50 years of age. The association offers various group insurance benefits, discount travel, and community services such as crime prevention, tax assistance, and retirement planning. The AARP, with a membership of more than 16 million, lobbies for programs and services for retired and about-to-retire individuals.

AMERICAN BANKERS ASSOCIATION (ABA), organization founded in 1875 to promote the welfare and development of banks and the banking system. The ABA serves the industry by providing various training and education programs, lobbying for favorable legislation, and publishing a magazine and bulletins. Its membership represents approximately 95 percent of the banking industry.

AMERICAN BAR ASSOCIATION, a professional association comprised of attorneys who have been admitted to the bar in any of the fifty states. A registered lobby, the organization's basic objectives are to advance the science of jurisprudence, ensure the fair administration of justice and uniformity of legislation throughout the country, and maintain the standards of the profession. Headquarters are in Chicago.

AMERICAN CIVIL LIBERTIES UNION (ACLU), founded in 1920 with the purpose of defending the individual's rights as guranteed by the Constitution. Toward this end, the group's primary activities are direct involvement in test cases, organized opposition to legislation considered unconstitutional, and public protests.

Among the many prominent cases in which the ACLU has participated are the Sacco-Vanzetti and the Scopes "monkey" trials. The ACLU played a vital role in decisions citing the unconstitutionality of prayer in public schools, state-administered loyalty oaths for teachers, and illegal police search and seizure. In recent years the organization has been involved in the fight for black civil rights, opening a southern regional office in Atlanta, Ga.

Privately sponsored, the ACLU has a membership of nearly 150,000, with offices in forty-five states. In addition to a regular legal staff, vital to its successful operation are 2,000 lawyers who represent ACLU without fee in over 300 cities.

AMERICAN DAIRY ASSOCIATION (ADA), business organization, established in 1940. The ADA is a federation of some 20 state and regional dairy associations. Its primary activity is the promotion and advertising of milk and milk products, as well as lobbying federal and state government.

AMERICAN ENTERPRISE INSTITUTE (AEI), a research and educational organization that is supported by grants and endowments from private donors. The institute does policy-oriented research on national and international issues. AEI, considered to be Washington's conservative think tank, disseminates to politicians, other researchers, and the public in-depth analyses on important issues.

AMERICAN FARM BUREAU FEDERATION, a registered lobby and the largest U.S. farm organization, composed of farm bureaus in the 48 contiguous states and Puerto Rico. Bureau membership is composed of farm families. After studying agricultural problems, the federation formulates courses of action, which it may then actively promote for legislative enactment. In presenting members' views to Congress, officials are guided by resolutions adopted at the annual convention. In recent years the federation has supported the reduction of government price supports and acreage controls, the expansion of overseas markets for American farm products, and the establishment of uniform policies of federal land acquisition. Headquarters are in Chicago.

AMERICAN FEDERATION OF LABOR AND CONGRESS OF INDUSTRIAL ORGANIZATIONS (AFL-CIO), an alliance of national and international labor unions representing nearly every kind of trade, industrial, and service occupation.

This enormous union, with a membership of over 13 million workers, was formed in 1955 with the merger of the American Federation of Labor and the Congress of Industrial Organizations. The AFL, founded in 1866 by Samuel Gompers, was a federation of craft unions, unions of workers skilled in a particular craft, such as plumbing, carpentry, or brick-laying. The CIO was founded by John L. Lewis, president of the United Mine Workers, in 1938 and was comprised of unskilled workers in particular industries, such as the steel business.

The AFL-CIO works to advance the cause of union members through collective bargaining, public appeals, and lobbying. The official political arm of the federation is the Committee on Political Education (COPE), which works to educate union members and their families as to the importance of political participation. COPE is active in local, state, and national political campaigns and has been influential in electoral politics. The AFL-CIO's COPE has had success in such areas as workers' health conditions, social security, housing, and civil rights.

See also Labor Unions.

AMERICAN INDIAN MOVEMENT (AIM), a civil rights interest group for native Americans. It was originally established to combat discriminatory practices of the Minnesota police in 1968. Chapters soon developed across the country in order to encourage Indian self-determination, international recognition of American Indian treaty rights, and maintenance of traditions and customs. AIM conducts research, provides educational services, maintains historical archives, and supports a school providing programs for individuals from kindergarten to adult extension.

AMERICAN JEWISH COMMITTEE, an interest group with members of the Jewish faith from more than 600 U.S. communities. The committee is concerned with developing educational and informational programs to combat racism, to protect religious tolerance, and to promote civil rights.

AMERICAN LABOR PARTY, a labor-dominated political movement active in New York State during the 1930s and 1940s. Founded in 1936 to build support for Franklin Delano Roosevelt and his "New Deal," the party was largely organized by David Dubinsky of the International Ladies Garment Workers Union and Sidney Hillman of the Amalgamated Clothing Workers of America.

In 1936 the party endorsed Roosevelt as candidate for president and helped elect Herbert Lehman as governor of New York. In New York City elections that year, American Labor candidates won five council seats and party-endorsed Fiorello La Guardia became mayor.

In 1944 growing Communist influence prompted Dubinsky and others to withdraw from the organization. Despite this loss, the party's best year was 1948, when Henry A. Wallace, the Progressive candidate for president, received over 500,000 votes on the American

Labor party line. Its influence steadily declined thereafter, and the party was formally dissolved in 1956.

See also Political Parties in the United States; Presidential Elections.

AMERICAN MEDICAL ASSOCIATION (AMA), professional group founded in 1847, the largest organization of medical professionals in the world. The AMA funds research, publishes, and distributes medical and scientific information to its members and to the public. It assists in setting standards for medical schools, residency programs, and continuing education projects. A powerful lobbying group, it has been successful in influencing the nature of most medical and related legislation. Although it was unsuccessful in defeating Medicare, a health care program for the elderly, it has been successful in opposing programs that would nationalize health care for the general population and has preferred private health care insurance as an alternative.

AMERICAN PARTY. See Know-Nothings; Political Parties in the United States.

AMERICAN PETROLEUM INSTITUTE (API), interest group that represents and lobbies for major American oil producers. Members include all segments of the oil industry from the wells to the pump. The API is the major source of information and data on oil in the United States and abroad. It conducts extensive research into energy production, consumption, imports-exports, and related technology.

AMERICAN SECURITY COUNCIL, an independent research and information center whose primary interest is in the furtherance of a strong military and foreign policy. Supported by contributions from private individuals and businesses, the council serves as a research and information center on national security needs. The group, headquartered in Chicago, maintains a bureau in Washington, D.C., where its weekly Washington Report is published, and broadcasts a daily news report over 900 radio stations across the country. The Security Council also periodically produces rankings of members of Congress on how they voted on key conservative military and foreign policy issues.

AMERICANS FOR CONSTITUTIONAL ACTION (ACA), group organized in 1958 at the urging of a group of conservative U.S. senators, initially for the purpose of electing "constitutional conservatives" to Congress. The ACA is best known for its rating of U.S. representatives and senators in terms of the percent they vote in accordance with ACA's conservative positions.

AMERICANS FOR DEMOCRATIC ACTION (ADA), a nonpartisan political organization founded in 1947 to formulate liberal domestic and foreign policies and to support progressive candidates for elective office. The ADA works actively from its Washington, D.C. headquarters to encourage the passage of liberal legislation. It has particularly stressed the need to reduce defense and military spending. Though avowedly nonpartisan, the ADA has long been associated with the liberal wing of the Democratic party.

The ADA periodically issues rankings of members of Congress on key liberal policy areas.

AMICUS CURIAE (Lat., friend of the court), one who is permitted, or invited, by a court to participate in a legal proceeding but who is not a party to it. In cases involving civil and criminal rights where a question of general applicability is being decided, courts have increasingly allowed "amicus briefs," which give legal arguments or facts. The practice can be of value in providing the court with a clear analysis of the factors it should consider in making its decision and of the possible implications of that decision.

AMNESTY, the constitutional prerogative of the president to grant a universal pardon to all those who have broken a specific national law (Article II, Section 2). The leaders and forces of the Confederacy were amnestied by presidents Abraham Lincoln and Andrew Johnson.

AMTRAK, railroad corporation created by the Rail Passenger Service Act of 1970, providing most of the U.S. passenger rail service. Established as a result of the significant decline in rail service and the possible elimination of such service in areas around the country, this semipublic corporation is financed by membership fees from participating railroads and by federal grants and loans. In the mid 1970s, there was an increase in passenger use, in part due to the energy crisis. However, in the 1980s, Amtrak experienced a steady financial decline.

ANARCHISM, a social philosophy and political movement that advocates the abolition of all government and maintains that voluntary institutions are best suited to express the natural social tendencies of mankind. Anarchists believe all government is authoritarian and seek to substitute for it cooperative groups working freely in each sphere of human activity.

The way that government is to be eliminated varies among anarchist writers. Hostility towards any form of authority has inhibited the creation of effective anarchist organizations. Modern proponents of anarchism have been Proudhon, who wanted peaceful change; Blanqui, who advocated violent change; and Bakunin, who continued the Blanquist line.

ANNAPOLIS CONVENTION. Through the efforts of the Virginia legislature, an invitation was extended to all the states to meet at Annapolis in Sept. 1786, and consider common interests that would lead to permanent harmony within the Confederation. Rival claims to western lands, commercial relations, and other controversies precipitated the recognition that the Articles of Confederation prevented any significant action in dealing with these problems. With only five state delegations in attendance, the convention accepted a report, written by Alexander Hamilton, that called attention to the critical situation of the Confederation and proposed a convention of all the states to meet at Philadelphia May 2, 1787, to consider adequate measures in coping with Confederation problems.

See also Constitutional Convention.

ANTHONY, SUSAN B(ROWNELL) (1820-1906), reformer, feminist, crusader and organizer for women's equal rights. She was born a Quaker in Adams, Mass. She taught school in New York until 1850. An austere, morally zealous and aggressive woman, she never married, devoting her life to a career of social protest. Concerned with the temperance and abolitionist movements, she realized that in these areas there could be but slow progress until women had equal rights, including the franchise.

She started the first women's temperance society in 1852. In collaboration with Elizabeth Cady Stanton, a woman of similar persuasion and ability, Susan B. Anthony participated in the first organizations for women's rights, later founding the National American Women's Suffrage Association in 1869, and serving as its president from 1892 to 1900. She fought for the inclusion of women in the "male inhabitants" provision

Susan B. Anthony pioneered for women's rights.

of the Fourteenth Amendment to the Constitution. When this effort failed, she and fourteen other women registered and voted in Rochester, N.Y., in the presidential election of 1872. She was arrested, tried without jury, and fined. She wrote and lectured throughout the world. In 1888 she started the International Council of Women. She died in Rochester in 1906.

During her lifetime she saw the adoption by several states of legislation according limited rights to women, but the full legal status she espoused did not come un-

til the passage of the Nineteenth Amendment in 1919. Susan B. Anthony contended that equal rights for women must include opportunity for education and employment, control over their own property, guardianship of children after divorce and the right to vote in all elections. As a pioneer organizer of social protest, she developed the techniques of mass petitions and demonstrations, anticipating the women's liberation movement of today.

See also Woman Suffrage.

ANTI-FEDERALISTS, those opposed to the ratification of the Constitution. Largely comprised of small farmers, shopkeepers and laborers, they contrasted with the propertied pro-Constitutional Federalists. They feared that the Constitution would destroy state sovereignty, increase the power of the upper classes, and offer insufficient protection to individual rights.

ANTI-KU KLUX KLAN ACT. *See* Civil Rights Acts: Act of April 20, 1872.

ANTI-MASONIC PARTY, a short-lived United States third party movement. It was organized in Ontario, New York in 1827 by Thurlow Weed, a journalist, in response to the disappearance and alleged murder of a Mason who had threatened to expose the group's secret procedures.

In 1831 the Anti-Masons held the first national party convention in Philadelphia, which marked the shift from party caucuses to the convention nominating system. In 1832 their presidential candidate, William Wirt, opposed National Republican Henry Clay and Andrew Jackson of the Democratic-Republicans, and received seven electoral votes. William H. Harrison was the joint presidential nominee of the Anti-Masons and the newly formed Whigs in 1836. After Democrat Martin Van Buren's victory in this election, the Anti-Masons were gradually absorbed by the Whigs.

The Anti-Masonic Party achieved greater success on a local level, sending fifteen members to the New York State Assembly in 1827 and winning the governorships in Vermont and Pennsylvania.

See also Political Parties in the United States; Presidential Elections.

ANTI-MONOPOLY PARTY, an independent reform movement of the early 1880s. Organized in eleven states, it favored strong regulation of railroads and reduction of taxes. The party eventually merged with the Greenback-Labor movement.

See also Political Parties in the United States; Presidential Elections.

ANTIPOVERTY PROGRAM. *See* Poverty Program.

ANTITRUST. *See* Business Regulation in the United States.

ANTITRUST ACTS. *See* Clayton Antitrust Act; Robinson-Patman Act; Sherman Antitrust Act; Webb-Pomerene Export Trade Act.

ANZUS PACT, agreement signed in San Francisco in 1951 by Australia, New Zealand, and the United States, pledging mutual support in the event of an armed attack in the Pacific area against any one of the signatories. Although the pact was first proposed as a means of preventing possible Japanese aggression, the United States came to see the alliance as part of a broader protection against Communism in the Pacific region. The alliance has been strained because New Zealand refused (1985) to allow a U.S. naval vessel to use the country's ports because of the possibility that the ship might be carrying nuclear weapons.

APARTHEID, an Afrikaans expression applied to the system of racial separation practiced in South Africa. Separation of the races is the goal of the system. The policy includes the forced relocation of millions of blacks from land designated for "whites only" and their resettlement in so-called black homelands. Blacks are treated as aliens; their movements are strictly regulated; and they are denied the right to vote.

International pressure on South Africa to end its racial policy has intensified during the last twenty years. In the United States, the antiapartheid protest movement helped to bring about economic sanctions (such as the elimination of U.S. investments in South Africa) and to increase political pressure on the South African government to allow non-whites equal status and full participation in the government and society.

APPALACHIA, a poverty-stricken region of over 15 million persons in the eastern United States. Primarily in the Appalachian Highlands, the area includes parts of thirteen states from northern Pennsylvania to central Alabama. Decline of the farming and coal mining economy has left many unemployed; health, housing, and education are substandard. In 1965, Congress passed the Appalachian Regional Development Act, which had a planned expenditure of $1.2 billion. About 80 percent of the funds was used for a 5-year road-building program. The rest of the money was used for hospitals, schools, land rehabilitation, and sewage treatment plants. States receiving aid are: Alabama, Georgia, Kentucky, Maryland, Mississippi, New York, North Carolina, Ohio, Pennsylvania, South Carolina, Tennessee, Virginia, and West Virginia.

See also Appalachian Regional Program.

APPALACHIAN REGIONAL PROGRAM (1965), the comprehensive antipoverty program aimed at helping the rural poor in the thirteen states designated Appalachia. The plan uses federal and state funds to prime regional programs to improve employment opportunities, raise average incomes, and stimulate socioeconomic development. Nearly half the program's funds are earmarked for highway construction to open the area to itself.

APPEAL, loosely applied to the appellate review of an inferior court final decision or even to the initial judicial review of an administrative body's decision. Appeal is an ancient proceeding, adopted by equity from the civil law, in which a case is removed from an inferior to a superior court and retried as to law and fact. Most appellate proceedings are now governed by statute. The term is now used to connote any form of appellate review of errors of law and not fact or serves to distinguish appellate review as a matter of right from appellate review as a matter of the appellate court's discretion (certiorari).

Most appellate courts decide for themselves which cases they will hear (discretionary jurisdiction). Only a small percentage of lower court decisions will ever be heard by an appellate court. There are also a few types of cases that the U.S. Supreme Court is required to accept (obligatory jurisdiction), including cases where the highest court of a state has found a federal law to be unconstitutional.

See also Certiorari, Writ Of.

APPEALS, COURT OF, one of the present appellate courts of the United States. Because the Constitution itself provided for only one court, the Supreme Court, and left to Congress the creation of inferior courts (Article III, Section I), the courts of appeal are creatures of Congress. Nevertheless, they are called constitutional courts because they exercise part of the judicial power of Article III of the Constitution. The courts of appeal have appellate jurisdiction over most administrative agencies and over final decisions of district courts, except in the few cases where there is a right of direct appeal to the Supreme Court. Appeal from district court decisions is a matter of right. These courts do not have any original jurisdiction. Since the availability of Supreme Court review is limited, the courts of appeal function as courts of last resort in most instances.

There are eleven courts of appeal, one for each judicial circuit—the First through the Tenth and the District of Columbia ("Circuit" is a historical term, derived from the old circuit courts. It simply designates a geographical area at present). Cases in the courts of appeal are heard before three judges.

See also Circuit Court; District Court.

APPEASEMENT, sacrifice of the interests of a country, ally, or innocent third party to forestall a serious military threat or militant diplomatic move. The term has a dishonorable connotation and usually refers to concessions made in violation of treaties or moral obligations. Perhaps the most infamous example of appeasement in the twentieth century is the 1938 turnover of the Czechoslovakian Sudetenland to Germany in spite of British and French treaties with Czechoslovakia to protect her in case of German attack. Great Britain and France went along with this Munich pact in hopes of satisfying Hitler, but he took the rest of Czechoslovakia in 1939 and then moved toward Poland.

APPELLATE COURT. *See* Appeals, Court of.

APPELLATE JURISDICTION, the authority of certain courts to hear cases "on appeal" from lower courts. As distinguished from original jurisdiction, courts with appellate jurisdiction hear cases that were first heard elsewhere and that are now being appealed to a higher court for review. Appellate courts usually render decisions based on errors of a lower court or administrative tribunal in applying or interpreting principles of law or the Constitution, and not on factual errors, although on occasion they may deal with questions of fact.
See also Appeal; Jurisdiction.   —*Mary L. Carns*

APPOINTMENT, PRESIDENTIAL, the prerogative of the president to fill offices in the executive and judicial branches of the federal government, in the armed forces, and in the regulatory commissions. In some cases the president's appointment power is unrestricted; in other cases he is limited to nominating candidates that the Senate may approve. Cabinet officers are appointed in this manner.

In practice the president's nominees are usually confirmed, because of the traditional president's privilege to appoint the officials of his administration. The grounds for senatorial opposition to a presidential appointee are usually moral; if the nominee had committed some past indiscretion that reflects on his integrity, he may not be approved by the Senate. The privilege of making numerous appointments gives the chief executive the important power of patronage—the ability to do favors for political allies, which strengthens his position.

APPORTIONMENT, LEGISLATIVE, the allocation of legislative seats to constituencies. The term is therefore applied to Congress, to state legislatures, and to city councils. The basis for the allocation of seats is laid down in constitutions, statutes, and judicial decisions. In the apportionment of representatives, several important questions arise: How many people shall be contained in each district? Should each representative represent the same number of constituents? Is population size the sole criterion in determining representation, or should the physical size of a district be considered? How does one draw district boundaries? What is the best machinery to administer fair principles of representation?

The Constitution provides that each state, regardless of population, shall have two senators. The result is that small states have a disproportionate influence in Senate affairs, especially where a two-thirds majority is required for action.

The Constitution also provides that seats in the House of Representatives are to be apportioned among the states according to population, as determined every ten years by the census. The original sixty-five members of the House were apportioned in the Constitution. Thereafter, assignments were made after each census, excepting that of 1920, on which Congress failed to act. The Reapportionment Act of 1929 set the permanent number of House members at 435 and provided for automatic reapportionment if Congress failed to act.

Nowhere does the Constitution require the election of representatives by single-member districts; but this provision was imposed by an 1842 law, which remains in effect. Originally requiring that each district be composed of contiguous territory, in 1872 the law added that districts must be of substantially equal population. In 1901 a requirement of compactness was introduced. Compactness, contiguity, and equality were not included in the law of 1929, but the Supreme Court restored the requirement of equality in its 1964 decision, *Westberry v. Sanders.*

Problems of Reapportionment. The drawing of congressional districts is the task of state legislatures. In many states, the party in control has engaged in gerrymandering, that is, in setting the boundaries to secure as many representatives as possible. The major consequence of permitting state legislatures to define congressional districts was to reduce the number of competitive seats in the House and to overrepresent rural areas, mostly at the expense of the suburbs. Because of the movement from rural to urban and suburban areas, failure to redistrict strengthened disproportionate rural representation.

The Supreme Court first intervened in the reapportionment question at the state level. In a Tennessee case—*Baker v. Carr* (1962)—the Court ruled that cases involving state legislative representation might be raised under the equal protection clause in federal courts. *Reynolds v. Sims* (1964) established that population must be the basis for representation in both houses of a state legislature, and *Westberry v. Sanders* (1964) declared that congressional districts must be substantially equal in population. As nearly as practicable, the Court said "one person's vote in a congressional election is to be worth as much as another's." This principle remains the established doctrine.

The judicial actions have ended gross population inequalities among both congressional and state districts. Suburban representation has been increased in Congress and in state legislatures, usually at the expense of rural areas, but sometimes at a loss to the inner city. The problem of gerrymandering, however, remains unresolved.   —*Murray S. Stedman, Jr.*
See also Gerrymander.

APPRENTICESHIP AND TRAINING, BUREAU OF, a component of the Employment and Training Administration of the Department of Labor. It formulates and promotes the furtherance of labor standards necessary to safeguard the welfare of apprentices and cooperates with state government in the promulgation and promotion of such standards. Through field representatives in each state, the bureau works with employers, labor unions, vocational schools, community planning groups, and others concerned with apprenticeship. Programs must meet standards established by the bureau or the recognized state apprenticeship councils.

APPROPRIATION, a grant of money by Congress to carry out a governmental program; also one of a number of stages leading to the expenditure of funds. The appropriation process for major portions of the budget includes separate stages, known as authorization and appropriation. Substantive legislative committees first authorize specific programs, while appropriation grants the actual funding up to the ceiling set at the preceding authorization stage. Funds generally cannot be appropriated until the program has been authorized and signed into law, although there are exceptions. Tensions often arise between authorization and appropriation committees, and programs that have been authorized may not be fully funded. Generally, appropriation bills originate in the House. While authorization bills are considered by the substantive legislative committees, such as agriculture, education, and labor, appropriation bills are considered in each chamber of a separate appropriation committee. Since the Budget and Accounting Act of 1921, the president presents an annual budget to Congress indicating proposed expenditures, and appropriation committees work from this.

If Congress has not completed the budgetary process by the beginning of a new fiscal year, temporary funds may be provided in the form of a continuing resolution. Occasionally, sums may be appropriated after the start of a fiscal year to cover the difference between an agency's needs and its original grant (known as a deficiency bill). This "power of the purse," which also includes the power to levy taxes, played an important role in the development of legislative bodies and is one of their controls over the executive branch.

See also Power of the Purse.

APTHEKER v. SECRETARY OF STATE, 378 U.S. 500 (1964), involves a challenge to a section of the Subversive Activities Control Act of 1950, which makes it a felony for a member of a Communist organization registered under the act or under final order to register, to apply for, use, or attempt to use a passport. Aptheker applied for a passport and was denied one on the ground that he was allegedly an active member of a Communist organization. The Court held this section of the act unconstitutional, because it too broadly restricted the right to travel and therefore abridged a liberty guaranteed by the Fifth Amendment.

See also NAACP v. Alabama; Zemel v. Rusk.

ARBITRATION, in labor, third-party settlement of a labor dispute. When the labor and management parties engaged in collective bargaining cannot reach agreement, they may agree to be bound by the decision of a third party, the arbitrator. They agree on the issues that the arbitrator is to decide, and the arbitrator is limited by the parties or by the court and may be one person or an arbitration panel of three, five, or seven members who may all be neutral or may represent labor and management with one neutral member acting as chairman.

Once the arbitrator has made his decision, it is final and binding (but it may be appealed according to the specifications of state arbitration statutes). Generally, fraud, corruption, denial of a fair and impartial hearing, and awards made outside the scope of the arbitrator provide grounds for appeal.

Compulsory Arbitration is arbitration required by state and federal law. A party to a labor dispute may also be forced into arbitration not by law but by pressure from public opinion, a government agency, or the press.

Justiciable Arbitration is used for the settlement of employee or employer grievances under an existing labor contract. In this case, an arbitrator acts in a quasi-judiciary capacity in deciding the interpretation and application of a labor contract in regard to the grievances brought to him.

History. As early as 1898 the Erdman Act provided for voluntary arbitration and mediation with the railroad unions. In 1909 a two-month strike of the International Ladies Garment Workers Union was settled by providing a board of arbitration, and in 1919 the United Mine Workers agreed to arbitration by a presidential commission. Since then Congress has acted when necessary to provide arbitration in long-standing labor disputes. Since 1969 federal employees have had binding arbitration settle their disputes over new contracts.

See also Collective Bargaining; National Labor Relations Board (NLRB).

ARISTOCRACY, a system of government in which control is exercised by a small ruling class, based on social, economic, military or ecclesiastical position. The term also means any hereditary group enjoying superior rank.

ARIZONA v. YOUNGBLOOD, (1988), Supreme Court decision dealing with a man arrested for abducting and molesting a 10-year-old boy based on the boy's identification; Youngblood claimed mistaken identity. The police had found evidence of semen on the boy's clothing but failed to conduct a thorough test or to preserve evidence properly.

Expert witnesses testified that Youngblood might have been exonerated had the police acted correctly, but Youngblood was convicted. Chief Justice Rehnquist wrote for the majority that "unless a criminal defendant can show bad faith" by the police, he cannot claim a violation of his Fourteenth Amendment right of due process. The Constitution does not require that all potentially significant material be preserved.

ARMS CONTROL AND DISARMAMENT. *See* Atomic Weapons, International Control of; Disarmament.

ARMS, RIGHT TO BEAR, a provision of the Second Amendment that prohibits Congress from interfering with the right of the people to arm themselves. Enacted at a time of strong popular distrust of standing mercenary armies and a fear of the creation of an overly powerful central government, the Second Amendment allowed the establishment of state militia free of congressional restraints. The amendment and the inherent power of the states to control firearms have bred considerable contemporary controversy over gun control.
See also Gun-Control Legislation.

ARMY, DEPARTMENT OF THE. *See* Defense, United States Department of.

ARTHUR, CHESTER A(LAN) (1829-1886), 21st president of the United States (1881-1885), born in Fairfield, Vt. He entered New York politics as a conservative Stalwart, serving as New York quartermaster during the Civil War and as customs collector of New York (1871). When Republican nominee James Garfield offered the vice-presidency to the Stalwarts in 1880, Arthur accepted and, partly due to his efforts, the Republicans carried both state and nation. After Garfield's assassination, he became president (Sept. 19, 1881). A competent executive, Arthur prosecuted the Star Route frauds, vetoed Chinese immigration restrictions, tried to reduce "pork barrel" legislation, authorized a modern Navy, and cut national indebtedness. He shocked both Stalwarts and reformers by demanding civil service reform and signing the Pendleton Act (1883).
See also Presidential Elections.

ARTICLES OF CONFEDERATION. In 1776 during the American Revolution the Articles of Confederation and Perpetual Union were created at the behest of the Second Continental Congress. Approved by the Congress on November 17, 1777, and with the ratification of the last state, Maryland, in March 1781, the first Constitution of the United States went into effect.

Contents. Structurally, the articles provided Congress with authority to (1) declare war and make peace; (2) enter into treaties and alliances; (3) fix uniform standards of weights and measures; (4) create a postal system; (5) borrow money and issue bills of credit; (6) regulate coinage; (7) establish and control the armed forces; (8) create admiralty courts; (9) guarantee the citizens of each state the rights and privileges of citizens

in the several states when in another state; (10) regulate Indian affairs; (11) requisition men and money from the states; and (12) upon state petition adjudicate disputes between the states.

In its composition the Articles of Confederation conjoined the executive, legislative and judicial in one body—the Congress. Although state delegations varied from two to seven representatives, the Congress was unicameral, with each state possessing one vote. There was no provision for an executive, as such, but a presiding officer was selected by a committee of states and authorized to preside as "president" provided that he did not serve in that capacity for more than one year in any term of three.

Evaluation. Students of the period are usually divided into two groups in assessing the effectiveness of the articles. The supporters of the document admit the evident weaknesses: the lack of power to regulate interstate and foreign commerce, collect taxes directly from the people, or compel states to pay their share of the costs of government; and the requirement of nine states' approval in passing important bills, and the consent of all the states to amend the articles. But supporters hold that the document was designed with specific limitations in mind and, under the circumstances, that it fulfilled the objectives of its creators: considering the climate of distrust in centralized authority, one of the causes of the Revolution, the Articles of Confederation functioned as intended. Moreover, they accomplished certain common objectives and, most importantly, kept alive the idea of union. The articles were, they concluded, a necessary prelude to the adoption of the Constitution of the United States.   —*Samuel Raphalides*
See also Continental Congress.

ASHWANDER v. TENNESSEE VALLEY AUTHORITY (TVA), 297 U.S. 288 (1936), is one in a series of suits in which a number of power companies challenged the constitutional power of the federal government to develop the Tennessee River area. The Alabama Power Company had contracted with the TVA to provide for the sale of transmission lines and other property and the purchase of power. When this contract was challenged, the Court upheld it but limited its decision to the validity of the contract and pointedly avoided a consideration of the constitutionality of the TVA's program. In doing so it would also have had to consider abstract questions which the Court did not feel were within its realm. However, Mr. Justice Brandeis, who agreed with the conclusion of the Court, dissented in part, saying that the Court had been unwise in reviewing and deciding this case. He then outlined the function of the Court and the circumstances under which it should accept a case for review.
See also Luther v. Borden.

ASIAN DEVELOPMENT BANK (ASDB). Under the sponsorship of the United Nations Economic Commission for Asia and the Far East (ECAFE), the bank has a membership of 42 nations. Beginning operations in 1966, the bank's aims are the promotion of economic and agricultural development in Asia.

ASYLUM. Every sovereign state has the right to grant asylum to a persecuted alien, by permitting him to enter and remain on territory under its protection. Asylum is generally based on the refugee's having a "well-founded fear of being persecuted for reasons of race, religion, nationality, or political opinion" (Geneva Convention on the Statutes of Refugees, 1951). The determination is made by the host state, which would then deny any request to extradite the refugee.

Diplomatic asylum is a special category of asylum and occurs when persons seek protection in their own country at a foreign embassy or legation. The practice is widespread in Latin America but most states, particularly the United States, try to restrict asylum to situations in which a person's life is in immediate danger. In some unusual cases, diplomats have aided in the safe departure of persons whose lives were threatened. That occurred in 1979 when the Canadian and Swedish governments helped several U.S. consular officials to leave Iran after the seizure of the U.S. Embassy.

See also Extradition.

ATLANTIC CHARTER. *See* United Nations.

AT LARGE, a term used to refer to candidates who are elected from an entire area rather than from districts. Members of the U.S. Senate are elected at large in each state. Members of the House of Representatives are usually elected by district, but occasionally may be elected at large if the state was not redistricted following the federal census. Members of local legislative bodies, such as city commissions, are frequently elected at large to represent an entire city.   *—Mary L. Carns*

ATOMIC ENERGY ACTS (1946, 1954), acts of Congress that created the Atomic Energy Commission in 1946 and placed atomic energy under civilian control. The 1954 act permitted limited private entry into the growing field of nuclear power, under government regulation. The Atomic Energy Commission was abolished in 1974. Licensing and related regulatory functions were transferred to the newly-formed Nuclear Regulatory Commission, which was established as an independent regulatory agency under the Energy Reorganization Act of 1974 and by Executive Order 11834, signed January 15, 1975. Research and development functions were transferred first to the Energy Research and Development Administration and later to the Department of Energy.   *—Mary L. Carns*

See also Atomic Weapons, International Control of.

ATOMIC WEAPONS, INTERNATIONAL CONTROL OF, attempt by the nations of the world, through

conferences and treaties, to avoid nuclear catastrophe by controlling the testing and use of nuclear weapons. Current agreements in force include the Test-Ban Treaty, the Nuclear Nonproliferation Treaty, the Strategic Arms Limitation Treaty (SALT), the Hot-Line Agreement, and treaties banning nuclear weapons in Antarctica and in space.

A mushroom cloud forms in the Pacific after France detonates an experimental Atomic bomb.

U.N. Atomic Arms Control. Attempts at international controls began at the end of World War II, when the awesome power of atomic weapons was revealed at Hiroshima and Nagasaki. In November, 1945, the United States suggested that the U.N. oversee all nuclear energy production. The resulting U.N. Atomic Energy Commission, headed by Bernard Baruch, and representing twelve nations, issued a plan in June 1946 to outlaw atomic weapons and allow only the peaceful use of atomic energy. Among the proposals of the Baruch committee were the use of U.N. inspectors with unlimited inspection authority and the withdrawal of veto protection in the Security Council for nations who violated the ban on atomic weapons; once the system was established, the United States would have been required to destroy its atomic stockpile. The U.S.S.R. and Poland were the only two countries on the commission to disagree with the final decision. The U.S.S.R. rejected the inspection and veto plans; consequently, the United States refused to destroy its atomic stockpile. Then the United States had second thoughts about the plan and rejected it.

In another attempt to provide atomic arms control through the U.N., President Dwight Eisenhower submitted an Atoms for Peace proposal to the U.N. in 1953. In this plan, the United States and U.S.S.R. would have contributed uranium from their stockpiles to the U.N. and an atomic energy commission would have channeled the uranium into peaceful projects, such as electric power stations. Again no agreement was reached.

Open Skies. Although atomic arms production by the major powers continued, proposals for complete atomic disarmament persisted, but a major conceptual change developed in 1955. The Russians had finally accepted an English-French memorandum based on a complete disarmament plan with staged, balanced reductions governed by safeguards. However, the United States, pursuing a foreign policy of containment of the Russians, now favored a plan in which atomic weapons production would be stabilized rather than banned—in effect, a partial arms-limitation program. An Eisenhower "Open Skies" proposal at this time favored surveillance, disclosure of information, and mutual assurance that there would be no surprise nuclear attack by either side, but no agreement was reached.

Nuclear Test-Ban Treaty. In the early 1960s some substantial progress was made in international controls. There was some concern over the dangers of radioactive fallout from atmospheric nuclear testing; President Kennedy had appointed an Arms Control and Disarmament Agency, and in 1962 an eighteen-nation Disarmament Committee held meetings on this question. On August 5, 1963, the United States, the U.S.S.R., and Great Britain signed a nuclear test-ban treaty, which went into effect on October 10, 1963, and has been signed by almost all U.N. members except China and France. The signatories agreed not to hold any open-air or open-water nuclear tests. The danger of impulsive nuclear attack was lessened considerably the same year with the installation of the Hot-Line, a crisis communications link for direct contact between the United States and the Soviet Union.

Nonproliferation Treaty. The Disarmament Committee met again in Geneva in 1966 to consider a Nuclear Nonproliferation Treaty to prevent the spread of nuclear weapons. The committee met through 1967, but it could reach no final agreement. The inspection issue was the major problem, with nonnuclear nations protesting that inspection proposals were for themselves and not for the major nuclear powers. Finally the United States and Great Britain agreed to inspection of all of its nuclear facilities except those for direct defense. After more than four years of negotiations the treaty was ratified by the U.N. on June 12, 1968, and signed by the United States, the U.S.S.R., and sixty other nations on July 1.

The Senate ratified the treaty on March 13, 1969. The treaty prohibits nuclear states from giving nuclear weapons or their control to nonnuclear states, prohibits nonnuclear states from manufacturing or acquiring nuclear weapons, and provides safeguards that would prohibit a state from diverting peaceful nuclear energy to nuclear weapons. The treaty is administered by the International Atomic Energy Agency.

SALT. Soon after the ratification of the Nuclear Nonproliferation Treaty, the United States and the U.S.S.R. agreed to discuss the possibilities of limiting the produc-

tion of nuclear arms systems. The purpose of these Strategic Arms Limitation Treaty talks (SALT talks) was to stabilize the nuclear arms race to avoid the enormous expenditures needed by both countries for the development of these new systems. In 1972 an agreement was signed limiting antiballistic missile production and freezing the number of offensive missiles on land and sea. In 1974 President Ford met with Leonid Brezhnev of the Soviet Union to decide the general outline of a SALT II agreement. Continued negotiations resulted in a proposed treaty that the critics charged would have little practical effect on the arms race. Senate approval was doubtful, however, and debate was suspended in 1980 following the Soviet invasion of Afghanistan.

The Reagan administration continued discussions, but they broke down (November 1983) over the question of deployment of American Cruise and Pershing II missiles in Western Europe. Following President Reagan's reelection, the United States and the U.S.S.R. announced that they would meet in early 1985 to start new negotiations for controlling nuclear arms. Discussions were complicated by President Reagan's "Star Wars" proposal but culminated in ratification in 1988 of the INF Treaty, the first Soviet-American arms agreement since SALT I in 1972. It called for mutual reductions of missile forces. The Bush administration and Congress continued to fund "Star Wars" research. Strategic Arms Reduction Talks (START) also continued between the superpowers.

Analysis. Although in 1945 there were hopes of producing complete disarmament of nuclear weapons, this concept has been replaced by one of partial arms limitations in which the existing military balance is preserved. The increasing cost of developing nuclear systems, the new orbiting satellites for inspection and surveillance, and the specter of smaller nations settling their squabbles with atomic weapons have all had a sobering effect and have done much to produce the current agreements. Moreover, recent changes in Eastern Europe along with Gorbachev's need to reform the Soviet economy created a climate conducive to progress on arms reductions.

See also Disarmament; Intermediate Nuclear Forces; Nonproliferation Treaty; Star Wars; Strategic Arms Limitation Talks.

ATTACHÉ. *See* Foreign Service.

ATTORNEY GENERAL OF THE UNITED STATES, official who heads the Department of Justice and acts as the chief law officer of the federal government. The attorney general represents the United States in legal affairs and acts in an advisory capacity to the president and other executive departments. He is a member of the president's cabinet. In significant cases, he will represent the U.S. government before the U.S Supreme Court.

AUTHORITARIANISM, a doctrine that asserts the right of rulers to maintain the order and security of the state by whatever means necessary, despite any opposition. The doctrine opposes the freedom of political action espoused by democrats on the grounds that any kind of internal division produces weakness, disorder and disruption of political authority. Common to all authoritarian doctrines is the view that someone or something embodies the will of the state that should be imposed as the right pattern of thought and behavior. Doctrines have held this will lie with one man, a small group, an economic class, or with the people. Most commonly, authoritarians insist that power be possessed by one man or a few.

See also Absolutism; National Socialism; Totalitarianism.

AUTHORIZATION, the stage in the budgetary process that precedes the actual appropriation of funds. Substantive legislative committees, such as Agriculture or Education, authorize specific programs with ceilings on expenditures before funds are appropriated. Authorization committees consider proposed programs and recommend funding. Expenditures must be authorized and signed into law before the Appropriations Committees can act.   — *Mary L. Carns*

See also Appropriations.

BAIL SYSTEM, developed in the early common-law courts to secure the defendant's apperance in court at law. Originally required in civil and criminal cases, bail eventually came to be used primarily in criminal cases. Under the bail system, the defendant is released to his surety, who undertakes to produce him at trial, usually giving a "bail bond" to secure that obligation.

The bail system has come under increasing attack as a violation of civil liberties and due process. "Excessive" bail is prohibited under the Eighth Amendment. Nevertheless, with the bond's nonrefundable cost being approximately 10 percent of the face amount, it has served to keep many defendants in jail pending trial, depriving them of their liberty before having been found guilty of any crime.

See also Speedy Trial Act.

BAKER, JAMES (1930-   ), U.S. Secretary of State (1989-   ). Educated at Princeton and the University of Texas Law School, Baker practiced law before entering politics at the urging of his friend George Bush. Baker managed Gerald Ford's 1976 campaign and then returned to Texas.

Baker managed George Bush's attempt to secure the 1980 presidential nomination, but advised against continuing the campaign. He then joined the Reagan forces. After the election, Baker was asked to serve as President Reagan's Chief of Staff.

Baker became Secretary of the Treasury in January 1985 but left in August 1988 to manage Bush's presidential campaign. Following the election, Baker was picked to be Secretary of State.

BAKER v. CARR, 369 U.S. 186 (1962), one of the most important cases decided by the Warren Court. The issue remains important and troublesome despite the Court's landmark decision.

Traditionally the Court has shied away from dealing with political questions. This doctrine was usually expressed in statements to the effect that the court lacked jurisdiction over political problems such as the malapportionment of state legislatures. Therefore, the federal district court in this case felt compelled to deny judicial relief to Baker, a registered Tennessee voter who brought suit against the Tennessee Secretary of State alleging a violation of a federal constitutional right. The lower court recognized that there were large differences in the numbers of voters in rural and urban districts in Tennessee, but felt powerless to protect the right or correct the violation. On appeal, the Supreme Court held that the federal courts did have jurisdiction in this particular kind of political problem and that the courts should provide relief to the voter under the equal protection clause of the Constitution.   — *Philip J. Hannon*

See also Apportionment, Legislative; Colgrove v. Green; Reynolds v. Sims.

BAKKE CASE. *See* Regents of the University of California v. Bakke.

BALANCE OF PAYMENTS, the international commercial and financial transactions of a country's citizens and government. These transactions include the total payments made to foreign nations and the total receipts from foreign nations. The balance of payments is computed by figuring the difference between these two items during a specific period of time. Included in the computation are gold, merchandise, loans and their repayment and interest charges, services, and money spent by travelers.

When a country's foreign purchases (imports) exceed its sales abroad (exports), the nation has a balance of payments deficit. When the reverse situation occurs, a balance of payments surplus results.

See also International Monetary Fund.

BALANCE OF POWER, term used since ancient times to describe the relative distribution of power between states or alliance systems. Political theorists and policy makers are concerned about situations where power is concentrated on one side, thus creating an imbalance in international relations. At times states have aligned to preserve equilibrium and thus prevent conflict.

In modern times, the rise of the superpowers and the advent of the nuclear age have changed the character of international politics. The balance of power refers to the relative strength of the Communist and non-Communist alliance systems. The phrase "balance of terror" is often used to describe this alignment in the nuclear age.

BALANCED BUDGET AND EMERGENCY DEFI-CIT REDUCTION ACT OF 1985, a legislative compromise, necessitated by years of budgetary reforms that failed to reduce federal deficits. The law set maximum permissible deficit levels on a declining scale from 1986 to 1991. The Congress subsequently extended the "no deficit" deadline until 1993. Only Social Security and interest on the national debt were exempt from cuts.

Critics and even many supporters of the measure were concerned that requiring the president to bring the budget into conformity with a mandatory deficit-reduction schedule gave the executive branch too much power. Nevertheless, the law forced budget priorities and decisions.

BALLOT, the method by which an individual records his vote. There are various types of ballots. In the past ballots were usually made of paper upon which the voter would record his choice; today the U.S. voter typically pulls a lever on a machine to record his vote.

In national elections a short ballot is used, because at a maximum the voter is electing only four men—president, vice president, senator, and representative. The short ballot is also used in some state elections where a governor, lieutenant governor (on the same ballot), state senator and representative, and a handful of local judges are elected. However, many states and counties employ the long ballot, where a great number of offices are filled on both the state and county level.

There are two other important kinds of ballots, the office-block ballot ("Massachusetts ballot") and the party-column ballot ("Indiana ballot"). In the office-block ballot all candidates are listed under the office for which they are running; in the party-column ballot candidates are listed under their party designation. In the latter it is possible for the voter to cast his ballot for all the candidates of a party by depressing a single lever on the voting machine. Thus the office-block ballot encourages voting for the individual and the party-column ballot encourages voting for the party. About 60 percent of the states use the party-column ballot, and the rest use office-block ballot.

See also Voter Participation.

BANKING ACT OF 1933. *See* Business Regulation in the United States.

BANTAM BOOKS, INC. v. SULLIVAN, 372 U.S. 58 (1963), questions the constitutionality of a Rhode Island law creating the Commission to Encourage Morality in Youth with the aim of stopping the circulation of certain obscene publications. Several publishers and distributors brought suit against the State of Rhode Island, alleging that removal of their publications from the markets, without notice or hearing, violated the right of freedom of the press. In holding the acts and practices of the commission unconstitutional, the Court was of the opinion that the informal system of censorship effected by the commission, devoid of the constitutional safeguards against arbitrary and capricious state regulation of obscenity, abridged the First Amendment liberties protected against state action by the Fourteenth Amendment. The Court also found that in its attempt to protect youth, the commission unconstitutionally deprived adult readers of its listed publications as well.

BARENBLATT v. UNITED STATES, 360 U.S. 109 (1959), concerns the conflicting constitutional claims of congressional power and individual rights. Barenblatt was held in contempt of Congress for refusing to answer certain questions put to him by the House Un-American Activities Committee during the course of an inquiry concerning alleged Communist infiltration into the educational field. Contradicting its previous ruling in *Watkins v. United States,* the Court concluded five to four that the legislative authority of the Committee to conduct the inquiry was unassailable, because the pertinence of the questions directed to Barenblatt was clearly established. The Court also held that in this inquiry the petitioner's First Amendment rights had not been violated, as the amendment does not afford a witness the right to resist inquiry when public interest is at stake. The Court has, in subsequent cases, both sustained and struck down convictions for contempt of Congress depending on whether or not the congressional committee was authorized to investigate a particular activity and whether or not the questions were pertinent to that investigation.

See also Watkins v. United States.

BARN BURNERS. *See* Hunkers.

BARRON v. BALTIMORE, 7 Peters 243 (1833). In this case Chief Justice Marshall, on behalf of the Court, declared that the Fifth Amendment's provisions prohibiting the taking of private property for public use without compensation applied to the government alone and did not prohibit states or their political subdivisions from taking private property without just compensation. By this reading, the Court indicated its view that the entire Bill of Rights served as limitations on the power of the federal government alone. The states and their subdivisions were in no way circumscribed by these limitations of federal power. As a result, if citizens sought protection from official action by a non-federal official, they must look to their own state's laws. This is still the general rule of law, but later cases moved far in the direction of making the Bill of Rights applicable to state action. Later justices achieved this end in large part by giving a broad reading to the due process clause of the Fourteenth Amendment. Thus the Fourteenth Amendment is said to have incorporated parts of the Bill of Rights.   —*Philip J. Hannon*

BARTKUS v. ILLINOIS, 359 U.S. 121 (1959), concerns the constitutionality of prosecution by a state under state law after an acquittal for the same offense by a federal court under federal law. Bartkus had been tried and acquitted in a federal court for robbery of a federally-insured savings and loan association. He was then tried and convicted under an Illinois statute for the same offense, which he contended was in violation of the due process clause of the Fourteenth Amendment. The Court, in a controversial five to four decision delivered by Mr. Justice Frankfurter, refused to apply the double jeopardy provision of the Fifth Amendment to the states through the Fourteenth, holding that federal acquittal does not bar subsequent prosecution and conviction in a state court for the same crime. The dissenters stated that the federal authorities had participated so actively in the state prosecution that it violated the Fifth Amendment double jeopardy clause to uphold the conviction.

See also Palko v. Connecticut; United States v. Lanza.

BATES v. LITTLE ROCK, 361 U.S. 516 (1960), concerns the constitutionality of a city statute requiring local chapters of the National Association for the Advancement of Colored People to disclose their membership lists for taxing purposes. Bates, the custodian of the records of a branch of the NAACP in Little Rock, Ark., refused to supply these lists. The Court, in a unanimous decision, reasoned that freedom of association, like freedom of speech and press, is protected by the due process clause of the Fourteenth Amendment, and found no significant reason for encroaching on personal liberty through the enforcement of ordinances which could cause community hostility and economic reprisals. Also, the Court held that there was no reasonable relationship between membership disclosure and the determination of liability for the taxes involved.

See also NAACP v. Alabama.

BATTLE ACT (1951), or **MUTUAL DEFENSE ASSISTANCE CONTROL PROGRAM.** *See* Containment Policy.

BAY OF PIGS CRISIS, United States-sponsored invasion of Cuba by 1,200 to 1,400 Cuban refugees organized, trained, and supplied by the CIA. The refugees landed ninety miles south of Havana on April 17, 1961, in an attempt to overthrow the Castro regime. However, they were defeated and imprisoned within three days. Air cover that had apparently been planned for the refugee invasion was withdrawn and the refugees were left unaided. The 1,113 prisoners were freed by Christmas 1961 through the efforts of private negotiators for a ransom of money and medical supplies.

Planning for the invasion began under Eisenhower and continued under Kennedy. President Kennedy took full responsibility for the invasion's failure, but CIA activities were reviewed and Director Allen W. Dulles was replaced by John A. McCone.

Because of the Bay of Pigs crisis, President Kennedy suffered a serious loss of prestige which he did not regain until the Cuban missile crisis in 1962. He was criticized for trying to conceal United States participation in the invasion and for allowing Ambassador Adlai Stevenson to be unaware of these circumstances as he argued that the United States had nothing to do with the invasion in the U.N. Security Council. After the invasion United States-Cuban relations deteriorated, and the United States stopped trade with Cuba.

BENTON v. MARYLAND, 395 U.S. 784 (1969), makes the prohibition of double jeopardy by the Fifth Amendment applicable to the states by the due process clause of the Fourteenth. Benton was tried on charges of burglary and larceny. He was convicted on the burglary count, but acquitted of larceny. Benton's conviction, however, was set aside because the jury had been improperly selected. He was then retried and convicted on both counts. The Court held that retrial on the larceny count violated the constitutional prohibition against subjecting persons to double jeopardy for the same offense, and reversed the conviction on this count. The Court also noted that it "increasingly looked to the specific guarantees of the [Bill of Rights] to determine whether a state criminal trial was conducted with the due process of law."

See also Palko v. Connecticut.

BERGER v. NEW YORK, 388 U.S. 41 (1967), concerns constitutional restrictions on electronic surveillance, and tests the validity of New York's eavesdropping statute, which permits trespassing on private premises with prior court approval. Berger was convicted on two counts of conspiracy to bribe the chairman of the New York State Liquor Authority on evidence obtained from an electronic recording device placed in his office. The court held, in reversing the conviction, that although the New York statute went part of the way toward meeting the requirements of the Fourth and Fourteenth Amendments by placing a detached authority between the public and the policy, it so broadly authorized indiscriminate use of electronic devices as to be constitutionally defective. This opinion effectively overruled the requirement of *Olmstead v. United States* that some tangible thing be taken in order for the protections of the Fourth Amendment to be invoked.

See also Mapp v. Ohio.

BETTER BUSINESS BUREAUS. *See* Consumer Protection.

BETTS v. BRADY, 316 U.S. 455 (1942). Early in United States legal history the Supreme Court held that the first ten amendments to the Constitution applied to the federal government but not to the state governments. Thus the Bill of Rights served for many years as a limit only upon the powers that were exercised by the federal government.

For many years the Supreme Court has struggled with the problem of to what extent, if any, the due process clause of the Fourteenth Amendment incorporates the Bill of Rights' protections and applies them to state criminal proceedings. In the case of *Betts v. Brady* the Court was petitioned by an indigent whose request for a trial lawyer had been denied by a state court. The judges found that the right to counsel at trial was not an absolute right and was not an inherent part of the Fourteenth Amendment's due process requirements. The Sixth Amendment had been construed previously as requiring the appointment of counsel for all indigents in federal cases, but the Court declined to incorporate this requirement into the Fourteenth Amendment. Thus the state courts were left free to convict indigents without counsel in noncapital cases, provided the other facts revealed a fair trial.   —*Philip J. Hannon*

See also Gideon v. Wainwright; Mapp v. Ohio.

BICAMERALISM, consisting of two elective legislative houses or chambers. On the federal level there are two houses or chambers that comprise the bicameral structure of the Congress: the House of Representatives, or lower house, and the Senate, or upper house. Each of the lower house's 435 members is elected in a congressional district of approximately equal population. The Senate's one hundred members are elected two to a state, regardless of population. All the state legislative bodies are bicameral, except for Nebraska, which adopted its unicameral plan in 1937.

See also Unicameralism.

BILATERALISM in international politics, joint action by two states in response to a particular situation. In international trade, bilateralism is the practice of promoting trade between two countries through specific trade agreements.

BILL, the draft of a proposed law that is subjected to the legislative process before it can become law. On the national level the origin of a bill may be either house of Congress, executive agencies, private pressure groups, special interests, individuals or the White House. However, in all instances the bill is presented in the legislative branch in accordance with Article I, Section 7, of the Constitution.

Ordinary bills are designated with the initials "H.R." or "S." to reflect the house of origin and are consecutively numbered during a Congress. If a bill is jointly sponsored, it is designated "H.J.Res." or "S.J. Res." and termed a resolution. A joint resolution differs from ordinary bills in that it is intended as a temporary measure. Resolutions that pertain to matters of an internal nature in one house or both houses are not submitted to the president for endorsement.

A contemporary Congress entertains some 20,000 bills, but fewer than 1,100 are passed. Bills not acted on during two consecutive sessions are dropped from the record and must be reintroduced for future consideration.   —*Samuel Raphalides*

See also Legislation and the Legislative Process.

BILL OF ATTAINDER, by Supreme Court definition, a legislative act that inflicts punishment without a judicial trial. Attainder, the forfeiture of all property and civil rights after condemnation for treason or a felony, was common practice in Medieval England, and applied to the heirs of the condemned as well. The proscription against bills of attainder under Article I, Section 10 of the Constitution, was meant to ensure that legislatures would define crimes by general statute, leaving the interpretation and application of the law to the courts and the judgment of one's peers.

BILL OF RIGHTS, the first ten amendments to the Constitution, ratified in 1791, protecting certain liberties of the people against encroachment by the national government.

History. The Continental Congress outlined a brief bill of rights when it established the Northwest Territory in 1787. When the Constitutional Convention met in 1787, however, it failed to adopt a bill of rights. The Constitution itself, it was thought, being a bill of rights, there was no need to define further specific rights in a separate listing. It was also assumed that an explicit bill of rights might imply that what was not written down was thereby not a right. George Washington, however, felt constrained to promise that a Bill of Rights would be added to the Constitution, thus bringing support from several of the states for ratification. Following ratification of the Constitution, the states proposed over one hundred amendments to the new Congress, and the first ten amendments were the result.

Analysis. The Bill of Rights refer only to the people's rights against the national government. This doctrine has been affirmed many times since *Barron v. Baltimore,* 1883. The Supreme Court, however, in recent years has made extensive use of the Fourteenth Amendment's due-process clause to "incorporate" selectively most of the specific prohibitions of the first eight amendments against the states themselves. The Court has also broadly construed the Fourteenth Amendment's provision that no state shall deny to people within its jurisdiction "the equal protection of the laws." In a sense the latter clause has also brought to bear the people's rights against the states too.

Thus, constitutionally, the people are today protected in their fundamental rights and liberties against both the national and the state governments. In the final analysis, however, the Court determines the definition and limitations of those rights and liberties and thus the relation-

THE BILL OF RIGHTS

First Amendment

Congress shall make no law respecting an establishment of religion, or prohibiting the free exercise thereof; or abridging the freedom of speech, or of the press; or the right of the people peaceably to assemble, and to petition the Government for a redress of grievances.

Second Amendment

A well regulated Militia, being necessary to the security of a free State, the right of the people to keep and bear Arms, shall not be infringed.

Third Amendment

No soldier shall, in time of peace be quartered in any house, without the consent of the Owner, nor in time of war, but in a manner to be prescribed by law.

Fourth Amendment

The right of the people to be secure in their persons, houses, papers, and effects, against unreasonable searches and seizures, shall not be violated, and no Warrants shall issue, but upon probable cause, supported by Oath or affirmation, and particularly describing the place to be searched, and the persons or things to be seized.

Fifth Amendment

No person shall be held to answer for a capital, or otherwise infamous crime, unless on a presentment or indictment of a Grand Jury, except in cases arising in the land or naval forces, or in the Militia, when in actual service in time of War or public danger; nor shall any person be subject for the same offence to be twice put in jeopardy of life or limb; nor shall be compelled in any criminal case to be a witness against himself, nor be deprived of life, liberty, or property, without due process of law; nor shall private property be taken for public use, without just compensation.

Sixth Amendment

In all criminal prosecutions, the accused shall enjoy the right to a speedy and public trial, by an impartial jury of the State and district wherein the crime shall have been committed, which district shall have been previously ascertained by law, and to be informed of the nature and cause of the accusation; to be confronted with the witnesses against him; to have compulsory process for obtaining witnesses in his favor, and to have the Assistance of Counsel for his defence.

Seventh Amendment

In Suits at common law, where the value in controversy shall exceed twenty dollars, the right of trial by jury shall be preserved, and no fact tried by a jury, shall be otherwise re-examined in any Court of the United States, than according to the rules of the common law.

Eighth Amendment

Excessive bail shall not be required nor excessive fines imposed, nor cruel and unusual punishments inflicted.

Ninth Amendment

The enumeration in the Constitution, of certain rights, shall not be construed to deny or disparage others retained by the people.

Tenth Amendment

The powers not delegated to the United States by the Constitution, nor prohibited by it to the States, are reserved to the States respectively, or to the people.

---

ship of the individual to both governments in the federal system is in constant flux.   —*Erwin L. Levine*

See also Amendment, Constitutional; Barron v. Baltimore; Constitution of the United States; Federalism.

BIPARTISANSHIP. Emerging at the close of World War II, bipartisanship is essentially a consultation between the executive branch and the leaders of both parties in Congress in which the administration shares the responsibility for important decisions in foreign policy making. The Tonkin Gulf Resolution (1964), for example, was purposely sought by President Johnson and adopted by Congress as an indication of the nation's united leadership, or bipartisan support on the issue of policy in Vietnam. Although presidents desire bipartisan support on their domestic programs, it is confined almost exclusively to foreign policy.

BLACKLISTING, in labor, an employer's list of "undesirable" employees who are not to be hired. Usually these workers are considered to be agitators or active union supporters, and employers exchange these lists to effectively ban such workers from an industry. Blacklisting is prohibited by law in many states, and passage of the National Labor Relations Act (1935) made blacklisting a federal offense. However, it is difficult to prosecute or to prevent the exchange of blacklist information between employers.

Blacklisting was used first in labor during the turbulent economic and labor conditions of the 1860s and 1870s. Employers had a bitter view of labor unions and the blacklist was an effective method of excluding unions from their plants. The result was the secret-society nature of many labor unions at this time and the appearance of the professional union organizer—a man employed by the union and so immune to the blacklist. The widespread unionism of the twentieth century has made blacklisting an outmoded method.

Blacklisting was also prevalent in the 1950s as a means of denying employment to individuals accused of "communist affiliation" or "sympathy." A national campaign against presumed communist influence in the United States was led by Sen. Joseph McCarthy. Individuals identified by McCarthy, principally in the arts, government, and academia were blacklisted. Blacklisting while illegal is difficult to uncover and prove.

See also Labor Movement in the United States; McCarthy, Joseph.

BLACKMUN, HARRY ANDREW (1908-), associate justice of the Supreme Court (1970-). Born in Illinois, he was educated at Harvard University, receiving his law degree in 1932. He served as a law clerk for the U.S. Court of Appeals for the 8th circuit, taught law at St. Paul College of Law and the University of Minnesota, and served as counsel for the Mayo Clinic. Appointed judge of the 8th Circuit Court of Appeals by President Dwight D. Eisenhower in 1959, he was nominated to the Supreme Court in 1970 by President Richard Nixon. Known for his scholarly and thorough opinions, he spoke for the majority in *Roe v. Wade* (1973), which struck down anti-abortion laws, maintaining that the Fourteenth Amendment protects a woman's right to privacy regarding abortion. He was generally conservative but also an independent.

BLACK PANTHERS, a militant black group founded in 1966 in Oakland, California. The Panthers initially described themselves as a self-defense organization for protection from police harassment. Demanding control of their own institutions, the Panthers called for all-black juries, an end to police brutality, better education and housing, the release of all black prisoners, and full employment.

BLACK SHIRTS, name commonly applied to members of the Italian fascist movement. *See* Fascism.

BLOC, a coalition of legislators interested in fostering or obstructing legislative action. Generally, blocs reflect interest group pressure and transcend party lines. An example of such a group is the farm bloc, comprised of representatives from largely agricultural states, which seeks to gain support for legislation beneficial to farmers.

BLOCK GRANT. *See* Revenue Sharing.

BLUE-RIBBON JURY, or special jury is a petit jury selected for its special qualifications to try a particular case, either because the case is too complex for a regular jury, or because some expert knowledge is required. Special juries existed from the earliest period of development of the common law and were common in London by the mid-fourteenth century. Because of the modern emphasis on impartial selection of jurors, special juries have fallen into disfavor. They were abolished in the United States federal courts in 1968.

BOARD OF EDUCATION v. ALLEN, 392 U.S. 236 (1968), concerns a New York State law which required local public school authorities to lend textbooks free of charge to all students in parochial and private schools in the grades seven through twelve. A local board of education sought to bar Allen, a state education official, from apportioning state funds to school districts for the purchase of such textbooks. In the opinion of the Court, the statute did not entail unconstitutional assistance of religious instruction by the state, nor was it a law respecting the establishment of religion. The Court also disagreed with the board's contentions that secular textbooks furnished to parochial school students become instruments in the teaching of religion. Instead, the Court adhered to its "child benefit theory," which permits those forms of aid to parochial school students whose purpose is primarily to benefit the child and his education rather than religion.

See also Abington School District v. Schempp; Everson v. Board of Education.

BOLLING v. SHARPE, 347 U.S. 497 (1954). In this case, black children challenged the constitutionality of enforced segregation in the public schools of the District of Columbia. The challenge presented a different legal problem from that of the state segregation cases *(Brown v. Board of Education)* decided the same day. The equal protection clause of the Fourteenth Amendment, which the Court used to strike down state-imposed segregation, did not apply to the federal government in the District of Columbia.

Chief Justice Warren, speaking for a unanimous Court, declared that the due process clause of the Fifth Amendment rendered federally segregated schools unconstitutional. In doing so, Warren resurrected a substantive definition of due process, namely that the content of certain laws (their "substance") can be determined by the Court to run counter to the Fifth Amendment's prohibition against taking "life, liberty or property without due process of law." In 1937, the Supreme Court had rejected this view of due process. But in this case, Warren revived the clause as a safeguard against unacceptable social legislation. —*David Forte*

See also Brown v. Board of Education.

BOSS. *See* Machine, Political.

BOYCOTT, in labor, economic pressure by a union against an employer; union members refuse to patronize or do business with the employer or handle his products or supplies. The term originates from Captain Charles Boycott, an agent for an Irish landlord in the 1880s: his tenants, angered by harsh treatment, refused to speak to Boycott, work for him, bring him supplies, or help him. Boycott action may be extended to parties not directly involved (secondary boycott). Secondary boycott is an unfair labor practice under the Taft-Hartley Act (1947) and has been virtually outlawed by the Landrum-Griffin Act (1959).

The Order of the Knights of Labor used the boycott, rather than strikes, against troublesome employers. By the distribution of "unfair" lists, the order effectively boycotted certain stores, saloons, and food and clothing suppliers. These successes moved employers to form the Antiboycott Association in 1902 as part of the campaign against unionism.

A particularly famous example of a boycott was the Pullman strike. A more recent boycott in support of unionism was the consumer boycott of grapes shipped by nonunion California growers. The boycott was organized by Cesar Chavez in the late 1960s to emphasize the need for unionization of agricultural workers.

See also Labor Movement in the United States; Landrum-Griffin Act; Taft-Hartley Act.

BRANDEIS, LOUIS D. (1856-1941), served as associate justice of the United States Supreme Court from 1916, when he was appointed by President Woodrow Wilson, until 1939. Born in Louisville, Ky., Brandeis was educated in public schools, and in the severe academic discipline of Dresden, Germany, and at Harvard Law School. He gained recognition for his expertise in litigation when he undertook the practice of law in Boston. Brandeis disdained the traditional lawyer's belief, which was filled with narrow procedural points. Instead, he filled his legal presentations with social and economic arguments. "The Brandeis brief" became the label given to his type of argumentation. While he was a lawyer, he became an ardent Zionist. Once on the Court, Brandeis became immediately associated with Justice Oliver Wendell Holmes, Jr., for his advocacy of judicial restraint. Brandeis believed that legislative regulations in the economic sphere were necessary but he held that the judicial branch had to remain aloof from them (*Truax v. Corrigan,* 257 U.S. 312 [1921], dissenting). The thorough scholar, Brandeis' opinions were filled with cross-references and footnotes, for the man never shook himself of the importance of the facts involved in any social or legal issue.

Brandeis is also associated with Holmes in the formulation of the "clear and present danger" test in regard to laws restricting speech and press, although, if anything, Brandeis was more emphatic in his defense of the First Amendment freedoms (*Whitney v. California,* 274 U.S. 357 [1927]). Nonetheless, Brandeis is still generally placed in the tradition of judicial restraint. He consistently argued for a limited role in judicial decision-making (*Ashwander v. TVA,* 297 U.S. 288 [1936]), and he was a dedicated defender of federalism.

—*David Forte*

BRANDENBURG v. OHIO, 395 U.S. 444 (1969), concerns the constitutionality of Ohio's Criminal Syndicalism Act, which purported to punish mere advocacy and to forbid assembly with others merely to advocate illegal action. Brandenburg, a leader of a Ku Klux Klan group, was convicted under the Ohio statute for his participation in and speech at a KKK rally at which some members carried weapons. The Court held that the constitutional guarantees of free speech do not permit a state to forbid or proscribe advocacy except where such advocacy is directed to inciting or producing imminent lawless action and is likely to do so. Accordingly, the Ohio statute which, by its own words and as applied, purports to punish mere advocacy and to forbid assembly with others on pain of criminal punishment, falls within the condemnation of the First and Fourteenth Amendments. This decision overrules the contrary teaching of *Whitney v. California.*

See also Dennis v. United States.

BRENNAN, WILLIAM JOSEPH, JR. (1906-   ), associate justice of the Supreme Court (1956-1990). Born in New Jersey, he studied at the University of Pennsylvania and Harvard Law School before entering private law practice and specializing in labor law. He was appointed to the New Jersey Superior Court (1949-1952) after his leadership in a movement for state judicial reform and, during this time, moved to the appellate division. From 1952 he served on the state supreme court. Appointed by President Dwight D. Eisenhower to the U.S. Supreme Court in 1956, he became known as an articulate judicial scholar on the activist Warren Court. A liberal, he advocated upholding rights under the First Amendment, opposing restriction of rights of witnesses appearing before the House Committee on Un-American Activities (*Barenblatt v. United States,* 1961) and defending the rights of revolutionary groups (*Scales v. United States,* 1961) and subversive groups (*Communist Party v. Subversive Activities Control Board,* 1961). He also voted to uphold the constitutionality of the Voting Rights Act of 1965 (*Katzenbach v. Morgan,* 1966). On the more conservative Burger Court he was largely confined to writing dissents, as in *Regents of the University of California v. Bakke* (1978).

BRICKER AMENDMENT PROPOSAL (1953), a constitutional amendment submitted by John W. Bricker, three-term Republican governor and two-term senator for Ohio (1946). The proposal was expressly designed to nullify presidential power in the conduct of foreign affairs. The terms would have delegated to Congress, and in some cases the states, the job of enforcing within the United States all international agreements concluded by the President and not sanctioned by treaty. A McCarthy-era move to counteract "one-world" and "procommunist" deals and to prevent future Potsdam and Yalta "sellouts," the proposal was soundly defeated. However, it raised a major question of the postwar era that again crystallized around the Vietnam war: how can Congress assert its control over a president who chooses to run a virtually autonomous foreign policy?

BROOKINGS INSTITUTION, research and educational organization that analyzes economic, government, and foreign policy questions. Brookings, considered to be Washington's moderate-to-liberal think tank, seeks to provide independent research and criticism on public policy issues. Its activities are supported by grants and endowment.

BROWN v. BOARD OF EDUCATION, 349 U.S. 294

(1955). Having decided in *Brown v. Board of Education of Topeka* (1954) that state-imposed segregation violates the Fourteenth Amendment, the Court asked for reargument concerning the manner of state compliance which the Court should require. In this case, the rules of compliance were set forth.

The Supreme Court left the timing of desegregation up to federal district courts in the South with the following guidelines: (1) additional time may be granted to a district in carrying out desegregation; (2) the burden, however, was on the school district to show that it was acting in good faith; and (3) the district courts may also consider devices in their desegregation orders, including "the school transportation system, personnel, revision of school districts and attendance areas into compact units to achieve a system of determining admission to the public schools on a nonracial basis." Finally, the Supreme Court instructed the lower courts to require that "all deliberate speed" be used in desegregating school systems.

For many years after this decision, several Southern states delayed instituting desegregation orders. It was not until the end of the 1960s that a combination of congressional civil rights acts, executive pressure, and judicial exasperation marked the end of officially sanctioned segregation in the South. — *David Forte*
See also Civil Rights Acts; Civil Rights Movement.

BROWN v. BOARD OF EDUCATION OF TOPEKA,

347 U.S. 483 (1954), one of a series of cases in which several black children contested state laws permitting or requiring the establishment of separate school facilities based on race.

History. These cases were first argued in 1952, but following the death of chief Justice Frederick M. Vinson and his replacement by Earl Warren, the Court asked for reargument. In a unanimous opinion written by the new Chief Justice, the Court held that all state laws segregating children in public schools because of their race were invalid by virtue of the equal protection of the laws clause of the Fourteenth Amendment to the Constitution. Warren chose to base his opinion on contemporary sociological evidence. He did not assert that the Fourteenth Amendment was, since its ratification, designed to outlaw such discrimination. Rather, he stated, "To separate [Negroes] from others of similar age and qualifications solely because of their race generates a feeling of inferiority as to their status in a community that may affect their hearts and minds in a way unlikely ever to be undone." In *Plessy v. Ferguson* (1896), which this decision overruled, the majority said that separation did not imply inferiority. In this case, Warren said that it did.

Analysis. Warren not only suggested that legally required separation was unconstitutional, he stated that separation by any means was unconstitutional. This has led the Supreme Court into the difficult issue of deciding whether or not de facto segregation is as unconstitutional as de jure segregation and whether the constitution not only prohibits the legal separation of the races but also requires their social intermingling.

The decision in this case eventually brought about vast social changes in the South and, after Congress had enacted numerous civil rights acts, in the rest of the nation as well. — *David Forte*
See also Civil Rights Acts; Plessy v. Ferguson.

BRYAN, WILLIAM JENNINGS (1860-1925),

Democratic leader, popular orator, journalist, lawyer, religious writer and lecturer, three times unsuccessful candidate for president. An eloquent speaker in the flamboyant style of his time, Bryan voiced the sentiments of the common man beset by the forces of special privilege. Born in Salem, Ill., he obtained his law degree in 1883 and married Mary Baird, an educated woman who became his poltiical and business adviser.

After four years practicing law he moved to Nebraska, where he was elected to Congress in 1890 and 1892. Running for the Senate in 1893 and 1895 on a platform of free coinage of silver, tariff reform, and a tax on income, he lost to the Republicans. At the 1896 Chicago Convention of the Democratic Party his "cross of gold" speech won him the nomination and the en-

William Jennings Bryan, Democratic presidential candidate in 1896 and 1900, was a popular orator.

dorsement of three minor parties. The contest that year climaxed the conflict between the Southern-Western rural areas and the industrial-financial concentrations of the Northeast. William McKinley, a Republican, won by a narrow margin. Following the war with Spain, Bryan was again the Democratic candidate, attacking American expansionism. Again he lost to McKinley. From 1896 to 1913 Bryan led the progressive Democrats against the conservatives in his own party and the Republicans in office. He published the weekly *Commoner*, won nomination for the presidency in 1908, and lost to Taft.

In 1912 Bryan threw his influence to Woodrow Wilson, who upon election rewarded Bryan with the post of secretary of state. A neutralist, he opposed the "strict accountability" policy toward Germany and resigned in 1915. After war was declared he supported Wilson. Bryan favored the Eighteenth and Nineteenth Amendments but opposed entry into the League of Nations. His political influence declining, he published extensive religious commentaries, lectured on the Chautauqua circuit, and preached against the theory of evolution. Loved by evangelists and hated by scientists, in 1925 he joined the prosecution at the Scopes "evolution" trial in Tennessee, facing Clarence Darrow for the defense. He died five days later, a millionaire from real estate speculations.

BUCHANAN, JAMES (1791-1868), 15th President of the United States (1857-1861), born near Mercersburg, Pa. Initially a Federalist, he joined the Democratic Party in the 1820s and experienced many political successes, eventually becoming secretary of state in 1845. A compromise presidential candidate in 1856, he won the election by straddling the slavery question but was soon embroiled in the issues. He pleaded ineffectually for compromise when South Carolina seceded from the Union and stalled at reinforcing Fort Sumter when war was imminent.

See also Presidential Elections.

BUCHANAN v. WARLEY, 245 U.S. 60 (1917), concerns the right of a property owner to convey his property to a person of another race. A Louisville, Ky., city ordinance made it illegal for a black person to occupy a residence on a block predominantly inhabited by white persons, and vice versa. Buchanan, a white man, brought suit to enforce a contract for the sale of certain real estate to Warley, a black, who resisted, saying he would not be allowed to occupy the lot as a place of residence. The Court upheld the contract and found the city ordinance unconstitutional, stating that alienation of the property to a person of color violated the Fourteenth Amendment, which prevents state interference with property rights except by the due process of law. Here the Court pointed to the chief inducement to passage of the Fourteenth Amendment, which was the desire to extend federal protection to the recently emancipated race from unfriendly and discriminating legislation by the states.

See also Plessy v. Ferguson; Shelley v. Kraemer.

BUCKLEY v. VALEO, 424 U.S. 1 (1976), case in which the Supreme Court upheld the provision of the 1974 Federal Election Campaign Act which limits campaign contributions by individuals and groups, as well as its provision requiring public disclosure of all contributions over $100. These were marginal restrictions of First Amendment freedoms justified by the need to prevent corruption and the appearance of corruption. The Court also upheld public financing of presidential campaigns and spending limits on presidential candidates who accept that financing, but it struck down limits on spending by candidates not receiving public financing. The Federal Election Commission itself was declared unconstitutional because, with a majority of its officers appointed by congressional leaders, its structure violated the separation of powers.

BUDGET AND ACCOUNTING ACT (1921) set up a national Bureau of the Budget and a General Accounting Office (GAO). In 1939 the bureau was put under the office of the president and in 1970 the bureau's duties were shifted to the Office of Management and Budget. The GAO remains an independent regulatory agency in the legislative branch; the GAO's decisions are binding on the executive branch only, and their legality may be reviewed by the attorney general. By providing for an annual executive budget from the president and for a public and congressional review of expenditures via the comptroller general and the GAO, the law ended the prevailing anarchy in the determination of appropriations and established a system for measuring the relative performance and priority of competing government programs. As of June 1921 no department is permitted to submit budget estimates or to request funds directly from Congress, although the departments must appear with data before congressional fiscal committees when requested to do so.

See also General Accounting Office (GAO); Management and Budget, Office of.

BUDGET AND IMPOUNDMENT ACT OF 1974, legislation that set up a procedure and structure to allow Congress to overcome the fragmentation of the existing authorizing and appropriating process. In addition, the Congress enacted this law to restrict presidential use or misuse of impoundment.

The act moved the beginning of the fiscal year by one quarter (three months) from July 1 to October 1, allowing more time for congressional consideration of the budget. A budget timetable was established that included two concurrent resolutions (May and September) that allow Congress to set expenditure limits and priorities in each of the functional areas of the budget. These resolutions are used as guidelines that, when necessary,

would limit appropriations. Senate and House Budget Committees were established to prepare the resolutions for floor action. In addition, a non-partisan congressional agency, The Congressional Budget Office (CBO), was established to provide Congress with an independent analysis of the budget, including alternative budgets to the one prepared by the president. If the president wishes not to spend allocated funds (impoundment), he must receive within 45 days the approval of both houses of the Congress. If he does not receive such approval, he is obligated to spend the funds in the manner intended. The Budget and Impoundment Act was passed not only to allow Congress a comprehensive approach to the budget process, but to reassert or rebalance congressional and presidential power.
— *Guy C. Colarulli and Victor F. D'Lugin*

BUDGET BUREAU. *See* Management and Budget, Office of.

BUDGET MESSAGE. The president is required to submit the annual budget to Congress within the first fifteen days of each regular session spelling out the functions and activities of the government and reconciling actual and proposed expenditures with appropriations. The president must include budgets for Congress and the Supreme Court as submitted to him, and must provide information and recommendations on the national debt. The Office of Management and Budget assists the president and coordinates budgets from all government agencies and departments.

See also Budget and Accounting Act; Economic Message, President's.

BULL MOOSE PARTY. *See* Progressive, or Bull Moose, Party.

BUNCHE, RALPH (1904-1971), U.S. government and U.N. official. Bunche was born in Detroit and educated at U.C.L.A. and Harvard, from which he received a doctorate in 1934. He served as chief assistant to the renowned Swedish sociologist Gunnar Myrdal and entered government service during World War II with the Office of Strategic Services and the U.S. State Department. Bunche joined the United Nations as an international civil servant to direct the Trusteeship Division. He was then appointed to the U.N. Palestine Commission and became its chief mediator in 1948. His efforts at negotiating the Arab-Israeli conflict won him the Nobel Peace Prize in 1950. Bunche was the first black to receive the award. Bunche continued to hold a number of high-level U.N. posts until his retirement in 1967.

BUREAU OF . . . *See* second part of name.

BURGER, WARREN EARL (1907-   ), 15th Chief Justice of the Supreme Court (1969-1986). Born in

Warren Earl Burger, 15th Chief Justice of the Supreme Court.

Minnesota, he graduated from St. Paul (now Mitchell) College of Law. He was admitted to the Minnesota bar (1931); taught law at Mitchell (1931-1948), at the same time practicing law privately; and became active in state Republican politics. Under President Dwight D. Eisenhower he served as assistant attorney general (1953--1955) and on the U.S. Court of Appeals for the District of Columbia (1955-1969). There he was known as an advocate of "law and order," a conservative, and a strict constructionist, stressing the need to follow the established rules regarding evidence rather than adapting and changing the rules for each case.

Chief Justice. Named chief justice of the Supreme Court by President Richard M. Nixon in 1969, Burger fought for equality of justice, especially concerning criminal justice, and for judicial reform, to be achieved by more efficient administration of the system. He upheld the limitation of defendant's rights in criminal cases in *Harris v. New York* (1971), and he dissented in *Furman v. Georgia* (1972), disagreeing with the Court's majority opinion that capital punishment in its then-present form was unconstitutional. It was a unanimous Burger Court that ruled that President Nixon make available incriminating White House tape recordings to the special prosecutor of the Watergate hearings (1974). In 1981 *(Chandler et al v. Florida)*, Burger wrote the opinion that television cameras inside the courtroom did not violate the Constitution. The Burger Court became less conservative through the 1980s. Justice Burger retired in 1986 and headed the Commission on the Bicentennial of the United States Constitution.

BURKE, EDMUND (1729-1797), British Whig politician, philosopher, writer, and conservative reformist. Burke was born in Ireland but went to London in 1750 to prepare for the law. He turned to politics and was elected in 1765 to Parliament, where he served until shortly before his death.

Burke was critical of British policy in Ireland, India, and the American colonies. Although he advocated reformist principles, Burke believed in a limited franchise in which power was exercised by the wealthy, educated upper classes. Burke's reverence for the state and established institutions led him to condemn the French revolution in his most famous work, *Reflections on the Revolution in France* (1790). He argued that the revolution had changed society without preparation by destroying its established institutions. Burke's thesis provoked a number of pro-revolutionary works, the most famous of which was Tom Paine's *Rights of Man*.

BUSH, GEORGE (HERBERT WALKER) (1924-   ), 41st President of the United States (1989-   ). Vice President (1981-1989). Born in Milton, Mass., he was the son of a wealthy stockbroker. After service in the Navy during World War II, he attended Yale University (1948), then set up a successful oil and gas business in Texas.

Active in the Republican Party in Texas, Bush lost a

George Bush, 41st President of the United States.

contest for the U.S. Senate in 1964, but was elected to the House of Representatives in 1966. After losing another Senate bid in 1970, he was selected by President Nixon to be U.N. ambassador. Appointed chairman of the Republican National Committee in 1973, Bush served during the darkest days of the Watergate scandal, and it was his duty to advise Nixon to resign. President Ford appointed Bush to direct the Central Intelligence Agency in 1976.

Bush announced his candidacy for the presidency in 1979, but could not deter the momentum of Ronald Reagan's campaign. Bush was selected as Reagan's running mate at the convention, and the two went on to win a landslide victory over the Carter-Mondale ticket. Initially widely distrusted by Republican conservatives, Bush worked hard to demonstrate his loyalty to the President and gradually assumed a prominent role in the administration. Reelected in 1984, Bush easily won the Republican presidential nomination in 1988. He handily defeated his Democratic opponent Michael Dukakis. Early in his administration he won general public approval for meeting with Soviet leader Gorbachev and for the invasion of Panama.

BUSINESS REGULATION IN THE UNITED STATES. Business enterprises in the United States are extensively regulated by all levels of government. Government has always regulated American business practices, beginning with court decisions under common law and subsequently progressing to statutory laws. For example, states have been regulating banking since 1838, railroads since 1844, and insurance companies since 1854. By 1877 the states had statutes requiring certain safety conditions of employment. In 1890 the federal government passed legislation aimed at preserving competition. Direct protection of the consumer was undertaken in the early part of the twentieth century by a series of federal laws.

Government regulation of business stems from the inherent need for rules and regulations under which competition is to be exercised by institutions in a free society, the undesirable concentrations of economic power resulting from monopolies, the unethical practices by unfettered businessmen that result in economic or personal loss by individuals, and inherent conflicts of the business firm and the public interest, for example, pollution of a river or the atmosphere.

Methods of Government Regulation commonly employed are:

1. Statutory Laws These laws are specific ones passed by legislative bodies, such as Congress, a state legislature, or a city council. Such laws cover either general business practice or deal specifically with a particular industry. A law applicable to all industries is the Clayton Antitrust Act of 1914, which prohibits monopoly and collusion. An example of the second type is the Pure Food and Drug Act, applicable to the food processing industries.

2. Establishment of Governmental Agencies. For effective enforcement of statutory laws governmental agencies are established to perform as watchdog and act as interpreter of the provisions and applicability of these laws. An example of a federal regulatory agency would be the Federal Trade Commission. A state bureau of weights and measures is an illustration of a state regulatory agency.

3. Promulgation of Administrative Rules, Regulations, and Guidelines. As pointed out, governments pass regulatory laws and then set up agencies to enforce them. In many cases, regulatory laws are general in character and regulatory agencies must make specific rules for the guidance of business institutions, subject to judicial review. An example of administrative law would be a ruling by the Food and Drug Administration on the procedure of a pharmaceutical firm in testing a newly developed drug before its final release.

4. Court Rulings interpreting either statutory laws, administrative laws, or adjudication arising under common law. The most common regulatory functions of the judiciary are interpretation of laws and punitive actions for failure to comply with specific laws.

Methods of Regulatory Enforcement used by governments are:

1. Revocation of the license or privilege to do business. This measure is the ultimate weapon at the government's disposal. It is particularly effective in the area of such highly regulated industries as banking, finance, transportation, and communication. In the case of a new business, this type of compliance technique may take the form of refusal to grant a license until such time as the business complies with the requirements of the law.

2. Cease and Desist Orders. Such orders are issued formally by regulatory agencies and specifically forbid a business to continue a practice that is contrary to the law.

3. Jail Sentences, secured through the courts and imposed on the businessman who fails to comply with the law. Jail sentences can be used only under certain conditions and at the discretion of the courts.

4. Fines may be levied against the firm or the businessman independently or in conjunction with a jail sentence.

5. Publicity. Most businessmen attempt to avoid adverse publicity because it shows a company or its products in an adverse light and hurts sales. The mere threat of public hearings may be sufficient to bring about compliance with the law.

Common Areas. The thousands of examples of regulation of business by federal, state, and local governments might usefully be grouped under seven major headings.

1. Preservation and Promotion of Competition. Various laws promoting competitive conditions can be grouped under three headings: (a) the prevention of monopoly (Sherman, Clayton, and Celler-Kefauver acts), (b) the prevention of collusion between businesses, particularly in pricing practices (Federal Trade Commis-

sion and Robinson-Patman acts), and (c) the prevention of unfair competitive practices such as patent infringement, deceptive advertising, and selling below costs (Wheeler-Lea Act).

2. Protection of the Consumer. Various statutory laws designed to protect the public could be grouped under two broad categories as follows: (a) quality level of products as related to public health and safety (Food and Drugs, Flammable Fabrics, and National Traffic and Motor Vehicle Safety acts), (b) protection of public from fraud and deception (Wool Products Labeling, Consumer Credit Protection, and Securities acts).

3. General Environmental Quality (Water Pollution Control and National Air Quality acts).

4. Direct Regulation. A major form of regulation of business institutions by government is the power of licensing and certifying firms to do business. Although requirements are usually not difficult to meet, all business must be licensed, and if a corporate form of organization is used, they must be chartered. State and local governments generally control licensing and chartering. In addition to being licensed, some types of businesses must be certified to do business (commercial banks, radio and television stations, and public utilities, for example). Certification requirements are often stringent. In addition, governmental agencies regulate rates and services of many quasi-public corporations, such as electric utilities, telephone utilities and transportation companies.

5. Labor Relations and Working Conditions (National Labor Relations, Civil Rights, and Landrum-Griffin acts).

6. Comprehensive Overall Economic Emergency Controls. In times of national emergency, as defined by Congress, the federal government has been given overall economic powers to set and control all prices charged and wages paid by business firms and to allocate scarce materials and commodities to firms. These direct control regulations have been imposed three times since 1940: during World War II (1942-1946); the Korean War (1950-1953); and the Vietnam War with the imposition of a wage-price freeze (1971).

7. Regulation of International Trade. For businesses having international oeprations or importing goods, there are a variety of governmental controls in the forms of tariffs, import duties, and import quotas.

One of the announced policy concerns of the Reagan administration was to decrease the amount and kind of government regulation of the private sector. To this end, President Reagan appointed as administrators of many federal agencies individuals who sought to narrow the scope and jurisdiction of the agency and proposed legislation that would eliminate statutory obligations or limit the area of authority of many federal agencies. Much of the statutory deregulation that has been achieved to date, however, results from the Carter administration's efforts such as the Carrier Deregulation Act of 1978 and the Monetary Decontrol Act of 1980.

—*Algin B. King*

See also articles on individual regulatory agencies, statutes, and rulings.

BUSINESS ROUNDTABLE, an interest group coalition consisting of the chief executive officers of major U.S. corporations. The Roundtable produces reports on public policy issues that have an impact on the business economy. The Roundtable also attempts to develop and articulate economic principles that reflect the views of major business organizations.

CABINET, term commonly used to denote the heads (secretaries) of the fourteen current executive departments of the United States (state, treasury, defense, justice, interior, agriculture, commerce, labor, health and human services, housing and urban development, education, energy, transportation, and veterans affairs). The meeting of all the secretaries to advise and consult with the president is known as a cabinet meeting. The president may, at his discretion, name other government officials (such as the ambassador to the U.N.) as cabinet-level officers. The cabinet has no legal or constitutional function being rooted rather in custom and usage of the presidents. The heads of the executive departments are appointed by the president, with Senate confirmation. The clause "he may require the opinion in writing, of the principal officers in each of the executive departments" (Article II, Section 2) is the constitutional justification of direct presidential, administrative control over the secretaries and their departments. Traditionally, the secretaries of the departments serve at the president's pleasure.

Functions. The secretaries have two primary functions. First, the secretaries preside over the work of their departments as authorized and funded by Congress but under presidential direction of broad policy. Second, the secretaries present the views of the hierarchy of their departments to each other and to the president. For the most part cabinet secretaries are political appointees with views generally in line with those of the president and often drawn from the clientele groups with whom the departments have direct relationships, reflecting American pluralism.

History. Presidents have used their cabinets differently. President Dwight D. Eisenhower (1953-1960), for example, often used the cabinet as a fully developed body of advisors on a wide range of governmental policies, in line with his team approach. Presidents since John F. Kennedy have made little use of the cabinet as a collective body of advisers, preferring to deal more personally with individual secretaries and their departments.

Historically, the most recent cabinet posts created are the heads of the departments of Energy, Education,

PRESIDENTIAL CABINET

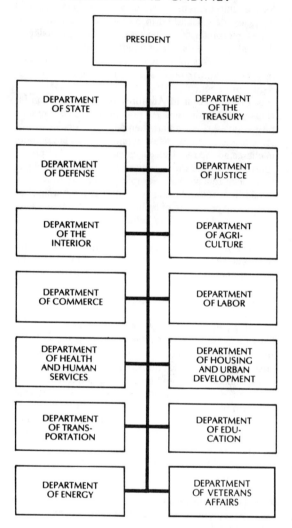

and Veterans Affairs. President Bush proposed in 1990 to elevate the Environmental Protection Agency to cabinet rank.

—*Erwin L. Levine*

See also Executive Branch.

CALENDAR, a list of the bills to be considered in the Senate or the House. In the House when a bill is reported out of committee, it is placed on one of five calendars: noncontroversial bills are placed on the *Consent Calendar;* bills withdrawn from committee by petition, on the *Discharge Calendar;* nonfiscal public bills, on the *House Calendar;* private bills, on the *Private Calendar;* and appropriation and revenue bills, on the *Union Calendar.* In the Senate all bills go on a single calendar, except for treaties and confirmations, which go on the *Executive Calendar*. The House of Representatives follows a procedure whereby Wednesdays (Calendar Wednesdays) may be used to call the roll of the standing committees in order to bring up bills for consideration from the calendars.

CALHOUN, JOHN CALDWELL (1782-1850), Vice President of the United States, legislator, political philosopher and leader, advocate of states' rights and the extension of slavery. Representative with Daniel Webster and Henry Clay of the diverse post-revolutionary leaders who debated the issues leading into the Civil War, Calhoun was born in Abbeville, S.C., of a poor farming family. He graduated from Yale in 1804 and was admitted to the bar in South Carolina, where in 1807 he began law practice. He was elected to the state legislature in 1808. He married Floride Bonneau Calhoun, a wealthy cousin whose social snub of a cabinet officer's wife later infuriated President Andrew Jackson.

Calhoun was elected to Congress in 1811 and joined the young hawks favoring war with England. His bellicose nationalism earned an appointment as Secretary of War in Monroe's cabinet in 1817. In 1825 he became Vice President under John Quincy Adams and was elected to the same office in 1828 in the Jackson administration. Calhoun's earlier position had changed to one of sectionalism, and in defending the Southern planters against high tariffs, he broke with Jackson. Calhoun introduced his doctrine of nullification, holding that a state might interpose its sovereignty to overrule an act of Congress. Calhoun resigned from the vice-presidency in 1832 to run for the senate, where he remained until 1843. As Secretary of State under Tyler in 1844, Calhoun, seeking more slave territory, favored the annexation of Texas, a policy which led to war with Mexico. A year later he returned to the Senate, where he stayed until his death in 1850.

Although he served the South as an apologist for chattel slavery and sought to extend it westward, he was not a secessionist: his final address to the Senate concerned the preservation of the Union. Calhoun supported the "peculiar institution" of slavery when it was already an unpalatable anachronism. An otherwise attractive and influential leader, he tried to fashion a strong federal government of states unwilling to renounce independence.

CAMPAIGN, POLITICAL, an effort to secure the designation or election of a candidate or the adoption of proposals. Parties mount extensive publicity and precinct efforts to sell their nominees, programs, and the parties themselves.

Do Campaigns Really Change Votes? In July 1948 Dr. George Gallup's pat negative answer to this question led him and other pollsters to misread the signs during the Dewey-Truman campaign. Gallup felt that events between elections and habitual loyalties were much more decisive. Uncommitted voters were assumed to go eventually in about equal members to the two parties.

Although voters listen to campaigns mostly to confirm what they already think, campaigns do serve to increase the voter turnout and to arouse latent loyalties. Truman in 1948 and Humphrey in 1968 appealed to traditional voting patterns; large turnout ordinarily favors the Democrats, whose supporters are hard to mobilize.

To Run for Office or to Stand for Office? It has become an aspect of Americana to conduct vigorous electoral campaigns. The Federalists died in part because they could not stoop to huckstering. John Quincy Adams' dignified appeal did not stand a chance against Jacksonian rabblerousing.

There are occasions, though, when the public responds to an above-the-battle stance. An incumbent president, especially during wartime, is able to pose as statesman, being too busy for a fulltime campaign.

Strategies, Slogans and Songs: Naturals and Washouts. While the factors that influence the outcome of elections are complex and varied, campaign managers often seek a theme to sway great numbers of voters. Such standbys as "It's time for a change," "You've never had it so good," and "Law and Order" are perennials but each campaign has its search for what will get a gut reaction from voters.

In 1840 the Whigs succeeded in transforming a patrician candidate into the embodiment of the common man while painting his rival as "Van, Van the used up man." In 1884 the Democrats exploited a Republican misfire (alleging that the Democratic party stood for "Rum, Romanism and Rebellion") while hammering away at "Blaine, Blaine, Continental Liar from the State of Maine."

Short slogans like the Republican 1896 pledge of a "full dinner pail" (after the depression of 1893) or the Democrats' 1916 assertion that Wilson "kept us out of war" (implying that his reelection would perpetuate neutrality) or the GOP's 1920 evocation "back to normalcy" provide comfort without being commitments to specific policies.

In 1932 the Democrats could resurrect Republican slogans ("Two chickens in every pot," "Prosperity is just around the corner") to cook the opposition in its own juice.

In 1940 the party in power urged: "Don't change horses in the middle of the stream." By 1946, after fourteen years of Democratic ascendency their opponents intoned: "Had enough? Vote Republican." Still in the opposition in 1952, the GOP's crusader, Eisenhower, vowed to "clean up the mess" and "go to Korea."

By 1960 the Democratic critic of the Eisenhower years, Kennedy, pledged to "get America moving again" and to correct "the missile gap."

Direct Approach or Media Approach? In 1896 the two presidential candidates used quite distinct modes of campaigning. McKinley presented himself on his front porch to visitors who journeyed to see him. The underdog Bryan made a cross-country whistle-stop tour to bring his case to the voters. In both instances the object was exposure without overexposure.

Today's candidates and their managers have the same need to fashion an image. Walkathons and talkathons, campaign biographies (as well as "truth teams" to follow opposition candidates around), special appeals (to ethnic, regional, economic, and cultural groups), and smear tactics (candidates are fair game; retractions come too late, and organizations to referee fair campaign practices lack appropriate sanctions) are all means to this end.

There has been a revival of the "great debates." Presidential candidates from 1964 through 1972 shied away from the debate; however, in 1976, Gerald Ford, an unelected president, agreed to meet Jimmy Carter in three debates. Their running mates, Robert Dole and Walter Mondale, also confronted one another. In 1980, Jimmy Carter avoided crossing verbal swords with Edward Kennedy during the nomination season. With a close election in prospect and with the precedent of the Carter-Ford debates, Carter and challenger Reagan had a televised debate in which Reagan appeared to be the winner. In 1984, challenger Mondale, who participated in a series of debates with the Democratic contenders, advocated a set of exchanges between himself and Reagan. The more stage-sure President agreed to two. Debates have become a fixture in presidential elections. The 1988 debates between Bush and Dukakis and the vice presidential candidates, Quayle and Bentsen, were characterized by considerable rancor.

A modern campaign has both centripetal and centrifugal tendencies. The new politics, making use of opinion polling and computer analysis tell the candidate when, where, how, and whom to woo, is based on centralized resources. In order to circumvent laws limiting amounts of campaign funds, as well as to generate a broad range of support, a number of temporary, specialized, localized campaign committees are created.

Campaign Financing and Its Implications. The high cost of campaigning has in recent years driven incumbents into retirement and parties into virtual bankruptcy. The 1925 Federal Corrupt Practices Act and the 1940 Hatch Act had glaring loopholes, making a mockery of attempts to regulate funding and spending. Primary campaigns and the presidential nomination process were not covered. Dummy organizations and delayed reporting concealed the sources and amounts of contributions. Penalties were rarely invoked.

The Revenue Act of 1971 adopted two long-advocated steps to encourage more small contributions to political campaigns by permitting limited tax deductions and by authorizing the financing of presidential elections (beginning with 1976) through $1 tax check-offs for one's party or for a non-partisan fund.

In 1972 a new Federal Election Campaign Act included improved contribution-disclosure and reporting provisions and covered prenomination campaigning. Realizing that previous legislation contained easily evaded ceilings on individuals' contributions and total party expenditures, the Congress opted for severe limits to expenditures for television, radio, telephone campaigns, newspapers, magazines, and billboards.

Public funding of presidential elections and restrictions on individual contributions led interest groups to put their economic muscle behind Political Action Committees (PACs). These conduits for contributions were criticized for distorting the political process through buying influence on Capitol Hill or through negative campaigning. Common Cause noted that the 20 members of the Senate Finance Committee received over $10 million from PACs in their most recent election. Although PACs are limited by law to a maximum contribution of $5,000 per candidate, there are some 4,000 PACs from which congressmen may solicit funds. Some reformers have proposed partial public funding for political contributions. However, most incumbents are reelected and have little enthusiasm for legislation that would encourage opposition.

Do Election Day Projections Bias the Results? Election night 1980 witnessed the phenomenon of a presidential candidate conceding defeat while the polls were still open in parts of the country. Early returns from the eastern states, coupled with exit polls from the rest of the country, foreshadowed the defeat that the Carter camp had come to expect from poll findings the weekend before election day. Even before the concession statement, the networks vied with one another to prophesy the election outcome. Afterwards, critics, mostly but not exclusively Democrats, speculated on what could be done to prevent a recurrence of this situation. Some felt that restrictions of election coverage were in violation of the First Amendment. Others felt the networks should participate in a voluntary agreement to forgo projecting winners and losers. Yet others urged a common 24-hour election period throughout the country, with polls opening and closing simultaneously nationwide so that no early results would contaminate the decision to vote in the western states. In 1984 and 1988 the networks and candidates exercised more caution than in 1980 in announcing victory and defeat.

Should Campaign Time Be Shortened? Because of the escalation of campaign expenses, distractions from the business of government, and voter loss of interest, it has been suggested that campaign time should be curtailed. The example of Britain, where elections occur within a month of the dissolution of Parliament, has been given as an alternative to the United States' virtually continuous campaigning.

A first-term congressman in a marginal seat is likely to begin his reelection efforts as soon as his term starts. Presidential candidate efforts to win endorsement by primaries and convention delegates are often launched far in advance of the eve of the March New Hampshire

primary; some drives commence as soon as the last presidential election results are known.
—*Martin Gruberg*
See also Convention, Political; Presidential Elections in the United States.

CAMPAIGN COMMITTEES, party instrument organized to coordinate the national campaign and provide financial assistance for congressional candidates. In the House each party's campaign committee consists of one member from each state. In the Senate each party's campaign committee is appointed by a party caucus chairman.
See also Committee System of Congress.

CAMPUS UNREST, PRESIDENT'S COMMISSION ON, nine-member panel commissioned on June 13, 1970, to explore the causes of campus violence and to recommend ways of peacefully resolving student grievances. The impetus for the commission, chaired by William Scranton, former Republican governor of Pennsylvania, was the shooting of students by National Guardsmen and police at Kent State University in Ohio and Jackson State University in Mississippi in May 1970. On September 26, 1970, the commission issued separate reports on each of those shootings, pointing to an "unparalleled crisis" on the nation's campuses. The studies saw the prolonged agonies of the Vietnam War and domestic economic instability as causes of student violence, which the commission vigorously condemned.

CANTWELL v. CONNECTICUT, *See* Jehovah's Witnesses Cases.

CANVASSING BOARD, an official and normally bipartisan group on county, city, or state level that receives the vote-counts from every precinct in its area. The state canvassing board obtains the voting results from all local boards, tabulates the figures, and certifies the winners.

CAPITAL GAINS. *See* Taxation.

CAPITALISM, a mode of economic production that is characterized by the control by private individuals or groups of the instruments of production (such as land, raw materials, and factories). Under capitalism, sales occur for profit. While markets are variously organized, capitalistic theory holds that they are all free markets because entrepreneurs are able to enter or leave, to expand or contract, at will. Consumers are similarly at liberty since they may choose to buy or not to buy.

To the capitalist, national and individual production are greatest when property is private, when individuals can buy and sell labor, and when the accumulation of capital, that part of money and wealth used in production, is unlimited. Capitalists believe that by the constant increase of capital, and therefore, production, both

goods and services will increase, employment will keep up with population growth, and the well-being of all will be improved.

The ethical foundation upon which capitalism is based is the notion that inequalities of income and wealth are a rough measure of the economic contributions of the men and women engaged in the productive process. This system, in modified form, exists today in most of Western Europe, the United States, Japan, and other parts of the world.
See also Conservatism; Laissez Faire.

CAPITAL PUNISHMENT means punishment by death. It is one of the most ancient of penalties, and has been used in every society, probably, because it seems to satisfy most of the rationales man has assigned for invoking criminal penalties. In addition to being quick and inexpensive to administer, it provided a spectacle for the masses. Capital punishment is the ultimate form of the most primordial reason for penalizing undesirable conduct: revenge. Capital punishment also decimates the ranks of archfelons, eliminating them as problems. Once, capital punishment was thought one of the best vehicles with which to deter the emulation of malefactors, but it now appears that this penalty is so severe—and so seldom imposed in modern times—that its deterrent effect may be minimal. Of course, it completely eliminates the possibility of rehabilitating the criminal; as rehabilitation increasingly becomes the prime goal, capital punishment falls into disfavor.

In July 1972, the Supreme Court held (5-4) in *Furman v. Georgia* that capital punishment as then applied was cruel and unusual punishment in violation of the Eighth and Fourteenth Amendments. Today, only a few offenses are subject to the death penalty, and they are, basically, some crimes against the state, especially treason, and some against the person, such as first-degree murder.

Five methods have been sanctioned for carrying out the death penalty: electrocution (used by most states), hanging, the gas chamber, lethal injection, and the firing squad.

From 1930 to 1967 there were 3,859 recorded executions in the United States. After the *Furman* case there was a pause while states revised their laws to meet the Supreme Court's concerns. Post-Furman capital statutes included requirements for a two-stage trial to determine guilt and then the sentence, a weighing of possible "aggravating" factors in the case against any "mitigating" factors, and automatic review of the sentence by the state supreme court.

In January 1977, Gary Gilmore became the first person since 1967 to be executed for a crime in the United States. There have subsequently been numerous executions, primarily in southern states. However, long legal delays have resulted in about 2,200 prisoners (1989) being held under sentence of death. Close to half have been in jail over four years since sentencing.

CAPITAL PUNISHMENT

State	Death Penalty?	No. Under Sentence of Death (1989)
Alabama	Yes	93
Alaska	No	0
Arizona	Yes	86
Arkansas	Yes	31
California	Yes	247
Colorado	Yes	3
Connecticut	Yes	1
Delaware	Yes	7
District of Columbia	No	0
Florida	Yes	294
Georgia	Yes	102
Hawaii	No	0
Idaho	Yes	16
Illinois	Yes	120
Indiana	Yes	50
Iowa	No	0
Kansas	No	0
Kentucky	Yes	28
Louisiana	Yes	39
Maine	No	0
Maryland	Yes	19
Massachusetts	No	0
Michigan	No	0
Minnesota	No	0
Mississippi	Yes	45
Missouri	Yes	73
Montana	Yes	10
Nebraska	Yes	13
Nevada	Yes	45
New Hampshire	Yes	0
New Jersey	Yes	25
New Mexico	Yes	0
New York	No	0
North Carolina	Yes	81
North Dakota	No	0
Ohio	Yes	92
Oklahoma	Yes	98
Oregon	Yes	15
Pennsylvania	Yes	115
Rhode Island	No	0
South Carolina	Yes	46
South Dakota	Yes	0
Tennessee	Yes	69
Texas	Yes	283
Utah	Yes	8
Vermont	Yes	0
Virginia	Yes	40
Washington	Yes	7
West Virginia	No	0
Wisconsin	No	0
Wyoming	Yes	2

CAPITOL, UNITED STATES, situated on a plateau 88 ft. above the Potomac River, covering an area of 175,170 sq. ft. or approximately 4 acres. Its height above the base line on the east front to the top of the Statue of Freedom is 287 ft. 5½ in. Its length, from north to south, is 751 ft. 4 in.; its greatest width, including approaches, is 350 ft.

After a site for the capital city was selected, the commissioners offered a prize of $500 for the "most approved plan" for a Capitol building. Sixteen plans were submitted, none of which was satisfactory. It was after the close of the competition that Dr. William Thornton, a versatile physician of Tortola, West Indies, requested permission to present a plan, and his was ultimately accepted by President Washington.

Plan. On September 18, 1793, the cornerstone was laid in the southeast corner of the north section of the building with Masonic ceremonies. Thornton's plan provided for a nearly square central section surmounted by a low dome and flanked on the north and south by rectangular wings, 126 ft. by 120 ft. The northern wing was completed by November 1800, in time for Congress to meet. For seven years this small building housed the Senate, House, Supreme Court, Library of Congress, and courts of the District of Columbia.

In 1807 the House moved into its new legislative chamber, and the Capitol was composed of two rectangular wings connected by a covered wooden passageway. In this stage of completion, the Capitol was gutted by fire set by the British on August 24, 1814. Congress was unable to occupy the building again until 1819, when it was rebuilt. It was another ten years until the central section, containing the rotunda and small dome, was finished.

The Capitol was built of Aquia Creek sandstone from Virginia. The structure was 351 ft. 7½ in. by 282 ft. 10½ in., including the east portico and steps. The cost of this original building, including landscape and repairs, was $2,432,851.34.

Additions. By 1851 the expanding needs of Congress made additions to the Capitol necessary, and famed Philadelphia architect Thomas U. Walter's plans were selected. On July 4, 1851, President Millard Fillmore laid the cornerstone, and Daniel Webster, Secretary of State, delivered the oration. The exterior of the extension is Massachusetts and Maryland marble. The House chamber was occupied December 16, 1857, and the Senate met in its new chamber in the north end of the building on January 4, 1859.

The addition of the Senate and House wings made the construction of a new dome necessary for the preservation of good architectural proportions. Between 1856 and 1865 the old, low, wooden dome was replaced with the familiar cast-iron structure designed by Walter. The overall width of the dome at the base is 135 ft. 5 in. The rotunda, or interior of the dome is 96 ft. in diameter, and the height from the floor to the apex of the Brumidi fresco in the canopy is 180 ft. 3 in.

The Capitol building, Washington, D.C.

Capping the huge iron dome is the Statue of Freedom, modeled by American sculptor Thomas Crawford in Rome. The statue is 19 ft. 6 in. in height. The plaster model was cast in bronze in nearby Maryland at a total cost of $23,796.82. The last section was raised into position on Dec. 2, 1863.

In 1897 the Library of Congress left its overcrowded quarters in the Capitol and moved to its own building adjacent to the Capitol grounds. Since 1935 the Supreme Court, also, has been accommodated in its own building. Thus the Capitol now houses only the Senate and the House of Representatives.

The exterior of the Capitol remained unchanged until 1956, when legislation authorized the extension of the east central front in marble. The original sandstone walls remained in place and became part of the interior wall construction. Work began in 1958 and was completed in 1962. The growth of the Capitol caused growth of the grounds surrounding it. The original 22½ acres have grown to nearly 60 acres.   *—George M. White*

CARDOZO, BENJAMIN NATHAN (1870-1938), lawyer and jurist of distinction whose liberal but balanced judgments profoundingly influenced the Supreme Court in its consideration of New Deal legislation. He was born in New York City, descendant of colonial settlers who were Sephardic Jews. His private tutor was Horatio Alger. Cardozo was educated at Columbia University and admitted to the bar in 1891. For twenty-two years he practiced specialized law, unknown except to his profession, where he was esteemed for his learning, sensitivity and tolerance. His elections and appointments to prominent positions in the Court of New York state met with the approval of his colleagues and both major political parties.

When Justice Oliver Wendell Holmes retired from the Supreme Court in 1932, President Hoover appointed Cardozo as the obvious successor. He adjusted rapidly to the demands of the highest court, which during his tenure of less than six years dealt with the controversial legislation of the New Deal. He wrote 150 opinions, notable for their legal reasoning and skill in adapting traditional principles to changing social values. In addition to his frequently cited judicial expressions, he wrote *The Nature of the Judicial Process* (1921) and related works. He died in Port Chester, N.Y.

Justice Cardozo held that the intent of historical law, not its form, should guide justice through successive generations. Government of a modern industrial society by a constitution written for an agrarian land invited legal conflicts that could only be resolved by the flexible application of law to the problems of new generations. In demonstrating responsiveness to change, the law should not abandon the wisdom of the past; the law must evolve in accordance with social necessity. The value of the Constitution lies in its intrinsic generality: it is the function of the judiciary to apply established principles to current trends.

CARNEGIE ENDOWMENT FOR INTERNATIONAL PEACE, a privately funded, independent educational and research foundation whose objective is the abolition of war. The foundation directs studies on causes of war and international tensions and seeks practical means to achieve peace. The organization conducts programs in newly developing nations in diplomatic training, technology, adult education, international law, and arms control.

CARTER, JIMMY (JAMES EARL, JR.) (1924-   ), thirty-ninth President of the United States (1977-1981). Born in Plains, Georgia, Carter graduated from the U.S. Naval Academy in 1946 and served in the Navy until 1953, when he returned to Georgia to run the family peanut business.

A Democrat, Carter failed to gain the nomination for governor of Georgia in 1966, but in 1970 he won both the primary and general election. His term as governor drew national attention when he called openly for an end to racial discrimination in Georgia.

President. Carter made a bid for the presidential nomination in 1976, and by winning all the early primaries established a stronghold within the party. By the time of the Democratic convention, he had enough delegates to win the nomination. Carter won the 1976 presidential election against Gerald Ford; his running mate was Walter Mondale.

The coming of the 1980 election signaled problems for Carter. Divisions within the party and opposition to Carter's policies weakened his support. A challenge for the nomination from Senator Edward Kennedy created further discord and threatened the success of Carter's campaign. This, coupled with popular dissatisfaction with Carter's economic policies, cost him the 1980 election.

As President, Carter took a strong stand on issues concerning human rights. Noted during his governorship for "bureaucratic streamlining," Carter signed a bill for massive government reorganization that consolidated agencies and offices, and established the new cabinet-level departments of energy, education, and health and human services. His wife Rosalynn was an outspoken supporter, and traveled around the world campaigning for his programs dealing with human rights. Another

Jimmy Carter, 39th President of the United States, who was criticized for his handling of the Iranian crisis.

important event during his administration was the signing of the Panama Canal Treaty of 1977. It provided for the establishment of a commission to oversee operation of the Panama Canal until 1999, when the Panamanian government would assume full responsibility for the canal.

After leaving office, Carter lectured and traveled but did not play a major role in national party politics. He recounted his political experiences in *Keeping Faith* (1983).

CASES AND CONTROVERSIES, the words used in Article III, section 2 of the U.S. Constitution to describe the judicial power of national courts. Through interpretation of this clause, federal courts will consider only "justiciable questions" involved in actual disputes involving two or more parties. They will not intervene in areas considered by the courts to be "political questions" that may properly be settled only by the executive or legislative branches. In addition they will not give advisory opinions, because the jurisdiction established in the Constitution is limited to "cases" and to "controversies."   —*Mary L. Carns*

See also Advisory Opinion; Justiciable Question; Political Question.

CATEGORICAL GRANTS. See Grants-In-Aid.

CAUCUS, a meeting of members of a political party for the purpose of making important political decisions. In the early nineteenth century members of Congress "caucused" to choose their party's nominee for the presidency, hence the term "King Caucus." The caucus was also the way state legislators and local party leaders selected national, state, and local candidates. By about 1840 the convention replaced the caucus as the primary method for nominating party candidates at state and national levels. "King Caucus" was discontinued because of the widespread criticism of its undemocratic and manipulative features.

Today the party caucus—called the "Caucus" by House Democrats and known as the "Conference" by Senate Democrats and by House and Senate Republicans—is used by party members to select party leaders and make decisions on pending issues. Decisions on bills made in caucus, however, are not binding on individuals, since party discipline is weak. The caucus is also used in national conventions when a state delegation may confer in private to decide whom to support for the presidential nomination. State and local officials also caucus when an important decision on legislative action is pending, and there are numerous informal groups in Congress—many centered around specific interests—such as the Congressional Black Caucus and the New England Congressional Caucus.

CEASE-AND-DESIST ORDER, an order issued by a state agency or the National Labor Relations Board to an employer or a labor organization to stop unfair labor practice that is in violation of a law. Such a command describes the action that must stop and the solution that must be taken. Cease-and-desist orders are subject to court appeal.

CELLER-KEFAUVER ANTIMERGER ACT (1950) strengthened the Clayton Antitrust Act of 1914. Although Section 7 of the Clayton Act barred mergers or acquisitions that restrict competition, court interpretations weakened the act. Because the Clayton Act appeared to outlaw only the acquisition of direct competitors, the acquisition of a noncompetitor did not seem to be illegal, even when the effect was to lessen competition. The purpose of the Celler-Kefauver Act was to make clear that Section 7 applied not only to mergers between competitors but to any merger that would lessen competition. The act tried to curb monopolistic tendencies before their trend would necessitate governmental Sherman Antitrust Act proceedings.

See also Business Regulation in the United States; Clayton Antitrust Act; Sherman Antitrust Act.

CENSURE, in political terms, official reprimand or condemnation of the activities of a member of the United States government. Censuring resolutions are instituted by Congress generally against a specific action or related actions undertaken by a particular individual and may or may not be accompanied by a removal of privileges and authority. Historically, censuring resolutions have been enacted against the President of the United States, notably in 1833 against Andrew Jackson's National Bank policy. Recent instances of censure have involved

the House's and Senate's own membership. In 1957, a resolution of censure was adopted against Sen. Joseph McCarthy of Wisconsin in regard to his investigative tactics against alleged subversives. Although congressmen have been reluctant to censure their colleagues, recent public concern over political ethics has led to increased scrutiny. Often, adverse publicity is sufficient to bring about a resignation. This occurred when Speaker of the House Jim Wright resigned in 1989 over conflict of interest charges. Censure is a milder form of disciplinary action than expulsion and requires only a simple majority vote.

the U.N. General Assembly against actions of a particular nation deemed hostile or aggressive.

See also Abscam; Expulsion.

CENSUS, BUREAU OF THE, carries out the enumeration of the population every ten years and also tabulates a wide range of statistics about the people and the economy of the United States. These statistics cover agriculture, industry, state and local government, transportation, and foreign trade. The bureau issues data and projections based on collected information, including the monthly unemployment figures. The information the bureau collects can only be used statistically and must by law be kept confidential.

The Census Board was established in May 1849 to carry out the 1850 census, and legislation in 1879 and 1880 created the Census Office in the Department of the Interior. The permanent Census Bureau was created in 1902 first in the Department of Commerce and Labor and then in the Department of Commerce. Many of the census positions were patronage appointments, but in the 1930s the bureau was overhauled and professional personnel were brought in. Since then, the bureau has become a scientific instrument of the federal government.

See also Census, United States.

CENSUS, UNITED STATES, a counting of the United States population every ten years, as authorized by Article I and United States law, to determine apportionment in the House of Representatives and for purposes of taxation. In addition to actually counting the people, the Bureau of the Census also tabulates a wide range of statistics about the country's people and economy. Census statistics are important in the development of various federal programs.

The earliest colonial census occurred in Virginia during 1624-1625. The first United States census began August 2, 1790, and ended March 3, 1792; six hundred marshals counted 3,893,635 Americans. The act providing for the 1790 census continued in force until 1850. Until the end of the Civil War a slave was counted as three-fifths a freeman, and until 1936 Indians who were not taxed were not counted. Legislation in 1879 and 1880 created a Census Office in the Department of the Interior.

40   Center for International Studies

THE UNITED STATES CENSUS, 1900-1980

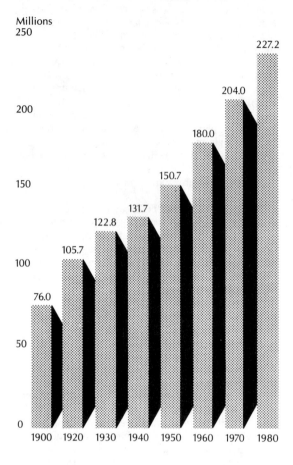

Millions

Year	Value
1900	76.0
1920	105.7
1930	122.8
1940	131.7
1950	150.7
1960	180.0
1970	204.0
1980	227.2

Traditionally, the Census Bureau has carried out a door-to-door counting of people in their places of residence, but the 1970 and 1980 censuses featured a do-it yourself census by mail with enumerators calling only on people who did not fill out their questionnaires. The questionnaires were tabulated by computer processing. Final statistics are confidential.

Anyone over seventeen years old who refuses to answer the census questions truthfully is subject to fine and imprisonment.

CENTER FOR INTERNATIONAL STUDIES, a research unit of the Woodrow Wilson School of Public and International Affairs at Princeton University. The center sponsors studies in national defense and military policy, comparative international politics, and the general scope of United States foreign policy. The center's findings are published in professional journals, books, and reports.

CENTRAL INTELLIGENCE AGENCY (CIA), organization that coordinates the intelligence activities of various governmental agencies of the United States as a means of strengthening national security. The CIA is administered by a director and deputy director appointed by the president with senate approval. Created by the National Security Act of 1947, the CIA is technically under the authority of the National Security Council (NSC), to which it reports. Nevertheless, the CIA may act semiautonomously in investigating matters pertaining to the national interest. Information obtained from these investigations is used to advise the NSC in its policy-making functions.

Adverse public opinion about the activities of the CIA was generated by revelations in the 1960s and 1970s of the agency's involvement in foreign aid programs, its alleged role in deposing the Diem regime in South Vietnam, and subsidies paid to student organizations.

See also National Security Council.

CENTRALIZATION, assumption of both political power and authority by the central or national government rather than state or local governments. The replacement of the Articles of Confederation and the adoption of the Constitution was an act of centralization. A system of government with all power located in a national government is called a unitary system. Throughout American history the division of power and responsibility has been the subject of great controversy. Proponents argue that centralization means greater efficiency and equity in dealing with nationwide problems. Opponents state that decentralization prevents tyranny, permits experimentation, and allows state and local governments to be responsive to subnational needs and differences.

See also Federalism.

CERTIORARI, WRIT OF, a written court order issued from an appellate court to inferior (or lower-level) courts, ordering them to send up records of the case for possible review. Based on an ancient common law practice and authorized by the Judiciary Act of 1925, the writ of *certiorari* is the principal vehicle for review by the U.S. Supreme Court. Most petitions for *certiorari* fall under the discretionary jurisdiction of the Court, and the great majority will be denied. At the Supreme Court level, the so-called "rule of four" is used, whereby a vote of at least four justices is needed before a writ of *certiorari* will be issued.

CHAMBER OF COMMERCE OF THE UNITED STATES OF AMERICA, a private voluntary national organization seeking to promote the common interests of businessmen. Founded in 1912, the chamber represents over 4 million individuals and firms. Research is conducted at the group's Washington, D.C. headquarters to determine those issues on which organized business should make its views known to Congress and federal agencies. The chamber actively seeks to influence legislative proposals, particularly those regarding labor, trade, and consumer activities. Analyses and recommendations are reported in several publications, including *Nation's Business* and *Congressional Action*.

Devoted to the growth of the free enterprise system, the chamber supports the restriction of federal business controls.

CHAMIZAL BORDER SETTLEMENT, a 1963 agreement between the United States and Mexico over the ownership of the Chamizal area along the Rio Grande. Both countries agreed to rechannel the Rio Grande through this area and stabilize its course with concrete. Under the agreement, 437 acres were ceded to Mexico, and the United States agreed to pay the cost of relocating the 4,500 Americans living in the Chamizal area.

The ownership of the Chamizal area had been disputed for over a century, and in 1910 the United States agreed to submit to binding arbitration of the matter. However, the decision to divide the tract was not honored because of Texas' protests. An agreement between President John Kennedy and President Adolfo Lopez Mateos in 1962 led to the settlement.

The Chamizal Treaty is administered by the International Boundary and Water Commission. This commission, established in 1889, consists of a Mexican and an American commissioner. It oversees border agreements between the two countries, cooperates on border projects, maintains the Rio Grande boundary, and regulates the water supply of the Rio Grande and Colorado rivers.

CHANGE OF VENUE, change of the location in which a case is heard. Article III, section 2 of the U.S. Constitution stipulates that trials "shall be held in the State where the said Crimes shall have been committed," and Amendment VI guarantees defendants in criminal prosecutions the right to a trial "by an impartial jury of the State and district wherein the crime shall have been committed." However, defendants sometimes petition the court for a change of *venue*, or location, on the grounds that excessive pretrial publicity has prejudiced the case and would make it impossible or impractical to secure an "impartial jury" in the district where the crime occurred. Change of *venue* may also be granted, in unusual circumstances, for the convenience of the parties to the dispute. The judge has discretion to permit or deny a request for change of *venue*. Venue is different from jurisdiction, in that *venue* refers to locality while jurisdiction refers to the power of a court to hear a case. —*Mary L. Carns*

See also Jurisdiction; *Venue*.

CHARGE D'AFFAIRES. *See* Foreign Service.

CHASE, SALMON P(ORTLAND) (1808-1873), 5th Chief Justice of the Supreme Court, born in New Hampshire. A lawyer, he was also active in the abolitionist movement and defended fugitive slaves. In 1848

Chase moved onto the national political scene when he was elected to the Senate. On the death of Chief Justice Taney in 1864, Lincoln appointed Chase, who had recently been his treasury secretary (1861-1864). In 1868, during Reconstruction, Chase presided fairly over the impeachment trial of President Johnson. Chase was against quick reopening of federal courts in the South and favored some aspects of Radical Reconstruction. Two of the major decisions of his Court were *Ex Parte Milligan* (1866) and the *Slaughterhouse Cases* (1873). Having first sought the presidency in 1856, Chase tried again unsuccessfully in 1868 and in 1872.

See also Supreme Court of the United States.

CHECKOFF, the deduction of union membership dues and assessments from employees' paychecks. The voluntary checkoff, required by the Taft-Hartley Act, requires the employee to give written authorization to his employer for these deductions. In addition, under the Labor-Management Relations Act the authorization is limited to one year, or to the termination of the collective bargaining agreement, whichever occurs first. In the agency shop the checkoff is used to deduct payments from union and nonunion members. The automatic checkoff, made without prior written authorization of the employee, is illegal under the Taft-Hartley Act.

CHECKS AND BALANCES, a unique innovation in American democracy, the sharing of powers (legislative, administrative, and judicial) among separate institutions—Congress, the executive branch, and the judiciary. For example, while the locus of legislative power is clearly in the Congress, the president, according to the Constitution, is a major legislative participant as he endorses or vetoes congressionally-enacted legislation. The system of shared powers (separation of powers) is referred to as "checks and balances" because all three institutions are checked from excessive exercises of authority, since no one institution has exclusive control of any of the three governmental functions. This structure for American government, primarily credited to James Madison (Federalist #47), supplements Montesquieu's concept of division of power as a means of minimizing the probability of tyranny from government.

In accordance with the Constitution, each of the three major institutions (branches) of the national government exercises certain expressed powers. Article I defines the structure, organization, rules, method of making law, and powers granted to Congress. Similar provisions exist in Article II for the executive and in Article III for the judiciary. In addition, judicial review, explained by Alexander Hamilton in Federalist #78 and lodged in constitutional practice since *Marbury v. Madison* in 1803, makes the Supreme Court the interpreter of jurisdictional limitations of the other two branches. The court itself cannot enforce such decisions over the other branches without the cooperation of the executive and the acquiescence of the Congress. Judicial review has become an integral part of the system of checks and balances.

In practice, the check-and-balance system has not always functioned ideally. There have been instances when the executive was curtailed by a more effective and better equipped Congress (as during Reconstruction) or when the executive has accrued more power due to the relinquishment of certain congressional responsibilities (as in the Vietnam crisis). Nevertheless, the system of checks and balances is considered to be America's most significant contribution to government.

— *Guy C. Colarulli and Victor F. D'Lugin*
See also Separation of Powers.

CHIEF OF STATE. *See* President of the United States.

CHILD LABOR, the employment of children under sixteen and the employment of children under eighteen in occupations listed as hazardous by the Children's Bureau, according to the Fair Labor Standards Act (1938). More generally, child labor is the employment of children at unsuitable ages, for long hours, and under conditions that adversely affect their health and interfere with their education. State laws regulate child labor and set age and employment limits for minors. Although considerable progress has been made in the United States to eliminate oppressive child labor, it still exists with, for example, migratory farm children working long hours picking fruits and vegetables. There are also instances where children are illegally employed in hazardous occupations and suffer serious injuries as a result, but earlier in the century, children as young as seven and eight worked sixty hours per week in cotton mills, factories, and tenement sweat shops.

Early Abuses. In the United States, children worked from the beginning of the country either for their parents

Prior to passage of child labor laws, thousands of children, such as these boys in the coal mines, were employed in hazardous occupations.

or under the colonial poor laws and the indenture system. With the coming of industry, even more children were employed, especially in the textile industry. The lack of education and the depressed wage scale supported by child labor stirred up enough protest to move states toward passing legislation limiting child labor and setting education requirements. In 1842 Massachusetts passed a law setting a maximum ten-hour work day for children under twelve. Pennsylvania set a twelve-year minimum for working in textile mills in 1848.

The growth of industry after the Civil War and the beginning of mass immigration to the United States increased the child labor force, and by 1900 over 2 million children were working. Southern textile mill owners, who had young children working a sixty-hour week in their mills, were instrumental in having the child labor laws passed by Congress in the early 1900s declared unconstitutional, but by 1920 the upsurge of organized labor, a greater demand for skilled workers, and a change in parents' attitudes decreased the child labor force, and by 1929 every state had some type of fourteen-year age limit.

Federal Legislation. In 1933 the National Recovery Administration set its sights on child labor, and the same year President Roosevelt signed a blanket code with a sixteen-year minimum age for hazardous industries and an absolute fourteen-year minimum, with children under sixteen not being allowed to work during school.

The Fair Labor Standards Act set an age limit of sixteen, with a minimum eighteen-year age for hazardous occupations. The act prohibited the interstate transportation of goods from any place where child labor existed, and the minimum wage provision of the bill applied equally to adults and children. Loopholes in the bill enabled some types of child labor, such as agricultural work, to continue. Since then the Fair Labor Standards Act has been strengthened by amendment to prohibit the employment of agricultural workers under sixteen during school hours; the law was also amended to apply to all nonagricultural establishments engaged in interstate commerce.

See also Fair Labor Standards Act (1938); Industrial Revolution; Labor Movement in the United States.

CHILD WELFARE. *See* Welfare Legislation.

CHISHOLM v. GEORGIA, 2 Dall. 419 (1793), questions whether a state can, under the federal Constitution, be sued by an individual citizen of another state. Chisholm and other citizens of South Carolina, as executors of an English creditor of Georgia, brought a suit against the State of Georgia to enforce a property right that had been confiscated during the war. Georgia vociferously declined to defend the suit, but the Court held that the suit was properly brought and that a state could be sued in the Supreme Court by an individual.

The Court observed that the Constitution specifically extends the federal judicial power to controversies "between a State and citizens of another State," and that a controversy between A and B was also a controversy between B and A. Thus, it had no choice but to assume jurisdiction. Georgia still refused to appear, and a default judgment was entered against the state. Two days after this decision was handed down what was to become the Eleventh Amendment was introduced into Congress.

CIRCUIT COURT, one of the inferior constitutional courts created by the Judiciary Act of 1789. For a major portion of the country's history, these courts were the principal trial courts in the federal judicial system, having jurisdiction over federal criminal offenses and diversity jurisdiction (between citizens of different states) where over $500 was in dispute. There was no intermediate appellate court, and appeals went directly to the Supreme Court. The circuit courts also had appellate jurisdiction over the district court, but neither they nor any other federal court had general, original federal-question jurisdiction until 1875 when it was given to circuit courts by Congress. Prior to that time, such questions were left to the state courts—with right of appeal to the Supreme Court. Because Congress did not provide for any circuit judges, the district judges came to preside over the circuit courts, and with time, only the initiated knew which court was sitting. In 1891 Congress created the circuit courts of appeal, now called simply courts of appeal, to which the appellate jurisdiction of the circuit courts was given. The Judicial Code of 1911 abolished the circuit courts and gave their original jurisdiction to the district courts.

See also District Court.

CITIZENSHIP, the relation between the individual and the state to which he owes allegiance. A number of rights and obligations define such status. It may be acquired by birth (*jus soli,* through birthplace, or *jus sanguinis,* through blood relation) and by act of volition (naturalization).

In monarchial regimes, the term is sometimes replaced by "subject," with practically the same connotations. Generally every citizen is entitled to the full benefits deriving from citizenship; however, some limitations or special rights may be due to age, creed, and so on. Citizenship can be acquired automatically, when changing borders determine a switch in the allegiance of people affected. Statelessness is lack of any citizenship. Stateless people are generally political refugees.

In the United States, as stated by the Fourteenth Amendment, "All persons born and naturalized in the United States, and subject to the jurisdiction thereof, are citizens of the United States and of the state wherein they reside." Under certain conditions, children born abroad to at least one American parent are United States citizens by birth. They must, however, take up residence in the United States or declare their intention to be citizens before they are twenty-one.

CITIZENSHIP: TOPIC GUIDE

The articles on CITIZENSHIP defines several aspects of the term and describes the rights of citizenship in both monarchial regimes and the United States.

The related articles on citizenship may be divided into two groups.

Mechanics of Citizenship. The articles ALIEN, DUAL CITIZENSHIP, and EXPATRIATION define the status of individuals. The entry IMMIGRATION outlines its effect in the United States.

The role of the U.S. government is discussed in DEPORTATION, IMMIGRATION AND NATURALIZATION SERVICE, PASSPORTS AND VISAS, and NATURALIZATION. Test cases challenging U.S. laws regulating citizenship include AFROYIM v. RUSK, FEDORENKO v. U.S., GIROUARD v. U.S., TROP v. DULLES, and U.S. v. WONG KIM ARK.

Controls of Aliens. Entries on legislative acts outlining control procedures include ALIEN REGISTRATION ACT OF 1940 (Smith Act), IMMIGRATION AND NATIONALITY ACT OF 1952, and IMMIGRATION CONTROL AND REFORM ACT OF 1986. ALIEN AND SEDITION ACTS (1798) describes early U.S. hostility toward aliens.

A distinction should be made between the terms national and citizen. In the United States, a national is anyone owing permanent allegiance to the United States. A citizen is also a U.S. national.

The inhabitants of American Samoa are U.S. nationals but do not have the political rights of U.S. citizens. This situation also applied to Filipinos and Puerto Ricans until the 1940s.   —*Sergio Barzanti*

CITY. In contrast to the long history of city development in Europe, the American transformation from village to city took place in an unusually short period of time. In the 1770s 4 percent of the colonies' population lived in urban areas; today 70 percent of Americans are urban.

Early History. From the original five port towns of the seventeenth century—Boston, Newport, Charleston, Philadelphia and New York—there arose by the time of the American revolution an urban influence that was completely disproportionate to the small numbers of people that lived in these towns. Chicago in 1830 had forty people, yet some twenty-five years later it was a city of 60,000.

The Industrial Revolution set in after the Civil War, and rivalry between cities burst out and formed an inherent part of the city dynamic. The winners of the rivalry, such as New York, created great wealth for their businessmen. For the losers there was bankruptcy, depression, and large-scale emigration. From that time on, city administrations set their tax rates to attract business and financed the construction of educational, recreational, and cultural facilities, largely in response to competing attractions from neighboring cities.

Industrialization, with its technology and division of labor, brought fundamental changes from preindustrial city characteristics; population jumped often ten times its original size and modern transportation increased the commuting radius as much as one hundred times. This mobility and density led to the breakdown of the demarcation of city from country as urban spaces developed amidst open spaces. City politics became linked with vast obligations and opportunities concerning material production and services, residential areas became located at considerable distances from work areas, and as occupational techniques changed and became more sophisticated, upward social mobility led to a constant movement of both skilled and unskilled workers.

With the need for more labor came immigrant migration. The majority of the 18 million who came to the United States between 1880 and 1910 were South and East European Catholics and Jews. The cities, particularly on the East coast, became chopped up into institutional preserves, which led to Irish politics, Italian unionism, Jewish commercialism and professionalism, and so on.

Black Influx, White Exodus. Beginning with World War I there took place another major migration, the internal migration of the blacks from the Southern rural settings to the Northern cities. The blacks often moved into areas that had been ghettos. By World War II this movement had increased.

By the early 1950s the white immigrants had been succeeded by their first and second generation descendants, who were sufficiently financially secure to think about realizing their prewar dream of the privately owned home. Aided by a federal program that encouraged home building, the exodus of the city began. Within a ten year period New York saw a million of its white middle class move to nearby suburban areas. The blacks, with accelerated migration from the South, arrived in the cities to find the obstacles of racial prejudice, poverty, and blocked opportunities; the blacks' frustrations resulted, by the mid-1960s, in rebellion and riot in numerous cities, and this violence in turn spurred the middle-class whites' determination to leave the inner cities. The middle class was afraid and lacked confidence in the city's future.

Decline. By the early 1970s the city's prospects were bleak; revenues were lost as the middle class and both large and small business moved to suburban areas, removing the city's financial lifeline. Crime increased and city services, financially starved, began to decline drastically. Erratic financial aid from the federal government often failed to halt the process. Some cities such as New York and Cleveland were in danger of going bankrupt and had to be bailed out by the federal government.

Renewed hope. In the late 1970s the exodus of white citizens from cities slowed due to the energy crisis (which increased commuter costs), a renewed interest in rehabilitating older homes in cities, and successful large-scale revitalization projects in cities such as Boston and San Antonio.

See also Municipal Government; Urban Planning.

CITY OF RICHMOND v. J.A. CROSON COMPANY, (1989), Supreme Court decision that struck down, in a 6 to 3 ruling, a Richmond, Virginia, program that set aside 30 percent of its construction funds for minority contractors. The court ruled this practice constituted reverse discrimination and violated the constitutional right of equal protection. Such programs could only be justified where evidence pointed to "identified discrimination" and not merely because of "past societal discrimination."

The repercussions of this ruling could be widespread in that many communities have similar programs that would now be subject to scrutiny. The Reagan administration hailed the decision while civil rights groups expressed concern for the future of affirmative action programs. The decision threatened minority set-asides established under the 1980 *Fullilove v. Klutznick* decision.

See also Martin v. Wilks; United Steelworkers of America v. Weber.

CITY-STATE, an independent, self-governing, urban, political community that usually also encompasses rural lands. City-states are as old as civilization and made enormous contributions to its progress. City-states were particularly important in three periods of Western civilization: the ancient Near East, classical Greece, and Medieval and Renaissance Europe.

Ancient Near East. The oldest city-states were those in Sumeria, the region of lower Mesopotamia between the Tigris and Euphrates rivers. Among the city-states were Ur, Lagash, and Erech, which were founded by Sumerian and, later, by Semitic tribes sometime between 4,000 and 3,000 B.C. and lasted about 1,000 years. Each city-state theoretically was ruled by a god and his special servants, priests and kings.

Classical Greece. The Greek city-states, or *polis*, which developed from early Homeric tribal societies, emerged between about 1000 and 500 B.C. Classic Greek civilization flourished in these many independent political units. Perhaps the most famous of these was Athens, which was the largest, covering 1,000 square miles, and developed democracy. Each of the city-states felt intense civic pride, which led to much rivalry between them in architecture, the arts, athletics, and martial arts. This rivalry eventually caused the demise of most of the city-states. The tradition of the Greek city-state was carried into southern Europe by the Greek colonies and included Etruscan and other Italian city-states as well as Rome, which eventually conquered the Mediterranean area and ended the era of the ancient city-state.

Medieval and Renaissance Europe. At the close of

the eleventh century, city-states existed in both Italy and Flanders. Although the Flemish city-states eventually fell under the rule of territorial princes, Italian city-states, like Milan, Florence, Venice, and Genoa, flourished and became the cultural centers of Europe. Much like the Greek *polis,* they were characterized by civic pride, rivalry, and political diversity.

See also City.

CIVIL AERONAUTICS BOARD (CAB), formerly an independent government agency that regulated civilian aviation. The board was established in 1938 under the Civil Aeronautics Act and continued by the Federal Aviation Act in 1958. The CAB was concerned with granting operating permits to airlines, approving fares and rates, approving proposed mergers, and advising the State Department on foreign air routes. The provisions of the Airline Deregulation Act of 1978, designed to promote competition in the air transportation industry, phased out the regulatory powers of the CAB and eliminated the board on Jan. 1, 1985.

CIVIL DISORDERS, NATIONAL ADVISORY COM-MISSION ON, or Kerner Commission, established in 1968 to study the increasing number of civil disorders in the nation. Under the chairmanship of former Ohio governor Otto Kerner, the commission saw the nation as moving toward "two societies, separate and unequal." An attempt by vice chairman Mayor John V. Lindsay of New York, and Senator Fred Harris of Oklahoma to reconvene the body for further study failed, but a follow-up report was issued in 1969 by the Urban Coalition and Urban America, Inc.

The findings of the Kerner Commission related to those of the Eisenhower Commission on the causes and prevention of violence and to the Scranton Commission on campus unrest. All three panels saw the country becoming increasingly polarized as a result of the prolonged Vietnam War and the domestic inequalities inherent in a society that was described as racist, whether consciously or unconsciously. As a result of these reports, institutions such as the Minority Business Development Agency and ACTION were created to combat the divisiveness of the society.

CIVIL CONSERVATION CORPS (CCC). *See* New Deal Legislation.

CIVIL LAW originally referred to the system of jurisprudence developed in the Roman empire (Roman Law) and now usually refers to the legal system descended from Roman law and prevailing in most of continental Europe. In this system of law, cases are decided *a priori* applying highly abstract legal concepts known as codes. In this sense, civil law is opposed to common law. The Western world generally adheres to one or the other of these two legal systems. The term civil law is also used to distinguish the law of a political

entity from international law and natural law, but "municipal law" is a more proper term in this context. In other contexts, civil law has been distinguished from criminal law, canon law, and admiralty law. In this usage, civil law is used to regulate relationships between private individuals or companies. Since the action taken does not constitute a threat to the well-being of society, persons who feel they have been injured by another party must take action on their own to seek judicial relief. By contrast, criminal law assumes that society itself is the victim, and therefore a government will prosecute on behalf of the injured party in criminal cases but not in civil cases.

See also Admiralty Law; Common Law; Criminal Law.

CIVIL LIBERTIES, those freedoms or liberties found in the first ten amendments of the Constitution (Bill of Rights). In the American tradition civil liberties are not granted to individuals, but rather are restraints on government. They are areas in which government is, by law or custom, prevented from acting. This can be seen in the First Amendment's opening line: "Congress shall make no law respecting an establishment of religion . . ." Civil liberties are assumed to create, by government restraint, a sphere of privacy or freedom for individuals.

See also Accused Persons, Rights of; Civil Rights; Civil Rights Act; Civil Rights, Commission on.

CIVIL RIGHTS, COMMISSION ON, independent, bipartisan agency established in 1957 and reestablished by the United States Commission on Civil Rights Acts of 1983. The commission is composed of eight members (four appointed by the president, four by Congress) under the 1983 act. It collects and analyzes information and holds hearings on discrimination or denial of equal protection due to race, color, religion, sex, age, handicap, or national origin. The commission investigates complaints of voting rights violations, serves as a clearing house for civil rights information, and submits reports and recommendations to the president and the Congress. The commission has no enforcement authority and occasionally clashes with the Department of Justice over enforcement of corrective actions. The commission's primary factfinding efforts are in the areas of voting, education, employment, and housing.

CIVIL RIGHTS ACTS. In the post-Civil War dislocation, and in a mounting backlash against the resurgence of Black Codes in the South relegating blacks to near-serfdom, Congress passed seven civil rights acts during Reconstruction to guarantee the rights of the freed slaves and to implement the Thirteenth, Fourteenth and Fifteenth Amendments to the Constitution. Militant friends of the blacks were joined in the Reconstruction Congresses by practical Republicans who felt black suffrage would undercut Democratic domination of the

South and by pro-industry legislators who feared that Democratic domination meant the triumph of agrarianism. Despite the far-reaching egalitarian legislation, social and political equality remained far out of reach. Those provisions that were not declared unconstitutional in the next two decades by the Supreme Court were rendered ineffectual via exquisitely narrow rulings handed down by judges responding to broad sympathy for states' rights as well as broad sentiment against legislating equality between the races. Moreover, the rapid industrialization of 1875-1900 entrenched an attitude, North and South, favoring individual property rights over individual civil rights. (*See* Slaughterhouse Cases and Civil Rights Cases). By 1896 the "separate but equal" doctrine triumphed in *Plessy v. Ferguson.*

Reconstruction Acts

Civil Rights Act of April 9, 1866. Passed over the veto of President Andrew Johnson, the law extended citizenship to anyone born in the United States and gave blacks full equality before the law "as is enjoyed by white citizens." One section authorized the president to enforce the law with federal armed forces if necessary—a clause considered vindictive toward the South by many. Debate over the constitutionality of the 1866 act ended in 1868 with the adoption of the Fourteenth Amendment.

Civil Rights Acts of April 21, 1866, and March 2, 1867. These two laws implement the Thirteenth Amendment and are still on the books. The first sets punishment for kidnapping or delivering anyone into involuntary servitude or exporting blacks into slavery. The second prohibits the system of peonage.

Civil Rights Act of May 31, 1870, known as the Act of 1870 or the Enforcement Act. The law sets out specific criminal sanctions for interfering with suffrage as protected by the Fifteenth Amendment or the Civil Rights Act of April 9, 1866. Sections 3 and 4, forbidding the use of bribery, threats, intimidation, or force to abridge a person's voting rights by economic sanctions or violence to his person or family, was disallowed by the Supreme Court in 1903. Section 16, guaranteeing equality before the law "as is enjoyed by white citizens" in "every state and territory," was stricken in 1906. Section 6, imposing penalties upon two or more persons who go or conspire to go in disguise upon the public highway to violate the civil rights of another precursed the Ku Klux Act.

Civil Rights Act of Feb. 28, 1871. An amendment to the Enforcement Act of 1870, the statute calls for the appointment of two election supervisors and two deputy marshals—all paid, and in each case from different parties—in cities of more than 20,000 where two citizens have presented written application to the United States circuit judge. The appointees' duties in congressional elections include the supervision of voter registration, polling places, voting procedures, challenging voters, counting votes, and submitting returns.

Civil Rights Act of April 10, 1872, also the Ku Klux Act or the Anti-Ku Klux Klan Act. "An act to enforce the Fourteenth Amendment," the law stipulates that anyone using law or custom to deprive an individual of his rights, privileges, and immunities secured by the Constitution or by federal law is guilty of a federal crime and liable for damages. The very detailed Section 2 imposed penalties for depriving any person of equal protection of the law and for using or conspiring to use force to overthrow the government or to interfere with justice, public officers, or elections; this section was declared unconstitutional in 1883 and 1887.

Civil Rights Act of March 1, 1875, or the Second Civil Rights Act. "An act to protect all citizens in their civil and legal rights," the law declared that all persons are entitled to "the full and equal enjoyment of the accommodations, advantages, facilities and privileges of inns, public conveyances on land and water, theaters and other places of public amusement" and imposed penalties for violations. Section 4 declared that no person could be excluded from state or federal jury duty because of race, color or previous servitude and fined violators. The act was nullified by the Civil Rights Cases of 1883, and virtually no new civil rights legislation was passed until 1957.

Twentieth Century Acts

Civil Rights Act of 1957. Following the 1954 *Brown v. Board of Education of Topeka* decision of the Supreme Court disallowing the separate-but-equal doctrine, and in the wake of the Montgomery bus boycott, led by Rev. Martin Luther King, Jr., in 1955, public sentiment for stronger civil rights legislation exerted increasing pressure on Congress and President Dwight Eisenhower. The 1957 law responded by establishing a Civil Rights Commission, a nonpartisan temporary body appointed by the President with instructions to investigate and document cases where voting rights or equal protection were denied by fraudulent practice or by reason of race, color, religion or national origin. The act added an assistant attorney general to oversee the new Civil Rights Division within the Justice Department. In cases where rights had been tampered with, the law provided for injunctive action or intervention by the attorney general and eventual trial by jury or judge. All persons residing more than one year in a judicial district were declared qualified for jury duty in that district unless they are illiterate in English, have a criminal record, or are physically or mentally incapable. In the 1950s and 1960s the Supreme Court was disposed to extend rather than restrict existing civil rights laws.

Civil Rights Act of 1960. Growing numbers of demonstrations, sit-ins, and protests—countered by resistant acts of violence—led to further legislation in 1960 to protect voting rights. The act set penalties for obstructing a federal court order by threat of force and for illegally using and transporting explosives. The law prohibited fleeing to avoid prosecution for destroying "any structure, facility, vehicle, dwelling house, synagogue, church or religious center, or educational institution, public or private." Further, election officials were required to keep all records of federal elections for twenty-two months after elections. Other provisions appointed persons residing in judicial districts to serve as district voting referees to take evidence and to report to the courts instances of voting discrimination, including discrimination in registration or vote-counting. If a "pattern or practice" of discrimination is documented, the Justice Department, on behalf of the voter, can bring suit even against a state.

Civil Rights Act of 1964. Civil rights legislation in the mid-twentieth century aimed as much to end discriminatory application of nondiscriminatory law as to define individual rights. As the wave of protest mounted and as the government moved, even with armed forces, to counter noncompliance, equality before the law came to be, in the words of generally conservative Senate Majority Leader Everett Dirksen: ". . . an idea whose time has come." In July 1964 Republicans joined with liberal Democrats to invoke cloture on the Senate floor (for the first time on a civil rights issue) and to pass a far-ranging bill that expressly forbids discrimination on the basis of race, color, religion, national origin and, in employment, sex. Most effectively, Title VI provides for the cut-off of federal funds from any program administered in a discriminatory manner. Title I prohibits arbitrary voting disqualification and streamlines the procedures in voter-denial suits. Most controversial was Title II, outlawing discrimination in public accommodations and providing for court action by the attorney general when a "pattern or practice" of resistance is evident. Titles III and IV call for the desegregation of public facilities and schools. Other sections extend the duties and life of the Civil Rights Commission, specify the right to equality in employment opportunity and set up the Equal Employment Opportunity Commission, and establish the Community Relations Service to help solve community race problems. The emphasis is on encouraging voluntary compliance, in line with the Fourteenth Amendment's "due process" clause, to avoid testing the constitutionality of older laws.

Civil Rights Act of 1968. Seven days after the assassination of Martin Luther King, President Johnson signed this measure, providing protection for civil rights workers and forbidding discrimination in most housing. The act provides penalties for those who attempt to interfere with an individual's civil rights and for those who use interstate commerce for the purpose of organizing or furthering a riot. The open-housing provision was made obsolete in June, when the Supreme Court prohibited discrimination in the sale and rental of all housing, citing the century-old act of April 9, 1866.

Civil Rights Act of 1983. In November 1983, President Ronald Reagan signed a bill that extended for six years the life of the Civil Rights Commission and refashioned it so that it consisted of four congressional and four presidential appointments. The bill established fixed terms of six years for half and three years for half of the commissioners, with all subsequent appointments for six-year terms. It provided that members could be removed only for cause, that no more than four commissioners could be members of the same political party, that two of the congressional appointees be named by House and Senate leaders, and that the staff director be appointed by the president. A majority of commissioners must concur in the designation of chairman, vice chairman, and staff director. While reaffirming its commitment to the principles of nondiscrimination and affirmative action, the commission rejected the use of quotas as "another form of unjustified discrimination" and embarked on a review of all previous commission policies.

See also Equal Employment Opportunity Commission (EEOC); Voting Rights Act.

CIVIL RIGHTS CASES, 109 U.S. (1883), tested the scope of the Civil Rights Act of 1875, which Congress had passed to ensure continued federal power to prevent racial discrimination in the South after the Reconstruction. Two of the cases concerned incidents in which blacks were denied accommodations in an inn or hotel, and two involved the denial to blacks of the privilege and accommodations of a theatre.

In the opinion of the Court, although states do not have the power to make or enforce laws which abridge the privileges or immunities of citizens without due process of law, the Fourteenth Amendment does not prevent such action by private individuals. In a forceful dissenting opinion, Mr. Justice John M. Harlan argued that those who operate inns and places of amusement are not "private persons," and that because they carry on business under state authority, they are agents of the state. Therefore, discriminatory action on the part of these persons was tantamount to discrimination on the part of the state that permitted them to operate in such a manner. This decision has since been overruled.

See also Heart of Atlanta Motel v. United States.

CIVIL RIGHTS MOVEMENT. The 350-year attempt to obtain equal rights for black Americans is the aspect of civil rights most recognized by Americans. Many other groups, including religious and political minorities, criminals, labor unions, the military, other ethnic minorities, and women have often been an unrecognized part of the American attempt to define and preserve civil rights for all citizens.

Beginnings. The beginnings of the modern civil rights movement are directly traceable to the Civil War and Reconstruction periods. The omission from the Declaration of Independence of guarantees of freedom for slaves and the inclusion in the Constitution of recognition of slavery had to wait for the adoption of the 13th Amendment after the Civil War to begin the period of redress. The Civil Rights Act of 1866 was the first federal legislation to attempt to give blacks equal rights under the law. The legislation was the forerunner of the 14th Amendment that guaranteed equal protection under the law to all citizens and granted citizenship to ex-slaves. Other legislation of the period made earnest efforts to secure equal rights for blacks. These included the Civil Rights Act of 1875; the Force Act of 1871; and the 15th Amendment, granting equal voting rights.

None of the these measures was able to secure the goal of equal justice under the law for black Americans. A combination of conservative judicial opinions, as exemplified by the *Plessy v. Ferguson* decision (1896) that resulted in the legal doctrine of "separate but equal," and the social failure of Americans to accept the validity of equal rights and opportunities for blacks brought an end to an era of reform in civil rights.

20th Century. *Brown v. Board of Education*(1954) reversed the separate but equal doctrine and helped initiate new legislation, court decisions, and a changing climate of public opinion that broadened civil rights for black Americans. It also helped create a demand for expansion of equal rights and opportunities by other minorities. In 1957, Martin Luther King, Jr., achieved overnight fame when he led a black boycott of the Montgomery, Ala. bus system. King and his organizational vehicle, the Southern Christian Leadership Conference, challenged the leadership of the older civil rights groups, such as the NAACP and the Urban League, in the new fight for civil rights. Congress, in its first major attempt at civil rights legislation since the act of 1875, passed a civil rights act in 1957. Although generally considered weak in its final effect, the act attempted to reinforce the voting-rights guarantees of the 15th Amendment and provided for the establishment of a Civil Rights Commission and a Civil Rights Division in the Department of Justice. A stronger, but still ineffective Civil Rights Act was passed in 1960. Its influence was less important than the effect of the newer organizations such as SNCC and CORE on the American conscience.

The Civil Rights Act of 1964 dealt largely with the granting of equal rights for public accommodations. The Voting Rights Act of 1965 was a forceful bill serving to effectively supplement the voting-rights guarantees of the 15th Amendment. It was modeled on, and more radical than, the Force Act of 1871, and it changed the ability of blacks to participate in the electoral process in the South.

Following the violence set off by the assassination of Martin Luther King in 1968, a new civil rights act was signed by the President which guaranteed fair housing opportunities for all citizens. In the 1970s Mexican-Americans, American Indians, and women's rights groups became more active in the movement to ensure their civil rights.   —*David C. Geliebter*

CIVIL SERVICE, the term applied to the body of employees working for a government. In the United States, employees of publicly owned business-type

CIVIL SERVICE

Year	Federal Civilian Employment	State Civilian Employment
1950	2,117,000	1,057,000
1960	2,421,000	1,527,000
1965	2,588,000	2,028,000
1970	2,881,000	2,755,000
1975	2,890,000	3,271,000
1980	2,898,000	3,753,000
1983	2,875,000	3,816,000
1987	3,091,000	4,115,000

The growth in state civil service employees has continued to increase as federal levels have stabilized. Shifting responsibilities for some federal programs to the states has contributed to this trend.

enterprises are included; in many countries they are not. Universally excluded are elected officials, judges, and the uniformed military.

History. Important governments, such as those of Rome and China, have always had groups of officials who helped a ruler govern, but it is only within the last two centuries that the idea of a permanent body of officials devoted full time to impartial and professional service has become the rule rather than the exception. Indeed, the term "civil service" was probably first used by the British in the late eighteenth century to characterize their civilian administrative officials who governed India. The experience of the United States in developing a modern civil service has been fairly typical, although reforms have come a little slower than in the most advanced European states.

President Washington and the Federalists realized the need for an efficient, incorruptible, and permanent group of federal officials. This goal was not difficult, as the national civil service in 1800 consisted of only some 3,000 persons. With the expansion of the government and the development of political parties, public offices became political plums. The spoils system, under which partisan service outweighed technical qualifications for appointment to office, began in a small way under Jefferson and came to a climax in the period from Jackson through Lincoln. This patronage system came under attack during the post-Civil War scandals. The result was reform of the federal civil service through the Pendleton Act (Civil Service Reform Act of 1833), which has also provided the model for state and local services.

The Pendleton Act accomplished three main things. First, it established a merit system, characterized by competitive examinations for entrance into the public service, partisan neutrality while in office, and, in return for giving up civic rights of partisanship, the granting of relative security of tenure. In fact, the merit system concept provides the central theme of the most effective civil services of today.

Second, the Pendleton Act permitted the president

to extend the system to most federal employees and established the United States Civil Service Commission. Successive presidents expanded the merit system from the 15 percent covered directly by the act to the present 95 percent or more. Except among top offices, appointments to which are viewed as the function of the president and his political party, old-fashioned spoils appointments have vanished from the federal service. The Civil Service Commission has gradually come to be the principal personnel agency of the federal government.

During the Carter administration the Civil Service Commission was reorganized. The Civil Service Reform Act of 1978 abolished the old commission structure and established the Office of Personnel Management (OPM) and the Merit System Protection Board (MSPB). The OPM is responsible for recruitment and examination of potential government employees. The Protection Board has authority to review and adjudicate on questions of personnel practices.

Questions of union-management relations were centralized under the Federal Labor Relations Authority. The Senior Executive Service was created to oversee conditions of employment for the three highest levels of federal government civil service. It establishes procedures for recruitment, placement, and compensation for workers at those levels.

Open Personnel System. In these respects the personnel system of the United States parallels those of other advanced nations, but the comparison ends there. The Pendleton Act also set in motion for the bulk of the civil service a type of personnel system known as an open system, which is unique in the modern world.

An open personnel system is characterized by considerable movement back and forth from governmnent into private enterprise and vice versa (lateral entry). In providing for entrance into the civil service at any age by means of examinations as practical as possible, the Pendleton Act suggested and supported such a system. Most other countries have developed closed career systems like those of the American military and the foreign service, where one enters only at an early age and remains for a lifetime career.

Some countries are moving gradually toward the more open American system because of its compatibility with ideas of social mobility and equality of opportunity. Indeed, many immigrant and other minorities, as well as women, have found in the United States public services an avenue to upward mobility.

State and Local Employees. Nearly one out of seven of the total civilian labor force of about 105 million persons is a public employee. Most of the larger state and local jurisdictions are operating under merit and open system principles. Progress toward the elimination of patronage has been slowest in the nation's counties, townships, and special districts.

However, much federal grant-in-aid legislation requires that state and local employees paid in whole or in part with federal funds be placed under merit procedures. The passage of the Intergovernmental Personnel Act brought an infusion of federal funds into state and local personnel agencies for their further improvements. —*Paul P. Van Riper*

See also Merit System Protection Board; Office of Personnel Management.

CIVIL SERVICE COMMISSION. *See* Civil Service.

CIVIL SERVICE REFORM ACT (1883), or **PENDLETON ACT.** the law established the principle of regulating federal employment on the basis of merit and competitive examination. The act, which replaced the old "spoils system" with one aimed at political neutrality, created a bipartisan Civil Service Commission to administer the personnel service. The reform was drafted by the National Civil Service Reform League and adopted on a wave of public discontent after the assassination of President Garfield by Charles Guiteau, a disappointed office seeker. Originally the law covered only 10 percent of federal employees, but eventually covered more than 90 percent of federal workers. The Pendleton Act adopted certain British practices, such as partisan neutrality of civil servants.

The Civil Service Commission was abolished by provisions of the Civil Service Reform Act of 1978, but the concept of basing employment on merit examinations has been retained as a central element of the new law. The merit principle has since been applied at the state level in many cases but less consistently in city government.

See also Civil Service; Civil Service Reform Act (1978); Spoils System.

CIVIL SERVICE REFORM ACT (1978), law incorporating a number of reforms proposed by President Jimmy Carter and Alan K. Campbell, head of the Civil Service Commission. The 1978 act abolished the Civil Service Commission and transferred its functions to the newly-created Office of Personnel Management (OPM) and the Merit System Protection Board (MSPB). The OPM administers competitive merit examinations and is responsible for establishing recruitment and employment procedures. The OPM continues to use the so-called "rule of three" that was adopted by the former Civil Service Commission, in which the names of three qualified applicants are submitted to an agency for consideration and from which the selection must be made. Members of the OPM are appointed by the president and confirmed by the Senate. The MSPB is an independent agency that was established to investigate infractions of personnel practices and civil service regulations. The MSPB has legal authority to prosecute violators of civil service regulations.

The Civil Service Reform Act of 1978 contains the most substantive revisions of the civil service system since the practice of merit examinations was adopted in the Pendleton Act of 1883. This law expedites employee complaints through the MSPB, increases management flexibility in firing incompetent employees, and establishes cash bonuses for the newly-created Senior Executive Service (who also have less job tenure protection).   —*Mary L. Carns*

See also Civil Service; Civil Service Reform Act (1883).

CLAIMS, COURT OF. *See* United States Claims Court.

CLASS ACTION, or representative action, an action by one or more persons on behalf of themselves and all others similarly situated or injured. Although the device had existed for some time in equity, class action has only become prominent in the last three decades. It has proven a very useful device for the enforcement of liabilities where the interest of any one person is too small to render a suit by him alone economically viable. A court will usually award lawyer's fees out of the aggregate judgment on behalf of the class.

CLAY, HENRY (1777-1852), statesman, several times unsuccessful candidate for president, expert compromiser in efforts to avert a civil war over slavery. Clay was born in Virginia. Despite a limited education, he was admitted to the bar in Richmond in 1797. He moved to Kentucky, practiced criminal law, married Lucretia Hart, and was elected to the state legislature 1803-1806. In 1807 he became Speaker of the Kentucky Assembly.

Between 1806 and 1811 he filled two unexpired terms in the United States Senate. From 1811 to 1820 he served in Congress and was immediately elected Speaker of the House. He led the "War Hawk" faction, urged Madison into war with England, and helped negotiate the Treaty of Ghent. An influential orator and politician, he developed the "American System" of high protective tariffs and internal improvements built at federal expense. He was responsible for the Missouri Compromise of 1820, temporarily resolving sectional disputes over the expansion of slave territory.

Clay then resigned as Speaker, but returned from 1823 to 1825. He was a candidate in the presidential election of 1824, which was decided against him by vote in the House. As Speaker, he threw his influence behind John Quincy Adams, who appointed Clay Secretary of State in 1825. He served in the Senate from 1831 to 1842, and ran as a Whig against Andrew Jackson in 1832. Clay lost because his identification with privileged property interests did not appeal to the emerging Democratic electorate. In 1844 Clay was defeated by James K. Polk. Clay returned to the Senate from 1849 to 1852. His last important work was the compromise of 1850, which again forestalled division over the question of slavery in the new Western states. Clay died in Washington in 1852.

Statesman Henry Clay's efforts to avert civil strife earned him the nickname "Great Compromiser."

A charismatic but impetuous man—he fought several duels with his political critics—his talent for compromise cast doubt on his principles and probably prevented him from attaining the highest office. He answered his doubters: "I would rather be right than be President."

CLAYTON ANTITRUST ACT (1914), the law forbidding practices that "substantially lessen competition or tend to create a monopoly," such as joint agreement to fix prices, boycott goods, overlap directorates, or acquire stock in a competitor with the aim of restraining trade. Corporate officers were made personally liable for abuses. The act is enforced by the Federal Trade Commission with the help of the Department of Justice. Known as "labor's Bill of Rights," the statute was "designed to equalize before the law the position of workers and employers as industrial combatants. Although Section 20 withdrew the Sherman Antitrust Act's interdict from specific union practices that had been halted by anti-labor injunctions, the courts interpreted the section in its most narrow sense to cover only union activities against an employer by his employees, and the consciously pro-labor legislation was ineffectual for eighteen years. The Norris-La Guardia Act of 1932 redressed the situation by immunizing labor to the antitrust laws.

CLEAN AIR AMENDMENTS (1970) transferred all HEW air pollution-control functions to the Environmental Protection Agency and ordered that office to develop programs for the prevention and control of air pollution. The EPA administrator was ordered to designate as Air Quality-Control Regions any areas necessary for the maintenance of federal standards.

The act restricted the discharge of major pollutants into the atmosphere, set emission standards for aircraft, and ordered additional reductions for automobile emissions beyond the levels set by regulations adopted in the 1960s. It ordered states to submit to EPA by January 1972 their plans to meet these new standards and specified that state controls must be at least as stringent as federal regulations. Further, the act enabled individual citizens as well as the federal government to bring civil action against polluters, including any American government. The bill was severely weakened by resistance from industry and local governments. Amendments passed in 1977 extended the original deadline for air quality standards and delayed the deadline for automobile emission reductions.

CLEAR AND PRESENT DANGER, a court test used in determining the limits of free expression guaranteed in the First Amendment. This yardstick was first formulated by Justice Oliver Wendell Holmes in the Supreme Court decision *Schenck v. United States* (1919), just after World War I. In upholding the conviction of the secretary of the Socialist party for distributing antidraft pamphlets to war recruits, Justice Holmes said that speech could be punished if there were a serious and imminent danger that it would result in illegal action. Although the First Amendment guarantees free expression unequivocally, the courts have tried to balance the First Amendment with the community's best interests.

The clear-and-present-danger test is applied in times of crisis. Other tests include the more limiting bad-tendency test (speech that has a tendency to bring about bad results), the preferred-position test (more rigorous standard of review required for First Amendment cases because of its importance), and the sliding-scale test (careful examination of facts of each individual case).

CLEVELAND, (STEPHEN) GROVER (1837-1908), 22nd and 24th President of the United States (1885-1889, 1893-1897), born in Caldwell, N.J. Long active in local Democratic politics, he became reform mayor of Buffalo, New York (1881) and governor of New York (1882). Cleveland's honest administration led him to repudiate Tammany Hall, and his "enemies" were one reason he obtained the Democratic presidential nomination in 1884. During his first term he advocated sound money and reduced inflation. He forced repeal of the Tenure Office Act and withdrew land for conservation purposes. He attempted to curb party patronage, lost political support from veterans by vetoing private pensions and the Dependent Pension Act, and alienated businessmen by suggesting a lower tariff. All these led to his defeat by Benjamin Harrison in 1888.

In 1892, Cleveland won the election, but he had to face the depression of 1893. Insisting on sound money,

Cleveland led repeal of the Sherman Silver Purchase Act and negotiated three loans that saved the gold standard. In foreign affairs he was criticized for withdrawing the annexation of Hawaii (1893) and intervening in the boundary dispute between Britain and Venezuela (1895).
See also Presidential Elections.

CLOSED SHOP, a labor arrangement in which an employer must employ only people who are continuing union members. Closed shops have been sought by labor unions in America as early as 1791, at the demand of local craft unions in Philadelphia, New York, and Boston. The closed shop is now illegal under federal labor statutes. Closed shop agreements are also illegal in labor contracts under the Taft-Hartley Act (1947); as a result, the union shop (non-union members can be hired, but they must then join the union) has supplanted the closed shop in collective bargaining.

A closed shop situation can be combined with a closed union. Here the union has a closed shop agreement with the employer, but it also controls the membership numbers of the union with extremely high entrance fees and dues and the device of closing the books to new members.
See also Union Shop.

CLOTURE, in the U.S. Congress, a method of cutting off debate to force a vote on a particular question. Cloture may be invoked in the Senate under provisions of Senate Rule XXII, first adopted in 1917 and amended several times since (most recently in 1975 and 1979). Current rules require a petition signed by one-sixth of the senators and a subsequent vote by three-fifths of the entire membership (60 senators). Each senator is then limited to one hour of speaking time prior to the vote. Opponents of the bill may still be able to delay the vote by use of the "post-cloture filibuster," a procedural tactic that includes numerous amendments and quorum calls, although the 1979 amendment to Rule XXII restricts debating time to 100 hours maximum after the vote for cloture.

The cloture rule was adopted to prevent the filibuster, a ploy that was frequently used by Southern senators to obstruct passage of civil rights legislation. Between the adoption of the first cloture rule and 1965, cloture was invoked only seven times, but the possibility of cloture often proved successful in itself to end debate. By the end of 1981, cloture had been attempted 168 times; 53 votes were successful.

In the House of Representatives the Rules Committee stipulates the time for debate on important measures. A call for the previous question also serves to restrict discussion of a particular bill and is sometimes referred to as "House cloture." —*Mary L. Carns*
See also Filibuster; Previous Question.

COALITION, the formulation of a political party from

disparate political factions. Both the Republican and the Democratic parties are amalgams of various political elements. The American tradition of the broad coalition is essential in preserving the two-party system. In local politics coalitions are sometimes formed by reform-minded individuals of both parties to challenge the city machine. The Fusion party of New York City, which elected Fiorello La Guardia mayor in 1933, was such a combination. In non-Communist Europe coalitions often include a shifting alliance of several political parties with the purpose of either winning an election or controlling a majority of delegates in the national assembly.

COAST GUARD, UNITED STATES. *See* Transportation, United States Department of (DOT).

COATTAIL EFFECT, a political phenomenon that results from straight-ticket voting in national elections. When voters cast their ballots for a presidential candidate they sometimes routinely vote for congressional and state candidates from the same party as the presidential choice. The latter candidates are then said to have ridden to office on the "coattails" of the presidential candidate. However, the case may apply in reverse, when a very popular senator or governor wins a landslide vote and thereby aids the presidential candidate.

CODE OF MILITARY JUSTICE. *See* Military Law.

COHENS v. VIRGINIA, 6 Wheat. 264 (1821), concerns the division of power between the federal and state governments. Congress had authorized a municipal lottery in the District of Columbia, and the Cohens sold tickets in Virginia. Virginia forbade the sale of the lottery tickets, and convicted the Cohens for selling them. The Virginia legislature passed a resolution protesting the jurisdiction of the Supreme Court in this case, and enlisted Daniel Webster to argue for the Commonwealth. The Court took jurisdiction in spite of the protest. It determined that Congress had not intended to provide for the sale of lottery tickets outside the District, held that the Supremacy clause had not been involved so as to invalidate the Virginia legislation, and affirmed the convictions. With this case, the Court clearly established its power to review federal questions arising in state courts.

COLD WAR, the ideological, political, and economic impasse that has existed between the United States and the Soviet Union, and to some extent between the United States and the People's Republic of China, since World War II. Although Russian territorial ambitions were evident even during the war, Western leaders hoped that the U.S.S.R. would adhere to the agreements made at the Yalta Conference, but at the Potsdam meeting after Germany's surrender, the U.S.S.R. made no promises about European security.

One of the first U.S.-U.S.S.R. stalemates was disagreement over the postwar U.N. Baruch Commission report on controlling the production of nuclear energy. With the Russian refusal to accept the plan, there was an increase in international tensions and the beginning of the buildup of huge nuclear weapons systems as deterrent forces. Other early crises involved Soviet efforts to impose Communist regimes in Eastern Europe and the Berlin blockade in 1948. The United States responded to the crisis in Berlin by airlifting supplies to the western sector for 11 months until the Soviets abandoned their attempt to isolate the city. During this period, the United States instituted its containment policy, proposed the Marshall Plan for economic aid (1948), and formed the NATO Alliance (1949) to counter Soviet military threats.

Subsequent situations in which the Cold War assumed dangerous proportions were the Korean War, the Middle East and Suez crises, confrontations in Berlin culminating in the construction of the Berlin Wall, the U-2 Affair and the subsequent collapse of the U.S.-U.S.S.R. Paris summit, the Bay of Pigs and the Cuban missile crises, and the Vietnam War. Interspersed among these crises were events and decisions that lessened Cold War tensions, such as Premier Nikita Khrushchev's proposal for peaceful coexistence, the 1955 Geneva thaw, the 1963 Test-Ban Treaty, the Strategic Arms Limitation Talks, the China-U.S. thaw, including the admittance of Communist China into the U.N., and the liberalizing of U.S.-U.S.S.R. and U.S.-China trade agreements.

Recent events have further complicated East/West divisions. The emergence of politically significant, yet often unstable, Third World countries and the increased power of Communist China contrast with arms control progress and the spread of democratic movements throughout Eastern Europe. While some have proclaimed an end to the Cold War, others are concerned that economic problems and ethnic rivalries could be destabilizing.

See also Atomic Weapons, International Control of; Containment Policy; Marshall Plan; North Atlantic Treaty Organization.

COLGROVE v. GREEN, 328 U.S. 549 (1946). Historically the United States Supreme Court has practiced a form of judicial restraint in cases which, for one reason or another, seem inappropriate for settlement by the judicial process. In *Colgrove v. Green* Justice Frankfurter, probably the premier advocate of judicial restraint, said that the petitioners were asking the Court for something beyond the Court's power to grant. The petitioners were Illinois voters, and they asked the federal courts to enjoin the holding of a congressional election on the grounds that the voting districts were malapportioned.

On behalf of the Court, Frankfurter declined to provide relief. He noted that the question before the Court was of a peculiarly political nature and was an appropriate problem for Congress, not the courts. The courts lacked the power to affirmatively remap the congressional districts and at best could only enjoin the election. After outlining the dangers inherent in exercising such a power, Frankfurter eloquently warned the Court not to enter this "political thicket," and he strenuously argued that the ultimate remedy lay with the people, who could influence their representatives.

—*Philip J. Hannon*

See also Apportionment, Legislative; Baker v. Carr; Reynolds v. Sims.

COLLECTIVE BARGAINING, the negotiating of the terms of employment between labor and management with a goal of a labor contract setting the terms of work and pay for a specific period of time. In its broader sense, collective bargaining includes the interpretation and administration of a labor agreement in the daily life of the union and the employer. Collective bargaining demands are enforced by employees using the strike and by employers using the lockout.

The scope of collective bargaining varies from a single union in a single company to an entire industry. Industry-wide bargaining does not exist completely, because all companies in a particular industry may not be organized. However, labor talks in the coal mining and steel industries, for example, come close to this type. Quite similar to industry-wide bargaining is association bargaining, which is collective bargaining between one union and a group of employers. Area-wide bargaining is negotiation between a union and employers covering a wide geographical area, as in the case of the West Coast Longshoremen's Union.

History. The first recorded collective bargaining was between the Philadelphia shoemakers and their employers in 1799. Collective bargaining finally took hold in management-labor relations in the 1850s, and early labor organizations gained many advances using collective bargaining. During World War I the federal government encouraged labor and management to use collective bargaining to reach a peaceful agreement, but even in the late 1940s collective bargaining was relatively new in many labor situations. To more firmly establish collective bargaining, the Taft-Hartley Act (1947) set up the Federal Mediation and Conciliation Service to provide assistance to labor and management in arriving at a peaceful settlement of labor disputes. Since then collective bargaining has widened its scope to include more details than wages: benefits, working conditions and hours, seniority, grievances, unemployment, and technological changes that affect work.

See also Arbitration; Labor Disputes, Mediation of; Lockout; Strike; Unfair Labor Practices.

COLLECTIVE SECURITY, an agreement by a group of states to protect each other against aggression by any member of the group. The organization agrees on the status quo to be defended and makes the necessary military arrangements to ensure this defense and resolve differences peacefully. A collective security agreement is not formed to protect against a specific threat, but instead against any threat to the decided status quo. Examples of collective security arrangements are the League of Nations and the United Nations. NATO and the Warsaw Pact may also be considered collective security arrangements, but their real purpose is collective defense against outside aggression.

A collective security agreement is based on law rather than on a determination of power. There is no central power in the group; instead, the power is divided equally among the member states. Action against member aggression is on the basis of law that already has been established by the group.

The failures of collective security have probably overshadowed its successes. Collective security arrangements did not prevent World War II, the Korean War, the Middle East conflict, or the Vietnam War. Many of these lapses occurred because major powers were not members of the collective security agreements or because members did not carry out their share of responsibility in dealing with threats to the status quo.

COLLECTIVISM, as opposed to individualism, stresses the idea of a group or "collective" of people working cooperatively in a common cause for the benefit of the whole. Collectives may be viewed as an entire nation or there may be many collectives with a nation, such as the collective farms in the U.S.S.R. or the kibutz in Israel. Although the state may own the collectivized farm or factory, the workers may be paid or in some fashion remunerated on the basis of the production of their particular collective. Though collective organizations are based most commonly on economic activity, their purposes are likely to be defined broadly enough to encompass all aspects of private and social life.

See also Corporate State; Democratic Socialism; Leftist; Socialism.

COLLECTOR v. DAY, 11 Wall. 113 (1871), concerns the power of Congress to impose a tax on the salary of a judicial officer of a state. Day, a county judge in Massachusetts, sued Buffington, the collector of internal revenue, to recover the taxes he had paid, for the years 1866 and 1867 and interest on that amount. The Court held that the salaries of state officers were immune from federal taxation. Although there is no express provision in the Constitution that prohibits the federal government from taxing the officers of a state, the Court believed that to do so would interfere with the reserved rights of the states to maintain courts. However, with ratification of the Sixteenth Amendment in 1913, Congress was given the power to levy a tax on income derived from any source whatever.

COMMERCE, UNITED STATES DEPARTMENT OF, established in 1913, an executive federal department responsible for the economic and technological growth of the United States. The department helps the states and industry, gives financial aid to areas with a sluggish economy, and promotes export of United States products and travel to the United States.

The Commerce Department originally was contained in the Department of Commerce and Labor, created in 1903 to enable the government to inspect and supervise the major corporations.

The Office of the Secretary administers the department, and in his cabinet role, the Secretary of Commerce advises the president on policy for the industrial and commercial aspects of the economy. The Office of Economic Analysis reviews the current business situation and provides the basic measures of the nation's economy, such as the Gross National Product. The Economic Development Administration is concerned with overseeing the economic development of depressed areas, and the Minority Business Development Agency coordinates programs for minority businesses.

Other divisions of the Department are the Bureau of the Census, the National Bureau of Standards, the National Oceanic and Atmospheric Administration, the Patent and Trademark Office, the Telecommunications and Information Administration, and the U.S. Travel Service.

COMMERCE POWER, delegated by the Constitution to Congress to regulate trade among the states and with foreign countries. Commerce power has become one of the major bases of the immense growth of the power of the national government. Social and industrial change expanded commerce among the states, and technological change has widened its definition to include such innovations as telegraphy, radio communications, and television. When the Constitution was adopted, commerce referred to the goods that moved in trade, but successive redefinitions gave Congress authority over carriers and passengers—even over labor relations, which are in the "stream of commerce." So widely has the commerce power been extended that it has become the constitutional basis for such acts as the Mann Act, having to do with taking prostitutes across state lines; the Brooks Act, dealing with stolen cars transported across state lines; and the Lindbergh Act, allowing federal involvement in kidnappings, on the assumption that a kidnapper intends to cross state lines.
—*Theodore B. Fleming, Jr.*

COMMISSION FORM. *See* Municipal Government.

COMMISSION ON . . . *See* Second part of name.

COMMISSIONS, UNITED STATES REGULATORY. *See* Independent Agencies and Regulatory Commissions.

COMMITTEE OF THE WHOLE, the House of Representatives sitting as a committee, usually in considering especially important measures. The Speaker appoints a member of the majority party as chairman, then seldom participates any further except to cast a vote in the event of a tie.

Public bills are considered by the "Committee of the Whole House on the State of the Union" (usually referred to as the Committee of the Whole), while private bills are considered in the less-important "Committee of the Whole House." Revenue and appropriations bills must be considered first in the Committee of the Whole, and other legislative measures also may be considered first by this body.

Procedures in the Committee of the Whole are highly flexible and are intended to expedite business. Debate on amendments is usually limited to five minute for opponents and five minutes for supporters, and the quorum that is required for the Committee of the Whole (100 members) is smaller than the quorum for the House of Representatives (218 members). By tradition, the Sergeant at Arms' mace is on display at all sessions of the House of Representatives as a symbol of authority, but is removed during sessions of the Committee of the Whole.
—*Mary L. Carns*

See also Mace; Quorum.

COMMITTEE SYSTEM OF CONGRESS, method by which the Senate and House divide their legislative, appropriatory, and investigatory functions into specialized small groups. In the early Congress the whole body of both houses was too large to work effectively. Accordingly, work was parceled out among specialized commmittees that reported their findings and recommendations to their parent bodies for final action. Gradually the committee system became the hub of the organizational wheel of Congress. Woodrow Wilson applied the term "little legislatures" to the standing committees of Congress in the 1880s. The term is still appropriate: most of the legislative work of Congress occurs in the committees, especially the standing committees.

Four major types of committees are usd in Congress: standing committees; joint committees, including conference committees; special, or select, committees; and subcommittees. The four types of committees permit specialization of function; they have helped to develop areas of expertise within Congress; and they reduce the number of bills and resolutions to a more workable number. Most legislative proposals will die in committee and will never reach the floor of the House or Senate.

Standing committees are permanent committees that will continue from one session of Congress to the next unless a major reorganization occurs. Once a member begins service on a committee, seniority virtually assures tenure. Each of a house's committees is in the control of the majority party, and the senior member of the

COMMITTEE SYSTEM

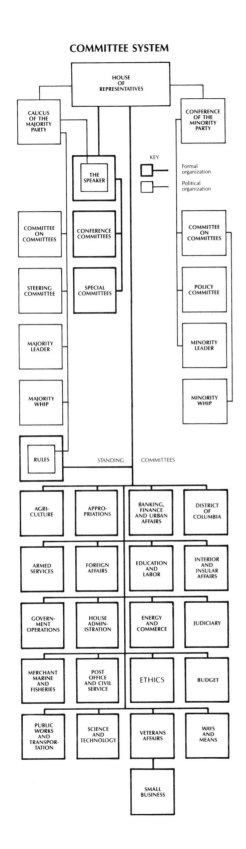

majority party normally will serve as chairman of the standing committee. Legislation introduced into the House or Senate is assigned by subject matter to one of the twenty-two House and sixteen Senate standing committees for review. If a standing committee reports legislation to the floor and the bill is passed, it goes to the other legislative body for approval.

Joint committees are drawn from members of both houses and may be formed to study specific problems as a single body, or to carry out oversight functions, or to coordinate action between the two houses. When the House and Senate do not agree on the wording and features of a bill that has passed both houses, the bill's particulars are ironed out by a specially-established joint conference committee, chaired by a member of the majority party and usually staffed equally by the two houses.

Special, or select, committees are established for specific purposes and for a limited period of time. A special committee goes out of existence once there is no further need for it. Occasionally a select committee may become a standing committee. Special and joint committees are controlled by the majority party.

Subcommittees are smaller units drawn from a full committee, and they permit much of the specialization that occurs in Congress. Hearings into proposed legislation are frequently conducted by subcommittees.

In addition to the legislative committees, both parties maintain campaign committees to help their members in elections and a committee on committees to select for party approval the proposed members of the standing, special, and joint committees. —*Mary L. Carns*

See also Legislation and the Legislative Process; Seniority System; Conference Committee.

COMMODITY CREDIT CORPORATION finances crop support and stabilization to protect farm income and to balance supplies of agricultural commodities. Acquired commodities are disposed of through foreign and domestic sales, exchanges, and donations. Needs of developing nations are met under the terms of the Food for Peace Act (1966). Organized in 1933, the corporation was operated in affiliation with the Reconstruction Finance Corporation until 1939, when the CCC was transferred to the Department of Agriculture.

COMMON CAUSE, a national citizen-action group founded in 1968 to achieve a reordering of national priorities and a greater responsiveness on the part of governmental institutions to the public. Membership is open to the general public for a small fee, and members are regularly polled to learn which local and national issues are in need of reassessment. The general goal of Common Cause is to open up the political process to greater involvement of citizens and to make government more accountable and efficient.

The organization uses various lobbying techniques to influence legislation. It has been active in such issues as limiting campaign financing, increasing voter registration, family assistance planning, U.S. withdrawal from Vietnam, and reducing the influence of political action committees (PACs) on Congress.

COMMON LAW, in its broadest sense, refers to the originally English legal system that has been adopted, in varying degrees, by most English-speaking countries. It is a system of judge-made law, although its principles theoretically derive from general usage and immemorial custom, which the judge only applies. Common law is often called "unwritten law," even though one looks to printed reports of decided cases to deduce its principles. No comprehensive listing of its legal rules is available, unlike civil law's "Codes." Because the legal rules depend on the nuances of the particular situation, decisions of cases are reached by reasoning inductively, comparing the cases' facts with those of previously decided cases. Within this legal system, the term "common law" is used both to distinguish judge-made law from statutory law and to distinguish the system of rigorously applied legal principles from the system of flexible, equitable remedies. The common law was codified inthe eighteenth century by a noted English jurist, Sir William Blackstone, following earlier compilation and analysis by Sir Edward Coke (later Lord Coke). Blackstone's *Commentaries on the Law of England* still stands as the definitive work on the common law.

See also Civil Law; Equity; Stare Decisis.

COMMON SENSE. *See* Paine, Thomas.

COMMUNICATIONS ACTS. The laws that govern the various communications media. The first federal regulatory measure was the Mann-Elkins Act of 1910, which gave the Interstate Commerce Commission (ICC) supervisory powers over the telegraph and telephone industries.

The act of 1934 created the Federal Communications Commission (FCC) to oversee cable, telephone, telegraph, and radio communications. The power to regulate television was added later. The purpose of the act was to give the United States a rapid, efficient communications system at reasonable rates and to regulate interstate and foreign communications. By the act, the FCC assumed the communications functions of the ICC, the Postmaster General, and the Radio Commission. The wiretapping provisions included in the 1934 act were later deleted.

See also Wiretapping.

COMMUNISM. The philosophical foundations of communism, as defined by Karl Marx, Frederick Engels, Vladimir Lenin, and some of their followers, lie in dialectical materialism. All reality is material; and matter is autodynamic, containing within itself elements of self-opposition that provide for its development; nature is not a conglomerate of things but an endless process.

Marx's Dialectic. According to Marx, history develops dialectically through class struggle, an irreconcilable conflict between property owners and propertyless, exploiters and exploited. The irreconcilability of that conflict resulted in emergence of the state, a class organization, a public unified force in the hands of the property owners, used for the protection of property.

In his monumental *Das Kapital,* Marx argued that the capitalistic society and its system of government are doomed, because although the process of production became as organized and collective as possible, its control, as well as appropriation of the fruits of production, are in the hands of a decreasing number of individuals motivated by profit. As a result, the productive forces cannot fully develop and the exploitation of the working classes becomes unbearable. Capitalism will be replaced by a socialist state in which the working class itself owns the means of production and distribution, controls and regulates the economy, and distributes the fruits of production according to its own needs.

Lenin's Contribution was a pragmatic continuation of Marx's communist theory. Lenin's work consists of voluminous writings on capitalist imperialism, on organization and leadership of the proletariat, on state and evolution, and on dictatorship of the proletariat.

— Jan Karski

COMMUNIST MANIFESTO. *See* Marx, Karl.

COMMUNIST PARTY OF THE U.S.A., an offshoot of the Socialist party formed in Chicago in 1919. Encouraged by the success of the Russian revolution, leftist members of the party rejected Socialist goals and advocated the immediate and violent overthrow of American capitalism. Upon their expulsion from the Socialist party, they organized as the American Communist party under the acknowledged leadership of the Soviet Union. Subject from the first to legal harassment, they operated for a time as the Workers Party of America, which they hoped would attract farmer-labor support.

In the 1930s, as the country felt the depression, the party was able to somewhat expand its influence, and in 1932 William Z. Foster, the Communist presidential candidate, polled over 100,000 votes. Competing with "New Deal" legislation however, the party failed to gain significant support from the urban working masses.

With the outbreak of World War II, legal harassment intensified. In 1940 the Smith Alien Registration Act was passed, which made it illegal to advocate overthrow of the government. In 1948 Foster and eleven other Communist leaders were sentenced to imprisonment for violation of the Smith Act. The Korean War caused a deepening of anti-Communist feeling, and in 1950 Congress passed, over President Truman's veto, the McCarran Internal Security Act, which required the party to register with the Attorney General. The McCarran-Walter Act of 1952, which allowed the deportation of foreigners for Communist activity, further undermined the legal status of the party.

Khrushchev's denunciation of Stalin, the Hungarian rebellion of 1956, and the move toward democratization in the East Bloc have split the party so deeply that it no longer presents a cohesive front.

See also Political Parties in the United States; Presidential Election.

COMMUNIST PARTY OF THE UNITED STATES v. SUBVERSIVE ACTIVITIES CONTROL BOARD (SACB), 367 U.S. 1 (1967), questions the constitutionality of the registration provision of the Subversive Activities Control Act as applied to the Communist party. The Communist party refused to register with the United States Attorney General, as ordered by the SACB. In a five to four decision, delivered by Mr. Justice Frankfurter, the Court held that the registration requirement was not unconstitutional or repugnant to the First Amendment, and that the Communist party, as a Communist action organization substantially directed, dominated, or controlled by a foreign power, was required to register. This decision concerning the membership section of the act was overruled in *Aptheker v. Secretary of State.*

COMMUNITY ACTION PROGRAM, a program created by the Economic Opportunity Act of 1964 to encourage communities to wage a war on poverty. This act stressed education and training of the poor. Federal aid is received by local public and private agencies to undertake antipoverty programs that involve poor people in operating the programs themselves. The act stressed "maximum feasible participation" by the poor in the planning and administration of programs; this process led, in many cases, to political conflicts with local government officials. Among the many activities that this act encourages are Volunteers in Service to America (VISTA) and the Job Corps.

VISTA volunteers live and work in such places as migrant-worker camps, Indian reservations, hospitals, schools, and slums. The volunteers are paid only a subsistence allowance. The Job Corps is a program in which unemployed and often seemingly unemployable young people from sixteen to twenty-one work, live, and study at training centers or in conservation camps. Education, vocational training, and work experience are stressed. Members receive living and travel allowances. Other programs funded by the Economic Opportunity Act include loans to farmers and small-businessmen.

See also Volunteers in Service to America.

COMMUNITY RELATIONS SERVICE (CRS), an agency of the Department of Justice. The CRS's primary duty is to assist in resolving disputes over violations of antidiscrimination statutes. CRS also may help in resolving any ethnic or socially-related problems.

COMPREHENSIVE ENVIRONMENTAL RESPONSE, COMPENSATION AND LIABILITY ACT (1980). *See* Superfund.

COMPTROLLER GENERAL OF THE UNITED STATES. *See* General Accounting Office (GAO).

COMPTROLLER OF THE CURRENCY. *See* Treasury, United States Department of the.

COMPULSORY TESTIMONY ACT OF 1954. *See* Immunity Act of 1954.

CONCILIATION, a French civil law procedure which requires the parties to appear before the judge who tries to persuade them to settle their differences and thus avoid further court proceedings. The common law lacks such a device. A "pretrial conference" can be held at the court's discretion, but with the lawyers, not the parties, only to simplify the trial, not settle the case. Conciliation is frequently used by U.S. courts in certain civil proceedings such as labor disputes. It is a voluntary and nonbinding process.

See also Arbitration.

CONCURRENT JURISDICTION exists when more than one court is entitled to consider the same case. This situation often exists in the United States due to its federal structure. The U.S. Constitution does not prohibit state courts from entertaining suits involving federal questions, although Congress does in specific instances, such as in national security cases and seditions. Article III of the Constitution grants federal courts jurisdiction where there is a diversity of citizenship. A person has the option of suing in state or federal court.

See also Jurisdiction.

CONCURRENT MAJORITY, a principle advanced by John C. Calhoun in the debates over slavery prior to the Civil War. Calhoun viewed all civil societies as composed of groups with differing and sometimes clashing interests. He argued that political decisions affecting these interests should not be made by a simple numerical majority of the individuals constituting all the groups. Rather, he argued, each group, by a majority from within itself, should have to agree to any decision affecting it. From these grounds, he held that the national government could not, through representatives supposedly representing a numerical majority of the whole country, decide to abolish slavery without at the same time a concurring majority of each state.

See also Democracy; Pluralism.

CONCURRENT POWER is held by both nations and states. The classic example is the power to tax: a state has the power to tax as does the national government, so long as the particular tax is not constitutionally prohibited and does not interfere with the taxing power of the national government.

See also Delegated Powers; Implied Powers; Reserved Powers.

CONFEDERATION, a decentralized, loose association of subnational governments with a weak national government. Sovereignty resides in the subnational government, and the national government is usually limited to national defense and police power.

CONFERENCE COMMITTEE, the most common form of joint committee, especially created to reconcile differences between House and Senate versions of the same bill. Most major pieces of legislation require action by a conference committee. Members of the conference committee, known as "managers," are appointed by the Speaker of the House and the President of the Senate. There is no specific number of members for a conference committee, but the usual number ranges from three to nine managers from each house. The majority party in each house must be represented by a majority of membership on the conference committee delegations.

—Mary L. Carns

CONFERENCE ON CONFIDENCE AND SECURITY-BUILDING MEASURES AND DISARMAMENT IN EUROPE (CDE), initiative begun in 1983 to achieve advances in the areas of non-nuclear disarmament. Membership includes all European states, except Albania, plus the United States and Canada. Talks began in 1984 and were stalemated by demands from Warsaw Pact members that conventional air forces be a part of the negotiations. After two and a half years of discussions in Stockholm, the conference adopted a final document. Among its historic provisions are measures requiring advance notification of military maneuvers and mandatory on-site inspections.

The success of this agreement, combined with recent events in Eastern Europe, led to calls for major reductions in defense spending and for the removal of large numbers of American troops from Western Europe.

CONFESSION, voluntary admission of guilt. To be accepted as evidence in a court of law, a confession must not have been obtained under duress. The right to be protected from forced confession and to stand mute rather than incriminate oneself stems from the Fifth Amendment assurance that no person "shall be compelled in any criminal case to be a witness against himself," and the Fourteenth Amendment guarantee of due process. The use of the Fifth Amendment by an accused person is not to be considered a confession of guilt. On the other hand, if a confession is freely given, its use cannot be prevented in court.

In a 1964 decision the Supreme Court decided that the judge must determine whether or not the confession has been properly obtained before it is admitted in evidence. Criteria he uses include: the time elapsing between arrest and arraignment; the defendant's knowledge at the time of the confession of the nature of the offense of which he was suspected; the accused's advisal of his rights; and the assistance of defense counsel when giving the confession.

As early as 1897 the Supreme Court ruled that a confession obtained by force, threats, or promises could not be used at a federal criminal trial. In 1954 the use of mental coercion in obtaining a confession was ruled illegal. The most important decision regarding confessions is the 1966 *Miranda v. Arizona* case. The Court ruled that the accused must be warned that he has the right to remain silent, to have a lawyer present when speaking and to be provided a lawyer if unable to pay. Otherwise, no statement the person in custody makes can be used against him in court.

A number of criminal convictions have been reversed because of the illegal manner in which confessions were obtained. "Law and order" advocates have protested these rulings in the belief that such rulings make it easier for criminals to escape prosecution. Subsequent crime-control bills have sought to weaken the impact of the Miranda case and similar decisions.

See also Accused Persons, Rights of.

CONFIRMATION, the process by which the U.S. Senate accepts or rejects presidential appointments, through the provision of the Constitution that gives the president powers of appointment "by and with the Advice and Consent of the Senate" (Article II, section 2). In actual practice, high-ranking officials known as "superior officers" are appointed with the advice and consent of the Senate. Those designated by the Senate as "inferior officers" may be appointed by the president alone, even though some listed as inferior officers actually hold position of considerable power and influence. There is also one confirmation process in which the House of Representatives has a role. The Twenty-fifth Amendment (section 2) stipulates that whenever there is a vacancy in the office of the vice president, the president shall nominate a new vice president, subject to confirmation by a majority vote of both houses of Congress.

The power to reject an appointment is rarely used, but the threat of rejection and the detailed and probing investigations that precede the actual vote for important officers are considered to be checks on possible presidential abuse of power. Appointments to judicial posts and to regulatory commissions generally receive closer scrutiny than do "political appointments" such as Cabinet officers. Under the tradition of "senatorial courtesy," the Senate customarily will refuse to confirm appointees who will serve within a single state unless the nominee is acceptable to the senator or senators of the president's party who represent that state.

—Mary L. Carns

See also Advice and Consent; Senatorial Courtesy.

CONFLICT OF INTEREST, behavior of a public official (appointed or elected) that may benefit or appear to benefit the official's private interest. Public officials are in a position to make decisions that will influence the value of property (stocks, bonds, land) or the success of particular corporations. If the official were to make such a decision that would result or would appear to result in the official's personal gain, such a situation is a conflict of interest. Procedures have been established on the state and federal level to minimize the chance of this occurring.

See also Congressional Ethics.

CONGRESSIONAL COMMITTEES. *See* Committee System of Congress.

CONGRESSIONAL DIRECTORY, the official government directory, published for each session of Congress by the Government Printing Office. The Directory outlines the organization of all three branches of government and gives biographical data on all members of Congress, their addresses, and committee assignments. There is also biographical information on the president and the vice president, and the members of the Supreme Court and other federal courts. The Directory gives the names of all foreign ambassadors, along with the address of their embassies, and the location of consular offices throughout the United States.

CONGRESSIONAL ETHICS, moral behavior of congressional members and employees, including proper use of political funds and power. After the 1960s' turmoil over Robert (Bobby) G. Baker, former secretary of the Senate majority leader, Sen. Thomas J. Dodd (D.-Conn.), and Rep. Adam Clayton Powell (D.-N.Y.), both houses formulated written rules regarding congressional ethics in general.

After Bobby Baker was charged with using his office to promote outside business interests, each house established a Select Committee on Standards and Conduct to investigate any breaches of congressional ethics. In 1968 both Houses adopted codes of Official Conduct. These rules covered congressional members, employees, and candidates. In the Senate version the rules declared that "a Senator should use the power entrusted to him by the people only for their benefit and never for the benefit of himself or a few."

The new ethics codes were not enforced against members of either house until 1976, although eight members of Congress were convicted in courts of law between 1968 and 1976, and several others were indicted. New House and Senate codes of ethics were again enacted in 1977. The new codes included restrictions on honoraria and outside income, established requirements for financial disclosures, and set strict limitation on the value of gifts that could be accepted by members of Congress. In 1978 the provisions of the House and Senate ethics codes were slightly amended and applied to high-ranking executive and judicial officers under terms of the Ethics in Government Act.

Various forms of discipline have been employed by the House and Senate, including expulsion, censure, reprimand, and loss of chairmanships. Several members have remained in office even after convictions on criminal charges. Dodd was the seventh senator in history to be censured, in his case for misuse of campaign funds. Other senators have been censured for security breaches, assault, and, in the case of Sen. Joseph McCarthy (R.-Wisc.), for abuse of senators. Only one senator has been expelled, but House members have been excluded for such varied causes as aiding the Confederacy, polygamy, and selling military appointments to West Point. Recent congressional scandals include the "Koreagate" scandal in 1976, which involved charges of influence-buying by South Korean agents; and the "Abscam" investigation of 1980 that led to the expulsion of one representative. Since then more than twenty members have been objects of ethics inquiries. Congressional honoraria are a major target of concern, but the practice was left open to continued abuse when reforms, tied to a pay increase, were defeated in 1989. *—Mary L. Carns*

See also Abscam; Censure; Ethics in Government Act; Expulsion.

CONGRESSIONAL INVESTIGATIONS. *See* Investigative Power of Congress.

CONGRESSIONAL RECORD, a daily publication of the U.S. Congress, when in session, carrying the official account of congressional proceedings. Each night approximately 32,000 copies of the *Record,* averaging 200 pages per copy, are printed and delivered by 8 a.m. the next day (at an annual cost of about $25 million). A large proportion of each printing of the *Congressional Record* is sent free of charge to individuals, government agencies, and departments authorized by the Joint Committee on Printing. Subscriptions are also available. The Joint Committee on Printing controls the style and arrangement of the *Record.*

Each day that Congress is in session, remarks made on the floor are reported by the official reporters of each house. Written remarks may also be submitted for inclusion in the "Extension of Remarks" section. At the back of the *Record* is the "Daily Digest," first published March 17, 1947, summarizing the daily events in each house. Corrections are made in the indexed biweekly and hardbound editions.

Although the law requires the *Congressional Record* to be "substantially a verbatim report of proceedings," major deviations from actual floor proceedings may appear in the *Record.* Through the process known as "interlining," members may add, delete, or edit remarks. The most famous example of this practice was in 1972 when House Majority Leader Hale Boggs was recorded as giving a speech—two days after he was presumed dead in a plane crash. In 1978 the Government Printing Office began using black dots, known as "bullets," to designate material that was added to the *Record* but which had not been spoken by the member on the floor.

CONGRESSIONAL RESEARCH SERVICE, professional research staff that gathers and analyzes data for members of Congress. A division of the Library of Congress, it was formerly known as the Legislative Reference Service.   —*Mary L. Carns*

CONGRESSMAN AT LARGE, a member of the House of Representatives who is elected from the entire state, rather than from a district. Prevalent in the early nineteenth century, election of congressmen at large is no longer a common practice. Election at large generally occurs in redistricting when no agreement can be reached on the boundaries of a new district or in a state entitled to only one seat.

CONGRESS OF INDUSTRIAL ORGANIZATIONS. *See* American Federation of Labor and Congress of Industrial Organizations (AFL-CIO).

CONGRESS OF RACIAL EQUALITY (CORE), a civil rights organization founded in Chicago in 1942. As early as 1946, CORE leader James Farmer utilized the sit-in to challenge segregation in a Chicago restaurant.

CORE gained national prominence in May 1961, when hundreds of black and white freedom riders traveled South, hoping to break down segregated transportation facilities. In September of that year, the Interstate Commerce Commission issued an order banning segregation in interstate travel terminals. In the mid-1960s the group led intensive voter registration drives in the South. Having endorsed black power, CORE has since 1968, under its national director, Roy Innis, emphasized its role as a black nationalist organization.

CONGRESS OF THE UNITED STATES, the legislative branch of the federal government authorized by Article I of the Constitution. Congress' division into two houses resulted from the Great Compromise of the Constitutional Convention, where it was agreed that representation in the House should reflect the population of each state and that each state would have two votes in the Senate.

Congress has the power to assess and collect taxes, regulate interstate and foreign commerce, declare war, establish courts and a post office, coin money, raise and maintain an army and navy, call up the militia, make laws regarding the preceding areas, and propose amendments to the Constitution. In addition, the Senate has the rights of advise-and-consent on presidential appointments, ratification of treaties, and trial of impeachment. The House has the power of originating all bills to raise revenue and the power of impeachment. For

---

CONGRESS OF THE UNITED STATES: TOPIC GUIDE

The article on CONGRESS OF THE UNITED STATES defines the powers of Congress, summarizes its history from 1789 through the twentieth century, and briefly describes the organization of Congress today.

The related articles on the Congress of the United States may be divided into three groups.

Components of Congress. The activities of Congress' divisions are covered in articles on SENATE OF THE UNITED STATES, whose senior member is PRESIDENT PRO TEMPORE OF THE SENATE, and HOUSE OF REPRESENTATIVES OF THE UNITED STATES, whose most powerful member is the SPEAKER OF THE HOUSE. The majority party is headed by the MAJORITY LEADER; the minority party by the MINORITY LEADER. Each is assisted by a WHIP.

The COMMITTEE SYSTEM OF CONGRESS, in which the SENIORITY SYSTEM dominates, plays a key role in the legislative process. Through STANDING COMMITTEES AND SELECT COMMITTEES, consideration of a BILL is often controlled. Among the influential committees are the WAYS AND MEANS COMMITTEE and RULES COMMITTEE.

The INVESTIGATIVE POWER OF CONGRESS gives it a wide-ranging ability to probe, although the extent of these powers was limited by WATKINS v. U.S. Efforts to thwart Congress can result in CONTEMPT OF CONGRESS.

Special Features. A congressman generally represents a DISTRICT. Attempts to create a district with particular characteristics may result in a GERRYMANDER. Congressional seats are alloted by APPORTIONMENT. While in office a Congressman must be aware of CONGRESSIONAL ETHICS, abuses of which may bring CENSURE or IMPEACHMENT. An un-reelected Congressman whose term has not ended is a LAME DUCK.

Legislative Features. General features of legislation are discussed under LEGISLATION AND LEGISLATIVE PROCESSES, which has a Study Guide, while articles describing specific features include ACT OF CONGRESS, APPROPRIATION, CALENDAR, PORK BARREL LEGISLATION, QUORUM, and AMENDMENT, CONGRESSIONAL. Opponents of a bill in the Senate may FILIBUSTER, but supporters can end debate through CLOTURE. SENATORIAL COURTESY sometimes determines actions in the upper house.

---

legislation to be passed in Congress, bills and joint resolutions must pass both houses and then be signed by the president—or else be passed over veto by a two-thirds vote of both houses.

Early History. Congress first met in 1789 at the Federal Hall in New York City with with twenty senators and fifty-nine representatives present. As envisioned by the framers of the Constitution, the House was to be

CONGRESSIONAL LEADERSHIP

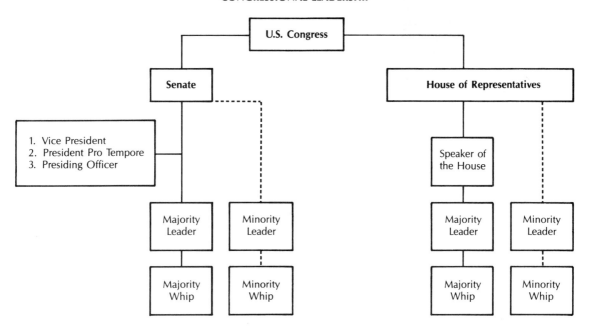

"the grand depository of the democratic principles of the Government," while the Senate was to represent state sovereignty. Representatives were elected by the people, but the Senators were chosen by the state legislatures. In the early years of the country, the House was the more important chamber of Congress and attracted members like James Madison and Henry Clay. The House originated the bulk of the bills and the Senate revised them. The Senate regarded itself as a deliberative body, and there were many fears that it would become an American House of Lords.

Surviving the early challenge, the Senate became a powerful legislative body and the main forum for discussing national issues. After the Civil War the Senate emerged as the dominant arm of the government. The increasing size of the House and its workload necessitated strict procedural rules limiting debate and emphasizing committee work, with a consequent weakening of the power of each representative.

A major change in the nature of Congress came at the turn of the century with voter dissatisfaction over the abuses of some state legislatures in electing senators. Many of the more progressive states had already adopted preferential elections for choosing senators, but it was not until the Seventeenth Amendment in 1912 that senators were elected directly by the people.

Twentieth Century. Congress in the twentieth century was marked by an increase in the power of the president. By passing reorganization acts, Congress tried to restore equal footing with the executive branch, but the role of the president in the Vietnam War, for instance, cast doubts on Congress' ability to overpower

the president. In addition, in demanding a more responsive Congress, the public has made serious, but so far unsuccessful, challenges to the congressional tradition of seniority, secrecy, and filibuster.

Today's senate is composed of one hundred members, with each elected to a six-year term. The House has 435 members, who are elected for two-year terms. Article I of the Constitution requires Congress "to assemble at least once in every Year," and the 20th Amendment sets January 3 as the first day of regular sessions. The president may convene Congress for extraordinary sessions.

"A Congress" also refers to the two-year period of time, used for organizational purposes and numbered consecutively, that coincides with the term of office for the House of Representatives. Each Congress has two sessions, beginning in January of each year. The Legislative Reorganization Act of 1970 sets July 31 as the date for adjournment "unless otherwise provided for by Congress."

See also House of Representatives; Senate.

CONNALLY AMENDMENT, also known as the Connally Reservation of 1946, is not strictly an amendment since a treaty cannot be amended unilaterally. In accepting the jurisdiction of the International Court in 1946, Chairman Thomas Connally of the Senate Foreign Relations Committee reserved the United States' right to determine what issues were strictly domestic and outside the court's jurisdiction. Connally loyally championed the foreign policies of Roosevelt and Truman, but like many Americans he had no deep commitment to internationalism. The amendment significantly indicates a limit to the abandonment of national interest during the establishment of the United Nations and the International Court. Attempts to repeal the reservation were defeated consistently in subsequent years.

See also Isolationism.

CONNECTICUT COMPROMISE, the great compromise of the Constitutional Convention of 1787 that resolved the debate over representation in the proposed bicameral legislature. The compromise resolved the clash between the large and small states, evident in the earlier Virginia and New Jersey plans. Suggested by Roger Sherman of Connecticut, the compromise also provided the solution to a fundamental question of democratic government—how to reconcile the sovereignty of the states with the rights of individuals to have a voice in the government. Sherman's basic proposal suggesting proportional representation in the lower house and one vote for each state in the upper house was adopted with modifications by the convention on July 16, 1787, thus removing the major obstacle to the formulation of the Constitution.

See also Constitutional Convention of 1787; New Jersey Plan; Three-Fifths Compromise; Virginia Plan.

CONSCIENTIOUS OBJECTION, resistance to state authority, particularly military service, on the grounds of religious or moral views. In the United States, conscientious objection to military service dates from the Civil War, when Quakers refused to fight. At that time, however, one could avoid military service by providing a substitute or paying a fee. When the United States entered World War I in 1916, however, general conscription was enacted and conscientious objectors were required to enter non-combatant service. A conscientious objector was defined as someone belonging to a recognized sect that specifically disavowed all wars. Under the 1948 Selective Service Act, the 1951 Universal Military Training and Service Act, and the Military Selective Service Act of 1967, persons who could not demonstrate such membership or who objected only to a particular war were segregated or imprisoned.

Testing of the Definition of conscientious objection and the requirement that conscientious objectors perform analogous nonmilitary service greatly increased in the late 1960s as a result of intensified United States involvement in the Vietnam War. Many notable individuals including Dr. Benjamin Spock and Fathers Philip and Daniel Berrigan, and hundreds of young men opted for prison terms rather than participate in that war. In 1970 a Massachusetts court ruled that a person who was not a member of a religious sect could be classified as a conscientious objector to a particular war without opposing war in general. In an apparent reversal of the trend to broaden the definition of conscientious objection, in 1971 the Supreme Court determined that the label applied only to those whose opposition to war in

general was based on deeply held religious beliefs (*Gilette v. United States*).

CONSCRIPTION. *See* Selective Service System.

CONSENT, POPULAR, the basis for nearly all modern governments. It stems from seventeenth-century contract theories. Classical and medieval political theories insisted that people were communal by nature and that government was ordained by natural law, God, or the cosmos: people were born to poltiical life and were bound by the laws of their city or state whether they consented to them or not. The contract theorists postulated a state of nature, prior to government, and in which all were free and equal: individuals created and entered into civil society only by giving their consent to doing so. From these views come the idea of popular consent, which hold that no law is legitimate without the direct or indirect consent of the people living under them.

See also Contract Theory; Democracy; Democratic Socialism; Limited Government.

CONSERVATISM, a political movement in opposition to theories or activities designed to effect change. Conservatism's substantive content will depend, therefore, upon the context in which it arises. Contemporary Western conservatism opposes the moral relativism, communal ideas and movements, and state planning and control over the economy advocated by contemporary liberalism. Conservatism looks to various forms of traditional moral philosophy or religion for universal political principles (for example, the natural right to private property) and espouses individualism and the free market economy. Modern conservative theory is based on the writings of English political theorist Edmund Burke. Burke believed in the *prima facie* validity of custom and tradition. Change, to be acceptable, must adapt to existing institutions or values.

See also Communism; Liberalism.

CONSERVATIVE COALITION, bipartisan alliance of Republicans and Southern Democrats in Congress, most powerful in the House. This coalition developed in the late 1930s in reaction to the New Deal and was a powerful force on major social and economic issues, blocking proposed measures or trimming them. Possessing little formalized organization, it relied on communication and cooperation among some of its recognized leaders to map a course of action. In addition to mobilizing votes, the coalition leaders showed considerable ability in the use of rules and procedures to block measures they opposed.   —*Dale Vinyard*

See also Democratic Study Group; Rules Committee.

CONSTITUENT, one who resides in a legislator's district. Contact with constituents—through the mail, the press, public opinion surveys, and political parties—

is a central feature of the "typical day" of a legislator. Most members of Congress find that the majority of their time will be spent on handling constituent problems and requests. —*Mary L. Carns*

CONSTITUENT POWER, functions that relate to amending the Constitution. The amendment power is shared by Congress and the states: the power of proposal belongs to Congress, while ratification rests with the states. Amendments may be proposed by a two-thirds vote of each house of Congress, or congress may convene a national constitutional convention if two-thirds of the state legislatures request it. The second method has never been used. Proposed amendments may be ratified by three-fourths of the state legislatures, or by ratifying conventions in three-fourths of the states. The latter method has been used only once, in the case of the Twenty-first Amendment. —*Mary L. Carns*

CONSTITUTIONAL AMENDMENT. See Amendment, Constitutional.

CONSTITUTIONAL CONSTRUCTION, a method of interpreting the various articles in the United States Constitution. "Strict" constructionists take literally the words of the Tenth Amendment: "The powers not delegated to the United States by the Constitution, nor prohibited by it to the States, are reserved to the States respectively, or to the people." A literal or strict interpretation leads to restrictions on federal power, granting to the national government only those powers explicitly awarded it in the Constitution. A "strict" constructionist attempts to interpret the Constitution as it was intended by its authors. "Loose" constructionists, on the other hand, maintain that the Constitution, in allocating certain powers and responsibilities to the federal government, meant the government to have the additional means to carry out those responsibilities. A "loose" constructionist attempts to interpret the Constitution in light of current needs while respecting historical precedent.

The controversy began as long ago as 1819, in the celebrated Supreme Court case *McCulloch v. Maryland.* In that case Chief Justice John Marshall originated the loose constructionist view when he affirmed the Federal government's right to establish a bank, although not expressly empowered to do so by the Constitution. Marshall argued that the financial duties imposed on Congress implied its right to create a bank. The loose construction of the Constitution has enabled it to survive for nearly 200 years with only twenty-six amendments. Strict interpretation would have necessitated many more alterations.

See also Marshall, John; McCulloch v. Maryland.

CONSTITUTIONAL CONVENTION OF 1787, an assembly of fifty-five delegates from twelve of the original thirteen states (Rhode Island excepted) that drafted the Constitution. The signal failure of the Articles of Con-

federation (1781-1787) to provide a workable form of government, particularly with regard to powers of taxation and control of trade, was the impetus for the convention. Originally the delegates planned only to revise the articles, but it was soon apparent that the problem of establishing the proper balance between the powers of the national government and those of the states, and between individual rights and governmental authority necessitated a new framework.

The often bitter debate over the essential question of federalism lasted from May 17 to September 25, in Independence Hall, Philadelphia. Under the chairmanship of George Washington, the argument was resolved initially through the adoption of the basic principles of the Virginia Plan. In large measure a summary of the theories of James Madison, known as the father of the Constitution, this plan envisioned a strong central government each of whose three branches—legislative, executive, and judicial—would maintain checks on the others to ensure the proper balance of power. The ensuing argument over representation in the bicameral legislature suggested in the Virginia Plan was settled by the Connecticut Compromise.

Other discussions centered on the power of Congress to tax and regulate foreign and interstate commerce, the slavery question, and the prohibition of bills of attainder and ex post facto laws. The final draft of the Constitution, engineered chiefly by Madison, Alexander Hamilton, and Gouverneur Morris, was ratified by thirty-nine of the delegates on September 17.

See also Articles of Confederation; Connecticut Compromise; Constitution of the United States; Madison's Journal; Three-fifths Compromise; Virginia Plan.

CONSTITUTIONAL COURT. See Legislative Court.

CONSTITUTIONALISM insists that there exist fundamental laws not subject to ordinary change that determine the organization and structure, divide the functions among the parts, and set the limits of a government. Aristotle compiled an anthology on constitutions. He viewed a constitution, or *politeia,* as including not only the organization of political offices, but also customs, habits, and the predominant spirit of a regime. Constitutionalism was predominant in Roman thought and practice. Modern constitutionalism stems from seventeenth-century political thought, especially the contract theory, and stresses a set of written or unwritten fundamental positive laws that must be agreed to by the governed. The consent of the governed is more important to the legitimacy of a constitution than its content is. The oldest written constitution still in effect is the United States'.

See also Contract Theory; Democracy; Limited Government.

CONSTITUTIONAL LAW, provisions having to do with the creation, amendment, operation, and interpretation of constitutions. With reference to a particular law, the term is used to indicate that the law is consistent with the provisions of the constitution(s) to which it is subordinate. In the United States, the term has come to refer most commonly to the body of case law created by almost two centuries of decisions in which the courts have considered various federal and state laws and executive acts to determine whether they are consistent with the applicable constitutions.

The power of the judiciary to evaluate acts of the other branches of government is not set forth in the United States Constitution but is implied therein, according to Chief Justice Marshall's opinion in 1803 in *Marbury v. Madison*. Because our legal system derives from that of England, it should be noted that English courts lack any power over acts of Parliament, nor does constitutional law in the American sense exist in England: the fundamental principle of the unwritten English constitution is its supremacy of Parliament.

Cases in Constitutional Law

Separate articles on many of these important cases will be found in this volume. In addition, the reader will find these cases organized chronologically in the listing accompanying the article on the Supreme Court of the United States.

Civil Rights and Liberties
Abrams v. United States (1919)
Adderly v. Florida (1966)
Alexander v. Holmes County Board of Education (1969)
Aptheker v. Secretary of State (1964)
Bantam Books, Inc. v. Sullivan (1963)
Bates v. City of Little Rock (1960)
Brandenburg v. Ohio (1969)
Brown v. Board of Education of Topeka (1954)
Brown v. Board of Education (1955)
Buchanan v. Warley (1917)
City of Richmond v. J.A. Croson (1989)
Civil Rights Cases (1883)
Communist Party v. Subversive Activities Control Board (1961)
Corrigan v. Buckley (1926)
Dennis v. United States (1951)
Dred Scott v. Sandford (1857)
Edwards v. South Carolina (1963)
Elfbrandt v. Russell (1966)
Feiner v. New York (1951)
Garrison v. Louisiana (1964)
Gitlow v. New York (1925)
Griswold v. Connecticut (1965)
Grove City College v. Bell (1984)
Guinn v. United States (1915)
Hazelwood School District v. Kuhlmeier (1988)
Heart of Atlanta Motel v. United States (1964)
Herndon v. Lowry (1937)
Hirabayashi v. United States (1943)

Jones v. Alfred H. Mayer Co. (1968)
Katzenbach v. McClung (1964)
Keyishian v. Board of Regents (1967)
Kingsley Pictures Corp. v. Regents (1959)
Korematsu v. United States (1944)
Kunz v. New York (1951)
Lamont v. Postmaster-General (1965)
Martin v. Wilkes (1989)
McGowan v. Maryland (1961)
NAACP v. Alabama (1958)
NAACP v. Button (1963)
Near v. Minnesota (1931)
New York Times v. Sullivan (1964)
Nixon v. Herndon (1927)
Plessy v. Ferguson (1896)
Reitman v. Mulkey (1967)
Roth v. United States (1957)
Scales v. United States (1961)
Schenck v. United States (1919)
Screws v. United States (1945)
Shelley v. Kraimer (1948)
Skinner v. Railway Labor Executive Assocation (1989)
Slaughter House Cases (1873)
Smith v. Allwright (1944)
Stanley v. Georgia (1969)
Sweatt v. Painter (1950)
Sweezy v. New Hampshire (1957)
Terminiello v. Chicago (1949)
Texas v. Johnson (1989)
Thornhill v. Alabama (1940)
Tinker v. Des Moines School District et al (1969)
United States v. Guest (1966)
United States v. O'Brien (1968)
Webster v. Reproductive Health Services (1989)
Whitehill v. Elkins (1967)
Whitney v. California (1927)

Rights of Accused
Aguilar v. Texas (1964)
Albertson v. Subversive Activities Control Board (1965)
Arizona v. Youngblood (1988)
Barenblatt v. United States (1959)
Bartkus v. Illinois (1959)
Benton v. Maryland (1969)
Berger v. State of New York (1967)
Betts v. Brady (1942)
Elkins v. United States (1960)
Escobedo v. Illinois (1964)
Ex parte Milligan (1866)
Gideon v. Wainwright (1963)
Harris v. New York (1971)
Hurtado v. California (1884)
In re Gault (1967)
Katz v. United States (1967)
Klopfer v. North Carolina (1967)
Mallory v. Hogan (1964)
Mapp v. Ohio (1961)
Miranda v. Arizona (1966)

Nardone v. United States (1937, 1939)
Nelson v. Los Angeles (1960)
Olmstead v. United States (1928)
Palko v. Connecticut (1937)
Pointer v. Texas (1965)
Powell v. Alabama (1932)
Ullman v. United States (1956)
Watkins v. United States (1957)
Weeks v. United States (1914)
Citizenship
Afroyim v. Rusk (1967)
Dred Scott v. Sandford (1857)
Girouard v. United States (1946)
Schneider v. Rusk (1964)
Trop v. Dulles (1958)
United States v. Wong Kim Ark (1898)
Religion
Abington School District v. Schempp (1963)
Board of Education v. Allen (1968)
Edwards v. Aguillard (1987)
Engel v. Vitale (1962)
Everson v. Board of Education (1947)
Illinois ex rel McCollum v. Board of Education (1948)
Kunz v. New York (1951)
Minersville School District v. Gobitis (1940)
Torcaso v. Watkins (1961)
United States v. Seeger (1965)
Zorach v. Clauson (1951)
Federal Union
Barron v. Baltimore (1833)
Chisholm v. Georgia (1793)
Cohens v. Virginia (1821)
Collector v. Day (1871)
Fletcher v. Peck (1810)
Genessee Chief v. Fitzhugh (1851)
Gibbons v. Ogden (1824)
Hammer v. Dagenhart (1918)
Home Building and Loan Assoc. v. Blaisdell (1934)
McCulloch v. Maryland (1819)
Marbury v. Madison (1803)
Missouri v. Holland (1920)
Pennsylvania v. Nelson (1956)
Texas v. White (1868)
United States v. Lanza (1922)
Politics
Baker v. Carr (1962)
Colegrove v. Green (1946)
Gomillion v. Lightfoot (1960)
Harper v. Virginia Board of Elections (1966)
Katzenbach v. Morgan (1966)
Luther v. Borden (1849)
Newberry v. United States (1921)
Nixon v. Condon (1932)
Nixon v. Herndon (1927)
Reynolds v. Sims (1964)
Smith v. Allwright (1944)
South Carolina v. Katzenbach (1966)
United States v. Classic (1941)

Wells v. Rockefeller (1969)
Wesberry v. Sanders (1964)
The Executive
Humphrey's Executor v. United States (1935)
Korematsu v. United States (1944)
Myers v. United States (1926)
United States v. Curtiss-Wright Corporation (1936)
Youngstown Sheet and Tube Co. v. Sawyer (1952)
Public Administration & Business Regulation
Adkins v. Children's Hospital (1923)
Ashwander v. T.V.A. (1936)
Bates v. City of Little Rock (1960)
Corn Products Co. v. FTC (1945)
Federal Trade Commission v. Colgate-Palmolive Co. (1965)
Lochner v. New York (1905)
National Labor Relations Board v. Jones & Laughlin Steel Corporation (1937)
Nebbia v. New York (1934)
Radovitch v. National Football League (1957)
Schecter Poultry Corp. v. United States (1935)
Steward Machine Company v. Davis (1937)
United States v. Butler (1936)
United States v. Darby Lumber Co. (1941)
United States v. E.C. Knight Co. (1895)
West Coast Hotel Co. v. Parrish (1937)
Wickard v. Filburn (1942)
International Affairs
Missouri v. Holland (1920)
United States v. Curtiss-Wright Corporation (1936)

CONSTITUTIONAL REFERENDUM. *See* Initiative and Referendum.

CONSTITUTIONAL UNION PARTY, a pre-Civil War party whose goal was the preservation of the Union. Also known as the American Party, it was organized in 1859 to counter both abolitionist and proslavery extremists. This evasion of the central issue of slavery earned members the popular title of "Do Nothings."

At the party's convention in Baltimore, John Bell of Tennessee received the presidential nomination, and the party polled thirty-nine electoral votes in the 1860 election before disappearing with the outbreak of the Civil War.

See also Political Parties in the United States; Presidential Elections.

CONSTITUTION OF THE UNITED STATES. The Articles of Confederation did not provide the centralizing force necessary for unity among the new states and were soon found to be so fundamentally weak that a different political structure was vital. Conflicts about money and credit, trade, and suspicions about regional domination were among the concerns when Congress on February 21, 1787, authorized a Constitutional Convention to revise the Articles. The delegates were selected and assembled in Philadelphia about three

CONSTITUTION OF THE UNITED STATES: TOPIC GUIDE

The article on the CONSTITUTION OF THE UNITED STATES covers the background of the Constitutional Convention, describes the basic features of the Constitution, and discusses its change and adaptation throughout U.S. history.

The related articles on the Constitution may be divided into three groups.

Historical Antecedants. Many principles were expressed earlier in the DECLARATION OF INDEPENDENCE, CONTINENTAL CONGRESS, and ARTICLES OF CONFEDERATION. Dissatisfaction with the Articles and a desire to create a better system led to the ANNAPOLIS CONVENTION (1786), followed by the CONSTITUTIONAL CONVENTION OF 1787. MADISON'S JOURNAL is an account of the Convention, which produced the Constitution after considering proposals like the NEW JERSEY PLAN and VIRGINIA PLAN and ultimately accommodating differences through the CONNECTICUT COMPROMISE and THREE-FIFTHS COMPROMISE.

Constitutional Principles. The framers of the Constitution were concerned with STATES RIGHTS and STATE SOVEREIGNTY and with FEDERALISM. To assure the strength of each they included CONCURRENT POWER, DELEGATED POWERS, EXCLUSIVE POWERS, and RESERVED POWERS in it. Less explicit were IMPLIED POWERS and INHERENT POWERS.

Legal aspects of the Constitution are discussed under CONSTITUTIONAL LAW, CONSTITUTIONAL CONSTRUCTION, and NATIONAL SUPREMACY.

Specific Features. Several of the powers defined are described in CONTRACT CLAUSE, FULL FAITH AND CREDIT CLAUSE, NECESSARY AND PROPER CLAUSE, and PRIVILEGES AND IMMUNITIES. The Constitution was left flexible through the ability to make an AMENDMENT, the first ten of which are called the BILL OF RIGHTS.

Constitution of the United States, signed in 1787, was ratified by the necessary nine states by 1788.

of the early arrivals, especially Madison, time to make preparations on substantive matters, and Gov. Edmund Jennings Randolph presented a plan early in the proceedings that formed the basis for much of the convention deliberations. The essentials were that there should be a government adequate to prevent foreign invasion, prevent dissension among the states, provide for general national development, and give the national government power enough to make it superior in its realm. The decision was made not merely to revise the articles but to create a new government and a new constitution.

One of the most crucial decisions was the arrangement for representation, a compromise providing that one house would represent the states equally, the other house to be based on popular representation (with some modification due to the slavery question). This arrangement recognized political facts and concessions among men with both theoretical and practical political knowledge.

Basic Features. Oliver Wendell Holmes, Jr., once wrote that the provisions of the Constitution were not mathematical formulas, but "organic living institutions [sic] and its origins and growth were vital to understanding it." The Constitution's basic features provide for a supreme law—notwithstanding any other legal document or practice, the Constitution is supreme, as are the laws made in pursuance of it and treaties made under the authority of the United States.

The organizational plan for government is widely known. Foremost is the separation of powers. If the new government were to be limited in its powers, one way to keep it limited would have been executive, legislative, and judicial power in three distinct and nonoverlapping branches. A government could not actually function, however, if the separation meant the independence of one branch from the others. The answer was a design to insure cooperation and the sharing of some functions. Among these are the executive veto and the power of

Continued on Page 74

months after the call. They concluded their work by September.

The delegates agreed and abided to secrecy. Years afterward James Madison supported the secrecy decision writing that "no man felt himself obliged to retain his opinions any longer than he was satisfied of their propriety and truth, and was open to the force of argument." Secrecy was not for all time. Madison, a delegate from Virginia, was a self-appointed but recognized recorder and took notes in the clear view of the members. Published long afterward, Madison's *Journal* gives a good record of the convention.

The delegates began to assemble on May 14, 1787, but a majority did not arrive until May 25. George Washington was elected President of the Convention without opposition. The lag of those few days gave some

THE CONSTITUTION OF THE UNITED STATES

We the People of the United States, in Order to form a more perfect Union, establish Justice, insure domestic Tranquility, provide for the common defence, promote the general Welfare, and secure the Blessings of Liberty to ourselves and our Posterity, do ordain and establish this Constitution for the United States of America.

ARTICLE I

Section 1. All legislative Powers herein granted shall be vested in a Congress of the United States, which shall consist of a Senate and House of Representatives.

Section 2. The House of Representatives shall be composed of Members chosen every second Year by the People of the several States, and the Electors in each State shall have the Qualifications requisite for Electors of the most numerous Branch of the State Legislature.

No person shall be a Representative who shall not have attained to the Age of twenty five Years, and been seven Years a Citizen of the United States, and who shall not, when elected, be an Inhabitant of that State in which he shall be chosen.

Representatives and direct Taxes shall be apportioned among the several States which may be included within this Union, according to their respective Numbers, which shall be determined by adding to the whole Number of free Persons, including those bound to Service for a Term of Years, and excluding Indians not taxed, three fifths of all other Persons. The actual Enumeration shall be made within three Years after the first Meeting of the Congress of the United States, and within every subsequent Term of ten Years, in such Manner as they shall by Law direct. The Number of Representatives shall not exceed one for every thirty Thousand, but each State shall have at Least one Representative; and until such enumeration shall be made, the State of New Hampshire shall be entitled to chuse three, Massachusetts eight, Rhode-Island and Providence Plantations one, Connecticut five, New-York six, New Jersey four, Pennsylvania eight, Delaware one, Maryland six, Virginia ten, North Carolina five, South Carolina five, and Georgia three.

When vacancies happen in the Representation from any State, the Executive Authority thereof shall issue Writs of Election to fill such Vacancies.

The House of Representatives shall chuse their Speaker and other Officers; and shall have the sole Power of Impeachment.

Section 3. The Senate of the United States shall be composed of two Senators from each State, chosen by the Legislature thereof, for six Years; and each Senator shall have one Vote.

Immediately after they shall be assembled in Consequence of the first Election, they shall be divided as equally as may be into three Classes. The Seats of the Senators of the first Class shall be vacated at the Expiration of the second Year, of the second Class at the Expiration of the fourth Year, and of the third Class at the Expiration of the sixth Year, so that one third may be chosen every second Year; and if Vacancies happen by Resignation, or otherwise, during the Recess of the Legislature of any State, the Executive thereof may make temporary Appointments until the next Meeting of the Legislature, which shall then fill such Vacancies.

No Person shall be a Senator who shall not have attained to the Age of thirty Years, and been nine Years a Citizen of the United States, and who shall not, when elected, be an Inhabitant of that State for which he shall be chosen.

The Vice President of the United States shall be President of the Senate, but shall have no Vote, unless they be equally divided.

The Senate shall chuse their other Officers, and also a President pro tempore, in the Absence of the Vice President, or when he shall exercise the Office of President of the United States.

The Senate shall have the sole Power to try all Impeachments. When sitting for that Purpose, they shall be on Oath or Affirmation. When the President of the United States is tried, the Chief Justice shall preside: And no Person shall be convicted without the Concurrence of two thirds of the Members present.

Judgment in Cases of Impeachment shall not extend further than to removal from Office, and disqualification to hold and enjoy any Office of honor, Trust or Profit under the United States: but the Party convicted shall nevertheless be liable and subject to Indictment, Trial, Judgment and Punishment, according to Law.

Section 4. The Times, Places and Manner of holding Elections for Senators and Representatives, shall be prescribed in each State by the Legislature thereof; but the Congress may at any time by Law make or alter such Regulations, except as to the Places of chusing Senators.

The Congress shall assemble at least once in every Year, and such Meeting shall be on the first Monday in December, unless they shall by Law appoint a different Day.

Section 5. Each House shall be the Judge of the Elections, Returns and Qualifications of its own Members, and a Majority of each shall constitute a Quorum to do Business; but a smaller Number may adjourn from day to day, and may be authorized to compel the Attendance of absent Members, in such Manner, and under such Penalties as each House may provide.

Each House may determine the Rules of its Proceedings, punish its Members for disorderly Behaviour, and, with the Concurrence of two thirds, expel a Member.

Each House shall keep a Journal of its Proceedings, and from time to time publish the same, excepting such Parts as may in their Judgment require Secrecy; and the Yeas and Nays of the Members of either House on any question shall, at the Desire of one fifth of those Present, be entered on the Journal.

Neither House, during the Session of Congress, shall, without the Consent of the other, adjourn for more than three days, nor to any other Place than that in which the two Houses shall be sitting.

Section 6. The Senators and Representatives shall receive a Compensation for their Services, to be ascertained by Law, and paid out of the Treasury of the United States. They shall in all Cases, except Treason, Felony and Breach of the Peace, be privileged from Arrest during their Attendance at the Session of their respective Houses, and in going to and returning from the same; and for any Speech or Debate in either House, they shall not be questioned in any other Place.

No Senator or Representative shall, during the Time for which he was elected, be appointed to any civil Office under the Authority of the United States, which shall have been created, or the Emoluments whereof shall have been encreased during such time; and no Person holding any Office under the United States, shall be a Member of either House during his Continuance in Office.

Section 7. All Bills for raising Revenue shall originate in the House of Representatives; but the Senate may propose or concur with Amendments as on other Bills.

Every Bill which shall have passed the House of Representatives and the Senate, shall, before it become a Law, be presented to the President of the United States; If he approve he shall sign it, but if not he shall return it, with his Objections to that House in which it shall have originated, who shall enter the Objections at large on their Journal, and proceed to reconsider it. If after such Reconsideration two thirds of that House shall agree to pass the Bill, it shall be sent, together with the Objections, to the other House, by which it shall likewise be reconsidered, and if approved by two thirds of that House, it shall become a Law. But in all such Cases the Votes of both Houses shall be determined by yeas and Nays, and the Names of the Persons voting for and against the Bill shall be entered on the Journal of each House respectively. If any Bill shall not be returned by the President within ten Days (Sundays excepted) after it shall have been presented to him, the Same shall be a Law, in like Manner as if he had signed it, unless the Congress by their Adjournment prevent its Return, in which Case it shall not be a Law.

Every Order, Resolution, or Vote to which the Concurrence of the Senate and House of Representatives may be necessary (except on a question of Adjournment) shall be presented to the President of the United States; and before the Same shall take Effect, shall be approved by him, or being disapproved by him, shall be repassed by two thirds of the Senate and House of Representatives, according to the Rules and Limitations prescribed in the Case of a Bill.

Section 8. The Congress shall have Power To lay and collect Taxes, Duties, Imposts and Excises, to pay the Debts and provide for the common Defence and general Welfare of the United States; but all Duties, Imposts and Excises shall be uniform throughout the United States;

To borrow Money on the credit of the United States;

To regulate Commerce with foreign Nations, and among the several States, and with the Indian Tribes;

To establish an uniform Rule of Naturalization, and uniform Laws on the subject of Bankruptcies throughout the United States;

To coin Money, regulate the Value thereof, and of foreign Coin, and fix the Standard of Weights and Measures;

To provide for the Punishment of counterfeiting the Securities and current Coin of the United States;

To establish Post Offices and post Roads;

To promote the Progress of Science and useful Arts, by securing for limited Times to Authors and Inventors the exclusive Right to their respective Writings and Discoveries;

To constitute Tribunals inferior to the supreme Court;

To define and punish Piracies and Felonies committed on the high Seas, and Offences against the Law of Nations;

To declare War, grant Letters of Marque and Reprisal, and make Rules concerning Captures on Land and Water;

To raise and support Armies, but no Appropriation of Money to that Use shall be for a longer Term than two Years;

To provide and maintain a Navy;

To make Rules for the Government and Regulation of the land and naval Forces;

To provide for calling forth the Militia to execute the Laws of the Union, suppress Insurrections and repel Invasions;

To provide for organizing, arming, and disciplining, the Militia, and for governing such Part of them as may be employed in the Service of the United States, reserving to the States respectively, the Appointment of the Officers, and the Authority of training the Militia according to the discipline prescribed by Congress;

To exercise exclusive Legislation In all Cases whatsoever, over such District (not exceeding ten Miles square) as may, by Cession of particular States, and the Acceptance of Congress, become the Seat of the Government of the United States, and to exercise like Authority over all Places purchased by the Consent of the Legislature of the State in which the Same shall be, for the Erection of Forts, Magazines, Arsenals, dock-Yards, and other needful Buildings;— And

To make all Laws which shall be necessary and proper for carrying into Execution the foregoing Powers, and all other Powers vested by this Constitution in the Government of the United States, or in any Department or Officer thereof.

Section 9. The Migration or Importation of such Persons as any of the States now existing shall think proper to admit, shall not be prohibited by the Congress prior to the year one thousand eight hundred and eight, but a Tax or duty may be imposed on such Importation, not exceeding ten dollars for each Person.

The Privilege of the Writ of Habeas Corpus shall not be suspended, unless when in Cases of Rebellion or Invasion the public Safety may require it.

No Bill of Attainder or ex post facto Law shall be passed.

No Capitation, or other direct, Tax shall be laid, unless in Proportion to the Census or Enumeration herein before directed to be taken.

No Tax or Duty shall be laid on Articles exported from any State.

No Preference shall be given by any Regulation of Commerce or Revenue to the Ports of one State over those of another; nor shall Vessels bound to, or from, one State, be obliged to enter, clear or pay Duties in another.

No Money shall be drawn from the Treasury, but in Consequence of Appropriations made by Law; and a regular Statement and Account of the Receipts and Expenditures of all public Money shall be published from time to time.

No Title of Nobility shall be granted by the United States: And no Person holding any Office of Profit or Trust under them, shall, without the Consent of the Congress, accept of any present, Emolument, Office, or Title, of any kind whatever, from any King, Prince, or foreign State.

Section 10. No State shall enter into any Treaty, Alliance, or Confederation; grant Letters of Marque and Reprisal; coin Money; emit Bills of Credit; make any Thing but gold and silver Coin a Tender in Payment of Debts; pass any Bill of Attainder, ex post facto Law, or Law impairing the Obligation of Contracts, or grant any Title of Nobility.

No State shall, without the Consent of the Congress, lay any Imposts or Duties on Imports or Exports, except what may be absolutely necessary for executing its inspection Laws: and the net Produce of all Duties and Imposts, laid by any State on Imports or Exports, shall be for the Use of the Treasury of the United States; and all such Laws shall be subject to the Revision and Controul of the Congress.

No State shall, without the Consent of Congress, lay any Duty of Tonnage, keep Troops, or Ships of War in time of Peace, enter into any Agreement or Compact with another State, or with a foreign Power, or engage in War, unless actually invaded, or in such imminent Danger as will not admit of delay.

ARTICLE II

Section 1. The executive Power shall be vested in a President of the United States of America. He shall hold his Office during the Term of four Years, and, together with the Vice President, chosen for the same Term, be elected, as follows:

Each State shall appoint, in such Manner as the Legislature thereof may direct, a Number of Electors, equal to the whole Number of Senators and Representatives to which the State may be entitled in the Congress: but no Senator or Representative, or Person holding an Office of Trust or Profit under the United States, shall be appointed an Elector.

The Electors shall meet in their respective States, and vote by Ballot for two Persons, of whom one at least shall not be an Inhabitant of the same State with themselves. And they shall make a List of all the Persons voted for, and of the Number of Votes for each; which List they shall sign and certify, and transmit sealed to the Seat of the Government of the United States, directed to the President of the Senate. The President of the Senate shall, in the Presence of the Senate and House of Representatives, open all the Certificates, and the Votes shall then be counted. The Person having the greatest Number of Votes shall be the President, if such Number be a Majority of the whole Number of Electors appointed; and if there be more than one who have such Majority, and have an equal Number of Votes, then the House of Representatives shall immediately chuse by Ballot one of them for President; and if no Person have a Majority, then from the five highest on the List the said House shall in like Manner chuse the President. But in chusing the President, the Votes shall be taken by States, the Representation from each State having one Vote; A Quorum for this Purpose shall consist of a Member

or Members from two thirds of the States, and a Majority of all the States shall be necessary to a Choice. In every Case, after the Choice of the President, the person having the greatest Number of Votes of the Electors shall be the Vice President. But if there should remain two or more who have equal Votes, the Senate shall chuse from them by Ballot the Vice President.

The Congress may determine the Time of chusing the Electors, and the Day on which they shall give their Votes; which Day shall be the same throughout the United States.

No Person except a natural born Citizen, or a Citizen of the United States, at the time of the Adoption of this Constitution, shall be eligible to the Office of President; neither shall any Person be eligible to that Office who shall not have attained to the Age of thirty five Years, and been fourteen Years a Resident within the United States.

In Case of the Removal of the President from Office, or of his Death, Resignation, or Inability to Discharge the Powers and Duties of the said Office, the Same shall devolve on the Vice President, and the Congress may by Law provide for the Case of Removal, Death, Resignation or Inability, both of the President and Vice President, declaring what Officer shall then act as President, and such Officer shall act accordingly, until the Disability be removed, or a President shall be elected.

The President shall, at stated Times, receive for his Services, a Compensation, which shall neither be encreased nor diminished during the Period for which he shall have been elected, and he shall not receive within that Period any other Emolument from the United States, or any of them.

Before he enter on the Execution of his Office, he shall take the following Oath or Affirmation:—"I do solemnly swear (or affirm) that I will faithfully execute the Office of President of the United States, and will to the best of my Ability, preserve, protect and defend the Constitution of the United States."

Section 2. The President shall be Commander in Chief of the Army and Navy of the United States, and of the Militia of the several States, when called into the actual Service of the United States; he may require the Opinion, in writing, of the principal Officer in each of the executive Departments, upon any Subject relating to the Duties of their respective Offices, and he shall have Power to grant Reprieves and Pardons for Offences against the United States, except in Cases of Impeachment.

He shall have Power, by and with the Advice and Consent of the Senate, to make Treaties, provided two thirds of the Senators present concur; and he shall nominate, and by and with the Advice and Consent of the Senate, shall appoint Ambassadors, other public Ministers and Consuls, Judges of the supreme Court, and all other Officers of the United States, whose Appointments are not herein otherwise provided for, and which shall be established by Law: but the Congress may by Law vest the Appointment of such inferior Officers, as they think proper, in the President alone, in the Courts of Law, or in the Heads of Departments.

The President shall have Power to fill up all Vacancies that may happen during the Recess of the Senate, by granting Commissions which shall expire at the End of their next Session.

Section 3. He shall from time to time give to the Congress Information of the State of the Union, and recommend to their Consideration such Measures as he shall judge necessary and expedient; he may, on extraordinary Occasions, convene both Houses, or either of them, and in Case of Disagreement between them, with Respect to the Time of Adjournment, he may adjourn them to such Time as he shall think proper; he shall receive Ambassadors and other public Ministers; he shall take Care that the Laws be faithfully executed, and shall Commission all the Officers of the United States.

Section 4. The President, Vice President and all civil Officers of the United States, shall be removed from Office on Impeachment for, and Conviction of, Treason, Bribery, or other high Crimes and Misdemeanors.

ARTICLE III

Section 1. The judicial Power of the United States, shall be vested in one supreme Court, and in such inferior Courts as the Congress may from time to time ordain and establish. The Judges, both of the supreme and inferior Courts, shall hold their Offices during good Behaviour, and shall, at stated Times, receive for their Services, a Compensation, which shall not be diminished during their Continuance in Office.

Section 2. The judicial Power shall extend to all Cases, in Law and Equity, arising under this Constitution, the Laws of the United States, and Treaties made, or which shall be made, under their Authority;—to all Cases affecting Ambassadors, other public Ministers and Consuls;—to all Cases of admiralty and maritime Jurisdiction;—to Controversies to which the United States shall be a Party;—to Controversies between two or more States;—between a State and Citizens of another State;—between Citizens of different States;—between Citizens of the same State claiming Lands under Grants of different States, and between a State, or the Citizens thereof, and foreign States, Citizens or Subjects.

In all Cases affecting Ambassadors, other public Ministers and Consuls, and those in which a State shall be Party, the supreme Court shall have original Jurisdiction. In all the other Cases before mentioned, the supreme Court shall have appellate Jurisdiction, both as to Law and Fact, with such Exceptions, and under such Regulations as the Congress shall make.

The Trial of all Crimes, except in Cases of Impeachment, shall be by Jury; and such Trial shall be held in the State where the said Crimes shall have been committed; but when not committed within any State, the Trial shall be at such a Place or Places as the Congress may by Law have directed.

Section 3. Treason against the United States, shall consist only in levying War against them, or in adhering to their enemies, giving them Aid and Comfort. No Person shall be convicted of Treason unless on the Testimony of two Witnesses to the same overt Act, or on Confession in open Court.

The Congress shall have Power to declare the Punishment of Treason, but no Attainder of Treason shall work Corruption of Blood, or Forfeiture except during the Life of the Person attainted.

ARTICLE IV

Section 1. Full Faith and Credit shall be given in each State to the public Acts, Records, and judicial Proceedings of every other State. And the Congress may by general Laws prescribe the Manner in which such Acts, Records, and Proceedings shall be proved, and the Effect thereof.

Section 2. The Citizens of each State shall be entitled to all Privileges and Immunities of Citizens in the several States.

A Person charged in any State with Treason, Felony, or other Crime, who shall flee from Justice, and be found in another State, shall on Demand of the executive Authority of the State from which he fled, be delivered up, to be removed to the State having Jurisdiction of the Crime.

No Person held to Service or Labour in one State, under the Laws thereof, escaping into another, shall, in Consequence of any Law or Regulation therein, be discharged from such Service or Labour, but shall be delivered up on Claim of the Party to whom such Service or Labour may be due.

Section 3. New States may be admitted by the Congress into this Union; but no new State shall be formed or erected within the Jurisdiction of any other State; nor any State be formed by the Junction of two or more States, or Parts of States, without the Consent of the Legislatures of the States concerned as well as of the Congress.

The Congress shall have Power to dispose of and make all needful Rules and Regulations respecting the Territory or other Property belonging to the United States; and nothing in this Constitution shall be so construed as to Prejudice any Claims of the United States, or of any particular State.

Section 4. The United States shall guarantee to every State in this Union a Republican Form of Government, and shall protect each of them against Invasion; and on Application of the Legislature, or of the Executive (when the Legislature cannot be convened) against domestic Violence.

ARTICLE V

The Congress, whenever two thirds of both Houses shall deem it necessary, shall propose Amendments to this Constitution, or, on the Application of the Legislatures of two thirds of the several States, shall call a Convention for proposing Amendments, which, in either Case, shall be valid to all Intents and Purposes, as Part of this Constitution, when ratified by the Legislatures of three fourths of the several States, or by Conventions in three fourths thereof, as the one or the other Mode of Ratification may be proposed by the Congress; Provided that no Amendment which may be made prior to the Year One thousand eight hundred and eight shall in any Manner affect the first and fourth Clauses in the Ninth Section of the first Article; and that no State, without its Consent, shall be deprived of its equal Suffrage in the Senate.

ARTICLE VI

All Debts contracted and Engagements entered into, before the Adoption of this Constitution, shall be as valid against the United States under this Constitution, as under the Confederation.

This Constitution, and the Laws of the United States which shall be made in Pursuance thereof; and all Treaties made, or which shall be made, under the Authority of the United States, shall be the supreme Law of the Land; and the Judges in every State shall be bound thereby, any Thing in the Constitution or Laws of any State to the Contrary notwithstanding.

The Senators and Representatives before mentioned, and the Members of the several State Legislatures, and all executive and judicial Officers, both of the United States and of the several States, shall be bound by Oath or Affirmation, to support this Constitution; but no religious Test shall ever be required as a Qualification to any Office or public Trust under the United States.

ARTICLE VII

The Ratification of the Conventions of nine States, shall be sufficient for the Establishment of this Constitution between the States so ratifying the Same.

Done in Convention by the Unanimous Consent of the States present the Seventeenth Day of September in the Year of our Lord one thousand seven hundred and Eighty seven and of the Independence of the United States of America the Twelfth   IN WITNESS whereof We have hereunto subscribed our Names,

G⁰· Washington	Presid'. and deputy from Virginia
New Hampshire	John Langdon
	Nicholas Gilman
Massachusetts	Nathaniel Gorham
	Rufus King
Connecticut	Wm. Saml. Johnson
	Roger Sherman
New York	Alexander Hamilton
New Jersey	Wil: Livingston
	David Brearley
	Wm. Paterson
	Jona: Dayton
Pennsylvania	B Franklin
	Thomas Mifflin
	Rob' Morris
	Geo. Clymer
	Thos. FitzSimons
	Jared Ingersoll
	James Wilson
	Gouv Morris
Delaware	Geo: Read
	Gunning Bedford jun
	John Dickinson
	Richard Bassett
	Jaco: Broom
Maryland	James McHenry
	Dan of S' Thos. Jenifer
	Dan' Carroll
Virginia	John Blair–
	James Madison Jr.
North Carolina	Wm. Blount
	Rich'd Dobbs Spaight
	Hu Williamson
South Carolina	J. Rutledge
	Charles Cotesworth Pinckney
	Charles Pinckney
	Pierce Butler
Georgia	William Few
	Abr Baldwin
Attest:	William Jackson, Secretary

Articles in addition to, and Amendment of, The Constitution of the United States of America, proposed by Congress, and ratified by the legislatures of the several states, pursuant to the fifth article of the original Constitution.

AMENDMENT I

Congress shall make no law respecting an establishment of religion, or prohibiting the free exercise thereof; or abridging the freedom of speech, or of the press; or the right of the people peaceably to assemble, and to petition the Government for a redress of grievances.

AMENDMENT II

A well regulated Militia, being necessary to the security of a free State, the right of the people to keep and bear Arms, shall not be infringed.

AMENDMENT III

No Soldier shall, in time of peace be quartered in any house, without the consent of the Owner, nor in time of war, but in a manner to be prescribed by law.

AMENDMENT IV

The right of the people to be secure in their persons, houses, papers, and effects, against unreasonable searches and seizures, shall not be violated, and no Warrants shall issue, but upon probable cause, supported by Oath or affirmation, and particularly describing the place to be searched, and the persons or things to be seized.

AMENDMENT V

No person shall be held to answer for a capital, or otherwise infamous crime, unless on a presentment or indictment of a Grand Jury, except in cases arising in the land or naval forces, or in the Militia, when in actual service in time of War or public danger; nor shall any person be subject for the same offence to be twice put in jeopardy of life or limb; nor shall be compelled in any criminal case to be a witness against himself, nor be deprived of life, liberty, or property, without due process of law; nor shall private property be taken for public use, without just compensation.

AMENDMENT VI

In all criminal prosecutions, the accused shall enjoy the right to a speedy and public trial, by an impartial jury of the State and district wherein the crime shall have been committed, which district shall have been previously ascertained by law, and to be informed of the nature and cause of the accusation; to be confronted with the witnesses against him; to have compulsory process for obtaining Witnesses in his favor, and to have the assistance of counsel for his defence.

AMENDMENT VII

In Suits at common law, where the value in controversy shall exceed twenty dollars, the right of trial by jury shall be preserved, and no fact tried by a jury, shall be otherwise reexamined in any Court of the United States, than according to the rules of the common law.

AMENDMENT VIII

Excessive bail shall not be required, nor excessive fines imposed, nor cruel and unusual punishments inflicted.

AMENDMENT IX

The enumeration in the Constitution, of certain rights, shall not be construed to deny or disparage others retained by the people.

AMENDMENT X

The powers not delegated to the United States by the Constitution, nor prohibited by it to the States, are reserved to the States respectively, or to the people.

AMENDMENT XI
(1795)

The Judicial power of the United States shall not be construed to extend to any suit in law or equity, commenced or prosecuted against one of the United States by Citizens of another State, or by Citizens or Subjects of any Foreign State.

AMENDMENT XII
(1804)

The Electors shall meet in their respective states and vote by ballot for President and Vice-President, one of whom, at least, shall not be an inhabitant of the same state with themselves; they shall name in their ballots the person voted for as President, and in distinct ballots the person voted for as Vice-President, and they shall make distinct lists of all persons voted for as President, and of all persons voted for as Vice-President, and of the number of votes for each, which lists they shall sign and certify, and transmit sealed to the seat of the government of the United States, directed to the President of the Senate;—The President of the Senate shall, in the presence of the Senate and House of Representatives, open all the certificates and the votes shall then be counted;—The person having the greatest number of votes for President, shall be the President, if such number be a majority of the whole number of Electors appointed; and if no person have such majority, then from the persons having the highest numbers not exceeding three on the list of those voted for as President, the House of Representatives shall choose immediately, by ballot, the President. But in choosing the President, the votes shall be taken by states, the representation from each state having one vote; a quorum for this purpose shall consist of a member or members from two-thirds of the states, and a majority of all the states shall be necessary to a choice. And if the House of Representatives shall not choose a President whenever the right of choice shall devolve upon them, before the fourth day of March next following, then the Vice-President shall act as President, as in the case of the death or other constitutional disability of the President. The person having the greatest number of votes as Vice-President, shall be the Vice-President, if such number be a majority of the whole number of Electors appointed, and if no person have a majority, then from the two highest numbers on the list, the Senate shall choose the Vice-President; a quorum for the purpose shall consist of two-thirds of the whole number of Senators, and a majority of the whole number shall be necessary to a choice. But no person constitutionally ineligible to the office of President shall be eligible to that of Vice-President of the United States.

AMENDMENT XIII
(1865)

Section 1. Neither slavery nor involuntary servitude, except as a punishment for crime whereof the party shall have been duly convicted, shall exist within the United States, or any place subject to their jurisdiction.

Section 2. Congress shall have power to enforce this article by appropriate legislation.

AMENDMENT XIV
(1868)

Section 1. All persons born or naturalized in the United States, and subject to the jurisdiction thereof, are citizens of the United States and of the State wherein they reside. No State shall make or enforce any law which shall abridge the privileges or immunities of citizens of the United States; nor shall any State deprive any person of life, liberty, or property, without due process of law; nor deny to any person within its jurisdiction the equal protection of the laws.

Section 2. Representatives shall be apportioned among the several States according to their respective numbers, counting the whole number of persons in each State, excluding Indians not taxed. But when the right to vote at any election for the choice of electors for President and Vice President of the United States, Representatives in Congress, the Executive and Judicial officers of a State, or the members of the Legislature thereof, is denied to any of the male inhabitants of such State, being twenty-one years of age, and citizens of the United States, or in any way abridged, except for participation in rebellion, or other crime, the basis of representation therein shall be reduced in the proportion which the number of such male citizens shall bear to the whole number of male citizens twenty-one years of age in such State.

Section 3. No person shall be a Senator or Representative in Congress, or elector of President and Vice President, or hold any office, civil or military, under the United States, or under any State, who, having previously taken an oath, as a member of Congress, or as an officer of the United States, or as a member of any State legislature, or as an executive or judicial officer of any State, to support the Constitution of the United States, shall have engaged in insurrection or rebellion against the same, or given aid or comfort to the enemies thereof. But Congress may by a vote of two-thirds of each House, remove such disability.

Section 4. The validity of the public debt of the United States, authorized by law, including debts incurred for payment of pensions and bounties for services in suppressing insurrection or rebellion, shall not be questioned. But neither the United States nor any State shall assume or pay any debt or obligation incurred in aid of insurrection or rebellion against the United States, or any claim for the loss or emancipation of any slave; but all such debts, obligations and claims shall be held illegal and void.

Section 5. The Congress shall have power to enforce, by appropriate legislation, the provisions of this article.

AMENDMENT XV
(1870)

Section 1. The right of citizens of the United States to vote shall not be denied or abridged by the United States or by any State on account of race, color, or previous condition of servitude.

Section 2. The Congress shall have power to enforce this article by appropriate legislation.

AMENDMENT XVI
(1913)

The Congress shall have power to lay and collect taxes on incomes, from whatever source derived, without apportionment among the several States, and without regard to any census or enumeration.

AMENDMENT XVII
(1913)

The Senate of the United States shall be composed of two Senators from each State, elected by the people thereof, for six years; and each Senator shall have one vote. The electors in each State shall have the qualifications requisite for electors of the most numerous branch of the State legislatures.

When vacancies happen in the representation of any State in the Senate, the executive authority of such State shall issue writs of election to fill such vacancies: *Provided,* That the legislature of any State may empower the executive thereof to make temporary appointments until the people fill the vacancies by election as the legislature may direct.

This amendment shall not be so construed as to affect the election or term of any Senator chosen before it becomes valid as part of the Constitution.

AMENDMENT XVIII
(1919)

Section 1. After one year from the ratification of this article the manufacture, sale, or transportation of intoxicating liquors within, the importation thereof into, or the exportation thereof from the United States and all territory subject to the jurisdiction thereof for beverage purposes is hereby prohibited.

Section 2. The Congress and the several States shall have concurrent power to enforce this article by appropriate legislation.

Section 3. This article shall be inoperative unless it shall have been ratified as an amendment to the Constitution by the legislatures of the several States, as provided in the Constitution, within seven years from the date of the submission hereof to the States by the Congress.

AMENDMENT XIX
(1920)

The right of citizens of the United States to vote shall not be denied or abridged by the United States or by any State on account of sex.

Congress shall have power to enforce this article by appropriate legislation.

AMENDMENT XX
(1933)

Section 1. The terms of the President and Vice President shall end at noon on the 20th day of January, and the terms of Senators and Representatives at noon on the 3d of January, of the years in which such terms would have ended if this article had not been ratified; and the terms of their successors shall then begin.

Section 2. The Congress shall assemble at least once in every year, and such meeting shall begin at noon on the 3d day of January, unless they shall by law appoint a different day.

Section 3. If, at the time fixed for the beginning of the term of the President, the President elect shall have died, the Vice President elect shall become President. If a President shall not have been chosen before the time fixed for the beginning of his term, or if the President elect shall have failed to qualify, then the Vice President elect shall act as President until a President shall have qualified; and the Congress may by law provide for the case wherein neither a President elect nor a Vice President elect shall have qualified, declaring who shall then act as President, or the manner in which one who is to act shall be selected, and such person shall act accordingly until a President or Vice President shall have qualified.

Section 4. The Congress may by law provide for the case of the death of any of the persons from whom the House of Representatives may choose a President whenever the right of choice shall have devolved upon them, and for the case of the death of any of the persons from whom the Senate may choose a Vice President whenever the right of choice shall have devolved upon them.

Section 5. Sections 1 and 2 shall take effect on the 15th day of October following the ratification of this article.

Section 6. This article shall be inoperative unless it shall have been ratified as an amendment to the Constitution by the legislatures of three-fourths of the several States within seven years from the date of its submission.

AMENDMENT XXI
(1933)

Section 1. The eighteenth article of amendment to the Constitution of the United States is hereby repealed.

Section 2. The transportation or importation into any State, Territory, or possession of the United States for delivery or use therein of intoxicating liquors, in violation of the laws thereof, is hereby prohibited.

Section 3. This article shall be inoperative unless it shall have been ratified as an amendment to the Constitution by conventions in the several States, as provided in the Constitution, within seven years from the date of the submission hereof to the States by the Congress.

AMENDMENT XXII
(1951)

Section 1. No person shall be elected to the office of the President more than twice, and no person who has held the office of President, or acted as President for more than two years of a term to which some other person was elected President shall be elected to the office of the President more than once. But this Article shall not apply to any person holding the office of President when this Article was proposed by the Congress, and shall not prevent any person who may be holding the office of President, or acting as President, during the term within which this Article becomes operative from holding the office of President or acting as President during the remainder of such term.

Section 2. This article shall be inoperative unless it shall have been ratified as an amendment to the Constitution by the legislatures of three-fourths of the several States within seven years from the date of its submission to the States by the Congress.

AMENDMENT XXIII
(1961)

Section 1. The District constituting the seat of Government of the United States shall appoint in such manner as the Congress may direct:

A number of electors of President and Vice President equal to the whole number of Senators and Representatives in Congress to which the District would be entitled if it were a State, but in no event more than the least populous State; they shall be in addition to those appointed by the States, but they shall be considered, for the purposes of the election of President and Vice President, to be electors appointed by a State; and they shall meet in the District and perform such duties as provided by the twelfth article of amendment.

Section 2. The Congress shall have power to enforce this article by appropriate legislation.

AMENDMENT XXIV
(1964)

Section 1. The right of citizens of the United States to vote in any primary or other election for President or Vice President, for electors for President or Vice President, or for Senator or Representative in Congress, shall not be denied or abridged by the United States or any State by reason of failure to pay any poll tax or other tax.

Section 2. The Congress shall have power to enforce this article by appropriate legislation.

AMENDMENT XXV
(1967)

Section 1. In case of the removal of the President from office or of his death or resignation, the Vice President shall become President.

Section 2. Whenever there is a vacancy in the office of the Vice President, the President shall nominate a Vice President, who shall take office upon confirmation by a majority vote of both Houses of Congress.

Section 3. Whenever the President transmits to the President pro tempore of the Senate and the Speaker of the House of Representatives his written declaration that he is unable to discharge the powers and duties of his office, and until he transmits to them a written declaration to the contrary, such powers and duties shall be discharged by the Vice President as Acting President.

Section 4. Whenever the Vice President and a majority of either the principal officers of the executive departments or of such other body as Congress may by law provide, transmit to the President pro tempore of the Senate and the Speaker of the House of Representatives their written declaration that the President is unable to discharge the powers and duties of his office, the Vice President shall immediately assume the powers and duties of the office as Acting President.

Thereafter, when the President transmits to the President pro tempore of the Senate and the Speaker of the House of Representatives his written declaration that no inability exists, he shall resume the powers and duties of his office unless the Vice President and a majority of either the principal officers of the executive department or of such other body as Congress may by law provide, transmit within four days to the President pro tempore of the Senate and the Speaker of the House of Representatives their written declaration that the President is unable to discharge the powers and duties of his office. Thereupon Congress shall decide the issue, assembling within forty-eight hours for that purpose if not in session. If the Congress, within twenty-one days after receipt of the latter written declaration, or, if Congress is not in session, within twenty-one days after Congress is required to assemble, determines by two-thirds vote of both Houses that the President is unable to discharge the powers and duties of his office, the Vice President shall continue to discharge the same as Acting President; otherwise, the President shall resume the powers and duties of his office.

AMENDMENT XXVI
(1971)

Section 1. The right of citizens of the United States, who are eighteen years of age or older, to vote shall not be denied or abridged by the United States or by any State on account of age.

Section 2. The Congress shall have power to enforce this article by appropriate legislation.

Continued from Page 66

the Congress to have its way if it musters a supermajority to override that veto. The direction of foreign affairs and the war power are both dispersed and shared. The appointing power is shared by the Senate and the president; impeaching of officers and financial controls are powers shared by the Senate and the House.

A second major contribution by the convention is the provision for the judiciary, which gave rise to the doctrine of judicial review. There is some doubt that the delegates comprehended this prospect but Alexander Hamilton considered it in *Federalist* No. 78: "The interpretation of the laws is a proper and peculiar province of the Courts . . . Wherever a particular statue contravenes the Constitution, it will be the duty of the judicial tribunals to adhere to the latter and disregard the former."

Another contribution is the federal system, an evolution from colonial practice and the relations between the colonies and the mother country. This division of authority between the new national government and the states recognized the doctrine of delegated and reserved powers. Only certain authority was to go to the new government; the states were not to be done away with and much of the Constitution is devoted to ensuring that they were to be maintained even with the stripping of some of their powers.

It is not surprising, therefore, that the convention has been called a great political reform caucus composed of both revolutionaries and men dedicated to democracy. By eighteenth-century standards the Constitution was a democratic document, but standards change and the Constitution has changed since its adoption.

Change and Adaptation. The authors of the Constitution knew that provision for change was essential and provided for it in Article V, ensuring that a majority could amend, but being restrictive enough that changes were not likely for the "light and transient" causes Jefferson warned about in the Declaration of Independence.

During the period immediately following the presentation of the Constitution for ratification, requiring assent of nine states to be effective, some alarm was expressed that there was a major defect: there was no bill of rights. So, many leaders committed themselves to the presentation of constitutional amendments for the purpose. Hamilton argued that the absence of a bill of rights was not a defect; indeed, a bill was not necessary. "Why," he wrote, in the last of *The Federalist Papers,* "declare things that shall not be done which there is no power to do?" Nonetheless, the Bill of Rights was presented in the form of amendments and adopted by the states in 1791.

Since 1791 many proposals have been suggested to amend the Constitution. By 1972 sixteen additional amendments had been adopted. Only one, the Twenty-first, which repealed the Eighteenth, was ratified by state conventions. All the others were ratified by state legislatures.

Even a cursory reading of the later amendments shows they do not alter the fundamentals of limited government, the separation of powers, the federal system, or the political process set in motion originally. The Thirteenth, Fourteenth, Fifteenth, and Nineteenth amendments attempt to ensure equality to all and are an extension of the Bill of Rights. The others reaffirm some existing constitutional arrangements, alter some procedures, and at least one, the Sixteenth, states national policy.

Substantial change and adaptation of the Constitution beyond the formal amendments have come from national experience, growth, and development. It has been from the Supreme Court that much of the gradual significant shaping of the Constitution has been done.

Government has remained neither static nor tranquil. Some conflict prevails continually. It may be about the activities of some phase of government or the extent of operations, and whether the arrangement for government can be made responsive to current and prospective needs of society. Conflict is inevitable in a democratic society. Sometimes the conflict is spirited and rises to challenge the continuation of the system. Questions arise whether a fair trial may be possible here or there; legislators are alleged to be indifferent to human problems and pursue distorted public priorities. Presidents are charged with secret actions designed for self-aggrandizement or actions based on half-truths. Voices are heard urging revolution again as the only means of righting alleged wrongs.

The responses continue to demonstrate, however, that the constitutional arrangement for government, the allocation of powers, and the restraints on government all provide the needed flexibility. The Constitution endures.   —*Adam C. Breckenridge*

CONSUL. *See* Foreign Service.

CONSULATE, the office of a consul and his staff. The consul operates in a consular district in a foreign country. The consulate protects the welfare of its country's nationals, commerce, and shipping. Passports and visas are issued at the consulate.

See also Embassy.

CONSUMER AFFAIRS, OFFICE OF, government agency, in the Department of Commerce, that represents consumer interests in the business community. The office works to improve business-customer relations through the development of voluntary cooperative projects between corporations and consumer groups.

CONSUMER CREDIT PROTECTION ACT OF 1968. *See* Truth in Lending Act.

CONSUMER PRODUCT SAFETY COMMISSION, an independent regulatory agency, established by the Consumer Product Safety Act of 1972. The commission's functions include the evaluation of the relative safety of consumer products and the development of uniform safety standards. The commission sponsors and promotes research into the causes and prevention of injuries, illnesses, and death resulting from the use or misuse of consumer products.

CONSUMER PROTECTION. As a result of the competitive conditions in the modern industrial society and the questionable ethical standards of a segment of the commercial community, the consumer needs protection. Some of the most common areas of abuse against which consumers need protection are:

1. emergence of monopoly, with its powers over pricing and the amount and quality of product offering;

2. misleading or false advertising efforts;

3. misleading or false personal selling practices, such as termite inspections resulting in unneeded home treatment;

4. excessive interest rates and carrying charges, as when small loan companies or retail stores tack on very high carrying charges by concealing them in the total payback price;

5. the marketing of harmful products, for example, cosmetics causing skin disorders, or foods packed under unsanitary conditions;

6. deceptive labeling or packaging of products, such as the failure to inform the consumer of the limitations or potential dangers associated with using the product;

7. environmental pollution by industries or consumers themselves.

Protecting the consumer. Local, state and federal governments act as rule makers and policemen, regulating various aspects of business by passing such statutory laws as the Sherman and Clayton Antitrust acts, the Food and Drug Act, and the Truth in Lending Act. In addition, administrative laws and regulations are handed down by agencies such as the Federal Trade Commission and the Pure Food and Drug Administration, which are charged specifically with regulating commercial activities.

Industry's own efforts to protect consumers from questionable business practices are exercised via trade associations, chambers of commerce, and better business bureaus through the adoption of codes of conduct and product standards.

Consumer advocates may study industry practices and product performance to determine if there are abuses against which the consumer should be protected. Their chief weapon is carefully documented publicity that is adverse to a company or a product. Consumer movements are sometimes formalized: delegates meet and attempt to exert pressure for legislation to protect the consumer.   —*Algin B. King*

See also Business Regulation in the United States.

CONSUMERS UNION OF THE UNITED STATES, a private organization that tests and rates competing brands of consumer goods, such as appliances, automobiles, food products, clothing, and household items. Founded in 1936, it derives the bulk of its income from the sale to one million subscribers of *Consumer Reports*, in which its evaluations of a variety of goods and services are featured monthly. The organization regularly represents consumer interests at government hearings and sponsors conferences and seminars to develop approaches and solutions to consumer-related problems.

CONTAINMENT POLICY, plans articulated by President Truman, Dean Acheson, and veteran diplomat George Kennan to resist Soviet expansion following World War II. President Truman explained this policy in a message to Congress on March 12, 1947. He asked Congress to appropriate $400 million for the Greek and Turkish governments in their effort to preserve independence from outside aggression. Congress appropriated the funds by a large majority. Some of the methods used to contain Russian expansion in Western Europe were the Marshall Plan (economic) and the 1949 NATO Treaty (military). Kennan formally articulated the policy of containment in an article that appeared in the July 1947 issue of *Foreign Affairs*. He stated that "it is clear that the main element of any United States policy toward the Soviet Union must be that of long-term, patient but firm and vigilant containment of Russian expansive tendencies."

Although the primary commitment was to resist aggression in Europe, the Truman administration was also concerned about Communist expansion in Asia. American forces occupied Japan in part to prevent Russia from gaining a foothold there. The United States also provided aid to the Nationalist government in China and to the French in Indochina. In 1950, President Truman obtained United Nations authorization to send military forces to Korea under U.N. auspices. Containment was used to justify the commitment of U.S. ground forces in Vietnam. The easing of Soviet-American tensions has all but ended talk of containment.

CONTEMPT OF CONGRESS, the refusal to answer pertinent questions before a congressional committee when summoned. Contempt of Congress is a misdemeanor punishable by a fine and imprisonment from one to twelve months. To cite a person for contempt, the committee concerned must introduce a resolution into the House or Senate. A simple majority is needed for approval, and if approved, the matter is referred to a United States attorney for presentation to a grand jury and prosecution in a federal court. Although Congress has the right to summon witnesses to testify, the witness may invoke the Fifth Amendment's protection against self-incrimination to avoid testifying.

Contempt of Congress was first ruled a criminal offense in 1857. Most of the more recent contempt citations have been associated with Senate investigations into organized crime and with hearings of the now-defunct House Un-American Activities Committee (HUAC).

See also Investigative Power of Congress; *Watkins v. United States.*

CONTEMPT OF COURT, any act that frustrates a court in the administration of justice or detracts from the authority or dignity of the court. The term applies to disobedience of a court order, disruptive acts, and the use of objectionable language in a courtroom. One need not be a party to an action pending before a court to be held in contempt. For example, attorneys have frequently been held in contempt for using trial tactics the court considers objectionable. Contempts are classified in two ways: civil/criminal and direct/constructive. Direct contempt is committed in the presence of the court, and indirect contempt is committed elsewhere. Civil contempt is a failure to do something ordered for the benefit of one's adversary, while criminal contempt is a failure to act as ordered for the court's benefit.

See also Injunction.

CONTINENTAL CONGRESS, legislative body that guided the thirteen American colonies from their assertion of independence to the establishment, by the Constitution, of the United States of America. The Congress sat in two major sessions from 1774 to 1789.

First Congress. The First Continental Congress, composed of fifty-six delegates from all the colonies except Georgia, met in Carpenter's Hall, Philadelphia, from September 5, to October 26, 1774. The Congress sought the reinstitution of colonial rights violated by acts of the British Parliament and Militia. To this end, the Congress drafted a Declaration of Rights and a plan for colonial association.

Second Congress. On May 10, 1775, the Second Continental Congress met to act on Great Britain's refusal to acknowledge the petition. Lexington and Concord were already hallowed battlegrounds, and the Congress authorized the establishment of the Continental Army as a defense measure, appointing George Washington as commander in chief. Frustrated in attempts at reconciliation with the mother country, the delgates finally adopted the Declaration of Independence on July 4, 1776. The Congress continued to supervise the conduct of the war and in 1781 authorized the creation of the Articles of Confederation as the foundation of the new government.

Under the articles the Congress embodied all legislative, executive, and judicial functions. The weaknesses of the articles were almost immediately apparent, but it was not until February 21, 1787, that the Congress called for a convention to revise them. This meeting led finally to the Constitutional Convention of 1787. Still under the authority of the Articles, on July 13, 1787, the Congress enacted one of its most significant achievements, the Northwest Ordinance, providing for the government and future inclusion into the Union of the territory north of the Ohio River.

See also Articles of Confederation; Declaration of Independence.

CONTRACT CLAUSE, a provision in Article I, Section 10, of the Constitution, prohibiting states from passing laws that interfere with the obligations of contracts, either by weakening them or by making them more difficult to enforce. No contracts, however, may endanger the public's health, safety, or welfare.

CONTRACT THEORY asserts that the only legitimate grounds for government is a mutual contract created by the governed. Contract theory's modern form was developed in seventeenth-century England by Thomas Hobbes and John Locke and in eighteenth-century France by Jean Jacques Rousseau.

The contract theorists analyzed man's basic nature, from which they derived the bases of political life: men were moved primarily by fear and pride. From man's fear came the natural right of self-preservation and related rights, such as liberty and property. Pride caused conflict, which in the absence of civil society (state of nature) would lead to war. Man's natural state was war, and to escape its horrors and secure man's natural rights

government was created by contract. All governments were limited by the purpose for which they were created, and if any government exceeded its purpose, the citizens had a right to revolt. Consent as the basis for government, the primacy of the individual over civil society and rights over duties, the preservation of natural rights as the end of government, and the right of revolution are among the principles of contract theory.

—*Robert F. Smith*

See also Consent, Popular; Limited Government; Popular Sovereignty.

CONVENTION, POLITICAL, for a century and a half the political parties have used conventions to select candidates, devise strategy, write platforms, choose party officers, and conduct other business. Perhaps equally significant have been the latest functions of conventions: encouraging and recognizing the faithful, providing a major stage in the generation of campaign publicity, and serving as arenas where conflicting sectional and interest groups can work out compromises. In theory, the parties employ a stairway of conventions leading from the local to the state and national levels, a hierarchy of bodies that consider candidates and issues.

Origins. Presidential candidates have been nominated by the convention method since 1831-1832. The first party to use a convention for this purpose was the Antimasonic Party. Previously, candidates for state and federal office were designated by caucuses of legislative members of the party. "King Caucus" was attacked for failing to give adequate attention to the rank-and-file while giving undue influence to legislators. By the turn of the century, reformers were faulting the convention system for many of the same flaws.

Criticisms. Conventions have been taken to task for being unwieldy, going on too long, having a circus atmosphere, lending themselves to manipulation by small groups, and being facades for behind-the-scenes deals (with party machines "packing" and stampeding the conventions with their followers).

Television has brought the convention spectacle into the nation's homes, and the parties have learned it can be costly to air in public their disagreements over credentials, resolutions, rules, and organization. Such structural anomalies as unit-rule voting, the need for extraordinary majorities to achieve some purposes, fractional votes, calling the rolls of a state's delegates, and favorite-son noncandidates have also been questioned.

In our confederal party system some delegates are selected by local party conventions while others are chosen by committee or by direct primary elections. Furthermore, the parties are not uniformly strong throughout the country. Should the relative weight assigned to each state stress state population or party strength and past success? In the past, convention machinery has been dominated by older conservatives who appointed delegates long in advance.

Persistence of the Convention System. There have

been periodic movements away from the system—most states nominate both Senators and Representatives by direct primary election, but in some of these states one or both parties, by convention or action of the state committee, endorse candidates before the primaries. The convention has endured because it is a valuable place to work out party bargains, solidify ranks, and rally campaign forces. Furthermore, convention delegates are sometimes in a better position than the voters to judge the qualifications of candidates and to hold them accountable.

Ever since President Wilson first proposed it in 1913, the idea of one nationwide primary to select the presidential candidates has been mulled over. The latest version of the scheme, the Mansfield-Aiken constitutional amendment, envisions a single nationwide presidential primary in early August whereby each party polling at least 10 percent of the vote in the preceding presidential election would select its nominee from a field of candidates who would qualify for the ballot by filing petitions signed by a set percentage of voters nationwide. There would be a runoff election 23 days after the primary if no candidate won at least 40 percent of a party's vote. Vice-presidential candidates would still be chosen by national party conventions.

The national primary proposal is vulnerable to charges that it would contribute to the erosion of party organizations, result in an even greater campaign cost, and cause fratricidal warfare that would not be assuaged with the "drafting" of a unifying candidate.

After the turmoil of the 1968 Democratic convention, the party proposed reforms to expand participation of women and minorities. After George McGovern's defeat in 1972, party leaders questioned the wisdom of reforms that may have excluded other traditional Democratic constituents, such as union members and the elderly. While the practice of targeting certain groups was abandoned, the party reaffirmed its commitment to nondiscrimination. The Democrats continue to convene "commissions" after each election. Their efforts in 1986 reduced the threshold from 20 percent to 15 percent of the vote needed for the assignment of delegates, a response to complaints from supporters of Jesse Jackson.

The Republicans have felt less pressure from discontented factions and have traditionally supported the primacy of state/local organization over the national committee. Nevertheless, many of these changes, particularly those dealing with nondiscrimination, have become a part of many state laws. Perhaps most significantly, primaries now account for the selection of most convention delegates.

—*Martin Gruberg*

CONVENTION OF 1787. *See* Constitutional Convention of 1787.

COOLIDGE, CALVIN. 30th President of the United States (1923-1929), born in Plymouth Notch, Vt. A lawyer and politician who held virtually every type of local and state office, he showed himself a conservative legislator and a budget-cutting administrator. Because of backing by conservative politicians and favorable publicity given his actions to crush the Boston police strike of 1919, Coolidge became vice president in 1921. He succeeded to the presidency in 1923 upon the death of Warren G. Harding. He continued the Harding policies of reducing taxes and encouraging peace both at home and abroad. Coolidge's administrations were remarkable for the lack of legislation passed and the laxity in enforcing existing anti-business and prohibition laws. His most notable actions were vetoes—of the McNary-Haugen Bill to help farmers and of the Muscle Shoals scheme to develop government power plants on the Tennessee River.

See also Presidential Elections.

COOPERATIVE FEDERALISM. *See* Federalism.

COOPER-CHURCH AMENDMENT. Citing the constitutional right of Congress to determine where and how public funds are spent, the antiwar amendment prohibited funds allocated in the 1969 and 1970 defense appropriations bills from being used "to finance the introduction of American ground combat troops into Laos or Thailand." Similarly, in December 1970, as part of the Supplemental Foreign Assistance Authorization Bill, the clause prohibited financing United States adviser or combat troop introduction into Cambodia. The move by anti-war senators was designed to prevent the president from initiating military engagements outside South Vietnam, to prevent military obligations from being written into secret treaties, and to discourage covert military action by the CIA or guerrilla outfits.

COPPERHEADS, an epithet applied to those Northern or "Peace" Democrats who were opposed to Lincoln during the Civil War and were sympathetic to the Confederate cause. The Cooperheads were strongest in the Midwest, where agrarian interests feared the loss of the South as a market and resented New England's industrial enrichment from the war.

COPYRIGHT, the rights by which an author or artist can protect and profit from his work. Authorized by Article I, Section 8, federal law allows copyrights on books, works of art, lectures, musical compositions, motion pictures, and photographs for a period of twenty-eight years. Registration must be filed within the first twenty-eight-year period to provide a basis for renewal. Registration is also necessary to protect a copyright in case of infringement. Renewal of copyright can be made only during the last twelve-month period of the twenty-eight years. If alive, the author may renew; otherwise, his widow or children may renew. If there are no immediate survivors, the executor of the estate or the next of kin can renew.

A registered copyright certifies that the work meets the mechanical and technical requirements of the law. A copyright is made valid only by the fact that the work is original with the author. His protection is that no one may copy his work. Although the copyright owner has the exclusive right to publish, copy, sell, and perform his work for profit, the doctrine of fair use allows other authors to copy to a limited extent for such purposes as research and criticism.

The present federal copyright law, enacted in 1976, allows copyrights on literary works, musical works, dramatic works, dance works, works of art, motion pictures, and sound recordings for the life of the copyright owner plus fifty years after the owner's death. The 1976 revision also closely details the ability to photocopy an author's work. Libraries are limited in their right to produce multiple copies, while educators and researchers are permitted some greater flexibility. The Copyright Office in Washington, D.C. registers all copyright claims. Patents should not be confused with copyrights. Patents are temporary rights of invention granted to an inventor. Anyone wishing a copyright must file a claim with the Copyright Office within three months of publication of the work to be copyrighted.

COPYRIGHT OFFICE. *See* Library of Congress.

CORN PRODUCTS REFINING CO. v. FEDERAL TRADE COMMISSION (FTC), 324 U.S. 726 (1945), concerns the administration of the Clayton Act as it applies to the selling of goods in any part of the United States at prices lower than those exacted elsewhere in the United States for the purpose of destroying competition. The FTC instituted proceedings, charging that the company's use of a single basing point system, that is, selling at delivered prices obtained by adding to a base price an amount for "freight" which usually does not correspond to the freight charges actually paid by the company, resulted in discriminations in price between different purchasers of glucose. Variations in the price of candy manufactured from this glucose thus diverted business from one manufacturer to another. The court concluded that the single basing point system and other discriminations involved in the company's pricing system were prohibited by the act, because their effect was to lessen competition.

CORPORATE STATE, a state whose major industries are organized into self-governing corporations in which both workers and owners participate. A committee representing workers and owners makes decisions affecting the functions of the corporation. A national organization composed of representatives from the various corporations decides national economic policy. The corporation may be used as the basis for representation in the national government. Although democratic in principle, the corporate state as practiced in fascist Italy and Germany came to be a part of the totalitarian systems.

See also National Socialism; Totalitarianism.

CORPS OF ENGINEERS, office of the Department of the Army responsible for engineering and construction of army projects and of federal civilian projects. As a part of the army, the corps is concerned with engineering and building for army property and mapping of land for army intelligence. As a member of the Office of Civil Functions of the Army, the corps' civilian duties include engineering, construction, and maintenance of improvements for navigation and flood control on the nation's waterways. The corps also administers legislation that protects navigable waters and does the engineering and construction on such federal projects as the Bonneville and Alaska hydroelectric works and the John F. Kennedy Space Center. The chief of the Engineers, commander of the corps, is a member of the U.S. Army Special Staff.

CORRIGAN v. BUCKLEY, 271 U.S. 323 (1926), concerns a court's refusal to decide a case if it does not present substantial constitutional or statutory questions. The Corrigans, white persons, wanted to convey certain real estate in the District of Columbia to Curtis, a black. Corrigan was one of thirty white persons owning twenty-five parcels of land who had entered into a mutual convenant stating that no part of the property should ever be occupied by or leased or sold to blacks. Buckley sued to have the convenant specifically enforced.

The Court held that because there is no constitutional provision or statute prohibiting private individuals from entering into contracts respecting the control and disposition of their own property, the Court had no jurisdiction to hear an appeal. The equal protection clause argument used in *Shelley v. Kraemer* was not available to the defendant here because the Fourteenth Amendment is, by its terms, not applicable to the District of Columbia.

See also Jones v. Mayer.

CORRUPT PRACTICES ACTS are state and federal statutes aimed at eliminating campaign and election abuses. The movement to end these abuses, prevalent in the nineteenth century, began after the Civil War. New York's 1890 law against bribery, illegal registration and ballot-box stuffing was followed eventually by the other states.

The basis of modern federal legislation is the Corrupt Practice Act of 1925. It limited primary and general election expenses for Congressional candidates, made disclosure of election expenses mandatory, outlawed fraudulent practices, and put controls on contributions by certain organizations, such as corporations. These acts were successful in ending many flagrant illegal election practices, but some restrictions, particularly on contributions, were often ineffective. Later, the scope of the federal act was widened and amended significantly by implementation of the Federal Election Campaign Acts of 1972 and 1974.

See also Federal Election Campaign Acts; Hatch Acts.

COUNCIL OF ECONOMIC ADVISERS (CEA), one of the fifteen divisions of the Executive Office of the President; established in 1946 to succeed the more limited National Resources Planning Board (1939-1943). A three-member council appointed by the president, its duties are to develop economic plans and budget recommendations for maintaining the nation's "employment, production, and purchasing power," and to help the president prepare an annual economic report to Congress. A main source of recommendations for self-regulation by business, the CEA is a frequent source of controversy.

See also Economic Message, President's.

COUNCIL OF STATE GOVERNMENTS (formerly the American Legislators' Association), an association of all fifty states dedicated to improving the quality of state government activities and programs. The governing board is composed of the nation's 50 governors and two legislators per state. In addition to attempting to improve the effectiveness of state government, the council assists in intergovernmental relations among states and with the federal government. The council issues a number of publications on state government activities, including the *Book of States.*

COUNCIL ON ENVIRONMENTAL QUALITY, an organization that recommends to the president policies to improve the environment. The council, created by the National Environmental Policy Act of 1969, is composed of three members designated by the president with the approval of the Senate. The Office of Environmental Quality was set up in 1970 to provide staff for the council. The council is further aided in its policy review and formulation by the Citizens' Advisory Committee on Environmental Quality.

COUNSEL, RIGHT OF ACCUSED PERSON TO. *See* Accused Persons, Rights of.

COURT-MARTIAL. *See* Military Law.

COURT OF . . . *See* second part of name.

COURT SYSTEM. *See* Judicial System.

CREDENTIALS COMMITTEE, an organizational framework maintained by both parties at their national conventions. The credentials committee inspects the claim of each prospective delegate to be seated as a legitimate representative of his state. Occasionally seats are contested, as in the Democratic convention of 1968, when a black group challenged the all-white Mississippi delegation. As a result, the challengers received a portion of the seats.

CRIME CONTROL ACT. *See* Omnibus Crime Control and Safe Streets Act.

CRIMINAL LAW, the branch of law dealing with crimes and their punishments. A crime is an act that is important enough to be considered an offense against public authority or a violation of a duty owed to the public. A tort on the other hand, is a violation of a private right. Crimes are usually classified as *mala in se*—immoral and wrong in themselves—or *mala prohibita*—illegal only because proscribed by statute. Crimes are also graded according to their gravity as felonies, misdemeanors, or offenses. To distinguish its procedural rules relating to proof of crime and protection of the accused, the body of law grading, defining and prescribing penalties for crimes is referred to as criminal, or substantive criminal law. Criminal law is both common and statutory, although the former aspect has been of decreasing importance in the United States.

CROSSER-DILL ACT. *See* Railway Labor Act.

CROSS-FILING, the practice permitted by some states of allowing an individual to become a candidate of more than one political party in a presidential primary election.

CRUEL AND UNUSUAL PUNISHMENT, prohibited by the Eighth Amendment to the Constitution, which states "Excessive bail shall not be required, nor excessive fines imposed, nor cruel and unusual punishments inflicted." At the time of the original congressional debate over the Bill of Rights, some delegates objected that the provisions of the Eighth Amendment were vaguely defined, and, in practice, the courts have determined the amendment's applications and limitations. The Court has held that Eighth-Amendment guarantees apply to the states by the due-process clause of the Fourteenth Amendment.

CUBAN MISSILE CRISIS, U.S.-U.S.S.R. confrontation (Oct. 22-28, 1962) over Soviet ballistic missiles in Cuba. On October 22, President Kennedy made a televised address to announce the presence of the missiles and the action he was taking—a quarantine (in reality a blockade) on military equipment shipped to Cuba, retaliation against the U.S.S.R. if any Cuban missiles were launched at the United States, the alert of American forces, action in the U.N. Security Council, and a demand to Premier Nikita Khrushchev to withdraw the missiles.

President John F. Kennedy at meeting of the Executive Committee of the National Security Council, Oct. 29, 1962, about the Cuban Missile Crisis.

The sense of confrontation was heightened by the announcement that the U.S. Navy might visit and search vessels bound for Cuba to determine whether they were bringing additional missiles. Khrushchev ordered Soviet ships to change course and offered to withdraw the missiles in exchange for the U.S. commitment not to invade Cuba. Since Kennedy was anxious to avoid a military confrontation, he was willing to offer Khrushchev a face-saving solution to the crisis. However, before Kennedy could respond, a new message arrived from the Soviet leader demanding removal of American missiles from Turkey. Attorney General Robert Kennedy suggested ignoring the demand and responding favorably to the first Soviet note. President Kennedy agreed and a message was sent (October 27) containing a pledge not to invade Cuba if Soviet missiles were removed. The next day Moscow agreed, and the crisis ended. President Kennedy's standing in public opinion polls went up along with his stature as a world leader. Khrushchev claimed that the American promise not to invade Cuba vindicated his actions, but many observers saw the crisis as a defeat for Soviet foreign policy. Khrushchev was removed from power in 1964 in part because of his handling of the missile crisis.

CUSTOMS AND PATENT APPEALS, COURT OF, is a specialized court created by Congress and given appellate jurisdiction over decisions of the Customs Court, Patent Office, and Tariff Commission. Such appellate review is by appeal, avilable as a matter of right. There is no appeal from the decisions of this court, but they may be reviewed by the Supreme Court on writ of *certiorari.*

CUSTOMS COURT has exclusive jurisdiction to review decisions of collectors of customs on questions affecting imports and import duties. Formerly the Board of General Appraisers, the Court's name was changed by the Congress in 1926, but no change was made in functions, which are quasi-judicial and quite similar to those usually performed by an administrative agency. Its decisions can be appealed to the Court of Customs and Patent Appeals.

CUSTOMS DUTIES. *See* Taxation.

CUSTOMS SERVICE, U.S., determines and collects duties and taxes on merchandise imported into the United States, controls exporters and importers and their goods, and works to control smuggling and revenue fraud. Created as a division of the Department of the Treasury in 1927, the Customs Service is authorized to collect customs and revenue by the second, third, and fifth acts of the First Congress (1789). The service helps enforce environmental protection programs regarding the discharge of oil or refuse into coastal waters, the safety standards of imported motor vehicles, and the regulation by quarantine of animals and plants entering the country. The service works closely with the Drug Enforcement Administration and the Immigration and Naturalization Service.

CUSTOMS UNION, also called tariff union, free trade areas established by agreement between two or more countries, who agree to be one customs territory, usually because of frequent exchange of merchandise and services. The members agree to adopt a common trade policy toward countries outside the union. For example, the General Agreement on Tariffs and Trade (1947) requires the elimination of duties and other restrictions on almost all trade between members; and the duties and restrictions affecting countries outside the union generally must not be increased beyond preunion levels. Customs unions tend to create trade and produce a better distribution of resources and output in the customs area. The European Common Market is an example of a customs union.

DANGEROUS TENDENCY TEST, a court test used in determining the limits of free expression guaranteed in the First Amendment. In *Gitlow v. New York* (1925) the Supreme Court rejected Oliver Wendell Holmes' clear and present danger test for interfering with freedom of speech, as enunciated in *Schenck v. United States* (1919) and *Abrams v. United States* (1919), in favor of a bad or dangerous tendency test. More limiting than the clear and present danger test, the dangerous tendency test makes punishable, by the government, those responsible for publications and speeches that, even though they create no immediate danger, have a "tendency" to bring about results dangerous to public safety—corrupting public morals, inciting to crime, or disturbing the public peace. In *Dennis v. United States* (1951), a Supreme Court case involving organization of the Communist party in the United States, the Court attempted to reconcile the two tests by a yardstick that measured the gravity of an evil against its probability.

See also Abrams v. United States; Clear and Present Danger; Dennis v. United States; Gitlow v. New York; Schenck v. United States.

DARK-HORSE CANDIDATE. *See* Primary Election.

DARTMOUTH COLLEGE v. WOODWARD, 4 Wheat. 518 (1819), concerns the contract clause of the Constitution. Dartmouth College, chartered by the English Crown in 1769, was controlled by a group of trustees led by Woodward. In 1816 the New Hampshire legislature passed a law entirely reorganizing the government of the college and changing its name to Dartmouth University. In doing so, the state maintained that the college had become public in character and as such was subject to public control. The court held that a college's charter is a contract which may not be impaired by a state's legislative enactment. The Constitution specifically states that "no state shall pass any . . . law impairing the obligation of contracts," and the trustees, as representatives of the founders and donors of Dartmouth, retained those rights set forth in the charter granted to the college.

DAVIS, JEFFERSON (1808-1889), President of the Confederate States of America (1861-1865). Davis graduated from West Point (1828) and spent the pre-Civil War years in public service. He was elected to the House from Mississippi but resigned to fight in the Mexican War in 1846. Davis was elected to the Senate (1847-1851, 1857-1861) and also served as Secretary

Jefferson Davis, president of the Confederacy.

of War under President Pierce (1853-1857). During his Senate terms, Davis became the acknowledged leader of the South, upholding states' rights and slavery. He resigned from the Senate when Mississippi seceded and became chief executive of the Confederate States. Davis was blamed for many failings, including his interference with military operations. After the war, he was jailed briefly and then spent his long retirement defending the cause of the South in such works as *The Rise and Fall of the Confederate Government* (1881) and *A Short History of the Confederacy* (1890).

DAY-CARE CENTER, a place outside the home where preschool children are supervised while their parents work. The need for centers increases as more women return to work and as the importance of early childhood education is recognized. In the private sector day-care centers may be run by employers or churches, or be organized by parents' cooperatives or private entrepreneurs. For middle-class children nursery school provides many of the educational and custodial functions of day care. The 1964 Economic Opportunity Act (Poverty Program) subsidized day-care facilities for the poor and launched the remedial Headstart program. Expansion of the day-care concept is integral to any Family Assistance program to enable mothers on public assistance to receive training and return to work. While social service programs have experienced uncertainty in funding, some level of federal support for child care continues.

DEAD-LETTER LAW, a law still in effect but generally disregarded and not enforced.

DEATH PENALTY. *See* Capital Punishment.

DEBS, EUGENE VICTOR (1855-1926), trade union leader whose early advocacy of industrial unionism anticipated the organization of the CIO, founder of the Socialist party and five times its candidate for president. Debs was born of immigrant parents in Terre Haute, Ind.

Trade Unionist. A railway worker at fourteen, he became an officer of his local in 1875, worked unselfishly to build his union, and by 1880 became secretary-treasurer of the National Brotherhood of Railway Firemen. He was active in Democratic politics as city clerk of Terre Haute (1880-1884) and member of the state legislature (1885-1887).

In 1893 Debs founded the American Railway Union, organized on industrial lines and open to all crafts. His efforts brought him into conflict with the established labor bureaucracy. In the Pullman strike of 1894, which was broken by violence and the courts, he was jailed six months for violating an injunction.

Socialist Leader. In jail Debs studied socialism, and upon release he worked with Victor L. Berger to consolidate radical factions to form the Socialist party. Debs ran as Socialist candidate for president in five elections, starting in 1900; in 1912 he received 6 percent of the popular vote.

Convicted in 1918 for speaking against participation in World War I, he was sentenced to ten years imprisonment. He campaigned from inside Atlanta Penitentiary and received 919,801 votes for president. In response to public pressure President Warren G. Harding commuted Debs' sentence in 1921. After his release and the decline of his party, Debs wrote on prison conditions and edited the socialist weekly *American Appeal*. He died in Elmhurst, Ill. Although Debs supported bolshevism in Russia and was considered a radical, his industrial unionism was influenced by the syndicalist ideas of Daniel De Leon, and his Socialist party was reformist, not revolutionary. Most of its program was later adopted by the Democrats.

DEBT, NATIONAL , the debt taken on by the central government to finance expenditures in the federal budget that cannot be met by available money. The national debt has been carried by the U.S. government since the early days of the republic. The Revolutionary War and the establishment of the new government produced a debt of $75 million. The debt rose to $259 billion in 1945, but increased dramatically during the Cold War and Vietnam. Escalating costs and higher interest on the debt led to a gross federal debt of more than $2.5 trillion in 1988.

The largest group of investors in the national debt are the individuals, funds, and businesses that buy government securities. The interest on the federal debt alone now is over $150 billion per year.

As An Economic Tool. The manner in which the debt is paid off can be used as a tool in controlling the economy. Because the national debt increases the money supply and the level of economic activity, the national debt supports a large part of the total money supply. The huge increases in debt in the last few years have raised fears that government borrowing will reduce real investment and cause a recession.

The Balanced Budget and Emergency Deficit Reduction Act of 1985 was designed to force government to address the problem of the deficit.

See also Balanced Budget and Emergency Deficit Reduction Act of 1985; Taxation.

**PUBLIC DEBT
OF THE FEDERAL GOVERNMENT**

	Gross Debt		Interest Paid	
	Total (in billions of dollars)	Per Capita (in dollars)	Total (in billions of dollars)	Percent of Federal Outlays
1900	1.3	$ 17	*	7.7
1905	1.1	14	*	4.3
1910	1.1	12	*	3.1
1915	1.2	12	*	3.0
1920	24.3	228	1.0	15.9
1925	20.5	177	.9	28.8
1930	16.2	132	.7	19.2
1935	28.7	226	.8	12.6
1940	43.0	325	1.0	11.5
1945	258.7	1,849	3.8	3.7
1950	256.1	1,688	5.7	14.5
1955	272.8	1,651	6.4	9.3
1960	284.1	1,572	9.2	10.0
1965	313.8	1,613	11.3	9.5
1970	370.1	1,814	19.3	9.9
1975	533.2	2,475	32.7	10.2
1980	907.7	3,985	74.9	13.0
1981	997.9	4,338	95.6	14.5
1982	1,142.0	4,913	117.4	16.1
1983	1,377.2	5,870	128.8	16.2
1988	2,602.3	10,534	151.7	16.1

*Less than $50 million

DECLARATION OF INDEPENDENCE. Virtually all of the Declaration of Independence was written by Thomas Jefferson, a member of an authoring committee appointed by the Continental Congress July 2, 1776. The Declaration was adopted by the Congress two days later.

No rights are established in this first significant for-

Declaration of Independence was signed on July 4, 1776.

THE DECLARATION OF INDEPENDENCE

WHEN in the Course of human events, it becomes necessary for one people to dissolve the political bands which have connected them with another, and to assume among the powers of the earth, the separate and equal station to which the Laws of Nature and of Nature's God entitle them, a decent respect to the opinions of mankind requires that they should declare the causes which impel them to the separation.—We hold these truths to be self-evident, that all men are created equal, that they are endowed by their Creator with certain unalienable Rights, that among these are Life, Liberty and the pursuit of Happiness.—That to secure these rights, Governments are instituted among Men, deriving their just powers from the consent of the governed.—That whenever any Form of Government becomes destructive of these ends it is the Right of the People to alter or to abolish it, and to institute new Government, laying its foundation on such principles and organizing its powers in such form, as to them shall seem most likely to effect their Safety and Happiness. Prudence, indeed, will dictate that Governments long established should not be changed for light and transient causes; and accordingly all experience hath shewn, that mankind are more disposed to suffer, while evils are sufferable, than to right themselves by abolishing the forms to which they are accustomed. But when a long train of abuses and usurpations, pursuing invariably the same Object evinces a design to reduce them under absolute Despotism, it is their right, it is their duty, to throw off such Government, and to provide new Guards for their future security.—Such has been the patient sufferance of these Colonies; and such is now the necessity which constrains them to alter their former Systems of Government. The history of the present King of Great Britain is a history of repeated injuries and usurpations, all having in direct object the establishment of an absolute Tyranny over these States. To prove this, let Facts be submitted to a candid world.—He has refused his Assent to Laws, the most wholesome and necessary for the public good.—He has forbidden his Governors to pass Laws of immediate and pressing importance, unless suspended in their operation till his Assent should be obtained; and when so suspended, he has utterly neglected to attend to them.—He has refused to pass other Laws for the accommodation of large districts of people, unless those people would relinquish the right of Representation in the Legislature, a right inestimable to them and formidable to tyrants only.—He has called together legislative bodies at places unusual, uncomfortable, and distant from the depository of their public Records, for the sole purpose of fatiguing them into compliance with his measures.—He has dissolved Representative Houses repeatedly, for opposing with manly firmness his invasions on the rights of the people.—He has refused for a long time, after such dissolutions, to cause others to be elected; whereby the Legislative powers, incapable of Annihilation, have returned to the People at large for their exercise; the State remaining in the meantime exposed to all the dangers of invasion from without, and convulsions within.—He has endeavoured to prevent the population of these States; for that purpose obstructing the Laws for Naturalization of Foreigners; refusing to pass others to encourage their migrations hither, and raising the conditions of new Appropriations of Lands.—He has obstructed the Administration of Justice, by refusing his Assent to Laws for establishing judiciary powers.—He has made Judges dependent on his Will alone, for the tenure of their offices, and the amount and payment of their salaries.—He has erected a multitude of New Offices, and sent hither swarms of Officers to harass our people, and eat out their substance. He has kept among us, in times of peace, Standing Armies without the Consent of our legislatures.—He has affected to render the Military independent of and superior to the Civil power.—He has com-

bined with others to subject us to a jurisdiction foreign to our constitution, and unacknowledged by our laws; giving his Assent to their Acts of pretended legislation:—For quartering large bodies of armed troops among us:—For protecting them, by a mock Trial, from punishment for any Murders which they should commit on the inhabitants of these States:—For cutting off our Trade with all parts of the world:—For imposing Taxes on us without our Consent:—For depriving us in many cases, of the benefits of Trial by Jury:—For transporting us beyond Seas to be tried for pretended offences:—For abolishing the free System of English Laws in a neighbouring Province, establishing therein an Arbitrary government, and enlarging its Boundaries so as to render it at once an example and fit instrument for introducing the same absolute rule into these Colonies:—For taking away our Charters, abolishing our most valuable Laws and altering fundamentally the Forms of our Governments:—For suspending our own Legislatures, and declaring themselves invested with power to legislate for us in all cases whatsoever.—He has abdicated Government here, by declaring us out of his Protection and waging War against us.—He has plundered our seas, ravaged our Coasts, burnt our towns, and destroyed the lives of our people.—He is at this time transporting large Armies of foreign Mercenaries to compleat the works of death, desolation and tyranny, already begun with circumstances of Cruelty & perfidy scarcely paralleled in the most barbarous ages, and totally unworthy the Head of a civilized nation.—He has constrained our fellow Citizens taken Captive on the high Seas to bear Arms gainst their Country, to become the executioners of their friends and Brethren, or to fall themselves by their Hands.—He has excited domestic insurrections amongst us, and has endeavoured to bring on the inhabitants of our frontiers, the merciless Indian Savages, whose known rule of warfare, is an undistinguished destruction of all ages, sexes and conditions. In every stage of these Oppressions We have Petitioned for Redress in the most humble terms: Our repeated Petitions have been answered only by repeated injury. A Prince, whose character is thus marked by every act which may define a Tyrant, is unfit to be the ruler of a free people. Nor have We been wanting in attentions to our British brethren. We have warned them from time to time of attempts by their legislature to extend an unwarrantable jurisdiction over us. We have reminded them of the circumstances of our emigration and settlement here. We have appealed to their native justice and magnanimity, and we have conjured them by the ties of our common kindred to disavow these usurpations, which would inevitably interrupt our connections and correspondence. They too have been deaf to the voice of justice and of consanguinity. We must, therefore, acquiesce in the necessity, which denounces our Separation, and hold them, as we hold the rest of mankind, Enemies in War, in Peace Friends.

WE, THEREFORE, the Representatives of the UNITED STATES OF AMERICA, in General Congress, Assembled, appealing to the Supreme Judge of the world for the rectitude of our intentions, do, in the Name, and by Authority of the good People of these Colonies, solemnly publish and declare, That these United Colonies are, and of Right ought to be FREE AND INDEPENDENT STATES; that they are Absolved from all Allegiance to the British Crown, and that all political connection between them and the State of Great Britain, is and ought to be totally dissolved; and that as Free and Independent States, they have full Power to levy War, conclude Peace, contract Alliances, establish Commerce, and to do all other Acts and Things which Independent States may of right do.—And for the support of this Declaration, with a firm reliance on the protection of divine Providence, we mutually pledge to each other our Lives, our Fortunes and our sacred Honor.

mal American state paper, but it is an expression of the American political mind at the time. Jefferson wrote many years later that the object of the Declaration was "to place before mankind the common sense of the subject, in terms so plain and firm as to command their [sic] assent, and to justify ourselves in the independent stand we are compelled to take."

The Declaration presents ideals with emphasis upon the "self-evident" rights of man, equality under the law. The document declares that government can exist only with the consent of the governed—a recognition of popular sovereignty. Government must be responsible to the people it governs and answerable for its acts. The end of government is the protection of the individual; his consent is a means to that end.

Philosophy of Government. The Declaration's philosophy about government outlines truths that are self-evident; that the purpose of a free government is the triumvirate of life, liberty, and happiness. These rights are not grants in any sense and come from no political source. Government's purpose is to make the rights secure. The government of England destroyed these fundamentals; thus it was a right to shed the abusive government and institute a new one. The colonists were revamping government, not to create new political institutions, but to reshape them, not to abolish them, but to have a government that gave full allegiance to stated fundamentals.

There is a warning from Jefferson that political bonds should be severed not for "light and transient" causes, but for only the most insufferable evils. Here majority rule is implied, for it is only when the majority feels the despotism that a government should be cast aside.

The allegations against the king are a potpourri of grievances large and small. But they are also a prelude to the deliberations eleven years later in the Constitutional Convention. While listing the charges, the compilation suggests those things which a freely constituted government, resting on agreed principles and rights, should not be permitted to do. The claimed abuses are not parallel in substance, but the total impact was both formidable and persuasive.

Conclusion. As if to lay a final appeal to men in and out of the Parliament, there is a restatement of circumstances familiar to all contemporaries: the colonists had been patient, sought redress, appealed, and petitioned, but these efforts had been in vain. Without a recapitulation of these endeavors, the Declaration summarily renounces the Parliament, too.

In a concluding paragraph the Declaration speaks of the United States of America for the first time. The colonies were now states and declared to be united. Their authority to do what other independent governments did was now available to them. The separation from allegiance to the Crown and the State of Great Britain was done. Thus free, the "united" states of America could carry out all acts that independent states "may of right do." —*Adam C. Breckenridge*

DECISION OF COURTS, the judgment of a court containing the "holding" (or determination) of the case, as well as the "disposition" (final settlement or sentencing) of the case. —*Mary L. Carns*

See also Opinions.

DECLARATION OF RIGHTS. See Continental Congress.

DE FACTO SEGREGATION, segregation of the races that has come about as a result of social and economic conditions rather than government action. Often, the distinction between *de facto* and *de jure* segregation is not a clear one, for policies of governmental housing agencies and school systems have reinforced private segregation patterns.

See also Civil Rights Cases; De Jure Segregation; Heart of Atlanta Motel v. United States; Katzenbach v. McClung; Jones v. Alfred H. Mayer Co.; Shelley v. Kraimer.

DEFENDANTS' RIGHTS. See Accused Persons, Rights of.

DEFENSE, UNITED STATES DEPARTMENT OF (DOD), largest of the 14 executive departments of the United States, responsible for the maintenance and the direction of the nation's military and defense forces. The DOD is headed by a civilian Secretary of Defense who has a deputy secretary and seven assistant secretaries. In addition, the secretaries of the army, navy, and air force are responsible to the Secretary of Defense. The

Seal of the Department of Defense.

coast guard is under the authority of the Transportation Department. The current organization of the DOD stems from the National Security Act of 1947, which established three coequal military branches. The first Secretary of Defense was James V. Forrestal.

The Secretary of Defense and the three service secretaries must be civilians by law. The military hierarchy, consisting of the military heads of the army, navy, air force, and marine corps as individual military departments and as coordinated in the Joint Chiefs of Staff (JCS), is subordinate by law to the civilian side. The secretary is responsible for conducting defense policy, representing the views of the military departments and services to the president and funneling presidential policies and directives to them. By law the secretary of defense is the final military decision-maker, subject only to the dictates of the president. The secretary must be an effective business manager, for the defense part of the annual budget amounts to many billions of dollars. He makes recommendations to the president about weapons needs, manpower needs, and estimates of the capability of potential military adversaries. Differences among the military branches related to budget requests and missions must be reconciled by the secretary of defense before budget requests are finally made by the president to the Congress.   —*Erwin L. Levine*
See also Joint Chiefs of Staff; Pentagon.

DEFENSE ASSISTANCE PACT. *See* Mutual Defense Assistance Pact.

DEFENSE DEPARTMENT REORGANIZATION ACT (1958), an amendment to the National Security Act, which furthered centralizing tendencies within the department and outlined civilian controls over the military establishment.

By the Act the secretary of defense was empowered to assign the development of new weapons systems and to consolidate supply and service systems. If the secretary made substantial functional changes, he was required to notify Congress, which could veto the change. The president was authorized to form joint commands for combat purposes. A 1949 provision of the National Security Act, denying the chairman of the Joint Chiefs of Staffs a vote, was repealed. Although the measure increased centralization, it also recognized the separate status of the military services and permitted their secretaries to make proposals to Congress.

DEFENSE INTELLIGENCE AGENCY (DIA), an agency of the Department of Defense under the supervision of the Joint Chiefs of Staff. DIA conducts intelligence operations within the department and supervises intelligence programs not assigned to it. DIA was established in 1961 under the provisions of the National Security Act (1947).

DEFERRAL. *See* Impoundment.

DE JURE SEGREGATION, segregation of the races that is the result of government action. By law, schools and public accommodations and facilities in the South were required to be segregated before the Supreme Court landmark decision in *Brown v. Board of Education of Topeka* (1954) that state-imposed segregation violates the Fourteenth Amendment.

See also Alexander v. Holmes County Board of Education; Brown v. Board of Education; Buchanan v. Warley; Plessy v. Ferguson.

DELEGATED POWERS, *or* **ENUMERATED POWERS,** in the federal divison of powers, those powers specifically granted to the national government by the Constitution. Whereas the Continental Congress had to depend on the states for the exercise of many of its important powers, some of them were spelled out in the Constitution of 1789, and the new national government was able to exercise them on its own authority. Most of the delegated powers are found in Article I, Section 8: most notable are the war power, the commerce power, and the power to tax and spend for the general welfare.

DEMOCRACY (Gr., rule by the people). In ancient Greek democracies all citizens gathered periodically to make laws directly. Administrators were chosen by lot or furnished by rotation from different groups in the city. Government by representative and election by ballot were considered undemocratic, since they denied full authority to all people. The right to participate was based exclusively on being born a citizen (as opposed to a slave).

Modern democracies trace their root to the seventeenth-century contract theories, which stressed natural rights, maximization of political equality and liberty, and government by consent. With the development of large nation-states, modern democratic practices include representative government, election by ballot, minimum qualifications for holding public office, inclusive suffrage, competitive elections, and free and open speech and press.

While freedom and equality have always been important conditions and ends of democratic regimes, liberal democratic systems stress the value of liberty at the expense of economic and social equality, while socialist democratic systems claim the reverse. The contract theorists emphasized life, liberty, and property as the ends of government. The later utilitarians defined government's purpose as the greatest happiness for the greatest number. More recently, theorists have defined democratic ends in terms of man's mind, spirit, or general potential.   —*Robert F. Smith*
See also Consent, Popular; Contract Theory; Democratic Socialism; Liberalism.

DEMOCRACY IN AMERICA. *See* Tocqueville, Alexis de.

DEMOCRATIC ELITISM. *See* Pluralism.

DEMOCRATIC-FARMER LABOR PARTY. *See* Farmer-Labor Party.

DEMOCRATIC PARTY, one of two major political parties in the United States. The present Democratic party traces its antecedents to the Democratic-Republican party of the late eighteenth century.

The Democratic-Republican Party, formed by Thomas Jefferson, the exponent of the Jeffersonian philosophy that the rights of the several states and their individual citizens be preserved against encroachments by the federal government. The party was thus pitted against the strongly centralist Federalist party dominated by Alexander Hamilton, which had controlled the government of the United States from its inception until Jefferson's election to the presidency in 1800.

The Democratic-Republican party early identified with small farmers and individual entrepreneurs attracted by the Jeffersonian ideal of participatory democracy. Emerging thus as the "party of the little man," the Democratic-Republicans engineered a political revolution of sorts by the time of the election of 1800. As a result of this election, the party established itself as the major focus of political power, replacing the Federalists.

Jackson's Democrats. In 1828, when the party had become known simply as the Democratic party, President Andrew Jackson revivified the philosophy and broadened the party base. Jackson, whose origins were in Southern poverty and illiteracy, enlarged the scope of the party's appeal as champion of individual rights and the voice of the poor in government, bringing more and more citizens under its philosophical umbrella, including many dissident factions.

Almost since its beginnings the party had drawn its strength from the South and Southwest, areas that had consistently allied themselves against the Republican strongholds of industry in the North. This entrenched regional position of the Democrats was shattered by the slavery controversy, and the party barely survived the effects of the Civil War, but by the end of the Reconstruction Era in 1876, the party was again a highly viable political influence, nearly regaining the White House under the standard borne by Samuel Tilden.

The Renaissance of the Party, like its birth, occurred in the South, which solidified around Democratic traditions in bitter opposition to the Republican administrations of Lincoln and the Reconstruction presidents, Andrew Johnson and Ulysses S. Grant. From 1876 the South produced regional bloc voting for the party for more than 70 years. Moreover, because of the party's ability to coopt third-party movements into its own, the Southern-based roots branched throughout the country, attracting both liberal and conservative elements.

William Jennings Bryan united the radical economic wing of the party under his free-silver banner in 1896, carrying on his unsuccessful bandwagon even dissidents

Cartoonist Thomas Nast (not a Democrat) made the donkey the party symbol, but this jackass represents Copperhead newspapers, which he also ridiculed.

from outside the party. Much of the Populist doctrine was adopted by the Democrats, as well as some of the Progressivist dogma of Theodore Roosevelt's Bull Moose party. But although the Democratic ideological diversity had historically heightened its broad appeal, the same diversity was often tantamount to dissension—and from 1896 it was not until the candidacy of Woodrow Wilson in 1912 that the Democrats were again able to capture the presidency. Wilson's liberal internationalist politics united the party and the country for a time, but from 1920 until 1932 the Democrats were out of power.

The New Deal. The Great Depression brought the party into national prominence again, guided by the masterful hand of Franklin Delano Roosevelt. Impelled by the exigences of the Depression, the Democrats under FDR's New Deal began reversing their time-honored traditions of individualism in favor of increased federal involvement in social welfare problems. The wave of isolationism that had swept the country in reaction to Wilson's abortive League of Nations was also gradually rejected in favor of a more internationalist approach to foreign politics. One legacy of the Roosevelt era was to make the Democrats statistically the majority party. Although the registration rolls testified to this majority, the party continued to be subject to ideological schisms that took their toll in the polling booth.

In 1948 two factions split from the main wing of the Democratic party in reaction to Harry Truman's candidacy. The Dixiecrats, led by Strom Thurmond of

South Carolina, expressed the conservative sentiment against "big government," and the advocates of increased socialism joined a second Progressive party (the first was Teddy Roosevelt's) in support of Henry Wallace. Wallace had served both as FDR's vice president and as Truman's secretary of commerce. Despite this factionalism, Truman was victorious in continuing the Democratic hold on the White House until 1952, when Dwight Eisenhower led the Republicans back to power.

Kennedy and After. The Democrats returned to the White House in 1960 under John F. Kennedy, and remained as a highly establishment party under Lyndon Johnson. The violence and dissension of the 1960s gravely affected the party, as dramatically evidenced at the Democratic Convention in Chicago in 1968. The enveloping chaos was paramount in defeating the Democratic candidate, Hubert H. Humphrey. One outcome was a radical attempt to revitalize party procedure, especially with regard to delegate selection and nomination procedures at the convention. Some of this revision was in response to drives by Southern black delegations to break the nearly all-white mold that had characterized the southern party membership. An opposite reaction to this reform tendency is the grass-roots conservatism of George Wallace of Alabama, which had attracted many adherents within the party. The election of Jimmy Carter in 1976 in the wake of Watergate did little to unite the party. Carter faced strong criticism and a sharp decrease in support, as well as a significant, although unsuccessful, challenge by Senator Edward Kennedy for the 1980 presidential nomination. The defeats of Walter Mondale in 1984 and Michael Dukakis in 1988 left the party in disarray and apparently unable to unite solidly behind a candidate.

See also Democratic-Republican Party; Jackson, Andrew; Jefferson, Thomas; Republican Party; Solid South; States' Rights Party; Two-party System.

DEMOCRATIC-REPUBLICAN PARTY, an anti-Federalist party founded in 1793 by Thomas Jefferson and James Madison. Party supporters called themselves "Republicans" to demonstrate their sympathy with the French Revolution. "Democratic" was a derisive label, then synonymous with radical, applied by scornful Federalists. The new party favored restriction of federal power to ensure personal liberties and a strict intepretation of the Constitution; they were opposed to high tariffs and the concept of a national bank.

With Jefferson's election in 1800, the Democratic-Republicans began a reign that ended with John Quincy Adams' election in 1824. The party returned to power with Andrew Jackson's election in 1828, when the name "Republican" was dropped and "Democratic" became the official party name.

See also Political Parties in the United States; Presidential Elections.

DEMOCRATIC SOCIALISM, the belief that socialism can be brought about by democratic means. In practice the actions of democratic-socialist political parties have tended to be pragmatic and evolutionary, effecting state ownership of the most important instruments of production (for example, the coal and steel industries) and leaving, at least for the time being, many other productive instruments in private hands.

The most important and successful socialist movements in Western Europe have been democratic, and Karl Marx toward the end of his life indicated the possibility that socialism could occur through peaceful democratic processes. The social-democratic political parties in West Germany, Italy, and France, and the Labor party in Great Britain have been major parties in their countries. Practically all capitalist countries, including the United States, have mixed economies in which some instruments of production are owned and operated by the community as a whole.

See also Capitalism; Collectivism; Economic Determinism; Socialism.

DEMOCRATIC STUDY GROUP, largely non-Southern, liberal, Democratic, House members formally organized to counter the Conservative Coalition and provide support for liberal legislation. Organized in 1959.

See also Conservative Coalition.

DENNIS v. UNITED STATES, 341 U.S. 494 (1951), considers the validity of the Smith Act of 1940, which attempts to protect the government from subversion and change by violence, revolution, and terrorism. In 1948 the top eleven leaders of the American Communist party were brought to trial and convicted for willfully and knowingly conspiring to advocate the overthrow of the government and to organize the Communist party for the purposes of so doing. The Court, in an opinion delivered by Chief Justice Vinson, said that the Smith Act, as applied in this case, does not violate the First Amendment rights of free assembly or speech, nor does it deny the defendants these rights. Here the Court applied Mr. Justice Holmes' "clear and present danger" test and found that the defendants, by their activities, created a "clear and present danger" aimed at the overthrow of the government by violence and force.

See also Schenck v. United States; Whitney v. California; Yates v. United States.

DE NOVO, "anew," frequently used to refer to trials in which the case must be tried "anew," or as if the case had not previously been heard. For example, appeals from state courts that are not courts of record (where no trial transcripts are kept) may have to be tried *de novo.*   *—Mary L. Carns*

DEPLETION ALLOWANCE, a legal tax deduction in the United States given to owners of exhaustible natural resources, such as oil, gas, metals, timberlands and minerals. The depletion allowance permits the owner to deduct from his income the costs of his investment in natural resources as the property becomes exhausted. There are two methods of computation: cost depletion, applied to timberlands, and percentage depletion, which is applied to oil and metals and is frequently condemned by economists. Efforts to eliminate the deduction as part of the 1986 Tax Reform Act were unsuccessful.

DEPORTATION, forcible removal of a person from the territory of the country of residence. As a form of punishment, deportation appears in history from very ancient times. In the United States several laws concerning deportation have been enacted since the Alien Act (1798), later repealed, which gave the president power to deport any alien he judged dangerous. Only aliens can be deported; American citizens cannot be expelled from the United States. However, naturalized (foreign born) citizens may be deported if they are first stripped of citizenship for falsifying their application.

See also Citizenship.

DEPRESSION, a part of the business cycle, normally following a period of prosperity, heavy (wartime) consumption, overextension of credit, overproduction, and speculation, and usually accompanied by financial panic or crash. Such a crash occurred in the United States for the first time in 1819, in part as a result of overextension during the Napoleonic wars. Crashes have occurred subsequently at fairly regular intervals: 1837, 1857, 1873, 1893, 1907, and 1929.

The Great Depression of 1929 began with a postwar slump in agriculture prices in 1921. The construction industry went into decline in 1926, and inventories of new cars and other consumer goods were high by the summer of 1929. Bank failures were common through the decade. The stock market had risen steadily, however, since 1921 and precipitously after 1926, the prices on the market bearing little or no relation to corporate earnings. Market prices were the result of rampant speculation, which came to an abrupt end with the crash of October 1929.

As production increased through the postwar decade, profits did not go to those in the economy who might consume the product, but to the wealthy few who often reinvested in plant and machinery to produce even more. Overseas markets were limited by the fact that most European nations were poverty-stricken as a result of the war and were heavily in debt to the United States. Tariff barriers further inhibited the flow of American goods overseas.

Unemployment was the most striking effect of the Great Depression. At one time nearly a fourth of the work force was unemployed. New Deal recovery programs tended to restore confidence and helped the

unemployed, but full recovery did not come until the outbreak of World War II. New Deal legislation regulating the stock market, insuring bank deposits, and strengthening the Federal Reserve System have helped prevent a recurrence of the postwar conditions. *—Alan Kifer*

See also New Deal Legislation.

DESEGREGATION. *See* Civil Rights Movement.

DESPOTISM, an ancient concept connoting the usurpation of legitimate political authority by a single individual, the despot, or the arbitrary use of the power seized by the despot solely for his own interests. The distinguishing characteristics of despotism were its illegitimacy, or violation of the legal grounds and limits of authority.

See also Authoritarianism; Fascism; Totalitarianism.

DÉTENTE, term of French origin associated with a relaxation of international tension. Détente is generally used to characterize the desire for improving relations between opposing nations and/or alliance systems. In contemporary international relations, détente is used primarily to describe efforts to improve relations between the superpowers.

DETENTION. *See* Preventive Pre-trial Detention.

DEVALUATION, an official lowering of the par value of a nation's currency relative to gold or to the currency of other countries. Countries that are members of the International Monetary Fund register the value of their currency in terms of gold or the United States dollar, and agree to maintain the value, plus or minus 1 percent. They also agree not to devalue their currency by more than 10 percent without agreement of the board of directors of the IMF.

The common cause of devaluation is that a country continually imports more goods than it exports, which means balance of payments difficulties. A major reason for a country's imports to be greater than its exports is that the prices of the country's goods are too high in terms of other currencies.

A government with frequent deficits in its balance of payments can use other financial measures and foreign policy changes to solve the problem, as devaluation payments deficit. A decrease in exports can cause a recessionary economy, while a large increase in exports can boost demand and lead to inflation. Another reason for devaluation is to regulate the supply of a country's currency in other countries.

See also Balance of Payments; International Monetary Fund.

DEWEY, THOMAS (1902-1971), lawyer and Republican politician. Dewey graduated from Columbia Law School and entered private practice. In 1933 he was appointed U.S. Attorney for the Southern District of New York and developed a national reputation for his prosecution of organized crime. He first ran for governor of New York in 1938. Dewey lost by a narrow margin, but was elected in 1942 and reelected in 1946 and 1950. During that period he ran for the presidency against Roosevelt in 1944 and Truman in 1948. Most experts predicted a Dewey victory in 1948, but they failed to anticipate that voters would be reluctant to reject an incumbent president in a period of peace and prosperity. After completing his third term as governor of New York, Dewey rejected further political ambitions and returned to private law practice.

DIPLOMACY, the art of conducting a country's international relations. Diplomacy is the means used to advance foreign policy goals and/or to resolve differences between states. Diplomacy can be conducted in several ways. Meetings may be held on a bilateral basis between the representatives of two countries. When world leaders meet, the phrase "summit diplomacy" is often used to characterize the meetings. Diplomatic relations are also conducted at a level in which many states participate, for example at an international conference or through an international organization such as the United Nations. The Department of State and the foreign service are charged with primary responsibility for carrying out the foreign policy objectives of the United States.

DIPLOMATIC IMMUNITY. Diplomats are exempt from local jurisdiction. They are free from arrest, trial in local courts, and police, fiscal, and ecclesiastical jurisdiction. Diplomats cannot be required to give evidence. They are entitled to freedom of communication. The diplomatic pouch is inviolate. The immunity extends to their families, documents, homes, and other personal belongings. Diplomatic immunity is based on common practice and is reciprocal. Because a diplomat cannot be tried in local courts, a host country may ask the diplomat's government to recall the offending official and to punish him. If a diplomat violates local laws, interferes in local affairs, or acts against the interests of the host state, he may be declared *persona non grata* and asked to leave the country to which he is accredited.

A diplomat is expected to pay due regard to local laws and regulations for the maintenance of public order and safety. He may not interfere in domestic matters; if he does he can be recalled.

DIPLOMATIC SERVICE. *See* Foreign Service.

DIRECT DEMOCRACY, a government in which all citizens vote collectively on all issues and pass legislation, as in ancient Athens and New England town meetings. In indirect, or representative, democracy, control is exercised by officials elected by a majority of voters. The minority's fundamental rights, however, are theoretically protected.

DIRECT LEGISLATION. *See* Initiative and Referendum.

DISARMAMENT, limitation of armaments, reducing their function to miminal defense and internal security requirements. In the present state of relations among nations, a stricter interpretation of the term would be unrealistic. General and complete disarmament, though, has been proposed at times, mainly for propaganda purposes. The idea of disarmament is not new; for centuries schemes to that effect have been produced by philosophers, writers, theologians, and statesmen.

Early History. The first timid attempts for serious negotiations about the limitation of arms occurred in the two Hague Conferences of 1899 and 1907. Germany's defeat in World War I brought about its forced disarmament, hopefully to be followed by the victors' disarmament, which never materialized. Article 8 of the Covenant of the League of Nations required the reduction of "national armaments to the lowest point consistent with national safety and the enforcement by common action of international obligations." The first concrete result of this covenant was the Five Power Treaty Limiting Naval Armaments of 1922, establishing a fixed ratio for capital ships between Great Britain, the United States, Japan, France, and Italy. After much preparatory effort, the World Disarmament Conference finally met in Geneva in 1932. New proposals soon replaced the original draft. France and Germany were unable to reach agreement, and the conference made no significant progress; Germany finally withdrew its representative. The coming to power of Adolf Hitler on January 30, 1933, prevented a return of Germany to the conference, which broke up inconclusively. Subsequent events proved how disastrous the lack of agreement had been.

The Atomic Age. The problem of disarmament acquired a great urgency after World War II, with the advent of atomic weapons. It fell on the United States, as the single repository of this devastating weapon, to make a proposal. In 1946 Bernard Baruch presented a plan before the newly-created Atomic Energy Commission of the United Nations to gradually relinquish control of atomic weapons to the U.N. Security Council. The United States would have retained its stockpile of atomic weapons, however, until the inspection and control of all atomic facilities everywhere became effective. The U.S.S.R. reacted by proposing an immediate halt in the manufacture of atomic weapons and the destruction of atomics already in stock. Mutual distrust brought to naught the chances to reach an agreement, and the momentous occasion slipped by. The U.S.S.R. went on to develop its own A-bomb, which was detonated in 1949. Hydrogen bombs followed in rapid succession: 1952 for the United States and 1953 for the U.S.S.R. Great Britain in 1951, France in 1960, and China in 1964 developed and tested their own nuclear weapons. The failure of the Baruch plan meant an acceleration of the armament race, both in atomic and in conventional weapons; it was now acknowledged that the two were inextricably linked. Numerous disarmament meetings, both within and outside the United Nations, for years failed to produce any agreement.

Agreements. In 1963 a Nuclear Test Ban Treaty was signed, banning atmospheric tests. However, the refusal of two of the nuclear powers, France and China, to sign the treaty, diminished its significance. Important limited disarmament agreements have since been concluded, prohibiting nuclear weapons in Latin America, Africa, and Antarctica, controlling atomic weapons in outer space, agreeing to nonproliferation, banning biological warfare, and prohibiting nuclear weapons in the ocean floor beyond a twelve-mile limit. Agreements signed by President Nixon at the Strategic Arms Limitation Talks (SALT I, 1972) between the United States and the Soviet Union began a series of negotiations that were at times sidetracked, as occurred after the 1979 Soviet invasion of Afghanistan. The INF Treaty, continued START discussions, and conventional forces agreements have led to optimism over further breakthroughs. —*Sergio Barzanti*

See also Atomic Weapons, International Control of; Intermediate-Range Nuclear Forces; Strategic Arms Limitation Talks (SALT).

DISCHARGE PETITION, *or* **DISCHARGE RULE,** a procedure by which a bill may be removed, or "discharged," from committee control and brought to the floor of a legislative chamber for consideration. Discharge rules in both houses are cumbersome, complex, and difficult to implement. Members of both houses hesitate to sign discharge petitions, which may appear to threaten the power of the party leadership.

In the House of Representatives, a discharge motion may be adopted for any bill that has been in a committee for thirty days, or in the Rules Committee for seven days. A discharge petition must be signed by an absolute majority of House members (218) and then is placed on the Discharge Calendar for seven legislative days. Any member who has signed the petition may move that the bill be discharged. A simple majority vote is required. This seemingly-simple procedure is in reality remarkably difficult and complex, and is rarely successful. However, the threat of such a petition has occasionally been successful in forcing a committee to release legislation. The discharge rule was adopted in 1910 as part of a movement to remove powers from the Speaker and was revised in 1935.

The discharge rule in the Senate permits any member to introduce a discharge motion during the morning session. The motion may be voted on after one legislative day and takes a simple majority vote. The Senate version appears to be simple, but is as difficult to invoke as the House procedure. It is seldom used. —*Mary L. Carns*

DISCLOSURE OF INFORMATION ACT (1966), *See* Freedom of Information Act.

DISTRICT, CONGRESSIONAL, the area of a state from which one member of the House of Representatives is elected. Under the terms of the Apportionment Act of 1929, House membership is limited to 435, so district lines change to reflect population shifts. A 1964 Supreme Court ruling, *Wesberry v. Sanders,* that districts should have approximately the same number of people helped eliminate wide disparities in population among districts.

See also Apportionment, Legislative; Gerrymander.

DISTRICT COURT usually refers to one of about ninety federal trial courts. There is at least one district court for each state. The larger states have several. Although originally created by the Judiciary Act of 1789, their jurisdiction was then essentially limited to admiralty. Jurisdiction over proceedings in bankruptcy was added later, but it was not until the circuit courts were abolished by the Judicial Code of 1911 that the district courts became courts of general jurisdiction, exercising original (trial) jurisdiction encompassed by the judicial power of the United States.

Ordinarily, cases in a district court are heard before a single judge, with or without jury, as appropriate. However, just after the turn of this century the Congress became concerned with district courts' injunctions restraining enforcement of statutes on grounds of unconstitutionality. That concern has nurtured provisions of law requiring any application for an injunction against a state or federal statute on constitutional grounds to be heard before a district court composed of three judges, at least one of which must be a circuit judge. There is a direct appeal to the Supreme Court from the decision of a three-judge district. Appeals from the decisions of single-judge district courts lie in the courts of appeals, unless an act of Congress is held unconstitutional in a civil suit to which the United States or an instrumentality thereof is a party, in which case the appeal goes directly to the Supreme Court.

DISTRICTING. *See* Apportionment, Legislative.

DISTRICT OF COLUMBIA. *See* Washington, D.C.

DIVINE RIGHT, a term denoting the theory that a sovereign's right to rule is derived from God. The theory says that sovereigns inherit the rights of their ancestors who had been divinely chosen to rule. After the Middle Ages many kings claimed their thrones by divine right. The theory of divine right must be distinguished from beliefs in the divinity of kings.

DIVISION VOTE. *See* Standing Vote.

DIXIECRATS. *See* States' Rights Party.

DOLE, ELIZABETH (1936-   ), Secretary, U.S. Department of Labor. After graduating from Harvard Law School, she entered private practice. She worked for a number of government agencies and became a Federal Trade Commissioner in 1973. Dole served as a presidential assistant in the Reagan administration from 1981 until her appointment as Secretary of Transportation in 1983. She was appointed Secretary of Labor by President Bush in 1989. Dole is married to Senate Minority Leader Robert Dole.

DOLE, ROBERT (1923-   ), Senator from Kansas and Republican minority leader. After seeing combat service in World War II, Dole received a law degree at Washburn University in 1952. He served briefly in the Kansas legislature before entering private law practice. He was elected to the U.S. House of Representatives in 1960 and the Senate in 1968. He assumed an early leadership role in the party and was appointed chairman of the Republican National Committee (1971-1973). His reputation as an outspoken supporter of Republican policies led to his selection as Gerald Ford's running mate in 1976. Dole became chairman of the important Senate Finance Committee in 1981 and was instrumental in shaping the Reagan budget. Dole became majority leader in 1985; but when the Republicans lost control of the Senate, he assumed the post of minority leader (1987). His wife, Elizabeth Hanford Dole, served as Secretary of Transportation in the Reagan administration and as George Bush's first Secretary of Labor.

Robert Dole, Senator (1969-   ), and Senate Minority Leader (1987-   ).

DOLLAR DIPLOMACY, use of American investment to stabilize strategic underdeveloped areas, chiefly in Latin America. The term was coined after a 1912 speech made by President William H. Taft in which he proposed a foreign policy of "substituting dollars for bullets." Investments in Cuba, the Dominican Republic, and Haiti were temporarily successful, but others, such as the reorganization of Nicaraguan finances, were failures. Dollar diplomacy had major faults as a foreign policy. How peace was maintained and how profits were distributed were not major considerations. The military and other American officials were often sent to enforce political and economic order. Although President Wilson and others attacked dollar diplomacy because it implied threats of "forcible interference," it was revived by a succession of presidents, including Harding, Coolidge, and even Wilson.

Dollar diplomacy gave way to the Good Neighbor Policy in the early 1930s. Presidents Hoover and Roosevelt were no less concerned for American interests in the hemisphere but saw the Good Neighbor Policy as a less controversial means of maintaining our influence.

See also Good Neighbor Policy.

DOMESTIC SYSTEM, also called the putting-out or cottage system, a method of manufacturing prevalent in Britain and Europe during the eighteenth century. A manufacturer distributed raw materials to laborers who worked at home at piece rates. Initially, the system was advantageous for the manufacturer, who minimized his investment, and for the workers, who were able to be at home with their families. Putting-out enabled many families and single women to earn a livelihood. Many fortunes were made by merchants who purchased raw cotton and had it picked, combed and woven by domestic workers.

Conditions, however, were uncomfortable, and rates eventually dropped; speed became a vital factor, and even children were forced to work. Often entire families went hungry and became ill while waiting for the next consignment. As more sophisticated machinery was invented, greater efficiency became possible in factories and the domestic system declined. Recent innovations in computer technology have increased the possibility of individuals working at home, connected to other workers and supervisors by a telephone communication network.

See also Factory System.

DOMINO THEORY, a political theory that if one independent state in Southeast Asia fell to communism, the rest would also fall, ultimately threatening the security of all of Asia. This theory was first enunciated by the U.S. National Security Council in February 1950 in explaining its decision to give military aid to the French in Indochina. This theory remained in force during the Eisenhower administration and became the cornerstone of United States policy in Southeast Asia. Hotly disputed in the 1960s by many congressional members and political theorists, the theory lost support in the early 1970s, with the American disengagement from Southeast Asia.

The Domino Theory has been mentioned in the 1980s as justification for American aid to Central American republics such as El Salvador and Honduras. American officials have expressed the fear that without continued aid the region could fall under Communist influence.

DOUBLE JEOPARDY, prohibited by the Fifth Amendment: "no person can be tried for the same crime twice. . . ."

Through the due-process clause of the Fourteenth Amendment, this constitutional immunity is binding upon the states, as well as the federal government. In practice, the protection is not absolute, for a state may prosecute an individual previously tried by the federal government. However, the state cannot order a second trial following an acquittal, nor can an individual be convicted more than once for the same crime. Similarly, a punishment imposed after conviction cannot later be increased.

DOUGLAS, STEPHEN ARNOLD (1813-1861), the "Little Giant," Democratic political leader, famed debater against Lincoln, presidential aspirant prior to the Civil War. Douglas was born in Vermont but moved to Illinois, was admitted to the bar there in 1834, and rose rapidly in Democratic politics to become congressman (1843-1847) and senator (1847-1861). As Chairman of the Committee on Territories he favored annexation of Texas and war with Mexico; he aided the expansion of slavery by his doctrine of "popular [squatters'] sovereignty," permitting local governments to determine their own positions. He drafted the important Kansas-Nebraska Act of 1854, which repealed the Missouri Compromise and realigned political parties on the slavery question.

In his campaign for reelection to the Senate in 1858 Douglas engaged Abraham Lincoln in the famous "stump speaker" debates. This personal contest was renewed in the presidential campaign of 1860, in which Douglas, favored by Democrats, lost Southern support and the election to Lincoln. Douglas died of typhoid fever in Chicago, while speaking in support of Lincoln and the Union. Douglas' presidential ambitions led him into compromises that satisfied neither the abolitionists nor the proprietors of slave plantations.

DOUGLASS, FREDERICK (1817-1895), civil rights leader, escaped slave, militant abolitionist, influential lecturer and journalist. In his understanding that the future development of America required an end to the outdated slave system, Douglass was more perceptive than his compromising contemporaries, including Lincoln.

His mother was a slave, and his father was an unknown white. In 1838 Douglass escaped North, where he worked as a stevedore and addressed gatherings of ex-slaves in the black communities. In 1841 he began to describe his experiences before antislavery meetings in New England but was often disbelieved, mobbed, and assaulted. With the endorsement of the leading abolitionists William Lloyd Garrison and Wendell Phillips, he published his *Narrative of the Life of Frederick Douglass* in 1845. Threatened after this exposure with return to his owner, he went to England and Ireland, where he earned enough money by lecturing to purchase his freedom in 1847. From Rochester he published *The North Star, Frederick Douglass' Paper,* and *The New Era.* In these widely circulated journals he advocated the abolition of slavery, education for blacks, and women's suffrage, a cause for which he attended the first convention, in 1848. A mature political figure by 1850, he attained an unprecedented status for a black person of that time.

Although he at first opposed violence, he operated a station on the underground railway to aid escaped slaves, was friend and adviser to John Brown, and after Harper's Ferry had to flee to Canada because of this association. Breaking with Garrison and the "persuasive" abolitionists, Douglass supported the Republicans and urged the reluctant Lincoln administration to emancipate the slaves. He was instrumental in recruiting black troops for the Union forces during the Civil War, and afterward supported reconstruction and urged full franchise for the former slaves. Underestimated by his contemporaries, he was rewarded by token appointments to minor posts. He died near Washington, D.C., in 1895. Only in recent times, with new evaluations inspired by the black liberation movement, has the historical import of Douglass been acknowledged.

DRAFT. *See* Selective Service System (SSS).

DRED SCOTT v. SANDFORD 19 How. 393 (1857), concerns the comity clause of the Constitution, the purpose of which is to prevent a citizen from one state from being treated as a foreigner when entering another. Scott, a Missouri slave, was freed in Illinois. Later, he returned to Missouri, whereupon he sued for his freedom and won. The question was, could Scott sue in federal court, a privilege granted to United States citizens? The Court, in an unfortunate decision which is said to have precipitated the Civil War, held that the descendants of African slaves were not included under the word "citizen" in the Constitution and could claim none of the rights and privileges which that instrument provides for and secures to the citizens of the United States, whether or not any one of the states had chosen to grant them citizenship for its own purposes. This deci-

The Drug Enforcement Agency in action.

sion was reversed with the ratification of the Thirteenth Amendment.

DRUG ENFORCEMENT AGENCY (DEA), federal agency created in 1973, to assume primary responsibility for enforcing narcotics and controlled substance laws. It has offices throughout the United States and in some 40 foreign countries. DEA is a part of the Department of Justice.

See also Office of National Drug Control Policy.

DUAL CITIZENSHIP, possession of dual nationality due to a jurisdictional conflict between two different countries. Dual citizenship may arise when (1) an individual takes citizenship in another state and this change is not recognized by the country of his previous nationality or (2) one country's *jus solis* conflicts with another country's *jus sanguinis*.

DUAL COURT SYSTEM, the separate jurisdictions of federal and state court systems in the United States. Federal and state courts are basically independent of each other and operate under separate bases of authority since federal courts are created under the authority of the national constitution and state courts are established in state constitutions.

Federal courts have exclusive jurisdiction over certain cases, including suits involving violations of federal laws. State courts also have sole jurisdiction over some cases, such as cases involving disputes arising from state law or state constitutions. Jurisdiction is concurrent (shared) for still other areas of law, including some diversity of

citizenship cases. The dual court system is an illustration of the principle of division of powers under a federal system of government.   —*Mary L. Carns*

DUBOIS, W(ILLIAM) E(DWARD) B(URGHARDT) (1868-1963), scholar, teacher, editor, black organization leader. He was born in Great Barrington, Mass., of free black and Huguenot ancestors, the year of ratification of the Fourteenth Amendment. His education was extensive, and the Ph.D. he received at Harvard was the first attained by a black person at that university. A linguist, historian, and prolific writer on sociological problems, he took an active part in the organization of successive popular movements, altering his tactics with the progress of black struggles and his own philosophical development.

Impatient with the gradualism of Booker T. Washington, the 1895 Tuskegee movement, and the Atlanta Compromise, DuBois searched for more effective forms to achieve full equality. As early as 1899 he demonstrated his political independence of Lincoln's Republican Party, traditional haven of the blacks, by supporting the Anti-Imperialist League and identifying with the victimized colored peoples of the Philippines. He cofounded the Niagara movement in 1905, claiming "for ourselves every single right that belongs to a free American." During this period DuBois distrusted trade unions and socialist parties for their disregard of black citizens. He believed then that the necessary black leadership would emerge through the education and promotion of the "talented tenth."

NAACP. Condemning lynching and Jim Crow, he joined in forming the National Association for the Advancement of Colored People (NAACP) in 1909, cooperating with white liberals to the extent that among its first executive officers he was the only black. He urged blacks to enlist in World War I and upon their return home advised them to continue fighting for democracy. He opposed Marcus Garvey's back-to-Africa movement with pan-African conferences, the first held in Paris in 1920, to unite the colored peoples of the world against colonial indignities. DuBois chided the black elite middle class for its vacillation and lack of militancy. He was ousted from the NAACP in 1932 and returned to Atlanta University as professor of sociology. After World War II he came back to the NAACP and served as consultant to the U.N.

Postwar Activity. Having visited the Soviet Union in 1928 and been impressed with its solution of the problems of multinationality, he became involved in the activities of the international peace and socialist movements. He received the Lenin Peace Prize in 1959. After nearly a century of struggle the logic of his life led him to join the Communist party in 1961. He went to Africa and became a citizen of Ghana.

DUE PROCESS OF LAW, a clause in the Fifth Amendment and the Fourteenth Amendment ensuring that laws are reasonable and that they are applied in a fair and equal manner. Essentially, due process guarantees that every person has a right to be fairly heard before he can be deprived of life, liberty, or property. Due process of law restricts the lawmaking powers of the government by banning laws and executive orders that are arbitrary or unreasonable. Due process of law was codified in 1215 in Article 29 of the Magna Charta and appears in an Edward III statute of 1354.

Because of the protection of the Bill of Rights against strictures of the federal government, the due-process clause of the Fifth Amendment, which applies only to the federal government, is not as important in actual practice as the Fourteenth Amendment's clause which applies to the states. In fact, this clause has been basic in enforcing the freedoms cherished by Americans; it has been the source of more constitutional law than any other language in the Constitution.

The Fourteenth Amendment was passed in 1868 in hopes of applying the Bill of Rights to the states, because it restricted only the federal government. The first major decision on due process did not come until 1925, when the Supreme Court ruled that the free-speech provision of the First Amendment should be brought within the scope of the Fourteenth Amendment and so bind the states. By 1937 all of the rights of the First Amendment were covered by the due-process clause. In that year Justice Benjamin J. Cardozo held that all Bill of Rights provisions essential to liberty and justice be included under the protections of due process.

Provisions. Since then the provisions of the Bill of Rights that have been included within the due-process clause, thereby applying also to the states, are protection against unreasonable searches and seizures (Amendment IV); protection against self-incrimination (Amendment V); the right to have counsel, confront hostile witnesses, and receive a jury trial in criminal cases (Amendment VI); and the prohibition of cruel and unusual punishment (Amendment VIII).

See also Accused Persons, Rights Of.

DUKAKIS, MICHAEL (1933-   ), the unsuccessful Democratic presidential candidate in 1988. He was first elected to public office as a liberal reform member of the Massachusetts legislature in 1962.

Dukakis was elected governor in 1974 and took office to find the state facing a large budget deficit. He cut spending for social programs but later relented and was forced to increase taxes. That violation of a "no new taxes" campaign pledge probably led to his defeat in 1978. Dukakis taught briefly at Harvard while planning another run for the state house. He was reelected by a wide margin in 1986 and announced his candidacy for president in April 1987.

Dukakis was victorious in the primaries, where he stressed his record of economic success and his ethnic background. However, he was unable to overcome George Bush's identification with the Reagan years and the relative prosperity of the American economy.

In January 1989, Dukakis announced he would not seek another term as governor. His decision may have been influenced by mounting fiscal problems in Massachusetts.

DULLES, JOHN FOSTER (1888-1959), international lawyer, diplomat, Eisenhower's Secretary of State, architect of the Western alliance, and crusader against communism. Dulles was born in Washington, D.C., and educated at Princeton, the Sorbonne, and George Washington University. His family had a tradition of diplomatic and public service and introduced him at the age of nineteen to the Hague Conference. He began law practice in New York in 1911 and was counsel to the American peace commission in 1918-1919 and United States representative at the war reparations conference in Berlin in 1933. Director of many large industrial and financial corporations conducting operations where he performed his diplomatic functions, Dulles was criticized for being partial to their interests.

Secretary of State. In 1945 he advised Sen. Arthur Vandenberg at the U.N. Charter Conference, becoming delegate to the General Assembly in 1946, 1947, and 1950. As author of the foreign policy platform of the Republican party in 1952, he was appointed Secretary of State by Eisenhower and held office from 1953 to 1959. In this capacity Dulles acted more as tactician than as policy maker, traveling extensively around the world to consolidate support for the United States during the Cold War.

He regarded communism as a moral evil with which there could be no honorable compromise. In the context of the confrontation between blocs of nations armed with nuclear weapons, his attitudes of "brinkmanship" and threats of "massive retaliation" helped preserve America's decisiveness and credibility. At the height of his influence Dulles died of cancer. His principal writings are *War, Peace and Change* (1939) and *War or Peace* (1950).

ECOLOGY: INTEREST GROUPS, private organizations working to preserve wildlife and other natural resources. Many of these groups have taken legal action in the courts and been instrumental in having Congress and state legislatures pass laws to curb environmental abuses. The groups often have distinguished memberships and are advised by boards of leading scientists and naturalists.

With headquarters in Washington, D.C., the National Wildlife Federation encourages both citizen and governmental action on environmental matters. One of the federation's main concerns is animals in danger of extinction. The Sierra Club, located in San Francisco, Calif., has a primary goal of protecting the nation's scenic resources. The National Audubon Society is particularly active in educating the public about conservation and wildlife.

A California-based group, the Friends of the Earth, uses lobbying and legal action as tools for making conservation gains. In 1970 the League of Conservation Voters was formed as a legal political action arm of this organization. Legal action is the main technique the Environmental Defense Fund uses against polluters. It campaigned actively against the use of DDT, offshore oil drilling, and oil spills.

Several conservation groups concentrate on the acquisition of natural land in an attempt to protect and preserve it. These include the Nature Conservancy, the National Parks Association, and the Wilderness Society, all with headquarters in Washington, D.C.

See also National Wildlife Federation; Sierra Club.

ECONOMIC AND SOCIAL COUNCIL (ECOSAC). *See* United Nations.

ECONOMIC DETERMINISM interprets all noneconomic ideas, institutions, and actions as determined, or caused, and understandable by the interaction of economic forces and relations. Knowledge consists of the history of economics. The best known exponent of economic determinism is Karl Marx, who viewed history as unfolding dialectically and ultimately ending with the triumph of the working class, or proletariat.

See also Democratic Socialism; Socialism.

ECONOMIC DEVELOPMENT ADMINISTRATION (EDA). *See* Commerce, United States Department of.

ECONOMIC MESSAGE, PRESIDENT'S, annual economic report submitted to Congress by the president as enjoined by the Employment Act of 1946. Composed by the Council of Economic Advisors and delivered every January, the report is a description of the state of the economy, with recommendations for future economic policy.

ECONOMIC OPPORTUNITY ACT (1964) created the Job Corps and VISTA, the first major piece of legislation in President Johnson's war on poverty. Although opposed by Republicans as an election-year giveaway, it was passed by Congress.

The Job Corps, for youths between sixteen and twenty-one, was designed to provide educational, vocational, and on-the-job training. It is administered by the Department of Labor. There was also federal aid for work-study and for state and local work training. VISTA, often called the domestic Peace Corps, authorized the recruiting and training of volunteers to help staff the antipoverty programs. VISTA has since 1971 been administered by ACTION. Other sections of the Act authorized federal grants for programs to provide better employment opportunities, education, small-business loans, and employment training for adults.

See also ACTION; Job Corps; Volunteers in Service to America.

ECONOMIC STABILIZATION POLICIES. Since the dawn of the industrial revolution, the capitalist system has experienced periodic economic crises, or business cycles. The American economy has, in the last hundred years, suffered about thirty recognizable business cycles, of which two—that in the 1890s and the Great Depression of the 1930s—were so profound as to cause severe economic and political strains. Until recently the prevention of business cycles was thought to be largely beyond reach; but gradually, and especially since 1945, the task of stabilizing the economy was recognized to be one of the most important and attainable tasks facing a modern capitalist economy.

Keynesian Background. In stabilizing the economy, prescribing an effective cure required prior knowledge of the causes of the malady: it was not until the 1930s, with the revolutionary ideas of the British economist J.M. Keynes, that the causes of cyclical difficulties came to be perceived with any clarity. The Keynesian doctrine holds that we must distinguish between the potential output of an economy and its actual output. Potential output is defined as what an economy could produce—with its given capital, resources, and techniques—if the labor force were four percent unemployed. Actual output is what the economy actually produced with, say, three, five, or seven percent of the labor force unemployed.

Keynes' revolutionary insight was to see that in the short run no automatic force ensures that actual output equals potential output. Although potential output is determined by the supply forces of the economy, actual output is determined by the aggregate demand of consumers, investors, and government. No automatic link exists to ensure that aggregate demand always moves quickly toward potential output. Consequently, the economy may experience extended periods when demand is insufficient (as in the Great Depression) or extended periods when demand is excessive (such as World War II).

Given this framework, the tasks of economic stabilization policy are straightforward. First, the policy makers must predict by how much actual and potential output will diverge. Second, once the divergence is estimated, policies must be taken to propel actual output toward potential.

Prediction. The improvement in the record of stabilization policy has been made possible by more accurate macroeconomic measurement and prediction. Historically, measurement came first with the development of national income accounting in the 1930s. Once the measuring rods had been adequately designed, they could then be applied to forecasting the short-run performance of the economy for six, twelve, or eighteen months into the future. These projections are crucial to adequate design of stabilization policies. Success is limited by imperfect vision into the future.

Policy. Once a prediction has been made of the short-term movement and the gap, a government of a modern industrial economy can rely on two general kinds of policies to influence actual output: fiscal policy and monetary policy. These policies work by affecting the expenditures of consumers, investors, and governments—the sum of which equals the Gross National Product. Fiscal policy consists of changes in the tax and expenditure policies of the government. The usual policies for stabilization are direct changes in Federal government expenditures on goods and services, changes in personal income tax and transfer payments (which induce changes in consumption), depreciation regulations and investment credits (affecting investment), and changes in indirect taxation.

Monetary Policy operates more indirectly by changing the structure of financial interest rates or stock market prices. The techniques of monetary policy consist of market intervention (buying and selling of securities) and of market regulation (such as setting ceilings on interest rates or regulating the terms of financial transactions). The most common form of monetary policy is the Federal Reserve's day-to-day regulation of the money supply. These policies affect the stream of spending mainly through investment, as they change the costs and benefits of an investment by changing interest rates.

One school—the monetarists—holds that the money supply is the most powerful determinant of the money value of output. Monetarists have used historical evidence to argue that if the monetary authorities would stabilize the growth of the money supply at a fixed growth rate (usually 3 to 5 percent per annum) the economy could experience reasonably full employment with stable prices.

The other school—comprised principally of the advocates of Keynesian analysis—would have the government employ a combination of monetary and fiscal policies—the particular policy mix depending on other policy needs, such as the balance of payments or the need for private investment and public expenditure.

Problems. Of the many issues concerning stabilization policy, the most important is whether—given the hazards of prediction and implementation—to stabilize at all. Some economists feel that, historically, stabilization policy has behaved perversely more often than correctly. Most economists, on the other hand, feel that the record has been improving and that with better use of monetary and fiscal policy actual output can be stabilized at a level very close to potential.

A paradoxical problem is that success in preventing the underutilization of resources has given rise to the opposite problem—a tendency to have excessive demand on national output, leading to persistent inflation. Economists generally believe that inflation arises when actual output exceeds potential: when excessive demands exist, the prices of labor, materials, and goods are bid up and a general inflation of the price level ensues. In recent years, a new form of stabilization policy has appeared, the income policy. These policies are designed to retard inflation, principally by reducing the growth of money wages but also by regulating price increases; these policies aim to reduce inflation by means other than causing national output to fall. Income policies have had temporary successes in some countries, but there are few cases where inflation has been reduced for long by this means.

—*William D. Nordhaus*
See also Gross National Product.

EDUCATION, U.S. DEPARTMENT OF, a cabinet-level department established to oversee policy concerning federal assistance to education. Until the department's creation in 1979, its functions were carried out by the former Department of Health, Education, and Welfare.

The office of the secretary directs and administers the entire department, and advises the president on matters concerning education programs of the federal government. The secretary also oversees the federal government's responsibilities concerning the American Printing House for the Blind, Gallaudet College, Howard University, and the National Technical Institute for the Deaf.

The Department of Education sets policy for the improvement of federal education programs, including those concerning bilingual education, desegregation, federal assistance for private schools, vocational and adult education, and special education.

EDUCATION ACT OF 1965. *See* Elementary and Secondary Education Act of 1965.

EDWARDS v. AGUILLARD, 482 U.S. 578 (1987), decision in which the Supreme Court struck down a Louisiana statute that required public schools teaching evolution also to teach "creation science." The statute was challenged as a violation of the establishment clause of the First Amendment. The court agreed and held the statute was a clear attempt to advance "a particular religious belief." They further rejected as a "sham" the state's argument that the statute had the secular purpose of providing a balanced scientific view of evolution. Most commentators read the 7 to 2 decision as representing a serious blow to the proponents of "creation science."

EDWARDS v. SOUTH CAROLINA, 372 U.S. 229 (1963), concerns the right of demonstration on public property. The 187 petitioners were black high school and college students who met on the morning of March 2, 1961 at Zion Baptist Church in Columbia,

South Carolina, and from there walked to the South Carolina State House grounds. Their purpose was to show the citizens and legislative bodies their dissatisfaction with South Carolina's segregationist policies. The group listened to a religious harangue, sang, stamped their feet, and clapped. They refused to disperse when so ordered and were arrested for breach of peace. The court ruled that the Fourteenth Amendment does not permit a state to make criminal the peaceful expression of unpopular views, and that South Carolina's actions infringed the petitioners' constitutionally protected rights of free speech, free assembly, and freedom to petition for redress of their grievances.

EISENHOWER, DWIGHT DAVID (1890-1969), elected 34th President of the United States (1953-1961) after a long and distinguished career in the Army, including command of the allied forces in Europe during World War II and culminating in the five-star rank of General of the Army.

Career. Dwight David Eisenhower was born of a poor family in Denison, Texas. He grew up in Abilene, Kansas, and was graduated from the Military Academy at West Point in 1915. By 1942 Eisenhower had become a Lieutenant General and in December 1943 was named Supreme Commander, Allied Expeditionary Forces in Europe. He accepted the surrender of Germany in May 1945. From November 1945 to February 1948 he was Chief of Staff of the Army. He served as president of Columbia University from June 1948 to December 1950 when he took leave to become Commander of NATO forces in Europe.

When Eisenhower was nominated for the presidency on July 11, 1952, by the Republican party, he resigned from the Army. He defeated Adlai E. Stevenson by a popular majority of 6,600,000 and an electoral margin of 353 votes. Eisenhower was reelected in 1956 over the same opponent by 9,500,000 popular votes and an electoral margin of 384. Upon his retirement from the presidency in 1961, he was again made general of the Army. He died in Washington on March 28, 1969, and was buried in Kansas.

Soldier. As a professional soldier, Eisenhower was apolitical. He eschewed engagement in politics until 1952. Assigned to many continental and overseas bases between 1915 and the beginning of World War II, he earned a sound reputation as an astute military planner and conciliator of conflicting views. President Roosevelt selected him above senior generals to command American troops in Europe and North Africa during the war.

President. As head of NATO forces after the war, Eisenhower was sought by many Republican leaders to become a candidate for the presidency. After an overwhelming victory in 1952, he reorganized the presidency along staff lines, a system with which he had been familiar all his military life. Eisenhower did not attempt to bulldoze Congress, which was controlled by the

Dwight D. Eisenhower, 34th President of the United States.

Democrats, for the last six of his eight years as president.

Eisenhower gave new leadership to American foreign policy but continued his predecessors' intentions to lead the nation as a major power against Communist aggression. He successfully faced down threats in the Far and Middle East. His vice president, Richard M. Nixon, was given a number of diplomatic assignments, and during Eisenhower's illnesses Nixon had opportunity to take part in domestic policy as well. A moderate conservative, Eisenhower was not usually a forceful president, but he was highly respected by the American people. The United States engaged in no major military conflicts during his administration.   —*Erwin L. Levine*

EISENHOWER DOCTRINE, announcement that the United States was "prepared to use armed force" to counter Communist-sponsored aggression in the Middle East. Eisenhower addressed a joint session of Congress on January 5, 1957 in the wake of the Suez Crisis. He stated the United States was ready to cooperate with its friends in the Middle East by providing economic and military aid in ways consonant with U.N. principles. His statement led to passage of the Middle East Resolution by Congress in March 1957.

Eisenhower invoked the doctrine twice during his administration. He sent the Sixth Fleet into the Eastern Mediterranean in April 1957 to prevent a Communist takeover of Jordan, and in 1958 Marines were sent to Lebanon to counter Communist threats.

ELASTIC CLAUSE. *See* Necessary and Proper Clause.

ELECTION, an act or process to choose a person to fill an office by vote. In the United States, elections are used in virtually every kind of organization. Elections are used more extensively to fill public offices in America than in any other country.

The Use of Elections. Elections came to America with

the early English settlers and have been a central facet of American political and governmental life ever since. England used elections to choose members of local councils and Parliament. The colonists, especially in New England, elected all sorts of civil, military, and judicial officers. The tradition survives, largely intact. The United States has a national government with 537 elective officials, fifty states with an aggregate of 13,000 elective officials, and 81,000 local governmental units with more than 500,000 elective officials. They include legislative, judicial, and administrative officers and boards, including such technical experts as coroners, surveyors, and auditors. The typical American voter may

---

ELECTION: TOPIC GUIDE

The article on ELECTION discusses the use of elections, nomination of candidates for elections, direct and indirect electoral systems, timing of elections, and election participation by various groups.

The related articles on election may be divided into three groups. See also POLITICAL PARTIES IN THE UNITED STATES and POLITICAL SYSTEMS, which have Study Guides.

Types of Elections. Some of the ways in which voters indicate preferences are described in PRESIDENTIAL ELECTIONS, PRIMARY ELECTION, NONPARTISAN ELECTIONS, PLEBISCITE, WRITE-IN CANDIDATE, and NATIONAL PRIMARY. Candidates' efforts to win elections are examined in CAMPAIGN, POLITICAL.

Voters exercise choices at several stages in the electoral process, beginning with VOTER REGISTRATION, in which VOTER QUALIFICATIONS may be examined. Normally a voter casts a BALLOT personally, but ABSENTEE VOTING, CROSS-FILING in the primaries, as well as voting a STRAIGHT TICKET or SPLIT TICKET, affects results. THE PUBLIC OPINION POLL may sway voters and politicians. Voters may also be involved in PETITION and RECALL strategems.

Group Politics. Political alliances, which have a pivotal role in elections, are discussed in TWO-PARTY SYSTEM, MULTI-PARTY SYSTEM, SOLID SOUTH, and COALITION.

The meetings of political parties are described in CONVENTION, POLITICAL. The NATIONAL COMMITTEE and CREDENTIALS COMMITTEE play key roles at national conventions. Some convention procedures are covered in CAUCUS, UNIT RULE, FAVORITE SON, and PLATFORM, PARTY.

Courts and Elections. The courts ruled against unjust practices in decisions such as GUINN v. U.S., which outlawed the GRANDFATHER CLAUSE; SMITH v. ALLWRIGHT, which invalidated the WHITE PRIMARY; and GOMILLION v. LIGHTFOOT, which set aside a GERRYMANDER. The right of Congress to regulate primaries was upheld in U.S. v. CLASSIC.

---

help elect dozens of officials. Sometimes the list becomes absurdly long, with ballots as big as bath towels. The size of the ballot has grown through the use of elections for related purposes. Since the Revolutionary War period, popular elections have been the standard device for designating the members of constitutional conventions, of which more than 200 have been held in the United States.

Popular referendum is another variant of election. Seventeenth-century New England assemblies referred some controversial measures to the voters for final approval. This device was revived during the Progressive Era around 1900 and is used widely by states, municipalities, and special districts, mainly for ratification of new constitutions and constitutional amendments, bond issues, and school budgets, but also for some laws. The Progressives extended the referendum concept to include popular initiative, whereby popular petitions may bring measures to the legislature or to referendum. The Progressives also introduced popular recall, through which voters can terminate an office holder's tenure by petition and special election.

Nominating Candidates for Elections. Another Progressive revival from early colonial days was the primary election as a means of nominating electoral candidates. Seventeenth-century New England often used preliminary elections to reduce the number of electoral candidates. Later, the method was displaced by other nominating means: (1) committees of correspondence, (2) party and legislative caucuses, and (3) local and state public meetings and conventions.

In 1830, national nominating conventions appeared and became the sole means of nominating major-party presidential candidates. Convention delegates, however, are designated by a variety of means. Delegates may be chosen by primaries or designated by state or local conventions, state or local committee caucuses, or a combination of means.

In the mid-nineteenth century the primary election was rediscovered and placed on a party basis. Since the Progressive Era, the primary has been the predominant mode of nomination for congressional, state, and local offices. For instance, in 1972, primary elections were scheduled in all states and the District of Columbia. Through most of our history popular petition has been an available alternative nominating device.

Electoral Systems. Most American elections use the uninominal plurality electoral system: each office is contested separately, and the candidate with the largest number of votes wins. The uninominal majority system is used in some Southern primary elections: the leading candidate must win a majority of the votes cast, or a later runoff election is held at which a plurality suffices. Some state legislature and municipal council elections use the plurinominal plurality system: each voter may cast as many votes in each contest as offices are at stake, and those offices are filled by the candidates receiving the largest number of votes. The proportional representation system has been used in the United States for only a few municipal council elections. The system distributes seats among party tickets in direct proportion to their share of the votes, using multimember districts.

Indirect Election Systems are equally rare in the United States. United States Senators were chosen by popularly elected state legislators before adoption of the Seventeenth Amendment in 1913. Some mayors are chosen by popularly elected city councils.

Presidents and vice presidents are elected indirectly in form, but directly in effect. Each state chooses "in such manner as the legislative thereof may direct," as many grand electors as it has members of Congress. Those electors cast ballots separately for president and vice president. A candidate who wins a majority of the electoral votes is elected. Failing a majority, the House of Representatives, voting by states, chooses the president from the top three candidates, and the Senate chooses the vice president from the top two candidates.

That system was a compromise among proponents of at least 21 different electoral systems proposed at the 1787 convention, of which the most popular were choice by (1) direct popular vote, (2) state legislatures, (3) state governors, or (4) Congress or one of its houses. The electoral college system permitted advocates of each of the first three methods to expect that the legislatures would designate the electorate they preferred. Advocates of Congressional selection believed that most elections would go to the House and Senate. In fact, except for 1800, half or more of the electoral college members have been popularly elected from the beginning, and only in 1800 and 1824 did the choice fall to the House. Otherwise, the electoral college has been little more than a vehicle for popular election.

Timing of Elections. American elections occur at regular, frequent intervals set by constitutional provisions and by laws. Presidential elections have occurred every leap year, and congressional elections, every even-numbered year since 1788. Most state elections coincide with congressional elections. Many local elections are held in odd-numbered years. Often, special elections are used to fill interim vacancies. The typical American voter is called to the polls for at least one primary and one general election each year.

Participation in Elections. Generally, the early colonists followed the English practice of adult, white, manhood suffrage with a "forty-shilling freehold" property qualification, although some colonies omitted the property qualification sometimes, and the ready availability of land attenuated its effect elsewhere. At times the religious unorthodox were disenfranchised. Poor transportation and communications, the use of voice voting in meetings rather than ballots, and voter apathy reduced participation further. Colonial voting data are scarce. Probably, turnout rarely exceeded 8 percent of the population. This figure compares to 14 percent in 1900, the last census-year presidential election before women's suffrage.

Property and religious tests disappeared, for some offices at least, in most states by the early 1790s. Virginia alone held back until the mid-nineteenth century. Racial bars fell next, at least constitutionally. The Fifteenth Amendment (1870) forbade denial of suffrage "on account of race, color, or previous condition of servitude." Subterfuges such as "grandfather clauses," literacy and educational tests, white primaries, poll taxes, complicated residency and registration requirements, and direct intimidation continued to disenfranchise many blacks, especially in the South, until the 1960s.

Twelve states introduced women's suffrage between 1890 and 1917. In 1920 the Nineteenth Amendment banned denial of suffrage "on account of sex" in all states. The Twenty-sixth Amendment (1971) forbids denial of suffrage to any citizen "18 years of age or older . . . on account of age." The Twenty-third Amendment (1961) permits District of Columbia residents to participate in presidential elections, and the Twenty-fourth Amendment (1964) outlaws disenfranchisement for failure to pay poll taxes. These amendments, unlike the Fifteenth, had the intended effect at once. Exclusions vary from state to state and are difficult to measure.

Several million adults remain excluded from the franchise by law because of their status as aliens or prison inmates. Larger numbers simply do not vote. In recent decades voter participation has declined to an average of less than 60 percent for presidential contests, even lower for non-presidential elections. This is far less than in other democracies. Apathy and the lack of perceived differences between the parties may be responsible.   —*William G. Andrews*

See also Electoral College; Presidential Elections; Primary Election; Voter Participation.

ELECTORAL COLLEGE, the constitutionally required method for the selection of the president and vice president.

Origin. In the desire to have the selection of the president and vice president indirectly elected by the people and in the hands of dispassionate, reasonable men, the framers of the Constitution devised the electoral college (Article II and Amendment XII). Each state was assigned as many electors as it has senators and congressmen. In addition, the District of Columbia has three electors (Amendment XXIII). To be elected, the candidates must have a majority of the electoral votes (currently, 270 out of 538).

Electors. Each state's electors are selected early in the presidential-election year by the state laws and applicable political party apparatus. The electors are pledged to the candidates chosen by their respective national party conventions in the summer of that year. In November the voters in the fifty states choose one slate of electors, pledged to both candidates of each party, from among those on the state ballot. If the slate of electors wins a plurality in a state, all the electors so chosen then cast their ballots (later in December at the state capital) for the presidential and vice-presidential candidates of the winning party. Neither the Constitution nor federal law requires the electors to cast their ballots in December for the candidate of their party, although only rarely does an elector bolt his party's ticket.

Process. If a majority of the electors have cast for one of the presidential and vice-presidential candidates, they are then declared to have been elected. If there is no majority for the president, the responsibility for selecting him from among the three top vote-getters falls on the House of Representatives, where each state has but one vote, and a majority of all the states is necessary to elect. If there is no majority cast for the vice president, the Senate then chooses him from among the top two vote-getters. A majority of all the senators is required to elect.

The president and vice president had to be chosen by Congress in 1801 (Jefferson and Burr), and in 1825 John Quincy Adams was chosen president by the House. It is mathematically possible for a president to be elected by a majority of electoral votes without a majority of popular votes cast in all the states. In the twentieth century this paradox has happened in the elections of Democrats Woodrow Wilson (1912, 1916), Harry S. Truman (1948), John F. Kennedy (1960), and Republican Richard M. Nixon (1968). Only once has a president lost the majority of the popular vote to one other candidate but won the electoral vote; in 1888 Benjamin Harrison defeated Grover Cleveland.

Reforms. Several reforms of the system have been proposed: (1) requiring by federal law the electors to vote for the candidates of their parties; (2) doing away with the electors themselves but keeping the substance of the college; (3) dividing the electoral votes in a state among the candidates in proportion to the popular vote cast in the state; and (4) electing the president and vice president by direct election of the people in the nation with a percentage requirement for victory. Although the last proposal made some headway in the Ninety-first Congress (1969-1970), the constitutional amendment required for such a change did not come to a vote in the Senate.   —*Erwin L. Levine*
See also Election; Presidential Elections.

ELECTRONIC VOTING, method of voting in the U.S. House of Representatives since 1973, whereby members insert a personalized plastic card, similar to a credit card, into a voting station and press a button to indicate "yea," "nay," or "present." Votes are immediately displayed on special electronic panels installed behind the Speaker's desk, and a running tally of votes is also visually displayed.

The procedure has speeded up the voting process and has resulted in a significant increase in recorded votes. Whereas a record vote in the House once required approximately thirty to forty-five minutes, rules for the new procedure close the vote after fifteen minutes. An average of approximately 600 votes a year are taken in the House of Representatives using electronic voting, as contrasted with fewer than 100 per year in the 1960s. Electronic voting is also used to establish the presence of a quorum.   —*Mary L. Carns*
See also Quorum; Record Vote.

ELEMENTARY AND SECONDARY EDUCATION ACT (1965). By basing its provisions on economic need, the Act avoided quarrels over aid to religious schools, in line with the 1964 Supreme Court ruling that defused the segregation issue. By stipulating that no federal official or office may interfere with any local or state school system in any way—including busing to overcome racial imbalance—the Act allayed fears that schools would lose local control. The "Great Society" act represented the first major legislation committed to quality education for all citizens and put an end to the myth of self-sufficient local schools.

Specifically, the "bootstrap" section offered local school districts federal aid allocated through state agencies, up to half the state's expenditures for children from families with incomes of less than $2,000. The Act offered further assistance for purchasing textbooks, expanding libraries and training librarians and generally bettering education. Provisions have been extended by subsequent amendments to include areas such as sex discrimination, education for handicapped persons, and adult education.

ELFBRANDT v. RUSSELL, 384 U.S. 11 (1966), questions the validity of a loyalty oath required by public employees in the State of Arizona. Elfbrandt, a public school teacher and a Quaker, decided that she could not take the state's oath in good conscience. The Court, in a five to four decision, held that the Arizona statute—the loyalty oath and an accompanying statutory gloss penalizing members of the Communist party—was in violation of the First Amendment protection of freedom of association, because it proscribed mere membership in the Communist party rather than "active" membership with specific intent to accomplish the unlawful ends of that organization. The dissenters felt that a state is entitled to require its employees to abstain from knowing membership in the party.
See also Whitehill v. Elkins.

ELKINS v. UNITED STATES, 364 U.S. 206 (1960), questions the constitutionality of using in a federal criminal trial evidence that was obtained through unreasonable search and seizure. Elkins and Clark were convicted of intercepting and recording wire communications and divulging such communications in violation of the Communications Act, and of conspiracy to violate the Act. The conviction was based on unlawfully obtained tape and wire recordings and a recording machine that had been seized by state law enforcement officers in Clark's home. In a five to four decision, the Court held that evidence obtained by state officers during a search which violated the defendant's immunity from unreasonable searches and seizures under the Fourth Amendment, made applicable to the states through the Fourteenth, is inadmissible over the defendant's timely objection in a federal criminal trial.

See also Mapp v. Ohio.

ELLSWORTH, OLIVER (1745-1807), statesman and 2nd Chief Justice of the Supreme Court, born in Windsor, Ct. He was respected by his contemporaries for his intelligence, common sense, diligence, and the major role he played in the Revolutionary period. A lawyer, Ellsworth represented Connecticut in the Continental Congress (1778-1783) and in the Constitutional Convention of 1787. He helped to frame the first draft of the Constitution and was instrumental in the adoption of the Connecticut Compromise. He was prominent in the Senate from 1787-1796.

Appointed to the Supreme Court in 1796 by John Adams, Ellsworth did not excel as a justice. His decisions were marked by common sense, not great legal learning. In 1799 he reluctantly left the Court to become a member of the commission sent to improve relations with France. When he returned in 1801, he felt that a possible war with France had been avoided.

See also Supreme Court of the United States.

EMANCIPATION PROCLAMATION. *See* Lincoln, Abraham; Slavery.

EMBARGO, a government restriction on trade, usually ordered during wartime. Under an embargo, ships of the embargoed nation are either detained in port or excluded from port. Aside from war, embargoes may be used to exert political or economic pressure or to protect against the landing of certain undesirable cargoes. Targets of recent United States embargoes include North Korea under the 1950 Trading with the Enemy Act and the Export Control Act, Cuba in 1960, the Soviet Union in 1980, and Nicaragua under the Sandinista regime.

EMBASSY, a word covering the function or position of an ambassador and his official residence, staff, and offices. In a strict sense, however, the term means his official residence.

A large embassy has an ambassador, sometimes a minister, counselors, diplomatic secretaries, attachés, and clerical staff. The ambassador, retinue, and premises enjoy diplomatic immunity and privileges. No officials of the host country may enter the premises without consent. If a crime is committed within the embassy, the offender is handed over to the local authorities. In some countries it is illegal to hold demonstrations within a specified distance from an embassy.

In Latin America, the right of an embassy to give asylum to political refugees is recognized. This right is no longer exercised in most European countries. An embassy has the right to have a chapel at which the rites of the religion of the ambassador may be celebrated.

In the nineteenth century, embassies and ambassadors were rare; only the great powers exchanged ambassadors, but many states exchanged ministers who functioned in legations. Today most capital cities have as many ambassadors as there are sovereign states.

A consulate is often attached to the embassy. It looks after the commercial interests of its country's citizens and also performs administrative functions, including the issuance of passports and visas.

A legation represents a lower level of diplomatic representation than an embassy. It is headed by an envoy and minister who also enjoy diplomatic privileges and immunities.

U.S. embassy in London.

EMERGENCY POWERS OF THE PRESIDENT. Although the Constitution does not provide for additional powers of the president during an emergency, there have been periods when the president has exercised rarely-used powers. In particular, the president possesses "inherent powers" in foreign affairs, even though the Constitution is silent on this matter. The president's control of foreign affairs derives from his responsibility for national security in an unsettled international community.

The inherent-powers doctrine was first enunciated by the Supreme Court's, *United States v. Curtiss-Wright Export Corporation* (1936). The case was precipitated when the president ordered an embargo on the shipment of weapons to two South American belligerents. In another case, *Youngstown Sheet and Tube Co. v. Sawyer* (1952), the Supreme Court rescinded as unconstitutional President Truman's emergency order for the seizure of steel mills.

See also Inherent Powers.

EMINENT DOMAIN, the right of a government to take private property for public use. The private owner must receive reasonable compensation for his property. In addition, the government's action must be in accord with the due process of law, outlined in the Fifth and Fourteenth Amendments.

EMPLOYMENT AND TRAINING ADMINISTRATION, formerly the Manpower Administration, an agency within the Department of Labor concerned with obtaining the greatest possible realization of the U.S. labor force potential. To this end the administration coordinates numerous training and employment programs, including those conducted by the Unemployment Insurance Service, the Bureau of Apprenticeship and Training, and the Job Corps, which focuses on socially and economically disadvantaged persons. The administration is composed of ten regional offices.

EMPLOYMENT SERVICE, U.S., federal agency that is responsible for providing placement services for unemployed persons seeking jobs. The service also provides employers with recruitment assistance and referrals of individuals seeking work. The agency also researches the economic forces that have an impact upon employment in order to plan and operate job training and vocational education programs.

EN BANC, "full bench," a reference to sessions in which the full membership of a court participates. In the United States, Federal Districts are single-judge courts. Cases in Courts of Appeal are normally heard by a panel of three judges, but important cases are occasionally heard by the full court *en banc*. All cases heard by the U.S. Supreme Court are decided *en banc*. Since the U.S. Constitution refers to "one Supreme Court," the Court has interpreted this to mean that the entire membership should participate as a "full bench" in each case.
—*Mary L. Carns*

ENERGY, U.S. DEPARTMENT OF (DOE), cabinet-level federal department, established in 1977 under the Carter administration to consolidate major federal energy functions under one organization. The goal of the DOE is to develop a foundation upon which a comprehensive national energy policy may be built. The agency provides funds for research and development of energy-related technology, promotes conservation measures, regulates various energy programs and industries, and collects data on energy-related areas. It also operates nuclear weapons facilities. It has suffered from serious management and safety lapses in recent years.

ENFORCEMENT ACT. *See* Civil Rights Acts: *Act of May 31, 1870.*

ENGEL v. VITALE, 370 U.S. 421 (1962), is one of the first cases concerning the recital of the so-called Regents' Prayer in the New York public school system. The parents of ten pupils challenged both the state law authorizing the school district to direct the use of prayer in public schools and the regulation ordering the daily recital of the Regents' Prayer. Although the prayer was intended to be religiously neutral as among various beliefs, the parents felt that it was contrary to the beliefs, religions, or religious practices of both themselves and their children. Mr. Justice Black, writing for the Court, stated that the State of New York, by using its public school system to encourage recitation of this prayer, had adopted a practice wholly inconsistent with the establishment clause of the Constitution. Mr. Justice Douglas, concurring, observed that once government finances a religious exercise, it inserts a divisive influence into our communities.
See also Abington School District v. Schempp.

ENGRAVING AND PRINTING, BUREAU OF. *See* Treasury, United States Department of.

ENROLLED BILL, the final copy of a bill that has been passed by both houses of Congress in identical form. The bill is printed on parchment, certified by the Clerk of the House if the bill originated in the House of Representatives or by the Secretary of the Senate if it originated in the Senate, signed by the presiding officers, and submitted to the President for his action.
—*Mary L. Carns*

ENUMERATED POWERS. *See* Delegated Powers.

ENVIRONMENTAL PROTECTION AGENCY (EPA), an independent agency in the executive branch, established in 1970 to permit coordinated and effective federal protection of the environment by controlling pollution in a systematic manner. The agency is responsible for limiting and eliminating pollution in the areas of air, water, solid waste, pesticides, radiation, and toxic substances. The EPA is responsible for a variety of research, standard-setting, and enforcement activities related to pollution abatement and control that, when properly integrated, are expected to provide for the treatment of the environment as a single ecological system.

The EPA supports and coordinates research and activities by state and local governments, private and public groups, and educational institutions. The responsibilities of the agency include regional air and water quality standards and pesticides, radiation, and solid waste management programs. The agency also conducts a national research program on the use of technology as a means of controlling pollution.

The EPA's dedication to the protection of the environment came under serious question for the first time during the first term of the Reagan administration. Among the issues discussed at that time was the administration of the Superfund, which had been enacted by Congress to provide funds to "clean up" dangerous chemical and toxic waste disposal sites.

President Bush has proposed elevating the EPA to Cabinet-level status.

—Guy C. Colarulli and Victor F. D'Lugin

ENVIRONMENTAL QUALITY. *See* Council on Environmental Quality.

EQUAL EMPLOYMENT OPPORTUNITY COMMISSION (EEOC), a bipartisan, independent agency established by Title VII of the Civil Rights Act of 1964. The purpose of the commission is to eliminate discrimination based on race, color, religion, sex, national origin, or age in conditions of employment. The commission also promotes voluntary action programs by employers, unions, and community organizations to foster equal job opportunity. The EEOC is responsible for compliance and enforcement of equal employment opportunity among federal employees and applicants. It may also exercise authority over private sector employers as well as state and local governments. The EEOC may issue notice of right to sue in employment discrimination cases and may recommend actions by the attorney general. Charges or complaints under the Age Discrimination in Employment Act or Equal Pay Act are under EEOC jurisdiction.

If the commission cannot eliminate the unlawful practice through informal modes of adjudication, it may take legal action. The commission consists of five members, appointed by the president with senatorial consent.

EQUAL PAY ACT (1963), an amendment to the Fair Labor Standards Act of 1938, enacted in 1963 and administered by the Equal Employment Opportunity Commission since 1979. The Act prohibits sex-based discrimination in employment practices or in wages paid for equal work. The Act regulates substantially equivalent jobs and does not deal with "comparable" jobs.

—Mary L. Carns

See also Equal Employment Opportunity Commission.

EQUAL PROTECTION UNDER THE LAW is guaranteed by Section 1 of the Fourteenth Amendment which states that no citizen of any state may be discriminated against by any act or condition. Areas in which equal protection has often been abused include jury selection, voting, use of public facilities, transportation, housing, education, and women's rights. Attempts to eliminate discrimination on the grounds of race, religion, political beliefs, and sex have taken the form of civil rights legislation in Congress and favorable Supreme Court decisions.

The equal protection provision, adopted in 1868, was at first interpreted as forbidding a state government from discriminating against any person within its jurisdiction. In 1954, the Supreme Court expanded this interpretation by making it the state's responsibility to remove discriminating conditions wherever they exist. The Court strengthened its position in 1964 by declaring that if a state did not do everything it could to eliminate discrimination, action would be enforced by Court decree.

See also Civil Rights Acts.

EQUAL RIGHTS AMENDMENT (ERA), a proposed amendment to the Constitution concerning equal rights for women. It was first introduced in Congress in 1923 and, although endorsed by the two main political parties and their presidential candidates since 1940, it did not pass in Congress until 1972. Early efforts were thwarted by those who felt that women needed special legal protections regarding employment and family status. Twenty-two states ratified it in 1972, and by 1975, the total reached 34, 4 short of the required number of 38. Proponents secured an extension of the deadline until June 30, 1982, but the amendment failed for want of the necessary ratifications.

Opponents of the ERA argued that it was unneeded since the Constitution also included the equal protection and due process clauses. They also alleged that its ratification would produce situations such as gay marriages, unisex toilets, husbands neglecting to provide for their families, and the sanctification of abortion. Proponents replied that the Supreme Court never treated sex as a constitutionally suspect classification and that nothing in the language of the ERA ("Equality of rights under the law shall not be denied or abridged by the United States or by any State on account of sex. Congress shall have the power to enforce by appropriate legislation, the provisions of this article") would result in the realization of any of the hypothetical situations.

EQUAL-TIME PROVISION, in broadcasting a law embodied in the Federal Communications Act of 1934 requiring that stations provide all candidates for public office with equal access to air time. Television networks and radio stations later became concerned because of the proliferation of minor party candidates for many offices. The first televised debate between Democrat John Kennedy and Republican Richard Nixon (1960) was held with the proviso that the equal-time provisions be suspended for minor party candidates. A bill to this effect was enacted, but it pertained only to the campaign of that year, permitting the "great debates" that political analysts feel had a far-reaching effect on the election results. A proposal to again waive the statutory requirement for equal time was made in the 1964 presidential campaign, but this request was rejected.

Debates were not held again until the 1976 election.

Then they were sponsored by the League of Women Voters as a means of circumventing the equal-time provisions. As a result of congressional action, the law was modified, and beginning in 1984, debates became part of the general election campaign under the sponsorship of the Commission on Presidential Debates.

Repeal of the "Fairness Doctrine" did not affect the equal time rule because it deals only with air time given to competing federal political candidates.

See also Campaign, Political; Fairness Doctrine.

EQUITY, apart from its broad meaning of natural, ethical justice, refers to a system of justice developed and administered by the English court of chancery. Equity continues to exist in the United States, but, due to the general abolition of the old dual system of courts, a sharp distinction is no longer made between actions of law and suits in equity. Common law was rigorously enforced by the law courts in England, with results that were often considered unjust. The only relief was petitions to the king, who tended to refer them to his chancellor. In time the petitions came to be addressed directly to the chancellor, and thus his authority to grant relief became institutionalized by the reign of Edward I (1272-1307). When the letter of the law was inadequate, an injured party looked to equity for relief.

Equity involves some concepts of "preventive justice" whereby a judge could either prohibit actions or order that actions be carried out to prevent harm from occurring. By contrast, most court procedures are "remedial," and corrective action can be taken only after the injurious act has occurred. Equity decrees are often issued in the form of a writ, such as the writ of *injunction,* which is a court order prohibiting an action.

See also Common Law.

ERDMAN ACT (1898). *See* Arbitration.

ESCOBEDO v. ILLINOIS, 378 U.S. 478 (1964). In this case the Court dealt with constitutional problems surrounding the use of confessions in criminal trials. The defendant, Escobedo, was arrested in connection with the killing of his brother-in-law. During the course of the questioning the police declined to accede to the defendant's request to be allowed to consult with his lawyer. The defendant subsequently made a confession that was used at trial by the state prosecutor to help convict Escobedo. On appeal the Supreme Court reversed Escobedo's conviction, but the grounds for the reversal were vague and the Court was sharply split on both the decision and the reasoning.

Justice Arthur Goldberg, speaking for a one-vote majority, apparently based his decision on the fact that the Court had recently used the Fourteenth Amendment due-process clause to incorporate the Sixth Amendment assistance-of-counsel provision as a protection in state criminal proceedings. On this basis Goldberg found that once a general criminal investigation shifts from an investigatory to an accusatory process, the suspect is entitled to counsel, even in a state proceeding. The dissenting judges sharply rebuked the majority's vague reasoning, alleging that the majority distorted the Constitution by using the Sixth Amendment's counsel provision to supersede the Fifth Amendment's self-incrimination provision.   *—Philip J. Hannon*

See also Accused Persons, Rights of; Confession; Gideon v. Wainwright; Miranda v. Arizona.

ESPIONAGE ACT (1917), an act prohibiting espionage, sabotage and obstruction of the war effort, with penalties up to $10,000 fine and twenty years imprisonment. This act was passed on June 15, 1917, to stamp out the mainly Socialist criticism of the United States' entry into World War I. In addition, anyone who willfully made false reports to help the enemy, incited rebellion in the armed forces or tried to obstruct draft recruiting was subject to prosecution under the act. The Espionage Act also gave the postmaster general the right to ban from the mails anything that he himself thought was seditious.

Soon after the Espionage Act came the Trading with the Enemy Act (1917), the Sabotage Act (1918), and the Sedition Act (1918). Wartime hysteria resulted in the vigorous enforcement of these acts, which continued in force after the armistice. One of the most famous cases prosecuted under the act was that of Eugene V. Debs, pacifist and Socialist leader. In *Schenck v. United States,* the "clear and present danger" test for the First Amendment was formulated to justify the conviction of the secretary of the Socialist party.

ESTABLISHMENT CLAUSE, clause in the First Amendment of the Constitution that states "Congress shall make no law respecting an establishment of religion, or prohibiting the free exercise thereof; . . ." There are two theories regarding the meaning and intention of this clause. The first, voiced by Thomas Jefferson, was that the clause's purpose was to build "a wall of separation between Church and State." This interpretation enabled the Supreme Court to strike down prayer and Bible-reading in the schools. The second theory interprets the clause's purpose as barring preferential treatment of any particular religion or sect by the government of the United States. Such an interpretation permitted the Warren Court to uphold Sunday closing laws for businesses and the Burger Court to allow nativity scenes on public property.

See also Freedom of Religion.

ETHICS IN GOVERNMENT ACT (1978), an act that established requirements for financial disclosure by top government officials and applied similar disclosure rules to high-ranking executive and judicial officials as had previously been applied to members of Congress in codes of ethics adopted in 1977. The Act, adopted in response to growing public and congressional criticism over a series of incidents involving congressional scandals and charges of misconduct, amended the House and Senate ethics codes, enacted them into law, and made provisions for assessing civil fines against violators. It also set provisions for appointing a special prosecutor in criminal cases involving high-ranking federal officers.

The Act required public disclosure of earned income, outside income including honoraria, gifts, and business and property holdings and made provisions for public access to information. The Act also placed some limitations on honoraria for members of Congress and presidential appointees and placed restrictions on employment and business activities of former senior-level government employees. Most of the restrictions were designed to reduce potential "conflict of interest" activities. The Office of Government Ethics was established to monitor and investigate compliance with disclosure requirements, order corrective action, and provide direction to executive policies relating to ethical standards and conflict of interest. Further restrictions on honoraria, tied to congressional pay increases, were rejected in 1989.   —*Mary L. Carns*

See also Abscam; Censure; Congressional Ethics; Expulsion.

EUROPEAN RECOVERY PROGRAM. *See* Marshall Plan.

EVERSON v. BOARD OF EDUCATION, 330 U.S. 1 (1947), involved a challenge by Everson, a New Jersey taxpayer, to a township board of education. The board, acting pursuant to a New Jersey statute, reimbursed parents of children attending both public and parochial schools for the cost of transportation to and from school on the public bus system. Mr. Justice Black, writing for the Court divided five to four, reviewed the history of the First Amendment, concluded that it was intended to prohibit assistance to any or all religions, but upheld the statute and board action. The decision was based on the "child benefit theory," which holds that state action primarily designed to aid the child, as opposed to the church school, is not prohibited by the First and Fourteenth Amendments.

See also Engel v. Vitale.

EVIDENCE, all means of giving information to courts trying cases involving factual disputes, including testimony, documents, and physical objects. In the common-law legal system the law of evidence principally determines when to admit or exclude evidence items, not how much weight to give them. Juries, or judges alone trying facts, do the latter, using their own experience and common sense as guides. Parties' attorneys obtain, select, and present evidence (the adversary system).

In Constitutional aspects of criminal cases, courts have in recent years greatly restricted evidence admissibility and created a criminal-law revolution, which is now beginning to recede. In other aspects, the trend is toward broader admissibility, with greater reliance on trial judges' discretion.

Evidence Terms. Direct evidence, if believed, establishes a fact directly, without needing inferences or presumptions. Circumstantial evidence, if believed, proves facts that may support an inference or presumption of the disputed fact. *Prima facie* evidence suffices to prove a fact until there is rebuttal evidence.

Relevancy. Only relevant evidence, which logically tends to prove or disprove a disputed fact, may be admitted. Many exclusionary rules may bar even relevant evidence, however. Substantial risk of misleading or prejudicing jurors, or unfairly surprising parties, or consuming excessive time, may outweigh relevant evidence's minor proof value and cause exclusion.

Competency. At one time, parties could not testify in their own lawsuits, nor could witnesses directly interested therein; convicted felons could not testify nor could spouses, for or against each other, in civil or criminal cases. A religious oath, and believing that God would punish false swearing, were witness requirements. Statutes have since abolished nearly all these incompetencies, but one—barring survivors, and persons interested in the outcome, from testifying to personal transactions or communications with someone deceased when suing his estate. Some variant states accept survivors' testimony but require corroboration to support judgments, or the states accept both survivors' testimony and decedents' written or oral statements on the subject. Spouses are now usually incompetent only to testify against the other in criminal cases, except for crimes against the witness spouse. Children, and even mental defectives, who can observe, remember, and narrate the facts, and understand their duty to testify truthfully, are competent witnesses.

Hearsay. Witnesses ordinarily give oral testimony telling what they have themselves seen, heard, or done. Evidence of other people's statements of facts, what these others saw, heard, or did, is hearsay if used to prove those facts. Documents containing such statements are also hearsay. Hearsay evidence is ordinarily excluded, because the declarants were usually not under oath and not cross-examinable. If all hearsay were barred absolutely, however, needed and trustworthy evidence of persons unavailable as witnesses would often be completely lost; hence, numerous hearsay exceptions have developed. These exceptions include admissions, declarations against interest, confessions, dying declarations, reported testimony, business and official records, spontaneous and contemporaneous declarations, and others. Hearsay admission is gradually broadening, pending closer scrutiny of its probative weight.

Opinion. Witnesses ordinarily testify to facts; opinions or conclusions are excluded. The fact-triers should form opinions and conclusions, but if special training or experience is needed for a reliable opinion (for example, on scientific, technical, and specialized subjects), experts' opinions are admissible if they assist fact-triers. Expert (especially medical) testimony is often biased and conflicting; the elaborate hypothetical questions are confusing; and solutions are being sought to improve this troublesome area.

Character. The accused in criminal cases may prove his good character, to imply unlikelihood of his committing the crime charged. If he does so, the prosecution may afterward show his bad character, but not initially. In civil and criminal cases, a witness's credibility may be attacked by proving his bad character for truthfulness or honesty, or his prior criminal conviction; only subsequently may his good character be shown, to bolster his credibility. Strangely, the character proof usually allowed is only his community reputation for the traits involved. The general rule in criminal cases is that proof of other crimes by the accused should not be received, but many exceptions allow admission when relevant to show more than simply the defendant's criminality.

Privilege. Though excluding relevant evidence thereby, the law's policy protects against compelled disclosure of confidential communications between spouses, attorney and client, and frequently between physician and patient and clergyman and penitent. Unless this privilege is waived by the other spouse, client, patient, or penitent, one may refuse to testify to such communications. Similar privileges exist for state secrets, government informants and, infrequently, accountants and journalists.

Writings. Documents are admissible without proof or concession of genuineness (authentication). All exclusionary evidence rules and some special doctrines apply to documents. The best evidence rule demands that original documents prove their contents; secondary evidence (copies, or testimony) are inadmissible unless the original's unavailability is properly explained. When persons make apparently complete writings to record their transactions or agreements, the parol evidence rule forbids receiving oral or extrinsic evidence showing prior contemporaneous agreements to vary or add to the writings' terms. Even if received without objection, such evidence has no legal effect, but extrinsic evidence is receivable to help interpret the documents, show conditional delivery, lack of consideration, fraud or illegality.

Real Evidence. Relevant physical objects properly authenticated are admissible, but gruesome, prejudicial, disruptive, or unnecessary ones are excluded to prevent abuse. Photographs, diagrams, and movies are admitted if shown to be accurate representations of relevant objects, places, or actions, as are physical demonstrations and tests.

Scientific Evidence. Expanding scientific knowledge and techniques keep enlarging this field. It now includes fingerprints, testing of questioned documents, ballistics, blood grouping, drunkeness tests, carbon dating, radar, lie detection, radiation recording, medicine, engineering, physics, chemistry, DNA matching and other tests. Comparison identifications are established for fact-triers with enlarged photographs, superimposed projector slides, spectroscopes, electron and comparison microscopes, and other devices.

Judicial Notice. Courts consider evidence unnecessary to establish certain obvious facts, like weights and measures tables or historical dates. Courts must judicially notice indisputable, universally known specific facts, even without request; courts may judicially notice facts so well known in the courts' jurisdiction as to be indisputable, as well as specific facts and generalized knowledge items capable of prompt, accurate determination from indisputably reliable reference sources. Courts must judicially notice the latter if a party asks, notify adverse parties beforehand, and furnish enough information, to comply. State courts also judicially notice national and their own state constitutions, statutes and law, but not those of sister states or foreign countries (except as widely adopted statutes permit). Federal courts judicially notice federal and state provisions. Statutes may declare administrative regulations and local ordinances judicially noticeable.

Presumptions. Trials often involve recurring facts difficult or impossible to prove directly. Probability or policy lead courts to allow the necessary inference once certain underlying facts are proved. These legally recognized inferences (presumptions) establish presumed facts *prima facie* for procedural purposes. Presumptions are permissible or mandatory, and rebuttable. For example, an individual unexplainedly disappearing and unheard from for seven years despite inquiry is presumed dead, or a properly addressed, stamped, and mailed letter is presumed delivered. So-called nonrebuttable presumptions of law, however, are really fixed legal rules. Thus a child under seven is conclusively presumed incapable of committing crimes; this presumption really means the law does not hold him criminally responsible. The presumption of innocence is not a real presumption but means that more convincing proof of guilt (beyond a reasonable doubt) is required than for civil cases.

What effect does a presumption have after credible rebuttal evidence is received? Under one widely held view, the presumption then disappears, and the question is decided only on the underlying facts proved and on the rebuttal evidence. Another view, now increasingly accepted, is that presumptions having a substantial backing of probability stand until the rebuttal evidence actually persuades the fact-triers contrariwise.

Burden of Proof. In trials the party having the burden of proof loses unless, on his whole claim or defense, he persuades the fact-triers that his fact allegations are true. A party having the burden of producing evidence must produce some, or additional, evidence supporting his allegations on controverted facts, or else have his allegations determined adversely. The burden of proof is fixed at the trial's start and continues unchanged, but the burden of evidence may shift between parties on different matters during trial.   —*Eli M. Spark*

EXECUTIVE OFFICE OF THE PRESIDENT

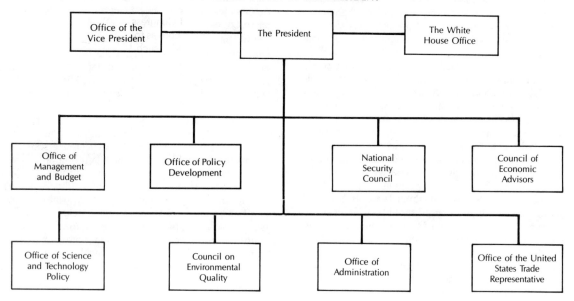

EXCLUSIONARY RULE, a rule that excludes the use of illegally-obtained evidence in all state and federal trials. In 1914 the Supreme Court in *Weeks v. United States* barred in a federal prosecution the use of evidence secured through an illegal search and seizure. This Fourth Amendment right was extended through the Fourteenth Amendment's due process clause to state criminal justice processes in the 1961 case of *Mapp v. Ohio*. The Burger and Rehnquist courts have created exceptions to the exclusionary rule to protect society against minor irregularities.

See also Due Process Clause; Weeks v. United States.

EXCLUSIVE POWERS, authority held by the national government and state governments. These powers, under the Constitution, belong exclusively to, and may be exercised only by nation or state. An example of an exclusive national power is the central government's power over foreign policy. An example of an exclusive state power is control of local government. Recently, power over welfare and civil rights decisions has changed from the sphere of state influence to the national.

EXECUTION. *See* Capital Punishment.

EXECUTIVE AGENCIES. *See* Executive Branch; Independent Agencies and Regulatory Commissions.

EXECUTIVE AGREEMENT. Under constitutional provision the president shares his treaty-making power with the Senate. In addition, Congress often extends authority to the executive to make agreements with other nations. Unlike treaties, executive agreements do not require senatorial approval. As with treaties, however, they may be set aside by the legislature. Although not binding on succeeding administrations without continued executive consent, executive agreements have been in use throughout American history as an important device in the president's molding of foreign policy and since 1900 have been used more frequently than treaties.

See also Treaty Power of the President.

EXECUTIVE BRANCH, that part of the government that applies the law. In a separation of powers system there is an attempt to distinguish the functions of rule initiation, rule application, and rule interpretation, and to assign the primary responsibility for each of these functions to the legislative branch, the executive branch and the judicial branch, though there is a marked sharing of these functions among the three branches.

The executive branch is a complex organization of various agencies, each more or less responsible to the chief executive. In a parliamentary system the executive branch, called a cabinet and headed by a prime minister or premier, is made up of members of the legislative branch and responsible to it. In the United States the president has a White House staff of aides who have a relatively intimate relationship with him and are entirely responsible to him; an executive office containing a number of agencies to give him information and advice; a cabinet, each member of which is the head of an executive department, such as treasury or defense; and some one hundred other agencies, boards, commissions and the like, with varying degrees of responsibility to the president.

Some agencies, such as the independent regulatory commissions, are almost completely free from control by the chief executive. Although the top officers of the executive branch are chosen by the chief executive and are clearly responsible to him, the bulk of their subordinates are usually selected under a merit system, giving them a large degree of job security and therefore a measure of autonomy in their decision making.

See also President of the United States; Separation of Powers.

EXECUTIVE DEPARTMENTS. *See* Cabinet; Executive Branch.

EXECUTIVE ORDER, a presidential directive that becomes law. Executive orders issued by the president or by administrative agencies must all be published in the Federal Register. Because of the complexity of American society, it is difficult for Congress to pass all necessary laws without being extremely overburdened. Hence Congress allows the president to issue executive orders (1) to establish or modify the practices of administrative agencies; (2) to give force to legislative statutes; and (3) to enforce the Constitution or treaties with foreign powers. The privilege of issuing executive orders contributes to the legislative power of the president.

EXECUTIVE PRIVILEGE, an accepted practice that prevents congressional committees and courts from interrogating executive officials without the express consent of the president. The concept evolved at a time when the president had a handful of close personal assistants who needed to be protected from congressional prying. In time the executive branch of government expanded, and with it, the number of presidential assistants. As a result, even lesser officials, with infrequent access to the president or to private information, have been protected by this doctrine.

See also United States v. Nixon.

EXECUTIVE SESSION, legislative session called to deliberate executive business. Because such sessions were held in secret until 1929, the term is now applied to any closed hearing, usually by a subcommittee on a particular bill. An executive session thus results in a determination of whether to table the bill in question or to report it favorably or unfavorably to the full committee in preparation for public hearings.

EX PARTE McCARDLE, 74 U.S. (7 Wall.) 506 (1869). Article III of the United States Constitution is devoted to the Supreme Court. This article describes in some detail the original jurisdiction of the Court, but leaves the appellate jurisdiction of the Court rather vague. More importantly, Article III places this kind of jurisdiction under the power of Congress by giving the Court "appellate jurisdiction, both as to Laws and Fact, with such exceptions, and under such Regulations as the Congress shall make." In the *ex Parte McCardle* case, the petitioner had been imprisoned by a state following the Civil War for publishing inflammatory articles. His petition for a writ of habeas corpus was denied by a lower court and appealed to the Supreme Court. After argument before the Court, but before the Court had handed down a decision, Congress passed a law which had the effect of denying the Court appellate jurisdiction in the case. In this period of congressional supremacy, the Court did not feel at liberty to look into the motives of the action, and it dismissed the case on the ground that it no longer had jurisdiction. —*Philip J. Hannon*

EX PARTE MILLIGAN, 4 Wall. 2 (1866), concerns military and executive invasion of individual rights. Milligan, a civilian and twenty-year resident of Indiana during the Civil War, was tried for treason by a military commission and sentenced to be hanged, even though he had never lived in one of the warring states and was not subject to the law of war. In a difficult decision, five of the justices held that Milligan had been unlawfully convicted, in that he was denied the right of a trial by jury, and that neither Congress nor the president had the power to set up military tribunals where civil courts were actually functioning. Four justices thought that Congress had the power to substitute a military tribunal for a civil one, but would deny that power to the president. All agreed, however, that Milligan had been unfairly convicted, and he was ordered released.

EXPATRIATION, the right to renounce one's own citizenship and become citizen of another country. The expression is also commonly used to indicate a citizen living abroad for prolonged periods who has not renounced his citizenship. The right to expatriate is still much contested, and some countries deny it. The United States consistently followed a policy of leaving to the individual the decision inherent to his national loyalty, irrespective of the will of the country having jurisdiction over him. America formalized its attitude in 1868 by act of Congress, and Great Britain passed similar legislation two years later, soon entering into an agreement concerning the matter with the United States.

A different kind of expatriation may be inflicted by totalitarian states upon some of their citizens—forcible expulsion or prohibition against return. If an expatriate cannot, or does not want to, take up the citizenship of another state, he becomes stateless. A citizen of the United States can easily divest himself of citizenship by formal renunciation filed with the American embassy, legation, or consul. An American woman, even residing abroad, who has married a foreign national, does not lose her American citizenship, unless she specifically renounces it. Although the U.S. does not recognize dual citizenship, many countries automatically confer their own citizenship to the foreign woman at the time of marriage. —*Sergio Barzanti*

   See also Citizenship; Extradition.

EXPORT-IMPORT BANK OF THE UNITED STATES (EXIMBANK), independent bank established in 1934 by Congress to promote and aid in the financing of the sale of U.S. goods and services in foreign markets. The goal of the bank is to expand U.S. exports through competitive financing. The programs developed by the bank to accomplish this goal include loans, loan guarantees, and insurance so that the financing of exporters by private lending institutions can be accomplished with fewer risks. Eximbank's direct lending activity is limited to support major sales. However, credit protection for U.S. exporters can be provided to businesses with smaller sales.

   The bank is managed by a five-member board of directors whose nominations require the approval of the Senate. At any one time, the bank can have as much as $40 billion outstanding in loans, guarantees, and insurance. The bank is authorized to have capital stock of $1 billion and to borrow from the U.S. Treasury up to $6 billion outstanding at any one time.

EXPORT-IMPORT BANK OF WASHINGTON, United States banking concern established in 1934. The bank is managed by a five-member board of directors whose nominations are approved by the Senate. The bank has a capital stock of $1 billion and may borrow up to $6 billion from the United States Treasury. The bank is designed to facilitate the financing of United States imports and exports, lending money to develop investment abroad to stimulate future trade; and to help United States businesses to sell abroad.

EX POST FACTO LAW (Lat., after the fact), a law retroactively making illegal a certain behavior, increasing punishment, or removing lawful protection. A basic principle recognized by civilized countries is that of *nulla poena sine lege* [Lat., no punishment without law]. Article I, Sections 9 and 10, forbids Congress and the states to pass any ex post facto law. The Supreme Court used this prohibiton to strike down the test-oath laws after the American Civil War; civil cases are not, however, affected by this protection.

EXPROPRIATION, the act of government confiscation of private property owned by resident aliens or foreign corporations. Expropriation is not illegal and may be compared to the right of eminent domain. Under international law, however, the government must meet specific obligations, including payment of fair, sufficient, and prompt compensation. In practice, governments have often ignored these obligations and seized foreign property without regard to international law.

EXPULSION, an extreme disciplinary action of legislative bodies. Article I, Section 5, states that each house may expel a member by a two-thirds vote. State constitutions often have similar provisions. However, because expulsion is regarded as an extreme measure, members are generally subjected to censure or deprivation of privileges if differences cannot be reconciled. Grounds for expulsion include moral turpitude, conduct unbecoming a member, and disloyalty.

   See also Censure.

EXTENSION SERVICE, established within the Department of Agriculture by the Smith-Lever Act (1914) as a joint federal-state-county organization to disseminate new technology in the fields of agricultural production, processing, and marketing, home economics, nutrition, rural development and youth (4-H) training. Closely allied with state land-grant colleges and agricultural research bureaus, the Extension Service reaches its target directly through the county agent, and by means of demonstrations, tours, publication, and the press. Despite his primary role in increasing agricultural productivity in the early twentieth century, the county agent, with his traditional personal contact, is being gradually pushed out as the USDA and state elements adapt to a highly technical and specialized agricultural industry.

EXTRADITION, the surrender by one state of a person accused or convicted of a crime to the state in which the offense was committed. The state having jurisdiction requests surrender through diplomatic channels.

   International law does not recognize extradition as a duty, except by treaty. Two states may sign an extradition treaty mutually agreeing to surrender any fugitive who has committed a specified crime in the other's territory. The offense must constitute a crime in both jurisdictions. Therefore, Americans who fled to Canada to avoid the draft during the Vietnam War could not be extradited in the absence of conscription in Canada.

   Extradition treaties do not generally apply in the case of political offenses. Political refugees who flee to a foreign country are usually granted asylum by that country.

   Some countries have immigration laws providing for the exclusion or deportation of aliens who are guilty of certain classes of offenses in other countries. These laws are intended for the protection of the country enacting the laws and are separate from laws and treaties relating to extradition.

   See also Asylum.

EXTRAORDINARY SESSION. *See* Joint Session.

EXTRATERRITORIALITY, term denoting the legal immunities accorded to sovereigns and diplomatic agents, their families and staff, and the premises they occupy. At one time, the term was used to apply to the practice of colonial powers, particularly in China during the late nineteenth century, who reserved the best sections of cities for exclusive European control.

FAIR LABOR STANDARDS ACT (1938), or **Wages and Hours Act,** set minimum wages and maximum working hours for employees engaged in interstate commerce. Introduced by Sen. Hugo Black on humanitarian grounds in 1937, the bill quickly passed the Senate but became stalled in the House. Northerners supported the bill as a counterweight to the artificially low wages of the South, which opposed the bill. After much political maneuvering, the bill was passed, and President Roosevelt signed it on June 25, 1938.

Some occupations were exempted in the final act, but it generally applied to workers engaged in interstate commerce or in producing goods for interstae commerce. Minimum wages were set at 40 cents an hour and the maximum work week at 40 hours, with time and one-half for overtime. Industries were given several years in which to meet the new standards. Although there were several weaknesses in the act, it provided a basis for reforms, such as increased minimum wages.

FAIRNESS DOCTRINE , a Federal Communications Commission (FCC) doctrine regulating broadcast media by requiring them to cover issues of public importance so as to reflect differing points of view. In practice, broadcasters could take editorial positions but were required to give the public an opportunity to respond. The FCC maintains a listing and a set of standards designating who may be covered by the Fairness Doctrine. The failure of a broadcaster to adhere to these guidelines could constitute grounds for nonrenewal of the station's license.

In 1987 the FCC abolished the 28-year-old Fairness Doctrine as an unconstitutional restriction of free speech. The commission felt that the rule made broadcasters avoid dealing with controversial issues. Many members of Congress threatened to reinstate the doctrine by amending the Communications Act of 1934.

See also Equal-Time Provision.

FAIR PACKAGING AND LABELING ACT OF 1966. *See* Truth in Packaging Laws.

FAIR TRADE ACT. *See* Miller-Tydings Act.

FANNIE MAE. *See* Federal National Mortgage Association (FNMA).

FARMER-LABOR PARTY, an alliance of agrarian and labor interests and former Theodore Roosevelt Progressives, formed in 1920. It called for government ownership of public utilities and national resources, relief for farmers, progressive labor legislation, and withdrawal of the United States from the Treaty of Versailles. P.P.

Christensen, the party's presidential candidate in 1920, made a poor showing, and the national organization soon disintegrated.

On the state level, however, the Farmer-Labor party became a major force in Minnesota politics. From 1922 through 1936 three United States Senators and seven Congressmen were elected on the Farmer-Labor ticket, and Floyd Olson was elected to three consecutive gubernatorial terms (1930-1934). Party strength began to wane with Harold Stassen's election as Republican governor in 1938. Its influence was further undermined by the wealth of progressive legislation enacted under Franklin Delano Roosevelt's "New Deal," and in 1944 the party merged with the Minnesota Democratic organization to form the Democratic-Farmer-Labor party.

See also Political Parties in the United States; Presidential Elections.

FASCISM is unique to the twentieth century. Nihilistic in character, it denies the reality of reason, truth, and objective political theory. Fascism pursues power for power's sake by appealing to the frustrations of men living in modern, mass, industrial societies. Fascism's greatest success was achieved in pre-World War II Italy and Germany. Free to use any ideas as merely tools of politics, fascist propagandists have extolled the state as the highest expression of reality and the only means by which individual lives could receive value. Propagandists stressed the supremacy of instinctive action, feelings of aggression, and glories of combat. Italian fascism depicted its aim as the restoration of the glory and greatness of imperial Rome. German national socialism, far more fascist than its Italian counterpart, proclaimed its aim as effecting the supremacy of the Aryan race, of which the German was the purest type, throughout the world. Inevitably, the arrogance, contempt, and irrational and aggressive spirit that characterized Italian and German fascism led to war.
—*Robert F. Smith*

See also Authoritarianism; Corporate State; National Socialism; Totalitarianism.

FAVORITE SON, the practice of state delegations at the national convention of nominating for the presidency their own political leaders, usually their governors. This device may be simply honorary, or it may be used to prevent any candidate from quickly obtaining a majority of the votes at the convention. The favorite son compels all of his state's delegates to vote for him, because he controls patronage in the state. If enough convention delegates are pledged to favorite sons, the leading candidate may not achieve a majority, thereby allowing each favorite son to play the role of power broker, throwing his support to one candidate or another. A favorite son who finally supports the eventual winner may hope to reap a reward of federal patronage from his future president.

FAA air traffic controller directs incoming planes.

At the Democratic convention in 1960, John Kennedy was the front runner. His opponents encouraged the governors of the larger states to become favorite son candidates, in order to prevent Senator Kennedy from obtaining a majority, but he was nominated on the first ballot.

FEATHERBEDDING, the practice of some unions to "make work" for their membership, generally in response to the increased mechanization of industry and the consequent reduction of jobs. In effect, featherbedding makes the employer pay for services that are not performed. An unfair labor practice according to the Taft-Hartley Act (1947), featherbedding is carried out by limiting the amount of work each union member performs so that more members can be employed or by insisting that workers whose jobs have been eliminated by machinery be retained. A classic example of featherbedding is the railroad union's insistence on the retention of firemen on diesel engines.

Some featherbedding has resulted in legislation. In one instance, the American Federation of Musicians required the use of stand-in musicians whenever non-live music was used. The Lea Act (Anti-Petrillo Act) of 1947 outlaws this featherbedding practice. However, in another instance, the Supreme Court in 1953 upheld the right of the union to demand that a local standby orchestra be employed when a traveling orchestra is hired for an event.

Essentially, featherbedding is a defensive tactic used by labor unions to maintain their membership and the status quo. Management considers featherbedding as an encroachment on its right to determine work assignments, crew sizes, and the like.

See also Unfair Labor Practice.

FEDERAL AGENCIES. *See* Independent Agencies and Regulatory Commissions.

FEDERAL AVIATION ADMINISTRATION (FAA). Set up as part of the Department of Transportation in 1967, the FAA assigns nearly half its staff to air-traffic control. FAA issues and enforces standards for all aircraft and for airline maintenance and repair stations. All pilots, key members of support crews and ground crews, and flight controllers must maintain FAA certification. FAA's 12 regional offices are also in charge of air transportation security, in particular the control of air hijacking, and of enforcing airplane noise controls. FAA's extensive research work is done mostly at the National Aviation Facilities Experimental Center in Atlantic City and at the DOT Transportation System Center in Cambridge, Mass.

FEDERAL BUDGET. *See* Budget and Impoundment Act of 1974.

FEDERAL BUREAU OF INVESTIGATION (FBI), the principal criminal investigative arm of the Department of Justice. The FBI is charged with the investigation of violations of all federal laws whose administration is not handled by other federal agencies. Its jurisdiction extends to activities such as espionage, sabotage, kidnapping across state lines, extortion, bank robbery, civil rights violations, fraud against the federal government, and assault upon or assassination of the President of the United States or a federal officer. Cooperative services of the FBI for other law enforcement agencies include fingerprint identification, laboratory services, and the National Crime Information Center.

FEDERAL COMMUNICATIONS COMMISSION (FCC). The 1934 successor to the 1927 Federal Radio Commission, the FCC regulates interstate and foreign communications via radio, television, telephone, telegraph, cable, and satellite. Specifically, the seven-member body, appointed by the president, controls all broadcasts and transmission licenses, enforces obscenity laws and strictures on political advertising, and, in cooperation with state utility commissions, oversees rates for "common carriers," that is, telephone, telegraph, and cable.

See also Communications Acts.

FEDERAL DEPOSIT INSURANCE CORPORATION (FDIC), a government corporation that insures deposits in member banks to a limit of $100,000. The FDIC was organized in 1933 to promote stability in the banking system by maintaining the confidence of depositors that their money is secure. Member banks of the Federal Reserve System are required to participate, and state banks have the option to join the program. The system is supported through annual assessments levied on privately-owned banks.

See also Federal Home Loan Bank Board (FHLBB).

FEDERAL ELECTION CAMPAIGN ACT. (1971). In order to lessen the national parties' and candidates' financial dependence on interest groups, Congress in 1971 passed campaign reform legislation and amended it in 1974, 1976, and 1979. The 1971 Act provided for a thorough disclosure of campaign contributions received after April 7, 1972, and a limitation on the amount of money that could be spent on media advertising. Enforcement was not very strict. It was felt that disclosure of the sources of a candidate's funds was an insufficient safeguard to reduce the influence of wealth on politics.

The 1974 amendments to the Act addressed the problems of excessive expenditures, improper fundraising practices, and public funding for presidential candidates. The legislation established a $1,000-per-person limit on contributions to any one candidate's primary, runoff, and general election campaigns, together with an overall limit of $25,000 on contributions by a single individual to all federal candidates in any one year. Organizations were limited to $5,000 per candidate per contest. However, there were no limits on the size of donating groups or on their number. This omission led

to the proliferation of political action committees (PACs) to fund campaigns. The Act also set candidate expenditure limits for the primary elections and limits in the general election for candidates who receive public funding. Candidates who accepted public funding in the primaries had to abide not only by the overall spending ceiling but also by individual state ceilings calculated according to the number of voters in the states. In order to be eligible for public funding during the primary season, candidates had to demonstrate their credibility by raising $100,000 in amounts of $5,000 or less from 20 or more states with contributions under $250. Minor party candidates got public money only if they received at least five percent of the popular vote in the previous election. The amount received was proportional to their voting strength in relation to the vote totals of the major party candidates. A new minor party could qualify for post-election public funding if it was on the ballot in at least 10 states, abided by the campaign finance law, and received at least five percent of the votes in the election.

The 1974 Act was challenged in the courts by an unusual alliance of those on the political right and left, including former senators James Buckley and Eugene McCarthy, wealthy contributor Stewart Mott, the New York Civil Liberties Union, and the American Conservative Union. The Supreme Court upheld most of the Act's provisions, but considered a limit on spending a violation of the First Amendment.

In the Federal Election Campaign Act amendments of 1976, Congress reestablished the Federal Election Commission. The Act was altered again in 1979 to allow state and local parties to do more and to reduce the reporting requirements.

See also Buckley v. Valeo; Political Action Committees.

FEDERAL EMERGENCY MANAGEMENT AGENCY (FEMA), federal agency with responsibility for coordinating all federal emergency preparedness activities. Working through a network of regional offices, FEMA is charged with planning relief operations and recovery assistance for natural, technological, or even attack-related destruction. FEMA was established in 1979 as an independent agency within the executive branch.

FEDERAL EMERGENCY RELIEF ACT (FERA) (1933). *See* New Deal Legislation: *Glossary.*

FEDERAL FARM MORTGAGE CORPORATION. *See* New Deal Legislation: *Glossary.*

FEDERAL HIGHWAY ADMINISTRATION (FHWA), a component of the Department of Transporation. The FHWA seeks to coordinate highways with other modes of transportation, to achieve the most effective balance of transportation systems, and to facilitate a cohesive federal transportation policy.

The FHWA is concerned with the total operation of the highway system, including highway safety. FHWA, in administering its highway transportation programs, gives full consideration to the impacts of highway development and uses transportation needs, engineering, safety, and costs. Since 1956, the FHWA's major activity has been the construction of a national system of interstate and defense highways. This system includes over 42,500 miles of highway, linking U.S. cities with populations over 50,000.

FEDERAL HOME LOAN BANK BOARD (FHLBB), an independent federal agency, originally established in 1932. The Bank Board was made an independent agency in the executive branch under the Housing Amendments of 1955. The Bank Board operated the FSLIC, which insured the savings of over 84 million Americans. The FHLBB was dismantled under the provisions of the savings and loan bailout. The FSLIC was replaced by the Savings Association Insurance Fund (SAIF). It will be run by the FDIC but separately maintained. Accounts will be insured to $100,000.

FEDERAL HOUSING ADMINISTRATION (FHA) insures under terms of the National Housing Act (1934) mortgages and housing loans made by private lending institutions. The FHA administers low-rent public housing (under the Housing Act [1937]) and a college housing program and has numerous housing programs for the elderly and handicapped. From 1934 FHA was under various authorities until transferred to Housing and Urban Development upon its creation in 1965.

FEDERAL INSURANCE ADMINISTRATION (FIA), a Department of Housing and Urban Development agency, directs a federal reinsurance program to protect against excessive losses from riots, crime, and natural disasters.

FEDERALISM, a method of governance whereby power is divided or shared between a central (national) government and its subdivisions (state and local governments).

State governments are historically rooted in the charters granted by the English crown in the colonial period. In 1776 the several colonial governments joined together as an independent nation. From 1781 until 1789 the nation was governed by a weak central government under the Articles of Confederation. The Constitution, however, established a stronger central (national) government with specific authority over the states and people, thus creating federalism.

Both the national (usually called federal) and the state governments have legislative, executive, and judicial powers, with the people subject to both authorities. The explicit powers of the states are derived from state constitutions, which must not contradict the United States Constitution. Local governments derive their powers from state constitutions. Some functions and powers (for example, to declare war, regulate interstate and foreign commerce, and coin money) are granted by the Constitution solely to the national government (exclusive jurisdiction). Several functions (such as taxation and public health rules) are shared by national and state governments (concurrent jurisdiction).

The relationship between national and state governments has undergone constant change as the national government has legislatively and judicially expanded its role. Yet, the nature of federalism remains; the electoral college, the division of the nation into states that in turn elect their own representatives to Congress, and the existence of separate judicial and law enforcement systems are fixed factors in maintaining the political identity of the states in the federal system. With the dramatic increase in grants-in-aid in the 1950s and 1960s, federalism was called Cooperative Federalism, and when such grants established relationships directly with private institutions and individuals it was labeled Creative Federalism. The actions of the Nixon and Reagan administrations to return areas of responsibility to the states are called New Federalism.   —Erwin L. Levine

See also Grants-in-Aid; National Supremacy; Revenue Sharing; States' Rights.

FEDERALIST, THE, also known as the *Federalist Papers,* written by Alexander Hamilton, John Jay, and James Madison in 1787. The papers were a series of essays addressed to the people of New York State. Appearing in a number of New York newspapers, *The Federalist* is one of the most brilliant and influential documents in American political theory. The papers' primary purpose was to inspire the New York State legislature to ratify the new federal constitution. Maintaining that the Articles of Confederation, which then held the thirteen states together in a very loose bond, were impractical, *The Federalist* argued for a strong and stable national government that would admittedly circumscribe the powers of the separate state governments.

FEDERALISTS, the designation first applied to supporters of the Constitution before its ratification. After the formation of the new government, the Federalist party quickly took shape under the leadership of Alexander Hamilton, Secretary of the Treasury, whose views clashed sharply with those of Secretary of State Thomas Jefferson.

Support. Federalist supporters were drawn mainly from the property-owning and merchant classes of New England and the mid-Atlantic states. Deeply conservative, they saw themselves as the only group qualified to govern, while the common man was fit only to follow. They favored a powerful central government, the expansion of manufacturing and trade, and a fiscal policy based on the establishment of a national bank and federal assumption of state debts. In foreign policy, they were pro-British and anti-French.

Decline. The Federalist-controlled Congress of 1798 passed the Alien and Sedition Acts, intended to quell criticism and cripple Jefferson's political organization. Instead, the measure contributed to the party's downfall and Jefferson was elected to the presidency in 1800. The Federalists also failed to recognize the growing democratic spirit of the country, and remained vehemently opposed to the extension of voting power to the masses. Their leaders, Hamilton and Adams, were at ideological odds, and could not match Jefferson's personal popularity. After its loss of national power, however, the Federalist party remained influential in New England until the mid-1820s.

Accomplishments. The contributions of the Federalist party to the American political system were definite and lasting. Its outstanding accomplishments were the organization of a central government with its separation of powers, the maintenance of ties with Britain, its support or a doctrine of neutrality, and the establishment of sound economic institutions.

See also Political Parties in the United States; Presidential Elections.

FEDERAL JUDICIAL CENTER, the investigative agency empowered by Congress to conduct policy research, systems development, and continuing education for judges and support personnel of the judicial branch. The center was created in 1967 by an Act of Congress after much public debate about crowded and poorly managed court calendars. Its goal is to improve judicial administration in the U.S. court system.

The center's policies and activities are determined by its board. The Chief Justice of the Supreme Court, a permanent member of the board, serves as its chair. The Director of the Administrative Office of the U.S. Courts is also a permanent member of the Board. Two judges from the U.S. Court of Appeals, three judges from the U.S. District Court, and one bankruptcy judge constitute the remainder of the Board. They are elected for four-year terms by the Judicial Conference of the United States.

FEDERAL MEDIATION AND CONCILIATION SERVICE (FMCS), an independent agency that assists in labor-management disputes to avoid disruptions in industries affecting interstate commerce. The service, created by the Taft-Hartley Act (1947), has no enforcement authority.

See also Labor Disputes, Mediation of.

FEDERAL NATIONAL MORTGAGE ASSOCIA-TION (FNMA), also known as "Fannie Mae," a government-sponsored corporation with privately held stock, which is regulated by the Department of Hous-

ing and Urban Development. The FNMA provides the housing industry with a secondary market in residential loans. It buys and sells loans in order to maintain the cash reserves necessary for the mortgage market. Created by Congress in 1938, the FNMA was split by the Housing and Urban Development Act of 1968, with the Government National Mortgage Association set up to administer only government-owned programs.

See also Government National Mortgage Association.

FEDERAL RAILROAD ADMINSITRATION (FRA), a division of the Department of Transportation. Its purpose is to develop and enforce rail safety regulations, and to consolidate government support of rail transportation activities.

The FRA conducts research to support improved railroad safety and the improvement of national rail transportation policy. The FRA provides for the rehabilitation of Northeast Corridor rail passenger service and operates the Alaska Railroad.

FEDERAL REGISTER, A United States government publication that prints presidential proclamations, reorganization plans, and executive orders. Notices of proposed rules and regulations and administrative orders of public agencies are published in the Federal Register as are the final rules and regulations of those agencies. The Federal Register Act of 1935 requires the publication of presidential proclamations, and the Administrative Procedure Act of 1946 requires compliance by public agencies.

Because of the constant increase in subject matter, the Federal Register is an extremely important and widely read publication. Before its existence citizens and business interests had no way of knowing what new rules applied to them. The publication gives all interested parties the opportunity to be heard before the enforcement of any rules and regulations. The Federal Register is published five times every week, and the documents are codified in the Code of Federal Regulations.

FEDERAL RESERVE SYSTEM, responsible for monetary policy within an economy with relatively full employment, stable prices, and economic growth. The services that the system renders and the means at its disposal are still evolving as domestic monetary policy and the role of central banking in today's world change.

Organization. The Federal Reserve Act (1913) established 12 regional banks whose policies were to be coordinated by a presidentially appointed Board of Governors. The regional grouping was necessary to allay fears that if one central bank were established, it might be unduly influenced by the money market and financial interests of its location.

In addition to the Board of Governors, the federal reserve system is comprised of the Open Market Committee, advisory committees, and member banks. Less than half the banks in the United States are members of the system, but these members control the largest share of banking assets. All national banks must belong, and state-chartered banks may join. Nonmember banks can avail themselves of some of the services provided by the federal reserve banks.

Functions. Federal reserve banks are banker's banks, and the services provided by them to the banking community are as follows: furnishing currency for circulation, supervising member banks, acting as fiscal agent for the government (U.S. Treasury), clearing and collecting checks, and holding member-bank reserves. Each federal reserve bank has a nine-member board of directors representing banking, business, and the public. The first two classes are elected by member banks; the latter class is appointed by the Board of Governors, and from this class the chairman and vice chairman are appointed; the chairman *ex officio* is the bank's federal reserve agent, the custodian of the federal reserve notes issued to the bank or the collateral behind them when they go into circulation. Currency is issued to banks upon request, and their reserve accounts are reduced. The reserve bank gets the currency from the agent by putting up collateral made up of gold certificates, short-term commercial paper, and government securities at least equal to the value of currency issued. Banking in the United States is based on a fractional reserve of demand deposits, which gives the federal reserve system great leverage in carrying out monetary policy. Changes in reserve requirements, discount rate changes in borrowing from a federal reserve bank and open-market operations are quantitative controls. The major qualitative control is that over margin requirements on stock purchases.

The Open Market Committee. Lending banks can lend no more than their excess reserve because of fear of adverse clearing. If the Open Market Committee wished banks to lend more, increasing the demand deposit component of the money supply, the committee's manager would buy securities in the open market,

a group of dealers in government securities in the financial district of New York City, who deposit receipts in the bank system. The committee meets at least once a month in Washington, D.C., and determines policy on the basis of carefully considered analysis.

—John R. Matthews

FEDERAL SAVINGS AND LOAN INSURANCE CORPORATION. *See* Federal Home Loan Bank Board (FHLBB).

FEDERAL SUPPLY SERVICE. *See* General Services Administration (GSA).

FEDERAL TRADE COMMISSION (FTC). A powerful, five-member independent, bipartisan commission established in 1915, the FTC exercises extensive quasi-judicial and quasi-legislative functions in enforcing most of the nation's laws related to industrial practices, pricing, food and drug purity, labeling and packaging, and fair credit. The FTC's main objective is to maintain the free enterprise system by preventing unfettered monopoly or corruption by unfair and deceptive trade practices. Much of its work is in guiding industry to voluntary compliance, but the FTC can institute legal cease-and-desist proceedings and impose penalties subject to court appeal. The members, including the chairman, are appointed by the president with senatorial consent.

FEDERAL TRADE COMMISSION (FTC) v. COLGATE-PALMOLIVE CO., 360 U.S. 374 (1965), concerns deceptive practices in television commercials. The FTC ordered Colgate-Palmolive to stop showing its Rapid Shave commercial in which shaving cream was applied to what appeared to be sandpaper and was then removed with a razor. In fact, the "sandpaper" was a plexiglass mock-up to which sand had been applied. The Court, in an opinion delivered by Chief Justice Warren, upheld the FTC order. The Court stated that

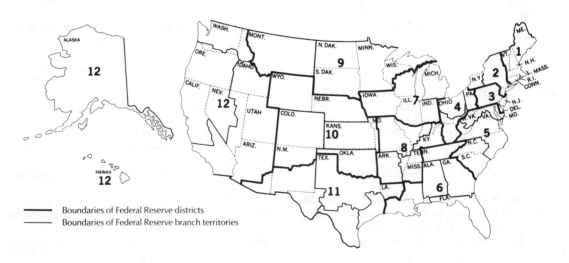

— Boundaries of Federal Reserve districts
— Boundaries of Federal Reserve branch territories

because Congress has given the commission the primary responsibility for eliminating unfair methods of competition and unfair or deceptive acts or practices in commerce, the courts should not "lightly modify" the discretion exercised by the FTC.

See also Corn Products Refining Co. v. Federal Trade Commission.

FEDERAL WATER POLLUTION CONTROL ACT, act first passed in 1955 to establish standards for treatment of municipal waste water before it could be discharged into public waterways; subsequently amended and broadened in 1965, 1967, 1969 and 1972. Revisions to the Act have significantly extended the impact of the original Act, but major goals set have not been met, including the stipulation that all discharges of pollutants into public waterways were to cease by 1985. Administered by the Environmental Protection Agency (EPA), the program has come under increasingly bitter attacks from critics, who charge lack of progress and noncompliance with basic goals. Supporters point to major achievements such as enforcement of stricter regulations for water quality. Environmental groups such as the Sierra Club have successfully used regulations established by the EPA to obtain court orders and injunctions to block commercial projects that would have resulted in damage to the environment.

— Mary L. Carns

FEDORENKO v. U.S., 449 U.S. 490 (1981), ruling by the Supreme Court that citizenship of a former concentration camp guard could be revoked because he concealed his wartime activities in his visa application. Fedorenko was born in the Russian Ukraine but served as a German concentration camp guard at Treblinka during World War II. He entered the United States in 1949 under provisions of legislation (Displaced Persons Act) that enabled European refugees to emigrate without regard to quotas, provided they had not "assisted the enemy in persecuting civilians." Fedorenko lied about his wartime activities when applying for a visa and again in 1970 when he became a naturalized citizen. In 1977 the government moved to revoke Fedorenko's citizenship because it was illegally acquired. Petitioner claimed he had been forced to serve as a guard and denied any personal knowledge of camp atrocities but did admit that he lied on his entry and citizenship applications.

The Supreme Court ruled that Fedorenko was ineligible for entry regardless of whether his service was voluntary or involuntary. Since citizenship was illegally acquired, it must be revoked. The Court rejected the idea that it had discretion to excuse Fedorenko's conduct because of his exemplary record since arriving in the United States. The Court specified that Congress had passed the legislation setting terms and conditions of entry and that, therefore, the Court must enforce the legislative will.

See also Citizenship Cases.

FEINER v. NEW YORK, 340 U.S. 315 (1951), concerns a charge of disorderly conduct stemming from a street-corner speech. Feiner, a Syracuse University student, was convicted of disorderly conduct while giving a speech urging blacks to rise up in arms and fight for equal rights. Two police officers, unable to handle the crowd, finally stepped in and asked Feiner to stop speaking. He refused and was arrested to prevent a fight. Feiner maintained that his conviction violated his right of free speech under the Fourteenth Amendment. In the opinion of the Court, the police used the means at their disposal in the exercise of their power and duty to preserve peace and order. In view of the existing situation, the imminence of greater disorder, and Feiner's deliberate defiance of the police officers, the Court felt that it should not reverse his conviction in the name of free speech.

See also Free Speech.

FERRARO, GERALDINE (1935-   ), politician and first woman to run for vice president. Ferraro graduated from Fordham Law School in New York City and then entered private practice. She moved to the public sector and served for a number of years with the New York district attorney's office before her election to Congress in 1978. Ferraro was active as a member of the House Democratic Caucus but came to national attention only when she was selected by Democratic presidential candidate Walter Mondale as his running mate in 1984. Ferraro campaigned vigorously but allegations of family and previous political financial irregularities hampered her efforts and did not prevent a Reagan landslide.

FILIBUSTER, in the Senate, a means of halting action on a particular bill by long speeches. The filibuster, which grew out of Senate rules that permit extended debate, is sometimes referred to as "nonstop speech." It is frequently an attempt to "talk a bill to death," or to force amendments that weaken or reduce the impact of legislation. Filibusters have in general been a tactic of Southern senators to frustrate passage of civil rights bills, but moderate and liberal senators made increasing use of the filibuster in the 1970s and 1980s. On occasion, the filibuster has been used to affect passage of non-related legislation, as occurred when the confirmation hearings of Attorney General-designate Edwin Meese were delayed by a group of farm bloc senators in 1985, in an attempt to gain support for a farm credit bill.

The filibuster was first used in the Senate in 1790; unlimited debate was also permitted in the House of Representatives until 1811. The longest recorded filibuster by a single senator, lasting more than twenty-four hours, was undertaken by South Carolina Sen. Strom Thurmond in 1957 against civil rights legislation. Again, in 1964 filibustering tactics were used by a number of senators against another civil rights bill. That debate, the longest in the Senate's history, lasted eighty-two days. Northern liberal senators participated in that filibuster in an attempt to preclude amendments that would limit the effectiveness of the legislation. Although the Senate has an effective remedy against filibustering in its rules of cloture to cut off debate, the senators rarely invoke it in order to preserve that body as a place for the unencumbered interchange of ideas.

An unrelated definition of filibuster derives from the Spanish *filibustero,* meaning a freebooter, and is applied especially to Americans who fomented revolutions in Latin America in the nineteenth century.

See also Cloture.

FILLMORE, MILLARD (1800-1874), 13th President of the United States (1850-1853), born in Locke, N.Y. A Whig, he served in the House of Representatives (1832-1843) and became vice president under President Zachary Taylor. Upon Taylor's death in 1850, Fillmore assumed the presidency and inherited the dispute over slavery. He reshaped the cabinet and supported the entire package of compromise measures that were ultimately enacted as the Compromise of 1850. He failed to secure the nomination in 1852 and ran unsuccessfully on the Know-Nothing, or American, party ticket in 1856.

See also Presidential Elections.

FISCAL POLICY. *See* Economic Stabilization Policies.

FISH AND WILDLIFE SERVICE, U.S., an agency in the Department of the Interior responsible for overseeing inland sport fishing, fishery research, wild birds, and mammals in the United States and their maintenance, use and understanding by the public.

FLAMMABLE FABRICS ACT OF 1953. *See* Business Regulation in the United States.

FLAST v. COHEN, 392 U.S. 83 (1968), concerns the use of federal funds for the purchase of textbooks and other instructional materials for use in parochial schools. The appellants alleged that this expenditure, under Titles I and II of the Elementary and Secondary Education Acts of 1965, violated the establishment and free exercise clauses of the First Amendment. The appellants rested their complaint solely on their status as federal taxpayers, and a three-judge district court dismissed their claim on the ground that they lacked standing to sue, as in the *Frothingham v. Mellon* decision. The Supreme Court reversed this ruling, stating that federal taxpayers had standing to sue to prevent such expenditures where the ground for their complaint was two-fold. Firstly, there must be a logical link between their taxpayer status and the legislation attacked, which was the case here. Secondly, there must be a nexus between the taxpayer status and the precise nature of the alleged constitutional infringement, not merely a contention that the legislation is generally beyond the powers delegated to Congress. The Court made a distinction between this

case and *Frothingham,* saying that the first ground for complaint was lacking in *Frothingham,* because the challenged statute was essentially regulatory and only incidentally involved the expenditure of tax funds.

See also Board of Education v. Allen; Frothingham v. Mellon.

FLEXIBLE RESPONSE, defense strategy initiated during the Kennedy administration to provide alternative methods for responding to Soviet threats without precipitating a general nuclear conflict. The policy was described by Secretary of Defense McNamara as giving the United States and its allies choices, and thus flexibility, in developing plans to counter Soviet aggression. The United States continues to subscribe to the general idea despite European critics who see the policy as allowing Europe to be sacrificed to a Soviet attack.

FLOOR LEADER. *See* Majority Leader.

FOLEY, THOMAS (1929-   ), Speaker of the House of Representatives (1989-   ). Foley was a prominent lawyer and assistant attorney general in his native state of Washington before his election to the 89th Congress in 1964. Foley moved up through the administrative ranks as Democratic whip and majority leader. He became the 49th Speaker of the House in June 1989, when Speaker James Wright resigned amid allegations that he violated House ethics rules.

FOOD ADDITIVES AMENDMENT OF 1958. *See* Business Regulation in the United States.

FOOD AND AGRICULTURE ORGANIZATION OF THE UNITED NATIONS (FAO), headquartered in Rome, established October 16, 1945, at the Quebec Conference. The FAO's members have undertaken to raise levels of nutrition and standards of living, improve production and distribution of food and agricultural products, contribute toward an expanding world economy and ensure freedom from hunger for all. To achieve its aims the FAO conducts research on nutrition and agriculture and advises on conservation of natural resources, improved methods of agricultural production and distribution, and the adoption of policies on agricultural commodity arrangements.

FAO keeps the world food and agricultural situation under constant review, issuing statistics on all major crop and livestock products, land use, agricultural populations, and farm requisites. The organization conducts a fertilizer program, assists in distributing high-yield strains of wheat, rice, and other staples, and cooperates in national programs to control insect pects. FAO sponsors projects on animal breeding, livestock management and animal disease control. FAO provides fisheries experts to developing countries and advises governments on forest management and wildlife conservation.

The FAO-U.N. World Food Program provides money, food, and services to governments to assist development projects and to meet local emergencies. FAO's membership totals more than 150 countries.

FOOD AND DRUG ADMINISTRATION (FDA), a law-enforcement agency established in 1907 within the Public Health Service of the former Department of Health, Education, and Welfare. The major responsibilities of FDA are directed toward protecting public health by ensuring that foods are safe and pure; drugs are safe and effective; cosmetics are harmless; and products are honestly and informatively labeled and packaged. These responsibilities are carried out by six bureaus of the FDA: the Bureau of Foods, the Bureau of Drugs, the Bureau of Veterinary Medicine, the Bureau of Radiological Health, the Bureau of Biologics, and the Bureau of Medical Devices.

See also Business Regulation in the United States.

FOOD, DRUG AND COSMETIC ACT OF 1938. *See* Business Regulation in the United States.

Gerald Ford, 38th President of the United States, who assumed office after the resignation of President Nixon.

FORD, GERALD RUDOLPH (1913-   ), Republican legislator and 38th President of the United States (1974-1977). Born in Omaha, Nebraska, he was originally named Leslie Lynch King, Jr. He took his stepfather's name when his mother remarried. Graduated from Yale University Law School, he served in the Navy in World War II and began his political career in 1949, when he was elected to the U.S. House of Representatives. He served as Republican minority leader (1965-1973), and was popular and respected for his staunch support of the party on all issues.

With the resignation of Vice President Spiro Agnew in 1973, President Nixon nominated Ford to take Agnew's place. Ford was the first vice president to enter office under the terms specified in the Twenty-fifth Amendment. As vice president, Ford strongly supported Nixon and stated his confidence that Nixon had no part in the Watergate scandal.

President. Upon Nixon's resignation in 1974, Ford became President. In an effort to maintain party stability, Ford retained most of Nixon's cabinet and advisors, and pledged to continue Nixon's foreign policy of easing tensions with the Soviet Union and China. Only one month into his term, Ford granted Nixon a general pardon, a move for which he was sharply criticized. In domestic affairs, Ford proposed limited government spending (except for defense), tax cuts, and heavy taxation of imported oil.

Much of Ford's effort was unsuccessful because he was strongly opposed in the Democratic Congress. Republican strength faltered in the wake of Watergate, and Ford lost the 1976 presidential election to Jimmy Carter. There was a movement within the party supporting Ford for the 1980 presidential nomination, but he declined and offered his support to Ronald Reagan.

In 1980 he lectured and campaigned for Republican candidates but, after the election of President Reagan, Ford was not a factor in national politics.

FOREIGN AGENTS REGISTRATION ACT (1938). The law requires full public disclosure via registration with the Attorney General of all propaganda activities and other activities on behalf of foreign governments or foreign principals so that the public may recognize and judge those activities. The law prohibits distribution through the mails of foreign propaganda not duly labeled and registered. Attorneys, diplomatic corps, guests of state, and individuals engaged in trade, industrial, financial, humanitarian, religious, academic, and cultural activities are exempt. "Agents" include public relations counsels, publicity agents, servants, political consultants, and information service employees. The fine for concealing the truth is now five years, or $10,000, and/or deportation.

See also Alien Registration Act.

FOREIGN AID, economic grants and military aid given to countries in need. The United States' foray into foreign aid began at the end of World War II, with such programs as the Marshall Plan; grants were made to countries that were resisting takeover, particularly from Communist countries. Foreign aid was one of the main tools of President Truman's containment policy. During the 1950s the focus of foreign aid was shifted to the underdeveloped nations and countries near the U.S.S.R. and Communist China, in lieu of military involvement, in order to produce healthy economies and in hope of concessions (allegiance, military bases, and so on). Aid to southeastern Asian countries was increased in the 1960s with the intensification of the Vietnam War. Foreign aid grants were channeled to Latin America during the 1960s as part of the Alliance for Progress program.

By the early 1970s foreign aid came into disfavor. In the late 1980s foreign aid accounted for only two percent of the nation's budget. Any expansion of aid to newly democratic East Bloc nations would require additional appropriations or a reduction in funds "earmarked" for other countries.

See also Alliance for Progress; Marshall Plan.

FOREIGN ASSISTANCE ACT OF 1948. *See* Marshall Plan.

FOREIGN POLICY ASSOCIATION, a private, non-partisan educational organization whose objective is to stimulate interest in domestic matters, develop understanding of United States foreign policy issues, and increase citizen participation in world affairs. The association attempts to educate public opinion through the distribution of pamphlets, reports, and suggested study topics for schools, as well as regularly scheduled meetings and annual nationwide "Great Decisions" discussion forums. Headquarters are in New York.

FOREIGN SERVICE, a branch of the State Department that represents the United States in foreign countries. The Foreign Service is not a part of the federal government's civil service system but a separate organization whose employees, foreign service officers, are selectively recruited and rigorously trained to represent the country effectively abroad. Stationed throughout the world at embassies, missions, and consulates, foreign service officers report on foreign developments, represent the country and its foreign policies, negotiate agreements, and administer such routine affairs as the granting of visas to foreigners. Foreign service officers are also stationed at the Department of State in Washington, D.C., where they evaluate information being forwarded from abroad and make recommendations on foreign policy matters for the consideration of the president and the secretary of state.

Diplomatic representatives in the Foreign Service may hold different types of posts. The *ambassador,* who is the diplomatic agent of the highest rank, heads the embassy of one country in another. The *attaché,* who generally has diplomatic rank, deals with press and with cultural, administrative, or financial matters. The *chargé d'affaires* heads the diplomatic mission when the ambassador or minister temporarily leaves his post. The *consul* is the official agent in a consular district. He looks after commercial interests and also performs administrative functions, including the issuance of passports and visas.

FOREST SERVICE, a division of the Department of Agriculture responsible for managing the more than 150 national forests and 19 national grasslands areas, protecting them from disease, insect pests, and wildfire. The service maintains these areas as refuges for wildlife and helps the forestry industry develop in a way that will prolong the yield of forest resources. The Forest Service was created in 1905 when management of the federal forest reserves (established 1891) was transferred from the Department of the Interior to the Department of Agriculture. Under the Wilderness Act (1964) about 14.25 million acres of the national forest lands have been set aside to comprise the National Wilderness Preservation System and the Primitive Areas System. Administered by the Forest Service, these rugged areas are open to the public for backpacking, canoeing, hunting and fishing in season, and study.

FORRESTAL, JAMES VINCENT. *See* Defense, United States Department of.

FOUR-PARTY POLITICS or **Burns' Thesis.** In *The deadlock of Democracy,* James MacGregor Burns describes the system of national politics as a "four-party pattern" with Democratic and Republican parties "divided into congressional and presidential structures." A congressman in a safe district identifies with the congressional party; in marginal and competitive districts he identifies with the presidential party.

See also Two-Party System.

FRANKING PRIVILEGE, the right by law of members of Congress to use the mails for free on official business by putting their mark or signature on mail. The privilege is extended also to territorial commissioners and delegates to Congress. After a member's term of office expires, his franking privilege is extended until the next June 30 so that he can complete his official business. By special acts of Congress, the franking privilege has been granted to former presidents and to the widows of former presidents.

FRANKLIN, BENJAMIN (1706-1790), printer, philosopher, scientist, inventor, diplomat, staunch supporter of the new republic, and popular symbol of the American bourgeois revolution. Born in Boston of a poor working family, Franklin educated himself by reading Locke, Newton, Addison, and Steele; by 1718 he was an apprentice printer and journalist. He ran away to Philadelphia in 1723 and then to England, where he found work as a master printer, returning to Philadelphia in 1726. By 1730 he had acquired his own printing business and published the *Pennsylvania Gazette*. He wrote *Richard Saunders' [Poor Richard's] Almanack* and published it from 1732 to 1757. A best seller at 10,000 copies per year, it expressed a witty homespun philosophy attuned to the standards of the emerging merchant class. Franklin organized the Junto, a group of Philadelphia burghers concerned with civic improvements, and held various posts in colonial administration. He retired from business at forty-two and lived for twenty years on the income from his publishing house. During this period he experimented with electricity, invented the lightning rod, the Franklin stove, and other practical devices. His experiments gained him international recognition as a scientist by election to the British Royal Academy and the French Academy of Science.

Patriot. A member of the Pennsylvania Assembly from 1751 to 1764, he was its agent in England from 1757 to 1762 and again from 1764 to 1775, when he became the leading spokesman from America in London. He attended Parliament, opposed arbitrary taxation, and joined with William Pitt in urging conciliation. By 1775 Franklin was convinced that British mismanagement of the colonies left them no choice but to revolt. Returning to America, he went to the Second Continental Congress, helped draft the Declaration of Independence, and signed it.

Dispatched as envoy of the new government to France in 1776, proclaiming "our cause is the cause of all mankind," he began the successful diplomatic mission that raised foreign support for the revolution. This contribution to the war is rated in importance next to Washington's. Franklin's uncouth garb and mercantile manners typified the revolutionary bourgeois and titilated Europe's effete aristocracy. He signed the first United States treaty with France in 1778 and the peace accord with England in 1783. Two years later he came home, a national hero, was elected president of Pennsylvania's executive council for three years, and worked on his unfinished *Autobiography*. He attended the Constitutional Convention in 1787, where, despite differences with the provisions, he urged ratification. One of his last acts was to petition Congress against slavery. He died in Philadelphia.

FREE CITY, a term used to describe cities that were politically independent from both a pope and an emperor. The first free cities were in Italy in the Middle Ages and included such republics as Milan, Florence, and Venice. All free cities conducted their own domestic governmental duties as well as carrying out trade and foreign relations, which included making treaties and waging wars. Free cities often joined together and formed alliances, such as the Hanseatic League of North German cities and the Rhenish League of South German cities. These alliances were the forerunners of the unifications of Italy and Germany. In the twentieth century the term has been used to describe cities over which there was international dispute; Trieste, Danzig (now Gdansk), and Tangier were the most important examples.

Trieste was contested by Italy and Yugoslavia after World War II and was occupied by Allied forces until 1954, when it was awarded to Italy. Danzig was internationalized after World War I and made a protectorate of the League of Nations, occupied by Germany in 1939, and returned to Poland after World War II. Tangier was given international status after World War II and is now part of Morocco.

FREEDMAN v. MARYLAND, 380 U.S. 51 (1965), illustrates the strict standards which any censorship plan involving prior restraint must meet in order to be valid. The appellant challenged the constitutionality of the Maryland motion picture censorship statute by exhibiting a film in Baltimore without first submitting the picture to the State Board of Censors, as required by the statute. The Court held, in reversing the conviction, that the statute unconstitutionally impaired the First Amendment right of freedom of expression. Prior restraint presents a danger of unduly suppressing protected expression, and the statute lacked sufficient safeguards for confining censorship within constitutional limits. The Court has carefully avoided saying that censorship per se is void, but has confined itself to the case under review.

See also Near v. Minnesota; Schechter Poultry Corporation v. United States.

FREEDOM OF ASSEMBLY, one of the fundamental rights guaranteed the individual under the First Amendment. Like other rights in the Constitution, the right of assembly is not absolute or unlimited. In interpreting the extent of these freedoms, the courts have ruled that although a meeting cannot be prohibited for advocating unpopular views, the right to assemble is subject to reasonable police regulation to ensure general safety and the maintenance of peace and order.

The right of assembly falls within the broader concept of freedom of voluntary association with other people, which is not specifically delineated in the Constitution. With the rise of the civil rights movement, the right of free association has been tested in a number of court cases. In *NAACP v. Alabama* (1958) the Supreme Court ruled that the state could not constitutionally force the NAACP to disclose the names of its members. This decision was the first in which the phrase "freedom of association" was used by the Court. However, legal interpretation has placed this right, too, within "reasonable" limits.

See also NAACP v. Alabama.

FREEDOM OF INFORMATION ACT (1967), a bill designed to give the public greater access to government records. The Act, signed by President Johnson, superceded the disclosure of Information Act (1966). Both of these measures amended Section 3 of the Administrative Procedure Act.

The original Section 3 allowed agencies great discretion in the requirement that most federal proceedings and policies be made public, but the new Act permitted exemptions only in nine specific areas. Among these areas were national defense, confidential financial information, law enforcement files and certain personnel files, in addition to information whose disclosure was prohibited by statute. Critics soon charged that the Act had had no visible effect because government agencies reclassified their policies under the permitted exemptions.

FREEDOM OF RELIGION, one of the basic liberties guaranteed by the First Amendment, which states that "Congress shall make no law respecting an establishment of religion, or prohibiting the free exercise thereof."

Designed to separate affairs of church and state, the issue of religious freedom has been the subject of a number of crucial Supreme Court decisions defining its nature and extent. In *Engel v. Vitale* (1962), the Court cited as unconstitutional a prayer adopted by the New York State Board of Regents for daily recitation in the schools, declaring that "It is no part of the business of government to compose official prayers for any group." In Abington School District v. Schempp (1963), the Court ruled that a Pennsylvania statute requiring Bible reading in the public schools violated the essence of the First Amendment, namely that the government "maintain strict neutrality, neither aiding nor opposing religion." The Supreme Court has upheld the right of individual states to give indirect aid to parochial schools in the form of bus transportation, textbooks, and reimbursement for certain services that are required by state statute.

See also Abington School District v. Schempp; Board of Education v. Allen; Edwards v. Aguillard; Engel v. Vitale; Everson v. Board of Education.

FREEDOM OF SPEECH AND PRESS, basic liberties guaranteed by the First Amendment, included among the fundamental rights protected by the Fourteenth Amendment from infringement by the states.

The scope of constitutional protection of free expression was dealt with in *Schenck v. United States* (1919), when the Supreme Court declared that the boundaries of free speech and press are not unlimited. Upholding the conviction of a socialist group for distributing antiwar material during World War I, the Court ruled that protection of free speech does not lend the right to speak words that create a "clear and present danger." Although the decision stressed the need for a free play of ideas within a free society, the "clear and present danger" criterion set down by Justice Oliver Wendell Holmes

was to be frequently applied by the Court in setting the lawful limits of free expression.

In *Roth v. United States* (1957) the Court considered the question of whether the distribution of obscene material was a basic freedom protected by the First Amendment. The Court ruled that obscenity, being devoid of "redeeming social importance," did not fall within the province of constitutionally protected speech or press.

A landmark decision regarding freedom of the press was made in *New York Times. v. Sullivan* (1964), when the Court, supporting the principle that "mass debate on public issues should be uninhibited, robust, and wide-open," stated that unless political advertisements are intentionally libelous, they are to be afforded the protections of the First Amendment. In 1978 the confidentiality of news files was lost when it was ruled that a news office could be searched by the police with a search warrant.

In deciding questions of free speech the Supreme Court is extremely reluctant to impose prior restraints. Any such request from the government would carry a "heavy presumption" against its constitutionality.

See also Clear and Present Danger.

FREE EXERCISE CLAUSE, part of the Establishment Clause in the First Amendment of the Constitution that states "Congress shall make no law respecting an establishment of religion, or prohibiting the free exercise thereof; . . ." It prevents compulsion by law of the acceptance of any creed or of the practice of any form of worship. Conversely, it safeguards the free exercise of the chosen form of religion. However, the free exercise provision does not embrace actions that are in violation of social duties or subversive in nature. This interpretation enabled the Supreme Court to uphold Congress's ban on polygamy in the territories and, on the other hand, to strike down Wisconsin's law that compelled Amish parents to send their children to formal high school.

See also Freedom of Religion.

FREE-SOIL PARTY, a political organization founded in 1848 to oppose the extension of slavery to new territories. The Wilmot Proviso had included such a proposal, but even after it was defeated in 1846 the issue continued to provoke factionalism. The Free-Soilers were not moral abolitionists, but were against slavery for economic reasons. They desired free land from the government for homesteading, while Southern interests needed more land to perpetuate the slave-based plantation system.

In 1848 the first Free-Soil convention was held in Buffalo, New York, and former president Martin Van Buren was chosen as the party's presidential candidate. The Free-Soil platform was an ambivalent document in which an initial antislavery plank was followed by the declaration that Congress had no right to interfere with slavery within a state's borders. In the election, Van Buren helped to split the Democratic vote and to elect Whig Zachary Taylor.

The Compromise of 1850 had the effect of weakening the Free-Soil cause, and after the 1852 election the party disbanded. Its members soon drifted into other political organizations, most notably the new Republican party.

See also Political Parties in the United States; Presidential Elections.

FREE TRADE, international trade unhindered by import and export duties and trade-restricting regulations. Free trade applies to a system in which trade between countries is governed by a tariff system that does not distinguish between goods produced domestically and goods produced abroad: all such goods may be either taxed equally or be exempt from payment of duties. Examples of free trade are trade among the states of the United States and trade among the member countries of the European Common Market.

FRIEND OF THE COURT. *See* Amicus Curiae.

FROTHINGHAM v. MELLON, 262 U.S. 447 (1923), challenged the constitutionality of the Maternity Act, which allotted federal monies to certain states for the purpose of reducing maternal and infant mortality and protecting health. Frothingham, a taxpayer, alleged that the effect of the appropriations would be to increase the burden of future taxation and thereby deprive her of her property without due process of law.

The Court held that any one taxpayer's interest in the monies of the Treasury—partly realized from taxation and partly from other sources—is comparatively minute, and that the effect on future taxation of any payment out of the funds is so remote, fluctuating, and uncertain that no basis is afforded for an appeal to the preventative powers of a court of equity. This decision effectively rendered most federal programs immune from constitutional attacks based on misuse of funds, although the Court will review state taxpayers' suits in which due process of law, under the Fourteenth Amendment, has allegedly been denied.

See also Flast v. Cohen.

FULBRIGHT, J(AMES) WILLIAM (1905-   ), former U.S. senator from Arkansas, and Chairman of the Senate Foreign Relations Committee (1959-1975), known for his defense of Senate prerogatives in foreign policy.

Born in Sumner, Mo., Fulbright grew up in Fayetteville, Arkansas, where he has made his home. He graduated from the University of Arkansas in 1925 and earned B.A. and M.A. degrees at Oxford Unviersity, where he was a Rhodes Scholar. After George Washington University awarded him his LL.B. degree in 1934, he worked for the Justice Department for a short time. Following two years of teaching law he became president of the University of Arkansas (1939). Elected as a Democrat to Congress from the Third District in 1942, he won a Senate seat in 1944 and was re-elected four more times.

Committee Chairman. Senator Fulbright assumed the coveted chairmanship of the Foreign Relations Committee in 1959. An ardent internationalist and moderate on segregation, Fulbright strongly supported development of international cooperation among nations. He originated the Fulbright Scholarship plan, which awarded scholarships and fellowships to American students and teachers for study and teaching overseas in order to further international understanding.

Fulbright supported Kennedy's and Johnson's policies in Southeast Asia, leading the Senate in support of the Tonkin Gulf Resolution in 1964. However, disenchanted with the rise of American military involvement and casualty rates, Fulbright chaired the Foreign Relations Committee in a long public hearing on American foreign policy in Southeast Asia in 1966. Recanting his former defense of American policy there, he continued as a formidable adversary to Johnson's and Nixon's alleged abuse of presidential power. In 1974 he was defeated in a primary bid for his sixth term.

—*Erwin L. Levine*

FULLER, MELVILLE W(eston) (1833-1910), 7th Chief Justice of the Supreme Court (1888-1910), born in Augusta, Me. Admitted to the bar in 1855, he became noted for astute handling of difficult cases. He was a delegate to the 1862 Illinois Constitutional Convention before becoming a member of the state legislature. The appointment of Fuller as chief justice in 1888 by President Cleveland caused an uproar because Fuller lacked national prominence. During Fuller's term the Supreme Court's popular esteem rose through his skill in assigning cases for opinions, promoting compromises, and discouraging bitter dissents. Fuller favored strict construction of the Constitution. As chief justice, he left no significant opinions of his own; his most important decision was rendered in *Pollock v. Farmers' Loan and Trust Company* (1895), which held the Income Tax Act of 1893 unconstitutional.

See also Supreme Court of the United States.

FULL FAITH AND CREDIT, constitutional obligation of one state to honor civil—as opposed to criminal—matters (such as statutes, charters, deeds, vital records, and judicial decisions) of other states. This obligation does not imply, however, automatic enforcement of one state's judicial decisions by another state. A court order must be sought in the second state to require enforcement of the first state's decision. The full faith and credit clause (Article 4, Section 1) of the Constitution makes viable a national commerce.

One area in which the full faith and credit clause has been interpreted ambiguously by the courts is divorce.

Although it is clear that one state must recognize another state's divorce decree, the Supreme Court has held that a state may decide if the parties to a divorce had *bona fide* domicile in the divorce-granting state. In one famous case, North Carolina held that it need not give full faith and credit to a Nevada divorce; the Supreme Court agreed, and therefore Nevada did not have the proper jurisdiction to grant the divorce.

—*Theodore B. Fleming, Jr.*

See also Privileges and Immunities.

FULLILOVE v. KLUTZNICK, 488 U.S. 448 (1980). *See* City of Richmond v. J.A. Croson Company.

FURMAN v. GEORGIA, 408 U.S. 238 (1972). In this case and related cases, the Supreme Court nullified all death penalty statutes in the country, even though a majority of the Court did not agree that capital punishment per se constituted cruel and unusual punishment. It held instead that the procedures used by the states at that time left so much discretion to the judge and/or the jury in deciding whether to impose the death penalty that the results were arbitrary and irrational (and possibly racially discriminatory), and for *that* reason constituted cruel and unusual punishment and deprived defendants of due process of law.

Four years later the court upheld a number of state death penalty statutes which controlled this discretion.

FUR PRODUCTS LABELING ACT OF 1951. *See* Business Regulation in the United States.

GABRIEL'S PLOT. *See* Slavery: *Slavery Institutionalized.*

GARFIELD, JAMES ABRAM (1831-1881), 20th president of the United States (1881), born in Cuyahoga County, Ohio. During the Civil War he raised a regiment and commanded it effectively, leaving the Union army with the rank of major general. Elected to Congress in 1862, he served in the House (1863-1880) and was elected to the Senate early in 1880, but he never served because of his dark horse nomination as Republican candidate for the presidency. Identified with Blaine's Half-Breeds, Garfield sought to ensure Republican unity by making Chester Arthur his running mate and by promising patronage to Roscoe Conkling's Stalwarts. During his brief term the appointment of James G. Blaine as secretary of state, Garfield's desire for executive independence in appointments, and his intention of prosecuting the Star Route frauds led to party schism. On July 2, 1881, Garfield was shot in Washington's railroad terminal by Charles Guiteau, a disappointed office seeker. Garfield, the last president born in a log cabin, survived the summer but died of infection on Sept. 19, 1881. He was succeeded by Vice President Arthur.

See also Presidential Elections.

GARRISON, WILLIAM LLOYD (1805-1879), prominent abolitionist editor and early organizer of the antislavery movement. He was born in Newburyport, Mass., of a poor family and apprenticed to a printer. By 1827 he was editing a temperance journal in Boston where he met Benjamin Lundy, an early Quaker antislavery organizer. Garrison began editing Lundy's *Genius of Universal Emancipation* in Baltimore. In 1830 he was jailed briefly for libel of a shipowner in the slave trade. Garrison returned in 1831 to Boston, where he began publishing the *Liberator,* calling for immediate abolition of slavery. The *Liberator* had a maximum circulation of 3,000, yet it roused the conscience of prominent intellectuals and agitated for emancipation so effectively that it was banned in the South.

In 1832, Garrison formed the New England Antislavery Society, for the first time uniting ex-slaves with Boston aristocrats in a common cause. In 1833 he founded the American Anti-slavery Society, insisting that women be encouraged to participate. Garrison attracted liberals like Lowell, Thoreau, Emerson, and Wendell Phillips to his cause, but conservative abolitionists were alienated by his fiery rhetoric. At its height in 1840, the society had 250,000 members, fifteen state chapters, and twenty-five journals.

Around 1850, with the unpopular enactment of fugitive slave laws, Garrison found wide support. He denounced the government, refused to vote, and publicly burned a copy of the Constitution in 1854. When the Civil War began, he supported Lincoln and recognized the need for armed struggle for emancipation. Following the war and adoption of Amendments Thirteen–Fifteen to the Constitution, he considered the battle over and turned his attention to women's suffrage, prohibition, and the cause of the Indians. He died in New York City.

GARRISON v. LOUISIANA, 379 U.S. 64 (1964), concerns the constitutionality of a Louisiana statute which makes it a crime to publish the truth with malicious intent. Garrison, the District Attorney of Orleans Parish, stated in a press conference that a large backlog of pending criminal cases was due to the inefficiency, laziness, and excessive absences of the judges. The Court, unanimously holding his conviction for criminal libel unconstitutional, stated that the same constitutional test must be applied in prosecutions for criminal libel as were recently announced for civil libel actions by public officials, that is, that criticism of an official for official conduct is protected by the First and Fourteenth Amendments unless there is proof of actual malice or gross negligence on the part of the speaker.

GENERAL ACCOUNTING OFFICE (GAO), an independent regulatory office created under Congress in 1921 to audit all government expenditures for executive purposes (except activities of the Federal Reserve Board and Banks, the Comptroller of the Currency, and certain intelligence operations). The Comptroller General of the United States and his deputy head the GAO, are appointed by the president with senatorial consent for 15-year terms, and can be removed only by a joint resolution of Congress for specified reasons or by impeachment.

The GAO prescribes forms, systems, and procedures for administrative appropriations and accounting; reports to appropriate congressional committees regarding government expenditures; reports violations of the fiscal law; supplies information to the Office of Management and Budget necessary for evaluating programs and preparing the budget; settles all claims against or by the United States; and analyzes expenditures for efficiency and propriety. All GAO rulings are binding on the executive branch, but may as a question of law be submitted to the Attorney General for an opinion. The GAO has become particularly important in watchdogging military funds, making many specific recommendations to Congress to improve efficiency and eliminate wastefulness.

GENERAL AGREEMENT ON TARIFFS AND TRADE (GATT), negotiated in Geneva by 17 nations to lower customs tariffs and to reduce other restrictions. GATT members, 90 contracting and 30 under special arrangements, meet at least once a year at their headquarters in Geneva. A recommendation by the 1947--1948 Havana Trade Conference that an international trade organization be established was not implemented, as it was doubtful that the United States would participate.

GATT calls for reciprocal rights and duties and sets rules for fair trading. It provides for equal treatment in the application of import and export taxes. Under GATT a country may protect domestic interests through customs tariffs, but not through import quotas. Quotas can, however, be imposed for such purposes as redressing balance of payments.

GATT talks that began in 1963 and ended in 1966 led to a further reduction of trade barriers. Agreements were reached providing concessions valued at $40 billion over a period of five years. These talks, known as the "Kennedy Round," were undertaken after the adoption of the United States Trade Expansion Act of 1962, which enabled the United States to participate in tariff reduction talks.

GENERAL SERVICES ADMINISTRATION (GSA), the chief agency responsible for attending to the physical needs of the federal agencies. The Federal Property and Administrative Services Act (1949), which created GSA, was the result of recommendations contained in the first Hoover Commission report and other studies aimed at effecting improvements and economies in government management practices. The act consolidated functions formerly assigned to various separate agencies. The original GSA organization included the Federal Supply Service, and the Public Buildings Service. Later in 1949 and in 1966 the Property Management and Disposal Service was formed. Each of these services is supervised by a commissioner and his staff.

The Public Buildings Service supervises the design and construction of most government buildings. GSA owns or maintains approximately 10,000 buildings and is responsible for thousands of leased locations used by federal agencies.

The Federal Supply Service procures and distributes to the government's civilian agencies some 40,000 items, which range from office furniture and paper to motor vehicles and civilian aircraft. The service determines specifications that must be met by products before they can be purchased by the government.

The National Archives and Records Service administers a system of federal record complexes that include the National Archives, fourteen federal records centers, and six presidential libraries, as well as designing and implementing efficient office management procedures for government agencies. Records from all federal agencies are maintained in the Records Centers.

The Federal Property Resources Service maintains a stockpile of critical raw goods used in the nation's major industries in order to guarantee availability during periods of national emergency. The service disposes of most of the government's surplus land, buildings, and equipment. During this process, the service has made surplus federal property available at no cost to local governments for park and recreation use.

Transportation and Public Utilities Service administers the federal transportation management, setting policies concerning the acquisition of transportation and public utilities for government use.

Automated Data and Telecommunications Service oversees the management and operation of automated data and telecommunications equipment services, which provide long-distance telephone services, as well as teletype and data transmissions for all government agencies.

Implied Powers. As the business arm of the federal government, GSA has responsibility for a network of federal information centers in federal buildings throughout the country and sponsors a Consumer Product Information Coordinating Center. As a major government contractor, both in the construction industry and through its procurement activities, GSA implements national policy by requiring contractors to prove their compliance with equal employment opportunity legislation.

—Rod Kreger

GENESSEE CHIEF v. FITZHUGH (1851) concerns the nation's power to regulate commerce over public navigable waterways. The vessel *Genessee Chief* was alleged to have run afoul of and sunk the schooner *Cuba* while engaging in commerce and navigation on the Great Lakes. The respondents maintained that the courts had no jurisdiction because both respondents and libelants were citizens of the same state and because the collision did not occur on the high seas or in tidewaters. Chief Justice Taney rejected both arguments, saying that admiralty jurisdiction extended to all navigable waters and that, admiralty jurisdiction being separate from the federal government's commerce power and exclusive in the federal courts, no diversity of citizenship is required.

GEOLOGICAL SURVEY, an agency created to conduct topographic and geologic mapping of the United States and physical and chemical research of the mineral and water resources of the nation. The survey enforces the gas, oil, and mining lease regulations. One of its best known publications is the *National Topographic Map Series.* Established March 3, 1879, the Geological Survey is in the Department of the Interior. In 1962, the survey was authorized to carry out research outside the United States.

GERRYMANDER, a legislative district shaped with excessive manipulation to produce a majority of votes for the controlling party in the state legislature doing the redistricting. The term is derived from wildly shaped districts created by the legislative redistricting of Gov. Elbridge Gerry of Massachusetts in 1812.

Congress has passed several laws to combat this practice. Most of these laws ruled that congressional districts should be of "contiguous territory" and should be "compact." These laws are no longer in effect, and actual redistricting is provided by state law. A Supreme Court ruling in 1964, in acting against malapportionment (districts with grossly unequal populations) and gerrymandering, stated that "as nearly as is practicable, one man's vote in a Congressional election is to be worth as much as another's."

See also Appointment, Legislative; Baker v. Carr; District, Congressional; Reynolds v. Sims; Wesberry v. Sanders.

GIBBONS v. OGDEN, 9 Wheat. 1 (1824). In the case of *Gibbons v. Ogden,* Chief Justice John Marshall availed himself of an opportunity to enhance and consolidate national power over commerce. The Constitution had specifically granted Congress the power to regulate commerce, but there was much more room for interpretation in this broad grant. Marshall interpreted "commerce" broadly and he further held the commerce power was complete in itself, with no limitations other than those specifically found in the Constitution.

As a result of this interpretation, the court found that a New York state law granting an exclusive right to operate steamboats in state waters was unconstitutional because it was in conflict with an act of Congress. The congressional power prevailed, not only because of the commerce clause, but also because Article VI of the Constitution makes the act of Congress the supreme law of the land. Thus the plaintiff, Ogden, who relied on the state grant of a monopoly, failed in his attempt to get an injunction against Gibbons to prevent him from using his steamboats in New York waters.

—Philip J. Hannon
See also Fletcher v. Peck; National Supremacy.

GIDEON v. WAINWRIGHT, 372 U.S. 335 (1963). In *Betts v. Brady* (1942), a sharply divided Supreme Court dealt with the problem of an indigent defendant's constitutional right to be represented by counsel in a state court criminal proceeding. The Court at that time made a distinction between federal proceedings, where indigents were entitled to counsel as a matter of right, and state proceedings, where in noncapital cases the right to counsel was more limited. Although the Court declined to incorporate the right, guaranteed by the Sixth Amendment in federal prosecutions, the judges continued to be troubled by the issue. In *Gideon v. Wainwright,* the Court once again faced the right-to-counsel problem. This time the Court overruled Betts and decided that Gideon, an indigent felony defendant, was entitled to have a counsel appointed to him at state expense. The Court now held that the right to counsel was fundamental to a fair trial. Thus the right became obligatory upon the states by virtue of the Fourteenth Amendment.

—Philip J. Hannon

GILLETTE v. UNITED STATES. *See* Conscientious Objection.

GINSBERG v. NEW YORK, 390 U.S. 629 (1968), concerns a violation of a New York statute which prohibits the sale of obscene materials to minors under the age of seventeen years. Ginsberg operated a lunch counter and sold, among other things, "girlie" magazines. He was convicted of selling two magazines, which contained graphic descriptions and narrative accounts of sexual activities, to a 16-year-old boy. The Court upheld the conviction because the statute did not invade the freedom of expression or other freedoms constitutionally guaranteed to minors and because the objective of the statute was clearly to safeguard minors from exposure to such material as potentially harmful to their development. Prior opinions establishing the right of the state to be especially solicitous of its minors and to safeguard them from "abuses" were noted.

GINSBURG v. UNITED STATES, 383 U.S. 463 (1966), is concerned with a federal statute which prohibits mailing of "hard-core" pornography. Ginsburg was convicted under that statute of advertising and mailing obscene matter. The Court, in a five to four decision, upheld the conviction. Although the matter was not "hard-core" in and of itself, the Court said nonobscene matter might become obscene if the advertising therefore pandered to prurient interests.

The dissenters said, in part, that the First Amendment forbids any governmental censorship over views as distinguished from conduct; that condemnation of the use of sex symbols to sell literature engrafts another exception onto First Amendment rights; and that the First Amendment protections mean that a man cannot be sent to prison merely for distributing publications which offend the esthetic sensibilities of a justice. This case is so devoid of any standards by which to measure conduct that it has no value as a precedent.

GIROUARD v. UNITED STATES, 328 U.S. 61 (1946), concerns the constitutional validity of denying the privilege of naturalization to those who, because of religious belief or other conscientious scruples, refuse to bear arms. Girouard, a Seventh Day Adventist, was willing to take the oath of allegiance to the United States, but was not willing to take up arms in defense of this country, although he said he would serve as a noncombatant. In the opinion of the Court, the oath of allegiance does not, by its terms, require that aliens promise to bear arms; nor has Congress, in passing the Naturalization Act, expressly or by implication made bearing arms a prerequisite to citizenship. In admitting Girouard to citizenship, the Court stated that to bar from naturalization those who object to military service on religious grounds would be to contradict the country's long-standing tradition of religious liberty.

GITLOW v. NEW YORK, 268 U.S. 652 (1925). Benjamin Gitlow, a member of the Left Wing Section of the Socialist party, was convicted of violating New York State's criminal anarchy statute by publishing and distributing a pamphlet urging the violent overthrow of the United States government. The Court said, "For present purposes we may and do assume that freedom of speech and of the press—which are protected by the First Amendment from abridgment by Congress—are among the fundamental personal rights and 'liberties' protected by the due process clause of the Fourteenth Amendment from impairment by the States." Up until this case, it was generally thought that the Fourteenth Amendment did not apply the protections of the Bill of Rights to the states.

Though the First Amendment afforded protection against state incursions, the Court said, the police power of the state could legitimately punish Gitlow in this instance. The Court was using a form of the "bad tendency" test, which allowed speech to be punishable if it tended to bring about evils which the state had a right to prevent.

In dissent, Justices Holmes and Brandeis preferred to apply the "clear and present danger" test *(Schenck v. U.S.),* and they would have found Gitlow's actions constitutionally protected. —*David Forte*

See also Schenck v. United States.

GLASNOST, a policy of "openness" through freer expression, associated with the leadership of Mikhail Gorbachev in the Soviet Union. Glasnost has resulted in widely ranging expressions of independence from strict Soviet control. Numerous ethnic groups have demonstrated for greater freedom, while Soviet artists, writers, and even the media have become increasingly outspoken.

See also Perestroika.

GOLD STANDARD, system upon which most countries base their currency. During the nineteenth century most European countries and the United States used the pure or classical gold standard, in which the currency must equal a certain weight of gold and may be converted into gold on demand. This system was abandoned for the most part during the 1930s. It was replaced by the gold reserve system. According to this system, a country's currency is still based on gold, but the state does not promise to convert paper money and coinage into gold, and the government can make laws regulating shipments and holdings. The advantages of this system are that governments are unable to issue excessive amounts of currency (price inflation) and that exchange rates in international trade are fixed.

The system's disadvantages are that a single nation has great problems in trying to remove itself from worldwide depression or inflation, that a country with a payment deficit has a long and difficult adjustment period, and that there may be insufficient flexibility in the supply of paper money. In addition to the internal gold systems there is the international system. Exchange values of countries are fixed in terms of gold or in terms of currencies whose value is fixed in gold.

GOLDWATER, BARRY MORRIS (1909-   ), former leader of Republican conservatives, presidential candidate against Lyndon Johnson in 1964, and United States Senator from Arizona.

Elected to the Senate in 1953, Goldwater became known as spokesman for the conservative wing of his party. Although he advanced no legislative program of his own, he established as his objectives the total victory over world communism and reduction of federal authority in all matters except military preparations and control of trade unions. His *Conscience of a Conservative* (1960), *Why Not Victory?* (1962), and *Where I Stand* (1964) reached millions of readers. He was a popular speaker and a successful fund raiser.

In the presidential campaign of 1964 he led many to believe that if elected he would swing the nation drastically to the right. Supported by some southern Democrats but not by liberal Republicans, he lost to Johnson.

He was reelected in 1969 to the Senate, where he continued to exercise considerable political influence. Goldwater retired in 1987.

GOMILLION v. LIGHTFOOT, 364 U.S. 339 (1960), questions the constitutionality of an act of the Alabama legislature that redefined the city limits of Tuskegee, not merely to the incidental inconvenience of the petitioners, but, the Court found, to purposely deprive them of the municipal franchise. Most of Tuskegee's 400 Negro voters lived in one area just inside the city's former limits. The legislature had redrawn the city limits to exclude this area. The petitioners complained that the legislature's action deprived them of the right to vote in municipal elections. Mr. Justice Frankfurter, delivering the opinion of the Court, said that when a legislature thus singles out a readily isolated segment of a racial minority for special discriminatory treatment, it violates the Fifteenth Amendment.

See also Colgrove v. Green; Guinn v. United States.

GOMPERS, SAMUEL (1850-1924), founder and president of the American Federation of Labor during its first 38 years. A proponent of pure-and-simple trade unionism, he improved the economic status of skilled workers through craft organization and stabilized unions on a business-like basis. He was born in London, emigrated to New York at the age of 13, and joined the Cigar Makers International Union in 1864, when cigars were made in tenement sweatshops by artisans working 16 hours a day for miserable wages. Although the young Gompers associated with Marxian Socialists schooled in European radicalism, he later distrusted economic theories and was apprehensive of "unruly Socialist elements" in the labor movement. He was active in Local 114, became its president, and after the business panic of 1873 rebuilt the cigar maker's union into a model for other crafts.

AFL. When the Federation of Organized Trades and Labor Unions came into being in 1881, at a time when manufacturing was shifting from handicraft to factory mass production, Gompers was chairman of the constitutional committee. He established organizational principles and forms that shaped the American Federation of Labor, formed in 1886 with Gompers as president.

The AFL was from its beginning a loose national federation of exclusive craft unions, the skilled aristocracy of labor. The AFL's purpose was to secure higher wages, shorter hours, economic benefits and better working conditions for its members through collective bargaining. To achieve these ends, Gompers constructed an efficient format patterned after commercial enterprises, with large treasuries financed by high dues, and activities conducted by salaried business agents. While the strike was recognized as the ultimate weapon, emphasis was on jurisdiction and negotiation of contracts. In politics, labor was to maintain neutrality between parties, free to reward its friends and punish its enemies. By 1900 the AFL numbered half a million members, and by 1915—two million.

Gompers, in opposition to Eugene V. Debs and the pacifists, supported Woodrow Wilson in World War I and urged labor-management collaboration for war production. In 1918 he was sent to Europe to counter the socialist-oriented international labor movement for a negotiated peace. Gompers is credited with winning from the government such reforms as workmens' compensation, a department of labor, and the exemption of unions from the Clayton Antitrust Act.

His "New Unionism" brought economic concessions for skilled workers, and the "House of Labor" that he built perpetuates his conservative economism. In his autobiography *Seventy Years of Life and Labor* (1925) and three earlier books Gompers defended and explained the emerging labor unions and gained for them a measure of public respectability. He died in San Antonio, Tex.

GOOD NEIGHBOR POLICY, a term applied to a series of United States foreign policy moves to cultivate the good will of Latin America in the 1930s and 1940s. The essence of the policy was to deal with the Latin American countries as diplomatic equals and assure them that the United States had no territorial intentions in Latin America. The term was invented by President Herbert Hoover, but much of the credit went to President Franklin Roosevelt.

The Good Neighbor policy was launched with the issuance of the Clark Memorandum in 1930 calling United States intervention in Latin American affairs an improper extension of the Monroe Doctrine; Hoover did not officially acknowledge the Clark Memorandum, but he did refrain from intervening in Latin American affairs. When Roosevelt assumed office in 1933, he continued this policy of noninterference. The United States took part in the Pan-American Conference in Montevideo in 1933; the next year, the marines were taken out of Nicaragua, Haiti, and the Dominican Republic. This action was followed by Roosevelt's 1934 disavowal of the United States right to interfere in Cuban affairs. The annuity to Panama for the Panama Canal was increased, and in 1936 Roosevelt attended the Inter-American Conference for Peace and promised to maintain mutual safety through consultation with the Latin American nations. Although the Good Neighbor policy resulted in hemispheric unity during World War II, continued disregard of the economic needs of Latin America fostered resentment toward the United States.

See also Alliance for Progress; Dollar Diplomacy; Pan-Americanism.

GOVERNMENT DEBT. *See* Debt, National.

GOVERNMENT NATIONAL MORTGAGE ASSOCIATION (GNMA), also known as "Ginnie Mae," agency regulated by the Department of Housing and Urban Development. It was authorized in 1968 as a spin-off from the Federal National Mortgage Association to provide secondary market financing for the majority of VA and FHA home loans (government-owned programs), assistance in financing certain federally underwritten mortgages, and management of three federal asset trusts.

GOVERNMENT ORGANIZATION. As set out in the Constitution, all legislative power is vested in the Congress (Article I), made up of the Senate and the House of Representatives; all executive power, in the president (Article II), and all judicial power, in the Supreme Court (Article III)—thereby codifying a deliberate separation of powers designed to prevent autocracy. The membership of the House of Representatives is determined by the population of each state, whereas each state is equal in the Senate, with two members.

Congressional Power encompasses the duty to set and collect taxes, declare war, raise, regulate, and support the armed forces, provide for the common defense, regulate commerce among the states, pay national debts, coin money, establish post office and road systems, set up courts below the Supreme Court, and make "all laws necessary and proper for carrying into execution the foregoing power." To become law, all bills must pass both houses of Congress and be presented to the president, who can sign the bill if he approves, let it pass without explicit approval by holding it for ten days, or veto it. A veto can be overriden only by a two-thirds majority of both houses of Congress.

The House of Representatives is empowered to originate all bills for raising revenue, although these bills, like others, must pass the Senate and the president. To the Senate is reserved the right to impeach or remove from office by a two-thirds vote government officials, including the president. The vice president is the president of the Senate and can cast his vote only to break a tie. Congress operates through committees—17 standing committees in the Senate and 21 in the House, plus various special, select, joint, and investigative committees and subcommittees—which control hearings on legislative issues and, more importantly, report bills out to be voted upon by the legislators at large. Membership on committees is rigidly controlled by the seniority system and is generally bipartisan.

Judicial Power. The Supreme Court has the right of judicial review in cases involving any state, ambassador, public minister, or consul; in all other cases it has appellate jurisdiction with regard to both law and fact. It is the Supreme Court's role to determine what shall or shall not stand as the law of the land under the Constitution.

Presidential Power. The president's duties are to carry out the laws enacted by Congress, with the help of appointed officials. He is commander in chief of the armed forces but cannot declare war. He makes treaties, but only with the advice and consent of two-thirds of the Senate; he names diplomats, Supreme Court judges, and other officials specified by law, but again with senatorial advice.

The list of duties is disarmingly simple, for the president is by far the most powerful man in the country, with enormous influence and prestige deriving from his place as head of his party, head of state, legislative leader, policy chief, top administrator, and chief foreign officer.

Bureaucracy. The major bureaucracy of government comes under the executive branch responsible to the president, through the departments of State, Treasury, Labor, Education, Housing and Urban Development, Energy, Health and Human Services, Transportation, Veterans Affairs—as well as through independent agencies, offices, commissions, and so on, authorized by Congress. The latter constitute what is critically referred to as the headless fourth branch of government. The Cabinet, made up of department heads, functions as an advisory body to assist and report to the president. Cabinet officers are political appointments not subject to civil service. The president is assisted by a free-wheeling personal staff within the Executive Office of the President called the White House Office; variously titled counselors, consultants, advisers, and special assistants. Some serve as liaison with other offices and Congress, some develop policy, and some are personal aides. The executive office includes several offices dealing with everything from the budget to telecommunications.

Balance of Power. At various points in history the checks-and-balances system has favored one or another branch of government. The second half of the twentieth century has marked a relentless growth in the power of the presidency, and the Warren Court's civil rights decisions have prompted complaints that the judiciary is usurping governmental control. The major problems of government are induced by size and cost as much as corruption, inefficiency, and inertia. However, there are deep philosophical questions under debate today relating to the advisability of Big Government and the proper relation of the state to the citizen. If the nineteenth and early twentieth centuries led to the supremacy of the centralized federal government over the states, the end of the twentieth century may well see a rebirth of decentralization and concomitant regionalism as a way to streamline government and return control to the people.

GOVERNMENT ORGANIZATION MANUAL. *See* United States Government Organization Manual.

GOVERNMENT PRINTING OFFICE (GPO) was established by Congress on June 23, 1860. A then existing commercial printing plant was purchased and named the Government Printing Office. It is now the largest and best equipped complete printing plant in the world. In Washington the GPO occupies 32 acres of floor space. The GPO provides the printing and binding services required by Congress, and the various government departments, independent establishments, and agencies. It furnishes blank paper, inks and similar supplies to government activities on order and distributes and sells over 25,000 different government publications and catalogs. The GPO has regional procurement offices in each of the federal regions. There are also five regional printing plants.   —*H.J. Humphrey*

GRAMM, RUDMAN, HOLLINGS DEFICIT REDUCTION ACT. *See* Balanced Budget and Emergency Deficit Reduction Act of 1985.

GRANDFATHER CLAUSE, device used by Southern states to exempt whites from state tax and literacy laws originally intended to disenfranchise black voters. The clause, inserted in seven state constitutions, enfranchised those individuals whose ancestors had voted before 1867. Since blacks received the right to vote after that date, the clause restored the vote to whites who had failed to meet the tax or literacy requirements. The Supreme Court ruled in 1915 *(Guinn v. United States)* that all grandfather clauses were in violation of the Fifteenth Amendment.

GRAND JURY, a body of persons selected according to law to serve as a type of investigative arm of a court. Being composed of 12 to 23 people at common law, a jury is "grand" because it is larger than a petit, or trial jury. The jury is an inquisitorial and accusatorial body that developed very early in the history of the common law. Originally being also a trial body, the grand jury's function is to investigate possible criminal activity and specific accusations generally made by a prosecuting attorney. A grand jury is intended to protect innocent persons against false accusations. If it determines that crimes have been committed, it files a formal accusation (called an "indictment"), the traditional method of commencing a criminal case with the court. Although considered an agency of the court for certain purposes, grand juries have been criticized for being dominated by the prosecutor.

See also Accusatorial Procedure; Inquisitorial Procedure; No Bill; Presentment; True Bill.

GRANT, ULYSSES S(IMPSON) (1822-1885), General of the Armies and 19th President of the United States (1869-1877), born in Point Pleasant, Ohio. He graduated from West Point in 1843 and served in the Mexican War. Resigning from the Army (1854), Grant unsuccessfully tried a variety of endeavors, but when the Civil War erupted he was quickly appointed colonel, then brigadier general (1861). In February 1862, Grant captured Forts Henry and Donelson. He took Vicksburg (July 1863), splitting the Confederacy. In late 1863 he was brought East as lieutenant general with orders to defeat Robert E. Lee. Grant's tactics brought final victory at Appomattox (April 1865). Grant was elected president in 1868 and easily defeated Horace Greeley to win reelection in 1872.

His Administration was run as an army headquarters,

which led to autonomy, which in turn led to scandals such as Black Friday, Crédit Mobilier, and the Salary Grab. His Administration ended inflation, funded the debt, resumed specie payments, and named the first Civil Service Commission.

See also Presidential Elections.

GRANTS-IN-AID, or categorical grants, federal funds allocated to the states for the support of services. Grants-in-aid have enabled the national government to fund such services as highway construction, flood control, and health-care centers.

Grants-in-aid have frequently been attacked as a way for the national government to annex the reserved powers of the states. Often applauded as a means of raising the level of some services in poor states, the grants have also been attacked as imposing priorities on the states. Policy decisions in such categorical grants are essentially made at the national level. The offer of federal funds is difficult to refuse, however, even though federal prescriptions may require a state to invest "matching" funds. The later development of alternative types of grants, such as general revenue sharing and block grants, return most or some (respectively) of decision-making power to sub-national governments. In the allocation of a grant to a state or local government, the national government attaches additional specifications that must be met in expending the funds, including non-discrimination requirements. The new federal-state relations, as a result of grant-in-aid programs, have been called Cooperative Federalism and Creative Federalism.

—*Guy C. Colarulli and Victor F. D'Lugin*
See also Federalism; Revenue Sharing.

GREAT COMPROMISE. *See* Connecticut Compromise.

GREAT DEPRESSION. *See* Depression; Roosevelt, Franklin Delano.

GREAT SEAL OF THE UNITED STATES is one of the nation's principal symbols. The seal's central figure is an American bald eagle clutching a bundle of 13 arrows—for armed might—in its left talon and an olive branch—for peace—in its right. In its beak is a streamer with the inscription *E Pluribus Unum* (from many, one). A red, white, and blue shield is superimposed on the eagle's chest. Above the eagle's head is a crest with 13 stars—for the original 13 states—against a blue sky. On the reverse of the seal, which appears on the back of the $1 bill, is an unfinished pyramid with the eye of God above it.

The seal is kept by the Department of State and is imprinted on certain official documents. Its design is used by many civil and military authorities. The search for a national seal began on July 4, 1776, but, because of the Revolutionary War one was not selected by the

The Great Seal of the United States.

Continental Congress until June 20, 1782. The present seal, made in 1904, has essentially the same design as the original.

GREENSPAN, ALAN (1926-   ), chairman of the Federal Reserve Board (1987-   ). Greenspan was appointed by President Reagan as chairman of the Federal Reserve Board in 1987. He had extensive experience as a consultant before becoming an adviser to Richard Nixon during the 1968 campaign. He did not assume a permanent government position until 1974, when he became the chairman of the Council of Economic Advisers. In 1977 Greenspan left government and returned to the consulting firm he helped found. When Paul Volcker announced that he was stepping down as chairman of the Federal Reserve Board in June 1987, President Reagan nominated Greenspan. He inherited the dilemma of balancing interest rates against inflation and the dangers of recession.

GRISWOLD v. CONNECTICUT,   381 U.S. 479 (1965), offers an unusual insight into the judicial

process in general and the role of the justices of the Supreme Court in particular. Griswold, the head of the Planned Parenthood Association, was convicted of violating a Connecticut penal statute which prohibited providing birth control information to married persons. The Court strained hard to find a means of knocking down this statute. The majority Court could not find a specific Bill of Rights violation, but they argued that the specific guarantees of the first ten amendments have penumbras which enlarge the rights guaranteed by the Bill of Rights. The so-called right of privacy is not found in the Constitution's words, but the Court felt that the penumbra of the Fourth Amendment included a right of privacy, and this statute violated that right.

See also Roe v. Wade.

GROSS NATIONAL PRODUCT (GNP), a measure of the market value of all commodities and services produced by a nation during a given period of time, usually one year. This value is measured only once, at the point of final sale. The value of inventories at the end of the period are included, but these inventories are subtracted from the subsequent period's product. In the United States, GNP figures are prepared by the Department of Commerce.

GNP is composed of four classes of goods: consumer goods (personal consumption expenditures), business capital (gross private domestic investment), government purchases of goods and services, and net exports of goods and services (exports minus imports). Although the great bulk of GNP represents sales in the market, it also includes estimated values of some forms of production that are not actually sold, such as the rental value of owner-occupied homes, wages paid in kind, and food consumed by the farmers who produced it.

National Income is the income earned by persons providing their labor or property for use in producing GNP. Basically, national income is GNP minus business depreciation (capital consumption allowances) and indirect business taxes. Some earned income is not received as personal income but rather is paid to the government as corporate profits taxes or contributions for social insurance or is retained by corporations as undistributed profits. On the other hand, transfer payments (such as pensions or unemployment compensation) are included in personal income although they are not part of GNP because they do not represent goods produced in the current period.

Interpretation. Because GNP represents the monetary value of physical output, it may rise because of an increase in physical goods or a rise in prices, or both. The GNP may rise even when real output actually falls, the whole increase resulting from inflation. It is possible to correct the dollar figures for price changes, and the resulting constant dollar GNP tells how much real output rose as if the price level had not changed. GNP does not measure economic welfare. It omits

GROSS NATIONAL PRODUCT

Billions of dollars

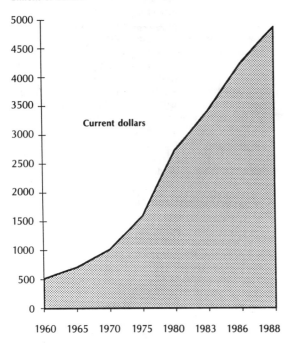

Current dollars

1960 1965 1970 1975 1980 1983 1986 1988

several forms of useful activity (homemaking, hobby activities, and voluntary social service, for instance). GNP does not consider social costs (such as pollution) as an offset to production; it may even add them on the positive side (more crime calls for more policemen, whose pay raises GNP). GNP does not measure such social gains as improvement of knowledge nor can GNP measure gains or losses in freedom, security, civil rights, and so on.

— *Walter W. Haines*

GROVE CITY COLLEGE v. BELL, 465 U.S. 555 (1984), concerned a private college that refused to certify compliance with Title IX of the Educational Amendments of 1972, which prohibits "sex discrimination in any education program or activity receiving federal financial assistance." The college argued it did not receive any federal funds, although a number of their students did claim federal aid directly from Education Department grants.

Grove City was threatened with termination of funding to the entire institution. However, the Supreme Court ruled narrowly that Title IX was "program-specific." It stated that for enforcement purposes "the program or activity at the college receiving federal financial assistance was the college's financial aid program, and not the entire college."

Critics of the decision were concerned that other institutions could discriminate in specific areas without fear of an institution-wide loss of federal funding.

GUARANTEED ANNUAL INCOME, a direct cash subsidy by the federal government to each needy citizen or family to provide a uniformly adequate standard of living. This proposal of income maintenance would replace public assistance (welfare).

GUINN v. UNITED STATES, 238 U.S. 347 (1915), concerns a "grandfather clause" in the Oklahoma constitution which affected suffrage. The clause read that "no person shall be registered as an elector of this state or be allowed to vote in any election held herein, unless he be able to read and write any section of the constitution of the state." The clause also specified that a person allowed to vote prior to January 1, 1866 would still be allowed to do so, regardless of his ability to read and write. The clause did not mention race or color, but before that date blacks had not been allowed to vote. The Court held that although the Fifteenth Amendment does not guarantee any citizen the right to vote, because voting qualifications are fixed by state law, it does protect him from denial of that right because of race or color, whether the statutory provision be directly or indirectly worded.

See also Katzenbach v. Morgan; Smith v. Allwright.

GUN CONTROL LEGISLATION, passed by Congress in 1968 to ban the interstate shipment of firearms and ammunition to individuals and to prohibit most individuals from buying guns outside their own states. This legislation is contained in Title IV of the 1968 Omnibus Crime Control Safe Streets Act, which applied to handguns, and in additional legislation enacted by Congress in 1968 to cover longguns and ammunition.

Strong gun control legislation has always been difficult to pass in the United States. In 1927, a law was passed which prohibited mailing concealable weapons (penguns and caneguns). Ammunition and explosives were also banned from the mails by postal laws. The National Firearms Act (1934) attempted to curb the traffic in and possession of automatic weapons, sawed-off shotguns and rifles, silencers, and concealable weapons. The 1938 Federal Firearms Act required that manufacturers and importers of firearms and of pistol and revolver ammunition obtain an annual license from the Internal Revenue Service. Weapons could only be shipped between licensed manufacturers and dealers, and in states that required purchase permits, the purchaser had to show his permit before purchase. The law made it a crime to ship firearms or ammunition knowingly to a fugitive from justice or anyone under indictment or convicted of a crime requiring more than one year imprisonment. Regulations of the State Department controlled the import and export of weapons.

All of these laws were difficult to enforce: until 1968 anyone could obtain even bazookas through mail-order houses. Gun control laws passed since 1963 were a result mainly of the assassinations of President John Kennedy, Senator Robert Kennedy, Dr. Martin Luther King Jr., and Medgar Evers.

Arguments. The main opponent of gun control legislation has been the National Rifle Association. This organization argues that gun control legislation would impose hardship on hunters and gun enthusiasts, while criminal and deranged persons would continue to obtain firearms illegally. The NRA quotes the Second Amendment's right to "keep and bear arms," but supporters of firearm legislation cite the differences between eighteenth- and twentieth-century life and the mounting crime statistics related to the use of firearms. Proponents argue that each citizen no longer needs firearms for protection and that the rights of the Second Amendment apply only in the context of the state militia or National Guard. Supporters of gun control contend that there should be national registration for every firearm and a national license for each gun owner because of the wide variance in state laws.

HABEAS CORPUS (Lat., you have the body), **WRIT OF,** a remedy for illegal confinement. The name was derived during the seventeenth century from the first words of an ancient writ directing a jailer to produce his prisoner so that the court could inquire into the legality of the detention. It enables anyone in custody to secure immediate inquiry by a court into the cause of detention, and if good cause is not established, to be freed. It provides a remedy for jurisdictional and constitutional errors without limit as to time and can be used to correct errors by military as well as civil courts. During the Civil War, President Lincoln suspended the writ of habeas corpus in the case of persons suspected of disloyal practices. This action was challenged in the cases of *Ex Parte Merryman* (1861) and *Ex Parte Milligan* (1866).

See also Ex Parte Merryman.

HAMILTON, ALEXANDER (c. 1755-1804), essayist, soldier of the Revolution, adviser to Washington, first secretary of the treasury, leader of the Federalists, and founder of the national monetary system. Hamilton was born in the West Indies, the illegitimate son of a British nobleman, later abandoned by his father, and brought to America in 1773 by sympathizers impressed with his potentials.

After a brief education he involved himself in the patriot movement, making his first anti-British speech in New York in 1774 and joining the Corsicans, a unit of voluntary militia. From 1776 to the end of the war he fought as an artillery officer. Wasington discovered him and in 1777 made him his aide and confidential secretary. He made friends with Lafayette and commanded one of his regiments at Yorktown. In 1780

Hamilton married Elizabeth Schuyler, daughter of the wealthy and influential general. Admitted to the bar in 1782, Hamilton opened an office on Wall Street and became a leading lawyer. In 1783 he was a delegate to the Continental Congress. In 1784 he founded the Bank of New York.

Hamilton sponsored the Annapolis Convention of 1786 and the following year attended the Constitutional Convention in Philadelphia, where he stood for strong executive powers in opposition to states' rights. He signed the Constitution and pushed for its ratification by the New York state legislature. In 1788, with Madison and Jay, he produced *The Federalist Papers,* a persuasive explanation of the Constitution.

When Washington took office in 1789, he appointed Hamilton Secretary of the Treasury. Hamilton worked to establish a standard currency, a mint, a federal banking system, excise taxes, protective duties, a national debt, and federal assumption of state and foreign debts resulting from the Revolution. His major accomplishment was the creation of a sound fiscal apparatus to sustain the new government. In the cabinet he often clashed with Jefferson on foreign policy and centralization.

In 1795 Hamilton resigned to resume his law practice. From 1798 to 1800 he was Inspector General of the Army. In the election of 1800 he backed Charles Pinckney against John Adams, splitting the Federalist party, but when the election was thrown into the House, Hamilton used his influence to secure the victory for Jefferson's candidate. In 1801 he founded the *New York Evening Post,* which he used to express his opinions. In 1804 he was challenged to a duel by his political enemy Aaron Burr, and died from a bullet wound.

HAMMARSKJOLD, DAG HJALMAR. See United Nations.

HAMMER v. DAGENHART, 247 U.S. 251 (1918), illustrates the obstacles raised by the Court to early attempts by the federal government to place controls on child labor. The Keating-Owens Act of 1916 denied the facilities of interstate commerce to those manufacturers who employed children within certain ages. Dagenhart, the father of two children under the age of sixteen who were employed in a North Carolina cotton mill, challenged the validity of the act. In a controversial five to four decision, the Court concluded that the law exceeded the constitutional authority of the Congress because the conditions in factories producing goods for interstate shipment did not affect interstate commerce directly enough to bring them within the commerce clause. Therefore, the regulation of such conditions was within the reserved power of the states. In 1941 the Court overruled this opinion when it upheld the validity of the 1938 Fair Labor Standard Act.

HAND, LEARNED (1872-1961), eminent jurist and long-term federal circuit judge, noted for the clarity and perception of his opinions which strengthened the development of public law. He was born in Albany, N.Y. of a family well known in the legal profession. An honor student at Harvard, he graduated in 1893 and obtained his degree at the Law School in 1896. He began to practice in New York in 1897.

In 1909 Hand was made judge of the U.S. District Court for the Southern District of New York. In 1924 he was raised to the U.S. Circuit Court of Appeals. When he retired in 1951, he held a record of tenure for a federal judge. In addition to nearly 3,000 legal opinions, his writings include *Bill of Rights* (1958) and *Spirit of Liberty* (1960). He was on the council of the American Law Institute. Although he never reached the Supreme Court and was limited in his jurisdiction, Hand was one of the best-known judges of his time. After his retirement he continued to sit on the bench.

HARDING, WARREN G(AMALIEL) (1865-1923), 29th President of the United States (1921-1923), born in Blooming Grove, Ohio. A newspaper man, he was a product of Ohio small-town politics who rose to become president. He was nominated by the Republicans in 1920 and swept to victory on the dissatisfaction with Woodrow Wilson. He succeeded in bringing an end to the agitations of the Wilson era and in laying a foundation for the business prosperity of the 1920s. Adept in human relationships, he attempted to mediate the industrial strife of the postwar era. Harding ended American involvement in World War I and set up a relatively successful disarmament meeting, the Washington Armament Conference. He stood for encouraging private investment by lowering government expenditures and reducing taxation, expecially of the rich. By 1923 industrial prosperity was well launched, and the Republicans followed Harding's policies for many years. However, he and his appointees failed to enforce laws vigorously, from Prohibition to antitrust. He is perhaps best remembered for the series of scandals that marred his term in office, notably the Teapot Dome affair.
See also Presidential Elections.

HARE PLAN. *See* Proportional Representation.

HARPER v. VIRGINIA BOARD OF ELECTIONS, 383 U.S. 663 (1966), concerns the constitutionality of poll taxes in state elections. Virginia residents challenged the state poll tax, which was a precondition to voting in the state. The Court held that a state violates the equal protection clause of the Fourteenth Amendment whenever it makes the affluence of the voter or payment of any fee an electoral standard. Voter qualifications have no relation to wealth or to the payment of any tax. Wealth, like race, creed, and color, is not germane to one's ability to participate intelligently in the electoral process.

HARRISON, BENJAMIN (1833-1901), 23rd President of the United States (1889-1893), born in North Bend, Ohio. The grandson of President William Henry Harrison, he rose to brevet brigadier general during the Civil War. A staunch Republican, he supported Radical Reconstruction while building one of the most lucrative law practices in the Midwest. His political career began in 1876, when he ran for governor of Indiana and lost. He served in the Senate (1881-1887) where he supported civil service reform, conservation measures, and railroad regulation. He was elected to the presidency in 1888. Harrison's first Congress authorized a steel navy, purchased land for conservation, increased veterans' benefits, and passed the Silver Purchase Act and much pork barrel legislation. Harrison also signed the Sherman Antitrust Act. By approving the prohibitive McKinley Tariff (1890), he reduced national income while increasing expenditures, thus bringing on the depression of 1893.
See also Presidential Elections.

HARRISON, WILLIAM HENRY (1773-1841), ninth President of the United States (1841), born in Berkeley, Va. He fought in the western Indian wars in the 1790s and was delegate from the Northwest Territory to Congress (1799-1800). Governor of the territory (1800-1813), he led the militia against the Indians at Tippicanoe (1811) and fought in the War of 1812. Before becoming president elected on the Whig ticket, he represented Ohio in the U.S. House of Representatives (1816-1819) and Senate (1825-1828). He died barely a month after his inauguration.
See also Presidential Elections.

HARRIS v. McRAE, 448 U.S. 297 (1980), concerns the constitutionality of Congress's right to limit federal funding of abortions. After a district court judge had struck down all versions of the Hyde Amendment, which prohibited states from spending federal medical care grant funds for abortions, the secretary of Health, Education and Welfare appealed. In 1980 the Supreme Court upheld the Hyde Amendment, ruling that Congress might choose to value the potential life of the fetus and to spend or not spend its money in support of that value. The four dissenters, Justices Blackmun, Brennan, Marshall, and Stevens, noted that the indigent were given public funds for all other medical expenses and that indigent women were being denied equal protection and were severely punished if the government subsidized childbirth but not abortion. Justice Potter Stewart, writing the majority opinion, noted that financial need alone did not warrant constitutional protection and that abortion itself had not been outlawed.

HARRIS v. NEW YORK, 401 U.S. 222 (1971), concerns the constitutionality of using a question and answer statement obtained while the petitioner was in police custody to impeach the credibility of the later testimony the petitioner gave in his own defense. Harris was charged with selling heroin to an undercover police agent. At the trial, Harris' testimony in his own behalf differed sharply from what he had told the police shortly after the arrest. The Court, in a 5 to 4 decision, held that if the statement's trustworthiness satisfies legal standards, it may be used to attack the credibility of a defendant's trial testimony.

In a dissenting opinion, Mr. Justice Brennan said that the Fifth Amendment's privilege against self-incrimination forbids the prosecution to use a tainted statement to impeach the accused. He also said that the Court, in affirming Harris' conviction, effectively sanctioned interrogation of accused persons incommunicado and without counsel.

See also Miranda v. Arizona.

HATCH ACTS (1939 and **1940),** prohibit the use of federal authority to affect nominations and elections or the use of rank to pressure federal employees to make political contributions. Federal civil-service employees and employees of any government office receiving federal funds may not actively engage in politics, no one contributor may give more than $5,000 in one calendar year to one candidate or political committee, and no committee may spend more than $3 million within the same period. No individual or firm under contract to the United States for services or materials may aid political parties or candidates. Relief rolls may in no way be used for political purposes.

The 1940 Act, which placed limitations on state and local employees working on projects that use federal funds, was repealed in 1974. The Hatch Acts were designed to reduce political influence on public employees. Critics claim the provisions are ineffective in controlling influence buying and that federal employees are reduced to the status of "second-class citizens." Recent attempts to modify the Hatch Act have not succeeded.

HAWLEY-SMOOT TARIFF. *See* Tariff.

HAYES, RUTHERFORD B(IRCHARD) (1822-1893), 19th President of the United States, born in Delaware, Ohio. During the Civil War he rose to brevet major general and was then twice elected to Congress (1864, 1866) as a Republican. In 1876, Hayes was named on the seventh ballot to oppose Samuel Tilden for the presidency. After a bitter campaign and disputed tallies from four states, the election was awarded to Hayes. As President, Hayes completed the withdrawal of federal troops from the South, ended Reconstruction, mobilized troops to suppress the railway strikes of 1877, and restored executive independence after a long period of congressional control.

See also Presidential Elections.

HAZARDOUS SUBSTANCES LABELING ACT OF 1962. *See* Business Regulation in the United States.

HAZELWOOD SCHOOL DISTRICT v. KUHLMEIER, 484 U.S. 260 (1988), Supreme Court decision that dealt with a high school newspaper, supervised by a teacher as part of a journalism class, that intended to publish articles describing the pregnancy of three students and the impact of divorce on some local families. The principal directed that these sections be removed because they did not properly protect the identity of the parties.

The students brought suit in federal court. The District Court ruled in their favor but the decision was reversed on appeal. The Supreme Court held that the newspaper was not a "forum for public expression." Rather, it was a part of the school's curriculum and the principal had the authority to reject materials that he considered inappropriate.

HEAD START, a nationwide program helping poor preschool children catch up to their middle class counterparts in social adaptation, intellectual skills, and emotional development. Project Head Start is a Community Action Program component of the 1964 Economic Opportunity Act. Recognizing the crucial role of early childhood experience in later development, Head Start attempts to fill the gaps in the life of a young child from a disadvantaged environment through verbal and social skill instruction, health and nutritional care, and emotional guidance. Active parental participation is encouraged. Originally a summer program, Head Start was soon expanded into a year-round project.

See also Poverty Program.

HEALTH, EDUCATION, AND WELFARE, U.S. DEPARTMENT OF (HEW), *See* Education, U.S. Department of; Health and Human Services, U.S. Department of.

HEALTH AND HUMAN SERVICES, U.S. DEPARTMENT OF (HHS), cabinet-level federal department, created in 1979 out of the Department of Health, Education and Welfare. It has a broad range of functions that deal with health, welfare, and income programs. The Offices of Human Development Services, Child Support Enforcement, Community Services, the Public Health Service, the Social Security Administration, and the Health Care Financing Administration are all under the general supervision of the secretary of HHS. Such major programs as Social Security, Medicare, and Medicaid are part of HHS. Educational programs, the remaining function of HEW, were placed in the Department of Education.

HEARST, WILLIAM RANDOLPH (1863-1951), editor and publisher, whose yellow journalism helped build a publishing empire and political career. He was born in San Francisco; his father was a rich mining magnate former senator.

In 1895 Hearst bought the New York *Journal* and competed with Joseph Pulitzer's *New York World* in a circulation contest characterized by scare headlines, exaggeration, and fabrication of news. Inflaming their readers over alleged atrocities in Cuba, the two journalists helped to push the country into the Spanish-American War.

Political Career. Hearst supported William Jennings Bryan for the presidency in 1896 and 1900. He then used his papers to further his political ambitions and was elected as a Democratic representative from New York (1903-1907). However, his political career ended when he ran unsuccessfully for governor of New York and mayor of New York City. Hearst remained politically active as a Democrat until he broke with Roosevelt over the New Deal.

Magnate. Hearst acquired ownership of *Cosmopolitan, Good Housekeeping, Harper's Bazaar,* and other nationally circulated magazines; bought up newspapers in major cities; and established International News Service. His journalistic empire allowed Hearst to live extravagantly. He spent $30 million on the construction of his palatial estate at San Simeon, Calif. He lost control over his holdings during the Depression, but regained them in the prosperity that followed World War II. Hearst then became identified with the ultraright. He hated Communism and the Soviet Union and used his publications to ignite the postwar political hysteria that culminated in McCarthyism.

Hearst's five sons all became executives in his newspapers, and one received the Pulitzer Prize in 1956. His granddaughter, Patricia Hearst, was abducted in 1974.

HEART OF ATLANTA MOTELS, INC. v. UNITED STATES, 379 U.S. 241 (1964). In recent years there has been a change in the manner and method by which the law is used in an attempt to further the cause of civil rights. At one time, the Thirteenth, Fourteenth, and Fifteenth Amendments were the primary tool used to prevent violations of civil rights based on race, but the commerce clause is increasingly being used to augment the impact of the Civil War amendments. In the Heart of Atlanta case, the constitutionality of Title II of the Civil Rights Act of 1964 was challenged on the grounds that Congress had exceeded its powers under the commerce clause. The hotel owners admitted that they refused to rent rooms to blacks. The only significant question the Court had to settle was whether or not Congress had exceeded its power. The Court upheld the exercise of power, finding that racial discrimination against transient blacks placed a burden upon interstate commerce and that Congress had the power to make the discrimination illegal in order to remove that burden. The Court recognized that Congress was really legislating against

moral wrongs rather than trying to facilitate the flow of commerce, but said this fact did not impair the constitutionality of the statute.   —*Philip J. Hannon*

See also Civil Rights Acts; Katzenbach v. McClung.

HELSINKI ACCORDS, agreement signed in August 1975 as the final document of the Conference on Security and Cooperation in Europe (CSCE). The United States, Canada, and 33 European states participated in signing a non-binding agreement to recognize existing European boundaries and to "respect human rights and fundamental freedoms." Critics contended that U.S. participation gave legitimacy to Soviet control over Eastern Europe and the Baltic states.

A conference was held in Madrid, Spain, in 1983 to review implementation of the accords. However, sharp conflicts developed over the human rights issue, which was further complicated by turmoil in Poland and the Soviet invasion of Afghanistan. Nevertheless, the conference closed by reaffirming the Helsinki principles.

A third conference was held in Vienna from 1986 to January 1989. The final document contained a Human Rights accord that emphasized specific freedoms (e.g., travel, religion, gender equality) along with methods of implementation. While the accord was not legally binding, all the signatories, except Romania, promised to abide. The conference also established the framework for further discussions aimed at reducing conventional forces in Europe.

HERNDON v. LOWRY, 301 U.S. 242 (1937), concerns the legality of a section of the Georgia Penal Code, which penalizes the mere advocacy of insurrection and restricts freedom of speech and of assembly. Herndon claimed his conviction in a state court deprived him of his liberty, contrary to the guarantees of the Fourteenth Amendment. He was charged with calling and attending public assemblies and making speeches for the purpose of organizing white and colored persons under the name of the Communist party of Alabama. The Court held that the statute, as construed and applied, amounted merely to a dragnet which could enmesh anyone who agitated for a change of government. So vague and indeterminate were the boundaries thus set to the freedom of speech and assembly that the law violated the guarantees of liberty embodied in the Fourteenth Amendment.

HIGH CRIMES AND MISDEMEANORS. *See* Impeachment.

HIGHER EDUCATION ACT (1965). The law gives unusual support to needy undergraduate institutions by increasing national teaching fellowships, expanding scholarships, adding to state and university loan reserves, supporting part-time undergraduate employment and earmarking funds for undergraduate as well as graduate laboratory, audiovisual, and library facilities.

The stress on aid to the needy, as in the Elementary and Secondary Education Act of 1965, is seen in Title I's providing matching grants to assist in solving community problems (housing, poverty, recreation, employment, youth opportunity, transportation, land use), and in Title V's establishing a National Teacher Corps to supply experienced teachers and teacher interns to schools in low-income areas. The program is administered by the Department of Education.

See also Elementary and Secondary Education Act.

HIGHWAY BEAUTIFICATION ACT (1965), a measure that sought to improve the beauty of federally aided highways by imposing controls on outdoor advertising, dumping, and landscaping. The act declared that outdoor advertising (primarily billboards) next to federally aided interstate highways and primary roads should promote safety and natural beauty. Junkyards were to be moved or screened from the road. Landscaping provisions authorized the construction of rest and recreation areas. To help enforce the law, up to 10 percent of a state's federal highway funds could be withheld for failure to comply.

Although the bill's aims seemed quite modest, it created much controversy, in large part because of its identification with President and Mrs. Johnson. Critics complained of "arm-twisting" and in subsequent years defeated appropriations for it.

HILL-BURTON ACT (1946), or Hospital Survey and Construction Act, established a national hospital construction program. The Act permitted the federal government to participate in financing and set standards for hospital construction for the first time. Originally intended to fulfill the postwar need for small community hospitals, health centers, and related facilities, the Act is now administered through HHS's U.S. Public Health Service. Initially funded at $3 million to aid the states in surveying their needs and $375 million to help finance construction for five years, with federal participation in each project limited to one-third the cost, financing has been periodically extended and greatly increased since 1946.

HIRABAYASHI v. UNITED STATES, 320 U.S. 81 (1943), concerns the right of government to impose a curfew on citizens of foreign ancestry in time of war. Hirabayashi, who had never been to Japan or had any association with Japanese residing there, was convicted under a 1942 act of Congress of violating a presidential curfew order. The order restricted all persons of Japanese ancestry in a military area of the West Coast to their residences between the hours of 8:00 p.m. and 6:00 a.m. In the opinion of the Court, the curfew order was necessary to prevent espionage and sabotage in an area threatened by Japanese attack and, as such, was within the boundaries of the war power of the govern-

ment. Although the curfew amounted to discrimination solely on account of race, which ordinarily would be rendered unconstitutional, the Court held that in time of war residents having ethnic affiliations with an enemy may be a greater source of danger than those of a different ancestry.

See also Korematsu v. United States.

HOLMES, OLIVER WENDELL (1841-1935). Appointed by president Theodore Rosoevelt to the Supreme Court in 1902, Oliver Wendell Holmes, Jr., would eventually rank with John Marshall as one of the two greatest justices ever to sit on the Court. Born in Boston, Holmes came to the Court already renowned. A veteran of the Civil War, Holmes was graduated from Harvard Law School in 1866, rapidly rose in the practice of law, and became a friend of many prominent scholars and philosophers, including William James. In 1881 he published *The Common Law.* The following year, he was appointed to the faculty of Harvard Law School, largely through the influence of Louis D. Brandeis. A few months later, however, he accepted a justiceship on the Massachusetts Supreme Judicial Court, serving almost twenty years, the last three as Chief Justice.

Supreme Court Justice. On the United States Supreme Court (1902-1931), Holmes became the most outspoken advocate of judicial self-restraint, dissenting time and again when the Court majority sruck down federal and state legislative regulations of business (*Lochner v. New York,* 1905; *Hammer v. Dagenhart,* 1918). Skeptical of all absolutist philosophies, Holmes believed the Constitution allowed wide latitude in social experimentation by the states and by Congress.

When Holmes first came to the Court, battles were already raging over the meanings of the due process and the interstate commerce clauses. However, it was he who began the Supreme Court's initial contact with freedom of speech and the meaning of the First Amendment. He formulated the famous rule that an utterance could be punished only if there was a "clear and present danger" that it would lead to an evil which Congress or the states could legitimately prevent (*Schenck v. U.S.,* 1919).

Because of his skepticism of all absolutes, this rule gave Congress somewhat less latitude in its ability to curb expressions than it had in economic regulations. At the same time, howver, Holmes' rule consciously fell short of giving speech an absolute inviolability, especially in regard to the states. Holmes' belief in experimentation and his defense of state legislation on economics and speech made him an ardent protector of federalism.

—*David Forte*

HOME BUILDING AND LOAN ASSOCIATION v. BLAISDELL, 290 U.S. 398 (1934), concerns the loss of homes and land through foreclosure during the Depression. The Home Building and Loan Association contested the validity of the Minnesota Mortgage Moratorium Law (1933) as being repugnant to the contract clause and to the due process and equal protection clauses of the Fourteenth Amendment to the Constitution. The act provided relief with respect to foreclosures of mortgages and execution of sales of real estate, in that such sales could be postponed and periods of redemption extended. In a five to four decision, the Court was of the opinion that the Minnesota statute did not violate the contract or equal protection clauses. The Court found that an emergency existed in Minnesota which furnished a proper occasion for the exercise of the police power of the state to protect the vital interests of the community.

HOME OWNERS LOAN CORPORATION (HOLC). *See* New Deal Legislation: *Glossary.*

HOME RULE, the power of a local government, usually a city, to manage its own affairs and to draft or change its charter. Under home rule a state legislature voluntarily renounces its power and authorizes cities to manage their affairs, subject only to broad state statutes. More than half of the states allow a varying degree of freedom for their cities. There has always been friction between state and local governments over the definition of their functions, which frequently change according to circumstance. Local governments are often unable to handle many modern problems, which are becoming increasingly more economical for the state to administer. These areas include education, highway construction, and welfare. State legislatures, on the other hand, are not responsible for handling many local problems, which are best solved by the groups affected by them. Home rule also strengthens local self-government and fosters interest in government on the part of individual citizens.

See also Municipal Government.

HOMESTEADING, right to gain title of public land by paying a filing fee and satisfying the legal requirements of settlement, residence, and cultivation. Homesteads of 160 or 320 acres can be obtained if the land is classified as suitable for cultivation by the Bureau of Land Management. At present there is not much vacant public land that can be cultivated, and homesteads are difficult to obtain through this bureau. However, homesteads do become available through the Water and Power Resources Service. These homesteads must be irrigated, and greater expense and farming experience are required to cultivate them successfully.

Homestead Act. Although there are many laws regulating the sale of public lands, the main legal basis of homesteading is the Homestead Act (1862). This bill was sought by the West and the Republicans to expand the nation's economy. Under this Act, any citizen or alien seeking citizenship could register a claim to 160 acres of public land. After living on the claim and cultivating

it for five years, he could receive title to the land on payment of a small fee. Even though the Homestead Act was intended as a democratic act to raise the living standards of the people, Congress did nothing to help poor people apply for these lands nor did it offer any guidance or credit to people during their first difficult years on the land.

Although 400,000 registrants received title to 48,225,000 acres of homesteaded land by 1890, there was widespread fraud under the Homestead Act and other land laws, with timber merchants, speculators, and mining and cattle companies claiming millions of acres of public land. Congress was forced to act against these abuses: by 1891 no person could obtain title to more than 320 acres of public lands under the land laws; forest reservations were also created on public lands.

HOOVER, HERBERT CLARK (1874-1964), 31st President of the United States (1929-1933), who was also noted for his humanitarian relief work after two world wars. He was born in West Branch, Iowa. In 1895 he graduated from Stanford University and began a successful career as a mining engineer.

After World War II, Herbert Hoover toured war-torn Europe to make recommendations for avoiding famine.

During World War I he helped Americans stranded in Europe to reach home and organized war relief in Belgium and France. This service led to his appointment as war-relief director for Europe after the war. He first entered government in 1921, when President Harding made him Secretary of Commerce. He served through the Coolidge administration and then became the Republican nominee for president in 1928. Emphasizing prosperity, prohibition, and a protective tariff, Hoover swept all but eight states and had the largest popular and electoral college vote of any candidate up to that time. His opponent, Alfred E. Smith, a "wet," was hurt by his Roman Catholicism.

President. The prosperity of the late 1920s proved only surface deep, and the United States plunged into the Depression during Hoover's first year as president. Believing in self-reliance, Hoover was at first reluctant to commit the federal government directly to the recovery effort. His administration's lack of success led to a Democratic triumph in the congressional elections of 1930. More significant efforts were then made to fight the Depression, and Hoover was renominated in 1932, but the country turned to Franklin D. Roosevelt and the Democrats.

Critic. After leaving office, Hoover was a vocal critic of the New Deal and adopted an isolationist stand on foreign policy. After World War II, however, he surveyed the world-wide relief crisis at the request of President Truman. Hoover's administrative experience was utilized in 1947-1949 and 1953-1955 on the Hoover Commissions, which made recommendations on reorganizing the federal government. He died in New York City.

A success as a businessman and sincerely committed to the relief of suffering, Hoover and his accomplishments were overshadowed by the Depression. As its memory faded, his popularity increased.

HOOVER, J(OHN) EDGAR (1895-1972), American public official who served as director of the Federal Bureau of Investigation (FBI) for nearly 50 years. Hoover was born in Washington, D.C., and after high school he worked as a messenger in the Library of Congress. After receiving a law degree in 1917, he began work at the Department of Justice as a file reviewer. Within two years, however, he was named a special assistant to Attorney General Palmer. He became the director of the FBI in 1924.

During his long career, Hoover turned the FBI into a symbol of law enforcement, established the world's largest fingerprint file, and created the FBI National Academy, which trains police from all over the country.

From the late 1940s, Hoover was increasingly well known for his uncompromising attitude toward suspected communists and subversives. In addition, the FBI and Hoover came under fire for exceeding their authority. Prominent leaders such as Robert Kennedy called for his resignation, but he was stoutly defended by others, such as President Nixon. Despite criticism,

J. Edgar Hoover, director of the Federal Bureau of Investigation, 1924-1972.

Hoover continued in office until his death. Hoover's books included *Masters of Deceit* (1958) and *On Communism* (1969).

See also Federal Bureau of Investigation.

HOOVER COMMISSIONS (Commission on the Reorganization of the Executive Branch, 1947-1949; 1953-1955), third and fourth of a series of commissions to study the paralysis, waste, and corruption of bureaucracy. Named chairman twice because of his eminence as a past president and his record of incorruptible public service, Herbert Hoover was particularly concerned with overlap and efficiency.

The earlier commission advocated widespread consolidation of agencies according to function. Basically, the reports specified that all executive departments should have a definite line of command, more executive freedom in administration and in hiring and firing, more staff assistants, higher pay for senior officers and more efficient budgeting and accounting. In all, about 70 percent of the earlier commission's 281 proposals submitted were acted on by Congress. Determined efforts by Sen. William Benton and President Truman saved the reform proposals from defeat by entrenched interests. Although reforms in the State Department were effectively implemented, changes in the Defense Department, the National Security Council, and the departments of the Interior and Agriculture were more successfully resisted. Neither commission reduced significantly the offices reporting directly to the President.

The question of the advisability of fostering Big Government came to the fore when the later commission interpreted its function to include not just a definition of how well an agency is functioning but whether or not it ought to function at all. Because of the controversy, fewer of the 375 recommendations put forth by the later commission survived pressure from special interests and threatened bureaucrats.

—Mary L. Carns

See also Government Organization.

HOPPER, a mahogany box that is placed close to the Clerk's desk in the House of Representatives. Bills are introduced in the House when a member drops a copy "in the hopper" or hands a copy to the Clerk.

HOSPITAL SURVEY AND CONSTRUCTION ACT OF 1946. *See* Hill-Burton Act of 1946.

HOUSE OF REPRESENTATIVES OF THE UNITED STATES, the lower house of the U.S. Congress, which represents individual congressional districts of the 50 states. The House represents the people on the basis of population, and in 1929 Congress limited the total number of congressmen to 435, regardless of the total population. Every ten years, on the basis of the shifts in population, congressional seats are reassigned by the census bureau to each state. If a state loses seats in the House because of a drop in population relative to other states, the state's legislature must redraw its congressional district lines. If a state gains seats, it may choose to select the extra congressmen in an at-large election, but usually the state's legislature will redistrict to accommodate the majority party's attempt to increase its representation in the House of Representatives.

Apportionment. Until 1962 state legislatures were free to apportion congressional seats in any way they saw fit *(Colgrove v. Greene);* within a state some

The United States House of Representatives.

districts contained many more of the electorate than others. This malapportionment resulted in gross underrepresentation of the urban areas in Congress. In 1962 the Supreme Court ruled that malapportionment could be disputed on constitutional grounds *(Baker v. Carr),* and as of 1964 congressional districts had to be as numerically equal as possible *(Wesberry v. Sanders).* Consequent redistricting has caused the House to represent the people of the 50 states on a relatively equal basis.

The House has sole jurisdiction to originate revenue measures (Article II, Section 7), and it has become the traditional point of origin for appropriations. Jealously guarding this prerogative, the committees on ways and means and appropriations are the most important of all 22 in the House.

Organization. Presiding over the House is the speaker. Nominally elected by the entire House, he is really chosen by the majority party. Each party in the House elects its own floor leaders (majority and minority leaders) and assistant leaders (whips). Each party has a campaign committee to help at election time, a policy committee to determine party policy, and a committee on committees to place party members on the standing, select, and joint committees.

Because of the size of the House, committees are particularly important. It is in committee that the bulk of the legislative work is done, and because so many bills must be cleared for action and voted upon, there is no unlimited debate (or filibuster), as in the Senate. The House Rules Committee controls the traffic of legislation in the House, giving each bill that goes to the floor a "rule" limiting debate and amendments from the floor.

The House is a highly complex institution of congressmen, representing a host of interests within their districts. Because each congressman is elected only by his district, it is difficult to maintain party discipline in voting. Because of the seniority ladder, the longer a representative remains in office, the more influential he becomes in helping his constituency.

Specialization of its members has become a hallmark of the House. Each member carves himself a special niche in the legislative process. The committee he is on influences his specialization. Thus one can view the House as an institution dividing its labor among its membership through a stabilized specialization of work. Because most seats (roughly 325) are won by at least 55 percent of the vote they are safe for their party.

The Congressman is in a delicate and complex position in the House. He must maintain a working relationship with (1) his party leadership in the House and in his own committee; (2) his own constituency; (3) his party's district hierarchy, usually needed for his renomination; (4) his executive agency and department contacts needed to do "favors" for his constituents; (5) the interest groups in his district and state that supply information, electoral support and, at times, guidance; and (6) miscellaneous supportive people used or need-

METHODS USED BY HOUSE TO SELECT BILLS FOR CONSIDERATION

PRIVILEGED MATTERS
Almost any time. Committees such as Ways and Means and Appropriations. May claim immediate consideration for privileged measure. (Few times each Congress.)

RULES COMMITTEE SPECIAL ORDER
Almost any time. Simple majority vote. May waive points of order, limit or ban amendments, set debate limits. (Sixty to eighty special rules each recent session.)

UNANIMOUS CONSENT
Almost any time. No objection. Measure taken up at once. (Rarely used separately.)

S	M	T	W	T	F	S
	X		X			
	X		X			
	X		X			
	X		X			

SUSPENSION OF RULE
First and third Mondays. Two-thirds vote required. No amendments. (Few times each Congress.)

CALENDAR WEDNESDAY
Any Wednesday. Committees called; chairman may take up bills from House or Union Calendars. (Often dispensed with by two-thirds vote or unanimous consent.)

CONSENT CALENDAR
First and third Mondays. No objection. Takes minor bills from Union and House Calendars. (Used for over one-third of all bills that pass House.)

DISCHARGE RULE
Second and fourth Mondays. 218 signatures and simple majority. If withdrawn from committee, considered at once. (Very few measures discharged in recent Congresses.)

ed constantly, such as the leaders of the public opinion media and his financial "experts."

A congressman maintains close personal touch with his district and heads his home office by a trusted aide. The representative's own office staff in Washington consists of an assistant, a legislative aide, a public relations aide, and several lesser aides and secretaries. Additional help comes from the staff of the congressman's committee and the Library of Congress.

Leadership in the House is fairly stable, regardless of electoral sweeps in the presidency and even radical changes in district lines. Thus the House tends to be slow-moving, and presidents have had difficulty moving legislative requests through it. The president can persuade and promise, but he has no ultimate power to require the House to act. Leadership in the House tends to rest with the small towns, despite new apportionment.

See also Apportionment, Legislative; Committee System of Congress; Legislation and the Legislative Process; Majority Leader; Seniority System; Speaker of the House; Whip.

HOUSING AND URBAN DEVELOPMENT, U.S. DEPARTMENT OF (HUD), established in 1965 to provide for sound development of the nation's communities and metropolitan areas. HUD is under the administration of a secretary who is appointed by and reports directly to the president. HUD administers programs that provide financial and technical assistance for housing, particularly to low-income groups, and currently sponsors over 70 programs that help states, counties, and communities solve urban problems. The department encourages private industry to produce more housing more efficiently, to build new communities, and to insure and finance housing construction.

Among the many programs the department supervises is the New Community Development Corporation, which provides grants and technical assistance to special programs for restoring blighted areas. HUD helps to provide housing at rentals lower-income families can afford through interest-assistance payments on Federal

Housing Administration-insured projects. HUD also has a variety of programs that help communities construct adequate water and sewer facilities; provide neighborhood community centers, senior-citizen housing, and nursing homes; provide long-term financing for public facilities; and help in the planning of public works projects.

Important to the financing of HUD programs is its Federal Housing Administration. FHA insures mortgages and loans made by private lending institutions for the purchase, construction, rehabilitation, repair, and improvement of single-family and multifamily housing. FHA mortgages and loans also provide housing for the elderly, group medical facilities, and non-profit hospitals. FHA administers housing production under HUD's low-rent public-housing program and college housing programs.

HUD was rocked by a scandal over charges that Samuel Pierce, Reagan's HUD Secretary for eight years, and his associates had granted favorable decisions to contractors and housing speculators with Republican connections. Pierce faced ongoing investigations into activities that apparently cost taxpayers billions of dollars.

HUGHES, CHARLES EVANS (1862-1948), American jurist and political figure, the tenth chief justice of the Supreme Court. Born in Glens Falls, N.Y., he took a law degree from Columbia University. He attracted public attention in 1906-1907 when he headed commissions investigating abuses in New York's gas utility and insurance industries. In 1906 he was elected governor of New York as a Republican and was reelected in 1908.

In 1910 Hughes was made an associate justice of the Supreme Court. Without his consent the Republicans nominated him for president in 1916, and he resigned from the court to run against Woodrow Wilson. Political feuding in California between the Republicans and the Progressives, of whom he was also the candidate, cost Hughes the election, 277 to 254 electoral votes. He then returned to private law practice.

Charles Evans Hughes served as Supreme Court justice, secretary of state, and chief justice.

Secretary of State. After Harding became president in 1921, Hughes was made secretary of state. He failed to secure United States entry into the League of Nations, but he did negotiate successfully to limit naval armaments, lessen tension in Asia, and improve United States relations in South America. Although he left government in 1925, he reentered public service in 1928 to sit on the Court of International Justice.

Chief Justice. President Hoover nominated Hughes for chief justice in 1930, and, after opposition in the Senate, he was confirmed. Hughes' rulings against the National Recovery Administration and other New Deal measures led to President Roosevelt's unsuccessful effort to "pack" the Supreme Court in 1937. Hughes retired from the court in 1941 and died in Osterville, Mass. Criticized and praised by both conservatives and liberals during his career, Hughes steered a middle course that emphasized constitutional liberties and curbed the power of administrative agencies.

HULL, CORDELL (1871-1955), Secretary of State under Franklin D. Roosevelt. A member of the House from Tennessee for a quarter of a century, and briefly chairman of the Democratic National Committee, Hull came to the New Deal as a representative of the Southern wing of the party.

A free-trade advocate and moralist-internationalist of the Wilsonian persuasion, Hull was primarily responsible for initiating and carrying out Roosevelt's Good Neighbor Policy and an elaborate program of reciprocal trade agreements through which tariffs could be systematically lowered.

Hull remained in the cabinet through 1944, actively participating in the establishment of the United Nations. Because Roosevelt often acted as his own State Department, it is difficult to sort out Hull's contributions, particularly in prewar relations with the belligerents and in wartime diplomacy.   —*Allen F. Kifer*

See also Good Neighbor Policy; Isolationism.

HUMAN DEVELOPMENT SERVICES, OFFICE OF (HDS), an agency within the Department of Health and Human Services, which develops and administers federal programs providing technical, consultative, and financial support to state and local communities in the areas of service to the aged and aging, children, youths, the handicapped, and Native Americans. Formerly part of the Social and Rehabilitation Service, which was dissolved in 1977, HDS works closely with other federal agencies in providing special services to the needy.

HDS consists of four component agencies. The Administration on Aging funds and administers programs designed to stimulate the development of public and private services and opportunities for older people at state and local levels. The Administration for Children, Youths, and Families develops and oversees programs that provide social services to children and their families, including adoption services and programs to deal with domestic violence. The Administration for Native Americans oversees programs dealing with the special concerns of American Indians, Alaskan natives, and native Hawaiians. The Administration for Public Services coordinates programs to help eligible persons attain self-sufficiency, assist in family planning, and improve the social functioning of the disabled.

HUMAN RIGHTS, UNIVERSAL DECLARATION OF, U.N. document proclaiming a common standard "for all peoples and all nations" in the areas of civil, social, economic, and political rights. The declaration, approved by the General Assembly December 10, 1948, was the product of discussions held by the Commission on Human Rights beginning in January 1947.

There have been major problems with subsequent U.N. attempts to strengthen the non-binding resolution. States are reluctant to ratify agreements that might give individuals U.N. protection against their own state.

The United States has pursued its own policy, most notably under the Carter administration. The president spoke out against human rights abuses, particularly in the Soviet Union. However, his critics complained that U.S. policy was selective since Carter rarely mentioned events in strategically located countries such as South Korea and the Philippines. In addition, the Congress has enacted legislation that makes continued economic and military aid contingent on human rights progress. The Reagan administration placed less emphasis on the issue, stating that these restrictions hinder the conduct of foreign policy.

HUMPHREY, HUBERT HORATIO (1911-1978), 38th Vice President of the United States. He was known as a vigorous campaigner with a reputation for versatility and volubility. He was elected mayor of Minneapolis in 1945 on a reform ticket and was reelected in 1947. A cofounder of Americans for Democratic Action (ADA), he first appeared on the national stage in 1948 by championing a liberal civil rights plank at the Democratic National Convention. Elected to the Senate that year, he served until 1964 as a leading voice of liberalism.

In 1961 Humphrey became Senate majority whip, and in 1964 Lyndon Johnson selected him as his running mate. As vice president he supported the cities, labor, and minorities, but his loyalty to Johnson's Vietnam policies tarnished his liberal appeal. With Johnson's sudden retirement announcement in 1968, Humphrey gained the presidential nomination but lost a close election to Richard Nixon. Returning to the Senate in 1970, he unsuccessfully sought the presidential nomination in 1972.

HUMPHREY'S EXECUTOR (RATHBUN) v. UNITED STATES, 295 U.S. 602 (1935), concerns the president's power to remove from office a member of the Federal Trade Commission. William E. Humphrey, the decedent, had been nominated to the commission by President Hoover for a seven-year term and his appointment was confirmed by the Senate. When Roosevelt took office two years later, he removed the commissioner on the grounds that his views were uncongenial to the President's. Humphrey's executor sued for the salary Humphrey would have received from the time he was removed until the time of his death several months later.

The Court held that Congress had intended the commission to be free from, and not subject to, the orders of the president. Therefore, Roosevelt did not have the power of removal. The president can still exercise the power of removal of officials of the executive branch, but not members of the "independent agencies" created by Congress to serve the legislative as much as the executive branch.

HUNG JURY, a jury that is unable to reach a decision, resulting in a mistrial. The U.S. Supreme Court has interpreted the Sixth Amendment to require unanimous verdicts in criminal cases heard by federal courts, but has accepted less than unanimous verdicts by state courts. The Court has not clearly indicated the minimum

vote needed, but it has accepted convictions based on a 9-3 vote in state courts.　　　—*Mary L. Carns*

HUNKERS, a group of conservative Democrats, influential in New York State during the 1840s, so-called for their alleged hankering after power. A rift between the proslavery Hunkers and the antislavery Barnburner faction splintered the Democratic party.

HURTADO v. CALIFORNIA, 100 U.S. 516 (1884), concerns the meaning of the due process clause in relation to state criminal cases. Hurtado, convicted of murder and sentenced to hang by the State of California, claimed that he had been denied due process of law because he had been charged by an "information," a document formally charging a person with a crime and submitted to the court by a public official, usually a prosecuting attorney. According to common law, he would have been entitled to be charged by an "indictment," which is the same thing as an information, except that it is submitted to the court by a grand jury. In the opinion of the Court, any legal proceedings supported by public authority which regards and preserves the principles of liberty and justice must be held to comply with due process of law. The substitution of an information for an indictment does not violate the clause because a person is not convicted until tried.

HYDE AMENDMENT (1976), amendments to appropriations bills that prohibit the use of federal funds for abortions. These amendments are named after their author, Rep. Henry Hyde, a Republican from Illinois. The Supreme Court in *Harris v. McRae* (1980) upheld this restriction. Without matching federal funds, many states discontinued using public funds for this purpose. The impact of this cutback was felt most severely by those receiving welfare aid.

ILLINOIS EX REL. McCOLLUM v. BOARD OF EDUCATION, 333 U.S. 203 (1948), considers the constitutionality of a system whereby children were regularly released from classes to receive religious instruction during school hours on public school premises. McCollum, a taxpayer and resident of Champaign County, Ill., and a parent whose child was enrolled in the Champaign public schools, questioned the state's power to aid religious instruction by utilizing its tax-supported public school facilities to assist in the dissemination of religious doctrine. In the opinion of the Court, the state did not have the power to aid religious groups in the spread of their faith through such means. The Court also said that governmental aid to religious teachings is in clear violation of the principle of separation of church and state as set forth in the First and Fourteenth Amendments.

See also Everson v. Board of Education.

IMMIGRATION, the free movement of people from

Woman being inspected by health official at Ellis Island.

one country to another, aiming at permanent resettlement. Migratory movements greatly accelerated after the geographical discoveries, and impetus was added by the industrial revolution and the political upheavals of Europe in the nineteenth century. A new ethnic configuration changed the Americas, Australia, New Zealand, and parts of Africa and Asia.

Immigration into the United States, initially a northern and western European phenomenon, assumed new dimensions from the 1890s until World War I, when many millions of immigrants came from southern and eastern Europe. Entering the United States became harder after the Immigration Act (1917) listed several categories of people not qualifying for immigration and revised a much-debated literacy test. New restrictive provisions were added in 1918; in 1921 and 1924 a quota system was established based on the ethnic composition of the United States in 1920, but excluding Asians and Africans. Not included in the quota system were people born in the other countries of the Western Hemisphere, whose admission had therefore no legal ceiling. Later some Asians were allowed entry. Communists and other subversive elements were excluded by the Internal Security Act (1950). Important modifications came in 1952 with the McCarran-Walter Act.

Easing the Quota System. Public Law 89-236 was enacted in 1965 and subsequently amended in 1976 and 1980. It set an annual limit of 320,000 refugees and immigrants, of whom no more than 20,000 should come from one nation. First priority was given to persons with family resident in the United States and to skilled workers.

The 320,000 limit had numerous exceptions and was further complicated by the problem of establishing

policies for admittance of political refugees. Congress passed the Refugee Act of 1980 setting a limit of 50,000 annually, but the president has additional discretionary power to admit groups who are of "grave humanitarian concern to the United States."

Congress has since passed legislation to provide amnesty for undocumented aliens. It also revamped the visa allocation system to permit more immigration from Western Europe. This would be accomplished by placing emphasis on special skills rather than on having family members already resident within the United States. The ceiling would also be raised to 630,000.   —*Sergio Barzanti*

See also Immigration Reform and Control Act of 1986; Refugee.

IMMIGRATION AND NATIONALITY ACT OF 1952
(McCarran-Walter Immigration Act), passed over President Harry S. Truman's veto (he said that the bad parts far outweighed the acceptable ones), essentially reaffirmed the national-origins quota system of 1924 under which quotas for admission were set in proportion to the number of former nationals of each country living in the United States at a given time. Under the Act, the annual quota for any quota area was "one-sixth of one percentum of the number of inhabitants in the continental United States in 1920." People born in the Western Hemisphere and spouses and children of U.S. citizens were exempt from the quota, and certain racial restrictions were eliminated. But new categories of ineligibles were added, with emphasis on political reliability.

The McCarran-Walter Act was amended by Congress in 1965 in response to criticism that the law was discriminatory. It was further modified in 1975 and 1980. The national origins quota system has been eliminated and ceilings placed on immigration. Preference is given to relatives of U.S. citizens and skilled workers.

See also Immigration.

IMMIGRATION AND NATURALIZATION SERVICE, a division of the Department of Justice that administers the procedures through which immigrants fulfill the qualifications of naturalized citizenship. The service further enforces the requirements regarding immigrants living in the United States as resident aliens, effects exclusionary and deportation laws against undesirable aliens, and guards the borders against illegal entry. Established as the Bureau of Immigration under the Treasury Department in 1891, the service expanded to include naturalization functions in 1933, finally moving under the Justice Department in 1940.

See also Immigration.

IMMIGRATION AND NATURALIZATION SERVICE v. CHADHA, 103 S.C. 2764 (1983), case in which the Supreme Court ruled unconstitutional the Congressional veto provision of the Immigration and Nationality Act of 1952. Since the early 1930s Congress had utilized a legislature veto whereby it delegated authority to the legislative branch while retaining the right to disapprove of the way that the authority was used. Presidential or administrative actions could be taken only if a majority of one or both houses of Congress did not vote to stop the action. In time, approximately 200 laws, ranging from environmental, consumer, and federal pay legislation to executive organization and national security had provisions for Congressional veto. This practice was struck down by the Supreme Court by a 7-2 vote in 1983 as a violation of the constitutional provisions for separation of powers. The challenge was brought to a section of the Immigration and Nationality Act by an alien (Chadha) facing deportation for overstaying his student visa, after a judge had suspended deportation and Congress vetoed that suspension.

See also Legislative Veto.

IMMIGRATION REFORM AND CONTROL ACT OF 1986, was passed after Congress had debated for years the question of how to deal with large numbers of primarily Hispanic aliens working illegally in the United States. Agricultural interests and Hispanic groups that were afraid that employers would avoid hiring all Hispanics if legal penalties existed opposed tighter regulations.

Congress responded with legislation designed to achieve a compromise. Undocumented aliens who could prove that they had lived continuously in the United States since January 1, 1982, would be given amnesty. Employers who knowingly hired illegals would be subject to fines under the act and repeated offenses could result in jail terms. Employers would also be subject to fines if they refused to hire aliens simply because they were foreigners.

Approximately two million aliens applied for amnesty prior to the May 4, 1987, deadline, but many did not because of their inability to document residence and/or fears that other family members might be deported. The act, therefore, did not completely resolve the problem of illegal aliens in the United States.

IMMUNITY. *See* Self-Incrimination.

IMMUNITY ACT (1954), a measure that forces witnesses appearing in national security cases to testify by granting immunity from prosecution for self-incriminatory testimony. If granted immunity, witnesses must testify or face jail terms. Introduced at the height of the Communist scare, the bill was aimed at witnesses who refused to testify under the provisions of the Fifth Amendment.

The law allows either the House or the Senate, by majority vote, to grant immunity in national security cases if an order has first been obtained from a United States district court judge. The attorney general must be notified in advance and given the chance to present any objections he might have. Congressional committees, by a two-thirds vote, may also grant immunity. In addition, the law permits United States district courts to grant immunity to witnesses coming before district courts or grand juries.

IMPEACHMENT, as authorized by Article I of the Constitution, action by the House and Senate to remove the president, vice president, or civil officers of the United States from office for crimes of "treason, bribery, or other high crimes and misdemeanors." Alexander Hamilton defined impeachment as a "method of national inquest into the conduct of public men." The procedure dates from fourteenth-century England and was adopted by the colonial government. Impeachment proceedings are initiated in the House of Representatives where it takes a simple majority vote "to impeach" (bring formal charges). If impeachment is approved by the House, the Senate tries the case. Conviction requires a two-thirds vote of those senators present. The Chief Justice of the U.S. Supreme Court will be presiding officer if the president or vice president is being tried; in all other cases, the vice president (as president of the Senate) will preside. If the Senate convicts, the penalty is removal from office and disqualification from holding further office. There is no appeal.

Impeachment proceedings have been initiated more than 50 times in the House, but only a small handful have reached the Senate. Of these cases, most have involved federal judges, who hold lifetime appointments to the bench and can be removed only by impeachment. Charges have ranged from loose morals and insanity to tyranny and advocating secession.

The two highest ranking officials to be impeached by

the House were Supreme Court Justice Samuel Chase—in 1805 for harsh and partisan conduct on the bench—and President Andrew Johnson—in 1868 for violation of the Tenure of Office Act. Both, however, were acquitted by the Senate. Impeachment attempts have also been made against Presidents Tyler (in 1847), Hoover (in 1932 and 1933), and Nixon (in 1974) and Vice President Schuyler Colfax (1873). The House Judiciary Committee voted three articles of impeachment against President Richard Nixon in 1974, involving charges of obstruction of justice, abuse of power, and contempt of Congress. The vote followed a lengthy investigation into allegations that the President was involved in a conspiracy to cover up the role of the White House in the Watergate break-in and charges that the White House had used federal agencies such as the Internal Revenue Service to put pressure on persons on a political "enemies list." The President resigned three days after the final committee vote, before the House could take further action.

IMPERIALISM, the extension of the power of a state through the acquisition, generally by conquest, of territories outside its recognized national boundary. This involves the subjugation of the native inhabitants to rule imposed by force and their economic exploitation by the imperial power.

The term was coined in the nineteenth century and came into popular usage as a description of Great Britain's efforts to create a colonial empire. Lenin viewed imperialism as a necessary last stage of capitalist development in its efforts to prevent its violent overthrow. The result, Lenin believed, is the division of all people into capitalist and proletarian classes, a final struggle between the two, and the emergence of a community of mankind.

See also Communism; Economic Determinism; Internationalism; Nationalism.

IMPERIAL PRESIDENCY, term used by some to describe the office of president as too powerful or too circumscribed. In the 1960s and early 1970s actions by the administrations of Lyndon B. Johnson and Richard M. Nixon supported claims of an unchecked imperial presidency that negated the constitutional separation of powers and arrogated authority in both domestic and international arenas. During the Nixon administration, Congress, in the War Powers Act, sought to assure that the president's ability to commit the nation to a war was restricted. The Supreme Court, too, dealt the imperial presidency several blows in the time of Nixon, ruling that the president could not arbitrarily impound funds appropriated by Congress and that "executive privilege" could not be claimed to justify resisting judicial demands for evidence to be used in a criminal trial.

IMPLIED POWERS, those powers of the national government not specifically delegated by the Constitution but deemed to be reasonably implied (and not otherwise unconstitutional) by the exercise of the delegated powers (McCulloch v. Maryland). If the national government had no other powers than those specifically delegated, it would be a government of extremely limited powers.

See also Delegated Powers; McCulloch v. Maryland; Necessary and Proper Clause.

IMPOUNDMENT, the power claimed by a number of presidents to refuse to spend money that had been appropriated by Congress for specific purposes. The practice of impoundment can be traced as far back as 1803, when Thomas Jefferson deferred expenditure of $50,000 that had been appropriated for purchasing gunboats, but the power was used only sporadically by presidents until the post-World War II era. Legislators perceived the increasing use of impoundment to be a threat to Congress' traditional "power of the purse." The Constitution is silent on the issue of whether a president could make independent decisions on spending, although the power of appropriation is delegated to Congress. However, several recent presidents—including Truman, Eisenhower, Kennedy, and Johnson—tied their refusal to spend appropriated monies to their own commander-in-chief authority, by refusing to spend money for weapons that they believed to be unnecessary.

The conflict between Congress and the president came to a head during the Nixon administration, when the President claimed new and unprecedented powers to withhold funds. President Nixon impounded monies in a number of areas involving domestic programs rather than defense, including education, highway construction, housing, water pollution control, and agriculture—some of which included funds for projects that had been repassed over his veto. Nixon claimed that the funds he was withholding would unnecessarily contribute to an increase in inflation if expended; members of Congress felt the President was attempting to seize financial controls from the legislative branch.

In an attempt to reassert its own authority, Congress included restrictions on withholding of funds in the Congressional Budget and Impoundment Control Act of 1974. The law required a president to submit a report to Congress on any funds that were to be withheld. Temporary withholdings (deferrals), used to delay expenditures, could be disapproved by resolution of either house of Congress; permanent withholding (rescission) would require the approval of Congress within 45 days. If approval was not forthcoming, the funds would have to be released.

Two Supreme Court decisions may have a major effect on the power of impoundment. After several members of Congress sued President Nixon over his refusal to release appropriated funds, the Supreme Court ruled that the President was obligated to spend appropriated money because of the constitutional requirement to "take care that the laws be faithfully executed." In a related development in 1983, the Supreme Court struck down the so-called "legislative veto" as a violation of the doctrine of separation of powers. Because the section of the 1974 act that gave a single house authority to disapprove of presidential withholding was generally considered to be a form of the legislative veto, Congress in recent years has instead included disapprovals in supplemental appropriations bills submitted to the president for signing. —*Mary L. Carns*

See also Congressional Budget and Impoundment Control Act (1974); Legislative Veto; Supplemental Appropriation.

INCOME MAINTENANCE. *See* Guaranteed Annual Income.

INCOME POLICIES. *See* Economic Stabilization Policies.

INCUMBENT, one who currently holds a public office. Incumbents enjoy a significant advantage over their challengers in reelection campaigns. Few incumbent presidential candidates have been defeated in their bids for reelection, while the rate of reelection is in excess of 90 percent for state legislators and members of the U.S. House of Representatives and more than 80 percent for members of the U.S. Senate. —*Mary L. Carns*

INDEPENDENT AGENCIES AND REGULATORY COMMISSIONS. The following list includes major federal agencies and regulatory commissions. All mailing addresses are Washington, D.C., N.W., unless otherwise noted.

ACTION—established in 1971 to bring together a number of voluntary action programs, including VISTA, the Peace Corps, Office of Voluntary Action, and others. 806 Connecticut Avenue 20525

Administrative Conference of the United States—improves upon the legal procedures by which federal agencies, in administering government programs, establish the rights and duties of private persons and business interests. 2120 L Street 20037

American Battle Monuments Commission—erects and maintains memorials in the United States and foreign countries where U.S. Armed Forces have served since 1917, and designs and maintains cemetery memorials at foreign burial sites. 5127 Pulaski Building, 20 Massachusetts Avenue 20314

Appalachian Regional Commission—develops plans and programs for the economic and social development of the 13-state Appalachian region. 1666 Connecticut Avenue 20235

Arms Control and Disarmament Agency (ACDA)—conducts research for arms control and disarmament policy formulation, and works toward U.S. participa-

tion in international control systems and arms control and disarmament activities. 320 21st Street 20451

Board of Governors of the Federal Reserve System—consists of seven members appointed by the president and confirmed by the Senate, who supervise Federal Reserve banks, exercise control over credit conditions and open-market operations, and issue Federal Reserve notes. Federal Reserve Building, 20th St. and Constitution Avenue 20551

Central Intelligence Agency (CIA)—coordinates U.S. federal intelligence activities by making recommendations to the National Security Council, and reports intelligence it has acquired and evaluated. Washington, D.C. 20505

Commission of Fine Arts—provides the government with expert advice on matters relating to art. 708 Jackson Place 20006

Commission on Civil Rights—promotes equal protection of the laws under the Constitution and investigates charges that citizens are being deprived of their right to vote by reason of their race, color, religion, or national origin. 1121 Vermont Avenue 20425

Consumer Product Safety Commission—established to protect the public from unreasonable risks of injury from consumer products, evaluates the safety of consumer products and establishes uniform safety standards. 5401 Westbard Avenue, Bethesda, MD 20207

Council on Environmental Quality—formulates and recommends to the president national policies to promote the improvement of the quality of the environment. 722 Jackson Place 20006

Environmental Protection Agency (EPA)—coordinates government activities for the protection of the environment through the control of pollution. 401 M Street 20460

Equal Employment Opportunity Commission (EEOC)—seeks to end job discrimination based on race, color, religion, sex, or national origin, and to promote voluntary equal-employment programs by community organizations, employers, and unions. 2401 E Street 20506

Export-Import Bank of the United States—facilitates the exchange of goods between the United States or its territories and foreign countries. 811 Vermont Avenue 20571

Farm Credit Administration (FCA)—supervises a cooperative credit system for agriculture and provides credit to farmers and their marketing, purchasing and business service cooperatives. 1501 Farm Credit Drive, McLean, VA 22102

Federal Communications Commission (FCC)—directs interstate and foreign communications by wire and radio, including amateur radio and TV, categorizes and orders the services of radio stations and controls operators' licenses. 1919 M Street 20554

Federal Deposit Insurance Corporation (FDIC)—functions to promote and uphold public confidence in banks and protects the money supply by insuring deposit accounts in commercial banks. 550 17th Street 20429

Federal Election Commission—oversees the enforcement of the Federal Election Campaign Act (1971), which finances the federal elections, provides for disclosure of the financial activities of federal candidates, limits expenditures and contributions regarding federal candidates, and demands the registration of political committees. 999 E Street 20463

Federal Emergency Management Agency (FEMA)—coordinates federal emergency preparedness as well as efforts at the state and local level. 500 C Street S.W. 20472

Federal Maritime Commission—regulates offshore commerce of the United States. 1100 L Street 20573

Federal Mediation and Conciliation Service (FMCS)—aids the disputant parties in industries affecting interstate commerce to reach settlements by mediation or conciliation. 2100 K Street 20427

Federal Reserve System (FRS)—consists of 12 Federal Reserve Banks, each serving member banks in a Federal Reserve District; the Federal Reserve Banks are supervised by the Federal Reserve Board. 20th Street and Constitution Avenue 20551

Federal Trade Commission (FTC)—supervises and regulates business competition through the investigation of price-fixing, misrepresentation in advertising, unfair competition, and monopolies and deceptive practices. Pennsylvania Avenue and 6th Street 20580

General Accounting Office (GAO)—audits government programs and examines the efficiency of public funds applied by the executive agencies. 441 G Street 20548

General Services Administration (GSA)—manages government property and records involving a variety of functions including such diverse ones as the maintenance of the nation's historical records and the maintenance of motor pools. GSA Building, 18th and F Streets 20405

Government Printing Office (GPO)—prints and binds for the federal government and distributes and sells government publications and catalogs. N. Capitol and H Streets 20401

Inter-American Foundation—strives to achieve for all people in the Western Hemisphere opportunity to achieve their potential, fulfill their aspirations, and live in peace and justice. Provides social and economic development aid to Latin American and Caribbean nations. 1515 Wilson Boulevard, Arlington, VA 22209

International Trade Commission—advises the President on tariff, commercial, and foreign trade matters. 701 E Street 20436

Interstate Commerce Commission (ICC)—regulates and supervises interstate commerce and foreign commerce to the extent that it takes place within the United States. ICC Building, 12th Street and Constitution Avenue 20423

Library of Congress—a national library for the United States which serves the entire governmental establishment and the public but has as its first responsibility service to Congress. 10 1st Street S.E. 20003

National Aeronautics and Space Administration (NASA)—conducts research concerning problems of flight within and outside the earth's atmosphere and works for the peaceful use of space. 400 Maryland Avenue S.W. 20546

National Archives and Records Service (NARS)—a branch of the General Services Administration which maintains federal records and collects and publishes important government documents. 7th Street and Pennsylvania Avenue 20408

National Capital Planning Commission—plans the development and redevelopment of the District of Columbia and the conservation of its important historical and natural features. 1325 G Street 20576

National Credit Union Administration—provides nationwide administration of the federal credit union program through charters, supervision, examination of federal credit unions, and a system of share insurance. 1776 G Street 20456

National Foundation of the Arts and the Humanities—supports creative scholarly endeavors in the humanities and the arts. 1100 Pennsylvania Avenue 20506

National Labor Relations Board (NLRB)—upholds the right of employees to self-organization and collective bargaining through representatives of their own choosing. The board recognizes bargaining agents and conducts secret ballots among employees to determine bargaining representatives. 1717 Pennsylvania Avenue 20570

National Mediation Board—established to see that commerce would not be interrupted, to uphold the right of employees to join a labor organization and to ensure their freedom of association, and to provide for the prompt and orderly settlement of disputes concerning rates of pay, rules, or working conditions. 1425 K Street 20572

National Railroad Passenger Corporation (AMTRAK)—charged with developing the full potential of modern rail service to meet the needs of intercity transportation. 400 N. Capitol Street 20001

National Science Foundation (NSF)—promotes and strengthens research and education in the sciences for the advancement of the national welfare. 1800 G Street 20550

National Transportation Safety Board—works to assure the safety of all U.S. transportation by investigating accidents, conducting studies, and making recommendations of safety measures. It also regulates the transportation of all hazardous materials in the United States. 800 Independence Avenue 20594

Nuclear Regulatory Commission (NRC)—oversees U.S. nuclear energy, regulates its uses to ensure public health as well as environmental safety, and inspects on a regular basis the activities of the companies licensed to use nuclear energy as a power source. 1717 H Street 20555

Occupational Safety and Health Review Commission—ensures timely and fair resolution of cases alleging exposure of workers to unsafe and unhealthy working conditions. 1825 K Street 20006

Office of Management and Budget (OMB)—Evaluates, formulates, and coordinates management procedures and program objectives within federal departments and agencies. It also administers the federal budget. Executive Office Building 20503

Office of National Drug Control—helps devise national strategies to implement federal, state, and local efforts to control drug abuse. Suite 1011, 1825 Connecticut Avenue 20009

Office of Personnel Management (OPM)—administers the merit system of employment in the federal government; recruits, examines, and trains federal employees on the basis of skill. 1900 E Street 20415

Office of U.S. Trade Representative—directs and coordinates most of U.S. foreign trade policy, administers the trade agreements program, and supervises U.S. participation in foreign trade negotiations. 600 17th Street 20506

Peace Corps—sends volunteers from the United States for two-year programs to work with people of developing countries and to help fill their needs for skilled manpower. *See* ACTION.

Postal Rate Commission—major responsibility to submit recommended rate increases decisions to United States Postal Service Governors. It may also conduct hearings on postal rates and services, and act on appeals of closings or consolidation of post offices. 1333 H Street 20268

Postal Service, United States—became in 1970 an independent agency to provide efficient postal service to individuals and businesses throughout the United States. The Postmaster General is no longer a Cabinet member. 475 L'Enfant Plaza West 20260

Railroad Retirement Board (RRB)—administers a retirement system for railroad employees which governs payment of their retirement and disability annuities, annuities to their spouses, and benefits to their survivors. It also administers unemployment and sickness benefits and secures reemployment of unemployed railroad workers. 844 Rush Street, Chicago, IL 60611

Securities and Exchange Commission (SEC)—protects the interest of the public and investors by the issuance of regulations for securities and exchanges, by the registration of securities available for public sale, and by penalizing violators of regulations. 450 5th Street 20549

Selective Service System (SSS)—prepared to supply the Armed Forces with manpower sufficient for the security of the United States and directs the registration, examination, classification and selection of men for induction. 600 E Street 20435

Small Business Administration (SBA)—aids and protects the interests of small business firms, ensures their fair proportion of government contracts, makes loans to small business concerns and victims of floods or other catastrophes, improves the management skills of small business owners and managers, and conducts studies of the economic environment. 1441 L Street 20416

Smithsonian Institution—founded in 1846, it conducts studies and scientific investigations and operates a zoo, museums, art galleries, an astrophysical observatory, a tropical research institute, a radiation biology laboratory, a center for scholars, an exchange service, a science information exchange, and a cultural center. 1000 Jefferson Drive S.W. 20560

Tennessee Valley Authority (TVA)—set up in 1933 to speed the economic development of the Tennessee Valley Region, it works there to develop rural electrification, establish flood control, and produce fertilizer. Woodward Building 20444

United States Agency for International Development (USAID)—carries out economic assistance programs in developing countries. 320 21st Street 20523

United States Information Agency (USIA)—responsible for the U.S. government's overseas information and cultural programs including the Voice of America (VOA). It also has responsibility for communication activities including libraries, film programs, and cultural exchanges. 301 Fourth Street S.W. 20547

Volunteers in Service to America (VISTA)—a program transferred from the Office of Economic Opportunity to be included in ACTION, it sends volunteers to poverty areas in the United States to help the poor break away from the cycle of poverty. *See* ACTION.

INDIAN AFFAIRS, BUREAU OF, a division of the Department of the Interior responsible for the governance of those Indian and Alaska native peoples living on reservations. The Bureau attempts to discharge its responsibilities through the fulfillment of the government's treaty obligations. Of the 650,000 Indians and native Alaskans (Indians, Eskimos, and Aleuts) in the United States, some 450,000 come under the Bureau's jurisdiction. The Bureau was established under the old War Department in 1824 and became part of Interior when it was created in 1849.

Until 1924 Indians were considered wards of the states in which they lived, and local field divisions of the bureau exercised ultimate control over reservation administration. Although made citizens in 1924, it was not until 1948 that the Indians were granted full voting rights. Since that time the bureau, administered from the central office in Washington, D.C., has been working to promote greater self-management, utilizing the monetary and personal resources of various other governmental and private agencies. The bureau coordinates these resources with those of the tribes to develop programs of social and economic benefit administered by the reservation population. To this end the bureau seeks the establishment of reservation-based and reservation-controlled schools.

The bureau further works to reconcile its programs of modernization with tribal desires to retain some of the ancient traditions. Despite the bureau's announced policy of greater self-management, however, Indians and native Alaskans remain under a trust relationship with the federal government, which to a large extent retains control of their lands and funds.

See also Indian Policy of the United States.

INDIAN CLAIMS COMMISSION, an independent agency created by Congress in 1946 to adjudicate cases brought by Indians against the United States. Cases decided by the commission involved abrogation of treaties, executive orders, or constitutional rights as they pertained to Indians individually or collectively. After 1978, cases still pending were transferred to the U.S. Court of Claims.

INDIAN POLICY OF THE UNITED STATES. In the 200 years since the founding of the United States, Indians have been regarded in a variety of ways by their white neighbors: as military threats, as military allies, as "savages"—noble and otherwise, as objects for economic exploitation, as scientific curiosities, as potential converts to particular religions, and as helpless children in need of protection and assistance. All these points of view have helped to shape Indian "policy" in the United States.

Early History. Following the Declaration of Independence, the political leaders of the rebelling colonies looked to the Indians as allies in the struggle against the British and Spanish. Although the contest over land was already under way, the initial policy of the colonies was to win the friendship of the Indians by negotiating treaties of "peace and friendship," treating the Indians as sovereign peoples, just as the British had done. The earliest treaty was concluded with the Delawares in 1778.

Another aspect of British policy copied by the Americans was that of centralizing control of Indian affairs. The Articles of Confederation squarely assigned control of Indian affairs to the federal government. The Constitution which followed placed with Congress the responsibility for regulating Indian trade and, through later judicial interpretation, the warfare, treaty making, and "general welfare" clauses of the Constitution were so construed as to make the federal government paramount in Indian affairs.

At least by the mid-1700s, the British had accepted the notion that Indians owned the lands they used and occupied. As the administration of Indian affairs became more centralized, the Crown assumed what amounted to a protectorate over the lands of the Indians, reserv-

Geronimo, Apache Indian chief.

ing to itself the exclusive right to "extinguish" Indian title. This concept, also, was borrowed by the Americans.

Thus, from the birth of the nation, the legal framework of United States Indian policy has included four elements: supremacy of the federal government in the field of Indian affairs; recognition of Indian title to land and the exclusive right of the federal government to extinguish that title through purchase and exchange; responsibility by the federal government to protect Indians in the ownership and use of land; and the recognition, under certain conditions and always subject to the supremacy of the federal government, of Indian sovereignty. The interplay between popular attitudes and this legal framework has been critical in deciding the course of Indian affairs in the United States.

Removal. The first federal agency to be exclusively concerned with Indian matters was the Office of Indian Trade, established within the War Department in 1806. Congress in 1812, responding to a strong lobby of private fur traders, abolished the office and did not create a new Indian department until 1834. In 1824 Secretary of War Calhoun took matters into his own hands and established without congressional blessings an Office of Indian Affairs, appointing Thomas McKenney, former superintendent of Indian trade, as its first director.

Following the War of 1812, with the British and Spanish threats both extinguished and with the fur trade increasingly controlled by private interests, the dominant factors in determining Indian policy became land acquisition and elimination of the threat posed by hostile Indian presence in areas coveted or already settled by whites. Gen. Andrew Jackson, Secretary of War John

Calhoun, and Gov. Lewis Cass of the Northwest Territory were three early political leaders who favored a policy of removing Indians from the eastern half of the United States to locations in what are now the states of Arkansas, Missouri, Nebraska, Kansas, and Oklahoma. Although Congress did not act to impose a nationwide removal policy until 1830, after Jackson became president, the removal program was well under way by the early 1820s, particularly in the Great Lakes area. During the 1830s its full impact reached the large tribes of the Southeast. The Cherokees resisted strongly until 1838, when they were forced by Gen. Winfield Scott to set out on the long "trail of tears," which led to settlement in Oklahoma. By 1850 the eastern half of the continent had been almost completely cleared of Indians. In 1849 Indian administration permanently moved to the Interior Department.

Concurrent with the final decade of Indian removal was the acquisition by the United States of vast western territories. In 1853 Commissioner of Indian Affairs George Manypenny abandoned the idea of further Indian removal in favor of a policy of "reserving" lands for Indians within the territories in which they had traditionally resided. He also emphasized permitting Indians to acquire individual title to land, rather than continuing to own it in community or tribal status. Manypenny firmly believed that "civilization" for Indians would never be possible until they adopted the Western European system of private landholding.

Commissioner Manypenny's term of office initiated a heavy increase in the number of Indian treaties, as tribes in the Pacific Northwest, Great Basin and Rocky Mountain areas—usually after a period of initial resistance— surrendered large tracts of land. In 1871 Congress legislated that no more treaties would be negotiated or ratified with Indian tribes. As a result, certain of the tribes—including some large ones in the Southwest—were never the beneficiaries of any treaty.

Much of the criticism of the Indian Bureau during the post-Civil War period came from religious groups and, under President Grant, the religious sects acquired almost complete control of Indian schools. Missionaries assumed administrative jurisdiction, in the name of the federal government, over many reservations. Grant's policy was to rely upon the army to force Indians onto reservations, while turning to the missionaries to "civilize" and pacify them.

Forced Assimilation. Much of the 1870s was devoted to subduing the remaining hostile tribes in the West and distributing rations to the reservation groups whose economies had been destroyed. To solve the problem of the expensive maintenance of the reservation system, most administrators decided to allot lands in severalty among the Indians, thus breaking up tribalism and permitting the Indians as individuals to "progress" toward civilization and self-sufficiency. Under the 1887 General Allotment Act (Dawes Severalty Act), Indian land was to be individualized as rapidly as possible, the federal

protectorate over this land removed, and the Indians made citizens. Any reservation lands remaining after allotment to each Indian tribal member were to be sold at public auction and the proceeds deposited to the credit of the tribe. By 1934, when the act was repudiated, nearly 100,000,000 acres of Indian land passed out of federal trust status, most of it going into the hands of non-Indians.

A second arm of the "forced assimilation" policy set forth in the Dawes Act was the off-reservation boarding-school program. Various religious sects had been operating off-reservation boarding schools for many years, but the idea caught on with the Indian Bureau only after the establishment of a school at Carlisle Barracks, Pennsylvania, in 1879. As assimilation became the dominant theme in Indian policy, Bureau officials came to regard the off-reservation boarding school as the best means of removing an Indian child from the traditions of his tribe and teaching him the ways of the white man. Against the wishes of both parents and children, many were forcibly taken from the reservations to large schools in such communities as Lawrence, Kan.; Phoenix, Ariz.; Carson City, Nev.; and Riverside, Calif. The rapid rate at which land disappeared from Indian ownership after 1900, and the harsh treatment of Indian children in boarding schools produced a backlash of opposition that motivated Commissioner Charles Burke in 1921 to abandon the policy of imposing fee titles on Indian allottees and thus removing the federal protectorate over their lands.

Citizenship. In 1924, both in response to the new wave of sympathy for the Indians and to honor the Indians who had volunteered their services in World War I, Congress passed the Indian Citizenship Act, conferring full citizenship rights on all Indians who had not been made citizens previously (Arizona and New Mexico did not recognize Indians as citizens until 1948). Concern about Indian affairs led to the commissioning of a special Indian research project, begun in 1926 by Lewis Meriam and Associates. Their final report, called *The Problem of Indian Administration* (1928), is one of the most significant policy documents on Indian affairs ever produced in this country.

A number of the recommendations of the Meriam report were incorporated into the 1934 Indian Reorganization Act (Wheeler-Howard Act), which terminated the allotment of Indian lands, provided for the establishment of democratic tribal governments, set up scholarship and revolving loan funds, and authorized the establishment of new reservations. Companion legislation, the Johnson-O'Malley Act, provided subsidies to states carrying out welfare and education programs for Indians.

Making use of the new legislation, and in spite of meager appropriations, the Indian Bureau, under Commissioner John Collier, carried out many administrative reforms during the late 1930s. This productive period was ended, however, by the advent of World War II.

Termination. The most significant piece of postwar federal legislation was the Indian Claims Commission Act of 1946, which provided tribes the opportunity to sue the federal government before a special tribunal to recover financial damages for grievances accumulated through the years.

For another ten years, the dominant policy in Indian affairs was what the Indians themselves have called "termination" —identification of the more self-sufficient and educated Indian tribes and dissolution of their special bonds with the federal government. "Federal withdrawal" is another term which has been used to describe this process. The principle policy declaration of this period was House Concurrent Resolution 108, endorsed in 1953 by both bodies of Congress. H.C.R. 108 declared it to be the policy of Congress ". . . as rapidly as possible to make the Indians within the territorial limits of the United States subject to the same laws and responsibilities as are applicable to other citizens of the United States, and to grant them all the rights and prerogatives pertaining to American citizenship."

The first major legislation to be enacted in furtherance of federal withdrawal provided for the transfer of civil and criminal jurisdiction on Indian reservations to the states. The Indians were finally successful in having it repealed in 1968, 15 years after its enactment. Nonetheless, it did change the legal status of a number of reservations.

Indians and many other citizens bitterly resisted termination and, in 1958 Secretary of the Interior Fred Seaton stated that he would no longer recommend termination for any group without its consent. Subsequent administrations have also disavowed the termination policy. However, two large tribes (the Menominee of Wisconsin and the Klamath of Oregon), along with some smaller ones, were subjected to legislation terminating their special Indian relationship with the federal government.

New Options. The 1950s produced a program for assisting Indians wishing to leave the reservation to relocate in the cities. Although often criticized by reservation leaders who have felt that relocation program takes away many talented young tribesman, Indians have responded in large numbers. In 1956 Congress authorized a vocational training component for the off-reservation placement effort.

The most important development of the 1960s was the entry of a variety of new federal agencies into the field of Indian programming. Notable among these have been the Housing Assistance Administration, the Office of Economic Opportunity, the Office of Education, the Economic Development Administration and the Department of Labor. This decade also produced the first Indian to serve as commissioner—Robert L. Bennett, an Oneida from Wisconsin, named to the post by President Johnson. Bennett was succeeded in 1969 by Louis Bruce, a Mohawk from New York.

The basic policy of the Kennedy and Johnson ad-ministrations was to provide options for Indians that would permit them to retain their Indian identity while striving for a better standard of living. Forced assimilation was specifically rejected. Federal appropriations for Indians in the areas of health, education, and welfare (including housing) increased spectacularly.

The option idea carried over to the administration of President Nixon, but new emphasis was placed on permitting Indians a greater role in decision making. The Indian Bureau was staffed with Indians at many high levels, and new ways were sought to involve Indians in policy formulation and implementation. National organizations of Indians residing both on the reservations and in urban areas contributed importantly to this effort.

The 1970s saw an increase in the numbers of suits filed against the government by Indian tribes for the reimbursement or the return of their lost lands. In 1978 the Narragansett was the first tribe to regain part of its ancestral lands. —*James E. Officer*

INDICTMENT. *See* Grand Jury.

INDUSTRIAL REVOLUTION, term applied to the basic changes in the system of manufacturing in Western societies following the application of mechanical, as opposed to human, power for the production of consumer goods at the end of the eighteenth century. The development of the factory system, the application of technology to agriculture, the speeding of transportation and communication, and the abundance of consumer goods are essential characteristics of the Industrial Revolution. Industrialization coupled with

Textile manufacture was among the first industries affected by the development of the factory system.

capitalism required ever-expanding markets, and industrialized nations embarked on a policy of imperialism in the eighteenth and nineteenth centuries.

The Industrial Revolution started in England, where conditions were particularly receptive, due to an advanced banking structure, the existence of a pool of skilled workers, good transportation, and widespread mineral resources. Other countries followed in succession: Belgium and France, the United States, most of remaining Europe, and then Japan. Most Latin American, African, and Asian states are today at various levels of industrialization. In the nineteenth and twentieth centuries, new political and economic philosophies emerged, Marxism by far the most significant, to challenge industrial order and capitalism.
— *Guy C. Colarulli and Victor F. D'Lugin*

INFLATION AND DEFLATION. *See* Business Regulation in the United States; Debt, National; Devaluation.

INFORMATION, in law a formal statement of charges against a defendant in a criminal case, supported by sworn statements or other evidence. It is similar to an indictment but is submitted by the prosecutor directly to a court of original jurisdiction, rather than going through a grand jury hearing. Information is a relatively efficient and economical procedure, as contrasted to the more involved grand jury proceeding.
— *Mary L. Carns*

INHERENT POWERS, the principle that argues that all states possess certain authority in addition to those enumerated or implied by a written constitution; also powers held by the national government by virtue of its being a sovereign state with the right to preserve itself. Although the Supreme Court has been willing to allow the national government to undertake certain activities in foreign affairs under this doctrine, the Court has been more reluctant to do so in domestic affairs. The classic denial was the decision by a federal district court in 1952 not to uphold President Truman's seizure of the steel mills in the face of a strike, the judge denying the government's argument that the President had an inherent power to protect the nation against a work stoppage that would threaten the national defense in a time of war. The Supreme Court upheld the district court judge, but it did not find it necessary to substantiate his denial of the President's inherent power.

INITIATIVE AND REFERENDUM, two methods by which state and local voters may participate directly in the governmental process. These actions limit the power of state and local authorities.

An Initiative is a procedure whereby voters can propose a law or a constitutional amendment. Special interest groups often draft initiatives and then circulate

petitions, which usually must be signed by 5-10 percent of the voters to be valid. In states or localities that permit indirect initiatives, the proposal is first presented to the legislature and goes to the electorate only if not passed by the legislature. Direct initiatives go straight to the voters.

A Referendum is the act of referring legislative (statutory) or constitutional measures to the voters for approval or disapproval. Constitutional referendums are less common. In some states there is a variant that allows voters, by submitting petitions, to challenge a law before it goes into effect. The law is then placed on the ballot to be accepted or rejected by the electorate.

INJUNCTION is a court order which forbids a threatened action that would irreparably injure the plaintiff. A typical example is an injunction against a public servants' strike. Violation of an injunction constitutes contempt of court. An injunction is available as an equitable remedy only where the remedy at law (money damages) would not be adequate compensation for the wrong being proscribed. Although generally prohibitory, an injunction can direct positive action and is then called a "mandatory injunction."
See also Contempt of Court; Equity.

INNER CABINET, a term used to describe those presidential cabinet offices dealing with the key concerns of national security and economic power and that have special access to the president and to one another. The secretaries of State, Defense, Treasury, and Justice constitute an inner cabinet. The other department heads are consulted less frequently and usually only with respect to the problems of their areas of jurisdiction.

INQUISITORIAL PROCEDURE, legal procedure that places emphasis on the rights of the state in criminal trials and on the judge's role in examining witnesses. Characterized by the French legal system, it is essentially the opposite of the accusatorial system and has sometimes been described as a system in which the defendant is "guilty until proven innocent."
— *Mary L. Carns*
See also Accusatorial Procedure.

IN RE GAULT, 387 U.S. (1967), concerns the basic right of children to be assured fair treatment in juvenile courts. 15-year-old Gault was sentenced by a juvenile court to up to six years imprisonment for making lewd and indecent remarks on the telephone. This offense usually carried a maximum sentence of two months when committed by an adult. Gault had been taken into custody from his home, no notice or other advice of his arrest was left for his working parents, and the many other elements of due process granted to adults were not observed—a typical incident in the juvenile court system. In the opinion of the Court, a juvenile court must adhere to the due process requirements of notice, advice of the right to counsel, advice of the right to remain silent to avoid self-incrimination, offer of the right to confront accusers, and proper procurement of confessions.

IN RE NEAGLE, 135 U.S. 1 (1890), concerns the president's constitutional duty to "take care that the laws be faithfully executed." Neagle, a deputy marshal, was hired by the President of the United States to protect a circuit justice whose life had been threatened by a litigant in a case previously heard by the justice. Neagle shot and killed the man when he attempted to attack the justice and was promptly arrested by the local authorities for so doing. In the opinion of the Court, the president has the power to take measures for the protection of a justice, without special statutory authority, in line with his constitutional duties. The Court also held that Neagle was acting under the authority of the law, and that he was not liable to answer in the state courts for an act done pursuant to a federal order, under the doctrine of supremacy of the national law.

INSTITUTE OF PUBLIC ADMINISTRATION (formerly Bureau of Municipal Research), the oldest United States center for research and education in public administration. Created in 1906 to introduce scientific management concepts to government, the IPA is financed by government and private foundation grants. Its primary interest at present is in urban studies, with emphasis on overall planning and administration and such specific problems as transportation systems and pollution control. Headquarters are in Washington, D.C.

INTER-AMERICAN DEVELOPMENT BANK (IDB), bank formed in 1959 as a regional lending authority; its objectives are socio-economic development and technical assistance through loans to the 42 member states. The bank, which has headquarters in Washington, D.C., was founded in response to long-standing Latin American discontent over the level of U.S. investment in the region. Membership has expanded to include a number of European countries. The bank has ordinary capital resources gathered largely from the issuance of securities in capital markets, and a special operations fund is the product of subscriptions from governments, primarily the United States, Brazil, and Mexico.

INTER-AMERICAN RELATIONS. See Pan-Americanism.

INTEREST GROUP THEORY OF DEMOCRACY, a descriptive and normative theory of social and political practice that argues that all politics is in and among groups. A group is composed of individuals with a shared characteristic(s). Similar to pluralist theory, interest group theory describes a process of group competition and resolution that is a version of a process theory of democracy. The public interest is simply whatever results from the competition of groups. As developed by David Truman, interest group theory requires access for all groups to policy decision making and competitive elections. Potential groups (groups not organized but having a shared interest) act as a check on excessive or potentially excessive policy by becoming organized to challenge established interests and the policy in question. The political system remains peaceful in part because individuals belong to many groups, which moderates positions and actions on behalf of any one interest or group.

See also Pluralism.

INTERIOR, U.S. DEPARTMENT OF THE, a department that oversees the nation's natural resources, the development of United States territories, and programs for Indians and Eskimos. Originally established in 1849, the department was once a catch-all for such agencies as the General Land Office, Office of Indian Affairs, Patent Office, Census Bureau, and others. The department's current responsibilities include the administration of over 500 million acres of federal land and the trust responsibilities for 50 million acres that include Indian reservations; conservation and development of mineral and water resources, including mine safety and hydroelectric systems and irrigation reclamation; and overseeing fish and wildlife resources and scenic and historic areas.

The Office of the Secretary oversees the entire department. Other departmental offices include the Office of Energy and Minerals, which plans to provide adequate supplies of metals, minerals, and solid fuels; and the Office of Water Research and Technology, committed to solve national water-resource problems.

Bureaus in the Department include the Fish and

Shasta Dam on the Sacramento River in central California was constructed by the Department of the Interior.

Wildlife Service, which oversees the sport and wildlife resources; Park Service, trustee for the national parks, recreation areas and monuments; Bureau of Mines, which oversees the production of minerals and fuels; Geological Survey, to map and classify United States land; Bureau of Indian Affairs; Bureau of Land Management, which administers the federal lands; Heritage Conservation and Recreation Service, to develop outdoor recreational facilities; Water and Power Resources Service, which is concerned with the reclamation of arid and semiarid land in the western United States; and Bonneville, Alaska, Southeastern, and Southwestern Power Administrations.

INTERMEDIATE-RANGE NUCLEAR FORCES (INF), a treaty ratified by the Senate on May 27, 1988. It represented the first arms agreement ratified between the United States and the Soviet Union since the Strategic Arms Limitation Treaty (SALT I) in 1972. The treaty called for mutual force reductions. Both countries would eliminate missiles with ranges of between 300 and 3,437 miles. In total, the U.S. would destroy 867 missiles and the Soviets 1,752. These reductions represent about 5 percent of their combined nuclear arsenals. The Soviets began the first INF weapons destruction in August 1988 with the United States following in September. The treaty contained provisions for on-site inspection and verification of weapons removal and destruction.

See also Atomic Weapons, International Control of; Strategic Arms Limitation Talks; Strategic Defense Initiative.

INTERNAL REVENUE SERVICE (IRS), agency within the Treasury Department responsible for administering internal revenue laws except for those related to alcohol, firearms, and explosives. Its basic responsibilities include the collection of taxes, providing education and service to taxpayers, and preparing rulings and regulations to supplement the Internal Revenue Code.

The IRS is a decentralized agency with three operational levels: the national, regional, and district. Each of the seven regional offices has its own commissioner and supervises the operation of district offices in its region. IRS data are maintained at the National Computer Center in Martinsburg, W. Va., and at each of the regional centers.

The district offices collect and deposit tax payments, determine tax liability, certify refunds, process returns, investigate criminal and civil violations of the tax code, and provide information and assistance to individual and corporate taxpayers. The Internal Revenue Bureau was created in 1792, disbanded in 1801, reinstituted and reorganized between 1813-1817, disbanded until 1861, and reopened in 1862.

— *Guy C. Colarulli and Victor F. D'Lugin*
See also Taxation.

Seal of the Internal Revenue Service.

INTERNAL SECURITY ACT (1950), or McCarran Internal Security Act. Enacted as a curb on Communist subversion, the act does not forbid the Communist party. Instead, the act provides for the registration of all Communist and totalitarian action or front groups, revokes their members' passports, and requires public labeling of these organizations' broadcasts, publications, and mailings. Government or defense employees cannot contribute money or services to these organizations and must not conceal membership in them. To enforce the law, Congress established a five-man Subversive Activities Control Board. Further, the act forbids the transmittal or receipt of classified information, regulates entry into defense plants, and strips infiltrated unions of their rights. The bill bans aliens who are connected in any way with Communist or totalitarian organizations. Title II sanctions preventive detention during internal security emergencies where "reasonable grounds" exist for the belief that a person may engage in espionage or sabotage.

The entire act raises distinct questions of constitutionality. Portions of the law dealing with self-registration and passport restrictions have been successfully challenged in court in a series of cases, beginning with *Aptheker v. Secretary of State* (1964) and *Albertson v. Subversive Activities Control Board* (1964). The Subversive Activities Control Board itself, which had been established to enforce the provisions of this act, was abolished in 1973.

In 1989 the House further narrowed the act by eliminating provisions used to exclude and/or deport foreign nationals whose political ideology or expressions were considered potentially subversive. A Colombian writer and winner of the Nobel Prize for Literature was denied a visa under provisions of the act.

INTERNAL SECURITY COMMITTEE, HOUSE. *See* Investigative Power of Congress.

INTERNATIONAL BANK FOR RECONSTRUCTION AND DEVELOPMENT (IBRD), planned at the 1944 Bretton Woods Conference and established in Washington, D.C., December 27, 1945, when 28 governments signed its articles of agreement. IBRD has two affiliates, the International Development Association (IDA) and the International Finance Corporation (IFC). Membership in the International Monetary Fund is a prerequisite to membership in IBRD. Switzerland, the U.S.S.R., and its allies did not join. The bank's headquarters are in Washington, D.C.

The bank's main task in its early years was to rebuild the damaged economies of European countries after World War II. Today IBRD lends money to countries throughout the world at an annual rate of about $1 billion for economic development. The funds come from capital subscribed by members and loans by private investors. The IDA, established in 1960, lends money at lower interest rates and for longer periods than the bank. The IFC, established in 1956, provides loans and equity capital for a share of the profits.

All member states are represented on the bank's Board of Governors. An agreed formula controls subscriptions to the capital stock, and each governor votes according to the number of shares his government holds. Most of the board's authority is exercised by twenty elected executive directors who elect the bank's president. Robert S. McNamara (United States), formerly Secretary of Defense, served as president from April 1968 until his retirement in 1984. The current president is former Congressman Barber Conable.

INTERNATIONAL BOUNDARY AND WATER COMMISSION, U.S.-MEXICO. *See* Chamizal Border Settlement.

INTERNATIONAL BOUNDARY COMMISSION, U.S.-CANADA, established in 1892 to settle boundary disputes, particularly in Alaska and the bay between Maine and New Brunswick. The commission also maintains markers on land and water boundaries.

INTERNATIONAL COURT OF JUSTICE (ICJ), successor to the League of Nations Permanent Court of Justice, established by the United Nations at the 1945 San Francisco Conference. The Court's statute is a part of the U.N. charter, and all U.N. members are members of ICJ. Each member undertakes to abide by ICJ decisions in cases to which it is a party. The Security Council has the right to enforce decisions of the Court.

The Court, seated at The Hague, has 15 judges, who are elected by absolute majorities in the General Assembly and the Security Council. The judges serve for nine-year periods.

Nine judges form a quorum. Rulings are by majority vote and are final, without appeal. Only states can be parties in cases before the Court, but a state can take up a case in which a national is involved. The court's jurisdiction includes all legal disputes which members refer to it, and all matters provided for in the charter, treaties, and conventions. The Court also gives advisory opinions to the General Assembly and the Security Council on request.

The Court has not been effective in resolving international disputes because its authority is limited to cases where states have consented to its jurisdiction. In May 1980, the Court ordered Iran to release the American hostages. The Iranians refused to participate in the proceedings or to accept Court jurisdiction to hear the case and ignored the ruling. In January 1985, the Reagan Administration announced it would not participate in proceedings to consider Nicaragua's allegations of U.S. aggression.

INTERNATIONAL CRIMINAL POLICE ORGANIZATION. *See* INTERPOL.

INTERNATIONAL DEVELOPMENT ASSOCIATION (IDA). *See* International Bank for Reconstruction and Development (IBRD).

INTERNATIONAL DISPUTES, PACIFIC SETTLEMENT OF. All members of the international community are now under conventional obligation to settle disputes among themselves peacefully. As stated in the U.N. Charter, Article 2 (3,4): "All Members shall settle their international disputes by peaceful means in such a manner that international peace and security, and justice, are not endangered. All Members shall refrain in their international relations from the threat or use of force against the territorial integrity or political independence of any state . . . "

Some methods of nonjuridical settlement include negotiation, mediation, political settlement by an international organization such as the United Nations, and good offices provided by a third party.

Juridical methods are not used frequently because states often refuse to accept jurisdiction by the World Court or ignore an arbitration award that favors the other party.

INTERNATIONAL FINANCE CORPORATION (IFC). *See* International Bank for Reconstruction and Development (IBRD).

INTERNATIONALISM stresses the interrelatedness and interdependence of nations and often opposes nationalism and the idea that the nation-state is the highest or final form of political organization. Internationalism may be expressed in the advocacy of the formation of world organizations, such as the United Nations, or a world government or state.

See also Nationalism.

INTERNATIONAL LABOR ORGANIZATION (ILO), a specialized agency of the U.N. ILO was created in 1919 following the Treaty of Versailles as an autonomous institution associated with the League of Nations. Originally located in Geneva, ILO moved to Montreal during World War II, becoming an agency of the U.N.

The objectives of the organization include attainment of full employment, improvement of working conditions, recognition of the right to collective bargaining, extension of social security measures, and improvement of living standards for workers and their families. The organs of ILO are the General Conference, the Governing Body, and the International Labor Office (Secretariat). In principle, member states are obliged to enact in their national legislation the decisions of the General Conference. Recommendations and conventions constitute an international labor code.

INTERNATIONAL MONETARY FUND (IMF), founded in Washington, D.C., December 21, 1945, by twenty-nine governments under agreements made at the 1944 Bretton Woods Conference. IMF's main functions are to promote international monetary cooperation, assist in establishing a system of multilateral payments, and help in matters related to international balances of payments. Membership in the fund is a prerequisite to membership in IBRD.

All members are on the board of governors. Each member has 250 votes, plus one vote for each $100,000 of its quota. Twenty appointed executive directors conduct operations and elect the managing director.

Members subscribe to the fund's pool according to assigned quotas based on national income, holdings of gold and convertible currencies, and volume of trade. A member pays 25 percent of its quota in gold and 75 percent in its own currency.

Par values for currencies are established with the fund's concurrence and are reviewed every five years. The fund sells gold and currencies to members and borrows from them when necessary. It does not hold a member's currency in excess of twice its quota. Members may withdraw up to half of their quota and make agreements to draw given amounts within a specified period.

Special Drawing Rights (SDRs) were introduced into the IMF general agreement in 1970. Their purpose is to increase the volume of resources for financing world trade by acting as an international system of debits and credits.

INTERNATIONAL TRADE ORGANIZATION. *See* General Agreement on Tariffs and Trade (GATT).

INTERNATIONAL TREATY ON THE PEACEFUL USES OF OUTER SPACE was signed by more than 80 countries, including the United States, the Soviet Union, and the United Kingdom. The provisions of the treaty stress international cooperation in outer space; the illegality of all national sovereignty claims and military bases, maneuvers, and weapons in space; the rights of countries to inspect nonorbiting installations; assistance to and the safe return of astronauts; and liability for damage caused by a nation's space activities. Negotiations between the Soviet Union and the United States began in July 1966, under the auspices of the U.N. Outer Space Legal Subcommittee; the U.N. endorsed the resulting treaty on December 19, 1966.

INTERNATIONAL WHALING COMMISSION (IWC), with headquarters in London, was established in 1946 by 16 nations. The Commission makes recommendations for conservation and utilization of whales, disseminates information on method of maintaining and increasing whale populations, and regulates whaling.

INTERPOL. Twenty states established an organization in Vienna in 1923, to facilitate cooperation in fighting international crime. The group transferred its headquarters to Paris in 1938 and became the International Criminal Police Organization (INTERPOL). INTERPOL's secretariat is staffed by French police officers. It keeps in daily contact with about 90 affiliates through its own radio network and provides assistance to national police within the terms of local laws. INTERPOL functions include requests for detention of a criminal until deportation orders are filed, information on criminal whereabouts, and on smuggled goods.

INTERPOSITION, originated in the compact theory embodied in the Virginia and Kentucky resolves against the Sedition Act of 1798. Enacted by a Federalist Congress to counter foreign danger, the act was eventually directed against Republican domestic disaffection. The Republicans, considering this interpretation a violation of the First Amendment, declared in the Virginia and Kentucky resolves that when Congress inordinately transcends its powers each state may "interpose" its authority between its citizens and the federal government, allowing the states to declare the Sedition Act and subsequent acts void. As recently as 1962, for example, Alabama and Mississippi invoked "interposition" in their attempt to void court-ordered integration. The doctrine has been rejected by the federal courts as contrary to the national supremacy clause of Article VI.

See also National Supremacy; Nullification.

INTERSTATE COMMERCE COMMISSION (ICC),

an independent regulatory agency established in 1887 under the Act to Regulate Commerce. The commission acts in the public interest to regulate carriers engaged in interstate commerce or transportation. The commission settles disputes over the rates and charges of the carriers and rules on proposed mergers, sales, bankruptcy rules, and railroad operation. ICC also grants the right to operate buslines, trucking companies, and must approve changes in railroad service.

INVESTIGATIVE POWER OF CONGRESS. The power to make inquiries and hold hearings is an essential aspect of the legislative power conferred on Congress by the Constitution. It enables Congress to gather information on the possible need for future legislation and to examine the effectiveness of existing laws and policies. In addition, Congress' investigatory power is an essential tool for legislative oversight—to check how executive agencies are interpreting and applying the law—and dissemination—to alert the public to issues and problems.

Some recent subjects of investigation attracted considerable public attention: the TFX fighter plane contract, Vietnam, conditions in nursing homes and the need for federal standards, the executive use of security classifications to prevent publication of information, Watergate, Koreagate, ABSCAM, and the Iran-Contra affair. The most controversial investigations have had a tenuous link to possible legislation or executive action: instead, they seemed designed to expose certain types of activities, such as investigation of alleged subversion by the House Internal Security Committee (formerly the Un-American Activites Committee). The courts have been reluctant to impose limits on such inquiries.   —*Dale Vinyard*

See also Contempt of Congress; Oversight.

INVOLUNTARY SERVITUDE, slavery, peonage, or forced labor to fulfill a contract or debt. The Thirteenth Amendment prohibits involuntary servitude, except as a criminal punishment.

IRAN-CONTRA AFFAIR, the most serious scandal of the Reagan Administration. It began with reports in November 1986 that the then-U.S. National Security Adviser, Robert McFarlane, had made a secret trip to Iran. He reportedly discussed providing spare parts to Iran in exchange for their help in securing release of American hostages in Lebanon. President Reagan accepted responsibility and admitted that arms shipments of "defensive weapons" in very small quantities had been transferred to Iran through Israel. Reagan later indicated that he had not been given full details of the operation. He announced the resignation of his assistant serving for national security affairs, Admiral John Poindexter, and the dismissal of Lt. Col. Oliver North, a key member of the NSC staff. It was further

disclosed by the White House that the profits from the arms sale had been transferred to the Contras, anti-government forces seeking to overthrow the Sandinista administration in Nicaragua.

Both Congress and a White House Commission, headed by former Texas Sen. John Tower, investigated the events. The Tower Commission report was released in February 1987. It was critical of President Reagan's lack of direct supervision over his subordinates, including White House Chief of Staff Donald Regan and other ranking members of the administration, and for failing to comprehend the serious legal and political implications of the affair.

President Reagan continued to insist that he had not known of the diversion of funds to the Contras. He stated that he simply wanted to undertake a "strategic opening to Iran," then involved in a protracted conflict with neighboring Iraq and possibly susceptible to Soviet pressure.

Joint congressional hearings were held in May-August 1987, and were highlighted by the appearances of such key figures as McFarlane and North. The committee's final report, issued in November 1987, placed primary responsibility on President Reagan for failing to curb overzealous subordinates who were encouraged by an atmosphere of "secrecy" and "disdain for the law."

As a result of ongoing investigations, a federal grand jury delivered a multi-count indictment against the key participants in March 1988. North and Poindexter were charged with establishing a secret network to provide military aid to the Contras when that was forbidden under U.S. law. They were also accused of theft of government property and conspiring to defraud the government. Separate trials were scheduled with North's beginning in January 1989. He was convicted in May on three of twelve charges but the most serious, including fraud and theft, had already been dismissed. North was fined and given a suspended three-year jail term. His former boss, Admiral Poindexter, began his trial in March 1990.

See also Investigative Power of Congress.

ISOLATIONISM, a policy in diplomatic relations of maintaining a state's rights and interests without entering into alliances with other states. Isolationism should be distinguished from neutrality, which is a policy of selective non-involvement rather than complete avoidance of alliances and commitments with other states. A country's geographical position sometimes enables it to avoid diplomatic alliances. Japan practiced isolationism for 1,000 years before it made a pact with Britain in 1902. Britain chose isolation from 1882 to 1902. The United States was intensely isolationist from 1800 to 1917. Pressure was generated by many segments of the political spectrum for a return to isolationist policies following World War I.

See also Neutrality.

JACKSON, ANDREW (1767-1845), seventh President of the United States (1829-1837). He was born in Waxhaw, S.C. Orphaned while young, he enlisted in the militia during the Revolution.

Jackson was a delegate to Tennessee's constitutional convention (1796) and was the state's first congressional representative. In 1797 he was elected senator, but he resigned in 1798 to become a Tennessee superior court judge, holding the post until 1804. During the War of 1812, his toughness won him the nickname of "Old Hickory."

In 1818 he fought in the Seminole War in Florida. Although criticized for overzealousness, his actions led to the United States acquisition of Florida. Appointed its first governor in 1821, he resigned six months later. In 1824 he ran for president: although he won a plurality he was defeated in the House of Representatives' vote by John Quincy Adams.

President. In 1828, after a bitter campaign, Jackson was elected president and served two terms. The enormous turnover in offices after his inauguration introduced widespread use of the spoils system. The party formed by his supporters during this election became the Democratic party. One of the key issues of Jackson's presidency was the theory of "nullification," by which states claimed the right to void federal laws they judged unconstitutional. Jackson upheld federal power and vigorously opposed attempts to nullify federal legislation.

JACKSON, JESSE (1941-   ), political leader and Baptist clergyman. Born in North Carolina, he became nationally prominent with Martin Luther King during the southern black protest movement in the early 1960s. Jackson was later instrumental in founding Operation Breadbasket and Operation PUSH (People United to Save Humanity), organizations dedicated to improving economic conditions for blacks. Jackson became the first serious black candidate for the presidency in 1984 and 1988. He ran in the Democratic primaries using his personal magnetism to attract followers to what he called a "Rainbow Coalition" made up of blacks, Hispanics, American Indians, and "progressive whites." Jackson campaigned energetically and received 18 percent of the votes in the 1988 primaries. His efforts were seen as giving additional political influence to minorities on the national level. Jackson continued to maintain a high public profile and was expected to run again in 1992.

JACKSONIAN DEMOCRACY, the changes toward democracy in the American political system that resulted from the presidency of Andrew Jackson (1829-1837). Jackson, from middle Tennessee, was the first American president not born on the eastern seaboard. Rough-hewn, aggressive, tough, and uneducated, Jackson was proud of his own qualities and

his humble background. He campaigned against Eastern "industrialists and aristocrats" and promised to restore the national government to "the people." As a politician and president, he led a movement that expanded the suffrage, nominated presidential candidates by convention, created the spoils system of appointing governmental officials, decentralized government control over money by eliminating national banks, and strengthened the party system to make parties more responsive to the people.

See also Democracy, Populism.

JAY, JOHN (1745-1829), American patriot, jurist, and diplomat who played several key roles in the first years of United States independence. Born in New York City and a graduate of King's College, he was admitted to the New York bar in 1768 and was secretary of the royal commission that settled the New York-New Jersey boundary dispute in 1773.

Patriot. He was involved early in the struggle for American independence, serving on the New York Committee of Correspondence and in the first and second continental congresses. He was chief justice in New York before becoming president of the Continental Congress in 1778-1779. He went to Europe as minister to Spain in 1779 and then joined Benjamin Franklin in Paris in 1782 to help negotiate peace with Britain. Jay returned to the United States in 1784 and served as secretary of foreign affairs until 1789, attempting to settle disputes with Britain over occupation of the Northwest and with Spain over Mississippi

John Jay, patriot, diplomat, and first Chief Justice of the Supreme Court.

River navigation. During this period (1787-1788), he collaborated with Alexander Hamilton and James Madison in writing *The Federalist Papers,* which urged ratification of the Constitution and explained its provisions.

Justice and Governor. In 1789 Jay became the first chief justice of the Supreme Court. While heading the court, he undertook a diplomatic mission to Britain in an effort to resolve long-standing differences. He negotiated Jay's Treaty (1794), which was bitterly criticized but helped maintain peace. On his return from Britain in 1795, he learned that he had been elected governor of New York and resigned as chief justice. He served as governor until 1801, when he retired from public life. One of his last acts of office was to refuse to cooperate with Alexander Hamilton in a scheme to defeat the Republicans in the election of 1800. Jay died in Bedford, N.Y.

His intelligence, strict morality, and diplomatic skill helped Jay to make great contributions to the early development of the American republic. As a strong believer in a centralized government, he defended the Constitution and sought to extend federal powers.

See also Federalist, The; Supreme Court of the United States.

JEFFERSON, THOMAS (1743-1826), third President of the United States (1801-1809) and author of the Declaration of Independence. He was born in Albermarle County, Va., the son of a wealthy farmer. He graduated from William and Mary College in 1762 and was admitted to the bar in 1767.

He was a member of the Virginia House of Burgesses after 1769 and was elected to the Continental Congress in 1775. In 1776 he wrote the Declaration of Independence—a clear, elegant, and stirring summary of American ideals. He soon returned to Virginia, where he was elected governor in 1779 and was widely criticized when British troops invaded the state. He returned to the Continental Congress in 1783 and from 1784 to 1789 served as minister to France.

In 1790 he entered George Washington's cabinet as the first secretary of state. During his term he opposed Alexander Hamilton's pro-British inclinations and his fiscal and centralizing policies, which precipitated Jefferson's resignation in late 1793. By this time he was the leader of the anti-Hamilton forces, known as the Democratic-Republicans. Jefferson retired to his home at Monticello until 1796, when he ran for president against John Adams. Finishing second, Jefferson became vice president.

President. Although he won the election of 1800 as the Democratic-Republican candidate, the selection of the president went into the House, as Jefferson's electoral votes were equaled by those of Aaron Burr, his running mate. After a delay, Jefferson's supporters prevailed, and he began a popular first term, followed by his reelection in 1804. The Louisiana Purchase,

doubling the size of the United States, was completed in 1803. His successes were balanced by the controversies engendered by his conflicts with the federal judiciary and by the unpopular Embargo Act of 1807.

After leaving office in 1809, Jefferson remained at Monticello. He founded the University of Virginia in 1819 and helped revive classical architecture. Jefferson was wary of the power of centralized government and was a strong supporter of individual liberty.

JEFFERSONIAN REPUBLICANS. *See* Democratic-Republican Party.

JEHOVAH'S WITNESSES CASES, a series of Supreme Court cases involving the Jehovah's Witnesses religious sect. The cases tested state restrictions on religious freedom and forced the Court to examine the scope of religious freedom under the First and Fourteenth Amendments. In *Cantwell v. Connecticut* (1940) Cantwell and his two sons, members of the Jehovah's Witnesses, were arrested and convicted for soliciting contributions without authorizations. The decision held unconstitutional the state statute prohibiting unauthorized solicitation of money for religious, charitable, or philanthropic causes. The case of *West Virginia State Board of Education v. Barnette* (1943) was brought by Jehovah's Witnesses whose children were being expelled from school for refusing to salute the flag and recite the pledge of allegiance. The Court held that the children could not be forced to salute the flag, this being in opposition to their religious beliefs.

Some cases resulted in decisions restricting activities of the group. Others granted the Witnesses greater freedom under the First and Fourteenth Amendments. In *Cox v. New Hampshire* (1941) it was held that the group could not hold a parade without authorization. *Chaplinsky v. New Hampshire* (1942) prohibited a breach of peace by the sect during a public meeting. *Murdock v. Pennsylvania* (1943) held unconstitutional laws imposing license taxes on peddlers of religious literature. Laws barring house-to-house distribution of religious pamphlets were held unconstitutional in *Martin v. Struthers* (1943). In *Prince v. Massachusetts* (1944) it was held that the Jehovah's Witnesses could not violate state child welfare laws by having a child peddle magazines on a street corner at night. Laws requiring official approval for the group to hold worship services in public parks were held unconstitutional in *Niemotko v. Maryland* (1951).

JIM CROW, a term descriptive of the laws and practices supporting the segregation and suppression of blacks in the United States. In the North, Jim Crow practices have usually been based on custom rather than law. In the South, however, both legislation and custom have been used to deny the use of public facilities to blacks by requiring the establishment of separate facilities for blacks. The Supreme Court upheld the right of the states to pass Jim Crow laws in the case of *Plessy v. Ferguson* (1896). More than half a century later, however, in the historic *Brown v. Board of Education of Topeka* (1954), the Court ruled, in effect, that racial separation by whatever means is unconstitutional. This ruling, together with changing public opinion as evidenced by the series of civil rights acts of the 1960s and numerous antidiscrimination laws passed at the state and local level, has effectively prohibited most Jim Crow regulations. But in many parts of the country, custom and a reluctance to enforce the new laws have had the effect of preserving Jim Crow practices.

See also Brown v. Board of Education of Topeka; Civil Rights Acts; Plessy v. Ferguson.

JOB ACTION. *See* Strike.

JOHN BIRCH SOCIETY, an ultraconservative, semisecret political organization founded in Belmont, Mass., in 1958 to fight Communist subversion. Named for a Baptist missionary killed by Chinese Communists at the close of World War II, the society holds that Communist influences have so deeply cut into American life that even high public officials have been affected and has gone so far as to call for the impeachment of certain individuals, including former Chief Justice Earl Warren. The Society is opposed to the U.N., NATO, foreign aid, and cultural and economic exchanges with Communist nations and has sought the repeal of social security laws and the graduated income tax.

JOHN F. KENNEDY CENTER FOR THE PERFORMING ARTS. *See* Smithsonian Institution.

JOHNSON, ANDREW (1808-1875), 17th President of the United States (1865-1869), born in Raleigh, N.C. In 1935, he entered politics as a Jacksonian Democrat and served successively as a U.S. representative, governor of Tennessee (1853-1857), and U.S. senator (1857-1862). During the secession crisis of 1860-1861, he was a Southern loyalist, which led to his reappointment as governor of Tennessee in 1862. In 1864 Lincoln chose him as his vice-presidential running mate. Upon assuming the presidency after Lincoln's assassination, Johnson at first made radical statements but quickly changed and initiated a mild Reconstruction program. However, Congress was more radical and began to formulate its own plan. Relations between Johnson and Congress deteriorated, especially after the President's supporters were defeated in the 1866 elections. The battle reached a climax in 1868, when he removed Secretary of War Stanton in violation of the newly passed Tenure of Office Act. The House impeached him, but, by a one-

vote margin, the Senate exonerated him in the trial that followed. In 1874 he won election to the U.S. Senate, but he died soon after taking his seat.

See also Presidential Elections.

JOHNSON, LYNDON BAINES (1908-1973), Democratic legislator and 36th President of the United States (1963-1969). Born to a political family—his father and grandfather were members of the Texas legislature—Johnson began his career as secretary to a congressman. He was an ardent New Dealer, serving as state director of the National Youth Administration and in Congress after 1937. He went to the Senate in 1948 and became Democratic floor leader in 1953. His considerable strength at the national convention in 1960 led John F. Kennedy to choose him as his running mate. He became president upon Kennedy's assassination.

President. Johnson's considerable legislative skill enabled him to carry out and extend the Kennedy programs as president. He sought a "Great Society" through civil rights laws and through antipoverty programs reminiscent of the New Deal.

His foreign policy included military intervention in the Dominican Republic (1965), which reminded Latin Americans more of gunboat diplomacy than the Good Neighbor policy, and escalation of the Vietnam War. He committed some 500,000 troops to the struggle and initiated extensive air operations.

His domestic policies were unable to prevent the

Lyndon B. Johnson, 36th President of the United States, largely blamed for the domestic consequences of the Vietnam War.

expression of black disillusionment. Urban rioting spread in 1964. His foreign policies bred dissent and riot as well. He did not seek reelection in 1968 in the face of a "dump Johnson" movement within his own party.   —*Allen F. Kifer*

JOINT CHIEFS OF STAFF, the principal military advisers to the President, the National Security Council, and the Secretary of Defense. The Joint Chiefs of Staff consists of the Chairman of the Joint Chiefs, the Chief of Staff of the Army, the Chief of Naval Operations, the Chief of Staff of the Air Force, and the Commandant of the Marine Corps (when Marine Corps affairs are considered).

JOINT COMMITTEES bridge the gap between the two houses. The composition of a joint committee is worked out by the party organizations. There are standing joint committees on atomic energy, defense production, the Library of Congress, and other subjects. Temporary joint committees are established to perform special short-lived duties, such as planning the nation's Bicentennial. The most common form of joint committee is the conference committee.
See also Committee System of Congress.

JOINT SESSION, a meeting of the House and the Senate together. An infrequent event, the extraordinary session is generally held to hear addresses by the President. It may also be convened to hear a visiting foreign leader or national heroes, such as the astronauts. Joint sessions are held in the House chamber, with the Speaker of the House and vice president on the dais.
See also Session.

JONES v. ALFRED H. MAYER CO., 392 U.S. 409 (1968), concerns private racial discrimination in the sale of property. Jones sued under a section of the Civil Rights Act of 1866, alleging that the Mayer Co. had refused to sell him a home for the sole reason that he was black. The Mayer Co. alleged that the section applied only to state action and did not concern private refusals to sell. In the opinion of the Court, the act bars all racial discrimination, private as well as public, in the sale or rental of property and is a valid exercise of the power of Congress to enforce the Thirteenth Amendment. Mr. Justice Harlan, in a well-reasoned dissent reviewing the legislative history here involved, concluded that it was far from certain either that the Civil Rights Act of 1866 was meant to apply to private action or that the Thirteenth Amendment permits federal interdiction of private acts of racial discrimination of this type.
See also Civil Rights Cases.

JOURNAL OF THE FEDERAL CONVENTION. *See* Madison's Journal.

JOURNEYMAN, skilled worker who has finished an apprenticeship and learned a particular skill or craft. In medieval Europe a worker became an apprentice and then a journeyman, finally entering a guild as a master who trained his own apprentices. A number of labor unions organized along craft lines still use the term.

JUDICIAL ACTIVISM refers to the proclivity of judges to overrule principles of law established by prior decisions and to enunciate new legal principles. On any scale, judicial activism runs counter to one of the prime social objectives of the law: the need for preestablished and certain rules in accordance with which men can order their affairs. Nevertheless, as society changes, so must the law. The difficulty is to strike a balance between certainty and justice. Insufficient judicial activism in England in the Middle Ages led to the development of equity, while the extreme judicial activism of the Warren Court led to President Nixon's call for "strict constructionism."
See also Stare Decisis.

JUDICIAL BRANCH. *See* Judicial System.

JUDICIAL CONSTRUCTION, considerations by legislators and judges that are taken in interpretation of the Constitution and legislation. Some questions asked are: Should paramount importance be given to the language used?; Should the intent of the framers be the test?; Should decisions be based on the broad principles that underlie the text, not just the specific wording?; Ought decisions to reflect the values of the community? Judicial conservatives argue that judges should be less willing to base interpretations of the law on public moods or personal political leanings. Activists respond that facts, judicial precedent, legislative intent, and life experience all must guide a judge's decision making.

JUDICIAL REVIEW, the power of a court to review actions of other public officials to determine whether the actions are constitutional or unconstitutional. Judicial review is not mentioned in the Constitution, but the Supreme Court asserted in *Marbury v. Madison* (1803) that the Court has the right—and even the obligation—to interpret both laws and the Constitution. Although the Supreme Court ruled that it did not have the power to issue a writ of *mandamus* in this instance, in actual fact it successfully laid the groundwork for the power to override acts of Congress by judicial review. The power is derived from interpretation of Article VI, Section 2, of the Constitution (the "supremacy clause") and the assumption that the courts were to be the final arbiter of the Constitution. Further, Alexander Hamilton specifically stated in *The Federalist Papers #78* that the courts were to ascertain the meaning of the Constitution and of acts arising under it.

Judicial review is used by state courts as well as federal courts. The decision of the highest state court is final on questions of whether action of state officials violates the state constitution. Federal courts have final jurisdiction over cases involving interpretation of the national Constitution. Judicial review should be distinguished from routine appellate, or appeals, jurisdiction of courts.   —*Mary L. Carns*

See also Appellate Jurisdiction.

JUDICIAL SELF-RESTRAINT, theory that the courts should defer, except where compelling circumstances exist, to the elected branches of the government. As expressed by Justice Louis Brandeis in *Ashwander v. Tennessee Valley Authority* (1936), the federal courts should limit their jurisdiction to actual cases and not give advisory opinions. The Supreme Court ought not to pass upon constitutionality in a friendly, nonadversary proceeding. It should not anticipate a question of constitutional law in advance of the necessity of deciding it. It should not formulate a rule of constitutional law broader than is required by the precise facts to which it is to be applied. The Court ought not to pass upon a constitutional question if there is also present some other ground on which the case may be disposed. It should not pass upon the validity of a statute at the insistence of one who has availed himself of its benefits. When the validity of an act of Congress is drawn into question and a serious doubt of constitutionality is raised, it is a cardinal principle, according to Brandeis, that the Court first ascertain whether a construction of the statute is possible by which the question may be avoided.

JUDICIAL SYSTEM. Taken together, the federal courts, state courts, and municipal courts form a complex judicial system in the United States. The regular federal court structure is in three tiers: The Supreme Court, eleven courts of appeals, and ninety-one district courts.

District Courts are the trial courts, or courts of original jurisdiction. They can hear cases involving the United States Constitution, acts of Congress, or treaties with foreign countries; civil suits between citizens of different states where the amount in controversy exceeds $10,000; cases involving admiralty or maritime jurisdiction; cases where the United States is a party; cases instituted by a state against residents of other states; cases between the state or its citizens, and foreign countries or individuals; and cases between two or more states.

There are from one to four districts in each state, one in the District of Columbia, and four in the territories. They are staffed by one to twenty-four judges, although each district usually has two. Decisions of a district court may be appealed to the

FEDERAL COURT SYSTEM

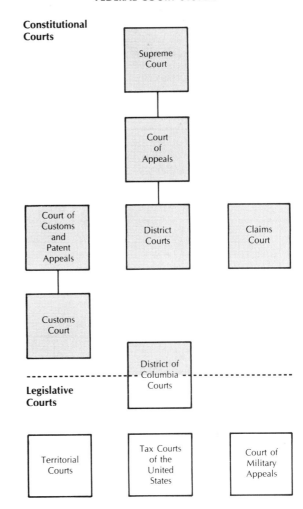

Supreme Court: (1) if a federal law is held unconstitutional; (2) if a decision in a criminal case goes against the United States; or (3) in certain cases having to do with particular congressional acts or independent agencies. Generally speaking, however, most appeals from district courts are lodged with the courts of appeals.

Courts of Appeals have appellate jurisdiction over cases from the district courts, from the regulatory commissions, and the Tax Court of the United States. There are from three to nine judges on each court of appeals, with larger circuits being subdivided into panels of three judges each.

The United States Supreme Court is the court of last resort for the nation. It hears appeals from the courts of appeals, the district courts and the highest state courts in cases where a federal question is raised. The Supreme Court can also hear appeals from the

THE FEDERAL COURTS

The Supreme Court of the United States

Nine justices, appointed for life by the President with the "advice and consent" of the Senate. Created by the Constitution, Article III. Interprets and applies the Constitution and all federal statutes, after decision by federal courts of appeal and state supreme courts. Hears argument in about 200 cases each year.

The State Courts

State Supreme Courts

Decides questions of law on briefs and oral arguments. Fifty states.

Intermediate Courts of Appeal

Discretionary review; 24 states.

State Superior Courts

Major cases, criminal and civil; trials with or without jury. One in each county.

Specialized Courts

Probate, Domestic Relations, Juvenile

State Local Agencies

Zoning boards, licensing boards, etc.

District Courts

In small towns; a justice of the peace; in large urban centers, a municipal or district court. Minor crimes and civil suits.

The Federal Courts

U.S. Circuit Courts of Appeals

Eleven circuits. Created by Congress in 1891. Each court decides questions of law on briefs and oral arguments.

Direct appeal

Specialized Courts

1. Court of Claims
2. Court of Customs and Patent Appeals
3. Court of Military Appeals

Federal Agencies

Interstate Commerce Commission, Tax Court, Securities and Exchange Commission, National Labor Relations Board, Federal Trade Commission, etc.

U.S. District Courts

Each district has from 2 judges (Wyoming) to over 40 judges (Southern District of New York). 93 districts.

Administrative Law Judges

Civil-service positions. Conduct hearings and submit reports and recommendations to administrative boards or agencies.

U.S. Commissioners

Conduct preliminary hearings; determine bail; assist district judges by serving as special masters and reporting suggested findings to judge.

special federal courts, but rarely does so. It has original jurisdiction when a state is a party and in cases involving ambassadors and ministers.

In the past, the Supreme Court has been staffed with four to ten justices, but has had nine for over a century. Its political power derives from judicial review, which allows it to be the final arbiter over decisions by other government agencies that purportedly conflict with the Constitution.

Special Courts. The federal judicial system also contains a number of special federal courts. The customs court reviews decisions of customs collectors. The court of customs and patent appeals hears appeals from decisions of the customs courts and the patent office. The court of claims hears cases instituted against the United States in civil, nontort areas. The court of military appeals reviews courts martial. The tax court, actually an executive agency, hears cases involving federal taxes.

Federal Judges (except those on the court of military appeals and the tax court) are appointed for life or "for good behavior"; the only procedure for removal is impeachment. Judges on the court of military appeal serve for 15 years; those on the tax court serve for 12 years. All judges are appointed by the president with the advice and consent of the Senate. The Senate Judiciary Committee and the American Bar Association are the two groups which have the most influence over whether or not a presidential nominee will be approved. Although more frequent in recent years, rejection by the Senate—either through formal vote or forcing the president to withdraw the nomination—is rare.

State Judicial Systems vary enormously, organizing their courts on from three to four levels. At the bottom are magistrate courts and those courts which have specifically limited jurisdiction. Magistrate courts are also known as police courts, justice of the peace courts, county courts and municipal courts. Examples of courts of limited jurisdiction include family courts,

probate courts, small claims courts, juvenile courts and domestic relations courts. These courts hear criminal and civil cases, where the crime involved is normally a misdemeanor or the civil claim is quite small.

The second level courts are usually labeled circuit, superior or district courts. In most states these courts possess both criminal and civil jurisdiction, although 16 states have separate courts for special kinds of jurisdiction. They are variously called courts of record, criminal courts, courts of common pleas, county courts, workmen's compensation courts, courts of industrial relations, corporative courts, hustings courts, law and equity courts, law and chancery courts and chancery courts. In addition, several cities have municipal courts at this level. Most states have only three levels of courts, but 14 states have an intermediate level of appellate courts above the circuit, superior or district courts but below the state's highest tribunal.

All states have a court of last resort, staffed with three to nine judges. Usually termed the state supreme court, this tribunal makes final determinations of questions of law on appeal from the lower courts. If a federal question is involved, a decision of a state supreme court may be appealed to the United States Supreme Court.

Selection procedures for state courts also vary. In ten states, the governor appoints judges above the magistrate level. There is a partisan election in 17 states, a nonpartisan election in 16, and a legislative election in four.

For the magistrate level, judges usually serve two or four year terms. Judges serving the major trial courts and intermediate appellate courts have four and six year terms, and state supreme court judges serve for six, eight, ten, 12 years, life, or until age 70.

—David F. Forte

See also Appeals, Court of; District Court; Supreme Court of the United States.

JUDICIARY ACT (1789) established the framework of the American judicial system and helped extend the powers of the federal government. The act provided for a Supreme Court, composed of a chief justice and five associate justices; 13 district courts; three circuit courts, each made up of two Supreme Court justices and a district judge; and an attorney general.

The act represented a compromise between two forces: one wanted a powerful judiciary to administer a uniform United States code of justice, and the other wanted existing state courts to enforce federal laws. Section 25 strengthened federal powers by permitting the Supreme Court to judicially review the states' highest courts when they upheld state laws that conflicted with federal statutes: the Constitution did not explicitly grant the Court these powers.

See also Judicial System; Supreme Court of the United States.

THE FEDERAL COURT SYSTEM: APPELLATE AND DISTRICT COURTS

Circuit	States Included	Federal Judges Appellate	District
1st	Maine, New Hampshire, Massachusetts, Rhode Island, Puerto Rico	7	32
2nd	New York, Connecticut, Vermont	16	77
3rd	Pennsylvania, New Jersey, Delaware, Virgin Islands	18	69
4th	Virginia, West Virginia, Maryland, North Carolina, South Carolina	14	60
5th	Texas, Louisiana, Mississippi	20	77
6th	Michigan, Ohio, Kentucky, Tennessee	21	74
7th	Illinois, Indiana, Wisconsin	15	55
8th	Missouri, Iowa, Minnesota, North Dakota, South Dakota, Nebraska, Arkansas	14	62
9th	California, Alaska, Hawaii, Washington, Oregon, Idaho, Montana, Arizona, Nevada, Guam, Northern Mariana Isl.	36	118
10th	Colorado, Kansas, Oklahoma, New Mexico, Utah, Wyoming	13	47
11th	Alabama, Florida, Georgia	18	70
D.C.	District of Columbia	13	21

JURISDICTION, the authority of a court over a particular question. There are several elements of jurisdiction. Subject-matter jurisdiction is the authority to consider a particular class of cases. Federal courts, for example, do not have the power to decide cases between citizens of the same state unless a federal question is involved. Jurisdiction *in rem* is jurisdiction over things, typically land. The third element of jurisdiction is the power to grant the relief requested. The most difficult element is jurisdiction over the person. At the common law, jurisdiction over the person is synonymous with power over him: it is necessary and sufficient to "serve" him within the territory over which the court has authority. The civil law, on the other hand, considers the person subject to the court's authority if the relationship that is the subject of the dispute is within the territory of the court.

Jurisdiction may also be original or appellate, civil or criminal. Jurisdiction may also refer to concurrent jurisdiction, where cases may originate in either state or federal court, or to exclusive jurisdiction, in which jurisdiction rests entirely with one level.

See also Appellate Jurisdiction; Civil Law; Criminal Law; Venue.

JURY SYSTEM *or* **TRIAL BY JURY,** a trial of issues of fact by impartial persons selected from the community and supervised by a judge to ensure fair trial according to the legal rules applicable to the case. A rudimentary jury system came to England with the

Conquest and evolved into an institution justly regarded as a bulwark of liberty. The system is considered so essential to liberty that it is guaranteed by the Seventh Amendment and the state constitutions. These provisions guarantee jury trial only where it existed at the common law; it is not applicable to suits in equity. Historically, the jury was made up of witnesses, selected because they knew the facts. As society became more complex, the jury evolved into trier of, not witness to, the facts, and elaborate rules of evidence were developed to ensure a fair presentation of facts. Trial by jury and the rules of evidence were peculiar to common-law countries.

JUSTICE, U.S. DEPARTMENT OF, a federal department responsible for enforcing federal laws and representing and advising the federal government in legal matters. The Justice Department was established in 1870 with the Attorney General as the head. The Office of the Attorney General had been in existence since 1789 with cabinet rank, but he did not head a department. The Justice Department also supervises federal penal institutions, investigates violation of federal laws, and supervises United States attorneys and marshalls. The department is organized into offices, divisions, bureaus, and boards.

Offices. The Office of the Attorney General, the offices of the Deputy Attorney General, and the Associate Attorney General oversee the entire department. The Attorney General is the chief law officer of the federal government, the Deputy Attorney General and the Associate Attorney General act as chief liaisons with other departments, recommend nominations for judicial appointments, and advise on pending legislation. Other offices include that of the Solicitor General, who represents the government in the Supreme Court; the office of Legal Counsel, which provides legal advice to the departments of government and the president; and the Office of the Pardon Attorney, who deals with pardon and executive clemency appeals to the president.

Divisions. Prominent divisions in the department include the Antitrust Division, which enforces federal antitrust laws and also represents the United States in judicial proceedings involving such agencies as ICC and FTC. The Criminal Division enforces all federal criminal laws not assigned to other divisions; these categories include mail fraud, organized crime, kidnapping, counterfeiting, and narcotics and dangerous drug laws. The Civil Division, which represents the United States in civil proceedings, has a wide range of responsibilities including the Customs Courts; patent, trademark, and copyright cases; foreign litigation; admiralty and shipping; and fraud cases. Other divisions are the Community Relations Service, which advises on minority problems; the Law Enforcement Assistance Administration, which works with local governments to reduce crime; the Civil Rights Division, which enforces federal civil-rights laws; the Land and Natural Resources Division, which conducts legal action on air and water pollution violations; and the Tax Division, which litigates for IRS.

Bureaus. Most famous of the bureaus is the Federal Bureau of Investigation (FBI), established in 1907 and charged with investigating all violations of federal laws. Two other particularly active bureaus are the Drug Enforcement Administration, established in 1973 to control drug abuse and regulate legal trade in narcotics and dangerous drugs; and the Immigration and Naturalization Service, created in 1891 to regulate immigration, patrol United States borders, and supervise the naturalization process. The Bureau of Prisons supervises federal penal institutions.

JUSTICIABLE QUESTION, areas of law that may properly be decided by a court. Justiciable questions involve real and substantial cases and controversies in which a genuine dispute occurs, the parties to the dispute have standing to sue, and the court has jurisdiction.   —*Mary L. Carns*
See also Cases and Controversies; Political Question.

JUVENILE COURTS. Juvenile courts emerged at the turn of the century to act in the best interests of children and, at the same time, to safeguard society. A juvenile court established in Illinois in 1899 was the first of its kind in the world. The system soon spread throughout the country. The goals were to investigate, diagnose, and prescribe treatment intended to divert the child from a possible life of crime. The offender's background was seen as more important than the facts of a given incident. Adversary tactics of the regular courtroom were thought to be out of place since the mutual aim was not to contest or object but to determine the best treatment plan for the child in a more informal atmosphere. The intention of the juvenile courts was to deal with the youths in their community under probationary supervision.

These courts have come under attack from the Supreme Court for denying children their constitutional rights. It has been argued that the juvenile courts have failed to have a positive impact on youths and that the problem of delinquency is too deeply rooted in society to be lessened effectively during a short court session. Probation remained inadequate to the task. A high proportion of children were sent to state reformatories or transferred to adult criminal courts.

Today the courts are faced with such problems as inferior status, overload, hurried trials, faulty recording practices, and limited funding. Two landmark cases, *Kent v. United States* (1966) and *In Re Gault* (1967), have given juveniles due process rights. As a result children now have the right to counsel, to adequate notice of charges, to remain silent, to confront witnesses, and to cross-examine. At the same time that these decisions established broader rights for juveniles, they did not abolish the informality of the juvenile courts that was seen as helpful to juveniles. Nor did they outlaw the practice of punishing children for status offenses (that is, determining that they were persons in need of supervision for actions such as truancy or running away, which would not be punished if done by adults).   —*Martin Gruberg*
See also In Re Gault.

KAISER ALUMINUM v. WEBER. *See* United Steelworkers of America v. Weber.

KANSAS-NEBRASKA ACT (1854), a landmark measure in the pre-Civil War political struggle between slavery and anti-slavery groups. The bill was introduced by Sen. Stephen Douglas as a method of ostensibly organizing Kansas and Nebraska as territories. By embracing "popular sovereignty" and leaving the question of slavery undecided, the act repealed the Missouri Compromise (1820), which prohibited slavery in Louisiana Purchase territory north of 36° 30′. Douglas' sponsorship has been linked to his desire for a transcontinental railroad through the area, his belief in self-government, and his effort to win Southern support for the presidency. Anti-slavery forces vehemently attacked the bill, but Douglas eloquently defended it in the Senate and saw the act through Congress. Opponents of the act banded together and formed the Republican party to fight slavery's extension.

See also Douglas, Stephen Arnold; Popular Sovereignty.

KATZENBACH v. McCLUNG, 379 U.S. 294 (1964). The Thirteenth, Fourteenth and Fifteenth Amendments, the Civil War amendments, were at one time the primary means the law provided for protection against racial discrimination. In the last few years, however, the commerce clause has increasingly been used to augment these amendments. In *Katzenbach v. McClung,* the owners of a small restaurant in Birmingham, Ala., challenged the constitutionality of the Civil Rights Act of 1964. The restaurant catered to a few transients, but it did discriminate against local blacks by refusing to serve them. The Court upheld the exercise of the Congressional power under the commerce clause on the grounds that the food the restaurant served had been shipped in interstate commerce. Thus, the Court said, Congress had the power to make the restaurant's discrimination illegal. The Court obviously recognized that Congress was really legislating against discrimination rather than trying to facilitate the flow of food in commerce, but felt this did not impair the constitutionality of the legislation.

See also Civil Rights Acts; Heart of Atlanta Motel, Inc. v. United States.

KATZENBACH v. MORGAN, 384 U.S. 641 (1966), questions the constitutionality of the section of the Voting Rights Acts of 1965, which states that no person who has successfully completed the six primary grades in a public or private school in Puerto Rico shall be denied the right to vote because of his inability to read and write English. A group of New York residents challenged the election laws of New York, which required an ability to read and write English as a voting condition. Under these laws, several hundred thousand New York City residents who had migrated from the Commonwealth of Puerto Rico were denied the right to vote. The Court held that the New York English literacy requirement could not be enforced because it was inconsistent with a federal statute enacted under the authority granted to Congress by the Fourteenth Amendment.

See also Harper v. Virginia Board of Elections.

KATZ v. UNITED STATES, 389 U.S. 347 (1967), questions whether a public telephone booth is a constitutionally protected area, so that evidence obtained electronically from such a booth is in violation of the right to privacy of the user of the booth, and whether physical penetration of a constitutionally protected area is necessary before a search and seizure can be said to be in violation of the Fourth Amendment. Katz was convicted, through the use of electronically ob-

tained evidence, of transmitting wagering information from a public telephone booth in Los Angeles to Miami and Boston, a violation of a federal statute. The Court held that the Fourth Amendment protects people and not simply areas. Therefore, the government's activities had violated the privacy on which the petitioner justifiably relied while using the telephone booth and thus constituted a "search and seizure" under the Fourth Amendment.

See also Nardone v. United States; Olmstead v. United States.

KENNAN, GEORGE (1904-   ), diplomat and scholar. Kennan graduated from Princeton University and entered the foreign service, where he held numerous posts throughout Europe. After World War II he served as head of the State Department's policy planning staff and as an adviser to Secretary of State Acheson. Kennan articulated the doctrine of containment and, because of his expertise on the Soviet Union, was appointed as ambassador there in 1952 but was soon recalled at Soviet insistence. He left the foreign service in 1953 and joined the Institute for Advanced Study at Princeton, returning briefly as ambassador to Yugoslavia (1961-1963). His memoirs won the Pulitzer Prize in 1968.

See also Containment Policy.

KENNEDY, ANTHONY M. (1936-   ), associate justice of the U.S. Supreme Court (1988-   ). Kennedy, a Harvard law graduate, practiced in California from 1961 to 1975 while also teaching a constitutional law course. He was then appointed by President Ford to a seat on the U.S. Court of Appeals for the Ninth Circuit. Kennedy spent the next 13 years as an appellate judge, earning a reputation as a conservative advocate of judicial restraint. He was unanimously confirmed to the Supreme Court in February 1988, following the defeat of Robert Bork, who was President Reagan's first choice for the seat. Kennedy generally sided with the Court's conservatives.

KENNEDY, EDWARD (1932-   ), Democratic political leader and senator from Massachusetts. Kennedy, like other members of his family, graduated from Harvard and went into politics. He was elected in 1962 to the Senate seat previously held by his brother John. Kennedy has held a number of leadership positions in the Senate and is known for his outspoken support of liberal causes. His reputation suffered from his involvement in the 1969 Chappaquiddick Island incident when he was charged with leaving the scene of a fatal road accident. Although Kennedy was often mentioned as a presidential candidate, he declined to seek the nomination until 1980, when he unsuccessfully challenged President Carter.

KENNEDY, JOHN FITZGERALD (1917-1963), 35th

John F. Kennedy, 35th President of the United States, 1961-1963.

President of the United States (1961-1963), and first Catholic to occupy the presidency, assassinated in the third year of his term. John F. Kennedy was born in Brookline, Mass., to Joseph P. Kennedy, a well-known Democrat who was to become ambassador to England, and Rose Fitzgerald Kennedy, the daughter of a prominent politician in Boston. A graduate of Harvard University in 1940, Kennedy entered the Navy the following year and distinguished himself in the South Pacific. He came to the House from Massachusetts in 1946 and was reelected in 1948 and 1950. He defeated Republican incumbent Henry Cabot Lodge, Jr., for the Senate in 1952 and was reelected in 1958.

President. Kennedy tried for the Democratic vice-presidential nomination in 1956, but he lost a close floor fight at the Democratic national convention to Estes Kefauver. In 1960 solid support at the convention gave him the Democratic nomination for the presidency. He was elected president in November, defeating Richard M. Nixon by only 112,000 popular votes and 84 electoral votes. The president was assassinated in Dallas, Texas, on November 22, 1963. He was buried with full military honors in Arlington National Cemetery. Kennedy authored three books: *Why England Slept* (1940), *Profiles in Courage* (1956), for which he won a Pulitzer Prize, and *Strategy for Peace* (1960).

John Fitzgerald Kennedy brought new youth to the presidency in 1961. Realizing that his victory over Nixon had been a narrow one, Kennedy set out to improve his public image. He surrounded himself with young, liberal, academically oriented assistants and set about to personalize the presidency by attempting to combine Roosevelt's technique of personal political control with Eisenhower's institutionalization of the office. Possessed of a strong charismatic personality, Kennedy put his press conferences on live television, which showed him as a witty, quickly responsive, and intelligent man.

His short term of office was marked with little success in domestic policy because of opposition from a conservative, although Democratic, Congress. His foreign policy continued to be based on containment of Communist expansion, culminating in a successful naval blockade of Cuba and forcing the Soviet Union to withdraw its missiles from Cuba in 1962. His most notable success with Congress was the passage of the Foreign Trade Act of 1962.   —*Erwin L. Levine*

KENNEDY, ROBERT (1925-1968), Democratic political leader, U.S. attorney general, and senator from New York. Kennedy graduated from the University of Virginia Law School in 1951 and entered politics. He managed his brother John's 1952 Senate campaign and was then counsel to several Senate committees. He received national attention as chief counsel to the Senate Rackets Committee. Kennedy managed John's 1960 presidential campaign and was then appointed attorney general. He actively enforced civil rights laws and also served as one of his brother's principal advisers. Kennedy was elected to the Senate from New York in 1964. In 1968 he entered the presidential primaries against Hubert Humphrey and, on June 4, 1968, following his narrow victory in California, was assassinated by Sirhan Sirhan, an Arab immigrant.

KENTUCKY AND VIRGINIA RESOLUTIONS. *See* Nullification.

KENT v. DULLES, 357 U.S. 166 (1958), questions whether or not a citizen can be denied a passport because of his political beliefs or associations. Kent, who wanted to visit England and to attend a meeting of the World Council of Peace in Finland, was denied a passport on the grounds that he was a Communist and had exhibited a consistent and prolonged adherence to the Communist party line. Mr. Justice Douglas, writing for a Court divided five to four, stated that the right to travel is a part of the liberty of which a citizen cannot be deprived without due process of law under the Fifth Amendment, but found it unnecessary to decide the extent to which that liberty might be curtailed. Examining the relevant history, he found that the only two grounds for passport denial were related to allegiance or criminal conduct, neither of which applied in this case. The Court therefore concluded that the Secretary of State did not have the authority to deny Kent a passport.

See also Aptheker v. Secretary of State; Zemel v. Rusk.

KERNER COMMISSION. *See* Civil Disorders, National Advisory Commission on.

KERR-MILLS ACT (1960), a forerunner of Medicaid, this amendment to the Social Security Act established a program of medical-care grants for elderly people too poor to pay for adequate care but not poor enough to qualify for aid under the Social Security Act's public assistance program. The Act provided increased benefits for the elderly through payments under the existing old-age assistance program and a new medical assistance to the aged (MAA) program. The former allowed additional federal matching payments to defray costs, while the latter paid 50-80 percent of the cost of setting up state programs. State participation was optional. Under Medicaid (1965), a section of the Social Security Act was rewritten to provide wider coverage than did the Kerr-Mills Act.

See also Medicare and Medicaid.

KEYISHIAN v. BOARD OF REGENTS, 285 U.S. 589 (1967), concerns the validity of New York's Feinberg Law, which as administered by the New York Board of Regents, required each member of the faculty of the state university, as a condition of employment, to sign a certificate stating that he was not a Communist and that if he had ever been a Communist he had communicated that fact to the president of the state university. The faculty defendants, each of whom refused to sign the required document and received dismissal notices, challenged the constitutionality of employment provisions which made Communist party membership, as such, prima facie evidence of disqualification. In the opinion of the Court, such provisions of the law are invalid insofar as they proscribe mere knowing membership without showing specific intent to further the unlawful aims, such as the overthrowing of the government, of the Communist party.

KEYNES, JOHN MAYNARD, FIRST BARON KEYNES OF TILTON (1883-1946), British economist who revolutionized economic thought. He was born in Cambridge and educated at Eton and Kings College, Cambridge, as a mathematician. He served in the India Office 1906-1908 and in the Treasury Department 1915-1919. As treasury adviser at the peace conferences after World War I, Keynes objected to the plans for reparations and the partition of Europe. He voiced these objections in his highly influential *Economic Consequences of the Peace* (1919), which, because of his attacks on Lloyd George and Woodrow Wilson, first put Keynes in the public eye.

For the rest of his life, Keynes remained a controversial and influential economist, especially in Britain and the United States. He sought answers in many current political areas, such as currencies and exchange rates, the gold standard, and economic reconstruction. In seeking to understand the causes of the depression of the 1930s, he showed that demand in total was determined by expenditures, and that full employment was necessary for recovery. Full employment, he argued, could be achieved only if governments and central banks encouraged investment and maintained a cheap-money policy during recession.

Keynes's most important work, *The General Theory of Employment, Interest and Money* (1936), divided economists into two political camps and had a profound effect on the economic policies of Franklin D. Roosevelt and war financing in the United States and Britain.

After World War II he played an important role in planning postwar policies. He served as chief British representative at Bretton Woods, where plans for the International Monetary Fund were decided, and was the chief negotiator of the large United States loan to Britain in 1945.

KING, MARTIN LUTHER, JR. (1929-1968), civil rights leader. The son and grandson of Baptist ministers, King was born into Atlanta's black middle class. His scholarly bent led him to a doctorate in systematic theology from Boston University (1955), and family tradition to a pastorate in Montgomery, Ala. (1954). It was there that he came to national prominence (1956) as leader of the Montgomery Improvement Association, which organized a successful boycott against bus

Martin Luther King, Jr., civil rights leader and president of the Southern Christian Leadership Conference.

segregation. The crusade for full citizenship for blacks led eventually to Memphis, Tenn., where he worked to support striking sanitation workers. There he was assassinated in April 1968 by James Earl Ray, who was convicted of the murder and sentenced to life in prison.

Arrests, bombings, and threats against his life did not divert him from a crusade against segregation and discrimination. With 60 black leaders in 1957 he organized what would later be called the Southern Christian Leadership Conference, which served to coordinate all his efforts and those of his followers. Although nonviolence and civil disobedience were not King's invention, he espoused them as the only devices available to an oppressed race. He felt the futility of violence, in that it met only with greater violence. His philosophy of action was a fusion of the thoughts of Jesus and Gandhi.

At the time of his death the efficacy of his teachings was being sorely tested by outbreaks of urban violence, which had begun in Harlem in the summer of 1964. His criticism of the Vietnam War during the last year of his life put an added strain on a badly splintered civil rights movement.

He was, in his last years, the most widely recognized black leader in the country. He was the star of the interracial and eclectic March on Washington, and he was *Time* magazine's man of the year in 1963. He was awarded the Nobel Peace Prize in 1964. His efforts helped bring to fruition the wide-ranging civil rights acts of the Kennedy-Johnson administrations.

Although the civil rights movement has come to concentrate on court actions, King's legacy remains strong. In 1983 the Congress passed and President Reagan signed legislation establishing Martin Luther King Day as a federal holiday on the third Monday in January.
—Allen F. Kifer

KINGSLEY INTERNATIONAL PICTURES CORP. v. REGENTS OF THE UNIVERSITY OF NEW YORK, 360 U.S. 684 (1959), concerns the impact of New York's motion picture licensing law on First Amendment liberties, protected by the Fourteenth Amendment from infringement by the states. Kingsley submitted *Lady Chatterley's Lover* to the New York Department of Education for a license required by the state law. The license was denied and the exhibition of the picture was prevented because it advocated an immoral idea—that adultery under certain circumstances may be proper behavior. The Court unanimously held that the state, quite simply, had struck at the heart of the First Amendment's basic guarantee of freedom to advocate ideas.
See also Freedman v. Maryland.

KIRKPATRICK, JEANE (1926-   ), political scientist and diplomat. Kirkpatrick received her doctorate from Columbia University and held a number of research and academic positions before becoming a professor of government at Georgetown University. She authored numerous publications on American party politics and became active in the Democratic party. Kirkpatrick was involved in the 1972 and 1976 Democratic national conventions as a member of the Credentials Committee and the Vice-Presidential Selection Committee. Her reputation as a conservative, anti-Communist proponent of a strong defense policy brought her to the attention of the Reagan administration. She served as ambassador to the United Nations (1981-1985), where she developed a reputation as an outspoken advocate of the Reagan administration's foreign policy and as a critic of alleged U.N. domination by Third World and Communist nations. Kirkpatrick, who enjoyed considerable support from conservatives, returned to Georgetown in 1985. She officially changed her party affiliation to become a Republican in the spring of 1985.

KISSINGER, HENRY ALFRED (1923-   ), secretary of state under Presidents Nixon and Ford. Kissinger was born in Furth, Germany. In 1938 his family fled to New York City to escape Hitler's persecution of the Jews. Kissinger served in the U.S. Army in World War II and then attended Harvard, where he graduated *summa cum laude,* in 1950. He became executive director of the university's International Seminar in 1951, and in 1954 he earned his Ph.D. His book *Nuclear Weapons and Foreign Policy* (1957) put him in the forefront as a theorist on foreign affairs and defense.

Kissinger was a full professor at the center for International Affairs at Harvard (1962-1969). He served as a consultant to the National Security Council (1961-1962) and the U.S. Arms Control and Disarmament Agency (1961-1967). Kissinger was principal foreign affairs adviser to Governor Nelson Rockefeller during the 1960s. He became President Nixon's Assistant for National Security in 1969, and was appointed secretary of state in 1973, a post he retained when Gerald Ford became president.

As Nixon's assistant and closest adviser, Kissinger headed the National Security Council and was in charge of its Senior Review Group, which had power over many interdepartmental bodies. He also served as the President's emissary in secret trips to Paris to discuss proposals for ending the Vietnam War, and flew secretly to China to arrange Nixon's trip to Peking. In 1973 he shared the Nobel Peace Prize with Le Duc Tho for efforts to end the Vietnam War.

After leaving public service, Kissinger traveled extensively as a foreign affairs consultant and continued to speak out on international developments. His views were sought by the media and he had considerable influence with the foreign policy establishment. Kissinger also authored two influential books, *White House Years* (1979) and *Years of Upheaval* (1982).

KLOPFER v. NORTH CAROLINA, 386 U.S. 213 (1967), concerns the right to a speedy trial guaranteed by the Sixth Amendment. Klopfer, a zoology professor at Duke University, had been tried on criminal trespass charges resulting from a 1964 sit-in demonstration. The jury was unable to agree and the trial judge entered a *nolle prosequi* (without leave): the case was discontinued, but it could be reopened by the state solicitor at some future time. Thus, Klopfer was continually under the threat of a new trial. The Court, in an opinion delivered by Chief Justice Warren, held that the right to a speedy trial is as fundamental as any of the rights secured by the Sixth Amendment and is, therefore, incorporated into Fourteenth Amendment due process. This right was denied by the discretion vested in the judge to hold Klopfer subject to trial, over his objection, for an unlimited period.

KNOW-NOTHINGS, an alliance of secret nativist societies which merged in the 1840s to form the Supreme Order of the Star-Spangled Banner. The arrival of growing numbers of Irish and German Catholic refugees had triggered a wave of resentment against foreigners. Fearing the loss of jobs and an added tax burden, the nativists called for restricting immigration, excluding Catholics and the foreign-born from public office, and a 21-year residency requirement for citizenship.

In 1854 they reorganized more openly as the American party. Horace Greeley of the New York Tribune dubbed them "Know-Nothings" because members, when questioned about the party, gave the stock reply, "I know nothing." The following year, Know-Nothing governors were elected in six states.

At its 1856 national convention, party delegates split over the issue of extending slavery. The debate had been reopened by the passage of the Kansas-Nebraska Act, which allowed residents of those areas to decide the slavery question for themselves. Northern delegates favored a declaration that Congress forbid slavery in territories north of the old Missouri Compromise line. Southern Whigs, many of whom had joined the Know-Nothings on the break-up of their own party, succeeded in tabling the proposal without a vote. The anti-slavery contingent then walked out of the convention, and those remaining nominated ex-Whig Millard Fillmore, who was to carry only Maryland in the election.

The party lost much of its influence after the election. Many charged that its raising the fear of foreign influences had helped the Southern cause by diverting attention from the slavery question.

See also Political Parties in the United States; Presidential Elections.

KOREMATSU v. UNITED STATES, 323 U.S. 214 (1944), concerns the right of the military, under a presidential order, to evacuate persons of Japanese ancestry from the West Coast during World War II. The petitioner, an American citizen of Japanese descent, was convicted for remaining in a "military area," San Leandro, California, contrary to a military order. The Court held that Congress and the president, during time of war, had the power to order the military to exclude persons from a particular area, thus overriding the customary civil rights of such persons. In this case, the United States was at war with the Japanese Empire, and the military authorities feared an invasion. The Court emphasized that residents having ethnic affiliations with an invading enemy might be a greater source of danger than those of a different ancestry.

See also Hirabayashi v. United States.

KU KLUX KLAN (KKK), a white supremacist organization founded in Pulaski, Tennessee, in 1865 by a small group of ex-Confederate soldiers to resist Reconstructionist policies and restore state sovereignty. Though a national group, founded in 1867, was short-lived, local chapters continued to be effective in terrorizing blacks and ensuring that they did not vote.

The Klan was revived in 1915, when the range of its enemies was broadened to include Jews, Catholics,

Northern view of the Ku Klux Klan in 1874.

and the foreign-born. The modern Klan employed the ritual and regalia of its predecessor and initiated the practice of cross-burning as a warning of impending violence, usually in the form of beatings, tarring and feathering, mutilation, and murder.

In 1924 Klan membership peaked at 5 million, and the KKK gained political control in many local areas. In 1928 the Klan was largely responsible for defeating the presidential ambitions of Al Smith, a Catholic Democrat, but by the 1930s the Klan had essentially lost all national influence. The civil rights movements of the 1960s spurred a revival of the Klan. Its membership, however, was scattered and not well unified. From the late 1970s through the mid-1980s the Klan attempted to regain followers and influence by protests against blacks, homosexuals, and other minorities.

See also Civil Rights Acts: *Act of April 10, 1872.*

KUNZ v. NEW YORK, 340 U.S. 290 (1951), illustrates the problems involved in imposing those "reasonable" limits on free speech, which the Constitution allows. Kunz, an ordained Baptist minister, was convicted and fined $10 for violating a New York City ordinance which makes it unlawful to hold public worship meetings on the streets without first obtaining a permit from the city police commissioner. His permit had been revoked in 1946, based on evidence that he had ridiculed and denounced other religious beliefs in his meetings, even though the ordinance mentioned no such power of revocation. In 1947 and 1948 Kunz had been denied permits for no stated reason. Here, the Court was concerned with an ordinance which gave an administrator discretionary power to control the right of citizens to speak on religious matters. In the opinion of the Court, such an ordinance is clearly invalid as a prior restraint on the exercise of First Amendment rights.

LABOR, U.S. DEPARTMENT OF, an executive department of the federal government that enforces federal labor laws and works to improve the working

Official seal of the Department of Labor.

conditions and opportunities of wage earners. The department was created in 1884 in the Interior Department and in 1903 was made part of the Department of Commerce and Labor achieving cabinet rank in 1913.

The Office of the Secretary of Labor, in addition to administering the department, advises the president on labor policy and the enforcement of labor laws. The Secretary's office includes the Wage Appeals Board, which decides wage disputes that come under several federal laws. The Undersecretary's includes the Employees' Compensation Appeals Board, which decides workmen's compensation disputes. The legal activities of the department, especially regarding the Fair Labor Standards Act, are handled by the Solicitor of Labor.

The Bureau of Labor Affairs is a division of the department that works closely with the Department of State and advises on the effects of international labor developments on American foreign and domestic policy. The bureau recommends programs that promote United States interests in the foreign labor field.

The Employment and Training Administration oversees several employment programs, including those of the U.S. Employment Service and the Office of Employment Development Programs, which maintain a system of public employment offices and coordinate employment programs on veterans, public service careers, on-the-job training, the Unemployment Insurance Service, and the Job Corps. The Labor Management Services Administration oversees welfare and pension program operations, helps unions and employees adjust to major economic and technological changes, and advises veterans and their employers of veterans' labor rights.

The Women's Bureau creates standards and policies concerning working women. It has ten regional offices that are responsible for promoting opportunities for professional working women and investigating matters that concern the welfare of working women.

The Employment Standards Administration deals with federal labor legislation covering minimum wage, overtime pay, equal pay, child labor, age discrimination, and working conditions. Responsibility for safe and healthful working conditions is held by the Occupational Safety and Health Administration.

The Bureau of Labor Statistics collects information on the standards of living and labor for compiling the Consumer Price Index and the Producer Price Index. Much of this information is published in the Bureau's *Monthly Labor Review.*

LABOR DISPUTES, MEDIATION OF, is accomplished by a neutral third party who is of assistance to both labor and management. Currently the terms "mediation" and "conciliation" are used interchangeably. However, in conciliation the third party, or conciliator, attempts to bring the parties together and allows them to resolve their problems. In mediation the third party plays a more active role, suggesting various proposals and resolutions to both sides. Neither the mediator nor the conciliator makes decisions.

Mediation usually occurs at an early stage in negotiations and is designed to prevent more serious and long-lasting disagreements.

Because serious labor-management disputes affect the general public, national governments are active as third parties. In the United States the first government intervention took place in 1886 in Massachusetts and New York, where public mediation boards were set up. One of the earliest federal mediation boards was established by the Erdman Act (1898): the chairman of the Interstate Commerce Commission and the commissioner of the Bureau of Labor were empowered to mediate railroad labor disputes. The most important agency for mediation was established in 1913 in the Department of Labor. From this agency grew the U.S. Conciliation Service, which was most active in the 1920s and 1930s; an independent agency, the Federal Mediation and Conciliation Service, was set up in 1947.

See also Federal Mediation and Conciliation Service; National Labor Relations Board (NLRB).

LABOR-MANAGEMENT RELATIONS ACT OF 1947. See Taft-Hartley Act.

LABOR-MANAGEMENT REPORTING AND DISCLOSURE ACT OF 1959. See Landrum-Griffin Act.

LABOR MOVEMENTS IN THE UNITED STATES. The term "labor movement" does not lend itself to precise definition, but in general it comprises the full range of the economic and political expressions of working-class interests in a particular country; the historical path traversed in the development of the present character and strength of this expression; and the trends and changes underway that give indication as to its emerging patterns and features. The concept of a labor movement, though dealing with generalizations about the ways in which workers respond to the economic and social pressures upon them, does not necessarily imply a unity of ideology, organizational form, and direction among workers. Labor movements are as likely to be fragmented as they are to be internally cohesive. Nor does the term pertain only to unionism and traditional economic activity; it includes as well the political expressions of workers' goals and the involvements that labor—as individuals and acting together in unions—has entered into in their pursuit.

The American labor movement, though its long and colorful history is replete with both political and economic action of varying degrees of organizational stability and success, in its modern era has been virtually synonymous with organized labor, and thus, for the most part, the labor movement has become the union movement. Accordingly, the American labor movement comprises something on the order of 18 million workers, or roughly one-third of the nonagricultural labor force and one-fourth of the total

LABOR MOVEMENT: TOPIC GUIDE

The article on LABOR MOVEMENT IN THE UNITED STATES defines various aspects of the term "labor movement" and discusses the early history of the U.S. labor movement. An analysis of political involvement of organized labor precedes an account of the formation and development of the American Federation of Labor, followed by the Congress of Industrial Organizations, and the subsequent merger of the two.

The related articles on Labor may be divided into three groups.

Organization of Labor. Problems created by the INDUSTRIAL REVOLUTION and abuses in such fields as CHILD LABOR and the DOMESTIC SYSTEM spurred the growth of LABOR UNIONS. The most powerful labor organization is the AMERICAN FEDERATION OF LABOR AND CONGRESS OF INDUSTRIAL ORGANIZATIONS (AFL-CIO).

For descriptions of specific labor terms, see individual entries. Among the most important are STRIKE, ARBITRATION, COLLECTIVE BARGAINING, UNFAIR LABOR PRACTICES, and BOYCOTT.

Labor and the Law. Some legislative developments are described in NEW DEAL LEGISLATION, which has a glossary, and there are also separate articles on key acts, such as TAFT-HARTLEY ACT, SOCIAL SECURITY, FAIR LABOR STANDARDS ACT OF 1938, and LANDRUM-GRIFFIN ACT. Court cases affecting the status of labor have separate entries, such as UNITED STATES v. DARBY.

Types of labor legislation are covered in WORKMEN'S COMPENSATION, INJUNCTION, and RIGHT - TO - WORK LAWS.

Government and Labor. The chief federal agency concerned with labor is LABOR, UNITED STATES DEPARTMENT OF, one of whose subdivisions is LABOR STATISTICS, BUREAU OF. The department's EMPLOYMENT AND TRAINING ADMINISTRATION is responsible for a number of programs, including the JOB CORPS and the services authorized by the MANPOWER DEVELOPMENT AND TRAINING ACT.

Independent federal agencies concerned with LABOR DISPUTES are the FEDERAL MEDIATION AND CONCILIATION SERVICE, NATIONAL LABOR RELATIONS BOARD, and NATIONAL MEDIATION BOARD.

labor force in the United States. These union members belong to approximately 200 national unions, most of which are members of the American Federation of Labor-Congress of Industrial Organizations.

There is, of course, substantial turnover at the edges of this figure, with workers entering and leaving union membership, just as there is constant entry into and withdrawal from the labor force. Furthermore, workers are shifting between jobs with union jurisdiction and representation and jobs without representation and collective bargaining. Also, those geographic, occupational, and industrial areas where unionism is relatively strong and those where it is weaker are changing in relative size and employment patterns; and the dividing line between the unionized and nonunionized sectors shifts one way, then another, under pressure of the interplay of worker, employer, and public attitudes toward unionism.

Early History. Although sporadic and occasional organizations of workers can be found earlier, the labor movement in the United States began toward the end of the eighteenth century and the beginning of the nineteenth century. As economic expansion occurred, and as first merchant and then industrial capitalism broadened the scale of production and widened the accessible markets, the sectorized markets of small-scale producers were broken down, and competition between producers in markets intensified, bringing wages into play as a competitive factor.

Labor's wage position was further threatened by the growth of the factory system and its utilization of unskilled and semi-skilled labor, often women and children. To protect their jobs and to fight against the deterioration of their wage position, workers organized and struck—to restore wage cuts, to achieve job security through the closed shop, and perhaps to gain some degree of permanent recognition by the employer.

Labor's response to the pressures of industrial expansion also took political expression. To keep open the path of upward economic and social mobility, labor pursued first one and then another political objective—the right to vote, free public education, the elimination of debtors' prisons, distribution of public lands to homesteaders, credit availability at low interest rates, antimonopoly legislation, mechanics' lien laws, and so on. During the first century of its life, the labor movement vacillated between economic actions—strikes, pickets, boycotts—directed against the employer, and political involvements—third party politics, reform movements, workingmen's political groups—to effect social change.

Generally, labor's economic action flourished when the demand for labor was high, when employers had favorable produce markets, and when the economy prospered. When economic activity fell in recession and depression periods, however, market conditions and employer resistance worked against the success of direct economic confrontation. Furthermore, worker acceptance of the capitalist system itself was shaken, in greater or lesser degree, in these periods of large-scale unemployment and declining wages. Together, these two factors led to aroused political consciousness and involvement by workers to alter the system, to provide more opportunity for escape from the wage system, and to improve worker status and hopes in other ways.

Conservative Unionism. Political involvement served to undermine the continuity and growth of labor organization in several ways, and, finally, with the decline of the Knights of Labor—an inclusive, heterogeneous, multidirectional, political, and economic organization with a strong moral or uplift ideology—in the mid-1800s, the labor movement shed itself of direct political action and chose conservative unionism, accepting capitalism, forgoing politics, and relying on collective action. This philosophy, articulated by Samuel Gompers and other founders of the American Federation of Labor, proved successful as the basis for a permanent labor movement. Thus, the founding of the AFL in 1886 and the acceptance of the conservative unionism espoused by its leaders marks the beginning of the modern era in the story of labor organization in America.

For the AFL, however, its basis of strength was also its most severe limitation. The AFL's form of unionism was craft unionism—unionism of skilled workers, with jurisdictional lines defined by those skills—and the federation openly rejected industrial unionism—with jurisdictional lines determined by industry, lumping together all workers in each industry regardless of degree or type of skill.

Craft unionism has a basis of strength that industrial unionism lacks, a skill that can be collectively withheld as a means of forcing recognition and compelling bargaining by the employer. But the major structural transformations taking place in the economy, particularly the growth of the major manufacturing industries with mass production processes that used large numbers of unskilled workers, was raising in importance the unskilled worker. For the most part these workers could not look to the AFL for organization and representation of the sort they wanted, and the small, though ardent, minority member unions that confronted and opposed the conservative leadership on the issue of industrial unionism found themselves suspended from the federation.

Schism and Merger. Finally, in 1936, led by John L. Lewis, this group founded a new federation, the Congress of Industrial Organizations, which, aided immeasurably by New Deal prolabor legislation, successfully organized millions of unskilled and semi-skilled blue-collar workers into industrial unions. From that time forward, industrial and craft unionism both have flourished. Economic prosperity, a growing maturity in labor-management relations, and a continued, if modified, public policy favorable to trade unionism have all contributed to that growth. The AFL and CIO merged in 1953 and as one federation now include most unions and union members.

The union movement in contemporary America still includes much less than a majority of all workers; as geographic changes in the pattern of economic activity favor areas where unionism is not strong, and as shifting employment patterns emphasize jobs where union organization is less common, the future growth of organized labor is less than assured. How well it responds to and appeals to the needs of white-collar workers, agricultural workers, and public employees will, in large part, determine the future of the organized labor movement in America.

LABOR REFORM ACT OF 1959. *See* Landrum-Griffin Act.

LABOR STANDARDS ACT OF 1938. *See* Fair Labor Standards Act of 1938.

LABOR STATISTICS, BUREAU OF (BLS), collects and analyzes labor economics statistics for the government. BLS is particularly concerned with foreign and domestic employment, productivity, wages, industrial relations, prices and standards of living. Established in 1884 as the Bureau of Labor, it took its present name in 1913, when it was placed in the new Department of Labor. The bureau has no enforcement powers and collects data on a generally voluntary basis. Its data is issued in special bulletins and in the *Monthly Labor Review.*

See also Labor, U.S. Department of.

LABOR UNIONS, organizations of workers that exist primarily to bargain collectively with employers over the terms—wages, hours, and conditions—of employment for the workers represented. Unions are permitted and protected by the National Labor Relations (Wagner) Act of 1935. The Labor Management Relations Act of 1947 (Taft-Hartley Act) spelled out the limitations on unions in the exercise of their power, particularly in their relationship with members, employers, and the public.

History. Although thus qualified, the protection for unionism that exists today is vastly different from the long history of legal obstacles and opposition to the emerging labor movement in America. From the beginnings of unionism in the late eighteenth century until the change in public and governmental attitudes toward labor organizations generated by the severe economic conditions of the Great Depression of the 1930s, the legislatures and courts of the land, with some notable exceptions, placed one barrier after another in the path of union development. Unions were viewed, at one time or another, as illegal combinations (conspiracies) in restraint of trade; as organizations whose existence and activities, if not outright illegal, were under a cloud of uncertainty depending on subjective interpretations of the legality of their purposes or intent; and as falling within the scope of the Sherman Antitrust Act and other antimonopoly laws.

Furthermore, the strength of the institution of private property, particularly as defined to include the employer's right to conduct business in an unrestricted fashion, put the courts squarely on the side of management in labor disputes. The courts backed management's position by issuing injunctions restraining unions in their striking, picketing, and other activities, and finding state laws and even federal laws passed to redress the labor-management imbalance or otherwise to benefit labor as unconstitutional abrogations of the private property of the employer or of the right of contract of employers and employees. Thus, the turn of public policy in favor of unionism in the 1930s, although later modified, marked an acceptance of organized labor denied to it for well over a century beforehand.

Modern Unionism. Unionism has grown at an uneven pace over the years, and at any moment total membership figures can only be estimated. However, there are about 18 million union members, who belong to about 200 national unions, most of which belong to the major federation of unions, the American Federation of Labor-Congress of Industrial Organizations. Thus, roughly one-third of the nonagricultural labor force and one-fourth of the total labor force are unionized.

Mere figures are poor measures of the strength of unionism. Many unions are strong, but many are not; some obtain gains for members that soon become the pattern for all labor, but other unions claim as accomplishments advances that would have come to their members anyway. Economists thus find it difficult to specify just what unions have obtained for their members, particularly in regard to wages. But if agreement exists, it is that unionism has made two great contributions to workers; job and income security, and fairness in industrial relations, under terms set forth in the contract and given life by the grievance procedure.

Internal Organization. The members belong to national unions, which may originally have been craft unions, with jurisdictions defined to include all workers of a particular trade or skill, cutting across industry lines, or to industrial unions, comprising all workers in a particular industry regardless of skill or craft. Now, however, unions are usually quite heterogeneous in membership. Although most nationals belong to the AFL-CIO, they have surrendered little of their autonomy to it. The nationals are each made up of numerous locals, which are their building blocks, in the sense that they recruit eligible members, have continuing contact with them, perform numerous services for them, and are the contact point between them and the national union leadership. In addition, there may be intermediate-level organizations between the locals and the national, and between the nationals and the federation. Each of these unions in the labor movement, from the smallest local to the 15 million member AFL-CIO, has its officers and functionaries, who make unions and federations viable and operating organizations, now very much a part of the total relationship between employees and employers.   —*Leonard G. Schifrin*

See also American Federation of Labor-Congress of Industrial Organizations, International Brotherhood of the Teamsters; Taft-Hartley Act.

LA FOLLETTE, ROBERT M(ARION) (1855-1925), U.S. congressman and governor of Wisconsin, noted for his progressive reform programs. He was trained in the law but entered politics as a Republican district attorney and was elected (1884) to the House of Representatives, serving until 1890. La Follette then returned to Wisconsin to practice law and became the leader of the progressive wing of the party. He advocated direct primary nomination, higher corporation taxes, control of railroads, and lower tariffs. His policies attracted support, and La Follette was elected governor in 1900.

In 1905, La Follette was elected to the Senate,

Robert M. La Follette, "Fighting Bob," sought liberal reform. He headed the 1924 Progressive party.

where he served until his death. His career was marked by continued support of the liberal causes he had championed in Wisconsin. La Follette, however, was opposed to entry into World War I and to the League of Nations. After the war he continued with his reformist goals and demanded investigations into the scandals of the Harding administration. In 1924 he ran for president on the Progressive ticket, polling 5 million votes. La Follette was a popular, iconoclastic politician with a strong commitment to basic economic and social reforms.

His eldest son was elected to the Senate after La Follette's death and led the Wisconsin Progressives until 1946, when they reentered the Republican party. His second son served as governor of Wisconsin during the 1930s.

LA FOLLETTE SEAMEN'S ACT (1915), or Furuseth Act, was the first law to give sailors the same basic rights as factory workers. The bill abolished imprisonment for desertion by merchant seamen, reduced penalties for various disciplinary infractions, fixed wages, and ameliorated living and working conditions, including the right to join a union. The act also strengthened maritime safety requirements.

Andrew Furuseth, president of the Seamen's Union, had promoted seamen's legislation for many years before it was introduced in Congress, only to receive a pocket veto from President Taft in 1913. Sen. Robert La Follette reintroduced the measure, which was signed by President Wilson after much hesitation and a dramatic shift to support it by Senator Bryan. Critics asserted that it would abrogate numerous international maritime agreements, but La Follette pledged that the administration would be given ample time to renegotiate treaties.

LA GUARDIA, FIORELLO HENRY (1882-1947), congressman and mayor of New York City, where he was born and died. After the death of his father, an Army bandmaster, in 1898, he settled in Europe before returning to New York in 1907.

After attending law school, he became involved in politics as a Progressive Republican, running unsuccessfully for the House of Representatives in 1914 against the Democratic machine, Tammany Hall. He won an upset victory in the same district in 1916. After voting for United States entry into World War I, he left the House to enter the Army. Following heroic service, he returned to New York, where he was elected president of the Board of Aldermen in 1920.

La Guardia reentered the House in 1922 and was reelected until 1932. He was associated with liberal legislation and cosponsored the Norris-La Guardia Anti-injunction act, which outlawed antiunion practices. He was the Fusion party's successful candidate for mayor of New York in the 1933 election that followed Jimmy Walker's resignation. La Guardia continued as mayor until 1945, when he declined to run again. His administration was noted for its impartiality—he removed many jobs from political patronage—and for its improvement of municipal services, housing, and transportation.

In 1946 he became the first director of the U.N.'s Relief and Rehabilitation Administration (UNRRA), stepping down in December. Criticized as autocratic, La Guardia was a forceful politician who pushed through much-needed reforms in New York.

LAISSEZ-FAIRE (Fr., leave alone), the minimal government regulation of the economy. The doctrine was developed in Herbert Spencer's social Darwinism in late nineteenth-century England. Laissez-faire's spokesman in America was William Graham Sumner. The social Darwinists argued that the principles underlying a free market were similar to those of evolution: individual and group economic competition preserved the strong and eliminated the weak. In the process, the economy prospered and all men benefited. Government interference tampered with the laws of nature and therefore could only be harmful. Some advocates went so far as to argue that because God created nature, governmental regulation of the economy was sinful.

See also Capitalism; Socialism.

LAME DUCK, in United States political practice, an elected official who remains in office between his own defeat for reelection and the inauguration of his successor. The Twentieth Amendment (1933), the lame-duck amendment, moved the date of the inauguration of the president from March to January and stipulated January 3 as the opening day of congressional sessions, thereby eliminating ineffective lame-duck officials.

LAMONT v. POSTMASTER GENERAL, 381 U.S. 301 (1965), concerns the legality of the Postal Service and Federal Employees Salary Act of 1962, which required the detention and destruction of unsealed mail determined to be Communist political propaganda from foreign countries unless the addressee had submitted a card indicating his desire to receive such mail. Lamont, who was engaged in the publication and distribution of pamphlets, brought suit for detention of a copy of the *Peking Review,* alleging that such action infringed his rights under the First and Fifth Amendments. The Court, in a unanimous decision, held the statute unconstitutional in that it required an official act, that is, the return of the card, as a limitation on the exercise of the addressee's First Amendment rights.

LAND-GRANT COLLEGES. *See* Morrill Act.

LAND GRANTS, donations of public lands to subordinate governments, corporations, or individuals. In the United States, land grants have been made to railroads, settlers, and states, especially for educational institutions.

The federal government began giving land grants to states for educational support in 1802. In 1862 the Morrill Act provided land grants to states for the endowment and support of colleges that would "promote the liberal and practical education of the industrial classes in the several pursuits and professions of life." Agricultural and mechanical education was emphasized.

Beginning in 1850, railroads received land grants from the federal government in exchange for reduced rates on government traffic. These land grants, in addition to saving the government money, helped to lower construction costs and therefore encouraged the building of railroads in unsettled parts of the country. This arrangement was in effect until 1946. During the Civil War the Homestead Act (1862) was passed. It granted ownership of up to 160 acres without cost to anyone who lived on the land and cultivated it for five years.

LAND MANAGEMENT, BUREAU OF. *See* Interior, United States Department of the.

LANDRUM-GRIFFIN ACT (1959), also referred to as the Labor Reform Act or the Labor-Management Reporting and Disclosure Act. Passed as a result of the McClellan Senate Rackets Committee hearings in the mid-1950s, the Act aims to prevent misuse of union funds and pensions, to preserve union democracy, and to curb outside influence or coercion in labor-management disputes. With the Taft-Hartley Act, it represented a new trend in labor legislation designed to control rather than protect unions. The Act ensures free speech and free and periodical union elections; makes mandatory filing of signed financial and administrative reports, as well as the government-approved bonding of all officials handling union funds; bars from office individuals with criminal records or conflicting business interests; further codifies unfair labor practices; and defines NLRB jurisdiction. A provision to bar Communist party members was stricken by the Supreme Court in 1965. The Department of Labor's Office of Labor-Management and Welfare Pensions Reports enforces the reporting and disclosure provisions.

LAW ENFORCEMENT ASSISTANCE ADMINISTRATION (LEAA), established by the Omnibus Crime Control and Safe Streets Act (1968), LEAA is charged with helping states and local units improve their law enforcement personnel. LEAA is headed by an administrator and two assistants appointed by the president with senatorial approval, one assistant being from outside the president's party.

LAW OF THE SEA TREATY. Beginning in 1973, the United Nations sponsored negotiations to conclude a comprehensive Law of the Sea Treaty. These discussions culminated on Dec. 10, 1982, when 119 states signed the treaty. The United States was opposed to the agreement's final form despite pressure from Third World states that denounced its position as an obstruction of international cooperation. The Soviets joined in that criticism but have also expressed serious reservations about the treaty.

The Reagan administration supported provisions that allowed the free movement of all ships and planes beyond a 12-mile limit, codified a 12-mile territorial limit, allowed for free passage through straits used in international navigation, and dealt with environmental and fishing concerns. The administration was, however, opposed to a key provision that would create an International Seabed Authority to control the mining of cobalt, copper, manganese, and nickel deposits from the ocean floor beyond a 200-mile distance. The United States felt its mining interests would suffer and further objected to the administrative structure of the Seabed Authority, which would be controlled by a 36-member council. Since the question of access to resources on the ocean floor has divided the technologically advanced nations from developing Third World states, the United States feared the seabed authority might be dominated by radical Third World elements. The treaty was to be open for additional signatures for two years but would only take effect one year after ratification by 60 nations. The two-year period ended in December 1984 with 159 nations and organizations having signed. However, only a handful had ratified, with the United States, United Kingdom, and West Germany in continued opposition. By April 1989 only 40 of the needed 60 ratifications had been recorded.
— *Alexander Wellek*

LEAGUE OF NATIONS, the Paris Peace Conference, attended by 26 nations, adopted the Covenant of the League of Nations April 28, 1919.

Organization. The covenant provided for reduction of arms, suppression of private weapons manufacture, collective security without resort to arms, and respect for the sovereignty of states. The covenant provided for collective action—economic sanctions and military measures—against an aggressor.

The main organs of the league were the assembly (of all members) and the council (France, Italy, Japan, the United Kingdom, the United States, and nine members elected by the assembly). Germany joined the council in 1927. The United States' seat on the council was never occupied. Members had the right to withdraw from the league after two years' notice. The league had a secretariat and subsidiary bodies, dealing with economic and social affairs. Headquartered in Geneva, the secretariat had the task of registering and publishing all treaties.

LEAGUE OF NATIONS

(Original members marked with an asterisk)

adm—admitted
anx—annexed
wd—withdrew

Afghanistan—adm 1934
Albania—adm 1920;
  anx by Italy 1939
* Argentina
* Australia
Austria—adm 1920;
  anx by Germany 1938
* Belgium
* Bolivia
* Brazil—wd 1926
Bulgaria—adm 1920
* Canada
* Chile—wd 1938
* China
* Colombia
Costa Rica—adm 1920;
  wd 1925
* Cuba
* Czechoslovakia
* Denmark
Dominican Republic—
  adm 1924
Ecuador—adm 1934
Egypt—adm 1937
* El Salvador—wd 1937
Estonia—adm 1921
Ethiopia—adm 1923
Finland—adm 1920
* France
Germany—adm 1926;
  wd 1933
* Greece
* Guatemala—wd 1936
* Haiti—wd 1942

* Honduras—wd 1936
Hungary—adm 1922;
  wd 1939
* India
Iraq—adm 1932
Ireland—adm 1923
* Italy—wd 1937
* Japan—wd 1933
Latvia—adm 1921
* Liberia
Lithuania—adm 1921
Luxembourg—adm 1920
Mexico—adm 1931
* Netherlands
* New Zealand
* Nicaragua—wd 1936
* Norway
* Panama
* Paraguay—wd 1935
* Persia
* Peru—wd 1939
* Poland
* Portugal
* Rumania—wd 1940
* Siam
* Spain—wd 1939
* Sweden
* Switzerland
Turkey—adm 1932
* Union of South Africa
Union of Soviet
  Socialist Republics—
  adm 1934; expelled
  1939
* United Kingdom
* Uruguay
* Venezuela—wd 1938
* Yugoslavia

History. The covenant came into force, together with the Paris Peace Treaty, January 10, 1920. Although President Woodrow Wilson had called for an association of nations to guarantee political independence, the Senate did not ratify the covenant, and the United States did not join the league. All states that were neutral in World War I joined the league, which by 1927 had 52 members. Germany became a member in 1927, but it withdrew in 1933. The Soviet Union joined the league in 1934.

Japan attacked Manchuria September 1931 and made it the state of Manchukuo. The league appointed a commission to examine the problem, and the commission's recommendation that Manchuria be returned to China was rejected by Japan. A few weeks later Japan withdrew from the league. When Italy invaded Ethiopia in 1935, the league imposed economic sanctions against Italy and continued to recognize Ethiopia as an independent state.

The league failed to contain the actions of Japan, Germany, and Italy and held no meetings during World War II. The league, however, settled disputes between Finland and Sweden over the Aland Islands, frontier disputes between Albania, Greece, and Yugoslavia, border problems between Germany and Poland over Upper Silesia, Czechoslovakia-Poland border disputes, and controversies between the United Kingdom and Turkey over the Mosul area.

After the creation of the United Nations October 24, 1945, the league met for the last time in Geneva April 19, 1946.

LEAGUE OF WOMEN VOTERS, a voluntary nationwide organization of female citizens of voting age, whose objective is "to promote political responsibility through informed and active participation . . . in government." The league was founded in 1920 as an outgrowth of a female suffrage group. Members study selected issues at the local, state, or federal level to provide the public with reliable information on specific candidates. Though it may take a stand on legislative matters it favors, the league is nonpartisan and will neither oppose nor support specific candidates or parties. Headquarters are in Washington, D.C.

LEGAL AID, any of a number of programs designed to provide legal and quasi-legal assistance to persons who cannot afford to hire their own attorney. The term is frequently used to include only legal assistance of a civil—as opposed to criminal—nature, particularly since 1963, when *Gideon v. Wainwright* required a publicly appointed defense counsel in criminal cases. With increasing concern for the inability of the poor to obtain adequate legal representation, a large number of organizations, both privately and publicly sponsored, have been established to render this type of legal service. One of the oldest is the Legal Aid Society. In addition, the federal government sponsors the Legal Services Corporation with headquarters in Washington, D.C. One of the most promising developments is union-sponsored legal insurance, which keeps a law firm on retainer for a fixed annual fee to handle union members' problems without additional charge.

The Legal Services Corporation was established in 1974 to provide legal services in noncriminal cases to persons with limited incomes. It has come under increasing criticism for accepting cases involving social and political causes and for bringing lawsuits against government agencies. The criticisms were followed by sharp reductions in its budgets.

LEGATION, a second-class diplomatic establishment (inferior to an embassy). It is headed by an envoy extraordinary and minister plenipotentiary—minister for short. The minister and his legation, as in the case

---

LEGISLATION AND LEGISLATIVE PROCESSES: TOPIC GUIDE

The article on LEGISLATION AND LEGISLATIVE PROCESSES introduces the legislative process, and discusses legislative initiative and the powers of both Congress and the President, appropriations for bills, and investigation of these bills.

The related articles on legislation and legislative processes may be divided into two groups.

General Features. Articles that cover the federal legislative branch include CONGRESS OF THE UNITED STATES, which has a Study Guide, HOUSE OF REPRESENTATIVES OF THE UNITED STATES, and SENATE OF THE UNITED STATES.

Legislatures in the United States have generally been based on BICAMERALISM rather than UNICAMERALISM. Allocation of legislative seats is discussed in APPORTIONMENT, on which BAKER v. CARR had drastic effects. It is still possible to GERRYMANDER districts, however. Many lower-level legislatures provide for INITIATIVE AND REFERENDUM procedures that permit voters to register their opinions on issues.

Operations. The majority party in each house of a legislature is headed by a MAJORITY LEADER; the minority party by a MINORITY LEADER. Each may be assisted by a WHIP. As in Congress, the SENIORITY SYSTEM is a key feature of the process. Opponents of a measure may FILIBUSTER, but supporters can end debate through CLOTURE. Members who commit illegal or offensive acts may face CENSURE or IMPEACHMENT. An unreelected legislator whose term has not ended is a LAME DUCK.

A QUORUM must be present to vote on a BILL, many of which require an APPROPRIATION and some of which are classified as PORK BARREL LEGISLATION. Legislation is often presented according to a CALENDAR. ADJOURNMENT closes a legislative session.

---

of an embassy, enjoy diplomatic immunity and privileges and are extraterritorial.

See also Embassy.

LEGISLATION AND THE LEGISLATIVE PROCESS. The Congress of the United States consists of the Senate and the House of Representatives and derives authority from Article I of the Constitution. A reading of the powers enumerated in the first article will show a vast array of national responsibilities requiring diligence, study, and seriousness of purpose on the part of the Congress. Besides these enumerated powers, Congress has implied powers stemming from the clause "to make all laws which shall be necessary and proper for carrying into execution the foregoing [enumerated] powers, and all other powers vested by the Constitution in the Government of the United States, or in any Department or officer

LEGISLATIVE PROCESS

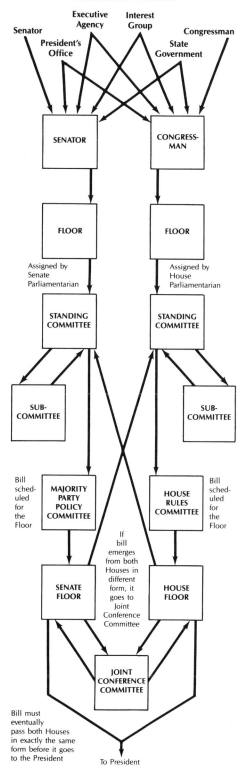

thereof" (Article I, Section 8). The legislative output of Congress is relatively small compared with the thousands of bills that are introduced in every Congress. (Congresses are numbered consecutively every two years following the election in even-numbered years.) In a recent Congress more than 11,000 bills and resolutions were introduced; fewer than six percent were enacted into law.

Legislation. A literal reading of the Constitution would lead one to believe that Congress holds the legislative initiative, with the president holding veto power over congressional bills. Bills can be introduced only by the Congress, but since the depression of the 1930s, much of the initiative for legislative leadership has been shifted to the president. Franklin D. Roosevelt's New Deal proposals, designed to lift the country from the depression, were the start of focusing the initiative in the president. The exigencies of World War II (1941-1945) and the disposition of President Harry S. Truman to deluge Congress with bills continued the trend of increasing the legislative role of the president. Even during the terms of Dwight D. Eisenhower (1953-1960), who was not a strong president, Congress continued to accept executive initiative, and it can be rightly said today that the president "proposes" and the Congress "disposes." Most of the important bills that are eventually passed by Congress are formulated, shaped, and guided through the congressional maze by the president. Bills are introduced in either house of Congress by a senator (in the Senate) or congressman (in the House) on behalf of himself, the executive branch, an agency or department, an interest group, or a state. Constitutionally, revenue bills must originate in the House of Representatives. Often a bill has several cosponsors. It is assigned to a standing committee and then must go through the labyrinth depicted in the accompanying chart. If a bill eventually passes one house, it must go through the same process in the other. Bills that pass the two houses in different forms are sent to a conference committee, which will attempt to draft a compromise version. If a bill passes both houses in the same form, the president may sign it, let it become law without his signature following ten days, or veto it. Unless both houses override his veto by a two-thirds vote, the bill is dead.

Appropriation. Most new bills, amendments of older bills, and extensions of acts of Congress require funding. The raising of money through taxation and the spending of money through appropriations have become even more important as legislative initiative has shifted to the president. Even though a president might get the legislation he wants, unless the Congress funds the agency or department designated to carry out the provisions of the bill, it is relatively useless. Ostensibly following the president, Congress holds this club over him.

In the beginning of each session, the president

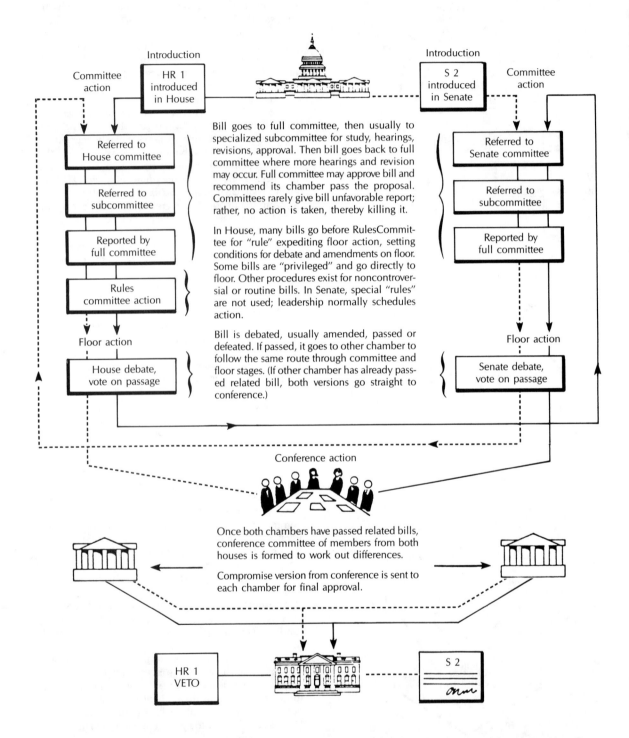

Introduction
HR 1 introduced in House

Committee action

Referred to House committee

Referred to subcommittee

Reported by full committee

Rules committee action

Floor action

House debate, vote on passage

Introduction
S 2 introduced in Senate

Committee action

Referred to Senate committee

Referred to subcommittee

Reported by full committee

Floor action

Senate debate, vote on passage

Bill goes to full committee, then usually to specialized subcommittee for study, hearings, revisions, approval. Then bill goes back to full committee where more hearings and revision may occur. Full committee may approve bill and recommend its chamber pass the proposal. Committees rarely give bill unfavorable report; rather, no action is taken, thereby killing it.

In House, many bills go before RulesCommittee for "rule" expediting floor action, setting conditions for debate and amendments on floor. Some bills are "privileged" and go directly to floor. Other procedures exist for noncontroversial or routine bills. In Senate, special "rules" are not used; leadership normally schedules action.

Bill is debated, usually amended, passed or defeated. If passed, it goes to other chamber to follow the same route through committee and floor stages. (If other chamber has already passed related bill, both versions go straight to conference.)

Conference action

Once both chambers have passed related bills, conference committee of members from both houses is formed to work out differences.

Compromise version from conference is sent to each chamber for final approval.

HR 1 VETO

S 2

Compromise version approved by both houses is sent to President who can either sign it into law or veto it and return it to Congress. Congress may override veto by a two-thirds majority vote in both houses; bill then becomes law without President's signature.

presents his "budget," which contains money requests for carrying out what he deems important. His budget is gathered from agencies, departments, the military, executive office requests, and interest groups by his Office of Management and Budget. It is traditional for the House to consider the budget first: historically, the House cuts the overall budget, the Senate restores most of the cuts, and then both houses even out their differences in a joint conference committee. Because Congress must re-fund previous actions, it is able to maintain controls over the executive power.

Investigation. Congress has the constitutional power to investigate anything remotely tied to legislative purpose. Investigations can take several avenues. When a bill is being handled by a standing committee, it investigates the merits of the bill by holding hearings on it or several similar bills. Such committees as the Senate Foreign Relations Committee and the House Internal Security Committee often hold hearings to determine if some new legislation is required. These investigations are accompanied by open hearings to hear interested persons' contributions. A third kind of investigation is called legislative oversight. This type of investigation is carried out usually by either of the government operations committees with General Accounting Office help to determine whether or not the executive branch is doing what the Congress intended when it passed and funded a bill; the Senate foreign relations and House foreign affairs committees use this ploy to focus publicity on the executive's handling of foreign policy. In the fourth type of investigation, either house investigates the ethical conduct of one of its members: the inquiry is handled by a standing committee or, at times, a special committee.

The investigative function has grown in the past several years. In its quest to influence American society in general and the executive branch in particular, Congress has attempted to enter many spheres of domestic life.

Congressional Organization. Congress is divided according to the two-party system. When one party is the majority of a house, all of its committees are in control of the party, and control of the Rules Committee in the House and the Majority Policy Committee in the Senate means control of the legislative traffic. The congressional committee system is a powerful one, and through the seniority system the chairmen of committees hold a great deal of power. The Speaker of the House heads the majority party and presides in the House. The Vice President of the United States presides in the Senate. Leadership is shared by the committee chairmen and the elected floor leaders. Party leadership is thus decentralized in the Congress. It must also be remembered that the Democrats in Congress are often divided between their Southern and non-Southern wings. Thus the Congress can sometimes be considered a three party system— Republicans, Democrats, and Southern Democrats.

See also Act of Congress; Bill; Committee System of Congress; Conference Committee; Congress of the United States.

LEGISLATIVE BRANCH, a part of the government primarily responsible for the making of law, for example, the Congress of the United States. The legislature need not be so separated from the other branches of government as in the United States, where a fear of tyranny limited the power of any one branch. Even in such a system, there is a mixture of functions; for example, the executive wields such lawmaking functions as the power to veto bills passed by Congress. This sharing of powers by the other branches enables them to check the exercise of power by the legislative branch.

In parliamentary systems, however, the legislative branch may be subject to little or no check by the other branches and may even be the source of supreme legal power. In Great Britain, for example, there is no check to the legal power of the legislative branch. The legislature may be bicameral, as in the House of Representatives and the Senate in the United States or the House of Commons and the House of Lords in Great Britain; or the legislative branch may be unicameral, as in Nebraska.   —*Theodore B. Fleming*
See also Congress of the United States; Executive Branch; Judicial Branch; Separation of Powers; Parliamentary Government.

LEGISLATIVE COURT, court created by Congress pursuant to its legislative powers. Legislative courts are to be distinguished from constitutional courts, created by Congress pursuant to its constitutional power to provide for federal courts inferior to the Supreme Court (Article III, Section 1). There are two principal differences between the courts: the Constitution protects the tenure and salary of judges of Article III courts only; and because their jurisdiction is not limited to "cases and controversies," legislative courts are not prohibited from exercising administrative or legislative functions, and their judgments are not free from legislative or executive revision. The Customs Court, Court of Claims, and Court of Customs and Patent Appeals are hybrids because although the Supreme Court has held them to be legislative, Congress has declared them to be constitutional.

LEGISLATIVE DAY, in the U.S. Senate, the period of time between a recess and an adjournment. Thus, a legislative day may not coincide with a calendar day if the Senate decides to recess (rather than adjourn) at the end of a daily session. Several of the rules of procedure in the Senate are based on legislative days, such as the requirement that proceedings of the Senate listed in the *Journal* shall be read at the beginning of each legislative day. Senate leadership has occasionally attempted to break a filibuster by invoking the rule that no member may speak more than twice during a legislative day. —*Mary L. Carns*

LEGISLATIVE OVERSIGHT. *See* Investigative Power of Congress; Oversight, Legislative.

LEGISLATIVE REORGANIZATION ACTS (1946, 1970), major acts that made provision for procedural and structural changes in the legislative branch. The 1946 Act was an attempt to modernize the committee system of Congress. It provided for the establishment of professional staffs for congressional committees, reduced the number of standing committees, and included provisions under Title III for regulation of lobbying. The Act requires public disclosure of spending by groups engaged in spending primarily to influence legislation, as well as identification and registration of lobbyists. The 1946 Act also provides that Congress shall adjourn annually no later than the end of July unless otherwise specifically provided for by Congress—a date that proved unrealistic, and in 1963 Congress even went into a year-long session. In an apparent recognition of the impracticality of the July adjournment, the 1970 Act calls for a 30-day recess in August.

The 1970 Legislative Reorganization Act increased committee staff allowances, required at least three minority employees on most staffs, and made major changes in voting procedures. Recorded teller votes may be demanded by one-fifth of the quorum for the Committee of the Whole (twenty members); provision is made for electronic voting in the House of Representatives; and proxy voting is prohibited unless a committee's written rules permit it on a specific issue.

Both Reorganization Acts recognize the authority of either house to amend rules of procedure in their own manuals. Thus, the House and Senate still have separate rules with regard to proxy voting despite the limitation set in the 1970 Reorganization Act.
—*Mary L. Carns*

LEGISLATIVE VETO, a procedure whereby one or both houses of Congress would disallow an order or regulation from the executive branch by a simple majority vote. The so-called "legislative veto" was first added to legislation in 1932 but was infrequently used until the 1970s. It was usually found in statutes that delegated authority to the executive branch while retaining the power of Congress to restrict its use. By 1981, more than 200 statutes contained provisions for the legislative veto. Although the veto was not often implemented, it was seen as a potential check to executive action.

All presidents since Herbert Hoover questioned the constitutionality of this practice, considering it to be an infringement upon executive authority. The legislative veto was declared unconstitutional by the U.S. Supreme Court in 1983 in a 7-2 decision in *Immigration*

and Naturalization Service v. Chadha, which found the procedure to be a violation of the doctrine of separation of powers. Legal experts are in disagreement as to what the final effect will be on certain laws that contain provisions for a legislative veto, such as the 1973 War Powers Resolution. —*Mary L. Carns*
See also Oversight, Legislative.

LEGISLATURE. *See* Legislation and Legislative Process; Legislative Branch.

LEND-LEASE PROGRAM, a plan proposed by President Franklin Roosevelt in January 1941 to provide war materials for the Allies and to circumvent the limitations of United States neutrality legislation. Under the plan the president had the authority to sell, lend, lease, or transfer war materials to any country whose defense was vital to the United States. At the time Roosevelt introduced the plan, Europe was already deeply embroiled in the fight against fascism, and Britain and the other Allies were quickly running out of cash for the purchase of war matériel. After long and bitter debate by isolationists, Lend-Lease became law on March 11, 1941. The United States began to shift industry to war production, and neutrality was abandoned; Lend-Lease was a major step toward war. The plan was extended to Russia in June 1941 with Hitler's declaration of war on Russia. China was also brought into Lend-Lease in 1941 and supplied through the Burma Road under the protection of the Flying Tigers. Under Lend-Lease the United States provided more than $50 billion in aid to the Allies.

LEWIS, JOHN L(LEWELLYN) (1880-1969), American labor leader, president (1920-1960) of United

John L. Lewis, mine workers' and AFL leader.

Mine Workers of America (UMWA) and a founder of the Congress of Industrial Organizations (CIO). He was born in Lucas, Iowa, the son of a Welsh immigrant coal miner. Young Lewis became a coal miner and began his association with UMWA in 1909 as a legislative agent.

He became an organizer for the American Federation of Labor (AFL) in 1911, vice president of UMWA in 1917, and president in 1920. An astute bargainer, Lewis led bitter, successful coal strikes in 1919 and 1922. During the 1920s, a time of depression in the coal industry, he fought vigorously to maintain the union's viability and his own leadership.

In the early 1930s, Lewis launched an organizing campaign in the coal fields. In 1935, he and other AFL dissidents formed the CIO with Lewis as president to organize the mass-production industries, thereby fragmenting the union movement. Following the Little Steel Strike (1937), his cordial relations with President Roosevelt deteriorated. Lewis opposed Roosevelt's third-term bid and resigned as CIO president after Roosevelt's reelection. During World War II, Lewis continued the miners' struggle for increased benefits. The coal strike of 1946 led to government seizure of the coal mines and was a prime reason for passage of the Taft-Hartley Act (1947), but the miners achieved their aims. Until his death in Washington, D.C., Lewis was a bulwark of the labor movement. Frequently accused by business and government leaders of seeking personal power, he was revered by many union members.

LIBEL AND SLANDER, respectively, printed and spoken defamation of character of a person or an institution. The laws of libel and slander concern the abuse of free expression guaranteed in the First Amendment. Usually civil offenses, libel and slander may be criminal. In a slander action it is usually necessary to prove specific damage by the spoken words to recover, but in a case of libel the damage is assumed to have occurred by publication. A slander conviction carries a small fine and a reprimand by the judge, but the more serious libel conviction carries greater penalties. As Justice Benjamin Cardozo stated, "the spoken word dissolves but the written one abides and perpetuates the scandal." Members of Congress, judges, executive officials of the federal government, and state officials are immune from defamation action in the performance of their duties.

Libel Laws are state statutes and usually vary from state to state. To be actionable, libel must be published and exposed so that a third person does or might see it—newspapers, magazines, billboards, posters, a letter or postcard sent through the mail, or even an unsealed letter left on one's desk all qualify under the third-person test. Truth and motives must also be decided in the action.

The landmark case in libel is the *New York Times v.*

Sullivan (1964). The *Times* had published an advertisement that was critical of police conduct in a Mississippi town. The police chief sued for libel and won his case; but the Supreme Court reversed the decision. The Court said, "No public official could recover for defamation, no matter how false the matter complained of, unless he could show that it was uttered in reckless disregard for the truth." This rule was then extended to cover all people in the public eye. In two decisions rendered in 1971, the Court extended the *New York Times* rule to cover publications that incorrectly report charges of criminal behavior by public officials or candidates for public office. Even though these charges do not relate to the officials' public conduct or political activities, any criminal conduct is relevant to the fitness of the person to hold office. In the other decision, the *New York Times* rule was extended to all people who are involved in any matter of public concern. Thus the defamed person in such cases can vindicate himself only if he can establish reckless disregard of the truth.

LIBERALISM has been divided into classical and modern forms. Classical liberalism of the nineteenth century developed as a protest against arbitrary government and sought to check government by the expansion of democratic procedures and the minimization of government involvement in the social and economic lives of individuals and groups. Modern liberalism, in contrast, is in part a protest against concentration of economic power produced by capitalism. It has sought to utilize democratic political power to achieve by law greater economic equality and security. Liberals believe that democratically controlled governments can use the physical and social knowledge of contemporary science to produce progress in the quality of individual and social life.

See also Contract Theory; Democracy; Limited Government; Populism.

LIBERAL PARTY, a labor-oriented political organization operating exclusively in New York State. It was founded in 1942 by David Dubinsky and others who had left the American Labor party in protest against Communist influence. The Liberal party has played a decisive role in nominating and endorsing candidates of other parties, generally Democratic, both on the local and on the national level. Each year the party issues a State Legislative Program delineating its goals. Its current recommendations include full employment, an increase in the minimum wage, a national health insurance, free education on all levels, greater consumer protection, the passage of gun control laws, and prison and judicial reforms.

See also Political Parties in the United States; Presidential Elections.

LIBERAL REPUBLICAN PARTY, a reform movement established in 1872 by a wing of the Republican party opposed to President Grant's renomination because of the corruption and extreme partisanship which had marked his first term. The movement originated in Missouri, where the liberal Republicans criticized the harsh treatment of former Confederates and demanded that their voting rights be restored. Led by Carl Schurz, they nominated and elected a full state ticket headed by Benjamin Gratz Brown.

The dissident Republicans were joined by others representing a diversity of interests—free traders, protectionists, western radicals, eastern conservatives—all united by their antipathy to Grant. At the 1872 convention in Cincinnati, the party chose Horace Greeley as its presidential candidate and drafted a platform calling for civil service reform, withdrawal of troops from the South, and lowering the tariff. The Liberal Republican party became defunct after Grant's reelection in 1872.

See also Political Parties in the United States; Presidential Elections.

LIBERTY PARTY, an anti-slavery movement formed in Albany, New York in 1840 by ex-slaveholder James Gillespie Birney. Adherents felt that slavery was not only immoral but also economically disastrous because it hindered the development of non-Southern commercial and industrial interests. Repudiating the political inaction of abolitionist William Lloyd Garrison, the Liberty party nominated Birney for president in 1840 and again in 1844. In the latter election, his candidacy split the Whig vote and aided in Polk's victory. In 1848 the Liberty party merged with the Free-Soilers.

See also Political Parties in the United States; Presidential Elections.

LIBRARY OF CONGRESS, the United States national library in Washington, D.C., established in 1800. The first Library of Congress, as well as the Capitol, were burned by the British when they captured Washington, D.C., in 1814. The Library was promptly restored by Congress but did not achieve the magnitude of a national library until the late nineteenth century under the librarianship of Ainsworth Rand Spofford. In 1897 the copyright department (now the Copyright Office) was created within the Library of Congress as the depository for copyrighted works.

Supported mainly by the appropriations of Congress, although also the beneficiary of thousands of other contributors, the library's foremost responsibility is service to Congress. Its Congressional Research Service operates solely for the legislature. The library's collection of over 60 million items includes more than 15 million books and pamphlets and vast manuscript collections, music collections, maps, photographs, prints and drawings, newspapers and periodicals, motion pictures, and microfilms.

Special services of the library include a generous

Main reading room of the Library of Congress.

interlibrary loan system; the sale of sound recordings, printed catalog cards, and cumulative catalog publications; the maintenance of a National Union Catalog; extensive services for the blind and the physically handicapped through 48 regional offices; and research facilities available to individuals, private organizations, and government agencies.

LIMITED GOVERNMENT, concept related to the development of modern liberal governments. It proposes specific limitations on the scope and authority of government and its officials, to minimize the probability of tyranny. According to John Locke, whose writings served as a principal foundation for the U.S. Constitution, government authority is circumscribed within specified areas as a means of maintaining the broadest possible scope of individual liberty. Depending on the beliefs and good intentions of officials is viewed as inadequate in protecting people from government. Limited government insists that institutional checks such as a written constitution, checks and balances, and periodic elections are necessary to ensure that government serves the public rather than the private interest.

See also Consent, Popular; Constitutionalism; Contract Theory; Democracy; Participatory Democracy.

Abraham Lincoln, 16th President of the United States (1861-1865).

LINCOLN, ABRAHAM (1809-1865), Civil War president and emancipator. Born in Kentucky, Lincoln moved to Illinois as a young man. Largely self-taught, he opened a law office in Springfield in 1837. Active and well-known as an Illinois Whig, he served in the state legislature (1834-1842) and in Congress (1847-1849). He joined the new Republican party in 1856 and ran unsuccessfully for the Senate in 1858. He came to national attention in the course of a series of debates with his opponent, Stephen A. Douglas. In 1860 Lincoln was selected by the Republican convention as a compromise candidate for president.

President. During the debates with Douglas, Lincoln adhered closely to the free-soil views which were to be those of Republican moderates in 1860. He was not an abolitionist, but after his election he retracted preinaugural promises that assured the South of the federal encouragement of slavery. Realizing that as a unionist he would have to take a stand on secession and the question of protecting federal forts in states which had seceded, he chose to provision Fort Sumter and thus forced the firing of the first shot of the Civil War. As the war expanded into a major conflict, he learned to be an effective commander-in-chief and became, by the last year of the struggle, a skilled military strategist. Furthermore, his skill as a master politician held the Northern states and the slave states which had not seceded together. He tightened federal control over state governments, as well as presidential control over his party and the armies.

Abolition and Reconstruction. Lincoln gradually moved toward an abolitionist position, issuing the Emancipation Proclamation in 1862, and sponsoring the Thirteenth Amendment, which became law after his death. He was the first president to confer with black leaders and to entertain black guests in the White House.

His plan for reconstruction of the Confederate states as they were brought under Union control called for peace, repudiation of secession, and abandonment of slavery. While many Confederates wanted only peace, Lincoln's plan fell far short of what Radicals in his party wanted: military occupation of the South and political rights for black people. He was assassinated in the midst of reestablishing the Union. —*Allen F. Kifer*

LIPPMANN, WALTER (1889-1974), newspaper commentator and author. A graduate of Harvard (1909), he was instrumental in founding the *New Republic* in 1914. President Wilson was influenced by Lippmann's writings and sent him to the Versailles peace negotiations after World War I as an aide to Colonel House. After the war, Lippmann joined the New York *World* and in 1932 the *Herald Tribune*, where his column "Today and Tomorrow" was widely read and respected, receiving Pulitzer prizes in 1958 and 1962. One of the most influential journalists of modern times, he cautioned against a return to isolationism after World War II but was a sharp critic of the policy of containment.

LITERACY TEST, a voter qualification test imposed by some states. Although the Fifteenth Amendment forbids the denial of the right to vote on account of race, denial was accomplished in some states by imposing a literacy requirement. The requirement was waived, however, by a grandfather clause for those who were already voters or descendants of voters registered before Jan. 1, 1867, thus denying the vote to recently freed blacks. The grandfather clauses were struck down by the Supreme Court in 1915, but literacy requirements, which did not seem unfair on the surface, were allowed.

In the 1964 Civil Rights Act, Congress made it a presumption that any person not judged as incompetent and who had completed the sixth grade in a public school possessed sufficient intelligence to vote in any federal election. The next year Congress empowered the courts to suspend the use of tests and devices used for the purpose of denying or abridging the right to vote on account of race or color. In 1970, Congress amended the Voting Rights Act by banning a literacy test in any national, state, or local election where such a test was not already proscribed by the basic Acts.

See also Civil Rights Acts; Grandfather Clause; Voter Registration.

LOBBY, a term used to describe an organization, an interest group (also known as pressure group), or an individual that attempts to influence the passage of legislation and the administrative decisions of government. The derivation of the term may be traced back over a century to the habit of certain private citizens who regularly congregated in the lobby outside legislative chambers before a session.

History. Lobbying reached an infamous peak in the latter part of the nineteenth century, when railroad and industrial interests openly bribed state legislators for the passage of beneficial legislation. Federal policy was in turn affected, for at that time senators were not directly elected but were picked for office by state legislators.

HOW PRESSURE GROUPS WORK

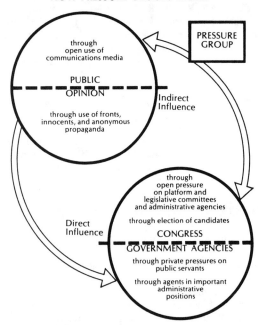

The increased complexity and specialization of twentieth-century society has seen an upsurge of interest groups and the creation of agencies and associations to present and promote their partisan views to the public and the government. Lobbyists may be full-time officials of companies of varying size and strength; individuals representing paying clients of a variety of interests and resources; or private citizens with a special grievance or goal to press.

The Standard Techniques employed by lobbyists are: (1) meeting privately with public officials to publicize the clients' interests, (2) monetary persuasion by contributions to campaign funds, (3) testifying before congressional committees; (4) membership on a federal advisory committee, and (5) working to rally public opinion by organizing telegram and letter-writing campaigns, and in some cases, considerable advertising and public relations efforts. Congressional committees, as part of the hearing process, attempt to serve as an educational arena in the process of formu-

lating laws and often also provide the setting for airing propaganda of interest groups. In calling for letters and telegrams from the public, the intention is to bring pressure to bear upon elected representatives by their constituents.

Perhaps less active on the state level than formerly, lobbyists are very much in evidence in Washington, D.C., where they far outnumber members of Congress. Probably the most influential are former public officials, who are not only familiar with procedure but who have the added advantage of personal contacts in both legislative and administrative areas.

See also Regulation of Lobbying Act.

LOBBYING ACT. *See* Regulation of Lobbying Act.

LOCAL GOVERNMENT. Local governments exist all over the world, but they cannot be given a precise definition. All of them, however, possess common characteristics:

1. a definite territory to which local authority is limited, except for such purposes as planning or nuisance abatement,

2. a definitely identifiable form of government separate both from the central government and its field offices,

3. a lack of sovereign powers of its own (in the United States, the United Kingdom, and the democracies of Western Europe, local governments are treated as corporations created by the higher government for its own convenience and that of the local citizenry's),

4. some form of local taxing power dependent, in most cases, entirely upon what the higher level of government is willing to permit,

5. some kind of authorization to enter into indebtedness or to allow for the long-term payment of the costs of expensive and long-lasting projects, such as buildings or parks, and

6. the power to choose at least some local officers.

Reasons for Existence. Local governments exist primarily for two reasons. The principal one is to provide for an administrative subdivision of the state or regional government. In this capacity the local government can serve both local residents and the more central government, as in the maintenance of records concerning real property, births, and deaths. The local government can also act to combine the powers of the state with local information about existing conditions, as in the maintenance of secondary roads or the application of public health laws under local conditions.

Local governments provide services for the comfort and convenience of local residents, businesses, and industries. In traditional American laws this second purpose was what characteristically distinguished cities and villages, that is, public corporations, from other local governments, the quasi-corporations. Var-

LOCAL GOVERNMENT GLOSSARY

Arrondissement. In France, this unit is the largest administrative division of a department, very roughly corresponding to a county. The administrative head is usually a subprefect. The term is also used in some other French-speaking countries.

Borough. In Great Britain this division is the standard term for an urban municipal government, roughly equivalent to a city in the United States. In the United States the term is used in a few states, where the borough is typically an urban community of a size somewhere between a village and city. In New York City the municipal government is divided into five boroughs, which are only administrative subdivisions with virtually no policy-making power.

City. In the United States this unit is the most common urban, municipal government. In some states municipal corporations can be formed under this title even though they have a population of only a few hundred or a few thousand people, a size that would usually be termed a village. In England a city is characteristically an urban municipal corporation in a community that also has a cathedral. Throughout history, it has been common to intermingle the terminology and institutions of religion and local government.

Commune. The basic unit of local government in France and some other countries, the commune was established after the French Revolution (1789) and, in an age when uniformity and equality were considered the ideal, was made the standard unit of local government throughout France, except for Paris. Communes, therefore, have the same basic structure and powers whether small and rural or large and urban. Communes are governed by a mayor and council.

County. The county is the chief local regional government drawn up as to area rather than as to rural or urban criteria. In England it descends from the Anglo-Saxon shire. In much of the United States the county's boundaries were determined naturally by terrain or arbitrarily by having the county seat within one day's horseback ride from any point within its boundaries. The county was primarily a unit for the administration of state functions, but it has in recent decades also become increasingly a unit for providing urban services.

County-borough. This unit of government in England is located in urban areas and combines the functions of both county and borough. The United States has a few, similar, city-county governments.

Department. In France the principal administrative district is the department. Although it has a locally elected council, the department's principal administrative officer is the prefect, who is appointed and paid by the Ministry of the Interior. Although some policy is made locally, the prefect serves as a coordinator and guide who keeps basic policy carefully aligned with that of the central government.

Parish. This unit, once based upon church attendance districts, still exists in rural areas of England, primarily to supply basic urban services to a village within a rural district. In the United States, parishes are found in Louisiana, where they correspond to counties.

Rural District. In England, these units are the successors to the parishes that once were common throughout the nonurban areas. Rural districts provide basic, local, government services similar to those of the township in the United States.

Special District. Units of local government providing, typically, only one governmental service, perhaps with services secondary to their principal objective, special districts exist in many countries for the provision of a great variety of local services. In most cases, the districts exist because of their ability to administer a function or to raise funds in an area that does not have boundaries identical to a number of other local governments'.

Town. This term is used loosely in Great Britain to indicate an urban area and in the United States to indicate either an urban area or a township. In New England the town is the principal unit of local government and includes an urban area and its rural environs all of which is administered under a single government. The town government is characterized by many elective officers and an annual meeting at which all adult citizens can participate and at which the budget and principal public policy is made.

Township. The township began as a unit for the surveying of land on the American frontier. Originally, the township consisted of an area of six miles by six miles. Because of its definite boundaries, it was easily recognized as a convenient basis for the establishment of a local unit of government. It became a subunit of the county for strictly local purposes in the Middle Atlantic states and the Midwest.

---

ious functions were once identified as being in the latter category, such as matters of parks, recreation, water supply, and public transportation, but the distinction between acting on behalf of the state and on behalf of local residents has become increasingly blurred. Today almost any local form of government can serve as a unit for providing the second type, or municipal, services.

Forms. The forms of local government do not differ greatly from one nation to another. Typically, there are general-purpose local governments of two types. The first is that of the municipality, ordinarily known as the city or village. A second type is based upon area, irrespective of whether it is urban or rural. The typical unit of this type is known in much of the English-speaking world as the county. It is sometimes divided into sub-units, such as the township, in order to provide grass-roots government at an even more local level. (See the glossary accompanying this article for more details.)

In addition to the general-purpose types of local government, there are special-purpose districts of great variety. These districts have existed for many centuries and defy inclusive description. For example, a sewage disposal district may engage in the manufacture and sale of fertilizer, or a forest district may provide recreational facilities. In the United States the most important and most common special district is that of the school district.

Development. Local government is the oldest form of government. After the family group, the first governments were probably those of the hunting party and the nomadic camp, where the hunters and their families lived between food searches. These early governments were moderately democratic. Leadership was probably informal, based upon consensus as to who was the most effective hunter and leader. Later as early man moved away from marginal existence, local governments came to be dominated less by the heroic leader of the hunt and more by the opinions of experienced older men, the elders, whence the term "aldermen" for local city councils.

As society developed, its government became increasingly complex. Additional, geographically broader governments were established as trade and commerce required. Eventually, the nation-state emerged and with it, the notion of sovereignty. Local governments lost their independent status, but the idea of preserving certain rights of decision at the local level remained. The practices of the ancient Greeks and the tribes of Germany reinforced the notion of the importance of local decision making.

In primitive societies local governments were essential and, furthermore, probably the only feasible kind, given the existing economy, transportation, and communication. In later times local governments became less essential, but practical reasons remained for their maintenance. Not only were local governments useful for the purposes of the central government and convenient for local citizens, but the grass-roots governments were of political value in allowing local variations in public policy in cases that were not of central importance to national leaders. As a result, local government has been preserved throughout the ages and has generally been encouraged for one reason or another.

In the Communist and the African nations, local government has remained an important and ideologically useful device for meeting local and tribal concerns, respectively, while encouraging greater allegiance to the national political organization. In frontier America, with its slow means of transportation and communication, local government became entrenched as an important institution and a revered tradition. Frontier attitudes and necessities established the belief in the desirability of electing a large number of officials and of emphasizing the importance of control over public policy at the local level by the general citizenry. Local government often serves as a bridge between the traditions of the past and the necessity of the present for national governments to cope with the problems of social change.

—*Charles R. Adrian*

See also Municipal Government.

LOCHNER v. NEW YORK, 198 U.S. 45 (1905), concerns a New York State statute entitled the Labor Law, under which no employee should be required or permitted to work in a biscuit, bread, or cake bakery or confectionery establishment more than sixty hours

in any one week. In this case, there was a conviction under the law in Oneida County, where a bakery worker was permitted to work more than sixty hours in one week. The Court found no adequate justification for the statute and held that there were no reasonable grounds for interfering with the liberty or right of free contract of a baker by determining his hours of labor. Mr. Justice Holmes, who took a more liberal stand toward the question of social and economic legislation, dissented. By the 1930s, the Court had adopted a more liberal view toward private affairs and upheld concrete labor laws enacted by Congress to protect the working people.

LOCKE, JOHN (1632-1704), English philosopher. He was educated at Westminster School and at Christ Church, Oxford, and taught at Oxford from 1660 to 1664. In 1667 he became adviser and physician to the Earl of Shaftsbury and accompanied him in exile to Holland (1682-1688). After he returned to England, he was appointed Commissioner of Appeals in 1689 and served as Commissioner to the Board of Trade and Plantations (1696-1700).

Locke's most important philosophical works are the *Essay Concerning Human Understanding* (1690) and *Two Treatises on Civil Government* (1690). In *Essay* Locke's thesis is that every human's mind is, at birth, a blank page on which experience makes its impressions, which are gradually formed into general ideas. He further states that no innate ideas exist and that an individual acquires all concepts through experience and that experience reaches him through his five senses. He argued that all that the untaught mind possesses is the power of comparing, distinguishing, judging, and willing.

In the first of his *Treatises,* Locke refutes the idea of the divine right of kings. In the second, and more important, Locke states that men are born equal with equal rights in nature. Men agree with one another to form a society, mostly to preserve property and obtain justice. As justice comes from laws, the highest power is the legislative. He adds that the legislative is limited by the original agreement and may not encroach on the powers of the judiciary. He further states that there should be an executive, also restrained by law. He closes with the idea that if the legislative is overthrown, the society is abolished and men may start again with a new mutual agreement.

Locke's writings strongly influenced Thomas Jefferson in writing the Declaration of Independence. In addition, many fundamental American political concepts, such as "separation of power," are based on the writings of Locke.

LOCKOUT, withholding of work by an employer. The lockout is last-resort action taken by an employer in a labor dispute to put economic pressure on the employees. The union's corresponding action is a strike.

Because it is often difficult to determine whether a lockout or a strike came first, the Labor Department classifies both under the heading "work stoppages" in its statistics. Under the Taft-Hartley Act (1947), the president can intervene in lockouts and strikes that endanger the national health or safety.

The lockout was a technique used quite frequently by employers during the turbulent 1870s, when labor unions were trying to gain a foothold in industry.

See also Labor Movement in the United States; Strike.

LOCOFOCOS, a radical faction of New York Democrats who were opposed to conservative Tammany party control in the 1830s. The name stemmed from an argumentative party meeting in 1835 at which the gaslight was turned off by Tammany regulars. Their radical opponents then produced Locofoco brand matches to provide candlelight and forced members to continue the meeting.

President Jackson had removed federal funds from the Bank of the United States and redistributed them to "pet" state banks. This led to the unrestricted issuance of paper money by individual banks and a resulting rise in inflation. Officially calling themselves the Equal Rights Party, the Locofocos led strong attacks against such banks, demanding a return to hard money and the separation of government funds from private banking. In 1837, they succeeded in passing state legislation for a "free banking" system to end the bribery of state legislators that had characterized the acquisition of state banking charters.

Martin Van Buren, after becoming president in 1837, sponsored the establishment of an Independent Treasury, an idea sparked by Locofoco principles. The Locofocos were eventually reabsorbed into the Democratic party.

See also Political Parties in the United States; Presidential Elections.

LODGE-GOSSETT PROPOSAL, a plan to alter the Electoral College system in national elections. At present the winning candidate in a state receives all of that state's electoral votes, no matter how tiny his plurality. The Lodge-Gossett system would eliminate electors and allocate electoral votes automatically in proportion to the popular vote. Under this plan even the loser in a state would receive some electoral votes.

See also Electoral College.

LOGROLLING, legislative practice whereby reciprocal agreements are made between legislators, usually in voting for or against a bill ("an aye for an aye"). Generally, logrolling is used to secure public works projects for a representative's constituency in order to reflect his performance, but not necessarily the needs of the constituents. Traditionally involving river-and-

harbor bills, logrolling has extended to aerospace projects.

See also Pork Barrel Legislation.

LONG, HUEY (PIERCE) (1893-1935), American political figure. Known as the "Kingfish," he was noted for his concern for the common man and for the ruthless, demagogic tactics he used to achieve his goals. He was born in Winfield, La., and left high school before graduating, worked as a salesman, and then took law courses, passing the Louisiana bar in 1915.

Long quickly became involved in politics and was elected state railroad commissioner in 1918. He transformed the commission, soon enlarged into the Public Service Commission, into a vigorous regulatory agency. He gained great popularity with his attacks on large corporations, particularly Standard Oil. His campaign for governor ended in defeat in 1924, but he won the election of 1928.

Governor. Despite conservative opposition that included an unsuccessful attempt at impeachment (1929), Long pushed through the legislature a comprehensive construction, public health, and education program. At the same time, he systematically crushed political opposition and created a "machine" that remained under Long family control for decades after his death. In 1930 he was elected to the United States Senate, but he did not take his seat until January 1932.

At first Long worked with President Roosevelt in the Senate, but deciding that the President's efforts to combat the Depression were insufficient, Long broke with FDR. In 1934 Long announces his Share Our Wealth program, which relied on heavy estate and income taxes and guaranteed families an annual income and a homestead. While active in the Senate, he retained a stranglehold on Louisiana politics and stated that he would be a presidential candidate in 1936 or 1940. On Sept. 8, 1935, he was fatally wounded in Baton Rouge, La., and died on September 10. Many felt that his death ended the threat of a United States dictatorship.

LOOSE CONSTRUCTION. *See* Constitutional Construction; Supreme Court of the United States.

LOYALTY OATH, swearing of allegiance to the government. In drafting the Constitution, the Founding Fathers expressed a desire for a declaration of loyalty from public servants, but the presidential oath was the only one specified in the Constitution.

With the inception of the Cold War after 1945, many government and private agencies and associations required special pledges of loyalty in an attempt to weed out subversives. The hunt for Communists came to a peak during the McCarthy era of the early 1950s, when charges of political disloyalty, often unfounded, were leveled against numerous individuals.

In seeking to ensure that the needs of national security do not negate basic civil rights, the Supreme Court has in a number of cases ruled that loyalty oaths are unconstitutional. In *Wieman v. Updegraff* (1952) the Court reversed Oklahoma's requirement that state employees submit to a loyalty oath, accusing the state of "asserting arbitrary power" and "offending due process." In 1966 a similar Arizona statute was invalidated *(Elfbrandt v. Russell)* as a threat to "the cherished freedom of association protected by the First Amendment."

See also Loyalty-Security Programs.

LOYALTY-SECURITY PROGRAMS, in the United States, programs on the federal, state, and local levels designed to uncover and investigate individuals or organizations held to be security risks because of questionable loyalty or simply questionable reliability and discretion. Such programs have existed since the American Revolution, when supporters of Great Britain were penalized by having their property confiscated. Loyalty oaths were required of secessionists after the Civil War. During World War I individuals suspected of pro-German sympathies were the target of many popular though unofficial reprisals, and American citizens of Japanese descent were placed in detention camps during World War II.

The most far-reaching loyalty-security programs have been directed against Communists or their sympathizers, particularly since World War II. A federal loyalty and security program was enacted by President Harry Truman's executive order in 1947, which required civil servants and teachers to take oaths affirming their loyalty to the United States. Persons who refused to take the oath or who were otherwise classified as security risks lost their jobs. The 1947 criteria for demonstrating loyalty were made more stringent in 1953, and the federal program was utilized by Senator Joseph McCarthy in his investigations of Communist agents in all walks of life. Since the mid-1960s, however, the Supreme Court has struck down many provisions of loyalty-security programs as violating the self-incrimination prohibition of the Fifth Amendment, including, in 1965, the provision of the Subversive Activities Control Act that required members of the Communist party to register with the Justice Department. The Court struck down various loyalty oath requirements, such as the New York State Feinberg Law, for teachers, students seeking loans, Medicare recipients, and labor union officials.

See also Self-Incrimination.

LUTHER v. BORDEN, 7 How. 1 (1849), concerns political differences arising from the approval of a new constitution for the State of Rhode Island in 1842. Although the case originated with a suit in which Luther sued Borden for trespass, the more important question which the Court was ultimately asked to decide was which of two governments—the charter government or the newly approved government— was lawful in Rhode Island in 1842. The Court declined to decide this issue, stating that it was a "political question," and under the Constitution Congress must decide which form of government is the established one in a state. Congress also has the responsibility to determine the proper means for handling the domestic violence arising from such political differences. The Court has generally remained unwilling to decide questions of a political nature.

McCARRAN INTERNAL SECURITY ACT OF 1950. *See* Internal Security Act.

McCARRAN-WALTER IMMIGRATION ACT. *See* Immigration and Nationality Act of 1952.

McCARTHY, JOSEPH R(AYMOND) (1909-1957), American senator, who was renowned for his accusations against alleged Communist influence in the United States. Born in Grand Chute, Wis., he worked his way through law school, was elected a circuit judge before and after serving in World War II, and was elected to the Senate in 1946 as a Republican.

In February 1950 he vaulted into national prominence with a speech in Wheeling. W. Va., in which he stated that he had a list of "card-carrying Communists" in the State Department. These charges remained unproven, and undocumented claims of "proof" became a trademark of later charges. McCarthy questioned the motives of those who doubted him and continued to accuse public figures of Communist associations and the Democratic party of "20 years of treason."

He was reelected to the Senate in 1952; in 1953, after his appointment as chairman of the Permanent Subcommittee on Investigations, he began probing communism in the Army. The Army-McCarthy hearings, televised in 1954, gave him further national exposure, but his charges were not supported. His abrasive guilt-by-association tactics, which led to the coining of the word "McCarthyism," brought a Senate investigation that ended with his condemnation on December 2, 1954. His political influence subsequently declined. He died in Bethesda, Md. Defended by some as a zealous patriot, McCarthy was criticized by most as demagogic and undemocratic.

McCOLLUM V. BOARD OF EDUCATION. *See* Illinois ex rel McCollum v. Board of Education.

McCULLOCH v. MARYLAND, 4 Wheat. 316 (1819), one of the most important cases decided under Chief Justice Marshall. There were two separate issues, and Marshall used both as an opportunity to enhance the power of the federal government. The first issue involved the power of the federal government to set up a national bank. The second involved the power of the states to tax a national bank located within its borders. Marshall recognized that the power to create banks was not one of the powers specifically delegated to the federal government by the Constitution, but he interpreted the "necessary and proper" clause of Article I broadly so that it enhanced those powers which were specifically delegated and enumerated by the Constitution.

By means of this interpretation, Marshall found the creation of the bank to be a necessary and proper exercise of congressional power. He also held that the State of Maryland lacked the power to tax the national bank. In Marshall's opinion, the power to tax included the power to destroy, and he held the state law providing this power to be unconstitutional and void, under Article VI of the Constitution, which makes federal law supreme.   —*Philip J. Hannon*

See also Gibbons v. Ogden; National Supremacy.

McGOWAN v. MARYLAND, 366 U.S. 420 (1961), questions the validity of Sunday closing laws which prohibit the sale on Sunday of all retail goods, with a few exceptions. McGowan and other employees of a large discount department store in Maryland were charged with selling prohibited goods on Sunday. The appellants argued that Maryland's Sunday closing statutes violated the equal protection clause of the Fourteenth Amendment, and that the classification of commodities which may or may not be sold on Sunday was without rational and substantial relation to the object of the legislation.

In the opinion of the Court, delivered by Chief Justice Warren, the closing laws did not bring about denial of equal protection of the laws. Whatever their original religious connections, they presently were designed to set aside a day of rest and recreation. Further, the establishment clause does not ban federal or state regulations of conduct for social good.

McKINLEY, WILLIAM (1843-1901), 25th President of the United States (1897-1901), born in Niles, Ohio. Elected to Congress as a Republican in 1876, he served as chairman of the House Ways and Means Committee (1889-1891) and was largely responsible for drafting the McKinley Tariff (1890), which raised duties to the highest levels up to that time. He was elected governor of Ohio in 1891. McKinley secured the party's presidential nomination in 1896. He had hoped to base his campaign on the tariff, but the rise of the silver crusade and the nomination of William Jennings Bryan by the Democrats and Populists dictated that silver would play a major role in the campaign. McKinley embraced the gold standard in 1896, defeated Bryan, and became the first presidential candidate in 26 years to win a majority of the popular vote. As President, McKinley backed the passage of a

higher protective tariff (1897) and an act officially putting the United States on the gold standard (1900). The most significant event of his administration was the Spanish American War. McKinley's decision that the United States should take the Philippines, Puerto Rico, and other Spanish possessions gave the United States a colonial empire and guaranteed that the nation would henceforth be a major world power. Reelected in 1900, McKinley was shot by an anarchist, Leon Czolgosz, on September 6, 1901. He died on September 14.

McNAMARA, ROBERT S(TRANGE), (1916-   ), American businessman and government official. He was born in San Francisco; intellectually gifted, he excelled at the University of California at Berkeley and at Harvard Business School, where he began teaching in 1940.

During World War II he served as an Army Air Force consultant and officer, developing systems control programs. In 1946 he was a member of a group of former Air Force officers, known as the "Wiz Kids," who joined Ford Motor Company. He rose quickly to become in 1960 the first company president who was not a Ford. Among his innovations were the development of Ford's luxury and compact models.

Soon after he was elected president of Ford, McNamara was appointed secretary of defense by President Kennedy. McNamara completely reorganized the Defense Department—streamlining and bringing business methods and civilian control to the Pentagon. He continued as secretary under President Johnson, overseeing the controversial military buildup during the Vietnam War. His misgivings about the course of the war grew, and he received increasing criticism for his role in it. He resigned as secretary to become president of the International Bank for Reconstruction and Development (World Bank) in 1968. He retired as president in 1984.

MACE, the traditional symbol of authority in the House of Representatives. The mace, which is 46 inches high and is composed of 13 ebony rods tied with silver, was carried by the Sergeant at Arms when he was called on by the Speaker to preserve order in the House. The mace is displayed on a green marble pedestal to the right of the Speaker during regular sessions of the House of Representatives and is placed on a white marble pedestal when the House meets as the Committee of the Whole.   —*Mary L. Carns*

MACHINE, POLITICAL, often considered a ruthless instrument wielded by a self-perpetuating leadership serving special interests, as in exposés by such reporters as Lincoln Steffens and analyses by such scholars as M. Ostrogorski and Edward M. Sait.

Other Views. Viscount Bryce, Alex Gottfried, and Robert Merton view the machine as an inevitable development, a response to the complexity of the party and governmental organizations and to the needs of clientele groups. The machine is an inner core of the party, the professionals who are concerned with party business and manage the array of offices, committees, and conventions at all levels of government. This group of writers sometimes uses "machine" to designate an organization associated with a particular party leader (the Byrd machine of Virginia, the La Follette machine of Wisconsin). The term, though indicating a strong leader's grip on his party, does not imply the use of sordid means to stay in power. For Theodore Lowi the new machines are outside the party: the rival bureaucratic hierarchies of police, sanitation, health, and other governmental agencies.

The Heyday of the Machine was in the period from the Civil War to the Depression, though there were prewar examples such as the Albany Regency. The local party organizations thrived by capitalizing on the needs of lower class and immigrant groups—humanizing government by providing jobs, a friend in court, welfare assistance, money for voting, expeditious naturalization, and entertainment—and by capitalizing on the needs of businessmen—by providing friendly legislation, construction contracts, sales to the government, municipal transportation franchises, licenses for saloons, entertainers, and race tracks, protection against police or inspectors, and favorable tax assessment. Machine strongholds included New York City (the Tammany Hall Democratic organization), Boston, Kansas City, Philadelphia, and Chicago. In the last two cities Republican machines were replaced by Democratic machines.

Decline. The metropolitan machines have fallen into decay. Among the factors that annihilated machine control were the government's taking over welfare functions, attenuation of ethnic group identifications, unions serving as rivals to the machines as sources of political education, and raids on the machine by reformers and wealthy or charismatic outsiders (abetted by the direct primary system, which weakened the machine's control over nominations).

As the electorate moved up the economic, social, and educational ladder, there was voter preference for independent candidates and for ticket splitting. Some machines tried to embrace certain new, social power groups (women, workers, and youth), and to use technological expertise (survey research and mass media), but it was usually the foes of machine dominance who capitalized on the techniques of the new politics. With a more mobile population, machines made infrequent direct contracts with the citizenry. The loss of patronage and other spoils resulted in fewer party workers, the erstwhile cogs of the machine.   —*Martin Gruberg*

See also Tammany.

James Madison, fourth President of the United States (1809-1817).

MADISON, JAMES (1751-1836), father of the Constitution, founder of the first political party and fourth President of the United States (1809-1817). Madison came from the planter class of Virginia. He served in the Virginia legislature and Congress during the Revolution (1778-1783) and helped draft Virginia's first constitution (1776).

He was active in bringing about the Constitutional Convention of 1787, and in Philadelphia he promulgated the Virginia Plan, stressing national supremacy, which became the framework of the new Constitution. He guided the Constitution through the ratification process in Virginia and was one of the authors of the *Federalist* papers. In Congress (1789-1797) he was one of the shapers of the Bill of Rights and led the opposition to Hamilton's fiscal programs.

Jefferson and Madison coauthored the Virginia and Kentucky resolutions in response to the Alien and Sedition Acts and, with Jefferson as titular leader, founded the first opposition party. As Jefferson's secretary of state, Madison was his principal adviser in all matters.

President. Elected president in 1809, he found himself commander in chief in a second war for independence with Britain, the War of 1812. Although support for the extension of the Napoleonic wars came from the South and West, concern over British interference with shipping was not enough to swing the Northeast to support "Mr. Madison's War." Primarily because Britain could not conduct a war across the Atlantic while fighting the French, the war ended with independence secure. Nationalist feeling was intense by the time of the battle of New Orleans (1815).

Near the end of his tenure, Madison edged toward the economic nationalism of Hamilton by supporting the Second Bank of the United States. More than any other individual, Madison laid the basis for constitutional government and for the American party system.
— *Allen F. Kifer*

See also Bill of Rights; Federalist, The; Madison's Journal.

MADISON'S JOURNAL, the notes of James Madison, describing the daily debates of the Constitutional Convention of 1787. The main source of information regarding the work of the Convention, the Journal was initially a private one. The secretary of the Convention, William Jackson (1759-1828), kept the formal record, but his sparse notes had little significance. Madison reconstructed in precise detail the bitter arguments over the nature of government and democracy that, once resolved, engendered the political theory underlying the Constitution. Because of a pledge of secrecy taken by the convention, the journal was not published until 1840.

See also Constitutional Convention of 1787; Madison, James.

MAGISTRATE COURTS. See Judicial System.

MAGNA CARTA, basic document in English constitutional law, granted by King John at Runnymede, Surrey, in 1215. Its main purpose was to confirm the privileges of the feudal barons, limiting the king's powers over them. Idealized in later interpretations, some of the features essential to a democratic government have been attributed to the Magna Carta. Repeatedly reissued and modified by John's successors, the document became a symbol of superiority of the law over the king and his prerogatives.

MAJORITY AND PLURALITY, terms that define the size of the winner's vote. A majority is in excess of 50 percent of the total vote; a plurality is less than 50 percent. In national elections an individual needs only a plurality of the vote in any state to win all the electoral votes of the state. Richard Nixon in 1968, running against two opponents, won only a plurality in many states, but he won by obtaining a majority of the electoral votes.

Most state elections can also be carried by a plurality. A few states require a runoff election in the event that no candidate receives a majority. The runoff is held between the two highest vote-getters, guaranteeing that one will obtain a majority.

See also Election.

MAJORITY LEADER, the most important party officer in the Senate. Selected by the party caucus, over which he comes to preside, the majority leader's duties include managing the legislative program of his party, planning and controlling the order of business, allocating speaking-time in debate, and directing party strategy. Robert Taft, Lyndon Johnson, Mike Mansfield, and Robert Byrd are examples of skillful Senate majority leaders. The House majority leader also plays a key role but is less powerful than the speaker of the House.

MALLOY v. HOGAN, 378 U.S. 1 (1964), concerns the applicability of the protection against self-incrimination contained in the Fifth Amendment to the states through the Fourteenth Amendment. Malloy, arrested during a gambling raid, had pleaded guilty to a state charge of pool selling, a misdemeanor. About 16 months later, he was ordered to testify in a county inquiry into alleged gambling and other criminal activities. He invoked the Fifth Amendment, refusing to answer on the ground that doing so might tend to incriminate him, and was held in contempt.

The Court, reversing a number of its older decisions, applied the Fifth Amendment's privilege against self-incrimination to the states through the Fourteenth Amendment, and rejected the contention that the federal privilege was to be measured by less stringent standards in a state inquiry that would be the case in a federal proceeding.

See also Gitlow v. New York.

MANAGEMENT AND BUDGET, OFFICE OF (OMB), one of the divisions of the executive office. On July 1, 1970, all functions assigned to the Bureau of the Budget were transferred to the president and delegated by executive order to OMB to increase the executive capacity for program evaluation and fiscal analysis and to apply sound management principles to the business of government. The office's main functions are to assist the president in preparing the annual budget; to clear and coordinate all department or agency budgets and advise on proposed legislation or executive orders; to help set fiscal policy; and to supervise the administration of the federal budget.

See also Budget and Accounting Act (1921); Executive Branch.

MANDAMUS (Lat., we command) **WRIT OF,** a court order commanding an inferior court, an executive, or administrative official to perform his duty. The order is not applicable if the official has the discretion to act. It merely compels action when that is the official's duty, to which he is not adhering.

MANPOWER ADMINISTRATION. See Employment and Training Administration.

MANPOWER DEVELOPMENT AND TRAINING ACT. Given urgency by the 1962 total of 4 million unemployed, the law was enacted as part of President John F. Kennedy's poverty programs. Following reports from the President's Committee on Manpower, the law was expanded in 1965 as part of President Lyndon Johnson's Great Society programs to eliminate unemployment. The initial act attempted to identify and remedy shortages of labor and trainable personnel, to study labor mobility, to reduce welfare and unemployment payments, and to retrain phased out specialists. Further, the secretary of labor was instructed to develop, collect, and disseminate information on the labor market.

Federal aid is provided to state programs for weekly training allowances (calculated as unemployment rates plus small incentives) and trained transportation and relocation costs. Training programs have been tailored to help farm workers earning less than $1,200 annually, high school dropouts and youths (after 1966, though, men under 22 years old are limited to less than 25 percent of all recipients), and men over 45 years old. The Department of Education trains and equips via state vocational agencies all cases referred to the Department of Labor, and the Department of Commerce supplements training programs in specially designated redevelopment areas. The act is administered through the Employment and Training Administration of the Department of Labor.

MAPP v. OHIO, 367 U.S. 643 (1961). This case is an example of the Supreme Court building or making law on a case-by-case basis in the traditional fashion. The issue in *Mapp* concerned the use at trial in a state court of evidence obtained by means of an unlawful search and seizure.

The majority of the Court felt that the use of such evidence was a violation of a federally protected constitutional right and henceforth a conviction based on such evidence would be subject to reversal. But this seemingly logical and even innocuous decision represented a departure from prior Supreme Court interpretations of the Constitution. Earlier decisions of the Court had held such evidence to be inadmissible only in federal courts. But even after it had decided to interpret the Fourteenth Amendment due process clause so as to incorporate the search and seizure provisions of the Fourth Amendment and apply them as limitations on the states, the Court in *Wolf v. Colorado* had specifically declined to prohibit on constitutional grounds the use of such evidence in state courts. Thus, before the Court changed its mind, Mapp, the defendant, could have his federally protected right violated and the evidence garnered by means of the violation might be legally used to support a conviction.   —*Philip J. Hannon*

MARBURY V. MADISON, 1 Cranch. 137 (1803). In this case Chief Justice John Marshall created a power of judicial review. The power is not provided specifically in the Constitution, but Marshall constructed an argument for this power so successfully that most Americans think it is found in the Constitution itself.

William Marbury was a political hack appointed by President Adams in his attempt to stack the courts with Federalist judges before leaving office. Thomas Jefferson, Adams' successor as president, was an Anti-Federalist, and he refused to allow his secretary of state, James Madison, to deliver the appointment. Federalist Marshall spent a large portion of his opinion in an attempt to embarrass the incumbent president, but the Chief Justice also wove a sophisticated argument creating a judicial review power: he ultimately declined to order the delivery of the appointment on the grounds that the act of Congress giving the Court the power to order the delivery was an unconstitutional attempt by Congress to enlarge the original jurisdiction of the Court. For the first time the Court reviewed and held an act of Congress to be unconstitutional.   —*Philip J. Hannon*
See also Judicial Review; Marshall, John.

MARITIME LAW. *See* Admiralty Law.

MARSHALL, GEORGE C(ATLETT) (1880-1959), American soldier and government official who played a key role in formulating World War II strategy and in shaping United States postwar policies. Born in Uniontown, Pa., he graduated from Virginia Military Institute in 1901. He won high marks for his grasp of tactics and became a close aide of General Pershing after World War I.

In 1936 he reached the rank of brigadier general and in 1939 was made Army chief of staff. Foreseeing war, he urged peacetime conscription and mobilization. During the war he was the chief allied strategist and directed United States forces in the Pacific and Europe. He was made general of the Army in 1944.

President Truman sent Marshall to China as his special ambassador in 1945, but Marshall was unable to resolve differences between the Communists and Nationalists. In early 1947 he returned to become secretary of state and helped mold the Truman Doctrine, which proposed to aid non-Communist countries. In June 1947 he announced the Marshall Plan, a program of unprecedented scope that provided direct economic aid to revitalize war-torn Europe.

Marshall left the government in 1949, but he returned a year later as secretary of defense during the Korean War crisis. He was responsible for American mobilization and for planning Korea's defense. He retired in 1951 and in 1953 received the Nobel Peace Prize. He died in Washington, D.C.

A brilliant staff planner and strategist, Marshall firmly believed in the necessity of armed preparedness and of overall civilian control. He resisted all offers to exploit his military fame through political channels.

MARSHALL, JOHN (1755-1835). John Marshall was given the sobriquet "the great Chief Justice" by Supreme Court Justice Benjamin Cardozo, and his right to the title is hardly ever questioned. Appointed in the last days of President John Adams' administration in 1801, Chief Justice Marshall battled with a series of presidents, nearly all of whom were vigorously opposed to Marshall's Federalist interpretation of the Constitution.

History. Marshall was born in Virginia in 1755. He joined the American Revolutionary forces at the first outbreak of hostilities and fought under George Washington until 1781, when he resigned his commission. After being admitted to the Virginia bar, he was elected to the Virginia House of Delegates, where he served during the years 1782-1785, 1787-1790, and 1795-1796. He also held a seat on the Virginia Executive Council from 1782 and 1784 and a minor judicial post as Recorder of the Richmond City Husting Court from 1785 to 1788. In the Virginia Ratifying Convention he argued eloquently for the Constitution and

John Marshall, third and most influential Chief Justice of the Supreme Court.

afterward became a Federalist leader in the state.

Though utterly devoted to George Washington, Marshall refused federal appointments until 1797, when John Adams appointed him minister to France. There he became involved in the XYZ Affair, which led to the undeclared naval war with France and the subsequent passage of the Alien and Sedition Acts by Congress. When these acts were being debated in the Federalist controlled Congress, Marshall was a member of the House of Representatives (1799-1800), and he vigorously opposed the legislation. He served as secretary of state to John Adams in 1800 and was then appointed to the Supreme Court. At the request of Martha Washington, he also wrote a biography of George Washington after the President's death.

Significance. Though there are some disagreements, it is generally held that Marshall strengthened both the Supreme Court and the Federalist interpretation of the Constitution. During his 34 years as chief justice, he maintained dominance over those justices appointed by presidents opposed to his policies. Marshall's clear control of the Court seems to have slipped only towards the last years of his term.

Marshall's expansion of the prestige of the Court was accomplished through formal changes, such as the establishment of a single opinion to express the Court's view. More important, he affected substantial changes in the law. He established the right of the Court to be the final arbiter of the Constitution and to declare congressional acts void (*Marbury v. Madison*, 1803). The Court also exercised the power to declare state laws invalid and to protect the right of contract (*Fletcher v. Peck*, 1810; *Dartmouth College v. Woodward*, 1819). He established the supremacy of the federal government and expanded the power of Congress through a broad interpretation of the "necessary and proper" clause (*McMulloch v. Maryland*, 1819). He also suggested a wide-ranging definition of federal control over interstate commerce (*Gibbons v. Ogden*, 1824). He solidified the right of the Supreme Court over the judiciaries of the various states *(Martin v. Hunter's Lessee*, 1816); *Cohens v. Virginia*, 1821).

In conclusion, John Marshall helped structure a distribution of the powers of government that has lasted to the present. His work has strongly influenced the political history of the United States. He died in office in 1835, still battling his adversaries in the other branches of government.   —*David Forte*

MARSHALL, THURGOOD (1908-   ), associate justice of the Supreme Court (1967-   ). Born in Maryland, he studied at Lincoln University and obtained his law degree from Howard University in 1933. For more than 20 years he headed the NAACP Legal Defense and Educational Fund, coordinating the legal attack on segregation in voting, housing, public accommodations, and education. During this time he argued the historic *Brown v. Board of Educa-*

Thurgood Marshall, first black associate justice of the U.S. Supreme Court.

tion (1954) case before the Supreme Court, which declared the "separate but equal" doctrine of segregation unconstitutional. Appointed by President John F. Kennedy to the U.S. Court of Appeals in 1961, he later served as U.S. Solicitor General (1964-1967) under President Lyndon B. Johnson before being appointed to the Supreme Court. The first black to serve on the Court, he continued to champion the rights of minorities, arguing that using local property taxes for funding public education poses inequality in education (*San Antonio Independent School District v. Rodriguez*, 1973) and advocating voting rights for 18-year-olds in federal elections (*Oregon v. Mitchell*, 1970).

MARSHALL PLAN, also called the European Recovery Program, a post-World War II foreign-aid plan to restore the economic stability of Western Europe. The plan lasted from 1948 to 1952 under a $13 billion appropriation by the Congress. Essentially, the United States supplied materials, technical advice, and money, while the participating countries were responsible for planning the details for recovery. Early in 1947 George Kennan, a veteran foreign service officer, proposed the plan to provide resources for the recovery of European nations, including Russia. The plan was formally presented by Secretary of State George Marshall on June 5, 1947. Six weeks later 16 European nations organized the Committee for European Economic Cooperation, which planned the amount of aid needed and the reconstruction details and goals. The participating nations were Austria,

Belgium, Britain, Denmark, France, Greece, Iceland, Italy, Luxembourg, The Netherlands, Norway, Portugal, Sweden, Switzerland, and Turkey. Russia did not take part because of the cooperative approach required as a condition for aid.

President Truman introduced the plan into Congress in December 1947. After the Communist takeover of Czechoslovakia in February 1948 Congress moved and passed the Foreign Assistance Act on April 4, 1948. This act provided an immediate $5.3 billion for the Marshall Plan and established the Economic Cooperation Administration. By 1949 industrial output of the participating countries was already above prewar levels. Steps toward European economic integration were taken during the second year, and by 1951 the United Kingdom was able to have its aid under the plan suspended.

MARTIAL LAW refers to control of civilian populations by a military commander. The commander is permitted to exercise this control because there is no power sufficient to stop him or to control the situation during war, insurrection, or violence. Martial law replaces all civilian laws, authorities, and courts. It is an exercise of military power that is totally arbitrary and unfettered: the commander is legislator, judge, and executioner.

See also Hirabayashi v. United States; Korematsu v. United States; Military Law.

MARTIN v. WILKS (1989), Supreme Court decision that involved white firemen in Birmingham, Alabama, who challenged an eight-year-old court-sanctioned plan to increase the number of blacks in the fire department. The whites claimed the plan constituted reverse discrimination and violated provisions of the 1964 Civil Rights Act that forbade employment actions based on considerations of race or sex.

Justice Rehnquist, writing for the five-member majority, concluded that white workers who were not a party to the original agreement could not be deprived of their legal right to bring suit. Justice Stevens, writing for the dissenters, argued: "It was inevitable that some white employees must share some of the burdens resulting from the redress of past wrongs." Civil rights groups and some congressmen saw this decision as a major setback for civil rights law.

See also City of Richmond v. J.A. Croson.

MARX, KARL (1818-1883), German economist and revolutionary socialist, one of the most important influences on twentieth-century political thought. He was born in Trèves and was educated at the universities of Bonn and Berlin, where he read Hegel. In 1842 he became a journalist in Germany, where his work was suppressed, and Paris. He was expelled from France in 1845 and moved to Brussels, where he helped to organize the German Workingmen's Association and the Communist League. In 1847 he and Engels wrote the famous *Communist Manifesto,* one of the most effective revolutionary documents ever written.

This work proclaims that historical change is caused by class struggles and that the modern struggle is between the owners of economic production (the capitalists) and the workers (the proletariat), who must overthrow the owners and redistribute the wealth.

Das Kapital. In 1849 Marx fled to London, where he spent the rest of his life studying and writing. He served as a correspondent of the *New York Tribune* and other newspapers. After 1873 he took no active part in politics and dedicated himself instead to the completion of *Das Kapital. Das Kapital* expounds Marx's theory of value: the way to measure a commodity is by the amount of labor necessary to produce it. He argues that in a capitalistic society the workers are exploited of what they produce over and above their wages (surplus value). Marx felt that in order to continually increase this surplus, workers would be forced to work harder and receive less of the fruits of their labors until they must rebel and seize the power. He urged the formation of revolutionary workers' parties to accomplish this end.

MAYFLOWER COMPACT, a covenant signed by 41 of the 44 men aboard the ship Mayflower on November 21, 1620. The Pilgrim leadership, recognizing that it was outside the jurisdiction of the London Company and fearful of losing political control, drafted a compact and by consent agreed, as members of a community, to form a government and obey its laws.

Although not a constitution, the document was a social compact reflecting the political thought of the seventeenth century. The document is historically significant as a prototype of many similar compacts having much influence with the development of American republican government and democracy.

MAYOR. *See* Municipal Government.

MEAT INSPECTION ACT OF 1901. *See* Business Regulation in the United States.

MEDICARE AND MEDICAID, programs of government participation in financing health care (1965 amendments to the Social Security Act). Medicare is a federal program of health and hospital insurance for the aged, and Medicaid is a federal-state program for care assistance for low-income persons of all ages. Medicare and Medicaid are administered by the U.S. Social Security Administration and by local social service departments, respectively. Medicare hospital insurance is a social security right for most persons 65 and over; its health care plan is voluntary. Medicaid is available to recipients of public assistance and in some

states to the medically indigent. Medicare benefits, uniform throughout the country, are limited (they exclude prescription drugs, eyeglasses, dental care, etc.); Medicaid programs, different in each state, can be very comprehensive.

The laws have no provisions for expansion of services or new health systems. They have greatly increased demand for medical services, resulting in escalating costs and insufficient health facilities. Congress attempted a solution by passing the Medicare Catastrophic Act in 1988. The law provided comprehensive coverage against long-term hospitalization and out-of-pocket expenses for doctors' services. However, many elderly persons complained because they were required to finance the extra costs. They pressured Congress, which responded by repealing the act in 1989.

Further new Medicare rules were included as part of the 1989 Deficit Reduction bill. They set limits on doctors' fees, prohibit charges substantially greater than the fee paid by Medicare itself, and include other provisions designed to prevent doctors from taking on extra patients or sending them to labs in which the doctor has a financial interest.

MEDICARE CATASTROPHIC ACT. *See* Medicare and Medicaid.

MERIT SYSTEM, a system used to measure workers' performances for promotions or transfers, thereby avoiding conflicts over granting promotions on the basis of length of service rather than ability and proven competence. Civil service appointments are handled by merit examinations instead of by political appointments (the spoils system).

See also Civil Service; Merit System Protection Board; Office of Personnel Management.

METROPOLITAN AREA, a term used to describe a large city and the suburban areas that surround it. The Census Bureau considers any civil division over 2,500 people an urban area. Using this definition, there are over 200 metropolitan areas, where approximately 73 percent of the population lives. These areas, however, occupy only 10 percent of the country's land area.

MIDDLE EAST RESOLUTION, congressional approval requested by President Dwight Eisenhower giving him authority to appropriate military and economic aid to the Middle Eastern nations resisting communism. Passage of the Resolution in 1957 supported the Eisenhower Doctrine. The Resolution gave the President the discretionary use of troops and $200 million to protect Middle Eastern nations, providing that Congress received 15 days' notice of such use. The Resolution was passed in the aftermath of the

1956 Suez crisis and the resulting power vacuum in the Middle East, to deter Russian action.

See also Eisenhower Doctrine.

MILITARY APPEALS, UNITED STATES COURT OF, the final court of appeals in the military justice system. It was established by Congress under Article I of the Constitution exclusively as an appellate criminal court. It occupies the same position within the system of military law as the Supreme Court occupies with regard to general judicial authority. The Military Appeals court is a court of last resort, from which there is no further appeal. The court consists of three civilian judges who are appointed by the president for 15-year terms. Decisions of the court affecting a general or flag officer or extending to death require presidential approval. Federal courts can examine the court of Military Appeals on questions of jurisdiction.

MILITARY-INDUSTRIAL COMPLEX, a term first used by President Dwight Eisenhower in his farewell address to describe the combination of military and industrial power, which exerts enormous political and economic power.

MILITARY LAW, any system of rules and regulations governing military forces. Both the president—by virtue of his authority as Commander in Chief of the Army and Navy (Constitution Article II, Section 2)— and the Congress (Constitution Article I, Section 8) with superior authority—may make military law. It also includes certain customary usages, which might be called "military common law." Military justice is administered by courts-martial with no concern to the judicial power or civil law of the United States. Courts-martial are convened for the duration of a particular case. The regulations governing military justice in the United States are set forth in the Uniform Code of Military Justice, 10 U.S.C. 47.

See also Martial Law; Military Appeals, Court of.

MILL, JOHN STUART (1806-1873), English social and political reformer, philosopher, and economist. Mill was educated at home by his father, the philosopher James Mill, and began working as a 17-year-old clerk for the East India Company. Mill retired after 35 years, was elected briefly to Parliament, and spent the remainder of his life writing. His best-known work, *On Liberty* (1859), remains a classic defense of free thought and discussion.

Mill was also a champion of women's rights and an advocate of a more equal distribution of profits. As an economist, he advocated a moderate socialist view that after his death became part of the tenets of the Fabian Society.

MILLER-TYDINGS ACT (1937), or Fair-Trade Act, permitted manufacturers to fix minimum retail prices

under certain conditions. The Act was ridered to an appropriations bill and reluctantly signed by President Roosevelt.

The Act was supported by merchants and manufacturers, who claimed that it would end destructive competition caused by price-cutting. Agreements setting minimum prices of advertised trademarked articles in interstate commerce were exempted from federal anti-trust laws if a state had fair-trade laws applying to intrastate commerce. Opponents of the bill argued that there was no justification for preventing buyers from seeking bargains. Although the Act applied to most states, the ability of mail-order houses to operate from states that did not have fair-trade laws made the Act largely ineffective.

MILLER v. CALIFORNIA, 413 U.S. 15 (1973), case in which the Supreme Court affirmed the right of states to regulate obscenity if the legislation is carefully drawn. The test of obscenity is whether the average person, applying contemporary community standards, would find a work as a whole appealing to prurient interest; whether the work depicts in a patently offensive way sexual conduct which has been specifically defined in the applicable state law; and whether the work as a whole lacks serious literary, artistic, political, or scientific value. The somewhat tougher "utterly without redeeming social value" test was rejected in favor of this looser standard which gives local communities somewhat more control over obscene materials. In a companion case, the Court narrowly rejected the "consulting adults" theory of consumption of obscene material.

MINERSVILLE SCHOOL DISTRICT v. GOBITIS, 310 U.S. 586 (1940), considers whether or not required saluting of the national flag as a daily school exercise, if contrary to one's religious convictions, constitutes an unconstitutional abridgement of the freedom of religion. The Gobitis family were Jehovah's Witnesses whose children were expelled from the Minersville public school for refusing to salute the flag. Gobitis sued for financial relief for the cost entailed of sending the children to private school. The Court, in an opinion delivered by Justice Frankfurter, held that the Minersville School Board was entitled to formulate its own policy concerning flag salutes, that the freedom of religion is not absolute, and that some compromises may be necessary in order to secure national unity to which the flag salute contributes. This decision was greatly criticized and was overruled in 1943.

See also West Virginia State Board of Education v. Barnette.

MINES, BUREAU OF, an agency in the Department of the Interior responsible for overseeing production of minerals and fuels in the United States, enforcing health and safety rules in mining, studying and controlling the effect of mining on the environment and researching and developing mineral resources. Created in 1910, the bureau oversees the production and sale of helium and administers the Federal Metal and Nonmetallic Mine Safety Act (1966) and the Federal Coal Mine Health and Safety Act (1969).

MINIMUM-WAGE LAWS. *See* Labor Movement in the United States.

MINORITY BUSINESS DEVELOPMENT AGENCY (MBDA), an agency of the Department of Commerce created in 1969 to aid in the development of businesses owned by and serving minority groups. MBDA coordinates public and private programs on the federal, state, and local levels to effect its national blueprint of minority business development. The office works particularly closely with the Small Business Administration, a federal agency that provides capital for Minority Enterprise Small Business Investment Companies (MESBICS), which in turn uses those funds to finance various minority business enterprises.

See also Small Business Administration.

MINORITY ECONOMIC IMPACT, OFFICE OF, part of the Department of Education, which advises the secretary of education on the effects that department policies have on minorities, their businesses, and their educational institutions. It also ensures minority participation in department programs.

MINORITY LEADER, the party officer in either house who commands the minority party's opposition to the policies of the majority party. His duties parallel the majority leaders in managing the legislative program of his party and directing party strategy.

See also Majority Leader.

MIRANDA v. ARIZONA, 384 U.S. 436 (1966). In the Miranda case the Warren Court consolidated four different criminal cases that each contained the use of a confession obtained from defendants who were not informed of their right to counsel or their right to

---

WARNING

The constitution requires that I inform you of your rights:

You have a right to remain silent. If you talk to any police officer, anything you say can and will be used against you in court.

You have a right to consult with a lawyer before you are questioned, and may have him with you during questioning.

If you cannot afford a lawyer, one will be appointed for you, if you wish, before any questioning.

If you wish to answer questions, you have the right to stop answering at any time.

You may stop answering questions at any time if you wish to talk to a lawyer, and may have him with you during any further questioning.

JDSR 4 Rev. 9-79

---

remain silent during the interrogation by the police. Although in these cases, as in the earlier *Escobedo v. Illinois,* the majority of the Court viewed the confessions as suspect, there was no showing of physical coercion or even psychological ploys.

The majority voted to reverse the convictions on the basis of the Fifth and Sixth Amendments, and the majority declared that henceforth the suspect should be immediately informed of his right to a court-appointed lawyer, of his right to remain silent under questioning, and of the fact that anything he does say may be used as evidence against him at the time of trial. The minority complained that the majority was distorting the Constitution by placing the rights of the individual criminal suspect above the rights of society as a whole.   —*Philip J. Hannon*

See also Accused Persons, Rights of; Escobedo v. Illinois; Gideon v. Wainwright.

MISSOURI PLAN, a method of selecting state judges. In Missouri a commission of attorneys and laymen draws up a list of three names from which the governor appoints a judge to the supreme court, to a court of appeals, or to a court in St. Louis or Kansas City. After one year of service the judge goes up for election. With voter approval he serves for six to 12 years. If he is defeated, another judge is appointed and the process begins again. The Missouri Plan has been welcomed as a satisfactory answer to the question of appointment versus election of judges. The plan preserves the power of the voters while at the same time freeing judges from campaigning for public office.

MISSOURI v. HOLLAND, 252 U.S. 416 (1920). It is generally understood that the federal government can exercise only those powers delegated to it by the Constitution. It is also understood that all other powers are reserved by virtue of the Tenth Amendment for the states and the people. In the area of foreign affairs however, these principles may break down. The United States Supreme Court has strayed from these principles in several cases, and nowhere further than in *Missouri v. Holland.* Previous to this case, an act of Congress concerning the regulation of migratory birds had been held unconstitutional by a federal court because it was not considered to be within the powers of the federal government. The act was passed by Congress a second time, pursuant to a treaty with Great Britain, and was then upheld by the Supreme Court. The state's Tenth Amendment challenge to the law was accepted the first time and turned down the second time, although the only significant factor that had changed was the adoption of the treaty. Thus the federal government was allowed to enhance its powers by virtue of passing a treaty and then passing a law giving internal effect to the international agreement.   —*Philip J. Hannon*

MONARCHY, a form of government in which power is vested in a single person. Absolute monarchs with hereditary rights were common particularly in Europe. However, in modern times there are few remaining monarchies, and they largely exercise symbolic power. England retains its monarchy, but effective power rests with Parliament and the prime minister.

MONDALE, WALTER (1928-   ), 42nd Vice President of the United States (1977-1981), Democratic candidate for president. He graduated from the University of Minnesota in 1951, served in the Korean War, and then returned to Minnesota, receiving his law degree in 1956. While in private law practice he started in politics by managing Governor Orville Freeman's 1958 campaign. Freeman appointed Mondale state attorney general in 1960. When Hubert Humphrey became vice president in 1964, Mondale was appointed to his U.S. Senate seat. He was elected in 1966 and reelected in 1972. Mondale was known for his support of liberal causes during his years in the Senate. He was chosen by presidential candidate Jimmy Carter as his running mate in 1976 and became a trusted adviser to the President. He ran again with Carter in their unsuccessful 1980 campaign. In 1984, Mondale was the Democratic presidential candidate running with Geraldine Ferraro against the Reagan-Bush ticket. After the election, Mondale lectured and resumed a law practice.

MONETARY POLICY. *See* Economic Stabilization Policies.

MONROE, JAMES (1758-1831), diplomat and fifth President of the United States (1817-1825), last president of the Virginia dynasty. Monroe served in the Virginia House and the Continental Congress (1782-1786), and in the Senate (1790-1794). Washington recalled him from his first diplomatic post in France (1794-1796) for agreeing with Republican and French criticism of Jay's treaty. He returned to Virginia to serve as governor (1799-1802) and was sent to France by the Jefferson administration (1802-1803). Before his appointment as Madison's secretary of state and heir apparent (1811-1817), he served in diplomatic posts in Britain and Spain (1803-1806).

Monroe entered politics as a protégé of Jefferson, remained a loyal Republican, and was chosen to succeed Madison as president. As a Virginia politician he followed a states' rights line, and in the Virginia convention (1788) he opposed the Constitution. His greatest diplomatic contribution was the purchase of Louisiana (1803).

His presidency was known as the "era of good feelings" because of the demise of the Federalists as a national party. His administration saw the acquisition of Florida (1819), the Missouri Compromise (1820), and the promulgation of the Monroe Doctrine (1823).

The Monroe Doctrine declared that the western hemisphere was no longer open for European colonization and that the United States would regard any European overtures as a threat. The doctrine was primarily the work of his secretary of state, John Quincy Adams, and contained elements contributed by Jefferson and Madison.   *—Allen F. Kifer*

MONROE DOCTRINE, a statement by President James Monroe in his annual message to Congress in 1823 that the American continents "are henceforth not to be considered as subjects for future colonization by any European powers" and that any such attempt would be regarded as "the manifestation of an unfriendly disposition toward the United States."

In return the United States would not "interfere in the internal concerns" of any European state. Recent applications of the Monroe Doctrine included the 1965 intervention in the Dominican Republic and President John Kennedy's actions in the Cuban missile crisis.

The Monroe Doctrine equated de facto with de jure government as a basis for United States recognition by the right of national self-determination. The doctrine marked the growing isolationist trend in the United States with its offer of escape from European entanglements and its stated desire for the western hemisphere to follow its own path in world affairs.

The Monroe Doctrine was expanded upon in 1904 with President Theodore Roosevelt's enunciation of the Roosevelt Corollary of the United States "international police power" in dealing with European threats to intervene in the finances of the Dominican Republic. The implications of the Corollary produced ill feeling in Latin America with fear of United States exploitation under the mantle of the Monroe Doctrine. The Roosevelt Corollary continued in force until the 1930 Clark Memorandum, which called it an improper extension of the Monroe Doctrine and stated that the basis for United States intervention should be "the doctrine of self-preservation." This statement was the start of the Good Neighbor Policy and decreased United States intervention.

MORRILL ACT (1862) established many technical and agricultural colleges through land grants in the Middle West and Far West. In response to long-term pressure for vocational training facilities, Rep. Justice Morrill introduced a land-grant bill in 1857, but it was vetoed by President Buchanan. A similar bill signed by President Lincoln on July 2, 1862, has been called the Morrill Act.

Under the Act, each state was endowed 30,000 acres per representative and senator. In some states the land went to existing schools, while in other states it proved an impetus for founding new institutions. The Act was amended in later years. Under the provisions of the Act over 13 million acres have been distributed and about 70 colleges have been founded.

MOST FAVORED NATION, a nondiscriminatory trade policy in which signatories to a trade treaty agree to give each other the most favorable trade concessions that they may separately grant to a third nation. This approach has been United States trade policy for much of the twentieth century. Essentially, the United States does not discriminate against the products of foreign nations in tariff rates as long as those nations do not discriminate against United States trade.

MOTOR VEHICLE MANUFACTURERS ASSOCIATION OF THE UNITED STATES (MVMA), an interest group whose members manufacture automobiles, trucks, and buses. The activities of MVMA include the compiling of statistics, research programs, and publishing books, reports, and technical journals relating to the industry. It also monitors legislative activities and lobbies for laws that benefit the industry.

MUCKRAKERS, the name given to a group of early twentieth-century writers who exposed public corruption and attacked slums, juvenile delinquency, prostitution, and the social evils that produced them. Popular magazines serialized these exposures, one of the most famous of which was Ida M. Tarbell's *History of the Standard Oil Company* (1903). Lincoln Steffens' *The Shame of the Cities* (1904) detailed political corruption on the state and local levels, citing how the drive for personal aggrandizement combined with the pressures of urbanization to depersonalize and impoverish the masses. Steffens' work and *The Treason of the Senate* by David Graham Phillips were instrumental in making politics synonymous with corruption. Few corporate enterprises were immune from the

Chief "muckraking" work of author Ida Tarbell was a detailed history of the Standard Oil Company.

muckrakers' investigations—finance, railroads, and insurance were all examined.

The evangelical and crusading impulses of these writers soon gave way to sensationalism, which was decried publicly by President Theodore Roosevelt in 1906. Roosevelt's speech first applied the term, which he took from an allegorical character in John Bunyan's *Pilgrim's Progress*. Nevertheless, the muckrakers were instrumental in arousing public concern, which in some cases was translated into programs to correct the exposed evils. Muckraking also affected the fictional literature of the time, most notably Upton Sinclair's *The Jungle* (1906), a novel about the meat-packing industry and the Chicago stockyards. By 1910, muckraking was on the decline. A resurgence of sorts began in the 1960s when attorney Ralph Nader began a drive for consumer protection that has attracted many adherents.

MULTILATERAL TREATIES. *See* Collective Security.

MULTIPARTY SYSTEM. The multiparty system is generally reflective of deep and persistent cleavages caused by religious or socioeconomic factors. Groups formed from these irreconcilable factors tend to be ideological in their orientation. In democratic societies the multiparty system, although highly dependent upon coalitions in order to form a government, operates much as a two-party system. France has twelve parties represented in the National Assembly; Italy has nine major parties in the Chamber of Deputies; and the Federal Republic of Germany has three major parties in the Bundestag.

See also Two-party System.

MUNICIPAL COURTS. *See* Judicial System.

MUNICIPAL GOVERNMENT, a type of local government, typically, a municipal corporation created by the national or regional government to serve as an administrative subdivision of that government and to provide local services for the comfort and convenience of citizens of the area. Ordinarily, municipal government exists separately from county and subcounty governments, not being responsible to them, nor reporting to their officers, dealing directly with the regional or central government and enjoying a coequal status with other local governments. Municipalities, as public corporations, have typically received charters from the central or regional governments. As corporations municipalities have a life of their own, independent of their citizens, can sue and be sued, own property, and make contracts.

Development. Even before the Norman Conquest in England, a few cities had been allowed to manage some of their own affairs, though under the general supervision of a representative of the king. Later other expanding cities were allowed to purchase from the crown a charter declaring their right to govern themselves within the rules established by the general laws of the nation. These cities, generally known as boroughs, had their own form of government and powers, as were agreed upon between the civic leaders and representatives of the crown in the negotiated charter. This practice of tailor-made charters, special powers for cities that were not enjoyed by rural areas, and the implied right of cities to have a special privilege to manage their own affairs became important in the United States as its urban communities began to emerge in colonial times.

Shortly after the proclamation of the Declaration of Independence, the legislature of New York State reaffirmed the New York City charter. The action set a precedent for all of the American states, and henceforth the legislature, seen as a representative of the people, determined the status of cities.

Organizational Types. Local government organization falls into three primary types. The first, descended from ancient English practice, emphasizes local autonomy on matters of local concern, although these matters are interpreted quite narrowly in both the United Kingdom and in the other nations that have followed its traditions, particularly the Commonwealth nations and the United States. The system characteristically includes a number of elective administrative officers as well as a one- or two-house council, elected for terms of from one to four years. The relationship with the central government tends to be functional in character. That is, the local health department tends to deal with the state or national health department, the highway departments at all levels with one another, and the like. Although there is some trend toward developing a ministry or department of local government to coordinate various functions and levels, this idea has had a limited amount of acceptance, going furthest in Great Britain itself.

The second type of government is the French system, which stems from the reforms that followed the French Revolution. The system is commonly found in the democracies of continental Europe and in the nations that were once colonies of those countries, as well as in Latin America and Japan. This system is highly centralized, with prefects hired and paid by the central government as the connecting link. Although there is usually a locally elected mayor and council, local policy discretion is less than in the Anglo-American system. Most policies and budgetary proposals must fit within the specific guidelines of central government policy or must be approved by the Ministry of the Interior before they can go into effect.

The third system is the Communist government, where local discretion is severely restricted by the regional and national governments. Effective intergovernmental relations and controls are coordinated through the Communist party machinery. Soviets (Russian councils) are elected popularly, although there is seldom more than one candidate for each office and all candidates are screened by the party. As under the French system, the actual routine administration of local government is in the hands of a professional bureaucracy.

Types of Charters. The powers and forms of city governments rest upon their charters. The practice of granting a special charter tailor-made for a particular city was adopted in the American colonies and, later, in the states. This *special act charter* is a grant of powers and structure only to a specifically-named city. In England, the United States, and the Commonwealth countries, the chartered municipality remains subject to the general laws. In the United States the special act charter allowed the state legislatures to dominate basic policy, including patronage and expenditure considerations, to such an extent that the method came to be highly criticized. In the 1840s serious efforts were made to find a new type of charter that would reestablish the principal of local self-government.

The result was the *general act charter,* which became common after 1850. This charter was based upon the French practice: after the Revolution all communes were provided with the same powers and structure of government, except for Paris. This charter was part of the French notion of equality, treating all citizens equally. In the United States the general act charter did not develop successfully because the problems and needs of the smallest and largest communities were much too different to operate under the same legal provisions. The general act charter survives in the United States because of two modifications. The first was the use of a *classification system* that assigned cities charters according to some reasonable method acceptable to the courts, most commonly by population. The other modification was the *optional charter system:* under this plan the legislature established a number of different types of charters, and the local city council or the voters by referendum chose the charter preferred.

A final type of charter, uniquely American, is that of the *home-rule charter,* which allows local voters to frame, adopt, and amend their own charters. In one-fourth of the American states, this system is available for some or all cities and villages. Typically, when a city or village is incorporated, the voters select a charter commission, which then prepares a charter that goes into effect only when a majority voting at a municipal referendum approve the document. Amendments are proposed by the council and sometimes by the charter commission, subject to referendum approval. In general, home rule charters do not have greater powers than do special or general act charters.

The powers that can be written into the municipal home-rule charter are limited by the universal use in the United States of Dillon's Rule, which says that, if in doubt, a municipality does not have power to act: the local charter is subject to the state constitution and to the general laws adopted by the state legislature. Dillon's Rule applies to home-rule cities as well as to others. The courts have tended to interpret general laws broadly, so that doubts are resolved in favor of the legislature rather than the municipality. Home rule has encouraged democratic experimentation in local government structure, and home rule's relative flexibility has been an attractive feature for municipal reformers.

Structures. The structures of municipal government in the United States fit into four types. The first type began to appear in the late eighteenth century and was a modification of the traditional English form. It is usually called *the weak mayor-council form* and evolved gradually over about two generations. By the end of the Civil War, it was virtually the universal form in the United States. The typical council was large by today's standards, sometimes consisting of more than 100 members. It was elected by wards, usually on a partisan ballot, and typically for two-year terms. The ceremonial head of the city, the mayor was weak because he had few administrative powers. The mayor had significant legislative powers, usually presiding over the council and often having the power to break ties. After the 1840s he commonly also had a veto power. At first the mayor was appointed, but after the wave of Jacksonian democracy in the 1830s, he became elective, usually on a partisan ballot for a two-year term. The personnel system was based upon patronage, for the merit system had not yet been developed in the United States. In the early years, administration was in the hands of council committees, but as committees grew larger and more complex, there was a strong tendency, beginning in the 1850s, to transfer administration to boards and commissions appointed by the council or by the mayor with the approval of the council. The weak-mayor plan is still commonly found in villages, in many medium-sized cities, especially in the South, and even in a few larger cities, Chicago and Los Angeles, for example.

The second form, *the strong mayor-council form,* grew out of the first. Many municipal reformers, beginning in the early 1880s, began to advocate this plan as being more in keeping with modern efficient business practices. Under this plan elections might be either partisan or nonpartisan. There was a definite tendency to lengthen the term to four years in hopes that this would allow the mayor and council members to concentrate more on civic duties and less on politics. The council was reduced in size and often made elective at-large. It was relieved of most of its administrative powers. The mayor was separated from the council, no longer presiding over it. He had a veto power and was given the power to appoint all or most department heads, with or sometimes without council

approval, and most of the boards and commissions were abolished. Emphasis was placed upon the merit system of civil service, and every effort was made to encourage professionalism. The strong-mayor plan is most commonly found in the nation's largest cities and in some of middle size. Increasingly, the mayor is assisted by a chief administrative officer.

The *commission plan* was devised in Galveston, Tex., in 1900. For a short time it became the target of interest for reformers looking for a plan that resembled the corporate structure in private business. The plan called for a small council, usually of three or five members and not more than seven. Collectively, its members acted as the legislative body; individually, they headed up departments or groups of departments. One commissioner, usually called the commissioner of public affairs, headed some agencies and also served as the mayor for ceremonial purposes. Commonly, he presided over council meetings but ordinarily had no veto power. This plan secured many adoptions from the time of its founding until about 1917, when it began to decline. There have been many abandonments but virtually no adoptions of the plan since then, owing to its internal weaknesses: the inability of the public to identify persons of administrative ability, and the lack of any institutionalized checks and balances. The plan, with modifications, is still used in a number of middle-sized cities and a few larger ones, but it is considered an anachronism, and the number of communities using it declines annually.

The *council-manager plan* was first put into use in 1913. It proved to be the long-sought parallel to the corporate structure in private business. Under the typical plan, there is a small council, usually five or seven members, rarely more than nine, elected at-large on a nonpartisan ballot for a four-year term. The council members are supposed to be responsible for basic policy making. They choose a professional city manager, who serves at their pleasure and names the department heads, often without the necessity for council approval. In the model plan, the mayor has no administrative powers, excepting in cases of emergencies, such as tornadoes or riots, in which case he is sometimes empowered to take over from the city manager, apparently on the assumption that in such times someone who is directly elected by the voters should be in the principal position of decision making. The manager plan spread rapidly after it was introduced. It became and has remained the favorite of municipal reformers and was widely adopted by the large number of new municipalities that were created in suburbia following World War II. Variations of the plan have also been adopted in Canada, Ireland, and the Federal Republic of Germany.

Municipal Courts. The court systems have generally been outside of municipal government, being primarily agencies of the national or regional governments. For practical reasons, however, courts are often limited to local jurisdictions and take care of minor cases, particularly those involving traffic offenses and violations of city ordinances, but courts in nearly all nations are agencies of a broader jurisdiction than that of the municipality.

Intergovernmental Relations. In the United States almost no major municipal policy is made unilaterally by the city government. The municipality must often work in conjunction with special districts, the county, the state, the national government, or even on an interstate or international basis. The same general pattern exists in most, if not all, nations of the world. Urban government is not declining in importance, but it is becoming more complex and costly. As a result, the pattern of decision making has become more complex and more difficult for the typical citizen to understand.   —*Charles R. Adrian*

See also Local Government.

MURRAY v. CURLETT. *See* Abington School Distict v. Schempp.

MUTINY, an uprising by sailors or soldiers against their commanders. Because of its need for discipline and obedience to authority, the military's most serious offense is mutiny. It has been defined a bit differently in American military law to mean action by two or more who, with intent to usurp or override lawful military authority, in concert disobey orders, shirk their duty, or create any violence or disturbance. The maximum penalty for mutiny is death.

MUTUAL DEFENSE ASSISTANCE ACT (1949, 1950), passed in an era of increasing fear of Communist power and aggression, was designed to improve the military strength of United States allies. The compromise bill reported out of Congress contained unrequested appropriations for China and, by assigning sums to specific nations, rejected the blank check President Truman wanted.

Of a total of more than $1.4 billion in military aid in 1949, $1 billion was authorized for NATO members who asked for aid. Greece and Turkey received a total of over $200 million, with smaller amounts assigned to Iran, South Korea, and the Philippines. The "general area" of China was given $75 million. In 1950 the act was extended for a year and applied to the same nations, with another $1 billion for NATO countries.

MUTUAL DEFENSE ASSISTANCE CONTROL PROGRAM. *See* Containment Policy.

MYERS v. UNITED STATES, 272 U.S. 52 (1926), questions the president's power to remove one of his appointees from office. Myers was appointed by President Wilson to a first-class postmastership in Portland, Ore., for a four-year term. He was removed from that office by the President 18 months before the term had expired, and he sued the government for the salary of which he was deprived.

In a 6-to-3 decision, Chief Justice Taft stated that the president has the unrestricted power to remove his appointed executive officers without the advice or consent of the Senate. Mr. Justice Holmes dissented, saying that the duty of the president to see that the laws be executed is a duty that does not go beyond the laws or the power given to him by Congress. This decision was overruled in 1935 by *Humphrey's Executor v. United States,* a decision which allowed Congress to limit the president's power of removal.

See also Humphrey's Executor v. United States.

NADER, RALPH (1934-   ), consumer advocate, known for his research in the field of automotive safety. He was educated at Princeton University's Woodrow Wilson School of Public and International Affairs (1955) and graduated with distinction from Harvard Law School (1958).

He wrote a 200-page report on auto safety in 1964 while serving as a consultant to the Labor Department. This report was the basis for his book *Unsafe At Any Speed* (1965). The book attacked the automotive industry, especially General Motors' Corvair. It was largely owing to Nader's actions that the National Traffic and Motor Vehicle Act (1966) passed into law. Nader subsequently founded the Center for the Study of Responsive Law, a legal advocate of public interest, and Nader's Raiders, a group of young lawyers and lay people who investigate and lobby for his causes, which have included reducing health hazards in mining, improving the safety standards of natural gas pipelines, and exposing baby foods for lack of nutritional value.

NARDONE v. UNITED STATES, 302 U.S. 379 (1937) and 308 U.S. (1939), concern the interpretation of the congressional intent of the Federal Communications Act of 1934, which provided that "no person not being authorized by the sender shall intercept any communication and divulge or publish the existence, contents, substance . . . of such intercepted communication to any person." The first time this case was before the Court, the question was whether evidence procured by a federal officer's wiretapping of telephone wires and intercepting of messages was admissible in a criminal trial.

The Court held that wiretapping invaded the right of privacy guaranteed by the Fourth and Fifth Amendments and that evidence obtained by that method was inadmissible in a federal prosecution. *Nardone II* questions whether the act also interdicts other use of evidence so obtained. Here the Court held that evidence discovered as a result of wiretapping could not be used in a federal prosecution in any manner.

NATIONAL ACADEMY OF SCIENCE (NAS), established in 1863 and approved by President Lincoln, an organization of distinguished scientists and engineers dedicated to furthering science and its uses for the general welfare. NAS, although under a congressional charter, is not a governmental agency. Its members, all United States citizens, are chosen for their continuing achievements in scientific or technological research. In 1964 NAS's council created the National Academy of Engineers, a parallel organization of engineering. The National Council of Research, whose members are selected by the NAS president, directly administers several million dollars annually to support conferences, committees, research projects, and fellowships in pioneering technology.

NATIONAL AERONAUTICS AND SPACE ADMINISTRATION (NASA), an independent governmental agency established in 1958 by the National Aeronautics and Space Act for the peaceful use of space. The agency is responsible for developing, building, testing, and operating aeronautical and space vehicles and for exploring space with manned and unmanned spacecraft. NASA also maintains cooperation between the United States and other countries on space activities for peaceful uses.

The offices that carry out NASA programs include the Office of Aeronautics and Space Technology, which conducts programs to develop advanced space technology and coordinates NASA research, and the Office of Space Science and Applications, which conducts research and investigations of the solar system, galaxies, and the planet Earth. This office is also responsible for efforts to understand microgravity, possibilities for life in space, and space communications. The Office of Space Flight is responsible for the space shuttle and other space transportation programs and coordinates all related research. The Office of Space Tracking and Data Systems monitors in-flight spacecraft with a worldwide system of tracking stations. NASA also maintains field offices around the country that facilitate the research and development necessary for its programs.

See also International Treaty on the Peaceful Uses of Outer Space.

NATIONAL AIR AND SPACE MUSEUM. *See* Smithsonian Institution.

NATIONAL ARCHIVES AND RECORD SERVICE (NARS), a part of the General Services Administration, established in 1949 to succeed the National Archive Establishment. The service selects, preserves, and makes available to the government and the public the permanently valuable noncurrent records of the federal government. NARS also administers the presidential libraries of Hoover, F.D. Roosevelt, Truman, Eisenhower, Kennedy, and L.B. Johnson. These libraries preserve presidential papers and collections, acquire related historical materials, prepare documentary and descriptive publications, and exhibit historic documents and museum items. The service also operates a library containing material on American history, government organization, archival science, and records management.

NARS regularly publishes the *Federal Register,* containing all federal regulatory documents; the *Code of Federal Regulations;* the *U.S. Government Organization Manual;* the *Public Papers of the Presidents of the United States;* and a variety of other historical documents. The service assists other federal agencies by promoting improved records management and paper practices.

NATIONAL ASSOCIATION FOR THE ADVANCEMENT OF COLORED PEOPLE (NAACP), the oldest and largest of U.S. civil rights groups. Founded in 1910 by W.E.B. DuBois, the black educator and writer, and seven white Americans, the organization devoted

Apollo 11 astronaut Edwin E. Aldrin stands on the moon during the first expedition to the lunar surface.

its earliest efforts toward ending the prevalent practice of lynching.

From its inception NAACP has advocated non-violence and eschewed extremist methods, working primarily through the courts to achieve black civil rights. Its Legal Defense and Educational Fund, which was for many years headed by Thurgood Marshall, brought to court cases involving discrimination in education, voting, travel and public facilities, and the racial composition of juries. Winning 29 of the 32 cases it argued before the Supreme Court, NAACP's greatest legal victory came in 1954 when the court, in *Brown v. Board of Education,* ruled segregation in the public schools to be unlawful.

Although the association has been criticized as being overly moderate, the NAACP continues to seek legal compliance with federal civil-rights laws.

NATIONAL ASSOCIATION FOR THE ADVANCE-MENT OF COLORED PEOPLE (NAACP) v. ALA-BAMA, 357 U.S. 499 (1958), concerns the freedom of association protected by the Fourteenth Amendment. Alabama was trying to compel the NAACP, a nonprofit membership corporation organized in New York, to qualify to do business as a foreign corporation in Alabama. In the course of Alabama court proceedings to require such qualification, the state demanded the names and addresses of all the NAACP's Alabama members.

In the opinion of the Court, the production of such a list would be a restraint on the NAACP members' exercise of their freedom to engage in association for the advancement of beliefs and ideas, part of the liberty assured by the due process clause of the Fourteenth Amendment. The Court could not discover any legitimate interest that Alabama might have in discovery of the names but suspected that the purpose was to harass the association.

See also Griswold v. Connecticut.

NATIONAL ASSOCIATION FOR THE ADVANCE-MENT OF COLORED PEOPLE (NAACP) v. BUTTON, 371 U.S. 415 (1963), questions the constitutionality of a chapter of the Commonwealth of Virginia Code which forbade the solicitation of legal business by any agent for an individual or organization who retains a lawyer in connection with an action to which it is not a party and in which it has no pecuniary interest. The NAACP maintained that the statute abridged the freedoms of the First Amendment by preventing the NAACP and its members and lawyers from associating for the purpose of assisting persons, not necessarily members, who seek legal redress for infringements of their rights.

The Court held that such NAACP activities are modes of expression and association protected by the First and Fourteenth Amendments which Virginia may not prohibit in the course of regulating the legal profession.

NATIONAL ASSOCIATION OF COUNTIES (NACO), a nationwide research and interest group representing elected and appointed county officials from 2,100 counties. NACO is the organization that lobbies for counties at the federal level.

NATIONAL ASSOCIATION OF MANUFACTUR-ERS (NAM), a voluntary nationwide organization representing the interest of private industry. Founded in 1895 to promote the cause of trade and commerce and to encourage the free enterprise system, NAM represents the views of its member companies on national and international questions to government. NAM has a number of standing committees to study such issues as economic policy, security, finance, agricultural cooperation, educational needs, and environmental matters. Recommendations to support or oppose proposed legislation are often made to members. In addition to producing numerous publications, bulletins, and reports, NAM's Industrial Information Committee operates as a public information body. Headquarters are in New York City.

NATIONAL BUREAU OF STANDARDS, founded in 1901 as part of the Treasury Department. In 1903 NBS was transferred to the Department of Commerce

National Bureau of Standards uses this anechoic chamber, whose porous walls minimize the reflection of sound, to test various acoustical products.

and Labor, and when that department was split into separate departments in 1913, NBS remained part of the Commerce Department.

The goal of NBS is to strengthen and advance the nation's science and technology and to facilitate their effective application for public benefit. To meet this responsibility, NBS conducts research and provides a complete and consistent system of physical measurements coordinating it with the measurement systems of other nations. For instance, NBS conducts materials research to improve ways of measuring the properties of substances and provides standard reference materials—samples thoroughly characterized according to composition or some other physical property—so that science and industry may bring their measurements into control.

NBS also develops standards and tests in such areas as housing, fabric flammability, and fire safety. NBS aids other government agencies in the selection and effective use of automatic data-processing equipment.
—*Lewis M. Branscomb*

NATIONAL COLLECTION OF FINE ARTS. *See* Smithsonian Institution.

NATIONAL COMMISSION ON . . . *See* second part of name.

NATIONAL COMMITTEE, a focal point of party organization in the United States. The Democratic national committee comprises one man and one woman from each state and territory. The Republican national committee has, in addition, the party chairmen of states that have voted Republican across the board in the previous national election. Committee members are selected in most cases by the national party conventions. In a few states members are chosen by the state committee in a convention or in a primary election. The national committee chairman is nominated by the party's presidental nominee, and the committee ratifies this choice pro forma.

Theoretically the committee is responsible for directing the presidential campaign, but in practice these duties lie with the campaign manager, who is the nominee's personal choice. The most widely publicized job of the committee is the planning and administration of the national convention—selecting the convention officers. Between elections the committee's authority to direct the national headquarters and deliberate on policy matters (without specific convention authority to make final decisions) is assumed by an executive committee chosen by the party national chairman. Over the last twenty years both major parties have made use of advisory councils to help formulate policy. Since 1952 the Republican advisory council to the committee has been a permanent body. Each state national committee member acts as liaison with the state organization, helping to ascertain grass-

roots opinion of policy matters. After the turbulence of the 1968 Democratic national convention in Chicago and the subsequent unsuccessful campaign of Hubert Humphrey, the Democratic national committee established a committee to reform delegate selection procedures and to reestablish communication with the masses.

NATIONAL COMMITTEE FOR AN EFFECTIVE CONGRESS (NCEC), an independent, nonpartisan, political action group founded in New York City in 1948. The organization's objective is to enhance the effectiveness of Congress by electing the most able candidates of either party to the House and Senate. NCEC surveys all congressional contests and then throws its support to those candidates selected by offering financial aid and public endorsements and doing field work. The committee has recently been concerned with campaign finance reform, Congressional procedures, and military versus domestic spending in the national budget. The committee's views on pertinent issues are found in its *Congressional Report.*

NATIONAL COOPERATIVE SOIL SURVEY. *See* Soil Conservation Service.

NATIONAL COUNCIL OF RESEARCH. *See* National Academy of Science.

NATIONAL COUNCIL OF SENIOR CITIZENS, an organization of some 4,000 senior citizen groups with over 4 million members. Its main activities include educational, recreational, and health programs. The council is also active in politics through lobbying for such concerns as Medicare benefits and low-cost public housing for the elderly.

NATIONAL DEFENSE EDUCATION ACT (NDEA) (1958), a $1 billion program directed toward science and foreign languages, enacted after the U.S.S.R.'s first satellite stimulated fears that the United States' education system was deficient. The bill moved through Congress with little opposition, and the act was subsequently amended and extended.

The bill established a low-interest loan fund for college students, permitting repayment over ten years. Repayment was reduced by half if borrowers taught in elementary or secondary schools for five years. The act provided matching grants to state schools and loans to private schools for science and foreign language facilities and created fellowships for graduate students who planned to teach at colleges or universities. There were smaller grants for advanced language study and for use of audiovisual media for education.

NATIONAL EDUCATION ASSOCIATION (NEA), a union and professional organization that represents teachers, professors, and administrators. The original purpose of the organization was to improve the working conditions of teachers and to upgrade the level of education in the United States. The NEA has been very successful in its lobbying efforts, particularly in increasing federal support of education. Participation in collective bargaining is also a key aspect of the union's activities.

NATIONAL ENVIRONMENTAL POLICY ACT (1969), established a Council on Environmental Quality to advise the president on environmental problems and technology. Under provisions of this Act, environmental impact statements must be filed with the Environmental Protection Agency before federal funds can be expended on any major project. Federal agencies are required to provide a written analysis of the potential effect on the environment of all significant activities and must prepare alternative recommendations. This Act was a reflection of growing concern in Congress over potential adverse impacts on public safety arising from environmental pollution and the development of new technology capable of creating long-range environmental consequences.

—Mary L. Carns

NATIONAL FARMERS UNION, also known as the Farmers' Educational and Cooperative Union of America, representing farm families, with membership concentrated in the wheat-growing areas of such Great Plains states as Oklahoma, Nebraska, and the Dakotas.

From headquarters in Denver, Colo., the union sponsors legislation and educational activities to promote farmer interests. A long-time supporter of political reformism and labor, the group upholds the tradition of the individual family farm. The union has successfully sponsored cooperative efforts in setting up storage terminals in the purchase of farm equipment and the sale of farm products and envisions the ultimate replacement of private enterprise by the cooperative movement.

NATIONAL FEDERATION OF BUSINESS AND PROFESSIONAL WOMEN'S CLUBS, an organization of business and professional women representing over 700 occupations. The group, founded in 1919, promotes the interests of women in business and extends their opportunities for growth through industrial, scientific, and vocational education. Headquarters are in Washington, D.C.

NATIONAL FOREST SYSTEM. *See* Forest Service.

NATIONAL FOUNDATION ON THE ARTS AND HUMANITIES. Created in 1965 as an independent agency responsible to the White House, the foundation promotes progress in and understanding of the

nation's intellectual and cultural life through grants to individuals, groups, and state offices to support projects, research, and the dissemination of information. The foundation consists of the National Endowment for the Arts and the National Endowment for the Humanities, each with its respective national council in charge of reviewing policies and grant applications. A 20-member Federal Council of the Arts and Humanities coordinates the work of the foundation with other agencies. Gifts are matched by the U.S. Treasury and given with an obligation to stimulate matching funds—thereby quadrupling each private dollar invested.

East wing of the National Gallery of Art, Washington, D.C.

NATIONAL GALLERY OF ART, a bureau of the Smithsonian Institution, created in 1937 as the result of Andrew W. Mellon's gift to the United States of his important art collection and a monumental gallery building. The gallery is responsible for assembling and maintaining a national collection of art representative of the best in American and European artistic heritage.

The collection included paintings, sculpture, prints, drawings, and items of decorative art. Several distinguished collections have been added to the gallery's original nucleus. In 1941 the Kress collection of Italian art was bequeathed to the gallery. The Widener collection of famous works was presented to the gallery in 1942. Also outstanding among the gallery's holdings is the Rosenwald Collection of over 23,000 prints and drawings. Two of the gallery's most famous works are *Portrait of Genevra de Benci* by Leonardo da Vinci and *The Artist's Father* by Paul Cézanne.

NATIONAL GOVERNORS' CONFERENCE, an organization composed of the governors of the 50 states and U.S. possessions such as Puerto Rico and Guam. The association is an interest group concerned with the development and implementation of federal government policy toward the states. It is involved in research activities on important issues and serves as a clearinghouse for information concerning new and innovative programs.

NATIONAL GRANGE, a nationwide fraternal organization of rural and farm families founded in 1867. Although it was initially somewhat radical, the grange today is a politically conservative group whose primary objective is the passage of legislation favorable to the agricultural interests of its members. There are over 7,000 local granges that offer social and economic programs such as youth activities, educational courses, and such services as buying cooperatives, low-priced insurance, and credit unions. The grange is opposed to efforts of labor unions to organize farm workers and advocates lifting trade restrictions to open more foreign markets to American farm products.

NATIONAL HEALTH INSURANCE. *See* Social Insurance.

NATIONAL HIGHWAY INSTITUTE (NHI), agency that is the vehicle through which the Federal Highway Administration instructs state and local highway agency employees who will be involved in federal-aid highway projects. The NHI also aids in the education of highway technicians.

NATIONAL HIGHWAY TRAFFIC SAFETY ADMINISTRATION, federal agency that establishes and carries out programs to promote the safety of motor vehicles, drivers, and pedestrians. The administration's aim is to reduce the number of deaths and injuries on streets and highways. Various research and development programs are pursued to increase motor vehicle safety, maintain clean air, and improve motor vehicle fuel economy. The administration also must maintain a uniform national speed limit.

NATIONAL INCOME. *See* Gross National Product (GNP).

NATIONAL INDUSTRIAL RECOVERY ACT (NIRA) (1933), one of the New Deal's most sweeping and controversial measures, designed to stimulate industry and trade and to relieve unemployment.

Under Title I the National Recovery Administration (NRA), directed by Gen. Hugh S. Johnson, was created. Supervised by the government, businesses were allowed to draft code agreements exempt from antitrust laws. Section 7a tried to safeguard labor by guaranteeing the rights of employees to bargain collectively through representatives of their own choosing. Title II of the act authorized a Public Works Administration (PWA), under Interior Secretary Ickes,

to construct roads, public buildings, and other projects. In 1935 Roosevelt asked that the NIRA be extended two years, but the Senate limited the extension to ten months. The Supreme Court declared NIRA unconstitutional in 1935 in *Schechter Poultry Corporation v. United States.* The National Labor Relations Act, a stronger version of Section 7a, was before Congress as the Court considered *Schechter Poultry.*

See also National Labor Relations Board; New Deal Legislation; *Glossary.*

NATIONAL INSTITUTES OF HEALTH (NIH), a separate division of the Department of Health and Human Services that provides leadership and direction to U.S. health programs, medical research, and health manpower training programs. Twelve research institutes conduct and finance research: National Cancer Institute; National Heart, Lung and Blood Institute; National Library of Medicine; National Institutes of Arthritis, Metabolism, and Digestive Diseases; National Institute of Allergy and Infectious Diseases; National Institute of Child Health and Development; National Institute of Dental Research; National Institute of Environmental Health Sciences; National Institute of General Medical Sciences; National Institute of Neurological and Communicative Disorders and Stroke; and National Institute on Aging.

In addition, NIH has six research divisions, including the John F. Fogarty International Center and the Division of Research Grants. Through these various institutes and divisions, the NIH conducts and supports biomedical research into the causes, prevention, and control of disease.

—Guy C. Colarulli and Victor F. D'Lugin

NATIONALISM, a political movement developed in Europe in the eighteenth century. Nationalism has been a moving force in most revolutions during the past 200 years. The one principle held in common by all nationalists is the right of people sharing an ethnic and cultural tradition to unify themselves into a single nation-state. Other than the right of self-determination, however, nationalists have varied widely in their political, economic, and social views. The earliest movements, typified by the American and French revolutions, were in general liberal, democratic, and middle-class in orientation. Toward the end of the nineteenth century, struggles for national unification, such as Germany's, acquired an autocratic and militaristic character. The worst form, aggressive nationalism, was expressed by the xenophobia and imperialism of fascist Italy and Nazi Germany. Today nationalism, combined with socialism and anti-colonialism, provides the impetus for wars of national liberation in the emerging states of Africa, Asia, and Latin America.   *—Robert F. Smith*

NATIONAL LABOR RELATIONS BOARD (NLRB),

independent, regulatory agency empowered under the Wagner Act (1935), the Taft-Hartley Act (1947), and the Landrum-Griffin Act (1959). The NLRB is made up of five members appointed by the president for five years and a general counsel appointed for four years. The board performs quasi-judicial and quasi-legislative functions aimed at preventing and remedying unfair labor practices by employers or by union organizations and at protecting fair union representation. In disputes it supervises secret-ballot union elections. The general counsel brings cases and complaints before the board for a ruling, and most are settled by voluntary action.

The board maintains 33 regional and several subregional offices. The NLRB has been crucial in formulating and altering national labor policy since the 1930s. It is the single agency most responsible for ending violent labor/management confrontations. A strong pro-labor reputation earned by the NLRB for its early and forceful action guaranteeing employees' rights to strike and to organize has been mitigated by forceful NLRB application of subsequent legal strictures on the unions.

NATIONAL LABOR RELATIONS BOARD (NLRB) v. JONES & LAUGHLIN STEEL CORPORATION, 301 U.S. 1 (1937), concerns unfair labor practices affecting commerce in violation of the National Labor Relations Act (Wagner Act). Jones & Laughlin had discharged some workers because of their union activities. The NLRB ordered the company to reinstate the men and to stop discriminating against members, or those who desire to become members, of a labor union. The company refused to do so and challenged the validity of the board's order and of the act itself. In a 5-to-4 decision, the Court held that the NLRB was acting within the sphere of its authority granted by Congress. Employees have the right to self-organization, representation, and collective bargaining, and discrimination and coercion to prevent this free exercise is clearly prohibited by the Constitution.

See also Hammer v. Dagenhart; United States v. Butler.

NATIONAL LEAGUE OF CITIES, an organization of over 1,100 cities. The league conducts research, holds conferences, and provides training to municipal officials to meet the needs and problems facing cities. It also lobbies for the cities in Congress and executive agencies in an attempt to increase federal aid. The organization maintains the National League of Cities Institute and publishes several periodicals dealing with urban affairs.

NATIONAL LEAGUE OF CITIES v. USERY, 426 U.S. 833 (1976), case in which the Supreme Court held, for the first time in four decades, that Congress had exceeded its powers under the Commerce Clause due to considerations of federalism. Congress cannot require the states as employers to abide by federal minimum wage and maximum hours regulations because that would "impair[ing] the States' integrity or their ability to function effectively in a federal system," and the states' determination of their employees' wages and hours is one of the "attributes of sovereignty attaching to every state government which may not be impaired by Congress."

NATIONAL MEDIATION BOARD, an independent federal agency that attempts to settle differences between railroads and airlines and their employees to avoid disruption of commerce or the operations of carriers. The Board was established in 1934 by a Railway Labor Act amendment that also gave these employees organizing and collective bargaining rights. The Board follows certain specified procedures to help maintain labor peace in the two industries. It also handles railroad and railway representation disputes. Other duties include financial supervision of the National Railroad Adjustment Board, which handles rail grievances relating to the interpretation and application of existing contracts.

NATIONAL MUSEUM OF NATURAL HISTORY. *See* Smithsonian Institution.

NATIONAL OCEANIC AND ATMOSPHERIC ADMINISTRATION (NOAA), federal agency, part of the Department of Commerce, NOAA is in charge of researching and assessing the atmosphere, global oceans, and the space environment. It examines the geographical structure of the oceans and monitors the consequences of changes in the environment, either natural or man-made. NOAA also reports the weather patterns across the nation and makes forecasts, issuing warnings for natural disasters such as floods and hurricanes. Considerable research is also done into harvesting the potential resources of the sea.

NATIONAL ORGANIZATION FOR WOMEN (NOW), an organization of women and men, founded in 1966, who seek "full equality for women in truly equal partnership with men." With over 260,000 members and 800 local groups, NOW is the largest women's civil rights group in the world. NOW's major goal is the elimination of sexual bias and discrimination in all aspects of public life. The organization is headquartered in Washington, D.C., and lobbies at all levels of government. NOW suffered a major defeat with the failure to ratify the Equal Rights Amendment (ERA).

NATIONAL PARK SERVICE, established in 1916 to oversee the nation's parks, recreation areas, and monuments. A division of the Department of the Interior, the service has 300 field areas that include over 26 million acres.

The role of the National Park Service is to conserve wildlife, scenery, and natural and historical objects and, at the same time, to enable the public to enjoy these elements. Construction of labeled nature walks, bicycle paths, horse trails, and camping facilities are some of the techniques the service has used to carry out its role. The National Park Service also works with the states in establishing archeological programs, providing grants for restoring historical properties, and establishing education and research programs.

Sculpture court of the National Portrait Gallery.

NATIONAL PORTRAIT GALLERY, a part of the Smithsonian Institution, located in the Old Patent Building in Washington, D.C. The gallery collects and exhibits likenesses of men and women who have made significant contributions to America's history. The concept of a national portrait gallery originated in 1782 with Charles William Peale, a Philadelphian painter and museum keeper who opened an exhibition room in which he hung a number of portraits of "worthy personages."

Attempts to establish some kind of gallery have been made periodically since Peale's day. In 1962 Congress passed an act creating the gallery as a free public museum to exhibit the portraits that had been accumulating in various governmental buildings for almost two centuries. The gallery maintains a selective reference library of books, prints, photographs, and other materials about the portraitists and the persons portrayed.

See also National Gallery of Art; Smithsonian Institution.

NATIONAL PRIMARY *or* **PRESIDENTIAL PRIMARY,** a statewide primary to help a political party determine its presidential nominee at the national convention. A national primary may be a delegate election, choosing convention delegates who are ei-

ther pledged to a particular presidential candidate or unpledged. In the second type of national primary the names of the presidential candidates themselves are entered in a popular preference test. The results of this type of primary are not binding on convention delegates but serve as an indicator of popular choice. Presidential primaries involve voters at an early stage in the candidate selection process. Nevertheless, in a delegate primary, elected delegates who are pledged to a particular candidate are generally bound only on the first convention ballot and may on subsequent ballots change their votes.

Often the eventual party nominee does not enter the primary races or is victorious in only a few of them because many delegates come to the convention unpledged and those who are pledged are soon released. In recent years, however, the primary has become crucial to the nominating process, as with Democrat John Kennedy in 1960 and Republican Barry Goldwater in 1964. In both instances the candidates were not the original choices of the national party committee members, but the convention was swayed by the primary results.

In 1980 the backers of Sen. Edward Kennedy attempted to change the Democratic party's rules to free elected delegates from their commitment to vote for a candidate. The reasoning was that many of the delegates had been selected months before and in the intervening period events had occurred that may have resulted in a different candidate choice. The petition was defeated at the convention, but a rule change in 1984 abolished the provision binding all national convention delegates to vote on the first ballot for the candidate they were chosen to represent. In 1986 the Democratic Party's Fairness Commission lowered the delegate "threshold" from 20 to 15 percent of the vote.

With the proliferation of primary states and the jockeying between New Hampshire and its rivals for the limelight that goes with the status of "first in the nation," reformers sought to improve the nomination process. One national primary per party was suggested to replace the piecemeal primaries. However, it was felt that this would favor early front runners and prevent the gradual emergence of dark horses, thus eliminating the survival of the fittest that the current system allows. National primaries would replace the national conventions and lead to a further weakening of the party system and to the appearance of extremist candidates.

Increasing numbers of states are using a caucus system to select delegates. A caucus generally focuses on the party organization. Delegates to the national convention are picked by town, district, county, and, finally, state caucuses. Each state may develop its own system. The Iowa caucuses were the first indicator of voter preference during the 1988 campaign.

NATIONAL RECOVERY ADMINISTRATION (NRA). *See* New Deal Legislation.

NATIONAL REPUBLICAN PARTY, a coalition of Republicans and Democrats who feared Andrew Jackson's radicalism. The group was organized after the 1824 election by President John Quincy Adams, Henry Clay, and Daniel Webster. Supporting such conservative policies as a high tariff and the Bank of the United States, the National Republicans lost to Jackson in 1828 and again in 1832, when they endorsed Henry Clay. By 1836 the group had been absorbed by the new Whig party.

See also Political Parties in the United States; Presidential Elections.

NATIONAL RESOURCES PLANNING BOARD. *See* Council of Economic Advisors (CEA).

NATIONAL SCIENCE FOUNDATION (NSF). Created in 1950, the foundation is made up of a National Science Board, a director, a deputy director, and assistant directors named by the president. Its purpose is to strengthen research and education in the sciences through targeted programs, grants, contracts, the maintenance of large facilities, and the wider dissemination of scientific information.

NATIONAL SECURITY ACTS (1947, 1949), reorganized defense agencies in the wake of World War II. The Act of 1947 replaced the War and Navy departments with a National Military Establishment made up of separate Army, Navy, and Air Force departments under a civilian Secretary of Defense. There was no provision for a Defense Department. The secretary and the Joint Chiefs of Staff were named as the president's principal military advisers, and the National Security Council, with a Central Intelligence Agency under it, was created.

The 1949 amendment renamed the National Military Establishment the Department of Defense. The three military departments were incorporated into the new department but were to be separately administered by their secretaries. The law also provided for a non-voting chairman of the Joint Chiefs of Staff. The service secretaries were removed from the National Security Council, and the vice president was added.

See also Central Intelligence Agency (CIA); Defense, U.S. Department of; National Security Council.

NATIONAL SECURITY AGENCY (NSA)/CENTRAL SECURITY SERVICE (CSS), federal security agencies, components of the Department of Defense. The NSA was established by a presidential directive as a separately organized agency within the Department of Defense in 1952; the Central Security Service was established in 1972 in accordance with a presidential memorandum. The director of the NSA is also the chief of the CSS. The NSA/CSS is responsible for centralized coordination, direction, and performance of highly technical functions in support of government activities to protect U.S. communications and to produce foreign intelligence data.

NATIONAL SECURITY COUNCIL, a congressionally authorized organization composed of the president, vice president, and secretaries of state and defense, which advises the president on matters of national security. The council, created by the National Security Act (1947), bases recommendations on an examination of all phases of United States policy—domestic and military—with an emphasis on foreign affairs. A vital role in the decision-making process is played by the presidential assistant for national security affairs, who acts as an adviser to the council.

NATIONAL SOCIALISM *or* NAZISM, the political movement that brought Adolf Hitler to power in Germany in 1933. He headed the National Socialist German Workers (Nazi) Party. Nazism exploited the frustrations, loss of pride, and economic dislocations caused by Germany's defeat in World War I and the 1929-1933 economic depression. Hitler promised to rectify the harsh provisions of the Treaty of Versailles, to rearm Germany, to rescue the economy, and to purify the German nation. Toward these ends, the Nazis eliminated all internal political opposition and established a totalitarian regime and state control over the economy. German Jews, deprived of all their rights, were eventually executed. A militaristic and expansionist policy was begun that led to World War II. During the war the Nazis' systematic destruction of all "inferior" races was continued in the territories occupied by the German armies.

Though Nazis pursued specific objectives, the movement was essentially nihilistic. It denied the existence of any rational norms, standards, or limits of political actions. All that mattered was the struggle for power. For the Nazi, might made right. The goal of Nazism was conquest of the world. —*Robert F. Smith*

See also Absolutism: Authoritarianism; Corporate State; Fascism; Totalitarianism.

NATIONAL SUPREMACY, doctrine whereby the authority of the national government takes precedence in conflict arising from concurrent jurisdiction. Ratification of the Constitution by the states began a prolonged, gradual shift away from state predominance. The Constitution and early Supreme Court interpretations of it clearly built a governmental structure that required a new emphasis and reliance on national authority and power, in place of the colonial and subsequent state governments.

Article VI, Clause 2, states that the Constitution, congressional laws, and national treaties are supreme over state constitutions and state laws. In some areas, such as education and regulation of political parties, the states can at times claim concurrent—if not exclusive—jurisdiction under the reserved powers clause (Tenth Amendment). The enforcement of national supremacy, however, was early established in *McCulloch v. Maryland,* 1819 (a state may not use its taxing power against the national government), *Gibbons v. Ogden,* 1824 (interstate commerce laws passed by Congress take precedence over conflicting state regulations), and *Missouri v. Holland,* 1920 (international treaties supersede state laws).

When Congress under its constitutional authority enters a field which it has previously left to the states (preemption), national law is supreme over state law, the reserved powers clause notwithstanding.

—*Erwin L. Levine*

See also Concurrent Power; Federalism; Reserved Powers.

NATIONAL TRANSPORTATION SAFETY BOARD, established by the Department of Transportation Act of 1966, received DOT administrative support but is an autonomous five-member, bipartisan body appointed by the president. The board must determine the causes of all civil aviation accidents and may investigate the most serious marine, railroad, highway, or pipeline mishaps. It reviews on appeal DOT administration's certificates or licenses.

NATIONAL TREASURY EMPLOYEES UNION v. RAAB. *See* Skinner v. Railway Executive Association.

NATIONAL URBAN LEAGUE, a voluntary community service agency founded in 1910 to end segregation and discrimination. The league's services are directed toward the creation of training and jobs, the building of better schools and housing, and the attainment of better opportunities for blacks in urban communities.

The league's Action Council has lobbied for increased federal funding of Model Cities urban renewal programs. Its Field Services Department is attempting to build a power base within urban black neighborhoods by developing grass-roots economic, social, and political strength and encouraging individual involvement in planning and decision-making processes.

NATIONAL WAR COLLEGE, a top-level inter-service school for senior military officers and State Department officials. Established in 1946, it functions under the Joint Chiefs of Staff and has its headquarters at Fort McNair, Washington, D.C.

Through studies of government agencies and the military, economic, scientific, political, and social components of power the college prepares students for senior policy, command, and staff positions and for planning national strategy. The school's ten-month academic program has a series of required interrelated courses on national security, plus individual elective programs that examine selected aspects of national security. The program culminates in intensive studies of specific problems and of areas of the world.

NATIONAL WILDERNESS PRESERVATION SYSTEM. *See* Forest Service.

NATIONAL WILDLIFE FEDERATION, a private conservation organization founded in 1936 to encourage the intelligent use and management of earth's resources and create a greater public awareness and appreciation of these resources. The federation gives administrative help and financial aid to local conservation projects, grants a number of fellowships for conservation studies, and sponsors a National Achievement Awards Program. Information on relevant ecological issues and suggested supportive measures is distributed in a series of pamphlets and

ALIEN NATURALIZATION
(no national data compiled prior to 1907)

	Total	Civilian	Military	Male	Female
	10,813,196	10,187,427	625,769	5,007,992	4,212,655
1907-1910	111,738	111,738	-		
1911-1920	1,128,972	884,672	244,300	-	-
1921-1930	1,773,185	1,716,979	56,206	1,166,199[a]	255,247[a]
1931-1940	1,518,464	1,498,573	19,891	968,410	550,054
1941-1950	1,987,028	1,837,229	149,799	941,491	1,045,537
1951-1960	1,189,946[b]	1,148,241	41,705	503,508	686,438
1961-1970	1,120,263	1,084,195	36,068	513,484	606,779
1971-1980	1,464,700	1,397,800	66,900	676,500	788,200
1981-1983	518,900	508,000	10,900	238,400	280,400

a) includes 1923-30 only.
b) includes aliens serving in the armed forces who were naturalized abroad.

newsletters published at the group's Washington, D.C., headquarters.

NATIONAL YOUTH ADMINISTRATION (NYA) (1935). *See* New Deal Legislation: *Glossary.*

NATIONAL ZOOLOGICAL PARK. *See* Smithsonian Institution.

NATIVE AMERICAN PARTY. *See* Know-Nothings.

NATURALIZATION, a process by which allegiance is transferred from one country to another, generally that of residence. Every sovereign state has its own attitude toward naturalizing aliens and adopts its own rules to confer citizenship. Article I empowers Congress "to establish a uniform rule of naturalization throughout the United States." Naturalization is administered by the Bureau of Immigration and Naturalization of the Department of Justice. The present procedure follows the Immigration and Nationality Act of 1952 (McCarran-Walter Immigration Act) as amended.

The requirements to obtain United States citizenship are rather simple: the applicant must be at least 18 years old, have entered the United States legally, have resided in the country at least five years, be of good moral character, be able to read and speak English, be ready to support the Constitution, and must know the fundamentals of United States history and government. He or she must renounce previous citizenship and swear allegiance to the United States. A father's naturalization is automatically extended to his children under 18 but not to his wife. The alien wife has to be naturalized individually. A female citizen of the United States retains her citizenship after marrying an alien. A native United States citizen taken abroad by parents who naturalize in a foreign country loses his/her citizenship unless he/she establishes a permanent residence in the United States prior to the age of 25. All the rights of a native United States citizen are acquired following naturalization, except eligibility to the presidency.

When territories are transferred, their inhabitants can be naturalized collectively, as in Texas, Alaska, Hawaii, Puerto Rico, and the Virgin Islands. Denaturalizaton, often preceding deportation, may occur in cases of disloyalty or fraudulent procurement of citizenship.   *—Sergio Barzanti*
See also Immigration and Nationality Act.

NATURAL LAW. Although present as a significant understanding of the source of law since the time of the Stoics, the school of natural law theory that has had the greatest impact developed in the eighteenth and nineteenth centuries and is best represented by the writings of English political theorist John Locke. Natural law theories assume that certain actions or restraints on action are required because they are a natural part of the condition of being human. For Locke these rights included protection of life, liberty, and property. Locke's theories are evident in the 1776 Constitution of the state of Virginia and the Declaration of Independence, both documents principally authored by Thomas Jefferson.

NAVY, DEPARTMENT OF THE. *See* Defense, United States Department of.

NAZISM. *See* National Socialism.

NEAR v. MINNESOTA, 283 U.S. 697 (1931), the first case in which a state law was found to violate freedom of the press, protected by the due process clause of the Fourteenth Amendment. The Minnesota law provided for the padlocking, by injunction, of the offices of periodicals, magazines, and newspapers for printing matter which is scandalous, malicious, defamatory, or obscene. The defendant published articles charging that a gangster was in control of organized crime in Minneapolis and that law enforcement officers, particularly the chief of police, were not energetically performing their duties. The court held that the statute, by preventing the defendants from publishing their newspaper, violated the due process law by censoring their right to publish rather than the nature of what they said.
See also New York Times v. Sullivan.

NEBBIA v. NEW YORK, 291 U.S. 502 (1934), concerns the establishment of a Milk Control Board in the State of New York to fix minimum and maximum retail prices for milk. Nebbia, the proprietor of a grocery store in Rochester, sold two quarts of milk and a five-cent loaf of bread for eighteen cents and was convicted for violating the board's order to sell milk for nine cents a quart. The question before the Court was whether the federal Constitution prohibits a state from so fixing the selling price of milk. In the opinion of the Court, a state is free to adopt whatever economic policy may reasonably be deemed to promote public welfare and to enforce that policy by legislation adapted to its purpose. The Court also held that price control, like any other form of regulation, is unconstitutional only if it is arbitrary or discriminatory or constitutes unwarranted interference with individual liberty, which this control did not.

NECESSARY AND PROPER CLAUSE, the conclusion to Article I, Section 8, of the Constitution and the basis of *McCulloch v. Maryland's* "implied powers doctrine," which greatly expanded the power of the national government. The framers of the Constitution, in granting power to the national government, recognized that Congress would need ways and means of carrying out the delegated powers. This "elastic clause" thus authorized Congress to legislate in areas beyond the specific grants of power it was given if such legislation was necessary to the carrying out of the delegated powers.

For example, Congress was delegated such fiscal powers as coining money, borrowing money, and taxing; Congress decided that a national bank was a reasonable agency for carrying out these fiscal powers, and though it had no delegated power to do so, Congress chartered a national bank. The Supreme Court, in *McCulloch v. Maryland,* decided that Congress had not exceeded its authority, since the bank was necessary to the performance of the fiscal functions and since there was nothing "improper," that is, otherwise unconstitutional, involved.

— *Theodore B. Fleming, Jr.*

See also Delegated Powers; Implied Powers; McCulloch v. Maryland.

NELSON v. COUNTY OF LOS ANGELES, 362 U.S. 1 (1960), concerns the constitutionality of a California statute requiring public employees to answer congressional subcommittee questions regarding subversive activities. Petitioners Nelson and Globe, county employees, were each discharged after refusing to answer questions relating to alleged Communist party membership and activities before a subcommittee of the House Un-American Activities Committee.

An equally divided Court affirmed Nelson's dismissal, which was not discussed. In a 5-to-3 decision, the Court also affirmed dismissal of Globe on the grounds of insubordination and violation of the statute. The California statute was not directed at the exercise of the Fifth Amendment privilege against self-incrimination, but rather covered all refusals to answer, a factor militating in favor of its validity.

See also Ullman v. United States.

NEUTRALISM, a political attitude of impartiality or noninvolvement. A position of neutralism can range from withdrawal or isolation from a particular international situation to a policy of independent action avoiding alliances. Countries may often resort to neutralism in a particular situation but not as a general policy because they do not want the legal obligations of neutrality.

NEUTRALITY, the legal status of a state that avoids support of any belligerent and gives no direct aid to any of the participants in a conflict. States can declare themselves to be neutral for a particular conflict, or they can become permanently neutral either by choice or by international treaty. There are few remaining neutral states today, but Switzerland and Austria are examples of states that are generally regarded as neutrals. Under international law, neutrality carries certain legal obligations for both the neutral state and the other countries.

Modern practice has witnessed the development of nonbelligerency. States provide material aid, as the United States did for Great Britain before Pearl Harbor, without direct involvement in the conflict.

NEWBERRY V. UNITED STATES, 256 U.S. 232 (1921), questions whether or not Congress has the power to make regulations affecting primary elections for congressional candidates. In 1918 Newberry won the Republican nomination for the Senate in the state of Michigan. In so doing, he spent a great deal more than the statutory amount specified for a congressional campaign under the federal Corrupt Practices Act of 1910 and was convicted for violating the federal statute. The court, in a 5-to-4 judgment, held that senatorial primary elections were not covered by the act because of a division within the majority. However, the Court was divided 4 to 4 and was therefore unable to rule on the question of whether or not such elections were susceptible to regulations under Article I, Section 4, of the Constitution.

See also United States v. Classic.

NEW DEAL LEGISLATION, the domestic program of President Franklin Roosevelt from 1933 to 1939, characterized by intense activity by the Congress, the executive branch, and the courts. Roosevelt was an active legislator, a principal author and sponsor of much New Deal legislation, though some items, like the Tennessee Valley Authority and the Wagner Labor Relations Act, were primarily congressional in origin. New Deal legislation was not consistent. It was often makeshift and self-contradictory—the product of many traditions, ideologies, and political groups.

The Early Weeks of the New Deal saw the President and Congress busily attempting to restore confidence. A special session of Congress endorsed a presidential program taking the nation off the gold standard, closing all banks, and providing for the judicious reopening of only the strongest banks. Congress passed an economy bill to balance the budget and legalize beer in anticipation of repeal of Prohibition.

The Next Hundred Days. Congress rubber-stamped Roosevelt's recovery measures, including FERA (federal emergency grants to the states for unemployment relief), CCC (work relief in conservation for young men), FCA and HOLC (mortgage refinancing for farmers and home owners), AAA and NRA (restriction of production in agriculture and industry). One early long-range reform was TVA, which provided electricity, flood control, and regional planning for the Tennessee River Valley. Another was FDIC to insure bank deposits. More far-reaching restrictions on banks, speculators, and the purveyors of securities followed. The Securities and Exchange Commission was established in 1934 to oversee many aspects of the stock market.

NEW DEAL LEGISLATION

Agricultural Adjustment Act (1938), attempted to stabilize farm prices; succeeded Soil Conservation and Domestic Allotment Act (1936).

Agricultural Adjustment Administration (AAA), created by Agricultural Adjustment Act (1933) and designed to reduce crop surpluses and to restore farmers' purchasing power.

Civilian Conservation Corps (CCC) (1933), agency to give employment on soil, road, and reforestation projects to males between eighteen and twenty-five.

Commodity Credit Corporation (1933), created under AAA to give loans to farmers on their crops.

Emergency Banking Relief Act (1933), gave Treasury control of bank openings and gave Roosevelt wide fiscal powers.

Emergency Relief Appropriation Act (1935), created apparatus for federally funded national works programs such as WPA, RA, and REA for unemployed.

Export-Import Bank, established in 1934 to help finance foreign trade.

Farm Credit Administration (FCA), under Farm Credit Act (1933) took over all federal agricultural credit programs.

Federal Communications Commission (FCC), established by Communications Act (1934) to regulate interstate and international telegraph, radio, and cable communications.

Federal Emergency Relief Act (FERA) (1933), authorized grants to states in proportion to amounts spent on relief by the states.

Federal Farm Mortgage Corporation (FFMC), set up in 1934 under FCA to refinance farm debts.

Federal Housing Administration (FHA), established by National Housing Act (1934) to provide home financing and to revive construction of homes.

Home Owners Loan Corporation (HOLC), created under Home Owners Refinancing Act (1933) to refinance non-farm mortgages.

National Industrial Recovery Act (NIRA) (1933), established NRA, PWA, and apparatus for fair trade regulation to revive business and reduce unemployment.

National Labor Relations Board (NLRB), created by National Labor Relations Act (1935) to supervise labor-management relations.

National Recovery Administration (NRA), administered key programs regulating industry that were authorized by NIRA.

National Youth Administration (NYA) (1935), division of WPA; designed to give employment to people between sixteen and twenty-five.

Public Works Administration (PWA) (1933), established under NIRA to increase employment through projects such as construction of roads and public buildings.

Reconstruction Finance Corporation (1932), Hoover's attempt to revive economy through government loans to financial institutions and railroads.

Resettlement Administration (RA) (1935), designed to reach poor farm families, not helped by AAA, through resettlement, loans, and land improvements.

Rural Electrification Administration (REA) (1935), created to bring electricity to isolated areas without private utility service.

Securities and Exchange Commission (SEC), established by Securities Exchange Act (1934) to regulate securities transactions.

Social Security Act (1935), established programs for retirement pensions, unemployment insurance, and other social welfare services.

Soil Conservation and Domestic Allotment Act (1936), unsuccessful substitute for AAA, declared unconstitutional in 1936.

Tennessee Valley Authority (TVA) (1933), corporation created to harness potential of Tennessee Valley and to aid its economic and social welfare.

Works Progress Administration (WPA) (1935), national relief program to use unemployed on public projects; called Works Projects Administration from 1939.

Reform. There was no clear-cut turn from relief to reform in the New Deal. Relief, much of it dependent on deficit spending, continued through to World War II. By 1935 FERA and other relief programs were revamped to provide massive aid to the unemployed and the poor. WPA, a variety of programs, aided millions of Americans. NYA was provided to assist young people who had not yet entered the labor market. FSA was established to provide help to migrant workers and farm labor—untouched by the benefits of AAA—and to sponsor experimental cooperative communities through which the rural poor might obtain farms and the knowledge to operate them.

In Section 7a of the National Industrial Recovery Act and the Wagner Act, Congress recognized for the first time the right of unions to bargain collectively.

Permanent reforms—producing a moderate welfare state—were legislated beginning in 1935: old-age assistance, retirement benefits and unemployment insurance for workers, aid to the blind and the disabled, and assistance to dependent mothers and children. Other reforms included an expanded, progressive, income tax and federally financed public housing.

Backlash. New Deal legislation was challenged early by the Supreme Court: AAA and NRA, among other measures, were struck down. An attempt by Roosevelt to seek legislation to enable him to pack the Court with his own appointees created a furor and had to be abandoned, but by 1937, retirements from the Court enabled the President to begin appointing New Deal sympathizers.   —*Allen F. Kifer*

See also Depression.

NEW FEDERALISM. *See* Federalism.

NEW JERSEY PLAN. On June 15, 1787, in a countermove to the Virginia Plan, William Patterson offered to the Philadelphia Convention the so-called New Jersey, or small-state, plan. The nine resolutions of the New Jersey Plan were a revision of the Articles of Confederation rather than a replacement of them as contemplated by the Virginia Plan. Although the resolutions specifically increased the power of Congress in addition to what it possessed under the articles by giving it the power to tax and to regulate trade and commerce, the plan retained the one-house legislature, in which the states were equally represented. The plan provided, also, for a plural executive appointed by the Congress but removable at the request of the majority of state governors and a Supreme Court. The justices of the Supreme Court were to be appointed by the executive and enjoyed tenure of office during good behavior.

The most significant contribution of the New Jersey Plan was the principle of the supremacy of the Constitution as the fundamental law of the land and that acts contravening it were void. The delegates of the smaller states and the confederationists supported the plan. However, after four days of debate the delegates voted to reject it in favor of the Virginia Plan.

—*Samuel Raphalides*

See also Constitutional Convention of 1787; Virginia Plan.

NEW TOWNS, attempts to alleviate modern urban problems by establishing new communities. *See* Urban Planning.

NEW YORK TIMES v. SULLIVAN, 376 U.S. 254 (1964). L.B. Sullivan, a Commissioner of the City of Montgomery, Alabama, brought a suit for libel against the *New York Times* and others who had printed an advertisement critical of actions of Montgomery officials in relation to the civil rights movement. Under Alabama law, if a jury found that the statements made were "libelous per se," general damages could be assessed without proof of the extent of the plaintiff's injury. The jury awarded Sullivan damages of $500,000, and this judgment was upheld by the Alabama Supreme Court.

The U.S. Supreme Court unanimously reversed the judgment, finding that Alabama's rule of liability as applied to public officials in the performance of their duty deprived critics of their rights of free speech under the First and Fourteenth Amendments. Justice Brennan, for the court, said that libel laws of this sort would inhibit free and unfettered discussion of public issues. The Court declared that a public official could not constitutionally gain damages for such a statement unless he could prove that the statement was made with actual malice. Thus the burden of proof was shifted from the defendant to the plaintiff, who now

had the difficult task of proving that the statement was made with actual malice.

In concurring, Justices Black, Goldberg, and Douglas believed that all statements about public officials, even those made with actual malice, should be protected by the First Amendment. —*David Forte*

See also Near v. Minnesota.

NIXON, RICHARD MILHOUS (1913-   ), Republican politician and 37th President of the United States (1969-1974). Nixon entered politics upon his return from naval service, winning a congressional seat in 1946. He moved through the Senate to the vice-presidency under Eisenhower. Unsuccessful in his bid to succeed the general, he achieved the presidency eight years later (1968).

Congressman. During his congressional period, Nixon became known as a militant anti-Communist and a domestic conservative. He was well-known for his role in the exposure of Alger Hiss in 1948. Chosen as a conservative to balance the Eisenhower ticket in 1952, he was an active vice president, traveling extensively and attacking the Democrats vigorously at every opportunity. He emerged as heir apparent upon the general's retirement from politics.

Defeated narrowly by John F. Kennedy in 1960 and in a 1962 gubernatorial race in his native California, Nixon retired from politics to practice law. In an unusual political comeback, he won the 1968 election by a narrow margin.

President. A law-and-order candidate supported by a "silent majority," Nixon appointed four conserva-

Richard M. Nixon, 37th President of the United States, who became the first president to resign from office.

tive justices to the Supreme Court and, as the 1972 election approached, sought federal antibusing legislation. He surprised many of his constituents, however, by establishing relations with Red China and instituting wage and price controls (1971). His Vietnamization policy reduced American ground forces to a fraction of what they had been under Johnson, though he did not abandon the air war until the start of his second term, when he completed negotiations for a ceasefire and the release of American POWs.

In 1974 scandal hit his administration. He was accused of a cover-up in the Watergate affair. On August 9, 1974, Nixon resigned from office, the first president in U.S. history to do so. Although some of his aides were convicted for their roles in the Watergate scandal and cover-up, Nixon was granted a general pardon by his successor, Gerald Ford.

After resigning in 1974, Nixon made infrequent public appearances and largely avoided involvement in partisan politics. In recent years, he has emerged as a respected voice in foreign affairs, and his counsel has been sought by Presidents Reagan and Bush.

See also Watergate.

NIXON DOCTRINE, defense policy announced in July 1969. President Nixon stated that the United States would continue to supply military and economic assistance but not troops to nations whose defense was threatened. The timing of the announcement was seen as an attempt to counter increasing public opposition to the Vietnam War by emphasizing its Vietnamization.

NIXON v. CONDON, 286 U.S. 73 (1932), is an illustration of several attempts by the state of Texas to disenfranchise blacks. The Texas legislature passed a statute authorizing the state executive committee of any political party to determine who may vote in its primary. The Democratic party then declared that only white Democrats were eligible to vote in primary elections. Nixon, a black member of the Democratic party, brought the question before the Court for the second time.

Justice Cardozo, in delivering the opinion of the Court, said that the party's resolution was in violation of the Fourteenth Amendment because the members of the executive committee of the party were acting as representatives of the state and thus were subject to the inhibition of the Fourteenth Amendment.

See also Nixon v. Herndon; Smith v. Allwright.

NIXON v. HERNDON, 273 U.S. 536 (1927), questions the constitutionality of a Texas statute which provided that "in no event shall a Negro be eligible to participate in a Democratic Party primary election." Nixon, a black and a member of the Democratic party, resided in El Paso and in every other way qualified to vote in the party primary but was denied the privilege because of his color.

In the opinion of the Court, delivered by Justice Holmes, it would be hard to find a more direct infringement of the Fourteenth Amendment. The amendment not only gives citizenship and the privileges of citizenship to persons of color, but it denies to any state the power to withhold from them the equal protection of the laws. The Texas statute was invalid because color alone cannot be made a basis of a statutory classification.

See also Slaughterhouse Cases.

NO BILL, a bill issued when a grand jury finds that there is not sufficient evidence to warrant holding a person for trial in a criminal case. —*Mary L. Carns*

See also Grand Jury; True Bill.

"NO KNOCK" SEARCH PROVISION. *See* Search and Seizure.

NOMINATION. *See* Caucus; Convention, Political; Petition; Primary Election.

NONALIGNMENT. *See* Neutralism.

NONPROLIFERATION TREATY, a treaty against the spreading of nuclear weapons, signed by 62 countries, including the United States, the U.S.S.R., and the United Kingdom, simultaneously in Washington, Moscow, and London, in 1968. Ratification was completed by the United States and the U.S.S.R. in 1969, and the treaty became effective in 1970. The signatories, other than the nuclear powers, undertook not to acquire nuclear weapons. Nonnuclear powers, which had entered into the commitments for a period of 25 years, also recognized the International Atomic Energy Agency as the authority exercising overall control over safeguards. Nonnuclear powers were guaranteed against aggression or the threat of aggression by a nuclear power; France and China, however, two of the five nuclear powers, had not signed the treaty.

See also Atomic Weapons, International Control of; Disarmament.

NORRIS-La GUARDIA (ANTI-INJUNCTION) ACT (1932) was a major New Deal victory for organized labor. The Act culminated 25 years of effort by labor to limit the use of injunctions in ending labor-management disputes. These injunctions severely limited the power and effectiveness of unions. Sponsored by Sen. George Norris and Rep. Fiorello La Guardia, the bill was signed on March 20, 1932.

The Act prohibited courts from issuing injunctions or restraining orders in many labor disputes. This Act outlawed previously common practices that had stopped strikes, picketing, and boycotts and had condoned yellow-dog contracts, which allowed antiunion employment. Although injunctions were still permitted if, after a court hearing, it was determined that illegal actions were threatened or imminent, the court orders had to be specific rather than general in nature.

NORTH ATLANTIC TREATY ORGANIZATION (NATO),
organization formed in 1949 to deter possible aggression by the Soviet Union against Western Europe, headquartered in Brussels, Belgium. Current members include Belgium, Canada, Denmark, France, Greece, Iceland, Italy, Luxembourg, the Netherlands, Norway, Portugal, Spain, Turkey, the United Kingdom, the United States, and West Germany.

Early Years. Immediately after its formation, NATO was content to rely on the threat of the American nuclear force to prevent Soviet attack. However, spurred on by the Korean War in 1950, the NATO powers tried to formulate plans to meet a Soviet conventional attack. The decision to defend Europe at the line dividing Germany rather than at the Rhine became known as the "forward strategy" and envisioned the use of German troops. The Pleven Plan would have brought Germany into the alliance through a European Defense Community (EDC), but France failed to ratify the project in 1954. Afterward British foreign minister Anthony Eden successfully negotiated German entrance into NATO as a separate member through the London and Paris Agreements of 1955.

In pursuit of a forward strategy, the NATO council in 1952 announced goals of 96 conventional divisions to be placed in Europe. Because of European reluctance to meet these goals and President Eisenhower's new emphasis on nuclear weapons, new goals were set in 1954 with a series of agreements emphasizing tactical nuclear weapons in response to a Soviet invasion. Conventional armed forces were to be simply a "tripwire" to trigger almost immediate nuclear response.

Recent Years. The American policy of maintaining total control of the alliance's nuclear capability failed with France's development of a nuclear force. In 1965 President de Gaulle ordered all NATO military forces out of France and withdrew France from military involvement in the alliance.

Over the last 20 years, the alliance has experienced growing internal differences. Greece and Turkey continue to feud over the 1974 Turkish invasion of Cyprus. Belgium, the Netherlands, and Denmark have expressed degrees of opposition to deployment of intermediate-range missiles on their territory. Domestic political opposition to continued NATO membership is strong in countries such as Spain and Greece. There is also continued frustration in the U.S. Congress over the alleged low levels of European spending on conventional forces. Despite these sharp and often vocal differences, the alliance is firmly established as the cornerstone of the Western defense system.

Organization. The major organs of NATO are (1) the North Atlantic council, made up of the foreign ministers of the member nations, charged with all major political military decisions, (2) a staff secretariat, headed by a secretary general, and (3) the military committee, made up of the chiefs of staff of the member countries, which formulates recommendations for military strategy for consideration by the council. In 1966 and 1967, in response to France's withdrawal from the military part of the alliance, NATO created: a division of defense, planning the policy within the international staff/secretariat; an international planning staff to advise the military committee; and two permanent nuclear committees, giving the allies some forum in which to influence American nuclear strategy.   —*David Forte*

NUCLEAR PROLIFERATION TREATY. *See* Nonproliferation Treaty.

NUCLEAR REGULATORY COMMISSION (NRC). *See* Independent Agencies and Regulatory Commissions.

NUCLEAR TEST-BAN TREATY. *See* Atomic Weapons, International Control of; Disarmament.

NULLIFICATION, the purported right of a state to nullify a federal statute. The idea of nullification emerged in the Kentucky and Virginia Resolutions of 1798, which asserted the principle of state sovereignty against the Alien and Sedition Acts of President John Adams. Nullification symbolized the controversy over the nature of the Union down to the time of the Civil War. Nullification's theoretical manifesto is John C. Calhoun's 1828 "South Carolina Exposition and Protest," which laments the adverse effects of the Tariff of 1828 upon his home state. This concept of nullification was based on the assumption that the "principals" that established the Constitution were not the American people, but the 13 sovereign states. Therefore, he reasoned, the states must individually decide the constitutionality of acts of Congress. Without the capacity to judge, the states would be reduced to a subordinate condition, contrary to Calhoun's goal of state sovereignty.

See also Alien and Sedition Acts; Interposition; States' Rights.

OBITER DICTUM (Lat., a remark by the way), usually abbreviated "dictum," a remark made by the judge that is relevant but that is not essential to the opinion or that strays from the central issue, as in a remark that begins "and by the way. . . ." Dicta are entitled to consideration by judges deciding later cases but are not precedent to which *stare decisis* applies because they are not directly related to the conclusions.

See also Stare Decisis.

OCCUPATIONAL SAFETY AND HEALTH AD-MINISTRATION (OSHA), a part of the Labor Department of the federal government. As its name implies, it develops programs and standards for worker safety and health. It receives recommendations on health standards from the Center for Disease Control in Atlanta; makes grants to provide education, training, and technical assistance and other health- and safety-related services to employers and employees; conducts public hearings on proposed occupational safety and health standards; and operates an enforcement program through workplace inspections, citing alleged violations of standards, assessing penalties, and assuring the abatement of any hazards noted. A recent priority has been to identify and regulate potential carcinogens (cancer-causing substances) in workplaces.

Caught between labor interests (which generally support extensive and precise regulations) and business interests (which do not), OSHA is one of the most frequently criticized agencies in the federal government.

O'CONNOR, SANDRA DAY (1930-   ), associate justice of the Supreme Court (1981-   ). Born in Texas and raised in Arizona, she held the office of Arizona assistant state attorney general (1965-1969) and for two terms was a member of the state senate (1969-1975), where she was the first woman to be chosen majority leader. She was elected to the superior court in 1974 and was appointed to the state court of appeals in 1979. Nominated to the Supreme Court by President Ronald Reagan, she became the first woman to serve on the Court. She is considered a mainstream pragmatic lawmaker and judge whose orientation is defense of the legislative branch and greater reliance on state courts for the protection of constitutional rights. She wrote the majority opinion for the Court in *Mississippi University for Women v. Joe Hogan* (1982), which ruled out sex discrimination in state-financed institutions of higher learning.

OFFICE OF NATIONAL DRUG CONTROL POL-ICY, part of the Executive Office of the President. It was established in January 1989 and charged with responsibility for coordinating federal, state, and local efforts to combat the flow of drugs. Former Secretary of Education William Bennett was named as the office's first director.

OFFICE OF PERSONNEL MANAGEMENT. *See* Civil Service.

OIL-DEPLETION ALLOWANCE. *See* Depletion Allowance.

OLD-AGE, SURVIVORS, AND DISABILITY IN-SURANCE. *See* Social Security.

OLIGARCHY, a form of government in which the right to participate in the governing processes is based on the possession of wealth or property. Aristotle defined an oligarchy as a perversion of aristocracy: rulers in an aristocracy govern for the benefit of the whole, but oligarchs govern for their own benefit or that of their class at the expense of the other subjects. Because only a few members of any regime are apt to be wealthy, an oligarchy is also the rule of the few. "Oligarchy" is used pejoratively by democrats to mean minority, in contrast to democratic majority rule.

See also Corporate State; Fascism.

OLMSTEAD v. UNITED STATES, 277 U.S. 438 (1928), concerns protection against unreasonable search and seizure. Olmstead was the leader of a smuggling conspiracy. For about five months, federal officers had his telephone wiretapped and recorded his conversations but did so without entering the office in which the telephone was located. These conversations were the only evidence of his guilt.

In a controversial 5-to-4 decision that was effectively overruled in 1967 by *Berger v. New York,* Olmstead's conviction was upheld. Chief Justice Taft said that wiretapping without entering the premises did not come within the meaning of the Fourth Amendment's prohibition because there was no unlawful search and seizure of "person, houses, papers, [or] effects." Holmes and Brandeis dissented, saying that the government ought not to use evidence obtained, and only obtainable, by criminal act.

OMBUDSMAN (Swed., representative), a kind of people's agent utilized in varying forms and under varying titles in many parts of the world. It is most appropriate to associate the term with Scandinavia. There the ombudsman holds an official office to which people bring their complaints about government. The ombudsman is, by tradition, held in great prestige, is knowledgeable about the ways of government, and is empowered to investigate the people's complaints. If he deems it necessary, he can publicize the results of his investigations, but he ordinarily lacks any official power and must rely on persuasion and public opinion. The ombudsman is expected to help individual clients resolve their differences with the government and is also supposed to make suggestions to improve administrative performance. The institution was in vogue in the United States, and a number of states and local communities were experimenting with ombudsmen. An unsuccessful attempt was made during the Carter administration to create a consumer's ombudsman in the Consumer Protection Agency.

OMNIBUS CRIME CONTROL ACTS, a series of acts passed by Congress to deal with the rise of crime in the United States. Heavily debated in Congress, the first of the Acts was passed in 1968. It established the Law Enforcement Assistance Administration to carry out a broad program of aid to the states and localities for crime control study—with particular attention to street crime, riots, and organized crime. Other provisions of the Acts and their subsequent amendments include a ban in federal court of evidence gained from wiretaps or listening devices; the regulation of firearm sales, transport, and possession; grants for the construction and renovation of correctional facilities, courtrooms, treatment centers, etc.; and the establishment of a Bureau of Justice Statistics, which disseminates statistical information to the criminal justice community.

O'NEILL, THOMAS (TIP) (1912-   ), Democratic Congressman and Speaker of the House of Representatives (1976-1987). O'Neill graduated from Boston College in 1936 and was elected the following year to the Massachusetts House, where he served until 1953, the last four years as speaker. He was then elected to Congress in 1952 from the Boston district represented by John F. Kennedy until he ran for the Senate. O'Neill became a consummate politician who placed great

Thomas P. (Tip) O'Neill, Speaker of the House of Representatives (1976-1987).

emphasis on party loyalty. As a result, he was elected House majority leader in 1973 and Speaker in 1976. After President Ronald Reagan took office in 1981, O'Neill stood out as a symbol of Democratic opposition to the President's policies. He retired from Congress in 1987.

ONE MAN, ONE VOTE. *See* Apportionment, Legislative; Baker v. Carr; District, Congressional; Reynolds v. Sims; Wesberry v. Sanders.

OPEN DOOR POLICY, equal treatment of foreign businessmen and shippers in a particular foreign country. The United States advocated the policy as a means of keeping China from being dismembered by European and Japanese interests at the turn of the century. The United States wanted to protect its economic interests in China, where internal weakness and the unsuccessful Boxer Rebellion (1899-1900) against foreign influence had led to increased foreign domination. American support for the preservation of Chinese territorial and administrative integrity represented one of the early changes from U.S. isolationist policies.

OPEN HOUSING, a civil rights goal of nondiscrimination in the sale or rental of dwelling space. Open housing opposes the racial bias that has helped keep minorities in inner-city ghettos. Open-occupancy and fair-housing laws have been passed by city, state, and federal governments. The 1968 Civil Rights Act prohibits racial discrimination by most sellers, renters, and financiers of real estate. The Supreme Court in *Jones v. Mayer*, 1968, barred all racial discrimination in the sale or rental of property. The Court upheld the first Civil Rights Act (1866), which gave newly freed southern blacks real and personal property rights. In the history of discrimination, however, private restrictive covenants and public racial zoning helped to create and maintain segregated neighborhoods. Federal policies of insuring home loans only in homogeneous or "stable" neighborhoods in the 1930s and 1940s encouraged growth of all-white suburbs. Today, low-density zoning, which precludes apartments and houses on small plots, keeps out persons of low income.

OPEN PERSONNEL SYSTEM. *See* Civil Service.

OPINIONS, written statements of an appellate court giving reasons why a particular decision was reached. The "majority opinion," which may be written by a single justice or by "the court" collectively (known as a *per curiam* opinion), may indicate constitutional or legal principles and arguments used by the court and may serve as precedent for future decisions. "Concurring opinions" and/or "dissenting opinions" may accompany the majority report. Concurring opinions

may be filed by justices who voted with the majority but who wish to show separate or different reasons. Dissenting opinions are reports of those who were in the minority, giving their reasons for disagreement.
—*Mary L. Carns*
See also Decisions of Courts.

ORGANIZATION FOR ECONOMIC COOPERATION AND DEVELOPMENT (OECD). Founded in 1961, OECD's objectives are to promote economic growth among member countries, to coordinate economic aid, and to develop world trade. OECD members are Australia, Austria, Belgium, Canada, Denmark, Finland, France, Greece, Iceland, Ireland, Italy, Japan, Luxembourg, Netherlands, New Zealand, Norway, Portugal, Spain, Sweden, Switzerland, Turkey, the United Kingdom, the United States, West Germany, and Yugoslavia. OECD replaced the Organization for European Economic Cooperation (OEEC), which was founded in 1948 in conjunction with the Marshall Plan. The impetus for founding the OECD came from the United States, which wanted some overall organization to aid North Atlantic economic integration. The membership has expanded, and the organization's concerns are global. It seeks to deal with such issues as liberalized international trade, Third World debt relief, and tariffs.

ORGANIZATION FOR EUROPEAN ECONOMIC COOPERATION (OEEC). *See* Marshall Plan.

ORGANIZATION OF AMERICAN STATES (OAS), established at Bogota, Colombia, December 13, 1951, replaced the Union of American Republics, formed in 1890. The Bogota treaty, signed by 29 western hemisphere states, calls for pacific settlement of disputes, collective security, and promotion of economic, social, and cultural cooperation. Headquartered in Washington, D.C., the OAS has a number of subsidiary organizations for specialized activities. Under the treaty inter-American conferences are held every five years. Foreign ministers of member states meet periodically. The Charter of Punta del Este (August 1961), created under OAS auspices, formed the Alliance for Progress.

ORGANIZATION OF PETROLEUM EXPORTING COUNTRIES (OPEC), cartel formed in 1960 for the purpose of establishing common oil production and pricing policies. The organization has headquarters in Vienna. Its members include: Algeria, Ecuador, Gabon, Indonesia, Iran, Iraq, Kuwait, Libya, Nigeria, Qatar, Saudi Arabia, United Arab Emirates, and Venezuela.

OPEC's members are divided over how to respond to decreased demands for crude oil and competition from major non-member producers such as Great Britain and Norway. The developments have affected the cartel's ability to set prices. The continued viability of OPEC will depend on world market conditions and cooperation among states whose governments are often bitterly divided over political questions.

OUTER CONTINENTAL SHELF ACT. *See* Submerged Lands Act.

OVERSIGHT, LEGISLATIVE, congressional review of the execution and administration of laws passed by Congress. It is derived from the legislative power of investigation. Legislative oversight is one of the oldest powers used by Congress but was first formalized by the Legislative Reorganization Act of 1946, which called for "continuous watchfulness" by congressional oversight committees. The Act established procedures for oversight committees and subcommittees to exercise controls over executive agencies that have been created by Congress to implement and administer statutes and legislative mandates. Oversight responsibilities were further refined and clarified by subsequent legislation, such as the Legislative Reorganization Act of 1970 and the Congressional Budget and Impoundment Control Act of 1974.

Oversight is used by Congress to assure that laws are administered in the manner in which they were intended. It is a major congressional check on the executive branch, intended to hold administrators accountable for their actions, but one that is often difficult to use effectively. Congressional oversight techniques may prove to be burdensome to the executive branch or may be impractical due to security problems, but lack of oversight paradoxically would leave the executive unchecked and possibly beyond legal controls.

Oversight controls have been traditionally exercised by committee hearings and investigations, such as the investigation into enforcement of the "Superfund" hazardous waste cleanup law and a series of investigations that uncovered abuses by the FBI and the CIA. Congressional claims of oversight powers have often come into conflict with presidential claims of executive authority.
—*Mary L. Carns*
See also Investigative Power of Congress; Watchdog Committee.

PACIFIC SETTLEMENT OF DISPUTES. *See* International Disputes, Pacific Settlement of.

PAINE, THOMAS (1737-1809), American revolutionary and pamphleteer. He was born in Thetford, Norfolk, England, and worked at his father's trade as a sleighmaker. In 1774 in London he met Benjamin Franklin, who gave him letters of introduction to leading citizens in the American colonies. In the same year Paine went to Philadelphia, where he became editor of the *Pennsylvania Magazine.* In 1776 he wrote his well-known pamphlet *Common Sense,* which recommended the separation of Great Britain and the colonies. In 1777 he joined the army under General Green and wrote the first of his political appeals, called *The Crisis,* which started with the words, "These are the times which try men's souls." These appeals continued to appear throughout the war.

After the Revolution, Paine traveled in Europe. First he went to Paris and then to England, where he wrote *The Rights of Man* (1791-1792), a defense of the French Revolution in answer to the criticisms of Edmund Burke. Paine fled the country but was tried in absentia and convicted of treason. He went to France, where he became a naturalized citizen and was elected to the French National Convention. Because he pleaded clemency for Louis XVI, Paine offended the extremists, who imprisoned him in 1793. He was released the following year at the request of James Monroe, the American minister. Paine was reelected to the Convention and served until 1795. He became increasingly unpopular because of his religious convictions, put forth in his *The Age of Reason* (1794-1796), which was regarded as an attack against organized religion. Paine returned to the United States in 1802 and retired to his farm in New Rochelle, N.Y., a piece of land given to him earlier in recognition of his services during the Revolution.

PAIRING, in a legislature, a method of nullifying opposing viewpoints on a particular measure: an agreement is made in advance of the vote between an opponent and a proponent of the bill to refrain from voting on a yea-and-nay roll-call vote. Therefore, if one is absent, the result of the vote will not be affected. The paired legislators are generally of different parties. Pairing often occurs on highly controversial issues where a legislator does not want his vote recorded but is unwilling to tip the scales one way or the other.

PALKO v. CONNECTICUT, 302 U.S. 319 (1937), undertakes to explain why some of the provisions of the Bill of Rights are essential to the due process of law and thus apply to the states through the Fourteenth Amendment. Palko, indicted for murder in the first degree, was found guilty of murder in the second degree. He was then retried on an appeal and found guilty of murder in the first degree. Palko claimed that because double jeopardy is forbidden by the Fifth Amendment, it is also forbidden by the Fourteenth. In an opinion that was overruled in 1969 by *Benton v. Maryland,* the court held that some provisions of the Bill of Rights, such as the right to counsel and freedom of speech, have been brought within the Fourteenth Amendment because they are fundamental principles of liberty and justice, but that the State of Connecticut had not violated any such principle. The Court observed that the state was asking no more than Palko would have asked had the legal error been in his favor.

See also Powell v. Alabama.

PAN-AMERICANISM, a doctrine expressing community of purpose between the countries of the western hemisphere and aiming at developing political, economic, and cultural ties between them. The doctrine has at times justified the hegemony of the United States over the hemisphere.

The Monroe Doctrine (1823) has been basic to relations between the United States and Latin America, rejecting the interference of European powers in the western hemisphere, implying United States supremacy over it. For many years, relations between the United States and Latin America were characterized by frequent open intervention of the "Colossus of the North" in the internal affairs of Latin American countries. The first attempt to present a united Latin American front, though limited, goes back to Símon Bolívar in the Congress of Panama (1826). Other conferences were later held, essentially for the same purposes, in Lima, Peru (1847 and 1864), and in Santiago, Chile (1856). The first International Conference of American States took place in 1889-1890 in Washington, D.C., at the invitation of the United States, resulting in the creation of the International Union of American Republics, whose secretariat became in 1910 the Pan-American Union.

Good Neighbors. Relations with Latin America remained basically unchanged until Franklin Roosevelt, in his 1933 inaugural address, defined the new good-neighbor policy. When World War II started, cooperation among American states for common defense, proclaimed in the Lima declaration (1938), was fully implemented. An Inter-American Conference

Pan American Union Building, Washington, D.C., home of the Organization of American States.

held in Mexico City (1945) resulted in the Act of Chapultepec, reiterating solidarity among American states. A conference in 1947 saw the signing of the Treaty of Reciprocal Assistance at Rio de Janeiro, Brazil, followed by the formation in 1948, at Bogota, Colombia, of the Organization of American States, which absorbed the Pan-American Union. The reverberations of the cold war in the western hemisphere provoked a strong condemnation of international communism in the conference held in Caracas, Venezuela, in 1954.

Bad Neighbors. Shortly thereafter the United States supported the overthrow of the leftist government of Guatemala. The goodwill tour of then-Vice President Richard Nixon in Latin America in 1958 encountered unforeseen hostility, and the victory of Fidel Castro in Cuba in 1959 provoked a new United States policy toward Latin America. Formulated by President John Kennedy in 1961 under the name of Alliance for Progress, it intended to be a common effort of the countries of the western hemisphere for social progress and economic development. A sense of continental solidarity followed the Cuban Missile Crisis of 1962 but was deeply shaken by the United States' intervention in the Dominican Republic in 1965. A trend to coordinate policies with extracontinental developing countries is gaining momentum in Latin America. Also, new forms of political and economic organizations have been increasingly appearing in the area.   —*Sergio Barzanti*

See also Good-Neighbor Policy; Organization of American States.

PAN-AMERICAN UNION. *See* Organization of American States (OAS); Pan-Americanism.

PARDON. Article II, Section 2, of the Constitution gives the president full pardoning power in all cases involving federal infractions. Within the Department of Justice there is an Office of the Pardon Attorney with responsibility for handling all administrative procedures concerning pardons. There are two kinds of pardons, the absolute pardon, which fully restores to the individual all rights and privileges of a citizen, and the conditional pardon, which requires a condition to be met before the pardon is officially granted. In most states the governor has full pardoning power, although in some states he must share this power with the state senate or some other body.

PARISH. *See* Local Government.

PARLIAMENTARY GOVERNMENT, a form in which the executive or government arises from and is responsible to the legislature. Parliamentary government's origins date to late seventeenth-century England. In contemporary usage, the concept refers to a system where legislators are democratically elected,

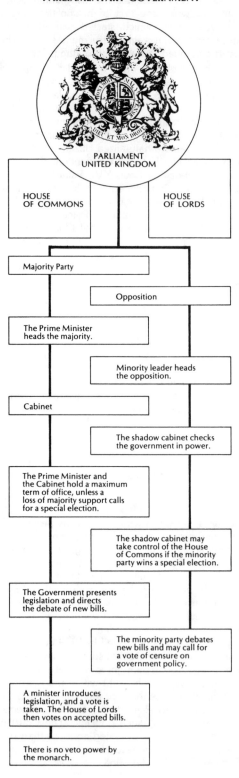

thus distinguishing it from a dictatorship.

Great Britain is the prototype of the modern parliamentary government. The legislature is bicameral, but the government is responsible only to the popularly elected House of Commons. Because the population is relatively homogeneous, only two highly unified major parties and one minority party are politically significant. The monarch formally requests the leader of the majority party in Commons to form a government. The leader in turn normally assumes the post of Prime Minister and appoints a cabinet and other ministers. The government is then approved by a majority vote in the House of Commons. Because the leader's party controls the majority, approval is automatic. Thus voters know prior to elections who will become the chief executive.

By custom the government must dissolve the House and hold new elections at a time most favorable to itself. If at any time, however, the majority of Commons fails to support major policies advocated by the executive, he must either resign or dissolve the legislature and ask for elections. If resignation occurs, the monarch asks for someone else in Commons to form a government. Through these processes, executive responsibility to the majority in the House of Commons is maintained. Where the population is sufficiently homogeneous to sustain a strong and unified majority party or a coalition of parties, an effective and stable government is ensured.

In contrast to the British experience, French parliamentary governments were characterized by disunity and ineffectiveness. The population had been too divided to elect a majority of one party to the legislature; and the parties were too disparate to form lasting coalitions. As a consequence, governments were constantly being forced to resign only to be replaced by ones equally important. Finally, in 1958 the Algerian crisis led to the adoption of a new constitution creating a presidential government somewhat similar to that of the United States. Experience suggests, therefore, that parliamentary governments, like other forms, require suitable circumstances.   —*Robert F. Smith*

See also Constitutionalism; Liberalism; Presidential Government; Representative Government.

PARTICIPATORY DEMOCRACY, a concept that appeared in the 1962 Port Huron statement of the founding convention of Students for a Democratic Society (SDS). This principle and objective of contemporary New Left politics developed in protest to the centralization and oligarchical distribution of power in current democratic institutions. Participatory democracy proposes the decentralization of power and decision making, permitting local authorities and groups to govern themselves wherever possible, and urges active participation in politics. The general purpose of participatory democracy is to restore to the individual some of the control over his life that has

been lost amid the complexities of modern industrial societies.

See also Concurrent Majority; Liberalism; Pluralism.

PARTY COMMITTEE, or Committee on Committees, bicameral party organ responsible for the assignment of party members to standing committees and the appointment of their chairmen. In conjunction with the party caucus, the party committee selects the speaker of the House and the president pro tempore of the Senate.

PARTY SYSTEM. *See* Political Parties in the United States; Two-Party System.

PASSIVE RESISTANCE, nonviolent demonstration and submission to arrest to effect a social, political, or economic change. The best-known practitioner of passive resistance was Mahatma Gandhi in his attempt to remove British rule from India. His spiritual resistance, manifest in his hunger strikes, is a typical tactic of passive resistance.

A long line of passive resistance and nonviolence runs through American history, beginning with the early Quakers' religion-based nonviolence. In the twentieth century the religious outlook has been tempered by a more political pacifism. Passive resistance has been an important force in changing the recent social and political climate. Sit-ins, bus boycotts, and demonstrations have affected the course of racial discrimination, the Vietnam War, and labor disputes.

Martin Luther King, Jr.'s campaigns for equality during the 1950s and 1960s are the most significant examples of organized passive resistance in American history.

PASSPORTS AND VISAS. A passport is a formal document issued by a state to one of its nationals, identifying him as a citizen or national of the state, with the right to protection while he is traveling and the right to return to his homeland. The word once meant permission for a ship to leave or enter harbor. Later, the term was extended to mean permission to pass. In time of war passports or safe-conduct papers were issued by countries at war. Passports are issued by a government to its nationals through its foreign office or state department and, abroad by the state's consular and, sometimes, diplomatic missions.

Rules. Countries issue passports for specified periods. In the United States, passports are valid for ten years for adults. Persons applying must have proof of citizenship. A certified copy of your birth certificate or naturalization certificate are most commonly used. In addition, current identification, two photos, and a basic fee are required to complete the application. Some countries require a passport to be stamped or a visa to be issued by the state to which travel is to be undertaken. The visa is considered evidence of permission to enter an issuing state under specified conditions for a specified period of time.

Passports are of many kinds. Ambassadors and officers of the foreign service having diplomatic status are issued diplomatic passports. Special passports are issued to officials who do not have diplomatic status and to their families. Regular passports are issued to eligible private persons. Some countries issue service passports to military personnel serving abroad and to their families. The *laissez-passer,* a travel document issued by the United Nations to members of its staff, is recognized by member states as a national passport.

In the United States, passports are required for exit and entry by United States citizens when traveling outside Canada, Mexico, Bermuda, and some other countries of the western hemisphere. Passports may not be denied without a hearing. Passports are not issued for travel in restricted areas or when foreign political considerations limit entry, and persons under indictment, or whose acts abroad may violate United States laws, are not issued passports.

History. The universal adoption of the passport as a travel document issued by sovereign states is a modern development. Before World War I many countries did not require passports from foreigners who entered their territory. After World War II many countries took steps to simplify the issuance of passports and visas. Western European countries made arrangements to permit tourists from certain countries to enter without visas. Some countries partially eliminated passports. Similarly, reciprocal arrangements were made between Commonwealth countries, and between France and its former colonies.

PATENT, temporary exclusive rights of invention granted to an inventor by the Patent Office, as authorized by Article I, Section 8, of the Constitution. The term "patent" originates from *literae patentes,* or the open letter, issued to the public first by Elizabeth I of England, granting royal protection to certain inventors' machines. A patent prevents anyone but the inventor or his/her licensees from making, using, and selling his/her invention in the United States for 17 years. In return, the inventor consents to make his/her invention public and available to anyone after the 17-year term of protection expires. If inventors want patent protection outside the United States, they must register separately with each country.

Patent should not be confused with copyright. Copyrights are those rights by which authors or artists can protect and profit from their work.

The first patent bill was enacted in 1790. Initially, the Department of State administered the provisions of the patent act, and patents were granted by the secretary of state, the secretary of war, and the attorney general. The modern patent system was established by the Patent Act of 1836. Originally, the patent

term was 14 years with a seven-year extension. The 17-year term was adopted by Congress in 1861. Patent laws were last revised in 1952. About 40,000 U.S. patents are issued annually, and since 1836 more than 3.5 million patents have been granted.

PATENT AND TRADEMARK OFFICE (PTO), a division of the Department of Commerce that implements the registration of trademarks and the issuance of invention or design patents. The PTO examines applications for design patents (issued for 17 years), and utility patents (issued for 17 years). Under provisions of the Patent Cooperation Treaty, the office also handles international applications.

See also Patent.

PATRONAGE, power of elected officials to increase their political strength by appointing people of their choice to governmental or public jobs. The term originated in fifteenth-century England and was associated with the protection and defense of the Church. At one time, members of Congress and the president had extensive patronage powers. Members of Congress could appoint local health inspectors, tax collectors, and postmasters. However, the establishment of the Civil Service has dissipated much of this power, and members of Congress have patronage over only their office staffs and jobs requiring no technical knowledge or special skills. The president still retains extensive patronage, including the cabinet, White House staff, and federal regulatory agencies. Patronage on the state and local levels continues at a high level. Elected officials who remain in office for long periods of time, such as did Mayor Richard Daley and Governor Nelson Rockefeller, can build substantial power bases through their patronage appointments.

Patronage in the United States government reached its high point after the Civil War, and senators spent a good deal of their time overseeing patronage appointments in their states. The results in many cases were dishonesty, nepotism, and outright favoritism in government. These abuses led to the passage of the Pendleton Act (1882), which set up the Civil Service Commission; under it, a system of competitive examinations certified applicants for federal jobs. The Civil Service Reform Act of 1978 abolished the old commission and established the Office of Personnel Management and the Merit System Protection Board. Today, about 80 percent of federal government positions are filled by a civil service merit system.

See also Civil Service; Merit System Protection Board; Spoils System.

PEACE CORPS, created by President Kennedy in 1961 to promote world peace and friendship through placement of volunteer men and women abroad to help developing nations fill their critical need for skilled manpower. Formerly under the Department of State, the Peace Corps is now under ACTION, an independent agency established in 1971 to bring all federal voluntary action programs together.

Peace Corps volunteers, who are carefully selected and trained, serve for periods of two years. Volunteers live in the communities to which they are sent to work. The Peace Corps is headed by a director appointed by the president with the advice and consent of the Senate. Each of the corps' geographical regions—Africa, East Asia and the Pacific, Latin America, and North Africa, the Near East, and South Asia—is headed by a director whose responsibilities include the operation of the region and the training of volunteers.

PENDLETON ACT. *See* Civil Service Reform Act of 1883.

PENN, WILLIAM (1664-1718), English Quaker, who was a political and religious leader in colonial America and the founder of Pennsylvania. The son of an admiral, Penn was born in London. He early espoused nonconformist religious beliefs and in 1667 adopted the unpopular Quaker faith.

He became a trustee of the American colony of West Jersey in 1675, when it was under Quaker influence, and was largely responsible for its liberal charter of government. In 1681 King Charles II granted Penn a large American tract named Pennsylvania after Penn's father and probably given to settle a family claim against the crown. The next year Penn arrived in America for a two-year stay, during which he made plans for Philadelphia, negotiated Indian treaties, and established the colony's government. Under Penn's Frame of Government, Pennsylvania had an appointed governor, elected council, and elected assembly. In 1682 the assembly passed measures assuring freedom of worship and individual liberties. In 1692, several years after Penn's return to England, his friendship with the deposed King James II led to Penn's replacement as governor.

Royal rule ended in 1694, and Penn returned to the colony as resident governor in 1699. In 1701 he granted a Charter of Liberties that established a unicameral legislature and, except for the appointment of a governor, ended English proprietary rule. Penn returned to England in 1701 to face years of financial trouble. In 1712 he suffered a stroke and died six years later.

Penn made landmark contributions to the political and religious development of colonial America. A humanitarian, he won the respect of the Indians by fair treatment of them, and he provided for the emancipation of his slaves at his death.

PENTAGON, a building located in Arlington, Va., that houses the Department of Defense. The name, derived from the five-sided structure of the building,

The Pentagon, home of the Defense Department.

has become synonymous with the U.S. military establishment itself. It is the largest office building in the world.

PENTAGON PAPERS, a secret study commissioned by the Pentagon to analyze United States involvement in the war in Indochina, particularly Vietnam. The existence of the study, initiated during the administration of Lyndon Johnson, was first revealed in 1971 by the *New York Times,* which had received anonymous copies of some of the documents. The source of these documents was later traced to Daniel Ellsberg, a Harvard professor who had worked on the study. The government sought to enjoin the *Times* and other newspapers from publishing the documents, but the courts upheld the principle of freedom of the press, in part on the ground that publication of the rationale behind 1968 policy decisions did not impair current national security. The subsequent controversy over the classification of certain materials as top secret led to a review of classification procedures and a declassification of certain other documents. The *New York Times* was later awarded the Pulitzer Prize for its reportage.

PEOPLE'S PARTY. *See* Populist People's, Party.

PEPPER, CLAUDE (1900-1989), U.S. congressman. Pepper became the country's most forceful advocate of programs and legislation to benefit the elderly. He was first elected to the U.S. Senate from Florida in 1936 as a strong supporter of the New Deal. However, Pepper's bid for a third term in 1950 was thwarted largely because his opponent used the anti-Communist hysteria of the time to label Pepper as a liberal supporter of blacks.

Pepper returned to the practice of law and made another unsuccessful run for a Senate nomination in 1958. He then ran for the House in 1962 from a district that covered the Miami area and included large numbers of blacks, Hispanics, and senior citizens. Pepper was consistently reelected by large margins. In

1977, he became chairman of the House Select Committee on Aging, which he used to champion the cause of the elderly. He was the architect of a landmark bill to modify and/or eliminate age as a factor in enforced retirement.

During the Reagan administration, Pepper resisted any attempts to reduce Social Security benefits. He traveled extensively, wrote a widely syndicated column of advice to the elderly, and became the single most influential proponent of the rights of the elderly.

PERESTROIKA, a term used to describe Soviet leader Mikhail Gorbachev's efforts to "restructure" and modernize the Soviet economy by stressing the need for improvements in technology and efficiency.
See also Glasnost.

PERMANENT COMMITTEES. *See* Standing Committees.

PERSONA NON GRATA. *See* Diplomatic Immunity.

PETITION. The First Amendment grants the privilege to "petition the government for redress of grievances." The petition is the principal means by which an American citizen can inform his political representative of his opinions; petition in the form of letters to members of Congress provides public officials with the opinions of their constituents.

PICKETING, labor's method of informing the public, employees, customers, and suppliers of the facts of a labor dispute. The striking union members patrol the employer's place of business with signs to demonstrate their strength, limit or prevent people from entering the plant, and prevent shipping and receipt of goods and materials. Peaceful picketing is a form of expression protected by the First Amendment, but picketing cannot obstruct or be for an illegal objective. Pickets that go beyond the limits of peaceful persuasion and use intimidation and violence to coerce the employer or other employees are acting illegally and forfeit their First Amendment rights. In organizational and recognition picketing, union members attempt to persuade workers to join the union or the employers to recognize the union for bargaining. In cross-picketing, two different picketing unions claim to represent the employees. Secondary picketing may also be used. In this method, places not directly involved in the labor dispute, such as related ownerships or other businesses that deal with the employer, are picketed by the striking union.
See also Strike.

PIERCE, FRANKLIN (1809-1869), 14th President of the United States (1853-1857), born in Hillsboro, N.H. A Democrat, he served in the House of Representatives and Senate (1833-1842) and was a compromise candidate for the Democrats in the 1852 presidential election. As President he supported proslavery forces in Kansas and made an abortive attempt to purchase Cuba from Spain. Not renominated by his party in 1856, he spent the following years in social and political obscurity.
See also Presidential Elections.

PIGEONHOLING a bill is a tactic used by legislators to avoid dealing with a measure at a politically inopportune time, such as an election year. In practice, pigeonholing sidetracks such unpopular issues as tax bills or labor laws, especially if the citizens' preferences and objections to a measure are known. A bill is pigeonholed when it is put aside for an indefinite period of time, usually with the intention of killing the bill. The term is derived from desks in the committee rooms of Congress, that once had a series of open compartments known as "pigeonholes" for filing papers.

PLATFORM, PARTY, a document drawn up by the platform committee at each national convention, citing the policies, positions, and principles of the party. It is then approved by the entire convention. Since neither the Democratic nor the Republican party are wholly unified, disagreements sometimes occur, and platform fights ensue. Sometimes presidential aspirants deliberately instigate platform struggles as a political tactic. Such was the case at the Republican convention of 1964, when anti-Goldwater forces unsuccessfully attempted to insert statements into the platform condemning the Ku Klux Klan and the John Birch Society. The hope was that a struggle on an issue that could evoke strong emotion would stampede the convention away from Sen. Goldwater. Platforms are usually propaganda documents excoriating the policies of the opposition party and promising to solve all national problems. In order to submerge differences and disagreements, the language of platforms may be deliberately general and vague. While presidential candidates are required to pay homage to the platform of their party, they seldom view it as important to their campaign.

PLEBISCITE (Lat., plebis citum, decree of the common people), an election that usually involves a simple "yes" or "no" vote on an issue, a territorial question, a person, or a party; a plebiscite differs from ordinary elections where political representatives are chosen. In the United States it is used to decide special questions or simply to allow the people to express their opinion on a controversial issue. In such cases, however, the vote is rarely referred to as a plebiscite.

One plebiscite was held in Florida in 1972 on the busing of school children to obtain racial balance in the state school system. In Europe the plebiscite has had a wider use: Napoleon Bonaparte used it to obtain a nationwide endorsement for his decision to crown himself Emperor; Adolf Hitler used the vote to obtain the support of the German people for his aggressive actions; Charles De Gaulle also used the plebiscite to receive a vote of confidence. Plebiscites were held at the end of World War I in areas like Schleswig, Silesia, and the Saar Basin to determine which government the local population preferred to live under.

PLESSY v. FERGUSON, 163 U.S. 537 (1896). Homer Plessy, of one-eighth black descent, had been convicted for violating an 1890 Louisiana statute that required railroads to provide equal and separate facilities for white and black passengers. Plessy requested from the Court a writ of prohibition to prevent Judge John Ferguson of a Louisiana district court from hearing the charge because the law was unconstitutional.

In an 8-to-1 decision, the Court upheld the statute. For the Court, Justice Brown said that the Fourteenth Amendment was intended "to enforce the absolute equality of the two races before the law," but not "to abolish distinctions based upon color, or to enforce social, as opposed to political, equality. . . . " So long as the statute required equal treatment, it did not violate the equal protection of the law clause of the Fourteenth Amendment. The majority went on to say that separation does not mean that one of the races is thereby stamped as inferior. Justice Harlan, in dissent, said that the Constitution contains an absolute prohibition against legislation discriminating between the races in their public or civil relations.

The majority decision in this case allowed for further state legislation in public schools, in transportation, and in public accommodations based on the "separate but equal" standard. The decision was overruled by *Brown v. Board of Education of Topeka* (1954). —David Forte

PLURALISM, a version of a process theory of democracy, sometimes called democratic elitism by critics. A system is viewed as democratic when public policy decisions are determined through some form of competition. Pluralist theory, thus, does not require the active participation of the majority of citizens. As developed by Robert Dahl, pluralism is a competition of elites in which different elites are involved and influential in different policy arenas (decision areas). Those citizens regularly involved in political or public policy decision making are called *homo politicus; homo civicus*, the majority of citizens, act as a check on excessive or potentially excessive decisions by becoming active only when disturbed to challenge individuals or groups in homo politicus.

See also Interest Group Theory of Democracy.

PLURALITY. *See* Majority and Plurality.

POCKET VETO. *See* Veto.

POINTER v. TEXAS, 380 U.S. 400 (1965), concerns the Sixth Amendment provision requiring that in all criminal prosecutions the accused shall enjoy the right of confrontation with the witnesses against him. Pointer, arrested for robbery, was convicted at a trial in which the chief witness was not available. The state court had accepted a transcript of the witness's testimony as evidence. The Court held that the Sixth Amendment's right of an accused to confront the witness against him is a fundamental right and therefore an element of due process applicable to the states by the Fourteenth Amendment. The Court noted that the use of a transcript did not give the defendant charged with the crime the opportunity to cross-examine the witness.

See also Palko v. Connecticut.

POINT FOUR PROGRAM, a plan to share scientific and technological advances with developing countries, introduced by President Harry Truman in his 1949 inaugural address. The plan was described in the fourth section of his address and was dubbed Point IV. Truman intended such sharing to result in stimulating investment in these areas. Funds for the program would come from the United States, United Nations, and beneficiary countries. In 1950, Congress authorized $26.9 million for the program, which expanded rapidly. It was integrated into the general foreign aid program during Eisenhower's first term.

POLICE COMMITTEE, each party's senatorial committee exercising considerable influence in shaping party position on legislative proposals. Republican policy committee members are elected by their conference committee. Democrats are appointed by their floor leaders.

See also Committee System of Congress.

POLICE COURTS. *See* Judicial System.

POLICE POWER, the authority to legislate for the protection of the health, morals, safety, and welfare of the people. In the United States, police power is a reserved power of the states. The federal government is able to legislate for the welfare of its citizens only through specific congressional powers, such as taxation and the regulation of interstate commerce.

Police power is the most important power exercised by individual state governments. Throughout United States history its use has been largely dependent on the judgment of the judiciary. During the twentieth century, however, the increasing power of corporations whose business crosses state boundaries has created a greater need for federal authority. The Eighteenth, or Prohibition, Amendment (1920) was the most extensive attempt to grant police power to the federal government. Prohibition was, however, repealed in 1933. In recent years further attempts have been made to exercise police powers on both national and state levels in regulation of some professions and in such matters as natural resources, zoning, prostitution, gambling, shipping impure drugs, mailing obscene literature, and advertising fraudulently.

See also Reserved Powers.

POLITICAL ACTION COMMITTEE (PAC), interest group, usually within an organization, that supports candidates or legislation that will act in the organization's best interests. Although political parties have always turned to interest groups to fund their candidates, political action committees, as known today, are a relatively new phenomenon. The number of PACs, the amount they contribute to congressional candidates, and candidates' reliance on PAC contributions have all grown substantially since 1974. The number of PACs rose from 608 in 1974 to more than 4,000 in 1989. Most PACs are started by established organizations—unions, corporations, trade associations, and "public interest" lobbying groups. A few are created by direct mail entrepreneurs.

Opponents, such as Common Cause, criticize PACs for having a negative impact on the legislative process, for magnifying the role of special interests, and for contributing to the growing fragmentation of the political process. They see them as a distortion of the process of representation, rewarding contributions with access not usually available to those who vote but do not contribute.

PAC supporters respond that PACs provide a convenient way for like-minded individuals to participate in the political process. They feel that PACs serve as a safeguard against undue influence by the government or by the media and that PACs have made more money available for political campaigns and that PACs have contributed to greater accountability in election campaign financing.

PAC contributions are most important in small states and in relatively inexpensive campaigns. In 1984, PACs provided only five percent of the $16 million raised by Republican Sen. Jesse Helms but 59 percent of the $884,904 reportedly raised by Democratic Sen. James Exon. PACs are more important to Republicans than to Democrats and contribute much more to incumbents than to challengers. In 1988-1989 contributions increased by 34 percent over the 1985-1986 cycle with $56.4 million going to congressional candidates. That accounted for 31 percent of all monies raised for the 1988 elections. Of the 535 members of Congress, nearly all accept some PAC money.   —*Martin Gruberg*

See also Common Cause; Federal Election Campaign Act.

POLITICAL ACTIVITIES ACTS OF 1939, 1940. *See* Hatch Acts.

POLITICAL PARTIES IN THE UNITED STATES. American political party development has gone through three stages. The first is the period from the creation of parties in the 1790s, and again in the 1820s, following a time of one-party rule, through the presidencies of James Monroe and John Quincy Adams. The second stage lasted from Andrew Jackson's presidency until the Civil War. During this period two national parties—the Democrats and the Whigs— were solidly established. The third period, following 1860, has featured competition between the modern Democratic and Republican parties.

For convenience, this third period is usually subdivided into the post-Civil War period, which ended in 1896, the Progressive movement, which was vigorous

---

**POLITICAL PARTIES:
TOPIC GUIDE**

The article on POLITICAL PARTIES IN THE UNITED STATES traces the development of the major political parties, and describes the political environment in which these parties function.

The related articles on political parties may be divided into two groups. See also ELECTION, which has a Study Guide.

Political Mechanics. Both PRESIDENTIAL ELECTIONS and local elections are usually dominated by the TWO-PARTY SYSTEM, but THIRD PARTY POLITICS often have a determining effect. The CAMPAIGN is often preceded by a PRIMARY ELECTION and a CONVENTION. At national conventions, party factions advance their views through the NATIONAL COMMITTEE and CREDENTIALS COMMITTEE and try to have them incorporated in the PLATFORM. Differences of opinion may be resolved in a CAUCUS.

Historical Role. The FEDERALISTS evolved during Washington's administration, as did their opponents, the DEMOCRATIC-REPUBLICAN PARTY. The DEMOCRATIC PARTY emerged in 1828 from the Democratic-Republicans and was soon opposed by the WHIG PARTY. They remained the major parties until the REPUBLICAN PARTY surpassed the Whigs after 1854.

Third party movements, often concentrating on a single issue, have been numerous. The first was the ANTI-MASONIC PARTY; others have included the FREE-SOIL PARTY, GREENBACK PARTY, KNOW-NOTHINGS, LOCO-FOCOS, and STATES' RIGHTS PARTY. Broader programs have been advanced by groups like the FARMER-LABOR PARTY; LIBERAL PARTY; LIBERAL-REPUBLICAN PARTY; POPULIST, OR PEOPLE'S PARTY; PROGRESSIVE PARTY; PROGRESSIVE, OR BULL MOOSE, PARTY; SOCIALIST PARTY; and COMMUNIST PARTY OF THE U.S.A.

GLOSSARY OF POLITICAL PARTIES

American Independent Party. George Wallace headed a third-party ticket under the label of the American Independent party in the 1968 presidential election. His followers were essentially Democrats who opposed the national administration of President Johnson. The emphasis was on race and nationalism. He received 9.89 million popular and 46 electoral votes.

Anti-Federalists. This name was given to those elements opposing the ratification of the Constitution. Eventually most of them became Jeffersonian Republicans.

Communist Party. See Marxist Parties.

Democratic Republicans. See Democrats; Whigs.

Democrats. The Democratic party had its origins in the Jeffersonian Republicans, who often termed themselves Democratic Republicans. Under Jackson's leadership, the party changed its name to the Democratic party. This party is the oldest continuing party in the Western world. Modern Democratic leaders have included Woodrow Wilson, Franklin Roosevelt, Harry Truman, John Kennedy, Lyndon Johnson, and Jimmy Carter. The party normally controls a substantial number of state governments and is dominant in the largest cities.

Farmer-Labor Parties. Various individual parties active in 1870-1900 are included in this term. The most prominent on the national scene were the Greenback party and the People's party, or Populists. The parties were generally reformist and in favor of government intervention. Many of the specific demands of such parties have subsequently been adopted by a major party and have become public law.

Federalists. The proponents of the Constitution were termed Federalists because they favored the proposed federal union. Subsequently they became a political party. Under the leadership of George Washington, Alexander Hamilton, and John Adams, they controlled the presidency and Congress during the first three administrations. The Federalists gave shape, direction, and vigor to the new government.

Greenback Party. See Farmer-Labor Parties.

Jacksonian Democrats. See Jeffersonian Republicans.

Jeffersonian Republicans. The origins of the first Republican party go back to the divisions in Congress between the followers of Alexander Hamilton and those of Thomas Jefferson. By 1800 the Republicans had become a national party and won the presidential election of that year under the leadership of Jefferson. From 1816 to 1828 most Americans were Jeffersonian Republicans. Distinctions eventually developed inside the party, with followers of John Quincy Adams and Henry Clay terming themselves National Republicans and followers of Andrew Jackson calling themselves Democratic Republicans. Under Jackson the organization became simply the Democratic party. Whence the terms "Jacksonian Democrats" and "Jacksonian Democracy."

Marxist Parties. The oldest of the Marxist parties is the *Socialist Labor party*, which was founded in the 1870s by German immigrants. Its chief theoretician was Daniel De Leon, a one-time Columbia University instructor. The program of the party calls for a syndicalist organization of society.

The *Socialist party* was officially founded in 1901 by persons who would not accept the leadership of De Leon. The party's most famous leaders were Eugene Debs and Norman Thomas. In three presidential elections between 1900 and 1948 the party polled nearly a million votes. In recent years the party has shrunk to a fraction of its former electoral importance.

The *Communist party* was formed as a result of a split in the Socialists following the victory of the Bolshevicks in Russia. The Communist party hasn't been important as an electoral force, although it has at times been influential in certain unions. In 1928 the Communists expelled the Trotskyites in their midst, who became the *Socialist Workers party*. This party regularly nominates presidential and other candidates.

National Republicans. See Jeffersonian Republicans; Whigs.

People's Party. See Farmer-Labor Parties; Populists.

Populists. The Populist, or People's party was active in national and state politics during the 1880s and early 1890s. Its base was agrarian, and the party's program was reformist. The party fused with the Democrats in 1896 when it endorsed the Democratic presidential candidate William Jennings Bryan. The party's best showing was in 1892, when its presidential candidate, James Weaver, received more than one million popular votes and 22 electoral votes.

Progressives (1912). In a major schism within the Republican party, former President Theodore Roosevelt ran for the presidency in 1912 as a Progressive. A three-way contest developed among the Democratic candidate Woodrow Wilson, the regular Republican candidate William Taft, and Roosevelt. The Progressive candidate took enough votes away from Taft so that Wilson was elected. He received 4.2 million popular and 88 electoral votes—more than Taft.

Progressives (1924). Robert La Follette of Wisconsin ran as a Progressive candidate for the presidency in 1924. He was endorsed by the Socialists, who did not run a candidate of their own. He received 4.8 million popular votes but only 13 electoral votes.

Progressives (1948). Former vice president Henry Wallace ran for the presidency as a Progressive in 1948. His followers were essentially Democrats who refused to support the Democratic candidate, Harry Truman. The primary emphasis was opposition to Truman's foreign policy. Wallace received 1.15 million popular votes but no electoral votes. The party did not survive the election.

Republicans (GOP). The second Republican party, sometimes abbreviated the GOP (Grand Old Party), was created in the mid-1850s from various groups seeking to fill the vacuum created by the collapse of the Whigs as a national party. The Republicans' first national convention was held in 1856, at which time they nominated John C. Fremont as their presidential candidate. Four years later under the banner of Abraham Lincoln, the party won the presidency. From 1860 to 1932 the Republicans were in the ascendancy, particularly in presidential elections. During that time only Cleveland and Wilson broke the string of Republican victories. Modern party leaders include Dwight Eisenhower, elected to the presidency in 1952 and again in 1956, and Richard Nixon, elected in 1968 and 1972. The Republicans normally control numerous state governments and are especially strong in the more prosperous suburbs of the large central cities.

States' Rights Party (1948). In 1948 J. Strom Thurmond of South Carolina headed the States' Rights party, which was essentially a regional spinoff of Southern Democrats dissatisfied with the Truman administration. Emphasis was placed on the contention that civil rights problems should be solved at the state, not the national, level. Thurmond received 1.69 million popular and 39 electoral votes.

Whigs. The Jeffersonian Republicans eventually split into two separate groups—the National Republicans under Henry Clay and Daniel Webster and the Democratic Republicans under Andrew Jackson. In opposition to Jackson, the National Republicans formed a new party, the Whigs. At the national level, the Whigs were able to elect only two presidents—William Harrison in 1840 and Zachary Taylor in 1848. Unable to maintain their unity over the slavery issue, the Whigs disintegrated as a national party during the 1850s.

until 1921, and the current phase, which began with the New Deal.

Federalists and Republicans. The initial partisan divisions occurred over the adoption of the Constitution, with the Federalists proposing adoption and the Anti-Federalists opposing ratification. The rival philosophies were represented by Alexander Hamilton, who was pro-Constitution, and by Thomas Jefferson, who was anti-Constitution. The Federalists lost the election of 1800 to the Jeffersonians (by then called the Republicans) and never returned to national power.

Democrats and Whigs. From 1816 to 1828 most voters considered themselves Jeffersonian Republicans, and two-party competition gave way to intraparty rivalry, but this balance proved to be unstable, and the followers of Henry Clay and of John Quincy Adams split with Andrew Jackson in the elections of 1824 and 1828. The factions rapidly became separate parties under the names of Democrats and Whigs. During this period the parties became institutionalized, for instance, in developing and using national nominating conventions to select the presidential and vice-presidential candidates.

From Lincoln to McKinley. The election of 1860 shattered the existing party system. With four major candidates in the presidential competition, Abraham Lincoln, as the candidate of the newly formed Republican party, received a majority of the electoral vote but only 39.9 percent of the popular vote. A new alignment grew up after the war, with the South becoming heavily Democratic and the North, heavily Republican. The next crucial election of the period was that of 1896, in which the Republicans under William McKinley severely defeated the Democratic and Populist candidate William Jennings Bryan. The Democrats were not able to recoup their losses significantly until Wilson's reelection in 1916.

The Progressive Era. The Progressive movement of the last part of the nineteenth and early part of the twentieth century had a direct influence on national party politics. In 1912 Theodore Roosevelt, in a major schism within the Republican party, ran as a Progressive against Republican William Taft and Democrat Woodrow Wilson. This division of the Republican vote made Wilson's victory possible. The Wilson administration enacted into law much of the Progressive party's platform, and that party rapidly disintegrated.

Republican Hegemony. From the Republican presidential victory under Warren Harding in 1920 through the election of Herbert Hoover in 1928, the Republicans were the dominant national party. In 1924 Robert La Follette broke with the Republican party and ran as a Progressive. Four years later Alfred Smith, a Catholic and a "wet," ran unsuccessfully against Herbert Hoover. It was the Great Depression and the failure of the Hoover administration to deal with it that ended Republican hegemony in the critical realigning election of 1932.

The New Deal. The impact of Franklin Roosevelt's electoral victories in 1932, 1936, 1940, and 1944 was profound. In terms of policy the New Deal began an era of positive government. Roosevelt used his position to give personal leadership to the Democrats. His fireside chats over the radio established a new form of direct communication between president and electorate.

Truman and Eisenhower. In April 1945 Vice President Harry Truman assumed the presidency on the death of Roosevelt. Truman won election in his own right in 1948, largely through keeping the labor, big-city, and minority votes. For the time being, the New Deal coalition persisted. It was shattered, however, in the election of 1952 and the triumph of Republican Dwight Eisenhower. The deterioration of Democratic strength was general, being reflected in congressional and gubernatorial races. Eisenhower was reelected in 1956 by a larger electoral vote than in 1952.

Kennedy and Johnson. The Democratic candidate in 1960, John Kennedy, narrowly defeated his Republican opponent, Richard Nixon. Kennedy received only a plurality of the popular vote. Following Kennedy's assassination, Lyndon Johnson assumed the presidency. In the 1964 election Johnson crushed the Republican Barry Goldwater. Because of difficulties stemming from his conduct of the unpopular war in Vietnam, Johnson declined to stand for reelection in 1968.

The Nixon Victory. After an interval of eight years Richard Nixon again ran for the presidency on the Republican ticket in 1968. His opponent was Johnson's Vice President, Hubert Humphrey. George Wallace ran as the candidate of the American Independent party. Nixon carried 32 states with a total of 301 electoral votes and received 31.7 million popular votes. Humphrey carried 14 states with 191 electoral votes and received 31.2 million popular votes. Wallace carried five states, all in the South, collected 46 electoral votes, and received 9.9 million popular votes. Nixon was elected with only a plurality of the popular vote.

Ford and Carter. Nixon's victory over McGovern in 1972 seemed a harbinger of a national turn toward conservatism, despite the continued Democratic control of both houses of Congress. The Watergate scandal changed the equation; Nixon resigned the presidency and Vice President Gerald Ford succeeded him. The Republicans (GOP) lost more ground in Congress in 1974 and relinquished the presidency in 1976 to Democrat Jimmy Carter. When the nation suffered stagflation and foreign humiliations, Carter was soundly defeated by Republican Ronald Reagan in 1980.

The Reagan Years. Ronald Reagan brought into office with him a gain in the number of Republicans in Congress, which gave the GOP control of the Senate, and was assisted by a group of conservative Democratic lawmakers, the "Boll Weevils." By 1982, "Gypsy Moths," as some Republican moderates and liberals were called, were showing their independence, and the Democrats gained back some of the House seats lost in 1980, enough to negate the coalition of House Republicans and conservative Democrats. Reagan's landslide victory over Walter Mondale in 1984, however, was accompanied by Republican gains across the country in state contests. The Republicans lost control of the Senate in 1986. The 1988 elections further solidified democratic control.

George Bush. The election of George Bush in 1988 further indicates the difficulty faced by the Democratic party in electing a president. Bush promised to maintain and expand on Reagan's conservative agenda. However, he has proven to be more of a pragmatist than an ideologue.

The National Two-Party System

The Political Environment. The national party system operates within a political environment that affects what the parties do and how they do it. One constraint is the attitude of the public toward parties. Another constraint is the constitutional framework. The separation of powers among executive, legislative, and judicial branches of government renders impossible in the United States the cabinet type of government found in parliamentary systems. Federalism, by dividing power between the federal government and the states, makes for a diffused governing system. This decentralization of political power has been accompanied by the decentralization of party power.

Causes of a Two-Party System. There are several reasons for the dominance of two major parties to the detriment or even exclusion of minor parties. The first of these is the electoral system itself. The use of a single-member district in choosing congressional representation means that whoever receives a plurality of the vote wins the contested seat. This system tends to work against smaller parties. The same principle is visible in the election of presidents, where the electoral college also has a bipolarizing effect. There are additional historical, cultural, and psychological factors that support a two-party system. The relative absence of ideology in American politics also tends to sustain a two-party system.

Minor Parties. Though the national parties receive the lion's share of the popular and electoral vote, there usually are minor parties that enter into national, state, and local contests. When these parties are secessions from a major party—like the Progressives in 1912—they may be formidable, if temporary, contestants. Where the parties are more interested in propaganda than in winning an election—like the Prohibition party—the results must be judged by changes in public law: the function of such parties is to raise issues that are eventually taken over by one of the major parties.
—*Murray S. Stedman*

See also Presidential Elections; Two-Party System; articles on individual political parties.

POLITICAL QUESTION, areas of law considered to be outside the jurisdiction of the courts because they do not involve "justiciable" issues. Political questions may properly be settled only by action of the executive or legislative branches. For example, federal courts refused to hear reapportionment cases until 1962 because representation and apportionment were then considered to be political questions best settled in the legislative branch. Also, courts will not rule on whether a foreign country is an independent nation because that is a political question to be decided by the president.   —*Mary L. Carns*

See also Baker v. Carr; Cases and Controversies; Justiciable Question.

POLK, JAMES K(NOX) (1795-1849), 11th President of the United States (1845-1849), born in Meklenburg County, N.C. A Democrat, he served in Congress (1825-1839; Speaker of the House from 1835) and as governor of Tennessee (1839-1841). During his presidency, the Oregon question was settled, dividing the region with the British at the 49th parallel. After he issued the Polk Doctrine (1845), an expansion of the Monroe Doctrine, he attempted to buy Mexico and California and then took the first opportunity to initiate the Mexican War (1846-1848).

See also Presidential Elections.

POLLOCK v. FARMERS' LOAN & TRUST COMPANY, 158 U.S. 601 (1895), questions the right of the federal government to tax the income from personal property, such as municipal bonds and real estate. Pollack, a citizen of Massachusetts, brought suit against the trust company to prevent it from complying with some of the provisions in the Income Tax Act of 1894, and questioned specifically the power of Congress to lay direct taxes on income derived from real estate, bonds, stocks, or other forms of personal property. The Court held that taxes on the income of real estate and personal property, being direct taxes within the meaning of the Constitution, are unconstitutional because they are not apportioned according to representation in the House of Representatives. It also held that the income from municipal bonds cannot be taxed because it is a tax on the borrowing power of the state. However, with the ratification of the Sixteenth Amendment in 1913, Congress was given the power to tax income from whatever source derived.

POLLS. *See* Public Opinion Poll.

POLL TAX, a state-imposed tax on voters required for exercising the franchise. The tax, usually $1 to $5, was widely used in Southern states as an effective barrier against poor, usually black, voters to ensure white control of the electoral process. The poll tax was rendered unconstitutional in national elections under the Twenty-fourth Amendment (1964). The Supreme Court invalidated the tax as a voting requirement in state elections by its 1966 decision in *Harper v. Virginia Board of Elections*.

POLL WATCHER, an individual appointed by a political party to scrutinize the voting process on election day. Usually there are two poll watchers at every voting place, representing the Democratic and Republican parties, and attempting to ensure the honesty of the election. The practice helps minimize voting fraud.

POPULAR SOVEREIGNTY stresses sovereignty or possession of ultimate power by the people and was popularized in the pre-Civil War debates over slavery. The concept's proponents insisted that the citizens of new Western states entering the Union should decide whether or not to permit slavery. Because the new lands were settled or "squatted upon" by newcomers to the West, "squatter sovereignty" was used to convey the same meaning. The principle was incorporated into national law in 1850. Its first application, to the Kansas-Nebraska territory, led to fierce fighting between citizens of Missouri and Kansas that helped precipitate the Civil War.

See also Consent, Popular; Democracy.

POPULATION, U.S. *See* Census, United States.

POPULISM, a political and social movement that began in the late 1870s in the United States as a protest by Western and Southern farmers against Eastern business interests. To the farmers, Eastern control of money, interest rates, and transportation costs was exploitative and kept the farmers poor. They depicted their protest as a struggle between the poor and the rich, the common man against the privileged few.

In 1891 the Populist party was formed. It demanded (1) the free coinage of silver; (2) the abolition of national banks; (3) a graduated income tax; (4) the government ownership of railroads, telephones, telegraphs, and steamship lines; and (5) the direct election of United States senators. Though the party soon disappeared from the national scene, many of its policies were adopted by the Democratic party and eventually became law.

Populism prepared the way for governmental policies designed to achieve greater economic equality and popular participation in politics. By articulating the political voices of poor whites in the South, populism contributed to the development of state laws discriminating against blacks. The idea of an Eastern "establishment" controlling the economy at the ex-

pense of the rest of the nation can still be found in American political life.   *—Robert F. Smith*

See also Jacksonian Democracy.

POPULIST PEOPLE'S PARTY, an agrarian protest movement formally organized as the People's Party in 1892 by Midwestern and Southern farmers who were still suffering the effects of the 1873 depression. Faced with falling farm prices, increased transportation rates, and foreclosures on their farm mortgages, they blamed Eastern banking and railroad interests for their plight.

At their national convention in Omaha in 1892, the Populists drew up an extensive platform that called for bolstering the circulation of money by free coinage of silver and increased paper currency, government ownership of railroads and other utilities, abolition of national banks and establishment of postal savings banks, a graduated income tax, direct election of senators, the secret ballot, civil service reforms, and an eight-hour working day.

James B. Weaver, the Populist presidential candidate in 1892, polled over one million popular votes, and in the 1894 Congressional elections party candidates received a total of about 1,500,000 votes. By 1896 the free silver issue had become the rallying cry for the "little man," and the Democratic party made the issue its own by calling for the immediate and unlimited coinage of silver and gold at a 16-to-1 ratio, the standard prevailing before the Panic of 1873. The Populists destroyed their chances of becoming a major independent party when they reluctantly supported the unsuccessful Democratic presidential candidate, William Jennings Bryan, in 1896. Although the party dissolved soon after, many of its proposals were to become law in the twentieth century.

See also Political Parties in the United States; Presidential Elections.

PORK BARREL LEGISLATION, a form of logrolling, primarily based on favor. Party lines have little or no bearing upon the practice of pork barrel legislation because popularity is the end sought by its practitioners.

As in logrolling, pork barrel legislation is commonly associated with river-and-harbor projects, highway construction, veterans' hospitals, military installations, and new post offices. Owing to its role as a lobby and participant in river-and-harbor projects, the Army Corps of Engineers is often associated with the practice.

See also Logrolling.

PORT AUTHORITY, a local administrative body that oversees the operation of port facilities. The power of port authorities varies from port to port. Some port authorities oversee the total operation of the port, and others merely maintain the port facilities, such as channel dredging and navigational aids, leaving the construction and maintenance of docks, piers, warehouses, and equipment to private companies.

POSTAL SERVICE, UNITED STATES, an independent establishment within the executive branch, responsible for the delivery of billions of pieces of mail each year. The world's largest mail system, with nearly 40,000 post offices and more than 700,000 employees, the Postal Service is also the largest civilian agency in the United States government and the nation's most important communications organization.

The Colonies. The U.S. postal system has its origins in the colonial mail service, first established on a rudimentary basis in the seventeenth century. In 1639 a Boston tavern owned by Richard Fairbanks was designated as the official repository for mail brought from or sent overseas. Fifty-two years later King William of England granted to Thomas Neale a patent to set up and maintain a postal system in the colonies. Following Neale's death in 1707, the British government assumed control over the American postal service.

In 1753, Benjamin Franklin and William Hunter were appointed by the Crown as joint postmasters general in the colonies. Franklin, who had formerly served as Deputy Postmaster General, effected many lasting improvements in the colonial posts, most notably extending the mail service throughout the colonies and facilitating communications with the mother country. As an active antiloyalist, however, Franklin was dismissed by the Crown in 1774. He was named by the Continental Congress as head of the American postal system the following year.

Early America. The Articles of Confederation, adopted in 1778, gave to the Congress exclusive control over the mail service. Following adoption of the Constitution the Congress in 1789 established a post office and created the office of Postmaster General under the Treasury Department. George Washington appointed Samuel Osgood of Massachusetts as the first Postmaster General under the Constitution.

In 1792 Congress passed legislation detailing provisions for the Post Office Department. Subsequent laws enlarged the duties of the department, strengthened and unified its organization, and provided rules and regulations for its development. In 1829 President Jackson's Postmaster General became the first head of the Postal Service to sit as a member of the cabinet, but it was not until 1872 that the Post Office Department officially became an executive department.

Modern America. In 1970 President Richard Nixon signed the Postal Reorganization Act, which removed the Postmaster General from the cabinet and provided for the conversion of the department to an independent agency within the executive. The agency, known as the U.S. Postal Service, was to be managed by a presidentially appointed, bipartisan Board of Gover-

nors and by a Postmaster General and Deputy Postmaster General selected by the Board. The new Postal Service officially began operations in 1971.

Since postal reform took effect, the Postal Service has embarked on a program of reorganization, modernization, and mechanization. A major investment in technological research and development, a progressive policy of labor relations, and a vigorous effort to respond to the needs of a rapidly changing market should enable the Postal Service to meet the challenges confronting it.   —*E.T. Klassen*

POULTRY PRODUCTS INSPECTION ACT OF 1957. *See* Business Regulation in the United States.

POVERTY PROGRAM, a broad attempt to combat poverty called the "War on Poverty" and proposed by Lyndon B. Johnson. Launched by the Economic Opportunity Act of 1964, the war on poverty was administered by the Office of Economic Opportunity (OEO). Work-training and work-study programs (Title I) included the Job Corps for untrained unemployed youths; job recruitment, counseling and placement services; hiring incentives for private employers; public works projects; and work-study opportunities for low-income college students. The Community Action Program (Title II) actively involved the poor in such multi-faceted projects as Head Start, legal services, comprehensive health services, family planning, and opportunities for the elderly. In the first year of the Reagan administration, Head Start was included in the group of programs that constituted the "safety net" and was protected from budgetary cuts. Poverty rural areas (Title III) was attacked by loans to farm families and broad assistance to migrant workers. Employment and investment incentives (Title IV) encouraged small businesses in low-income areas. Work experience, training and day-care programs (Title V) urged self-sufficiency for welfare families. Volunteer service programs (Title VIII) established VISTA. The Economic Opportunity Act also provided a National Advisory Council on Economic Opportunity to review progress and chart future directions.

Analysis. From its inception OEO was hampered by the complexity of its mandate and the shortage of domestic funds. In 1969 a reorganization spun off established programs to other federal agencies (Head Start to HEW, Job Corps to Department of Labor), leaving OEO a center for research, development, and innovation. Funds for many of the programs were sharply curtailed. Nevertheless, the Poverty Program had a tremendous impact on social policies in the United States. Head Start focused national interest on early childhood education. Broadened legal services for the poor protected the rights of low-income tenants, consumers, juveniles, and welfare recipients. The emphasis of the Community Action Program on neighborhood facilities and maximum participation of the poor influenced trends toward local control and decentralization of services. In addition, systems were innovated that may proliferate in the future: community development corporations for economic regeneration and neighborhood family health centers are two examples. OEO was eliminated by 1975, and its remaining functions were placed in a new agency, the Community Services Administration (CSA), and in the Legal Services Corporation. The Legal Services Corporation was later targeted for elimination for budgetary reasons.

See also Community Action Programs; Head Start; Office of Economic Opportunity.

POWELL, LEWIS FRANKLIN, JR. (1907-   ), associate justice of the Supreme Court (1971-1987). Born in Virginia, he received his law degree from Washington and Lee University in 1931 and a master's degree in law from Harvard University in 1932. He was deeply involved in the sensitive question of the desegregation of Virginia's public schools, first as president of the Richmond school board and later as a member of the state board of education. He served as president of the American Bar Association (1964-1965) and of the American College of Trial Lawyers (1968-1969). Nominated to the Supreme Court by President Richard Nixon, he was the only Democrat among Nixon's nominees. A moderate on the Court, he opposed a general anti-capital punishment rule (*Furman v. Georgia,* 1972), further arguing that the death penalty is not "cruel and unusual punishment" in itself (*Profitt v. Florida,* 1976). He was instrumental in establishing flexibility in racial quotas involving college admissions (*Regents of the University of California v. Bakke,* 1978). Justice Powell retired in 1987.

POWELL V. ALABAMA, 287 U.S. 45 (1932). This, the first Scottsboro case, revolves around the right to counsel in all criminal prosecutions, specifically granted by the Sixth Amendment. The petitioners, black youths charged with rape, were tried, found guilty, and sentenced to death in a single day, six days after the alleged crime and without appropriate counsel. The Court held that, in capital cases in both federal and state courts, the Sixth Amendment provides that it is the duty of the trial judge to assign counsel where the defendant is unable to employ counsel and is incapable of making his own defense adequately because of ignorance, feeblemindedness, illiteracy, or the like. This duty, moreover, is not discharged unless counsel is assigned in time and under circumstances designed to permit such counsel to give effective aid in the preparation and trial of the case.

POWER OF THE PURSE, the congressional power to control government finances. The "power of the

purse" is drawn from Article I of the U.S. Constitution, which authorizes Congress "to lay and collect Taxes, Duties, Imposts and Excises," and provides that "No Money shall be drawn from the Treasury, but in Consequence of Appropriations made by Law." Funds cannot be expended until they have been appropriated by Congress. The power of the purse permits significant congressional controls over the executive branch and is the oldest of the powers exercised by legislators. The growth of presidential power in the twentieth century has frequently rendered Congress's traditional power of the purse ineffective, as in the Vietnam crisis, but it is still considered a major limitation on executive authority.

—*Mary L. Carns*
See also Appropriation; Impoundment.

PRECEDENT, a principle of law that says that similar cases should yield similar decisions. Thus, judges may base decisions in current cases on a "line of precedent" established from prior cases. —*Mary L. Carns*
See also Stare Decisis.

PRECINCT, the smallest political unit in the country. The precinct is usually composed of no less than 200 and no more than 1,000 voters and contains a polling place where residents go to vote on election day. Both major national parties extend their organization to the precinct level.

PREFERRED POSITION TEST. *See* Clear and Present Danger.

PRESENTMENT, action of a grand jury when it conducts investigations under its own authority and returns a written accusation of criminal activities. Presentment is relatively rare. More commonly, "indictments" are returned, based on evidence brought to a grand jury by a government prosecutor. Nevertheless, grand juries have broad powers to investigate crimes, and presentment has been used in a number of important cases, including the "quiz show" scandals in 1959, the "Watergate" activities in the 1970s, and charges of tax evasion against Vice President Spiro Agnew in 1973. Provision for presentment is found in the Fifth Amendment to the Constitution.

—*Mary L. Carns*
See also Grand Jury; Information; True Bill.

PRESIDENT-ELECT. When a presidential candidate is elected in the November national elections, he/she becomes the president-elect until officially sworn into office on January 20. During this period the president-to-be has an opportunity to select the important officials of his/her administration and to plan a legislative program.

PRESIDENTIAL ELECTIONS. Article II of the Constitution established the election procedure for president and vice president. Each state was to choose, in any way its legislature determined, electors equal to the number of its members in Congress. These electors, meeting in their respective states, would cast ballots for two individuals. The results would be sent to the national government, where in the presence of Congress, they would be opened and counted. In the event of a tie, or if no candidate received a majority of the votes cast, the House of Representatives would decide, with each state acting as a unit having one vote. Where no candidate had a majority, the House would choose from the five leading contenders.

After the 1800 election tie between Jefferson and Burr, the Twelfth Amendment, providing separate voting for president and vice president, was enacted. If no presidential candidate receives a majority, the House selects from among the three highest candidates. Similarly, if no vice-presidential candidate secures a majority, the Senate chooses from between the two highest.

1789. The last Congress under the Articles of Confederation set the first Wednesday in January as the date for choosing state electors. They were to meet and vote on the first Wednesday in February; and the new Congress would assemble and tabulate the vote on the first Wednesday in March. Of the original 13 states, North Carolina and Rhode Island had not yet ratified the Constitution and could not vote, and the N.Y. legislature could not agree on procedure for selecting electors within the specified time. Most state legislatures determined their electors; only in Pennsylvania, Virginia, and Maryland were they directly selected by the voters.

As had been expected, George Washington, military hero and chairman of the Constitutional Convention, was unanimously elected first president. He received all 69 electoral votes, including the three Anti-Federalists; John Adams led over the other candidates with 34 votes to become vice president. The election was clearly a Federalist triumph.

1792. Congress decided state electors were to be chosen within 34 days of the first Wednesday in December, the day presidential electors would cast their votes. On the second Wednesday in February, Congress would tabulate the results. There were now 15 states, and only in Maryland, North Carolina, Pennsylvania, and Virginia were the electors chosen by popular vote.

This election saw the emergence of a strong opposition party in the Anti-Federalists (Democratic-Republicans, as they were later called). Led by Thomas Jefferson, Secretary of State, they accused the administration of monarchist tendencies and capitalist interests. The party was an alliance of the Southern Agrarian interests and the town mechanics of New

York (particularly Aaron Burr and the Sons of St. Tammany of New York City).

A reluctant Washington was again unanimously chosen president with an electoral vote of 132, but the contest for vice president reflected the increasing party solidarity. Adams received 77 votes; New York Governor Clinton, Anti-Federalist, 50; Jefferson, Anti-Federalist, four; Aaron Burr, Anti-Federalist, one.

1796. The French Revolution was in progress, and France had declared war with Spain and Britain. Washington's administration tried to maintain United States neutrality, but reactions were divided between Federalists (Monocrats), accused of English sympathy, and Democratic Republicans (Jacobins), felt to be pro-French. Reaction to the Jay Treaty with Britain, recall of the French Ambassador, Citizen Genêt, the Whiskey Rebellion in 1794, and the administration's use of militia to curb the defiant taxpayers—all helped solidify party lines.

Washington refused to accept the nomination and thereby established a precedent for two successive terms that lasted until 1940. At a meeting of congressmen and senators (first congressional caucus) John Adams and Thomas Pinckney (S.C.) were informally selected for president and vice president. Thomas Jefferson, leader of the opposition, and New York Governor Aaron Burr were chosen by the Democratic-Republicans. There were 16 states, but only six had a popular vote of electors. John Adams became president with a narrow majority of 71 votes and Thomas Jefferson became vice president with 68, the only instance when president and vice president were not of the same party. Thomas Pinckney had 59 votes; Aaron Burr, 30.

1800. Throughout Adams's administration constant threat of war with France culminated in the XYZ Affair, an attempted bribe by members of the French Directory to ensure peace between the two nations. War fever ran high. Preparations for war were in earnest, and the slogan "Millions for defense but not one cent for tribute" was coined. Dissension among the Federalists, particularly Adams and Hamilton, gave Jefferson, Madison, Gallatin, and Burr opportunity to consolidate a powerful alliance against the administration. Charging the Federalists with excessive taxation, they blamed the Jay Treaty with Britain as the cause of friction between the United States and France. They denounced the Alien and Sedition Acts as unconstitutional. The Federalists accused Jefferson of being a fanatic, a revolutionary, and an atheist.

Of the 16 states taking part in the election, only four chose their electors by popular vote. The Democratic-Republicans won. Adams was defeated (and with his defeat the era of the Federalist regime ended), but Jefferson and Burr (N.Y.-Dem.-Rep.) were tied with 73 electoral votes; Adams had 65; C.C. Pinckney (S.C.-Fed.) received 64; and John Jay (N.Y.-Fed.) had 1. The choice went to the House of Representa-

PRESIDENTIAL ELECTIONS

Year	Candidates	Parties	Popular Vote	Electoral Vote
1789	George Washington			69
	John Adams			34
	Others			35
1792	George Washington			132
	John Adams			77
	George Clinton			50
	Others			5
1796	John Adams	Federalist		71
	Thomas Jefferson	Dem.-Rep.		68
	Thomas Pinckney	Federalist		59
	Aaron Burr	Dem.-Rep.		30
	Others			48
1800	Thomas Jefferson	Dem.-Rep.		73
	Aaron Burr	Dem.-Rep.		73
	John Adams	Federalist		65
	C.C. Pinckney	Federalist		64
	John Jay	Federalist		1
1804	Thomas Jefferson	Dem.-Rep.		162
	C.C. Pinckney	Federalist		14
1808	James Madison	Dem.-Rep.		122
	C.C. Pinckney	Federalist		47
	George Clinton	Dem.-Rep.		6
1812	James Madison	Dem.-Rep.		128
	DeWitt Clinton	Federalist		89
1816	James Monroe	Dem.-Rep.		183
	Rufus King	Federalist		34
1820	James Monroe	Dem.-Rep.		231
	John Quincy Adams	Dem.-Rep.		1
1824	John Quincy Adams	Dem.-Rep.	108,740	84
	Andrew Jackson	Dem.-Rep.	153,544	99
	William H. Crawford	Dem.-Rep.	46,618	41
	Henry Clay	Dem.-Rep.	47,136	37
1828	Andrew Jackson	Democrat	647,286	178
	John Quincy Adams	Nat. Rep.	508,064	83
1832	Andrew Jackson	Democrat	687,502	219
	Henry Clay	Nat. Rep.	530,189	49
	John Floyd	Whig		11
	William Wirt	Anti-Masonic		7
1836	Martin Van Buren	Democrat	765,483	170
	William H. Harrison	Anti-Masonic		73
	Daniel Webster	Whig		14
	W.P. Mangum	Whig		11
	Hugh L. White	Whig		26
1840	William H. Harrison	Whig	1,274,624	234
	Martin Van Buren	Democrat	1,127,781	60
	J.G. Birney	Liberty	7,059	
1844	James K. Polk	Democrat	1,338,464	170
	Henry Clay	Whig	1,300,097	105
	J.G. Birney	Liberty	62,300	
1848	Zachary Taylor	Whig	1,360,967	163
	Lewis Cass	Democrat	1,222,342	127
	Martin Van Buren	Free-Soil	291,263	
1852	Franklin Pierce	Democrat	1,601,117	254
	Winfield Scott	Whig	1,385,453	42
	John P. Hale	Free-Soil	155,825	
1856	James Buchanan	Democrat	1,832,955	174
	John C. Frémont	Republican	1,339,932	114
	Millard Fillmore	American	871,731	8
1860	Abraham Lincoln	Republican	1,865,593	180
	Stephen A. Douglas	Democrat	1,382,713	12
	John C. Breckinridge	Democrat	848,356	72
	John Bell	Constitutional Union	592,906	39
1864	Abraham Lincoln	Republican	2,206,938	212
	George B. McClellan	Democrat	1,803,787	21
1868	Ulysses S. Grant	Republican	3,013,421	214
	Horatio Seymour	Democrat	2,706,829	80
1872	Ulysses S. Grant	Republican	3,596,745	286
	Horace Greeley	Dem., Lib. Rep.	2,843,446	66
1876	Rutherford B. Hayes	Republican	4,036,572	185
	Samuel J. Tilden	Democrat	4,284,020	184
1880	James A. Garfield	Republican	4,453,295	214
	Winfield S. Hancock	Democrat	4,414,082	155
1884	Grover Cleveland	Democrat	4,879,507	219
	James G. Blaine	Republican	4,850,293	182
1888	Benjamin Harrison	Republican	5,447,129	233
	Grover Cleveland	Democrat	5,537,857	168
1892	Grover Cleveland	Democrat	5,555,426	277
	Benjamin Harrison	Republican	5,182,690	145
	James B. Weaver	People's	1,029,846	22
1896	William McKinley	Republican	7,102,246	271
	William J. Bryan	Democrat, People's	6,492,559	176
1900	William McKinley	Republican	7,218,491	292
	William J. Bryan	Dem., Fusion Populists	6,356,734	155
1904	Theodore Roosevelt	Republican	7,628,461	336
	Alton B. Parker	Democrat	5,084,223	140
	Eugene V. Debs	Socialist	402,283	
1908	William H. Taft	Republican	7,675,320	321
	William J. Bryan	Democrat	6,412,294	162
	Eugene V. Debs	Socialist	420,793	
1912	Woodrow Wilson	Democrat	6,296,547	435
	Theodore Roosevelt	Progressive	4,118,571	88
	William H. Taft	Republican	3,486,720	8
	Eugene V. Debs	Socialist	900,672	
1916	Woodrow Wilson	Democrat	9,127,695	277
	Charles E. Hughes	Republican	8,533,507	254
	A.L. Benson	Socialist	585,113	
1920	Warren G. Harding	Republican	16,143,407	404
	James M. Cox	Democrat	9,130,328	127
	Eugene V. Debs	Socialist	919,799	
1924	Calvin Coolidge	Republican	15,718,211	382
	John W. Davis	Democrat	8,385,283	136
	Robert M. La Follette	Progressive	4,831,289	13
1928	Herbert Hoover	Republican	21,391,993	444
	Alfred E. Smith	Democrat	15,016,169	87
	Norman Thomas	Socialist	881,951	
1932	Franklin D. Roosevelt	Democrat	22,809,638	472
	Herbert Hoover	Republican	15,758,901	59
	Norman Thomas	Socialist	267,835	
1936	Franklin D. Roosevelt	Democrat	27,752,869	523
	Alfred M. Landon	Republican	16,674,665	8
	William Lemke	Union & Others	882,479	
1940	Franklin D. Roosevelt	Democrat	27,307,819	449
	Wendell L. Wilkie	Republican	22,321,018	82
1944	Franklin D. Roosevelt	Democrat	25,606,585	432
	Thomas E. Dewey	Republican	22,014,745	99
1948	Harry S. Truman	Democrat	24,105,812	303
	Thomas E. Dewey	Republican	21,970,065	189
	J. Strom Thurmond	States-Rights	1,169,063	39
	Henry A. Wallace	Progressive	1,157,172	
1952	Dwight D. Eisenhower	Republican	33,936,234	442
	Adlai E. Stevenson	Democrat	27,314,992	89
1956	Dwight D. Eisenhower	Republican	35,590,472	457
	Adlai E. Stevenson	Democrat	26,022,752	73
1960	John F. Kennedy	Democrat	34,227,096	303
	Richard M. Nixon	Republican	34,108,546	219
	Harry F. Byrd	Democrat		15
1964	Lyndon B. Johnson	Democrat	43,129,484	486
	Barry M. Goldwater	Republican	27,178,188	52
1968	Richard M. Nixon	Republican	31,785,480	301
	Hubert H. Humphrey	Democrat	31,275,165	191
	George C. Wallace	Independent	9,906,473	46
1972	Richard M. Nixon	Republican	47,168,963	517
	George S. McGovern	Democrat	29,169,615	17
1976	Jimmy Carter	Democrat	40,831,000	297
	Gerald R. Ford	Republican	39,148,000	240
1980	Ronald W. Reagan	Republican	43,201,220	489
	Jimmy Carter	Democrat	34,913,332	49
	John B. Anderson	Independent	5,581,379	
1984	Ronald W. Reagan	Republican	52,609,797	525
	Walter F. Mondale	Democrat	36,450,613	13
1988	George S. Bush	Republican	48,886,097	426
	Michael Dukakis	Democrat	41,809,074	111

tives, where after 35 ballots a majority was still not reached. Though it was understood that Jefferson was the intended Republican presidential candidate, the Federalists controlling the House decided to support Burr, as the lesser of two evils. However, Burr did nothing to gain the necessary support. Bayard, Delaware Federalist, was then instrumental in an "arrangement" breaking the deadlock. Federalist electors of Vermont and Maryland went to Jefferson, and Federalists from South Carolina and Delaware abstained. Jefferson was elected by ten out of 16 states. This election proved that with the advent of political parties this method of electoral voting was inoperable. Before the next presidential election the Twelfth Amendment, providing separate ballots for president and vice president was passed.

1804. The Jefferson administration was popular. The country was prosperous, the Alien and Sedition Acts had expired, taxes were repealed, the National debt had been reduced, agriculture and land migration were encouraged, and the Louisiana Territory was acquired. For the first time the Republican congressional caucus was not held secretly. The election was an assured victory for Jefferson and his vice-presidential nominee, George Clinton (N.Y.). Only in New England was there any opposition. The Federalists informally named C.C. Pinckney (S.C.), for president and Senator Rufus King (N.Y.), for vice president. Jefferson and Clinton received 162 of the 176 electoral votes. Seven of the 17 states voting selected their electors by direct popular vote.

1808. Jefferson, declining to run for a third term, named James Madison (Va.) his successor. George Clinton was renominated for vice president. Dissatisfaction with administration policies caused John Randolph and John Taylor of Virginia, leaders of a splinter group advocating stronger states' rights, to put forth James Monroe as Republican presidential candidate. Both France and England were harassing American shipping, and Britain, in particular, ignored neutral rights. The Jefferson administration had passed the Embargo Act, bringing trade with Europe to a stop and seriously jeopardizing the economy. The embargo became the major campaign issue, and Federalists, enjoying the brief revival, again named C.C. Pinckney (S.C.) and Rufus King (N.Y.) as their candidates. The Federalists regained control of New England, but Madison and Clinton, nonetheless, were elected by a substantial majority.

1812. Relations with Great Britain were deteriorating rapidly. American vessels were boarded, cargo was taken, and United States seamen were pressed into British service. Southern and Western expansionists urged war, hoping to end the English-Indian alliance and to annex more land in the West and Canada and ultimately gain Florida from the Spanish. On June 19, 1812, war was declared with Great Britain, and it became the single most important issue of the presidential campaign.

The congressional caucus renominated James Madison; Elbridge Gerry (Mass.) was chosen the vice-presidential nominee. Those New York Democratic-Republicans opposed to the war held a separate caucus at Albany, nominating De Witt Clinton for president and Charles Jared Ingersoll (Penn.) for vice president. They gained the endorsement of antiwar Federalists.

The results of the election were largely sectional. New England and the Middle States, except Vermont, Pennsylvania, and part of Maryland, voted for Clinton. Madison was reelected president with 128 electoral votes to Clinton's 89.

1816. The peace treaty between the United States and England was signed on Dec. 24, 1814. There were no strong political issues at stake, and the Republicans' only opposition came from those Federalist New England merchants who had been against the war and had even considered secession. The congressional caucus nominated James Monroe, another of the "Virginia Dynasty" and Madison's choice, for president. New York Governor Daniel Tomkins was selected for vice president. Federalists unofficially supported Rufus King (N.Y.) for president and John E. Howard (Md.) as his running mate. The Republicans carried the election with 183 electoral votes, and only Massachusetts, Connecticut, and Delaware cast their 34 electoral votes for King.

1820. Domestic, rather than foreign, issues were now in the forefront, and differences were less party than sectional. Controversies were over slavery, tariff, and internal improvements. Despite the financial panic of 1819 and the bitter struggle over admission of Missouri as a slave state, which led to the Missouri Compromise, Monroe was intensely popular, and his administration became known as the Era of Good Feelings. Monroe was reelected with only one dissenting vote, cast for John Quincy Adams, son of John Adams. Daniel D. Tompkins was again elected vice president.

1824. The Democratic-Republicans lost all appearance of party solidarity, and the attention focused on six sectional candidates. New England favored John Quincy Adams (Mass.), Secretary of State; the South, John C. Calhoun (S.C.), Secretary of War, and William H. Crawford (Ga.), Secretary of the Treasury; the West, Henry Clay (Ky.), House Speaker, Andrew Jackson (Tenn.), War of 1812 hero, and New York Governor De Witt Clinton. Adams and Jackson favored a tariff and internal improvements. Clay, in addition, advocated Western expansion, the U.S. Bank, and recognition of the South American Republics. Crawford, a states' rightist, opposed the tariff. In what proved to be the last congressional caucus, Crawford was nominated for president, and Albert Gallatin (Pa.), vice president. State legislatures had chosen Jackson and Clay; Adams was nominated at a Boston party; and in 1821 Calhoun had announced his candidacy. He withdrew to become vice-presidential candidate on the Adams-Jackson ticket. A paralytic stroke eliminated Crawford as a serious contender. Gallatin withdrew as Crawford's followers asked Clay to form a Crawford-Clay ticket, but Clay refused.

In 18 of the 24 states the people directly selected the electors. Jackson led the total popular vote, receiving 99 electoral votes; Adams, 84; Crawford, 41; and Clay, 37. Since no one received a majority, the vote went to the House, where the choice was among the three leading candidates. Clay, eliminated, wielding considerable power, released his votes to Adams, giving him the required 13 states for the presidency. Jackson received seven states' votes; Crawford, four. Jackson men claimed a corrupt bargain had been made between Clay and Adams and became more enraged when Clay was selected secretary of state. John C. Calhoun was chosen vice president by electoral vote. John Quincy Adams was the first president to take office with a popular vote minority.

1828. The Democratic-Republicans split into two rival parties. Supporters of Adams and Clay became National Republicans, and Jackson's followers formed the Democrats. In October 1825 the Tennessee legislature nominated Andrew Jackson for president. John C. Calhoun, Vice President under Adams, became Jackson's running mate. The National Republicans renominated John Quincy Adams and chose Richard Rush (Pa.), Secretary of State, for vice president.

Adams, advocating internal improvements and a high tariff, appealed to New England and Midwestern manufacturing interests, conservative Federalists and those Westerners favoring internal improvements. He also had support of the Anti-Masons, the first organized third party. Adams was identified with the aristocracy, and Jackson was the people's candidate, supported by Western farmers, Eastern laborers, and the South. William Crawford and John C. Calhoun allied with Old Hickory and through efforts of Martin Van Buren (N.Y.) the diverse anti-Adams factions were consolidated. Jackson supporters still maintained the charge of "corrupt bargain" between Adams and Clay. Racial, religious, and class prejudices played a major role in this campaign.

There was an unprecedented large popular vote. Jackson won with 647,276 votes against Adams's 508,064. Only South Carolina and Delaware selected their electors by legislature.

1832. The major issue of the 1832 campaign was the Bank of the United States. President Jackson, opposed to the renewal of its charter, vetoed it and rallied the sentiments of the people against it. The National Republicans allied with Nicholas Biddle, Director of the Bank, to defend it. The Anti-Masons held their first national convention of elected delegates to choose candidates for president and vice president;

the other parties quickly followed suit. Anti-Masons nominated William Wirt (Md.) for president and Amos Ellmaker (Pa.) for vice president. The National Republicans nominated Henry Clay (Ky.) for president and John Sergeant (Pa.), a chief legal and political adviser of the Bank, as his running mate. Jackson easily won the Democratic renomination, and Martin Van Buren (N.Y.), Minister to Great Britain and Jackson's choice for vice president, became his running mate. Jackson was reelected with 219 electoral votes; Clay received 49 from six states.

1836. President Jackson had tangled with the Senate over withdrawal of government funds from the Bank of the United States and was accused of assuming autocratic powers. His opponents rallied together as Whigs to defeat Martin Van Buren, his chosen successor. At the Democratic national convention, Van Buren secured the presidential nomination and Richard M. Johnson (Ky.), soldier and congressman, the vice-presidency. The Whigs, disagreeing among themselves, were unable to hold a national convention and left the choice of candidates to state legislatures, hoping the voting of favorite sons would divide the vote and throw the election to the House.

Martin Van Buren won with 170 votes against William H. Harrison (Ohio-Whigs), who emerged as the only serious rival with 73; Hugh L. White (Tenn.-Whig), 26; Daniel Webster (Mass.-Whig), 14; Willie P. Mangum, (N.C., a Calhoun man), 11. Lacking a majority, the vice-presidential election, for the first and only time, went to the Senate, where Richard M. Johnson was chosen vice president with 33 votes against the 16 votes of Francis Granger, (N.Y.-Whig).

1840. The campaign of 1840 was notable for its exuberance, its introduction of processions and rallies, and its party songs, banners and emblems. The Democrats renominated Van Buren but could not agree on a vice-presidential nominee. The first Whig national convention nominated William Henry Harrison (Ohio) for president. Harrison's ambiguous stance on all issues made him an acceptable candidate for the diverse Whig factions. He won over Henry Clay, whose long political career was felt to be a liability. John Tyler (Va.) was chosen for vice president. The Liberty party, or Abolitionist, held its first national convention, naming James C. Birney and Thomas Earl for president and vice president.

"Tippecanoe and Tyler, too" became one of the popular Whig slogans. The log cabin, hard cider, and coonskin cap became Harrison's symbols and helped create his image of a man of the people, while Van Buren represented the aristocracy. Harrison won by a very close popular vote but received 234 electoral votes against Van Buren's 60.

1844. The annexation of Texas and the controversy over the Oregon boundary were the most important issues of this election. Expansionism led the Democrats and the country onward to her Manifest Destiny.

The campaign of 1840 was notable for the use of banners and other displays.

Van Buren's attitude against annexation was unfavorable to the South, and thus the Democratic national convention finally selected James K. Polk (Tenn.) as the compromise and first dark horse candidate for president. George M. Dallas (Pa.) was the vice-presidential candidate. "All Oregon or None" and "Fifty-Four Forty or Fight" were the Democratic slogans. The Whigs nominated Henry Clay, 1824 and 1832 presidential candidate, for president and Theodore Frelinghuysen (N.J.) for vice president. John Tyler, who had succeeded to the presidency after Harrison's death, was the first president not to receive a nomination for a second term. James C. Birney, renominated by the Liberty Party with Thomas Morris (Ohio) as his running mate, took enough votes from Clay to make Polk president. Polk had 170 electoral votes against Clay's 105, but only a slim margin in the popular vote.

1848. The acquisition of Texas, New Mexico, Arizona, and California made slavery the leading issue. Zachary Taylor (La.), Mexican War hero, was the Whig candidate for president; Millard Fillmore (N.Y.) was the vice-presidential candidate. Polk did not run for reelection, and the Democratic convention chose General Lewis Cass, Michigan expansionist, for president and William O. Butler (Ky.) a slaveholder, as his running mate. The antislavery "Conscience" Whigs of New England, supported by the Barnburners of New York (antislavery Democrats) and Liberty party members, selected Martin Van Buren (N.Y.) and Charles Francis Adams (Mass.) their candidates. "Free soil, free speech, free labor and free men" became their slogan, and its proponents, Free-Soilers.

The New York Democratic split between Cass and Van Buren gave Taylor New York's 136 electoral votes, making him president. In 1845 Congress passed a law designating "the Tuesday next after the first Monday in the month of November" as election day, and for the first time all 30 states appointed their presidential electors on the same day.

1852. After President Taylor's death, Millard Fillmore, succeeding to the presidency, promptly endorsed the Clay Compromise. It established California as a free state, and all other territories acquired from Mexico would have no slavery restrictions; it contained a stringent fugitive slave law; and it abolished slave trade within the District of Columbia.

The Democratic convention after extended balloting selected the dark horse candidate, Sen. Franklin Pierce (N.H.) and Sen. William R. D. King (Ala.), Minister to France, as their choice for president and vice president. Pledging to support all aspects of the Clay Compromise, Pierce and King promised to resist efforts to renew agitation of this question. Overcoming sectional differences, the Whigs selected Winfield Scott (N.J.), Mexican War hero, (over Webster and Fillmore) and William A. Graham (N.C.), Secretary of the Navy, as their candidates. They acquiesced on the Compromise and vowed to maintain it until further legislation proved necessary. The dissatisfied Northern Whigs broke from the party to join the Free-Soilers, who nominated John P. Hale (N.H.) for president, and George W. Julien (Ind.) for vice president. They condemned both slavery and the Clay Compromise. Franklin Pierce won the presidency with a large electoral majority.

1856. The Kansas-Nebraska Act (1854) repealed the Missouri Compromise, thus intensifying the slavery conflict. James Buchanan (Pa.), Minister to England during the Kansas-Nebraska debates, was the least controversial candidate and became the Democratic nominee for president, winning over Franklin Pierce, Stephen A. Douglas, and Lewis Cass. John C. Breckinridge (Ky.) was Buchanan's running mate. The Democrats promised to avoid agitating the slavery question and condemned the Native Americans (or Know-Nothings), whose policies were directed against the foreign-born and Roman Catholics. The Know-Nothings chose former President Millard Fillmore for president and A.J. Donelson (Tenn.) for vice president. The Republican Party, comprised of antislavery Democrats, and Whigs, and Free-Soilers was formed in 1854. At their first national convention they chose John C. Frémont, explorer and soldier, candidate for president; William L. Dayton (N.J.) was his running mate. They argued that Congress should prohibit slavery in the territories. Their campaign was characterized by "Bleeding Kansas," and their slogan was "Free Soil, Free Men, Frémont."

The remnants of the Whig party endorsed the candidates but not the political principles of the Know-

Nothings. Buchanan was elected by all the slave states but Maryland, which went to Fillmore, and the free states of Pennsylvania, Indiana, New Jersey, California, and Illinois. Eleven free states voted for Frémont.

1860. The central figure of the Democratic convention, which met in Charleston, N.C., on April 23, was Stephen A. Douglas (Ill.) a firm believer in popular sovereignty and the Compromise of 1850. The convention adopted a platform reflecting Douglas' beliefs, and eight Southern states, demanding a repudiation of popular sovereignty and a guarantee of slavery in the territories, withdrew. After 57 ineffective ballots the convention adjourned to meet in Baltimore on June 18. There Douglas was nominated for president and Herschel V. Johnson (Ga.) for vice president, but not before another Southern withdrawal. The Southern Democratic delegates then assembled and chose John C. Breckinridge (Ky.) and Joseph Lane (Ore.) as running mates. Their platform repeated their demands for protection of slavery in all territories and threatened secession.

The Constitutional Union party, a remnant of the Whigs and Know-Nothings, nominated John Bell (Tenn.) and Edward Everett (Mass.). They advocated preservation of the Union. Republicans, meeting in Chicago, chose Abraham Lincoln (Ill.) their candidate, passing over party favorite William H. Seward. Hannibal Hamlin (Me.) was their choice for vice president. The Republicans proposed slavery prohibition in the territories, river and harbor improvements, higher tariffs, homestead law, and a railroad to the Pacific. After his nomination, the Rail-Splitter did not actively campaign; his election was almost assured by the Democratic split. The campaign was primarily a two-party fight with Lincoln against Douglas in the North and Bell against Breckinridge in the South. Lincoln carried the free states for 180 votes; Douglas 12; Breckinridge, 72 from 11 slave states; and Bell, 39.

1864. Casualties mounted as the war dragged on. The Radical, or anti-Lincoln, Republicans named John C. Frémont (Cal.) for president and General John Cochran (N.Y.) for vice president. The regular Republican convention renominated Lincoln on the first ballot and chose Andrew Johnson (Tenn.), war Democrat, as his running mate. The Democratic convention adopted a stop-the-war platform with George B. McClellan (N.J.), former commander-in-chief of the Union Army, as presidential candidate and George Pendleton, Ohio senator, his running mate. McClellan accepted the nomination but not the platform. With the Northern victories of General Sherman and Admiral Farragut, Frémont withdrew from the race, Lincoln's popularity heightened, and he was easily reelected.

1868. Four days after Andrew Johnson's acquittal of the impeachment charges levied by the Radical Republicans, the Republican convention met and unanimously selected Gen. Ulysses S. Grant its presidential

candidate; Schuyler Colfax (Ind.), House Speaker, was chosen for vice president. Reconstruction policy was the main issue of the campaign. The Republican platform called for equal suffrage and the payment of the public debt in gold rather than paper money. Horatio Seymour (N.Y.), the "Great Decliner," reluctantly accepted the Democratic nomination for president; Francis P. Blair (Mo.) was his running mate. The Democrats advocated the "greenback policy," the repayment of government bonds in paper currency rather than gold. Grant won the election because of the Southern black vote and the widespread popular confidence he inspired.

1872. The Liberal Republicans, a reform movement of the Republican party against the corrupt practices of the Grant administration, united the advocates of women's suffrage, tariff reduction, and civil service reforms. The platform condemned the spoils system and the harsh policies toward the South but were evasive about a tariff. Horace Greeley, *New York Tribune* editor and Missouri Gov. B. Gratz Brown were the nominees. The Republicans renominated Grant and voted Sen. Henry Wilson (Mass.) his running mate. The Democrats endorsed Greeley and Brown, but a group of dissatisfied Straight-out Democrats held a separate convention and nominated Charles O'Connor (N.Y.) and John Quincy Adams (Mass.). Both men refused the nomination, but their names were still used.

For the first time all 37 states held their elections by popular vote. Grant was easily reelected. Greeley died before the electoral vote was counted, and his votes scattered among other Democratic and Liberal Republican candidates.

1876. In December 1875 Congress passed a resolution upholding the two-successive-term precedent, ending any hope Grant may have had for a third term. The Republican convention nominated Ohio Gov. Rutherford B. Hayes for president, defeating former House Speaker James G. Blaine. William A. Wheeler (N.Y.), millionaire corporation lawyer, was the vice-presidential candidate. Samuel J. Tilden was elected the Democratic presidential nominee, and Thomas A. Henricks (Ind.) was the vice-presidential candidate. The Prohibition Reform party nominated Gen. Green Clay Smith (Ky.). The Independent National convention (Greenback successor to the Labor Reform and Granger movements) chose Peter Cooper (N.Y.).

The country was tired of the corruption of the Grant administration, the severity of the Reconstruction policies, and high unemployment since the 1873 depression. Both major parties wanted reform, and there appeared little difference between the candidates. Tilden received the popular-vote majority but lacked one disputed electoral vote to secure the electoral majority. In January, fearing the controversy's deadlock would leave the nation without a president, Congress submitted the problem to a Republican-dominated commission. The commission's vote was strictly partisan, and Hayes received 185 electoral votes against Tilden's 184. The Democrats accepted the commission's results rather than face the possibility of civil war, but only after a Southerner was placed in the cabinet and federal troops were withdrawn from the South.

1880. President Hayes did not seek reelection. Republicans were divided into two factions; Stalwarts, conservatives against reform, led by N.Y. Sen. Roscoe Conkling, and Half-breeds, more liberal, under James G. Blaine of Maine. The Republican party nominated James A. Garfield (Ohio) for president on the 36th ballot when former President Grant (backed by Stalwarts) and Blaine supporters were deadlocked. Chester A. Arthur, "gentleman boss" of New York, was nominated vice president as an appeasement to the Conkling faction. Democrats chose Winfield S. Hancock (Pa.) and William H. English (Ind.). James B. Weaver (Iowa) was the candidate of the National Greenback Labor party, and Neal Dow, a Maine Quaker, was the Prohibition candidate. No real political issues existed, and the campaign concentrated on the candidates' personalities. Garfield won the presidency with a very slim majority. Had either of the minor-party candidates supported Hancock, the Democrats could have won.

1884. The Republicans chose James G. Blaine (Me.), the "Plumed Knight," their presidential candidate and Gen. John A. Logan (Ill.) his running mate. The Republican reform movement, later called Mugwumps, rebelled against Blaine's nomination and met with Democrats to back a reform ticket. N.Y. Gov. Grover Cleveland and Thomas A. Hendricks (Ind.) were the Democratic candidates. Gen. Benjamin F. Butler (Mass.), former Radical Republican and Tammany candidate, became the Greenback candidate; John P. St. John (Kans.) became the Prohibition candidate. The campaign deteriorated into personal abuse of the candidates. Compromising business letters of Blaine were published, and Democrats and Mugwumps chanted: "Blaine! Blaine! James G. Blaine! The con-tin-nen-tal liar from the state of Maine." Republicans accused Cleveland of fathering an illegitimate child and sang: "Ma! Ma! Where's my Pa? Gone to the White House. Ha! Ha! Ha!" Grover Cleveland won the election by a very small majority. Blaine lost the important New York Irish-American vote when he did not immediately repudiate a supporter's reference to Democrats as the party of rum, Romanism, and rebellion.

1888. Cleveland's annual message to Congress in December 1887 advocated serious tariff reductions. The tariff became the major campaign issue, with Democrats urging lower rates and Republicans opposing. Cleveland was renominated by acclamation at the Democratic convention; Allen G. Thurman (Ohio) was named for vice president. The Republicans nomi-

Poster supporting Prohibitionist candidate Clinton B. Fisk in the 1888 campaign.

nated Blaine's choice, Benjamin Harrison (Ind.) and Levi P. Morton (N.Y.). Morton's red bandana became the Republican symbol. Clinton B. Fisk was the Prohibitionist candidate, and Alson J. Streeter ran for the Union Labor party. Enormous contributions from businessmen, afraid of losing the protective tariff, poured into Republican coffers. Vote buying and deal making were flagrant, and Harrison was elected president, though he lost the popular vote by 100,000.

1892. Republicans renominated President Harrison, Whitlaw Reid (N.Y.) was his running mate. Harrison's only possible rival, James G. Blaine (Me.) refused to run. Democrats nominated Grover Cleveland for the third successive time; Adlai E. Stevenson (Ill.) was their vice-presidential choice. The two parties differed only on the tariff; Democrats again advocated a tariff for revenue only, denouncing the Republican protective policy and the McKinley Tariff Law passed by the 51st Republican Congress.

The People's party, or Populists, formed in 1891 from rebelling farmers of the South and West, nominated James B. Weaver (Iowa) for president and James G. Field (Va.) for vice president. The party's radical platform blamed Republican monopolists for economic hardships of railroads, telegraph and telephone. The Populists won 8 percent of the vote, to make an impressive showing in the election. John Bidwell (Calf.) and J.B. Cramfill (Texas) were the Prohibitionist candidates; Simon Wing (Mass.) was the Socialist Labor party nominee. Cleveland easily won the presidency.

1896. The country suffered a severe depression. The free-silver coinage issue dominated the campaign, pitting the agrarian South and West against the financial East, the people against the privileged classes. The Republicans chose Ohio Gov. William

McKinley, whose campaign was managed by millionaire Mark Hanna. Garret A. Hobart was the vice-presidential nominee. A minority group led by Henry M. Teller (Colo.), opposed to the gold standard and protective tariff of the Republican platform, left the convention and later backed William Jennings Bryan. Bryan's cross-of-gold speech earned him the Democratic candidacy; Arthur Sewall, a rich Maine shipbuilder, was the vice-presidential nominee. Democrats advocated free and unlimited gold and silver coinage and a tariff for revenue only. Backing Bryan but not Sewall, Populists nominated Thomas E. Watson (Ga.) for vice president. Prohibitionists split over the silver issue: Narrow Gaugers, opposing free coinage, nominated Charles E. Bentley; Broad Gaugers (or National party), favoring free silver, chose Joshua Levering. The National Democratic party (Democrats for the gold standard) nominated John M. Palmer (Ill.) for president. C.H. Matchett (N.Y.) ran as Socialist Labor party candidate.

Bryan, denounced as an anarchist and revolutionary, toured the country making speeches, while McKinley spoke to delegations brought to his home. In a record turnout of 14 million, McKinley won the presidency with an electoral majority of 95.

1900. The economy revived, and the main concern of the campaign was imperialism. The United States, after the Spanish War of 1898, acquired Cuba, the Philippines, and Puerto Rico. Interest centered on annexation of Hawaii and building of an isthmian canal. Republicans renominated William McKinley; N.Y. Gov. Theodore Roosevelt was the vice-presidential nominee. William J. Bryan was again the Demo-

Poster supporting Theodore Roosevelt to succeed McKinley in 1900 shows McKinley holding a poster that was effective in his own 1896 campaign.

cratic choice for president; Adlai E. Stevenson, former vice president under Cleveland, was Bryan's running

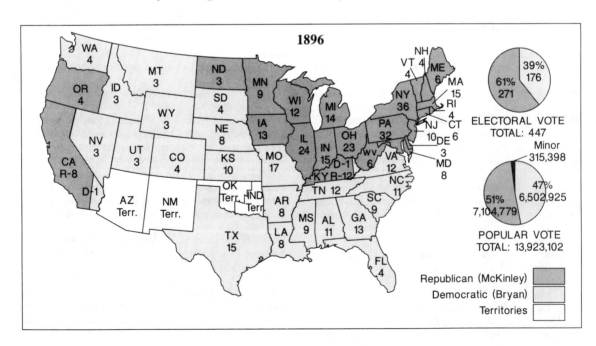

1896

ELECTORAL VOTE
TOTAL: 447

61% 271
39% 176

POPULAR VOTE
TOTAL: 13,923,102

51% 7,104,779
47% 6,502,925
Minor 315,398

Republican (McKinley)
Democratic (Bryan)
Territories

mate. Middle-of-the-road Populists backed Wharton Barker (Pa.). The Social Democratic party, holding its first national convention, nominated Eugene V. Debs and Ignatius Donelly. The United Christian, Socialist Labor, Union Reform, and National Prohibition parties named candidates. The Democrats denounced McKinley and the Republicans for their imperialist policies, but the promise of "Four Years More of a Full Dinner Pail" was effective, and McKinley was easily returned to the White House.

1904. After McKinley's assassination in 1901, Theodore Roosevelt became at 43 the youngest president. He unanimously won the Republican nomination; Indiana Sen. Charles Warren Fairbanks was nominated vice president by acclamation. Democrats passed over twice-defeated Bryan, choosing Judge Alton B. Parker (N.Y.); millionaire Henry G. Davis (W. Va.) was his running mate. Democrats advocated a "safe and sane" platform and accepted the gold standard. Eugene V. Debs was again the Socialist candidate, running with Benjamin Hanford (N.Y.). Prohibitionists nominated Silas C. Swallow (Pa.); Social Laborites, Corregan and Cox; Populists, Watson and Tibbles. Big business and Progressive reformers endorsed Roosevelt, and he won the election by an overwhelming majority.

1908. Roosevelt's "Imperial Years" were exciting; foreign affairs, vigorous and successful. Domestically many progressive laws were enacted. The Panama Canal was begun, and Roosevelt continued his crusade against trusts. Roosevelt did not seek a third term and chose William H. Taft, Secretary of War, as his successor. James S. Sherman was candidate for vice president. The Democrats nominated William J. Bryan for the third time; John W. Kern (Ind.) was their vice-presidential choice. Eugene V. Debs (Ga.) was Socialist candidate for the third time; Prohibitionists selected Eugene W. Chafin and Aaron Watkins; Populists nominated Thomas E. Watson; Socialist La-

These Republican candidates easily won the election of 1908.

borites, August Gilhaus; and Independents, Thomas L. Hisgen. Taft easily won the election.

1912. Taft, instead of carrying on Roosevelt's policies, became more conservative. Before the Republican convention, Roosevelt and Taft battled for the nomination. Party bosses favored Taft, and after a credentials battle most of the contested seats went to Taft. Republicans renominated him and James S. Sherman. Roosevelt left the convention to become the presidential nominee of the Progressive party; Hiram Johnson (Cal.) was his running mate on the Bull Moose ticket, which endorsed most of the current reform proposals. New Jersey Gov. Woodrow Wilson won the Democratic nomination on the 46th ballot over Champ Clark (Mo.), House Speaker Bryan refused to support anyone with Tammany connections and turned to Wilson. Indiana Gov. Thomas R. Marshall was the Democratic vice-presidential choice. Wilson's New Freedom did not differ much from Roosevelt's new Nationalism.

Eugene V. Debs again ran for the Socialists. Prohibitionists nominated Chafin and Watkins; Social Laborites, Reimer and Francis. Because of the split in the Republican party, Wilson easily won the election with 435 electoral votes over Theodore Roosevelt's 88, and President Taft's 8.

1916. War in Europe and American involvement were the primary issues. Wilson and Marshall were renominated in line with the Democrats' antiwar campaign slogan "He kept us out of war." Republicans chose Justice Charles Evans Hughes and Charles W. Fairbanks, vice president under Roosevelt, as their candidates. Roosevelt, refusing to run under the Progressive party banner, later supported Hughes and unsuccessfully tried to prod Hughes into a stronger war position. Allan L. Benson (N.Y.) and George R. Kilpatrick ran for the Socialists; Frank J. Hanly and Ira Landrith formed the Prohibition ticket. Wilson's peace attitude and progressive record won him the presidency by a slight majority. Republicans on election eve believed they had won and learned of their defeat the next morning, when California votes came in. Hughes had not asked for the support of California's Governor Hiram Johnson.

1920. Sen. Warren G. Harding and Gov. Calvin Coolidge ran for the Republicans. His health failing, Wilson did not run for reelection. Democrats nominated Gov. James M. Cox (Ohio) and Assistant Secretary of the Navy Franklin Delano Roosevelt. The Farmer Labor party nominated P.P. Christensen and Max S. Hayes; Prohibitionists, Watkins and Colvin. The socialist candidates Eugene V. Debs, serving a federal sentence for violating the Espionage Act, and Stedman attained their greatest vote in this election. The Nineteenth Amendment had passed, and women voted for the first time. The Republicans promised a "return to normalcy" and, advocating nationalism and isolationism, opposed the League of Nations. The

Democrats favored ratification of the Treaty of Versailles and endorsed the league. The country, suffering from high prices, labor disputes, and anti-Red hysteria swept in Harding as president, a conservative reaction to Wilson's progressive policies.

1924. Calvin Coolidge, succeeding to the presidency on the death of Warren Harding in 1923, easily won the Republican nomination. Charles G. Dawes (Ill.) was his running mate. The Democratic convention, setting a record for the longest convention in history, was split on the issue of the Ku Klux Klan. Anti-Klan delegates, largely from the East and large cities, fought Klan advocates from the South and West. Anti-Klan leader Gov. Alfred Emanuel Smith (N.Y.), whose liberalism and Catholicism were intolerable to the Klan, was pitted against pro-Klan William Gibbs McAdoo (Cal.). On the 103d ballot, John W. Davis was chosen by the Democrats as compromise candidate. Gov. Charles W. Bryan (Tenn.), brother of William Jennings Bryan, ran as vice president.

A new third party, the Progressives, nominated Robert M. La Follette (Wisc.) for president and Sen. Burton K. Wheeler (Mont.). Progressives attempted to merge farmers and laborers in one party to attack monopolies. Republican strategy identified Coolidge with prosperity and stressed economy. It was "Keep Cool and Keep Coolidge!" Republicans had a decisive victory; the Democratic vote was greatly reduced by the Progressives.

1928. Coolidge did "not choose to run for president," and the Republicans selected Secretary of Commerce Herbert Hoover as their candidate; Charles Curtis, Senate Majority Leader, was his running mate. New York Gov. Alfred E. Smith was Democratic choice for president. Sen. J. Taylor Robinson (Ark.) received the vice-presidential nomination. The Socialist candidate was Norman Thomas, former clergyman, pacifist, and editor of *The Nation*. The Workers nominated Foster; Socialist-Labor, Reynolds; Prohibitionists, Varney; and Farmer-Labor, Webb.

Republicans capitalized on the nation's continued prosperity. Prohibition was a major issue: Hoover advocated full enforcement, and Smith wanted modification of the laws. Religious bigotry directed against Smith, a Roman Catholic, played a large part in what became one of the most virulent campaigns. Though Smith, the "Happy Warrior," polled the largest vote ever given a Democratic candidate, he lost the election to Hoover by 357 electoral votes.

1932. Seven months after Hoover took office, the great crash occurred, and despite his optimism the depression deepened. Republicans renominated Hoover and Charles Curtis. Gov. Franklin D. Roosevelt was Democratic presidential nominee; John Nance Garner (Tex.), House Speaker, was his running mate. Norman Thomas and James H. Maurer were Socialist candidates; William Z. Foster and James W. Ford, Communist candidates; Reynolds, Socialist La-

Presidential candidate Alfred E. Smith campaigning for the 1928 election.

bor; Upshaw, Prohibitionists; Harvey, Liberty party; and Coxley, Farmer-Labor.

Republicans had no specific plans for combating the depression and advocated a protective tariff, sound money, a balanced budget, and self-determination by states on prohibition. Democrats promised unemployment and old-age relief, aid for farmers, conservation, development of power resources, regulation of securities exchanges, a balanced budget, sound currency, and repeal of the Eighteenth (Prohibition) Amendment. Roosevelt pledged himself to a "New Deal" to aid the "forgotten man," believing it the duty of government to regulate economic controls if private means failed. To Roosevelt's benefit, major speeches of candidates were heard over radio for the first time. Democrats won 42 states, Republicans, 6, placing Roosevelt in office.

1936. The nation was on the way to economic recovery. Democrats renominated Roosevelt and Garner without opposition. The President drafted the

Democratic platform, incorporating continuation of the New Deal. Republicans promised goals similar to the New Deal's but by "constitutional" means and with a balanced budget. Kansas Gov. Alfred M. Landon and W. Franklin Know, Illinois newspaper publisher, were the Republican candidates. The Union party denounced the New Deal and ran William Lemke (N.D.) and Thomas C. O'Brien (Mass.). They were supported by Father Coughlin's National Union for Social Justice and Dr. Francis E. Townsend, advocate of federal pensions for the aged. Socialists nominated Norman Thomas; Communists, Earl Browder; Socialist Labor, John W. Aiken; and Prohibitionists, David L. Colvin. Republican Sen. Norris ran as an Independent. The Liberty League attracted Republican and Democratic anti-Roosevelts and tacitly endorsed the Republican ticket. Roosevelt had the endorsement of Sen. La Follette and Labor's Nonpartisan League, formed by labor leaders siding with John L. Lewis.

Landon could not compete with growing evidence of economic recuperation, nor with Roosevelt's eloquence and personality. It was a landslide. Roosevelt won all but eight electoral votes.

1940. World War II had begun, and domestic issues were overshadowed by foreign affairs. Roosevelt ran for a precedent-breaking third term. Henry Agard Wallace (Iowa), Secretary of Agriculture, was Roosevelt's choice for vice president. Wendell L. Wilkie, New York lawyer and utilities executive, received the Republican nomination over party favorites Dewey, Vandenberg, and Taft. Wilkie, voting Democratic until 1938, had never held a political post; he was backed by big business and amateurs in a highly organized

campaign. Charles L. McNary (Ore.), Senate Minority Leader and an extreme isolationist, was the Republican vice-presidential candidate. Socialists nominated Norman Thomas; Communists, Browder; Prohibitionists, Babson; and Socialist Labor, Aiken.

Wilkie barnstormed the country in a battle against the concentration of power in one man. Many Democratic conservatives and isolationists turned to Wilkie. Though an internationalist, Wilkie attracted the isolationist vote. Both sides favored British aid, national defense programs, and hemispheric defense. Domestically, Wilkie agreed with New Deal goals but not their implementation. Roosevelt carried 38 states with 449 electoral votes to become the first third-term president.

1944. The war was drawing to a victorious finish. Roosevelt was the Democratic candidate for the fourth time. Sen. Harry S. Truman (Mo.) was his running mate, following a battle for nomination in which Vice President Wallace's radical policies were unacceptable to the conservatives. Republicans nominated New York Gov. Thomas E. Dewey and John W. Bricker, conservative Ohio Governor. Norman Thomas ran for the Socialists; Claude E. Watkins, Prohibitionists; and Edward A. Teichert, Socialist Laborites.

Democrats conducted their campaign primarily by radio because of newspaper hostility. There was little policy difference between the two parties. Dewey assailed the administration of "tired old men" with unpreparedness and mismanagement of the war and charged Roosevelt with Communist support. Rumors of his ill health were spread. Sydney Hillman, chairman of the Political Action Committee of the CIO,

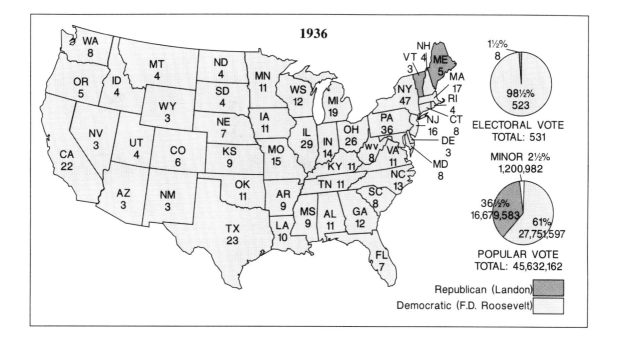

campaigning vigorously for Roosevelt, was the target of an assault in thinly disguised Ku Klux Klan terms, which boomeranged and brought out the labor vote. Because of the war, many voters did not wish to "change horses," and Roosevelt was easily reelected.

1948. The 1946 midterm election gave Republicans control of Congress. Harry S. Truman, succeeding to the presidency on Roosevelt's death in 1945, was Democratic choice for president; Alben W. Barkley (Ky.) was the vice-presidential nominee. In opposition to a strong civil rights plank, the Mississippi delegation and half of Alabama's left the convention and formed the States Rights (Dixiecrat) party with Governors J. Strom Thurmond (S.C.) and Fielding L. Wright (Miss.) as candidates. Before the convention, Henry A. Wallace left the Democrats to be the Progressive party candidate; Sen. Glen H. Taylor (Idaho) was his running mate. Advocating greater domestic reforms and diplomatic negotiations with Russia, the Progressives lost strength when their large Communist following became known. Republicans renominated Thomas E. Dewey for president; Gov. Earl Warren (Cal.) was his running mate. Thomas ran for the Socialists; Watson, Prohibitionist; Teichert, Socialist Labor; and Debs, Social Workers.

Truman stressed the inaction of the "do-nothing" Congress and compared Dewey's liberal campaign promises with the record of the 81st Congress. Barnstorming across the country, he won the Northern minority, labor, and farm votes as he spoke to the common man on specific issues. Truman's Fair Deal advocated social welfare measures, repeal of the Taft-Hartley law, civil rights legislation, and anti-inflation

proposals. Though mass media and public opinion polls were confident of a Republican victory, Truman won the election with a comfortable majority.

1952. Effects of Communist control of China and the start of the Korean War in 1950, plus rising prices and taxes and disclosures of governmental corruption and communism, justified Republican hopes for a presidential victory. Senator Robert A. Taft (Ohio), "Mr. Republican," in a third attempt to gain the Republican nomination, appealed to the conservatives. Liberal Republicans, led by Gov. Dewey, favored Gen. Dwight D. Eisenhower. After a credentials fight, Eisenhower became the presidential nominee; Sen. Richard M. Nixon (Cal.) was his running mate. The Republicans approved extension of Social Security and the Taft-Hartley law, stressed states' rights, and promised an early end to the Korean War.

Truman declined to run. Sen. Estes Kefauver (Tenn.) actively campaigned but lacked organizational approval, and Gov. Adlai E. Stevenson (Ill.), liberal and intellectual, was drafted as the Democratic presidential nominee. Sen. John J. Sparkman (Ala.) was the vice-presidential candidate. Stevenson was hampered by the Democratic administration's record and a hostile press. He upheld the civil rights platform and advocated federal control of offshore lands, losing the Southern conservative and states' rightists to Eisenhower. It was an Eisenhower sweep, but Republicans barely gained control of Congress.

1956. Adlai Stevenson, Democratic presidential nominee, left the choice of vice-presidential candidate to convention delegates. Estes Kefauver became the nominee, but the surprisingly large vote for Sen. John

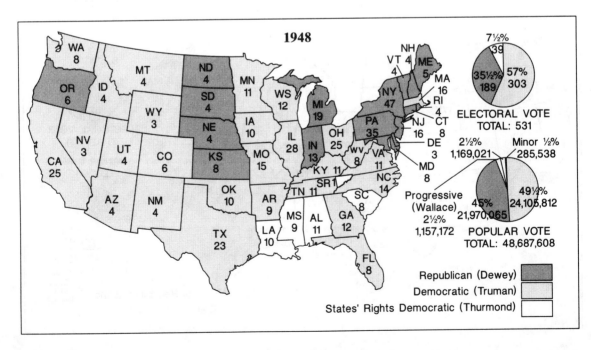

F. Kennedy made him a factor for future presidential plans. Republicans renominated Eisenhower and Nixon. There was little policy difference between the two major parties. School segregation was not stressed. Only Stevenson's proposal for an agreement with Russia for a ban on nuclear-bomb testing stirred any controversy.

Democrats stressed the uncertainty of Eisenhower's health following his recovery from a heart attack. Republicans cried "We like Ike," pointing to the end of the Korean War and a stabilized prosperity. Democrats countered that Stalin's death ended hostilities and that Eisenhower's ability to work with Congressional Democrats caused prosperity. It was a personal victory for Eisenhower: he was reelected by an overwhelming majority, but the country chose a Democratic Congress.

1960. The Twenty-second Amendment (1951) stated no president could accept a third term. Republicans nominated Vice President Richard M. Nixon for president after New York Gov. Nelson A. Rockefeller withdrew from competition; U.N. Ambassador Henry Cabot Lodge (Mass.) was his running mate. Democrats nominated Sen. John F. Kennedy following his skillfully run preconvention campaign. Sen. Lyndon B. Johnson (Tex.) was Kennedy's choice for vice president in a maneuver to gain Southern acceptance of a strong civil rights platform. Both candidates conducted intensive campaigns. Kennedy stressed a decline in the U.S. economy and in foreign prestige and presented the challenge of a "New Frontier" of the 1960s. The campaign climaxed in a series of four nationwide television debates. Kennedy was elected in

one of the closest popular contests in United States history with 34,226,731 votes to Nixon's 34,108,157 to become the first Catholic and the youngest elected President. Sen. Harry F. Byrd (Va.) received 15 electoral votes.

1964. Lyndon B. Johnson, serving as president following Kennedy's assassination, was chosen by acclamation as Democratic presidential nominee. Minnesota Sen. Hubert H. Humphrey was Johnson's choice for vice president to gain support by liberals and labor. Republican conservatives, led by Arizona Sen. Barry M. Goldwater, engaged in a power struggle with moderates before the Republican convention met. Attempts by the moderate-liberal wing, led by Governors Nelson A. Rockefeller (N.Y.) and William W. Scranton (Pa.), to pass a more liberal platform failed. Goldwater was nominated on the first ballot; Rep. William E. Miller (N.Y.) was his running mate.

Goldwater denounced encroachment of the individual's freedom by "big government," voted against civil rights, and urged acceleration of the Vietnam War, even to the use of nuclear weapons. Johnson's Great Society advocated additional government aid to help high school dropouts and worker retraining, support of the civil rights law, and responsibility in international affairs, especially in control of nuclear weapons. It was a Johnson landslide, and he carried every state but Arizona and five Southern states.

1968. Vietnam and violence were the major issues of the 1968 campaign. Rioting caused by racial unrest and U.S. involvement in the Vietnam War was spearheaded by the assassinations of civil rights leader Martin Luther King, Jr., advocate of nonviolence, and

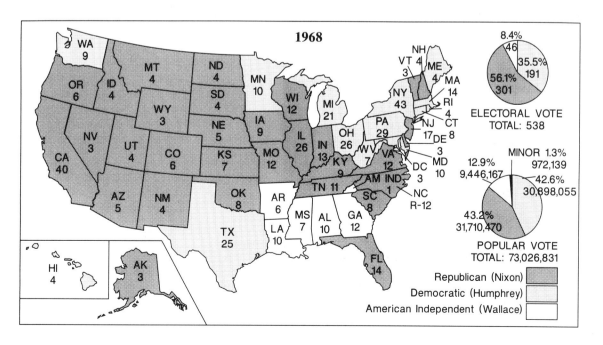

New York State Sen. Robert Kennedy, chief rival for the Democratic presidential candidacy. Former Vice President Nixon was Republican candidate; Gov. Spiro T. Agnew (Md.) was Nixon's choice for vice president. Following Johnson's decision not to run for reelection so that he could intensify his efforts to bring peace to Vietnam, Vice President Humphrey received the Democratic presidential nomination, winning over peace candidate Sen. Eugene McCarthy. Sen. Edmund S. Muskie (Me.) was his running mate.

Former Alabama Gov. George C. Wallace ran for president on the American Independent party ticket with Air Force Gen. Curtis LeMay as his running mate. Wallace's "law and order" campaign had strong racial overtones. Nixon's was a middle-of-the-road campaign. Humphrey tried to rally support of the Kennedy and McCarthy liberals without denying support of the administration's Vietnam policies. Nixon, in an extremely close race, won the presidency with 43.4 percent of the popular vote; Humphrey, 42.7 percent; and Wallace, 13.5 percent from five Deep South states. A Democratic Congress was reelected.

1972. An immediate assessment of the 1972 election was that it demonstrated the benefits of incumbency. Later on, though, the campaign was seen as having been flawed by the blight of the "imperial presidency." It was not necessary to have set in motion the dirty tricks (wiretapping of "enemies," manufactured polls and letters, hiring of hecklers and demonstrators) or the obtaining and laundering of illegal funds, all of which was revealed in the Watergate hearings; Richard Nixon could have coasted to victory just by being "presidential." As in 1944 and 1964 (and later in 1980), this incumbent would follow a "Rose Garden strategy," appearing to tend to his duties, avoiding press criticism, and reaping considerable publicity from meetings with his Russian and Chinese counterparts. (Despite continued involvement in Vietnam, Nixon could claim to be a "peacemaker.")

Meanwhile, the Democrats were choosing their candidate after a marathon primary season. When frontrunner Maine Sen. Edmund Muskie stumbled, anti-war candidate Sen. George McGovern (S.D.), repeating the Goldwater strategy of 1964, took advantage of a divided field of opponents, which was blind to his challenge until too late, and secured the nomination. Not that it was worth very much. Though the selection process, which he had helped structure, was far more democratic than what had existed previously, the alienated leaders of party and labor organizations, seeing his cause as forlorn, knifed the ticket. The GOP attacked its foe as the candidate of "acid, amnesty, and abortion." The hasty selection of running mate Sen. Thomas Eagleton (Mo.) was followed by an equally abrupt dropping of the Missourian when it was disclosed that the latter had a history of mental breakdowns. He was succeeded by Kennedy in-law Sargent

Shriver, who, like Eagleton, was a handsome campaigner and a Catholic.

There were heavy Democratic defections to Nixon from those who felt the moralist McGovern did not represent their views on economic, defense, and social issues. No one paid much attention to McGovern's charge that Nixon ruled "the most corrupt and immoral administration in history."

1976. The election of 1976 was strange, offering the reluctant voters a choice between a truly accidental president and an obscure ex-Governor of Georgia. Gerald Ford was the first beneficiary of the 25th Amendment's enabling the filling of a vice-presidential vacancy. The Michigan Republican House Minority Leader first replaced the disgraced Spiro Agnew and then the disgraced Richard Nixon. His September 1974 pardon of Nixon came back to haunt him in the 1976 election. Nonetheless, the trappings of the White House assisted in considerably narrowing the point spread between himself and his Democratic opponent.

Jimmy Carter, in what has become a familiar scenario, emerged from nowhere in the polls of political recognition and support to capture the nomination after surviving 31 primaries. Carter campaigned as an outsider against the Washington establishment. He projected an image of honesty, religious conviction, and efficiency. Issues were relegated to the sidelines, though he made a considerable number of specific promises. His running mate, Sen. Walter Mondale (Minn.), was a greater asset to the ticket than Ford's choice, Sen. Robert Dole (Kan.).

Ford, who had never been elected by a nationwide vote, was almost denied his party's nomination after a down-to-the-wire battle with former California Governor Ronald Reagan.

The election was extremely close, with Carter winning on the coattails of state and congressional Democrats. He would have failed had it not been for a series of televised debates with Ford, support from the South, and even more important, support from the black electorate. Carter also capitalized on economic discontent in several northern industrial states.

1980. The country prepared to go to the polls in 1980 unhappy with the choices and uncertain about its future. The man it had entrusted with its destiny in 1976, Jimmy Carter, had received the lowest job-performance ratings of any president since such polling began. Though regarded as decent and well-intentioned, he was faulted for political ineptitude and vacillation. He was an uninspiring speaker. What had at first seemed an asset, his being an outsider, came to be viewed as a liability as he had difficulty dealing with Congress and displayed too much loyalty to associates such as Budget Director Bert Lance and relatives such as his brother, Billy.

With Carter appearing to be a flawed candidate, Sen. Edward Kennedy was urged to wrest the nomination from him. The mythology of Kennedy invincibility received a jolt when he proved an unsellable candidate. The Iranian hostage seizure enabled Carter to act presidential in the Rose Garden and justify a failure to defend before Democrats his presidential record and departures from liberalism. In primary after primary, Kennedy dogged Carter. However, it was not until Carter had clinched the nomination that Kennedy began to get his message across. The Democratic convention gave Carter the nomination, but Kennedy its heart and platform.

Meanwhile, Ronald Reagan was overwhelming his Republican rivals in a primary season that now included 35 states, the District of Columbia, and Puerto Rico. Hopeful after hopeful, conservatives like Connolly, Dole, and Crane, moderates like Baker, all dropped from contention. The only liberal, Congressman John Anderson (Ill.), realizing how uncongenial were his prospects in wooing Republican primary voters, announced that he would run as an Independent. Finally, George Bush (Tex.) capitulated. He later was selected by Reagan as his running mate to balance the ticket.

Anderson's standing in the polls dropped after Labor Day, and the election outcome seemed a photo finish between Reagan and Carter—with the former likely to win the Electoral College vote, while the latter gained a popular plurality. Carter would not participate in a debate that included Anderson, not wanting to build up the latter at his expense. He counted on a return to the fold of dissident Democrats and on his

incumbency to capture nonpartisans. To general surprise, Reagan won an overwhelming majority of both the popular and electoral vote.

The party organizations by 1980 had lost their influence. Moving in to partially fill the void were the media (establishing the important battlegrounds, defining the viable candidates, and interpreting the results) and candidate and special-interest organizations (spending money, forming temporary coalitions of voters, and relying on computerized mailing and media experts).

1984. Although Reagan's first administration had produced a record budget deficit and some foreign policy and military disasters, such as Lebanon, the Democrats had slim prospects for defeating a popular president seeking reelection in a time of low inflation and a rebounding economy. They hoped that their old coalition would come together again and that registration of new voters and appeals to women would tip the balance in their favor.

The Democratic candidate with the best organization and most early support from party leaders and interest groups was Carter's vice president, Walter Mondale. Mondale easily triumphed over ex-astronaut Sen. John Glenn in the Iowa caucuses. However, the media built up Sen. Gary Hart as the new liberal candidate of 1984. Hart's stunning victory in New Hampshire and his appeal to young professionals did not, however, overcome his organizational difficulties. Rev. Jesse Jackson, the third candidate in the drawn-out Democratic primary season, shared the same fate

Televised debates, such as those between Ronald Reagan and Walter Mondale in 1984, have become important elements in presidential election campaigns.

as Hart, and Mondale won the nomination, thanks to the efforts of organized labor.

Mondale named Congresswoman Geraldine Ferraro (N.Y.) to be his running mate. For a brief time it appeared that the ticket had a chance at victory. However, the constant scrutiny of Ferraro's husband's business practices proved detrimental to the campaign. The Democrats' last hope of reversing statistics in their favor hinged on two presidential debates. Mondale was regarded as the winner of the first one, but the President held his own in the second debate, and the election outcome was never in doubt.

Ronald Reagan swept every electoral vote but those of Mondale's Minnesota and the District of Columbia. The Democrats won two more Senate seats and held their House losses to 15.

1988. With Reagan ineligible, George Bush had little difficulty securing the Republican nomination. His selection of Sen. Danforth Quayle (In.) as his running mate caused some controversy because of Quayle's youth and lack of national and international experience. Charges were also raised that Quayle had used family influence to secure an appointment to the National Guard rather than risk service in Vietnam.

The Democratic candidate, Michael Dukakis, prevailed over several primary opponents until only the Rev. Jesse Jackson remained, who also held delegates at the convention. Dukakis selected Sen. Lloyd Bentsen (Tx.) as his running mate because the senator's conservative views were seen as balancing those of the more liberal governor.

The Bush forces were particularly successful in portraying Dukakis as "soft on crime." Two debates between the presidential candidates were inconclusive. Dukakis failed to counter a public image of coldness and a lack of emotion. Despite images and rhetoric, eight years of economic growth under Reagan were more than enough to give Bush and Quayle a comfortable margin. They won 54 percent of the vote and 426 electoral votes.

In congressional races, the Democrats retained control of both the House and Senate. They also increased their edge in governorships.

—Martin Gruberg

See also Campaign, Political; Convention, Political; Political Parties in the United States; President of the United States; Primary Election.

PRESIDENTIAL PRIMARY. *See* Primary Election.

PRESIDENTIAL SUCCESSION, the constitutional provision for a successor to the president in the event of his death, incapacitation, or resignation. Article II, Section 1, names the vice president as his first successor and delegates choice of further successors to Congress. In 1947 Congress passed the presidential Succession Act, which specified that the Speaker of the House would be next in line for the presidential

succession, followed by the president pro tempore of the Senate, the secretary of state, and other members of the cabinet. Cabinet members serve only temporarily—until a Speaker or president pro tempore is selected.

The Twenty-fifth Amendment (1967) provides that the president may voluntarily transfer the powers of his office to the vice president by sending the Speaker and the president pro tempore written notification of inability to perform the functions of his office. The amendment also establishes that the president may be removed if he is held incapacitated by the vice president, sundry officials, and Congress. Although eight presidents have died in office, none have ever been declared unable to fulfill the functions of office.

See also Vice President of the United States.

PRESIDENT OF THE SENATE, the presiding officer of the U.S. Senate. The vice president of the United States is designated in Article I, Section 3, of the Constitution as president of the Senate. It is a position of little influence and is largely ceremonial in nature. Since the vice president is not a member of the Senate, he cannot participate in debate and can vote only in case of a tie (known as a "casting vote"). As presiding officer, he exercises only limited parliamentary powers, such as the power to recognize members to speak. The vice president's formal position in the Senate is so restricted that most vice presidents are seldom in attendance, and the president pro tempore or one of the other members designated by him usually presides.

Unlike the Speaker of the House of Representatives, the vice president is not the leader of the majority party and may even be a member of the opposition party. The real power in the Senate belongs to Majority and Minority Floor Leaders.

—Mary L. Carns

PRESIDENT OF THE UNITED STATES. The President of the United States is elected for a four-year term by the people of the 50 states through the Electoral College and is limited to two terms (see Article II, Section 1, and Amendments Twelve and Twenty-two). He is the chief executive officer of the United States and derives his authority, duties, and powers from Article II of the Constitution.

Constitutional Authority is both explicit (such as the appointment power, the command of the armed forces, and the power to grant reprieves and pardons) and ambiguous (such as guarding "that the laws are faithfully executed"). From both explicit and ambiguous sections of Article II, the president draws "resultant" powers; for example, as commander in chief of the armed forces, he can order the deployment of the military anywhere in the world without having Congress officially declare war as long as Congress has authorized enough military forces and money. The

The article on the PRESIDENT OF THE UNITED STATES illustrates the explicit, ambiguous, and resultant powers of the president, and explains the manner in which he exercises his political power in the legislative process and in the formulation of public opinion.

The related articles on the President of the United States may be divided into two groups.

Policies and Position. The President expresses his policies through such vehicles as the STATE OF THE UNION MESSAGE, PRESS CONFERENCE, WHITE HOUSE announcements, and statements on the BUDGET. Many presidential policies are implemented indirectly through the EXECUTIVE BRANCH or WHITE HOUSE OFFICE, or by CABINET members.

The President is protected by the SECRET SERVICE, but PRESIDENTIAL SUCCESSION remains a major political concern. The VICE PRESIDENT OF THE UNITED STATES is first in the line of succession.

Powers. The far-ranging powers of the President are discussed in EMERGENCY POWERS OF THE PRESIDENT, TREATY POWER OF THE PRESIDENT, and WAR POWERS OF THE PRESIDENT. The office's more specific powers include APPOINTMENT, PRESIDENTIAL; EXECUTIVE ORDER; VETO; AMNESTY; and PARDON.

Court decisions have upheld the President's power to remove appointees in certain cases, as in MYERS v. UNITED STATES, and denied it in others, as in HUMPHREY'S EXECUTOR v. UNITED STATES. A presidential intrusion into private industry was overthrown in YOUNGSTOWN SHEET AND TUBE CO. v. SAWYER.

clause that he shall oversee the faithful execution of laws gives the president much leeway in enforcing or not enforcing them as he sees fit. If a bill becomes law, there is nothing Congress can do to require the president to enforce some provision he deems unconstitutional. Nor is there any effective way for Congress to force a president to spend all the money it has appropriated. The president's authority to make treaties, with the approval of two-thirds of the Senate, his authority to make executive agreements with other nations simply as the executive head, and his authority to recognize the legitimacy of other nations make him ultimate spokesman for the United States on foreign policy. The Constitution makes the foreign policy of the president the foreign policy of the nation. Statutory authority is created for the president by Congress acting within the domain of its legislative function and role (see Article I). When Congress creates and funds a new independent agency to carry out some national function, Congress is adding authority to the presidency. When Congress empowers him to freeze wages and prices when he deems it economically necessary (such as in the Economic Stabilization Acts of 1970 and 1971), Congress is again increasing the president's overall authority by act of Congress. Numerous examples could be given to show the expansion of presidential power by legislative action.

Political Power is an extremely important facet of presidential authority. Particularly in this century, presidents have developed a myriad of techniques to persuade and induce the Congress to act as they suggest. By taking the constitutional duty to give Congress information on "the state of the Union" and "recommend to their consideration such measures as he shall judge necessary and expedient" (Article II, Section 3), twentieth-century presidents have as-

(continued on p. 258)

PRESIDENT'S ROLE IN THE LEGISLATIVE PROCESS

1.   George Washington (1732-99)
President (Fed) 1789-97
Commander in chief Continental
Army 1775-81; presided
Const. Convention 1787-89

2.   John Adams (1735-1826)
President (Fed) 1797-1801
Min. to Netherlands 1780-82
1st U.S. Min. to Britain
1785-88; Vice Pres. 1789-97

3.   Thomas Jefferson (1743-1826)
President (Dem-Rep) 1801-09
Gov. of Virginia 1779-81
Secretary of State 1789-93
Vice President 1797-1801

4.   James Madison (1751-1836)
President (Dem-Rep) 1809-17
Called "Father of Constitution"
House of Rep. 1789-97
Secretary of State 1801-09

5.   James Monroe (1758-1831)
President (Dem-Rep) 1817-25
Gov. of Va. 1799-1802, 1811
Secretary of State 1811-16
Secretary of War 1814-15

6.   John Quincy Adams (1767-
1848); Pres. (Dem-Rep) 1825-29
Senate 1803-08
Minister to Russia 1809-14
Secretary of State 1817-25

7.   Andrew Jackson (1767-1845)
President (Dem) 1829-37
House of Rep. 1796-97
Senate 1797-98, 1823-25
Tenn. Supreme Ct. 1798-1804

8.   Martin Van Buren (1782-
1862); Pres. (Dem) 1837-41
Governor of New York 1829
Secretary of State 1829-31
Vice President 1833-37

9.   William Henry Harrison
(1773-1841); Pres. (Whig)
1841; Gov. of Indiana Terr.
1800-12; House of Rep. 1816-
19; Senate, elected 1825

10.   John Tyler (1790-1862)
President (Whig) 1841-45
Gov. of Virginia 1825-27
Senate 1827-29, 1830-36
Vice President 1841

11.   James Knox Polk (1795-
1849); Pres. (Dem) 1845-49
Tenn. House of Rep. 1823-25
U.S. House of Rep. 1825-39
Gov. of Tennessee 1839-41

12.   Zachary Taylor (1784-1850)
President (Whig) 1849-50
Served 40 years in the Army
where he gained the name of
"Old Rough and Ready"

13.   Millard Fillmore (1800-74)
President (Whig) 1850-53
N.Y. State assembly 1829-31
House of Rep. 1833-35, 37-43
Vice President 1849-50

14.   Franklin Pierce (1804-69)
President (Dem) 1853-57
N.H. House of Rep. 1829-33
House of Rep. 1833-37
Senate 1837-42

15.   James Buchanan (1791-
1868); Pres. (Dem) 1857-61
Senate 1834-45
Secretary of State 1845-49
Min. to Gr. Britain 1853-56

16.   Abraham Lincoln (1809-65)
President (Rep) 1861-65
Kentucky legislature 1835-43
House of Rep. 1847-49
Emancipation Proc. 1863

17.   Andrew Johnson (1808-75)
President (Rep) 1865-69
Gov. of Tennessee 1853-57
Senate 1857-62
Vice President 1865

18.   Ulysses Simpson Grant
(1822-85); Pres. (Rep) 1869-77
Commander in chief of all
Union forces in the Civil
War 1864-65

19.   Rutherford Birchard Hayes
(1822-93); Pres. (Rep) 1877-
81; maj. general, Civil War
House of Rep. 1865-67
Gov. of Ohio 1867-77

20.   James Abram Garfield
(1831-81); Pres. (Rep) 1881
maj. general in Civil War
House of Rep. 1863-80
Elected to Senate 1880

21. Chester Alan Arthur (1830-86); Pres. (Rep) 1881-85; quartermaster of N.Y. State in Civil War Vice President 1881

22 & 24. Grover Cleveland (1837-1908); Pres. (Dem) 1885-89, 1893-97; elected mayor of New York 1881; elected gov. of New York State 1882

23. Benjamin Harrison (1833-1901); Pres. (Rep) 1889-93 brig. gen. in Civil War candidate for gov. of Ind. 1876; Senate 1881-87

25. William McKinley (1843-1901); Pres. (Rep) 1897-1901 major in the Civil War House of Rep. 1877-83, 85-91 Gov. of Ohio 1892-96

26. Theodore Roosevelt (1858-1919); Pres. (Rep) 1901-09 N.Y. state leg. 1882-84 Asst. Sec. of Navy 1897-98 Vice President 1901

27. William Howard Taft (1857-1930); Pres. (Rep) 1909-13; 1st civil Gov. of Philippines; Chief Justice U.S. Supreme Court 1921-30

28. (Thomas) Woodrow Wilson (1856-1924); Pres. (Dem) 1913-21; Ohio senate 1899-1903 Gov. of New Jersey 1911-13 Nobel Peace Prize 1919

29. Warren Gamaliel Harding (1865-1923); Pres. (Rep) 1921-23; Ohio senate 1899-1903 Lt. Gov. of Ohio 1904-06 Senate 1915-20

30. (John) Calvin Coolidge (1872-1933); Pres. (Rep) 1923-29; Ohio lt. gov. 1915-18 Ohio gov. 1918-21 Vice President 1921-23

31. Herbert Clark Hoover (1874-1964); Pres. (Rep) 1929-33; Sec. of Commerce 1921-29 Hoover Commission on Executive reorganization 1947-49, 1953-55

32. Franklin Delano Roosevelt (1882-1945); Pres. (Dem) 1933-45 N.Y. State Senate 1911-13 Asst. Sec. of Navy 1913-20 Gov. of New York 1929-33

33. Harry S. Truman (1884-1972) President (Dem) 1945-53 Jackson Co., Mo., judge 1926-34 Senate 1935-45 Vice President 1945

34. Dwight David Eisenhower (1890-1969); Pres. (Rep) 1953-61; Comm. Europe invasion, Army chief of staff 1944-48; SCAPE 1950-52

35. John Fitzgerald Kennedy (1917-63); Pres. (Dem) 1961-63 House of Rep. 1947-53 Senate 1953-61 Pulitzer Prize 1957

36. Lyndon Baines Johnson (1908-1973): Pres. (Dem.) 1963-69 Senate 1949-61 Senate Dem. leader 1953-61 Vice President 1961-63

37. Richard Milhous Nixon (1913-   ); Pres. (Rep) 1969-74 House of Rep. 1947-51 Senate 1951-53 Vice President 1953-61

38. Gerald Rudolph Ford (1913-   ); Pres. (Rep) 1974-77 House of Rep. 1948-74 Vice President 1973-74

39. James Earl Carter (1924-   ); Pres. (Dem) 1977-81 Georgia Governor 1971-75

40. Ronald Wilson Reagan (1911-   ) Pres. (Rep) 1981-89; California Governor 1966-75

41. George Bush (1924-   ); Pres. (Rep) 1989-   ; House of Rep. 1966-70; Amb. to UN 1971-73; Dir. of CIA 1976-77; Vice President 1981-89

sumed an all-important political position of establishing the president's legislative program at the beginning of each session of Congress. Thus the president has indeed become the chief legislator as he sets legislative priorites, through his State of the Union address, budget and economic messages, and follow-up measures introduced in Congress for him by his own party's congressional leaders. Political power can also be enhanced through his power of appointment. Furthermore, as modern legislation has become more and more tied to financial considerations and needs, the presidential Office of Management and Budget has become the chief executive's focal point for gathering even more political authority unto himself. The president's skill with the press, his television performances, and his personal rapport with other political leaders and the people also contribute to his political power.

The president is, then, the chief administrator of a large establishment, the head in essence of his political party, and formulator of public opinion. His is the most public of the three branches of government, with his daily routine, schedule, and policies the subject of much scrutiny by the press, radio-TV, the Congress, and the public. The vigor of a one-man office with its singleness of purpose, the fixed presidential term that keeps him in office for at least four years without danger of being replaced suddenly because of a controversial decision, and his having the only national constituency of the three branches of government establish for the president the indispensable platform from which to educate, persuade, and lead the nation.

—*Erwin L. Levine*

See also Appointment, Presidential; Economic Message, President's; Emergency Powers of the President; Executive Agreement; Executive Branch; Presidential Succession; Recognition; State of the Union Message; Treaty Power; War Powers.

PRESIDENT PRO TEMPORE presides over the Senate when the vice president is absent or assumes the presidency. The Senate is required by Article I, Section 3, of the Constitution to choose a second presiding officer. By tradition, the senior senator of the majority party is usually selected.

PRESIDENT'S COMMISSION ON CAMPUS UNREST. *See* Campus Unrest, President's Commission on.

PRESS, FREEDOM OF. *See* Freedom of Speech and Press.

PRESS CONFERENCE, PRESIDENT'S, the practice of the president of summoning the national press to discuss important matters. The president can use this opportunity to present his views on national issues or to make a statement on an important policy decision. Frequently televised, press conferences provide

the president with an extraordinary opportunity to reach a nationwide audience at almost a moment's notice. President John F. Kennedy made frequent use of the press conference, largely because of his skilled performances. It became a most effective means of publicizing his policies and intentions.

The format of the press conference is usually question-answer, with the president selecting individual newsmen for questions. The chief advantage of the press conference is that no other official or party spokesman can so readily command prime television time and the attention of so many millions. Thus, the press conference is one of the instruments that a president can use to command headlines, influence opinion, and dominate the news.

PRESSURE GROUPS. *See* Lobby.

PREVENTIVE PRE-TRIAL DETENTION, a procedure that would allow an individual to be held in police custody without benefit of bail. The practice of granting bail originated in thirteenth-century English common law and is guaranteed by the Eighth Amendment. Historically, the only condition for denying bail in other than capital cases has been that the accused might flee in order to avoid trial. Preventive detention would allow the courts to detain individuals without possibility of bail on another condition: that the accused might, if set free, commit serious crimes while awaiting trial.

In 1970 the United States Department of Justice enacted a preventive-detention statute for the District of Columbia, an area experiencing an increasingly high crime rate. The law claims to offer two basic safeguards: the accused is to have legal representation at a compulsory hearing, and the police must prove the potentially dangerous leanings or inclinations of the accused.

Critics of preventive detention claim that it would destroy the basic American legal tradition that an accused person must be presumed innocent until proven otherwise, imprisonment without trial presuming guilt. Furthermore, critics denounce the implication that the courts or police are capable of accurately predicting the future behavior of an individual. Civil libertarians hold that the judges' discretionary power to set or deny bail in capital cases is, in effect, a form of preventive detention.

PREVIOUS QUESTION, in congressional practice, a procedural motion to put the main issue under deliberation to an immediate vote without further debate or proposal of amendments. In the House a motion for a previous question is considered "House cloture" and operates under more complex rules than does the Senate's procedure. In both houses the practice recognizes the necessity for curbing debate.

PRICE SUPPORTS, complex economic system used by governments to keep market prices from falling below a certain level. This system is applied to agriculture in the United States. Because of weather conditions and crop diseases, farmers have little control over widely fluctuating prices and production. Because of these conditions, the United States government decided to guarantee farmers a uniform standard of living. The government chose a base period, when farmers had good purchasing power for their commodities, on which to maintain their support. The first of these base periods was 1909-1914. The price support program has been accomplished by limiting crop production to cut supplies and raise prices, by purchase-loan storage programs that guarantee to keep prices at a set level, and by a purchase and resale plan.

PRIMARY ELECTION, or direct primary, a preliminary election by registered voters to nominate a candidate for office. The primary was instituted to democratize the candidate selection procedures of party conventions, often characterized by cloakroom deals among a few of the party power wielders. Primaries, which are regulated by the states, have been in existence since 1842 on the local level. The first statewide primary was established in 1903 in Wisconsin after an intensive campaign for it by reform governor Robert La Follette. Some type of primary is now either the law or at least an option in every state in the country. In states that generally utilize the convention system, candidates who receive at least 20 percent of the convention vote may challenge the convention nominee in a postconvention primary.

Major Kinds. The most widely used primary is the closed primary, under which voters may participate only in the primaries of the parties with which they are registered. A few states maintain the open primary, where a voter may cast a ballot in the primary of either party without having to declare his registration, but once the voter chooses which party primary he will vote in, he must vote only for the candidates of that party. The state of Washington, however, uses the so-called blanket ballot. Under the blanket system, all candidate names are printed on the same ballot, regardless of party affiliation. The candidates are categorized only by the office to which they aspire. The voter may cast a ballot for the Democratic nominee for governor, for example, and the Republican nominee for lieutenant governor.

In general, candidates for party nominations must obtain a specified number of signatures to be entered on the ballot. In some states the candidates are required to pay a filing fee. Normally, the winner in a primary election need only obtain a plurality of the votes cast. In many Southern states, where Democratic nomination is tantamount to election, a runoff primary is held to determine the majority choice.

Cross-filing of candidates has been the practice in several states from time to time. From 1914 to 1958 in California, candidates were permitted to enter both the Republican and the Democratic primaries in an attempt to sew up an election. As attempts to democratize the election system have become more frequent, the practice of cross-filing has fallen into disuse.

In 1976 the Democrats adopted rules for the selection of future convention delegates stipulating that only declared Democrats could cast votes. States such as Wisconsin fought to retain the open primary, and their foot-dragging succeeded in 1980; however, for 1984, Wisconsin was required to comply with the new ruling. The effort to get the legislature to close the primary was unsuccessful; a "beauty contest" primary was retained, but the selection of delegates was achieved by a progression of party-member caucuses.

Variations. Some variations of the direct primary include the preprimary convention and the nonpartisan primary. Preprimary conventions are authorized in some states to screen prospective candidates for possible party endorsement in the primary. Candidates in nonpartisan primaries are entered on the ballot without party designation for a nonpartisan office on the state or local level. In some nonpartisan systems the candidate who wins the primary is declared elected. If there is no clear majority, the two candidates with the greatest votes engage in a runoff election.

See also National Primary.

PRINTING AND ENGRAVING, BUREAU OF. *See* Treasury, United States Department of.

PRIOR RESTRAINT, a type of censorship in the form of a restraining order that keeps information from being disseminated or published for various reasons. The courts have struck down restrictions on the publication of newspapers or magazines simply because their previous issues were held to be obscene or seditious. The Supreme Court has also overturned gag rules by judges intended to prohibit publication of information about particularly vicious crimes, materials whose content may make it difficult to select an unbiased jury. The Pentagon Papers case (1971) and a *Progressive* magazine H-bomb article case also involved efforts by the federal government to use national security as the basis for prior censorship. In each case the rationale was rejected and, usually, thought to be in violation of the First Amendment's guarantee of freedom of speech and of the press.

PRIVATE BILL, proposed legislation designed for the benefit of individuals or specific groups, such as private immigration bills. Most private bills are of such a limited nature that they are passed in Congress with little or no opposition. Because members do not have enough time to study all private bills, most will be passed without debate. (Private bills in state laws are prohibited under many state constitutions.)

In the House of Representatives, private bills must be placed on the Private Calendar for at least seven days. The Speaker calls private bills on the first Tuesday of each month and may also call them on the third Tuesday. If two or more members object to the bill, it is referred back to the committee that considered it.

In the Senate, all legislation is placed on the Calendar of General Orders. Noncontroversial measures, including private bills, are called up by unanimous consent. The Senate does not designate specific days for private bills, as occurs in the House.

—*Mary L. Carns*

See also Public Bill.

PRIVILEGES AND IMMUNITIES, obligations of individual state governments to their citizens, as set forth in Article IV and Amendment XIV of the Constitution. Article IV reads: "The citizens of each State shall be entitled to all privileges and immunities of citizens in several States." Amendment XIV reads: "No State shall make or enforce any law which shall abridge the privileges or immunities of the citizens of the United States."

Although neither provision defines a privilege or immunity, the courts distinguish them from rights, suggesting that privileges and immunities are fundamental. Examples are access to courts, making contracts, holding property, and tax equality. States may, however, make distinctions between their own citizens and other states': for example, residency may be prerequisite to voting.

PROBABLE CAUSE, term used in the Fourth Amendment of the Constitution that validates a warrantless search of private property when sufficient evidence shows that a crime has been or is being committed. It must be proven in court that there was "probable cause." Many court decisions focus on speculation about what an investigating officer knew, when and how the officer knew it, and whether the resulting course of action was reasonable.

PROBATE COURT *or* SURROGATE'S COURT, a state court having jurisdiction over probate (proving) of wills and administration of the estates of those who die intestate (without leaving a will), and supervision of financial matters relating to an estate. In some states probate courts have jurisdiction over the estates of minors and are thus called orphans' courts.

PRO BONO. *See* Public-Interest Law.

PRO-CHOICE MOVEMENT, the term used by those who believe women are entitled to make the decision of whether or not to terminate a pregnancy. Since a new conservative majority on the Supreme Court has issued a ruling modifying the landmark abortion rights decision in *Roe v. Wade* (1973), the pro-choice movement has concentrated on lobbying and national demonstrations. They hope to persuade the courts and state legislatures not to restrict access to abortion any further.

See also Right to Life, Roe v. Wade, Webster v. Reproductive Health Services.

PROCEDURAL RIGHTS, guarantees granted to every citizen by the Bill of Rights. Procedural rights are concerned with the methods by which citizens are protected against arbitrary actions by public officials. No one may be deprived of his life, liberty, property, or other rights granted him except according to carefully stated procedures. No person may be tried or condemned without due process of law, and convictions may be rendered void if procedural errors occur.

PROGRESSIVE *or* BULL MOOSE PARTY, a movement formed by Theodore Roosevelt when he lost the Republican presidential nomination to William Howard Taft in 1912. Roosevelt had described himself as feeling "fit as a bull moose" before the Republican convention, and this expression provided the popular name for his supporters. The Progressives nominated Roosevelt for president and drafted a platform advocating direct election of senators, tariff reduction, adoption of the initiative and referendum in formulating legislation, and female suffrage. Although Woodrow Wilson was victorious, Roosevelt received four million popular votes, making a better showing than Taft. Although the Progressives again nominated Roosevelt in 1916, he declined and left the party to support the Republican candidate, Charles Evans Hughes.

See also Political Parties in the United States; Presidential Elections.

PROGRESSIVE PARTY, a name common to several reform movements active during the first half of the twentieth century. In 1911 the National Progressive Republican League was formed by Republicans, who regarded President Taft's administration as overly conservative. Senator Robert M. La Follette of Wisconsin was their initial presidential choice, but they switched their support to Theodore Roosevelt in 1912 and 1916.

The party dissolved when Roosevelt broke his Progressive ties in 1916. Encouraged by the success of independent reform candidates in the 1922 congressional elections, the Progressives reassembled in Cleveland in 1924 and once again chose La Follette as their presidential candidate. Their program called for government ownership of railroads and natural resources, restriction of monopolies, prohibition of child labor, agrarian relief measures, and the right of labor to engage in collective bargaining.

In 1948 a new group opposing the Democrats adopted the name Progressive and nominated Henry A. Wallace to run against President Harry S. Truman. Wallace failed to receive any electoral votes, and his poor showing, coupled with alleged Communist infiltration, contributed to the party's failure.

See also Political Parties in the United States; Presidential Elections.

PROHIBITION generally denotes the ban of alcoholic beverages containing 0.5 percent of alcohol or more. In a broader sense, the term applies to the prohibition by law of the manufacture and use of certain foods, clothes, and other articles considered injurious to the population.

An example of a complete prohibition of the manufacture, transportation, and sale of liquor containing more than 0.5 percent alcohol was the Eighteenth Amendment, which was in force 1920-1933. It was preceded by restrictions on the local level since colonial times and the spreading of organized temperance movements, particularly in the rural areas, in the nineteenth century.

The amendment was repealed by the Twenty-First Amendment after the election of President Franklin Roosevelt, but prohibition continued on a state and local level.

Other countries that have enforced prohibition are Finland, Canada (during World War I), Russia (from World War I to 1925), Norway, Iceland, India, Sweden, and Denmark. The sale of deleterious liquor is forbidden in France, Netherlands, Belgium, Switzerland, and Italy.

PROHIBITION PARTY, the group considered largely responsible for the passage in 1919 of the Eighteenth (Prohibition) Amendment, which prohibited the manufacture, sale, or transportation of alcoholic beverages. Organized in Chicago in 1869, the Prohibition party was the national successor to a series of local temperance societies. It ran its first presidential candidate in 1872 and has entered a candidate in every national election since then, although it has never won an electoral vote.

See also Political Parties in the United States; Presidential Elections.

PROPORTIONAL REPRESENTATION (PR), an electoral system used more frequently in the European democracies than in the United States; only a small number of American cities have used the system. Proportional representation allows each political party representation in rough proportion to its percentage of the vote. This procedure permits minority parties to obtain some representation and often leads to a multiplicity of parties and groups in the legislature. In PR systems there is often a cutoff point below which a party receives no representation.

Most United States communities have single-member constituencies. In such constituencies each party runs a single candidate, and only the winner is sent to the legislature. Single-member constituencies reduce the minority voice in the legislature because one of the two major parties is generally successful in electing its candidate. Political fragmentation is thereby avoided.

PROPOSITION 13, a successful popular referendum in June of 1978, led by Howard Jarvis, which amended the California constitution so as to drastically limit the ability of localities to raise revenue through the property tax. Its success made it a symbol of, and model for, efforts nationwide to limit government spending. Opponents of it feared that severe curtailment of social welfare and educational programs, including massive teacher lay-offs, would result. In education, it appears to have increased state control (and hence diminished local control); helped to equalize spending among the state's districts; and made funding somewhat more susceptible to fluctuations in the economy.

PRO TEMPORE. *See* President Pro Tempore of the Senate.

PROTOCOL represents generaly accepted practices that have developed among nations in the course of consultations with one another. It is the recognized system of international courtesy.

The code that has developed prescribes deference to rank and strict adherence to correct procedure. Protocol is applied to official ceremonies and to immunities, privileges, and courtesies.

The word is used in connection with treaties and international agreements. A protocol is less formal than a treaty and is used to amend or qualify a treaty.

PUBLIC BILL, proposed legislation of general applicability. Unlike private bills, public bills are designed to apply to the general public rather than to specific individuals. Bills in Congress are designated with the initials "H.R." (House of Representatives) or "S." (Senate) to indicate the house of origin, and they are consecutively numbered during a two-year Congress. Public bills become public laws if passed by both houses of Congress and signed by the president.

— *Mary L. Carns*

PUBLIC DEBT. *See* Debt, National.

PUBLIC DEFENDER, an attorney appointed by a court to represent a person in a criminal proceeding who does not have the resources to provide his own attorney. The appointment of public defenders is now required in most criminal cases (unless the defendant has his own counsel) as a result of the Supreme Court's decision in *Gideon v. Wainwright* and the cases that followed it. Public defenders are not available for defense against civil suits.

See also Legal Aid.

PUBLIC FINANCE, the study of how governments obtain and spend money.

PUBLIC HEALTH SERVICE, originated in 1798 when it was responsible for authorizing hospitals for the care of American merchant seamen. Today its mission is to promote the protection and the advancement of the nation's physical health. The service is part of the Department of Health and Human Services. The service attempts to coordinate a national health policy with the states. The operating agencies of the service are the Food and Drug Administration; the Alcohol, Drug Abuse, and Mental Health Administration; the Center for Disease Control; the Health Resources and Services Administration; and the National Institutes of Health. The Public Health Service is also responsible for St. Elizabeth's Hospital and provides health services for American Indians.

PUBLIC HOUSING, federally subsidized low-rent dwelling units, traditionally owned and operated by local housing authorities. Earlier government activity in housing construction was made permanent in the 1937 Housing Act (Wagner-Steagall Act), a Depression measure to stimulate the economy and eliminate unsafe and unsanitary housing conditions. Under this act assistance for low-income units was usually contingent upon the elimination of a substantially equal number of slum dwellings. Subsequent housing acts of 1949 and 1954 stressed comprehensive programs of slum clearance and urban renewal, with public housing a component thereof.

The standard public housing formula calls for an authorized local government agency (housing authority) to finance projects by selling long-term low-interest bonds. Annual federal (or state) contributions cover the difference between the annual cost of housing obligations (bonds at maturity) and the net receipts of the project (rents tenants can afford minus maintenance). Municipalities provide tax exemptions, taking instead 10 percent of shelter rent.

The Housing and Urban Development Act of 1965 expanded this basic formula, allowing rent supplements in privately owned buildings and acquisition and rehabilitation of existing structures. These methods are favored alternatives to large-scale institutional projects, which often suffer from crime and vandalism. Low-density garden apartments are also advocated, although the greater land coverage (and greater real estate tax exemption) precludes this approach in many cities.

In 1977 the Supreme Court ruled that suburbs could restrict low-income housing if the reason for restriction was not discrimination. Thus, large areas of land that could have been used for low-income housing were lost because of strict zoning laws.

See also Open Housing.

PUBLIC-INTEREST LAW, not a branch of law, but a term that has come to be applied recently to legal and quasilegal (such as administrative) activities undertaken to protect an interest that concerns the community at large, but not any individual member thereof to a sufficient degree that he is willing or able to undertake legal action at his own expense. Another definition is the practice of law to achieve social change. Prime areas of public-interest law have been environmental and consumer protection, although a broader definition would include more traditional areas, such as legal aid. Ralph Nader has been one of the prime practitioners and is, perhaps, the founder of this type of legal practice.

PUBLIC OPINION POLLS. In the nineteenth century American newspapers and magazines often enlivened their coverage of politics by conducting straw polls or mail surveys of their readers. The *Literary Digest* developed the idea further by mailing large numbers of questionnaires to persons selected from telephone directories and from 1916 to 1936 had an impressive record of election forecasting. But in 1936 the *Digest* predicted, on the basis of two million tabulated returns, that Alfred M. Landon would capture the Presidency from Franklin D. Roosevelt. In fact, Landon carried only two states.

In that same year three newcomers to political polling accurately predicted the Democratic landslide. They were George Gallup, Elmo Roper, and Archibald Crossley, all of whom had helped develop modern polling methods in advertising and market research. They achieved their results by means of personal interviews with small but carefully selected samples of voters and dramatically demonstrated that a few thousand interviews, properly representative of the total electorate, were far more effective than millions of ballots collected in a biased or haphazard fashion.

World War II gave further impetus to polling, as government officials sought to keep informed of public satisfaction with the war effort and attitudes toward wartime restrictions. Methods of survey research spread quickly abroad, and by 1950 polling activities were common in Western Europe, Japan, Israel, and elsewhere. In the United States polling methods received increasing academic attention, and survey research centers were established on many university campuses.

Today polls are widely used by government, business, university scholars, political candidates, and voluntary groups of all kinds to provide reasonably accurate data on public attitudes, beliefs, expectations, and behavior. From census maps and data, probability samples are drawn of counties, localities, blocks, and households. Interviewers trained on the questionnaire are then sent to specific addresses to conduct personal interviews. Responses are coded, keypunched, and processed by computer.

Though polls are most highly publicized during election campaigns, they cannot predict public opinion or behavior but only describe it as of the time of the interview. In the 1948 election, for example, a late surge of support for President Truman overcame his opponent's lead, and the polls, not prepared to catch this change, were "wrong." Polls are easily biased and should be interpreted cautiously. They are most trustworthy when several different polls or question wordings produce the same result and when meaningful trends can be shown in repeated polls over time.

—Paul B. Sheatsley

PUBLIC PRINTER OF THE UNITED STATES. *See* Government Printing Office (GPO).

PUBLIC UTILITY, business or service that regularly supplies the public with goods or services vital to the entire community. Public utility areas include electricity, gas, telegraph and telephone services, water, and bridges. Public utilities enjoy such special legal privileges as the right of eminent domain for the purpose of building railroads or setting poles and the right to use highways in special ways. Public utilities involve exclusive franchises, natural monopolies, such as water, or virtual monopolies, caused by the excessive costs of starting and maintaining services and businesses (for example, railroads).

Because the interest of the entire community is concerned, public utilities are subject to obligations and regulations. A public utility must serve all who apply; give service without discrimination; furnish adequate service and facilities; and obey certain rules of liability for loss or injury. Regulations are commonly set and governed by special public utility commissions, which are usually appointed by state governors. Public utilities are, however, entitled to certain rights because of these obligations: the right to reasonable compensation for the service rendered and the right to make certain rules and regulations regarding the conduct of business.

PUBLIC WORKS ADMINISTRATION (PWA). *See* New Deal Legislation: *Glossary.*

PULLMAN STRIKE. *See* Labor Movement in the United States.

PURE FOOD AND DRUG ACT. *See* Business Regulation in the United States.

QUAYLE, JAMES DAN(FORTH) (1947-   ), Vice President of the United States (1989-   ). Born in Indianapolis, Indiana, to a prominent family of local newspaper publishers, he received a law degree from Indiana University in 1974. Quayle held several positions in state government and with a family-owned newspaper before winning election to the U.S. House of Representatives in 1976. Quayle served two terms, sought a Senate seat, and was elected in the Reagan landslide of 1980. Quayle was easily reelected in 1986. During his years in Congress, Quayle was considered a staunch supporter of Reagan's conservative programs. Quayle's selection for the Republican presidential ticket was controversial because of his youth and relative lack of national experience.

QUORUM, the number of officers or members of a deliberative or legislative body whose presence is required for the legal transaction of business. Under the Constitution a majority of the elected members of each house of Congress constitutes a quorum. In congressional practice much legislative business is carried on without the presence of a quorum, however, as long as a quorum count has not been demanded. A quorum count may be demanded by members present, usually in regard to a controversial question or bill. It is frequently used as a delaying tactic to preserve time for informal negotiations or for members to be "rounded up."

See also Committee of the Whole.

QUOTA SYSTEM. *See* Immigration.

RADICAL, in politics, one who espouses or exemplifies ideas fundamentally at variance with a given social, political, or economic order. The term is often used in political campaigns to attack an opponent.

RADICAL REPUBLICANS, a wing of the Republican party that regarded the Civil War as necessary to the abolition of slavery. They were highly critical of Lincoln for his handling of the war and clashed with conservative Republicans, who believed that the war was being fought primarily to restore the Union. Following Lincoln's assassination, the Radicals became furious at what they termed President Johnson's "soft peace" approach to Reconstruction and initiated impeachment proceedings against him.

See also Political Parties in the United States; Presidential Elections.

RADOVITCH v. NATIONAL FOOTBALL LEAGUE (NFL), 352 U.S. 445 (1957), tests the application of the antitrust laws (Sherman and Clayton Acts) to the business of professional football. Radovitch, an all-pro guard formerly with the Detroit Lions, contended that the NFL had entered into a conspiracy to monopolize and to control organized professional football in the United States. The Court, in a 6-to-3 decision, held that the volume of interstate business involved in organized professional football places it within the provisions of the antitrust laws. The Court said that the examption from the antitrust laws previously given to organized baseball was based on legislative history applicable to baseball alone. The dissenters could not find sufficient difference between organized baseball and football to indicate that Congress intended to exclude one but not the other. In 1951 bills were introduced into Congress to exampt all organized profesisonal sports from the antitrust laws, but none were enacted.

RAILROAD RETIREMENT ACT (1934) set up pensions for railroad workers, and was the first of the New Deal's social security measures and a forerunner of the Social Security Act (1935). In 1935 the Supreme Court, in *Railroad Retirement Board v. Alton Railroad,* found the Retirement Act unconstitutional. Railroad employees received a retirement and unemployment insurance system under a 1937 act.

RANDOLPH, A(SA) PHILIP (1889-1979), American black labor and civil rights leader. Born in Crescent City, Fla., he attended college in New York City while working at a variety of menial jobs. In 1917 he helped launch *The Messenger,* a radical journal that urged blacks to join labor unions and concerned itself with the plight of poor urban blacks.

He translated his theories into practical action in 1925, when he organized and became president of the Brotherhood of Sleeping Car Porters. Acceptance of the union came slowly, and it was not until after the Railway Labor Act (1934) that he could win a union contract. During the 1930s he was president of the National Negro Congress, but he resigned in 1940. To protest armed-forces segregation and the reluctance of industry to hire blacks for defense jobs, he organized a march on Washington in 1941, the threat of which led to President Roosevelt's support of fair employment practices.

Randolph continued his efforts to end segregation after the war. His 1947 campaign to end Jim Crow policies in the armed services prompted president Truman's assurance (1948) that they would be ended. Randolph was elected a vice president of the AFL-CIO in 1957. In 1963 he organized a march on Washington for jobs and freedom.

RANDOLPH PLAN. *See* Virginia Plan.

RATHBUN v. UNITED STATES. *See* Humphrey's Executor v. United States.

RAYBURN, SAM(UEL) (TALIAFERRO) (1882-1961), American Democratic congressman, known for his understanding of the mood of the House of Representatives. He was born near Kingston, Tenn., and moved to north Texas when he was five. After working his way through college, he was elected to the Texas House of Representatives and then went to law school. He was chosen Speaker of the Texas House in 1911 and successfully ran for the United States House in 1912. he served without interruption until his death.

During his first term he was named to the Interstate and Foreign Commerce Committee and from 1931 to 1937 was its chairman, responsible for shepherding through the House many of President Roosevelt's New Deal regulatory measures. In 1937 he was made House majority leader and in 1940 became Speaker. he served as Speaker until his death, except in 1947-1949 and 1953-1955, when he was minority leader.

A master of procedure, Rayburn exerted his power decisively in 1941, when he first pressed for passage of an extension of the Selective Service Act and then gaveled down opponents calling for its reconsideration. Although generally a supporter of Democratic presidents, he opposed federal price regulation of the natural gas industry and most civil rights bills. He died in Bonham, Tex. Sam Rayburn's tenure in the House was long and distinguished. He served the longest term in history as Speaker of the House. He spoke rarely, but he wielded enormous power behind the scenes, utilizing his comprehensive knowledge of politics and of the members of the House.

REACTIONARY, a person who favors a return to a political, economic, or social order of a previous era. He is opposed to recent changes. The term is also applied to political, economic, or social points of view that seek a return to earlier practices.

READINGS, in the U.S. Congress, the three readings of a bill required by traditional parliamentary procedure. The first reading occurs when a bill is introduced and printed by title in the *Congressional Record*. The second reading in the House is when floor consideration begins, and in the Senate on the legislative day after a measure was introduced. The third reading occurs after completion of floor action on amendments, but before the final votes. The first and third readings are usually by title only; the second reading may be a full reading of the bill in its entirety. State legislatures usually follow similar procedures.

The three customary readings were designed to assure careful consideration of legislation, but it is often of little significance today, and readings may even be dispensed with through the process of unanimous consent.   *—Mary L. Carns*

REAGAN, RONALD WILSON (1911-   ), 40th President of the United States (1981-1989). He was born Feb. 6, 1911, in Tampico, Ill. and graduated from Eureka College (Ill.) in 1932. He bacame famous as a

Ronald Reagan, 40th President of the United States, supported a military buildup.

motion picture and television actor (1937-1966), and served as president of the Screen Actors Guild (1947-1952, 1959).

Reagan was elected governor of California on the Republican ticket in 1966 and, although he was considered a conservative, his administration was more moderate than anticipated. He served until 1975 and in 1976 unsuccessfully challenged Gerald Ford for the Republican presidential nomination.

In 1980, however, he won the party's nomination. Reagan won an easy victory over the incumbent Jimmy Carter by garnering votes from traditional Democratic supporters such as Jews, Catholics, and blue-collar workers who were dissatified with the Carter administration.

As president he led a bipartisan coalition in Congress that produced large budget and tax cuts, while simultaneously promoting an enormous military buildup that enlarged the federal deficit to the highest levels in history. On foreign policy he pursued a hard line with the Soviet Union and leftist regimes, invaded Grenada, stationed Marines in Lebanon, and supported covert war against Nicaragua.

Reagan was reelected by a wide margin over former vice president Walter Mondale in 1984.

During his second term, Reagan continued his emphasis on a strong military but supported arms reduction talks with the Soviet Union. When he left office in 1989, the United States had huge budget deficits but a generally healthy economy. The Iran-Contra scandal did not diminish his popularity or that of his vice president and successor, George Bush.

REAPPORTIONMENT, LEGISLATIVE. *See* Apportionment, Legislative.

RECALL, a procedure for dismissing an elected official before his term of office has officially terminated. Several state constitutions specify that if a sufficient number of signatures have been gathered on a recall petition, an election will be held to decide whether the official involved shall be dismissed. Proponents of recall insist that it is most democratic, giving the citizenry the right to eject an unpopular official from his office. Opponents of the practice fear that its overuse could inhibit elected officials and reduce the effectiveness of government.

RECESS. *See* Adjournment.

RECESS APPOINTMENT, an appointment made by the President when the Senate is not in session. The appointment expires on the last day of the following congressional session unless the appointee has been confirmed by advice and consent of the Senate.   *—Mary L. Carns*

RECESSION. *See* Depression.

RECLAMATION, BUREAU OF. *See* Water and Power Resources Service.

RECOGNITION, the act of accepting the existence of a state, government, or state of belligerency. A state becomes a member of the family of nations only through recognition by other states. Recognition shows a readiness on the part of the recognizing country to enter into formal relations with a new state or government. A nation that recognizes belligerency accepts a revolt in another country as amounting to a state of war, imposing the rights and duties of the rules of war. Each state has the right to decide whether, and when, it will recognize a state, government, or state of belligerency. *De jure* recognition is complete and final; *de facto* recognition is for limited purposes only.

RECONSTRUCTION ACTS. On March 2, 1867, Congress passed the Reconstruction Act over President Andrew Johnson's veto. In the following twelve months, three supplementary acts were adopted to clarify the intent of the original legislation and to plug loopholes in the law.

The first Act provided that the ex-Confederate states be ruled temporarily by martial law. Five military districts were created, each under the control of a federal commander. Elections were to be held for a constitutional convention; blacks were eligible to vote, while all whites disqualified from officeholding under Section 3 of the proposed Fourteenth Amendment were ineligible. Black suffrage and disqualification of Confederate leaders had to be incorporated into the new constitutions, which then had to be ratified by a majority of the voters. Once this was accomplished and the new state legislatures had ratified the Fourteenth Amendment, a state could resume its place in Congress.

Efforts to Thwart the Law. The white South tried to thwart the law by refusing to call constitutional conventions. Congress responded on March 23, 1867, by requiring the military commanders in the South to initiate the proceedings. On July 19, 1867, Congress passed the third Reconstruction Act, a complicated statute that elaborated on the intent of the previous measures. Among other things, it provided that obstructionist state officials were to be removed, and voter registration boards were empowered to deny the franchise to those suspected of taking the loyalty oath in bad faith.

The failure of Southern white conservatives to vote in the elections for the ratification of the new constitutions necessitated the fourth and final Reconstruction Act. Since earlier legislation had specified that a majority of registered voters was needed for ratification, this tactic successfully prevented the adoption of the new constitutions. On March 11, 1868, Congress amended the law to allow ratification by a simple majority.

RECONSTRUCTION FINANCE CORPORATION (1932). *See* New Deal Legislation: *Glossary.*

RECORD VOTE, in legislative terminology, a recorded tally of each individual response for or against a particular motion or bill, known as a yeas-and-nays vote. A record vote is required on the demand of one-fifth of the members present of either house or when a vote is taken to pass a bill over a presidential veto. Prior to 1973, the record vote was infrequently used in the House of Representatives because the process of calling 435 names and recording their votes was too time-consuming. The present procedure, whereby members insert a plastic card similar to a credit card into a voting station and press a button to indicate "yea," "nay," or "present," speeded up the voting process and has resulted in a significant increase in recorded votes.

See also Roll-Call Vote.

REDISTRICTING. *See* Apportionment, Legislative.

REFERENDUM. *See* Initiative and Referendum.

REFUGEE, traditionally a person fleeing his or her country to avoid persecution or hardship. Individual states establish their own standards for the admission of refugees despite the obligations imposed by U.N. conventions. The problem continues to be global in scope with some 16 million refugees located in over 50 countries. The United Nations and private agencies provide considerable relief but are unable to cope with the drought and famine that have forced millions from their land, primarily in Africa.

Increasingly, some states, particularly the United States, have begun to distinguish between political refugees (who are admitted) and those fleeing for economic reasons (who are often refused entry).

REGENTS OF UNIVERSITY OF CALIFORNIA v. BAKKE, 438 U.S. 265 (1978), the first major Supreme Court case to address the question of "reverse discrimination" or "affirmative-action" programs. A special admissions program for a state medical school had set aside a portion of the available openings for minority students and had prevented white applicants from competing for them. The Supreme Court held that this rigid "quota" violated Title VI of the 1964 Civil Rights Act. But the Court held that admissions programs which consider race as "one of a complex of factors involved in the decision to admit or reject" an applicant are not necessarily unconstitutional. "Government may take race into account when it acts not to demean or insult any racial group, but remedy disadvantages cast on minorities by past racial prejudice."

REGIONAL CITY, a large city that dominates affairs within a larger geographical area. Examples of regional cities are Chicago and New Orleans. Regional cities were more common in the past, when railroads and rivers were the principal means of transportation.

REGISTRATION ACTS. *See* Alien Registration Act of 1940.

REGULATION OF LOBBYING ACT (1946), the first statute requiring lobbyists to register with the government. Part of the Legislative Reorganization Act of 1946, the law's constitutionality was upheld in 1954 by the Supreme Court.

Although the act did not restrict lobbyists' activities, it required paid lobbyists—people or firms hired by others to lobby in Congress—to file quarterly financial reports and to register with the House and Senate. Organizations that lobbied had to file financial reports but did not have to register. The reports were to list all contributions, expenditures, and the name and address of anyone who contributed over $500 or received payments. The act sought to remove the uncertainty surrounding the influence of lobbyists on legislation and to make lobbyists' activities known to Congress and the public. The act has been only partially successful because it lacks enforcement provisions and is open to conflicting interpretations.

See also Lobby.

REGULATORY AGENCIES. *See* Business Regulation in the United States; Independent Agencies and Regulatory Commissions.

REHNQUIST, WILLIAM HUBBS (1924-   ), 16th Chief Justice of the Supreme Court (1986-   ), associate justice (1971-1986). Born in Wisconsin, he received his law degree from Stanford University (1952). He served as law clerk to Supreme Court Justice Robert H. Jackson and practiced law privately before becoming assistant attorney general (1969). He was nominated to the Supreme Court by President Richard M. Nixon in 1971. An articulate pillar of the conservative bloc on the Court, he argued against abortion (*Roe v. Wade,* 1973) and affirmative action programs (*United Steelworkers of America v. Weber,* 1979). He wrote the majority opinion in *Rostker v. Goldberg* (1981), which held that exclusion of women from the draft was constitutional. Justice Rehnquist became Chief Justice in 1986.

REITMAN v. MULKEY, 387 U.S. 369 (1967), concerns the validity of an amendment to the California constitution which allowed private discrimination in the sale, rental, or lease of property. The Mulkeys sued Reitman, alleging that he had refused to rent them an apartment solely on the basis of their race. The Court, in assessing the ultimate impact of a statute that would encourage and significantly involve the state in private racial discrimination contrary to the

Fourteenth Amendment, held the California amendment unconstitutional.

See also Shelley v. Kraemer.

RELEASED TIME CASES. *See* Illinois ex rel. McCollum v. Board of Education; Zorach v. Clauson.

REPRESENTATIVE ACTION. *See* Class Action.

REPRESENTATIVE GOVERNMENT developed in England in the seventeenth century and has spread throughout the world. In this government representatives are empowered to act in behalf of those represented. Representative actions may be both legislative and executive. Representative governments developed prior to widespread suffrage and are not necessarily democratic. Modern forms, however, are associated with democracy and are based on the principles of political equality and government by consent. To be representative, therefore, equal numbers of a constituency must have equal representation and the representatives must be accountable to the represented. Periodic competitive elections are intended to serve as the means to provide accountability.

The American Founding Fathers justified a representative democracy as superior to direct democracy on the grounds that it would minimize the probability of self-interested factions (whether a minority or majority of the citizenry) from dominating the government, would produce a higher quality of governor, and would permit a larger geographic area and number of people to be incorporated in a single government.   —*Robert F. Smith*

See also Contract Theory; Democracy; Parliamentary Government; Popular Sovereignty.

REPUBLIC (Lat., public thing). That which is most public, in which all men in some fashion participate, is the state or commonwealth. A regime is public, however, only if it serves the common interest of all the people and not the private interest of the rulers. The modern view is that a state serves the common good in which large numbers of citizens participate and representatives are accountable the citizenry. Thus, modern usage tends to limit the republic to some form of democratic representative government.

See also Limited Government.

REPUBLICAN PARTY, one of the two major political parties in the United States. The party traces its name, if not its ideology, to Thomas Jefferson's Democratic Republican party of the late eighteenth century—the same origin as the contemporary Democratic party's.

Nineteenth Century. More direct philosophical antecedents date from 1854 when the forerunner of the present Republican party was founded to oppose the extension of slavery in the newly acquired territories of the United States. Abraham Lincoln was elected on a strong pro-union platform backed by abolitionists. The moderate Reconstructionist policies of Lincoln's successor, Andrew Johnson, were opposed by a radical wing of the party, which gained control during the first administration of Ulysses Grant. Opponents of Grant's hard line toward the South were further alienated by the scandals unearthed during his administration. The opponents were moved to form the short-lived Liberal-Republican party in 1872, but with the defeat of their candidate, this branch of the party virtually ceased to exist.

Rutherford B. Hayes succeeded Grant in 1876, continuing Republican control of the presidency, but the circumstances of that hotly disputed election (Samuel Tilden, the Democratic standard bearer, won the popular election but lost in the electoral college) and the excesses of the Reconstruction Era combined to break the Republican domination of the South, which thereafter voted consistently with the Democrats for more than 70 years. For nearly 20 years after Hayes' election, both the Republicans and the Democrats expounded virtually the same philosophy. Indeed, in 1884 many Republicans, known as Mugwumps, crossed party lines to vote for Democrat Grover Cleveland against the Republican candidate, James Blaine.

By 1896, however, ideological lines were clearly drawn, with the liberal economics of William Jennings Bryan pitted against the conservative gold standard and high protective tariff of William McKinley. The Republicans thus broadened the appeal to conservative big business interests that has continued to characterize a large segment of the party.

Interim. When these conservative interests denied him the nomination in 1912, Theodore Roosevelt, McKinley's successor, bolted the party to form the Progressive, or Bull Moose, party in an unsuccessful effort to retain the presidency. Except on the issue of race where they were consistently pro-integration, and therefore liberal, the Republicans entrenched themselves in conservative doctrines, particularly economic laissez-faire and isolationism. These doctrines had historically characterized the original liberal Democratic party under Thomas Jefferson.

This modern conservatism was strongly represented during the Republican administrations of Warren Harding, Calvin Coolidge, and Herbert Hoover. After the New Deal, opposition to the domestic programs of Franklin Roosevelt coalesced around this wing of the party. Nevertheless, the Republicans gave bipartisan support to Roosevelt's foreign policy under the leadership of Michigan Sen. Arthur H. Vandenberg. The party thus reversed the traditional isolationist stand that had successfully defeated the Democratic internationalism of Woodrow Wilson.

Eisenhower and After. Dwight Eisenhower's victory as Republican candidate for president in 1952 ended the 20-year Democratic dynasty. Although many political analysts view the Eisenhower victory as a personal rather than party triumph, the Republicans made their increasingly more moderate philosphy appealing to large numbers of the American people—so much so that Richard Nixon nearly defeated Democrat John F. Kennedy in 1960. Despite the fact that Eisenhower had guided the moderate wing of the party to prominence, his administration saw the rise of reactionary forces under Sen. Joseph McCarthy of Wisconsin, who exerted tremendous control over domestic politics with his campaign to root out subversives.

There had for many years been a liberal Republican wing centered in the northeastern part of the country. After McCarthy's demise, these elements exerted a broad influence on party policy under the leadership of Nelson Rockefeller, Jacob Javits, and Charles Percy, among others. A resurgence of the hard-line conservative doctrine was manifested in the unsuccessful candidacy of Arizona Sen. Barry Goldwater in 1964. Later this staunch conservative wing split off into a third-party movement, although Goldwater himself remained within the parent party, as did many other conservatives. Despite this indication of varying views, the dissensions that characterized the 1960s and virtually tore apart the Democratic party fabric had little effect on the Republican party structure.

Some observers view these schisms as a reflection of more clearly defined philosophical lines drawn between the two major parties. Except on the issue of race, reformers of whatever hue have tended to work at least within the Democratic party initially: the Republicans have maintained a more consistently conservative standard. This conservatism was perhaps modified under Eisenhower, who garnered enormous numbers of votes despite the party's statistical minority status, but the conservative wing evinced great power in the decision-making process during the administration of Richard M. Nixon, particularly on the domestic front and with regard to the conduct of the war in Vietnam.

The 1980 election of Ronald Reagan was viewed as a triumph of personality and conservative politics. Despite numerous scandals involving administration officials, the president maintained his popularity. The Republicans, however, lost control of the Senate in 1986. With Bush's election, it appeared that the Republican and Democratic parties had reached a contradictory and even illogical political impass. The Republicans prevail at the national level, while the Democrats control the Congress and a majority of state houses.

See also Democratic Party; Democratic-Republican Party; Eisenhower, Dwight David; Lincoln, Abraham; Two-Party System.

RESCISSION. *See* Impoundment.

RESERVED POWERS, or residual powers, powers not specifically "delegated to the United States by the Constitution, nor prohibited to the states respectively, or to the people" (Tenth Amendment). Although it is commonly believed that this clause is an exclusive reservoir of powers for the states, the reservoir is shared by the states and the people.

Once the colonies broke with the British and became sovereign states, they were individually the repository of sovereignty, or the ultimate power to rule. By adopting the Constitution, they delegated some of their sovereign powers to the national government. Although there is no list of the specific powers reserved in the states, the Tenth Amendment was adopted to elucidate the general principles of this federal division of power.

The principles of the Tenth Amendment have come into conflict with the Supremacy Clause, which states that the Constitution and federal statutes and treaties take precedence over any conflicting state law. Early Supreme Court decisions under the leadership of Chief Justice Marshall held to the Supremacy Clause. In later periods the Court leaned more heavily on the Tenth Amendment, looking upon nation and state as coequal sovereignties and holding that acts of states within their reserved powers could act as limitations on the powers of the national government. The later doctrine (dual federalism) was abandoned in the early 1940s. — *Theodore B. Fleming, Jr.*

See also Delegated Powers; Implied Powers; National Supremacy.

RESETTLEMENT ADMINISTRATION (RA). *See* New Deal Legislation: *Glossary.*

RESOLUTION, a formalized statement of an opinion or a decision. In Congress a resolution is simple, joint, or concurrent. A simple resolution deals with the rules of one chamber or expresses the sentiments of that chamber. Not requiring the approval of the other chamber or the signature of the president, a simple resolution does not have the force of law. Likewise, a concurrent resolution, which expresses the sentiments of both chambers, fixes time for adjournment, or deals with the rules or have the force of law. A joint resolution, however, if approved by both chambers and signed by the president, has the force of law. As contrasted with a bill, a joint resolution generally deals with a limited or specific matter, such as correcting errors in a bill already sent to the president. A proposed constitutional amendment takes the form of a joint resolution, but it requires a two-thirds vote of each house of Congress and does not require the president's signature.

See also Bill.

RESOLUTION TRUST CORPORATION (RTC), organization created in 1989 as a part of President Bush's plan to bail out and restructure insolvent savings and loan institutions. RTC is a private corporation charged with taking control of more than 300 insolvent S&Ls. The mission of the RTC is to determine if those S&Ls should be closed or sold. A second agency, the Resolution Funding Corporation, will issue $50 billion in 30-year bonds that the RTC will use to pay off the indebtedness of the S&Ls. The RTC board includes the Secretary of the Treasury, the chairman of the Federal Reserve Board, and other prominent government officials.

RESTRICTIVE COVENANT, an attachment to a property deed in which the buyer agrees not to sell the property to a member of certain minority groups. Though not in itself illegal, such a covenant has been declared unenforceable by the Supreme Court because enforcement would violate due process.

RESULTING POWERS, those powers of the national government derived from powers that have been delegated or implied. In other words, they are not powers granted directly by the Constitution. For example, the U.S. Criminal Code states that any individual who breaks a national law is subject to punishment. Nowhere does the Constitution directly specify this power; it results from all the powers delegated to the national government.

REVENUE SHARING, a response to the perceived need to maintain strong and independent state and local governments in the face of the federal government's relatively greater ability to raise revenue. First proposed by Walter Heller under the name "Tax Sharing," it seeks to "return" a large share of federally-raised revenue to the states on an essentially per capita, guaranteed, no-strings-attached basis. Once the formula for distribution of funds to the states is decided upon, general revenue sharing has few political or administrative implementation problems.

Federal aid to the states and cities tripled from 1965 to 1980, but most of this aid was in the form of categorical grants-in-aid that specified precisely how the money could be spent. By contrast, general revenue sharing, which Congress first approved in 1972 at the urging of President Richard M. Nixon, contains no restrictions beyond the prohibition of discrimination on the basis of race, sex, and handicapped status. In recent years, it has accounted for 10 percent of federal aid to states and cities. "Special revenue sharing" takes the form of "block grants" and falls somewhere between grants-in-aid and general revenue sharing with respect to specificity on the use of federal funds. The new federal-state relationship, as a result of revenue sharing and block grants, is called the New Federalism. — *Guy C. Colarulli and Victor F. D'Lugin*

REVERSE DISCRIMINATION, a term used to describe a form of discrimination against whites, males, or other members of traditionally chosen groups. Opponents of affirmative action programs cite the Fourteenth Amendment as extending equal protection of the laws to everyone and the 1964 Civil Rights Act as outlawing any form of discrimination in employment. They claim that reverse discrimination is being practiced when programs providing favored treatment for minorities pass over those people who are most qualified. The courts have interpreted the law in such a way that guidelines favoring the increased representation of minority groups have been upheld as long as rigid quotas are not used. However, recent Supreme Court actions have reopened the question of constitutionality and affirmative action.

See also City of Richmond v. J.A. Croson Company; Regents of the University of California v. Bakke; United Steelworkers of America v. Webster.

REYNOLDS v. SIMS, 377 U.S. 533 (1964), is one of several historic cases in which the Warren Court applied a one-man, one-vote principle to invalidate provisions of the constitutions of several states which apportioned the seats in one chamber of their bicameral legislatures on principles other than population. The Court held that the equal protection clause of the Fourteenth Amendment requires that both houses of a state legislature be apportioned on a population basis and that a state must make an honest effort to construct districts for both such houses which are as nearly equal in terms of population as practicable. The Court Stated that the "great compromise" of the Constitution, apportioning seats in the federal Senate equally among the states, afforded no basis for the states to avoid the one-man, one-vote edict of the equal protection clause here enunciated.

RIDER, an amendment, usually controversial, added to a legislative measure in the hope that the rider's opponents and the executive will accept the ridered bill rather than reject the entire package. Controversial riders frequently concern items unrelated to the legislation under consideration and are often attached to financial bills because of the pressure to support them. Most riders could not be passed as separate legislation.

In federal legislation the president cannot make item vetoes, so he must either accept or reject a bill with a rider. The House is more likely than the Senate to defeat riders that are not pertinent. Budgets for the District of Columbia have been a favorite target for riders—the Miller-Tydings Act (1937), involving national fair-trade standards, passed on one such budget.

See also Amendment, Congressional.

RIGHT-TO-KNOW LAWS, state laws that entitle genuine representatives of radio, television, newspapers, magazines, and certain citizens to access to official meetings, records, and other information. Although the First Amendment states that "Congress cannot make laws which threaten freedom of speech or freedom of the press," there is no enforceable constitutional right to know nor is there any specific regulation on what each branch of government may disclose.

In 1966 a bill was enacted that required records and information to be made available to the public, provided the information does not fall in nine specifically exempt categories. In addition, no records need be disclosed if Congress by statute prescribes secrecy. The president, by executive order, may exempt such data as facts pertaining to national defense and foreign policy.

See also Pentagon Papers.

RIGHT-TO-LIFE, theory that argues that human life begins at the moment of conception and that the taking of the life of the innocent unborn fetus by means of abortion is murder. Right-to-life advocates seek to reverse the Supreme Court decision of Roe v. Wade (1973), which invalidated a ban on abortion, except to save the mother's life. Advocates have tried in numerous ways to protect the unborn—through laws requiring that approval of husbands or parents be obtained before getting an abortion, that pregnant women receive indoctrination on the alleged consequences of abortion, that death certificates be issued for fetuses, that courts appoint guardians of the rights of the unborn, and that the use of governmental funds for abortions be prohibited. Ultimately right-to-lifers seek either a reversal of Roe v. Wade and a definition of legal life as beginning at the moment of conception or a constitutional amendment to outlaw abortions.

Recent Supreme Court actions may extend limitations on abortion rights.

See also Webster v. Reproductive Health Services.

RIGHT-TO-WORK LAWS, provisions in state laws that prohibit arrangements between a union and an employer requiring membership in a union as a condition of getting or keeping a job. The laws apply to union shops, closed shops, preferential hiring, or other security provisions. Under the Taft-Hartley Act, state legislatures have the right to pass more stringent legislation than the federal law's union security provisions. The courts have upheld the right of the state to pass and enforce such legislation. Some states have amended their constitutions to prohibit enactment of union security arrangements.

RIOT COMMISSION. See Civil Disorders, National Advisory Commission on.

ROBINSON-PATMAN ACT (1936), also called the Anti-Price-Discrimination Act. This amendment to the

Clayton Antitrust Act aimed at eliminating the preferential price treatments given large chain stores as a threat to small retailers, who had to pay higher prices for the same goods.

The bill was introduced after a 1935 FTC investigation revealed that chain stores were given discounts that far outweighed any savings the sellers could have realized from quantity orders. The Act outlawed quantity discounts unless they represented a reduction in actual cost to the seller and were available equally to all buyers dealing under similar conditions. The Act also prohibited advertising allowances and other payments unless they were available on proportionally equal terms.

See also Clayton Antitrust Act; Federal Trade Commission.

ROCKEFELLER, NELSON (1908-1979), Republican governor of New York and 41st Vice President of the United States. He was the grandson of John D. Rockefeller, the founder of Standard Oil. Until his appointment by President Roosevelt in 1940 as coordinator of Inter-American Affairs, Rockefeller had worked for the family business interests. He went on to hold a number of positions in the Eisenhower administration, but Rockefeller had always been interested in politics and used his experience and finances to run successfully for governor of New York in 1958. He remained as governor until 1973 but also made several unsuccessful attempts to gain the Republican presidential nomination, most notably in 1964.

After the resignation of President Nixon in 1974, Rockefeller was appointed vice president by Gerald Ford under provisions of the Twenty-fifth Amendment. Facing opposition from conservatives within his party, Rockefeller declined to run in 1976. An avid art collector, he was instrumental in founding the New York Museum of Primitive Art.

ROE v. WADE, 410 U.S. 113 (1973), case in which the Supreme Court established a qualified right to abortion as a part of the right of privacy grounded in the Fourteenth Amendment's due process clause. Having held that a fetus is not a constitutionally protected "person," the Court essentially balanced the pregnant woman's right against the interest of the state in her health and in the potential life of the fetus. This latter interest was said to increase as the fetus increased in "viability." Thus, the state may not interfere with a woman's decision to have an abortion during the first trimester of pregnancy, when viability is low and the risks to the woman of an abortion are less than those of a full-term pregnancy. During the second trimester, the state may impose reasonable regulations to protect the mother's health. And during the final trimester, the state may forbid abortions altogether except when the mother's life is endangered.

Roe v. Wade has been at the center of controversy over abortion rights. Recent Supreme Court actions have limited the scope of the ruling in *Roe* and may lead to state laws further restricting abortions.

See also Griswold v. Connecticut; Webster v. Reproductive Health Services.

ROLL-CALL VOTE, in a legislature, the calling of the name of each legislator to determine if a quorum is present or as a preliminary to a record vote. In Congress, roll-call votes are often used as delaying tactics by proponents or opponents of a measure in order to gain time to marshal their forces. The roll call is taken by the presiding officer of either house on the demand of one-fifth of its members.

See also Record Vote.

ROMAN LAW. *See* Civil Law.

ROOSEVELT, (ANNA) ELEANOR (1884-1962), social reformer and wife of Franklin Roosevelt. She married her distant cousin Franklin in 1905 and spent the next two decades raising a large family and assisting her husband in his developing political career. When FDR was struck down by polio in 1921, she encouraged his rehabilitation and his return to political life. Her political activities crested in 1928 with her vigorous role in her husband's gubernatorial campaign and in the presidential campaign of Alfred E. Smith.

Public Life. As first lady in Albany and Washington (1929-1945), she assumed a responsible role—writing, speaking, and serving as a liaison between her husband and the public. She was particularly committed to the special needs of young people and blacks in the Depression, and she took an active part in the

Eleanor Roosevelt confers with Fiorello La Guardia.

planning and administration of several New Deal programs.

With the war she turned, with the President, to an interest in foreign affairs, where her concern with the survival of democracy was predominant. After Franklin's death she pursued an active public career on her own. She was appointed a member of the U.S. delegation to the United Nations by President Truman, she continued to be active in party politics, and she was a founder of Americans for Democratic Action—a group that sought to perpetuate the New Deal. She spoke out on housing, labor, civil liberties, and other domestic issues while she worked in the United Nations and with its relief affiliates.   —Allen Kifer

See also Roosevelt, Franklin D.

ROOSEVELT, FRANKLIN DELANO (1881-1945),
32nd President of the United States (1933-1945), founder of the New Deal, and war-time leader. Franklin Roosevelt followed his distant cousin Theodore into politics, deliberately pursuing a like path through the New York state legislature (1911-1913) and the Department of the Navy (1913-1920). Temporarily frustrated by polio (1921), which left him unable to walk, he reentered the arena as a protégé and successor of Governor Al Smith (1929-1933). As a depression governor, he instituted a series of relief and reform measures which served as a rehearsal for much of the New Deal.

He was the principal author of the New Deal and molder of a new Democratic majority. The New Deal was characterized by improvisation, opportunism, and

The presidency of Franklin Roosevelt was marked by dramatic social and political change.

eclecticism in social experimentation, and political action. Increasingly hedged about by conservative resistance, Roosevelt was nevertheless reelected to unprecedented third and fourth terms and built a coalition of interest groups and ideologies which persisted through the programs of Truman, Kennedy, and Johnson.

Much of the early New Deal was aimed at the immediate emergency, but later Roosevelt reluctantly embraced Keynesian economics—in the form of deficit financing—and supported collective bargaining, social security, public power and regional planning, and farm price supports. Under the influence of his wife, Eleanor, and urban political leaders, he quietly sought to end racial discrimination in government agencies. His tenure was further characterized by a centralization of power in Washington, primarily due to the inability of states to meet problems.

In foreign affairs Roosevelt was at first an isolationist, emphasizing hemispheric solidarity and discretionary neutrality until 1939, when he actively sought to aid the democracies against the Axis. He sought defense funds and a selective service law in 1940. In 1941 he tried to commit the country as an "arsenal of democracy" to supply war matériel to the British—France and much of western Europe had fallen to the Germans the year before—and to proclaim a neutral zone in the Atlantic as far east as Iceland. In August Roosevelt met with Churchill to discuss goals, one of which was the "destruction of the Nazi tyranny."

When the Japanese attacked Pearl Harbor in December, Roosevelt was already committed to an Atlantic war, and American ships had engaged the Germans on a number of occasions. Roosevelt was an active commander in chief and diplomat: he met with Allied leaders at Casablanca, Cairo, Quebec, Teheran, and Yalta to determine wartime strategy and postwar arrangements. He expected the United States to assume much of the Allies' job in maintaining a power balance in the postwar world, but he did not live to attend the U.N.'s first meeting in San Francisco.

—Allen F. Kifer

ROOSEVELT, THEODORE (1858-1919), 26th President of the United States (1901-1909), first Progressive president. Theodore Roosevelt, a native of New York City, entered a political career almost immediately upon graduation from Harvard in 1880. His brief career as a maverick Republican member of the state legislature (1882-1884) was disrupted by the death of his wife, and he retired temporarily to a ranch in the Dakota territory (1884-1886). He reentered politics as unsuccessful candidate for mayor of New York and served over the next decade as federal civil service commissioner (1889-1895), president of the police commission in New York City (1895-1897), and assistant secretary of the Navy (1897-1898). He was a jingoist at the time of strained relations with Spain and

Theodore Roosevelt, 26th President of the United States (1901-1909).

helped organize and lead the Rough Riders in the Cuban campaign. Returning a hero, he captured the governorship.

His reforming zeal as governor alarmed Republican bosses sufficiently to kick him upstairs to the vice-presidency. He became president upon McKinley's assassination. As president he was an advocate of the use of power by the chief executive and by the federal government. His reputation as a trust-buster was tempered by his tolerance of bigness alone. Under what he later called the "New Nationalism," he sought the establishment of strong independent regulatory commissions and posed himself as mediator between coal operators and striking miners in 1902. He was an ardent conservationist and advocate of pure food and drug laws.

In foreign affairs he had preached the acquisition of an empire since before the Spanish War. As president he helped in securing an independent Panama that could negotiate with the United States over rights to an isthmian canal (1903). He was instigator of the Roosevelt corollary to the Monroe Doctrine, calling for intervention in the internal affairs of neighboring nations for strategic reasons (1905). Rejecting an isola-

tionist position, he actively sought a role in affairs outside the hemisphere. He was awarded the Nobel Prize for negotiating peace between Japan and Russia (1905) and advocated American responsibility in maintaining a balance of power in Asia and Europe.

He voluntarily left the presidency in 1909, and when he tried to reestablish his leadership in 1910, he was rebuffed by Taft and the conservatives. He led a third party movement of Bull Moose Progressives to second place in the 1912 election. His remaining years were spent in retirement, criticizing the isolationist, idealistic policies of Wilson and wielding some influence through supporters in Congress. Throughout his life he was a prolific author and publicist, producing books and articles on history, conservation, and politics.   —*Allen F. Kifer*

ROOSEVELT COROLLARY. *See* Monroe Doctrine.

ROTH v. UNITED STATES, 354 U.S. 476 (1957), questions whether federal obscenity statutes violated the provision of the First Amendment that "Congress shall make no law . . . abridging the freedom of speech, or of the press. . . . " Roth, who published and sold books, photographs, and magazines, was convicted of mailing obscene circulars and advertising and an obscene book. The Court, in affirming his conviction, held that obscenity is not within the area of constitutionally protected speech and press, and that implicit in the history of the First Amendment is the rejection of obscenity as utterly without redeeming social importance. Justice Douglas and Justice Black dissented, saying that government should be concerned with anti-social conduct, not with utterances (speech). Thus, the First Amendment's guarantee of freedom of speech and press should allow protests even against the current moral code accepted by the community.

See also Ginsburg v. United States.

RULE OF FOUR. *See* Certiorari, Writ of.

RULE OF REASON. *See* Sherman Antitrust Act.

RULES COMMITTEE, a standing committee of the U.S. House of Representatives that establishes special orders, or "rules," in scheduling legislative measures for floor action. "Rules" from this committee may set terms for debate, including specific time limitations; limit types and set conditions for amendments that may be proposed; and set dates for debate.

The Rules Committee is essential to sift through the myriad forms of bills and resolutions that are reported out of committee, set priorities, and reduce them to a workable number, but its powers are also open to abuse. One of the most powerful committees in the House, the Rules Committee has frequently used its powers to delay arbitrarily or even to kill legislation. In theory, a bill could be removed from control of the Rules Committee by adoption of a Discharge Rule, but in actual practice members have been reluctant to use this device. The power of the Rules Committee has been reduced somewhat in recent years by modifications in House rules and by giving the Speaker additional controls over the committee. —*Mary L. Carns*

See also Committee System of Congress; Discharge Petition.

RURAL ELECTRIFICATION ADMINISTRATION (REA), an agency of the Department of Agriculture that administers low-interest loan programs for rural electrification and telephone service. REA, created in 1935, furnishes borrowers with technical assistance and helps initiate programs to stimulate local economic development.

See also New Deal Legislation.

RUSK, DEAN (1909-), educator and Secretary of State. Rusk was a Rhodes scholar who then served as a colonel during World War II in the China-Burma-India theater. He held a number of administrative positions at the State Department and was also president of the Rockefeller Foundation, 1952-1960. In 1961, President Kennedy appointed him secretary of state, a position he held until 1969. Rusk acted as chief spokesman for President Johnson during the controversial military buildup in Vietnam and often defended administration policies before the Senate Foreign Relations Committee. After leaving government, Rusk became professor of international law at the University of Georgia.

RUTLEDGE, JOHN. *See* Supreme Court of the United States.

SABOTAGE, in labor, an intentional form of slowing down or discontinuing production by using illegal and often violent means, sometimes including machine wrecking. Sabotage may be used as a weapon against the employer to attain employee objectives or as a protest against the regime or the recipients of production (for example, sabotage against Germans in European factories during World War II). In international law, sabotage may be punished by jail terms or death if the perpetrators are not lawful combatants.

SAN ANTONIO INDEPENDENT SCHOOL DISTRICT v. RODRIGUES, 411 U.S. 1 (1973), in which a closely divided Supreme Court declined to establish the right to an education as a "fundamental" right or to hold that wealth is a "suspect" way of classifying people. As a result, the Court did not strictly scrutinize a state system of funding public schools essentially through local property taxes, even though the system resulted in wide disparities in the amount of money available to be spent per pupil. There was no absolute deprivation here, the majority said, and the system was not wholly irrational, but instead furthered a legitimate state interest in local control of schools.

SANCTIONS, in international law, steps taken by a nation or nations to enforce a law or discourage aggressive action by another nation. These steps include cutting off trade, severing diplomatic relations, and blockade. Individual states have also used force or its equivalent, such as naval demonstrations and shellings, as sanctions. While military sanctions may prove effective, economic sanctions are rarely successful.

SCALES v. UNITED STATES, 367 U.S. 203 (1961), concerns the constitutionality of a section of the Smith Act of 1940 which made mere membership in the Communist party a crime. Scales, a member of the party, argued that the membership section of the Smith Act had been repealed by the Subversive Activities Control Act of 1950, which provides that "Neither the holding of office nor membership in any Communist organization by any person shall constitute per se a violation of this section or any other criminal statute." In the opinion of the Court, this section of the 1950 act clarified, rather than repealed, the membership section of the Smith Act. The Court emphasized the difference between punishment for membership per se and punishment for membership with intent to aid in the violent overthrow of the government. The dissenters argued that the membership section of the Smith Act violated the First Amendment.

See also Dennis v. United States.

SCALIA, ANTONIN (1936-), associate justice of the Supreme Court (1986-). Scalia, a graduate of Harvard Law School, practiced law initially, then accepted a teaching position at the University of Virginia in 1967. His interest in politics and administrative law brought him to President Nixon's attention, leading to a series of appointments, including the post of assistant attorney general in charge of the Justice Department's Office of Legal Counsel, where he remained until Ford left office in 1977. Scalia resumed teaching law at the University of Chicago. His advocacy of judicial restraint brought him to the attention of President Reagan, who appointed Scalia to the bench of the U.S. Court of Appeals for the District of Columbia in 1982. Judge Scalia's opinions, in particular his strong support for presidential powers, made him President Reagan's nominee for the vacancy created when William Rehnquist became chief justice upon the unexpected retirement of Chief Justice Burger in 1989. Scalia was approved unanimously and has consistently sided with the conservative wing of the court.

SCHECHTER POULTRY CORPORATION v. UNITED STATES, 295 U.S. 495 (1935), deals with the extent to which the legislative power may be delegated to the executive branch. President Roosevelt promulgated a "Live Poultry Code" under authority granted to him by the National Industrial Recovery Act (NIRA). The code was designed to promote fair competition in the live poultry industry in the metropolitan New York area. The court held the President's code unconstitutional because Congress is not entitled to delegate the legislative power conferred on it by the Constitution, although it may delegate the right to make regulations designed to affect general provisions of enacted legislation if proper guidelines and limits of such rule-making power are contained in a statute. This decision voided the NIRA and was the last time an act of Congress was declared an unconstitutional delegation of the legislative power.

SCHENCK v. UNITED STATES, 249 U.S. 47 (1919), concerns several violations of the Espionage Act of 1917 and the Sedition Act of 1918. Schenck was charged with conspiring to have printed and circulated to military recruits a document allegedly designed to cause insubordination and to obstruct recruiting and enlisting. Schenck, general secretary of the Socialist party, maintained that the Acts abridged his First Amendment rights of freedom of speech and the press. Justice Holmes, for the Court, announced the now famous "clear and present danger" test: "The question is whether the words used are used in such circumstances and are of such a nature as to create a clear and present danger that they will bring about substantive evils that Congress has a right to prevent. It is a question of proximity and degree." Under this test, Schenck's conviction was upheld, the Court finding a clear and present danger that the pamphlets would bring about resistance to the draft.

See also Abrams v. United States; Gitlow v. New York.

SCHNEIDER v. RUSK, 377 U.S. 163 (1964), concerns the authority of the Congress to enlarge or abridge the rights of citizenship acquired by naturalization. Schneider, a German national by birth, came to the United States as a child and acquired derivative American citizenship through her mother at the age of sixteen. Subsequently, she married a German national and settled in Germany. Later, she applied for an American passport and was denied one on the grounds that she had forfeited her citizenship. In the opinion of the Court, the rights of citizenship of the native born and those of the naturalized person are of the same dignity and are coextensive. The Court also held that denationalization of naturalized citizens for living abroad in the country of their former citizenship or birth constitutes an unreasonable and arbitrary discrimination in violation of the Fifth Amendment.

See also Afroyim v. Rusk; Trop v. Dulles.

SCOTTSBORO CASE. *See* Powell v. Alabama.

SCRANTON COMMISSION. *See* Campus Unrest, President's Commission on.

SEARCH AND SEIZURE, the inspection and confiscation of property or person by authorities. American citizens are protected against unreasonable and unlawful search and seizure by the Fourth Amendment (applying to state and local officials). The Fourth Amendment was put in the Bill of Rights to prevent recurrence of the English Writs of Assistance, which gave authorities the right to enter the home of a citizen and search and seize his belongings. Today, if authorities obtain any evidence in violation of the Fourth or Fourteenth Amendment or any statutes, the evidence is generally inadmissible in court.

Property. Generally, police may search and seize only with a warrant, but there are instances in which no warrant is required. The warrant, which is issued by a judge, must be specific in describing the location to be searched and the items or people to be seized. Before the judge issues the warrant, he must decide whether there is probable cause and if the warrant meets the requirements of the Fourth Amendment and state laws. Once the officer has secured a warrant, he can seize only certain types of evidence: the proceeds of a crime, the tools by which the crime was committed and objects that make escape possible, and illegal items. The warrant must be executed within ten days of its issuance. The officer must announce himself at the premises unless there is a chance that narcotics evidence might be destroyed (no-knock provision) or there is danger to anyone. If he seizes anything, he must leave a copy of the warrant; otherwise, he is not required to show the warrant.

A search and seizure can be made without a warrant under certain circumstances, including emergencies and hot pursuit situations, and if a person clearly gives his consent to a search, knowing that he has a right to refuse. Also, public records may be examined without a warrant as long as the search is done in a reasonable manner, at a reasonable hour and day. A car may also be searched without a warrant when there is a chance the vehicle will be moved before a warrant can be obtained.

Person. The search and seizure protection also covers people and invalid arrests. A policeman may make an arrest without a warrant only if he actually sees the crime, if he has probable cause to believe a felony has been committed by a person he is arresting, and if there is no time to obtain a warrant.

In order to obtain an arrest warrant, there must be probable cause, and the warrant must contain a description of the crime and the alleged perpetrator. The arrest must be lawful or the items uncovered in the search incidental to the arrest are inadmissible in court. Also, the arrest must be made before the search unless a dangerous situation exists or there is an attempt to destroy the evidence.

In a stop-and-frisk situation, the policeman may frisk if he thinks a suspect is carrying a weapon and looking for trouble. The officer must be able to support his decision to stop and frisk with specific facts and observations. However, if the frisk is justified and incriminating evidence is found, it is admissible in court.

Electronic search and seizure is also permitted as long as a warrant is obtained beforehand. The judge issuing the warrant sets the limits under which the officer may eavesdrop. After eavesdropping, the officer must report what he heard to the court.

See also Accused Persons, Rights of; Evidence; Wiretapping.

SEARCH WARRANTS. *See* Search and Seizure.

SECOND CIVIL RIGHTS ACT. *See* Civil Rights Acts: Act of Mar. 1, 1875.

SECRET SERVICE, under the direction of the Secretary of the Treasury, is responsible for the protection of the president and members of his or her immediate family, the president-elect, the vice president or other officer next in the order of succession to the presidency, the vice president-elect during their lifetimes, major candidates for the offices of president and vice president and their spouses during the presidential campaigns, the minor children of a former president until they reach age sixteen, and visiting heads of a foreign state or government. The Secret Service is also authorized to detect and arrest persons committing offenses against the laws of the United States relating to coins, obligations, and securities of the United States and foreign governments, and persons who forge government requests for transportation to be furnished by a common carrier. The director of the Service is also responsible for the Executive Protective Service and the Treasury Security Force.

SECURITIES ACT OF 1933. *See* Business Regulation in the United States.

SECURITIES AND EXCHANGE COMMISSION (SEC), an independent government agency established in 1934 by the Securities Exchange Act. The commission protects the public against malpractice in the financial and securities markets by regulating security issues, the stock exchanges and investment and holding companies. SEC has five members, each appointed by the president for a five-year term. The main function is the administration of several acts,

including the Security Act (1933), the Public Utility Holding Company Act (1935), the Trust Indenture Act (1939), and the Investment Company and the Investments Advisers Acts (1940). As a quasi-judicial body, SEC advises the courts on Chapter X of the National Bankruptcy Act.

The SEC was established to protect investors after the crash of 1929, despite early protests by Wall Street. The SEC's requirements are quite extensive and specific concerning securities exchange. Securities and dealers must file a detailed report of their financial conditions each year and must comply with certain capital requirements so that customers and creditors are protected against unwarranted losses. Registration of securities, however, does not imply approval of the issue by the commission or that the commission has found registration disclosures to be accurate.

SEC requirements do not insure investors against loss but provide them with information upon which they can make informed and realistic evaluations of the worth of securities. The SEC may suspend the trading of certain issues on the stock exchange if there is adverse information about them.

SECURITY RISK. *See* Loyalty-Security Programs.

SEDITION. *See* Alien and Sedition Acts.

SEGREGATION. *See* Civil Rights Movement.

SELECTIVE SERVICE SYSTEM, an independent agency within the executive branch that coordinates the selection and registration of males for the U.S. Army. The initial system was created by Congress in 1948 and was revised by the Military Selective Service Act (1967). The system required that male citizens and alien permanent residents register for the draft at age eighteen. In general they were subject to the draft for a two-year term of service until age twenty-six.

Deferments and exemptions are granted for some types of study, hardship and dependency cases, physical or mental deficiency, conscientious objection, or participation in certain service organizations and vital jobs. Educational deferments were granted generally only through the first bachelor's degree. Medical and dental students were permitted to complete their postgraduate work but required to serve at a later date in either the U.S. Armed Forces or the U.S. Public Health Service. Also exempt were members of the diplomatic corps. Conscientious objectors were required to perform civilian service work. Some individuals were granted deferments but remained eligible until age 35.

The induction of registrants was terminated in 1973. In 1975 the registration process for the draft was suspended and an all-volunteer army was announced as a replacement for conscription. In 1980, as a response to perceived international tension, a system of compulsory registration was reinstituted. Registration presently is required for all males, and as a result of *Rostker v. Goldberg* the male-only status for military registration was affirmed.

SELF-INCRIMINATION, in constitutional terms, the process of becoming involved in or charged with a crime by one's own testimony. The Constitution prohibits forced self-incrimination under the Fifth Amendment. This amendment has been widely used by witnesses in congressional investigations of subversive or criminal activities in refusing to answer questions on the grounds that such answers would be self-incriminating.

During the McCarthy era it was often assumed that persons who "took the Fifth" were guilty of the specified charge. Thus, utilizing the constitutional prohibition against self-incrimination became in itself incriminating. During the 1960s there appeared to be a judicial trend in favor of strict adherence to the Fifth Amendment, as evidenced by the 1965 Supreme Court decision repealing the section of the Subversive Activities Control Act that required Communist party members to register with the federal government. However, in 1972 the Court upheld the constitutionality of the Organized Crime Control Law (1970), which protected a witness from prosecution only to the extent that what he says will not be used against him—he is still liable to prosecution on other evidence.

See also Loyalty-Security Programs.

SENATE OF THE UNITED STATES, the upper house of the U.S. Congress. Each state elects two senators, who serve a six-year term. The 50 states are represented in the Senate on an equal basis, regardless of the population or size. Originally the Constitution required the state legislatures to elect the senators, but in 1913 the Seventeenth Amendment changed the system to a popular election in the states. One-third of the Senate is elected every even-numbered year: the Senate is therefore considered to be a continuous body and does not have to adopt new rules for itself at the beginning of every Congress. There are no limitations on the number of terms a senator may serve, and it is not uncommon for a Senator to serve two to four continuous terms. The high likelihood of reelection and the six-year staggered-term system lends much to the stability, independence, and, at times, conservatism of the Senate. Its leadership, too, remains relatively stable, as Senate committee chairmen normally retain the chair for the length of their party's majority.

Filibuster. One aspect that makes the Senate quite different from the House is the Senate's tradition of unlimited debate, often enabling a determined minority to filibuster a bill to death. By refusing to end a debate, any number of senators can wear the majority

Senate in session, with visitors in gallery.

down to the point where their proposal simply dies without coming to a floor vote. Filibuster was prevalent in the nineteenth century. To cope with the problem, the Senate adopted Rule XXII in 1917, requiring a two-thirds vote of those present and voting to invoke "cloture" of debate. In 1949 the provision was raised to two-thirds of the entire Senate and in 1959 changed back to two-thirds of those present and voting, two days after submission of a petition by at least 16 senators. Rule XXII was subsequently amended again in 1975 and 1979. Current provisions require a petition signed by one-sixth of the senators, followed by a vote by three-fifths of the entire membership (60 senators). It is relatively difficult to obtain such a vote. Thus even if the House sends a bill to the Senate for its approval, there is no guarantee that a determined minority cannot thwart the will of the majority of both houses. Filibuster gives the Senate both strength—in upholding an unpopular view—and weakness—in thwarting the majority principle.

Powers. The Senate has some powers that the House does not. For example, the presidential power of appointment of justices and other officers of the government requires Senate approval; treaties must be approved by two-thirds of the Senate; and the Senate is the "court" on impeachment proceedings brought by the House, with the Chief Justice presiding. The first two powers give the Senate a leading voice over the House in the making of foreign policy, although the president himself is the dominant figure. The power of approval of appointment is rarely invoked to deny a president's appointee to office, but notable examples where nominations were rejected occurred when the Senate rejected one of President Eisenhower's appointees to the cabinet and two of President Nixon's appointees to the Supreme Court. The Senate Foreign Relations Committee takes a strong position in guarding the prerogatives of the Senate in the foreign policy area; the committee has often focused its investigatory spotlight on presidential action in foreign affairs.

Leadership. Because of the small size of the Senate (100) relative to the House (435) and the longer terms in office, senators get to know one another on a fairly close basis. Even partisan opponents respect the institution itself, giving it a certain sense of "clubbiness." Very often the ruling members of both parties on specific committees are very much alike: it is rare that the chairman of a committee makes an unusual move without advising his opposite number. Because the vice president is the presiding officer of the Senate, with the majority party choosing one of their elders as a temporary or "pro tem" presiding officer when the vice president is absent, the majority leader tends to be the most powerful figure in the Senate. The Democrats place much responsibility in their leader as party head, policy committee head, and committee selection chairman, whereas the Republicans tend to divide this party responsibility among two or more senators.

As in the House, Senate committee chairmen wield extreme power. Seniority and the safe state result in the Senate having a relatively stabilized leadership pattern. Even though it is true that today the legislative initiative is in the presidency, the Congress remains a formidable opponent.

Senators. The Senate, like the House, is organized along party lines, with the committees in the control of the majority party in the Senate. Too, the Senate has its division of labor and specialization. Most senators have at least one important committee on which they serve, giving them a solid base to advance their careers. Despite the six-year term, senators must continually maintain their ties to their home states, and because it is very difficult for the senator's party to deny him renomination if he seeks it, a senator tends to be a politician independent of the president and the national party organization.

The Senate has been a base for presidential aspirants. Since 1944 three senators (Truman, Johnson, and Nixon) have risen from the Senate to the vice-presidency to the presidency. Far more than governorships today, other than the presidency the Senate offers the widest platform for national prominence.

—*Erwin L. Levine*

See also Committee System of Congress; Congress of the United States; Filibuster; Legislation and the Legislative Process; Majority Leader; Senatorial Courtesy; Seniority.

SENATORIAL COURTESY, a Senate custom that gives members of the president's party control over presidential appointments to certain positions. By tradition, the Senate will refuse to confirm presidential nominees for offices such as district court judge and U.S. marshal unless the nominee has been approved by the senator or senators from the president's party who represent the nominee's home state. The courtesy does not extend to high-level offices like the cabinet.

The practical effect of senatorial courtesy is to transfer from the president to individual senators the distribution of patronage for their state. Senatorial courtesy gives the Senate the chance to influence and check the executive branch. Usually, the president will ask the appropriate senator his choice for a position. If the president submits an unacceptable name or if he fails to consult the senator, he will contest the nomination. An objection by one senator is customarily supported by the rest of the Senate.

See also Patronage.

SENIORITY SYSTEM, term given to the mode of determining rank on legislative committees. The system is employed in the two houses of the United States Congress and in a few of the state legislatures. Seniority is ordinarily not of much importance in making initial assignments to congressional committees. Other factors, such as party loyalty and geographic balance, are also taken into consideration by the party leaders. With a few exceptions, however, seniority is the only factor considered in retention on a committee. Should a party's majority on a committee decline because of electoral losses, it is the members with the least seniority who are dropped from the committee.

Seniority and Chairmanships in Congress. Seniority on a committee is virtually the only criterion used to determine rank on a committee, although reforms in the 1970s modified the seniority rule to permit committee members to elect or dismiss committee chairmen. Chairmen lost many of their "dictatorial" powers, and a few even lost their chairmanships under the new rules: in the House of Representatives, three committee chairmen were removed in 1975 and one in 1977; in the Senate, the ranking member of the Armed Services Committee was deprived of his position in 1985. This reduction in the power of committee chairmen has brought with it a corresponding increase in the role and influence of subcommittees. Nevertheless, a standing committee chairman is almost always the member of the majority party with the longest service on the committee. Because of this principle, the members of the majority party with the greatest seniority are likely to have chairmanships, and the most senior senators and representatives are likely to chair the most powerful committees. Another effect of the seniority rule is that most subcommittee chairmen are themselves senior members of the committee. Chairmen are, on the average, much older than their colleagues.

Another aspect of seniority is geographical, in that the chairmen come only from safe states or districts. Such one-party states and districts are likely to be conservative, isolated from liberal trends shown in national elections. Finally, the seniority principle limits severely the effectiveness of party leadership in Congress: the party leaders and the committee chairmen vie for authority. In defense of the seniority system, it is pointed out that it ensures that the committees will be strong, independent, and continuing centers of power.   —*Murray S. Stedman*

See also Committee System of Congress.

SEPARATE BUT EQUAL. *See* Brown v. Board of Education of Topeka; Plessy v. Ferguson.

SEPARATION OF CHURCH AND STATE. *See* Freedom of Religion.

SEPARATION OF POWERS, the separation and allocation of governmental functions to three branches of government—executive, legislative, and judicial—with each branch having a different method of selection and length of office. Based on the ideas of Montesquieu, the legislative branch makes the law, the executive branch implements and administers the law, and the judicial branch interprets the law. In this way, it was believed that tyranny of government over its citizens could be avoided or minimized. A modified version of separation of powers is incorporated into the U.S. Constitution and is an important element of the system of "checks and balances."

See also Checks and Balances; Judicial Review.

SESSION. Congresses are numbered consecutively, and each Congress consists of two sessions. Thus, for the 99th Congress, elected in 1984, the first session convened in 1985 and the second in 1986. In the nineteenth century a session might last no longer than three months, but since the Twentieth Amendment a session begins in January and runs most of the year. If action is not completed on some matter during the first session, it may be taken up at the second session at the stage it reached. Pending legislation dies at the end of a Congress. The president has the constitutional power to call Congress into special session after it has adjourned *sine die,* ending its regular session, but with Congress in more or less continuous session, there is less need for special sessions than formerly.

See also Adjournment; Sine Die.

SEX DISCRIMINATION. *See* Women's Liberation Movement.

SHELLEY v. KRAEMER, 334 U.S. 1 (1948), concerns a restrictive covenant in which private landowners agreed with one another not to sell or lease their land to blacks. Shelley, a black, contracted to purchase from Fitzgerald a parcel of land subject to the covenant. Kraemer sought to prevent Shelley from taking possession of the land. The court held that the state denied the petitioner the equal protection of the laws by granting judicial enforcement of the restrictive agreement, and the action of the state court was overruled. Freedom from discrimination in the enjoy-

ment of property rights was among the basic objectives of the framers of the Constitution, made applicable to the states by the Fourteenth Amendment. Judicial enforcement of such a contract by the state makes the state a guilty partner in racial discrimination and thereby violates the Fourteenth Amendment.

SHERMAN ANTITRUST ACT (1890), the first comprehensive legislation aimed at the industrial combinations that emerged in the late nineteenth century, particularly the Standard Oil Trust, formed in 1879.

The law banned all combinations that resulted in restraint of trade and prohibited monopolization or attempts at monopolization. Because the Act left undefined such key terms as "trust" and "restraint," at first the government had little success in prosecuting trusts, and courts failed to halt concentration of an industry among a few firms. Through the Clayton Act (1914) and the creation of the FTC (1914), the government strengthened the Sherman Act. The Celler-Kefauver Act (1950) added further restrictions on trusts. The Sherman Act is enforced by criminal prosecution, injunction, and private damage suit.

See also Celler-Kefauver Antimerger Act; Clayton Antitrust Act.

SHIELD LAW, a law that protects a journalist's communication status regarding informants. Although the Supreme Court does not find in the Constitution a basis for the claim to this right, it does agree that federal and state legislators can pass shield laws to extend the privilege to journalists. However, lawmakers and judges in each case have to weigh the public's right to know against a plaintiff's or defendant's right to a fair trial.

SHULTZ, GEORGE PRATT (1920-   ), U.S. cabinet officer. He began his career as a professor at the Massachusetts Institute of Technology, where he had earned a doctorate in industrial economics in 1949. He spent the next twenty years in academia, specializing in labor-management relations until he was appointed Secretary of Labor by President Nixon in 1969. In 1970 he was named to head the newly created Office of Management and Budget, a position he held until 1972 when he became Secretary of the Treasury. Shultz resigned in 1972 citing personal reasons, although he later admitted economic policy differences were at issue. After leaving government, Shultz became president of the Bechtel Group, which handled large construction and engineering projects around the world. In July 1982, President Reagan nominated Shultz to replace Alexander Haig as Secretary of State. Shultz maintained a close relationship with President Reagan, but critics questioned his claims of not having knowledge of the Iran-Contra scandal. After the election of George Bush in 1988, Shultz was replaced by James Baker.

SIERRA CLUB, organization formed in 1892 whose primary interests are to promote the enjoyment and protection of the environment. The club sponsors activities such as mountain climbing and camping and actively lobbies federal, state, and local governments for legislation designed to conserve the national environment. It is based in San Francisco and with 350,000 members is one of the largest ecology groups in the country.

SIMPLE MAJORITY. *See* Majority and Plurality.

SIMPSON-MIZZOLI ACT. *See* Immigration Reform and Control Act.

SINE DIE, adjournment that ends a session of Congress. *Sine die* means "without a day" and refers to the practice by which the legislature adjourns at the end of a session without setting a day for reconvening. The Legislative Reorganization Act of 1970 provides that Congress "shall adjourn *sine die* not later than July 31 of each year" unless Congress makes other provisions. —*Mary L. Carns*

SINGLE-MEMBER CONSTITUENCY. *See* Proportional Representation (PR).

SKINNER v. RAILWAY EXECUTIVE ASSOCIATION (1989), Supreme Court decision that held that Federal Railway Administration safety regulations mandating alcohol and drug tests without warrants did not violate the Fourth Amendment protections against "unreasonable searches and seizures." The Court ruled such tests were "searches" but were reasonable since workers involved with public safety had a lessened expectation of privacy. In sum, the government had a "compelling interest" to protect public safety by preventing drug use by railroad employees.

In a companion case (*National Treasury Employees Union v. Raab,* 1989), the Court also ruled that customs agents involved in drug interdiction were also subject to mandatory testing requirements without any Fourth Amendment violation.

SLANDER. *See* Libel and Slander.

SLAUGHTERHOUSE CASES, 16 Wall. 36 (1873), three cases arising from a Louisiana statute which granted a monopoly to a particular slaughterhouse company in New Orleans. This statute had the effect of putting a large number of butchers out of work, and these butchers sought an injunction on the grounds that the state law violated the privilege and immunities provision of the Fourteenth Amendment to the Constitution. This was the first case in which the Supreme

Court was asked to interpret and apply the privileges and immunities clause, and the Court gave it a very narrow reading which stands to this day. The Court ruled against the butchers' contention. The judges noted the distinction between state citizenship and United States citizenship in the first section of the amendment, and they decided that this amendment was not designed to protect a state citizen from actions by his own state. The Court decided this clause was intended only to protect those very limited privileges and immunities which stem from being a United States citizen.

SLAVERY, an ancient system of labor and property relations. It was originally a by-product of war and conquest, requiring whips and chains for organization. The cruel aspects of early slavery produced great uprisings, such as that headed by Spartacus in 73-71 B.C.; it was cut down without mercy. Civil law and religion reduced part of slavery's inhumanity. They allowed the emergence among slaves of teachers, skilled workers of every kind, entertainers, and favorite servants. Though slaves, they often received honor and respect in families and from the community. From their ranks developed classes of freed men and women who influenced Greek and, later, Roman civilization. Moslem nations also teemed with white, African, and native slaves and continued to maintain slavery even after Europe had transformed the slaves into semifree serfs attached to their estates but with a variety of privileges.

The Slave Trade. The systematic exploitation of the west African coast as a source of slaves accompanied the naval explorations of Spain, Portugal, the Netherlands, and Great Britain. Their seamen believed heathens deserved no consideration from Christians. After the fifteenth century the slave trade brought thousands of blacks in chains to South and North America and the Caribbean islands. The horrors of the Middle Passage—the transporting of slaves across the Atlantic Ocean—have never been defended. The ruthless packing of captives in shiploads resulted in insanity, disease, and death. White men and women in England and northern Ireland, among other countries, signed away their civil rights to obtain passage to the British colonies. As indentured servants, they were subject to the will of their masters for from four to seven years. The indentured, too, suffered a harsh Middle Passage before reaching Virginia or New York.

The first blacks who were brought by a Dutch man-of-war to Jamestown in 1619 were not slaves. No laws in Virginia covered such a condition. As servants, blacks experienced different fates, depending on their masters, Christian training, and personal abilities. Some early blacks became themselves masters, but the stigma of color remained. It created a caste of slaves, as court cases and local laws in Northern and Southern colonies separated blacks from other inden-

SLAVERY RECORD.

INSURRECTION IN VIRGINIA!

Extract of a letter from a gentleman to his friend in Baltimore, dated

'RICHMOND, August 23d.

An express reached the governor this morning, informing him that an insurrection had broken out in Southampton, and that, by the last accounts, there were seventy whites massacred, and the militia retreating. Another express to Petersburg says that the blacks were continuing their destruction; that three hundred militia were retreating in a body, before six or eight hundred blacks. A shower of rain coming up as the militia were making an attack, wet the powder so much that they were compelled to retreat, being armed only with shot-guns. The negroes are armed with muskets, scythes, axes, &c. &c. Our volunteers are marching to the scene of action. A troop of cavalry left at four o'clock, P. M. The artillery, with four field pieces, start in the steam boat Norfolk, at 6 o'clock, to land at Smithfield. Southampton county lies 80 miles south of us, below Petersburg.'

From the Richmond Whig, of Tuesday.

Disagreeable rumors have reached this city of an insurrection of the slaves in Southampton County, with loss of life. In order to correct exaggeration, and at the same time to induce all salutary caution, we state the following particulars:

An express from the Hon. James Trezvant states that an insurrection had broken out, that several families had been murdered, and that the negroes were embodied, requiring a considerable military force to reduce them.

The names and precise numbers of the families are not mentioned. A letter to the Post Master corroborates the intelligence. Prompt and efficient measures are being taken by the Governor, to call out a sufficient force to put down the insurrection, and place lower Virginia on its guard.

Serious danger of course there is none. The deluded wretches have rushed on assured destruction.

The Fayette Artillery and the Light Dragoons will leave here this evening for Southampton; the artillery go in a steamboat, and the troop by land.

We are indebted to the kindness of our friend Lyford for the following extract of a letter from the Editors of the Norfolk Herald, containing the particulars of a most murderous insurrection among the blacks of Southampton County,* Virginia.—*Gaz.*

NORFOLK, 24th Aug. 1831.

I have a horrible, a heart rending tale to relate, and lest even its worst feature might be distorted by rumor and exaggeration, I have thought it proper to give you all and the worst information, that has as yet reached us through the best sources of intelligence which the nature of the case will admit.

A gentleman arrived here yesterday express from Suffolk, with intelligence from the upper part of Southampton county, stating that a band of insurgent slaves (some of them believed to be runaways from the neighboring Swamps,) had turned out on Sunday night last, and murdered several whole families, amounting to 40 or 50 individuals. Some of the families were named, and among them was that of Mrs. Catharine Whitehead, sister of our worthy townsman, Dr. N. C. Whitehead,—who, with her son and five daughters, fell a sacrifice to the savage ferocity of these demons in human shape.

The insurrection was represented as one of a most alarming character, though it is believed to have originated only in a design to plunder, and not a view to a more important object—as Mrs. Whitehead being a wealthy lady, was supposed to have had a large sum of money in her house. Unfortunately a large number of the effective male popu-

* Southampton is bounded by the counties of Isle of Wight on the North, and Northampton, in North Carolina, on the South.

Abolitionist journal, *The Liberator,* reports insurrection of slaves in Virginia in 1831.

tured servants. However, the freeing of some blacks and the mixing of others with whites produced every gradation of color, permitting some of them to pass into white society over the generations.

A lost chapter in the early history of slavery in the colonies was the attempt made throughout the New World to enslave Indians. They did not respond well to slave conditions, except in their own tribal wars and family relations. By the end of the seventeenth century many Indian slaves in the Spanish colonies had been wiped out by disease and hard work of a kind they could not endure. In the North American colonies they were succeeded by blacks and a flood of toughened English, Scotch-Irish, and German servants who themselves eventually became freeholders of land.

Slavery in the Eighteenth Century. Black slaves continued to have an uncertain future in the colonial labor system, except in South Carolina, where they outnumbered the whites. Black enslavement proceeded without plan. A few humanitarian voices, especially among the Quakers, singled out slaves for special concern. The vigor of the free white labor force and the fact that free blacks promised to increase in numbers raised expectations that slave labor would disappear in time. In the North slavery did not flourish: it seemed fairly well-established in New York, and in Rhode Island a plantation-type of slave-farming became traditional, but, otherwise, black slaves tended to be mainly household servants.

Northern shipping formed a major association in the notorious Triangular Trade, which carried rum to the west coast of Africa in exchange for slaves. These slaves were transported to the West Indies and traded for highly prized sugar, which was used to manufacture more rum. A portion of the slave cargoes was increasingly landed in mainland ports.

Virginia became the largest of the Southern slave colonies and the foundation of Southern culture and economics. It produced an educated, outstanding aristocracy. Such leaders as Thomas Jefferson and George Mason ("father of the Bill of Rights") owned slaves but studied history and sought means for increasing free government. Virginians long remembered their efforts to end the foreign slave trade. They passed measures in their legislature that were disallowed by the British Board of Trade. The tidewater aristocrats—whose plantations lay among the Atlantic seaboard—were resented by their fellow Virginians of the hilly western counties, unable to utilize large numbers of slaves on their land. The inhabitants of what would later be West Virginia thus felt little stake in slavery.

Such facts, coupled with the rise of libertarian thought, combined to raise questions about the ethics of enslavement. Americans South and North were excited by expectations during the Revolution that slavery would crumble as a system. They foresaw a torrent of manumissions (voluntary freeing of slaves).

The loyal services of many slaves during hostilities did, indeed, increase the rate of emancipation. Also inspiring was the fact that Northern states began processes of gradual emancipation, setting dates when slavery must end. In 1783 the Massachusetts Supreme Court ruled that its new state constitution outlawed slavery. In 1787 the Northwest Ordinance stipulated that slavery was not to be permitted in what became the states of Ohio, Indiana, Illinois, Michigan, Wisconsin, and Minnesota.

Slavery Institutionalized. Slavery seemed on the road to extinction in the new United States: In 1808, the U.S. Congress barred the importation of slaves. It continued and even grew as an outlawed occupation. The fateful event was Eli Whitney's invention in 1793 of the cotton gin, which effectively separated the cotton from its seeds and made cotton a sensationally profitable crop. Cotton became king in the Southern economy. Manumissions fell. Although large plantations were relatively few, their success, coupled with the low status of blacks, permitted Southern intellectuals to refer to their "peculiar institution" in ways suggesting that slavery was a permanent feature in their lives.

Nevertheless, slavery was criticized on religious grounds and on grounds of humanity. Critics argued that its workings in the South contrasted unfavorably with the products of free labor in the North. Early abolitionists in North Carolina, Virginia, Tennessee, and Kentucky sought to educate blacks and encourage state laws favorable to emancipation. The American Colonization Society, initiated in 1816 in the North and South with federal encouragement, promised to send a stream of freed ex-slaves to Liberia as builders of civilization and Christian missionaries.

The battle in 1820 over the entrance of Missouri into the Union as a slave state revealed that North and South were not agreed on the future of slavery. In addition, the peace of the white South was shattered by rumors of slave conspiracies and uprisings such as Gabriel's Plot (1801) and the Denmark Vesey Conspiracy (1822), and as a result rigid state laws suppressed slaves. Nat Turner's Rebellion (1831) was a turning point. Although relatively small, it revealed the fears at the base of Virginia society. A crucial debate in the Virginia House of Delegates 1831-1832 on the proposition that slaves be freed or colonized elsewhere resulted in the complete victory of the pro-slavery forces. Thereafter, slaveholders in Virginia gave up the old idea that slavery was a burden and a problem to be solved. Throughout the Southern states slavery was held to be a positive good. In the border states slavery was less aggressively defended. "Southern feeling" and loyalty to the institution of slavery—as compared with loyalty to the Union—remained a major encouragement to Southern secessionists.

The constitutional compromise of 1787 had permitted the return of fugitive slaves. It had granted apportionment in representation to Congress to the amount of three-fifths per slave. Previously not mentioning slaves, as such, the Constitution now became the base for Southern demands that the chattel property be secured.

While free-soil and abolitionist sentiment flourished in the North, suppression of black attitudes and ambitions was firmly pursued in the South. The most spirited of the slaves sought freedom. They followed the North Star at night and hid to avoid slave-catchers by day. They were helped to safety by way of the Underground Railroad, a secret network of Northern anti-slavery workers and their sympathizers. Some of the runaways were led away from slavery by such ex-slaves as Harriet Tubman, the Moses of her people. Once fugitives were in the North, they created constitutional debates over how they were to be received. They helped abolitionize the North because otherwise law-abiding white citizens refused to help catch fugitives. Ex-slave and runaway Frederick Douglass became a living argument against the idea that blacks were naturally inferior or were satisfied to be slaves. Douglass, lecturing openly in defiance of slave-catchers, helped persuade many Northerners that their own civil liberties, as well as his, were in danger.

The Compromise of 1850 completely politicized the slavery question by giving Northerners a choice of obeying or breaking the strict Fugitive Slave Law. The Compromise ended the trading of slaves in Washington, D.C., but it did not end slavery there. It angered Northerners who wished to keep slavery out of the government domain by permitting slavery to move to the Southwest.

The End of Slavery. It now seemed to the sensitive North that slaveholders had turned the South into an armed camp. Southern leaders retorted that abolitionist agitation had forced them to end black education, meetings of slaves for religious services, and other traditions. The opening of Kansas to settlement began a border war that separated Free-Soilers and proslavery groups still farther. John Brown in Kansas became an extreme case of a Northerner determined to free the slaves by any means. The 1857 Dred Scott decision of the Supreme Court made it clear that slavery had a legal right to exist anywhere in the Union. The North, outraged, rallied to defend its way of life. The assault by John Brown and his men on Harpers Ferry in Virginia in 1859 was based on his naive faith that slaves would join him in a guerrilla war on their masters. The determination of Virginia authorities to hang Brown rather than treat him as insane persuaded Northerners that the South was guilt-ridden and insecure. The Civil War failed to produce slave uprisings, but slaves increasingly gave aid to Union troops. President Abraham Lincoln's Emancipation Proclamation (1863) was a war measure and did not free slaves in great number. Slavery was outlawed by the Thirteenth Amendment (1865).   —Louis Filler

SLIP LAW, a printed copy of Acts of Congress, separately published for distribution as soon as they are signed by the president. Slip laws are bound into the *Statutes at Large of the United States* after each session.   —*Mary L. Carns*

SMALL BUSINESS ADMINISTRATION (SBA). Set up in 1953 and expanded in 1958 to a permanent agency, the SBA is headed by an administrator named by the president. Through a network of field offices, the SBA provides the small business enterprise with low-cost loans and financial assistance, development planning, help in securing government contracts, and counseling services. SBA further aids victims of disasters, and minority-owned and managed enterprises. Most SBA loans are made in joint participation with a bank, and many through privately owned small-business investment companies.

SMALL CLAIMS COURT, a local court that has jurisdiction over cases where the amount in dispute is quite small. Generally, the limit would be below $500. A party need not be represented by an attorney and usually is not. Standard litigation procedures are drastically abbreviated, and the court clerk usually helps plaintiffs with their cases. The purpose of these courts is to reduce delay and expense as much as possible.

SMITH, ALFRED EMANUEL. *See* Presidential Elections: 1928.

SMITH ACT. *See* Alien Registration Act.

SMITHSONIAN INSTITUTION was established in 1846 under the terms of the will of James Smithson, of London, who bequeathed his fortune to the United States to found, at Washington, D.C., an establishment for the "increase and diffusion of knowledge among men." The institution is a federally chartered, nonprofit corporation. It is operated as a private institution, although it administers a number of government-funded programs.

The Smithsonian performs fundamental research; publishes the results of studies, explorations, and investigations; preserves for study and reference over 60 million items of scientific, cultural, and historical interest; and maintains exhibits representative of the arts, natural history, American history, technology, aeronautics and space exploration. The institute also participates in the international exchange of scholarly publications and engages in programs of education and national and international cooperative research and training. These and other programs and activities are carried out by the institution's many bureaus and museums.

The National Museum of Natural History serves as an international study center for the natural sciences.

The museum maintains a large reference collection and conducts a broad program of basic research on man, plants, animals, fossils, rocks, minerals, and materials from outer space. The National Zoological Park, a bureau of the institution, covers over 150 acres and contains about 3,000 living mammals, birds, and reptiles.

Other Activities. Also under the aegis of the institution are the Smithsonian Astrophysical Observatory in Cambridge, Mass.; the Smithsonian Tropical Research Institute; the National Air and Space Museum, which memorializes the development of the United States aviation and space flights; the Radiation Biology Laboratory; and the National Museum of History and Technology, which is the national museum of American cultural, civil, military, and scientific history. The institution has several other diverse activities: the National Armed Forces Museum Advisory Board, the Woodrow Wilson International Center for Scholars, and the Science Information Exchange.

Fine Arts. The Smithsonian is responsible for the National Collection of Fine Arts, which includes past and present arts of the United States; the Freer Gallery of Art, which houses a large collection of Near and Far Eastern art; the Hirshhorn Museum and Sculpture Garden, in which the emphasis is placed on twentieth-century art; and the Cooper-Hewitt Museum of Decorative Arts and Design, containing more than 85,000 decorative art items. The National Portrait Gallery, which collects and exhibits likenesses of persons who have made significant contributions to America's history, and the National Gallery of Art, which is responsible for assembling and maintaining a national collection of paintings, sculpture, and the graphic arts, are also bureaus of the Smithsonian Institution. The John F. Kennedy Center for the Performing Arts, formerly the National Cultural Center, was established as a bureau of the Institution in 1958 and is the only national memorial to the late President in the nation's capital area.

SMITH v. ALLWRIGHT, 321 U.S. 649 (1944), concerns an attempt by the State of Texas Democratic Convention in 1932 to disenfranchise blacks by adopting a resolution that all white citizens of the State of Texas shall be eligible for membership in the Democratic party and entitled to participate in the party's deliberations. It was maintained that because the Democratic party was private and not a governmental body, blacks were not denied the right to vote in the primary as a result of any state law or act of a state official. The Court said that although the privilege of membership in a political party may be of no concern to a state, when that privilege is also the essential qualification for voting in a primary to select nominees for a general election, the state had made the action of the party the action of the state. Such action is contrary to the provision of the Fifteenth Amendment forbidding the abridgement by a state of a citizen's right to vote.

See also United States v. Classic.

SOCIAL AND REHABILITATION SERVICE (SRS). *See* Human Development Services, Office of.

SOCIAL CONTRACT THEORY. *See* Consent, Popular.

SOCIAL INSURANCE, a legislative program that protects an individual and his/her dependents from unexpected loss of income due to sickness, injury, maternity, unemployment, old age, and death. A right of the working individual, social insurance is paid for by employer-employee contributions that are generally compulsory. Social insurance is often distinguished from public assistance, which is for the indigent and is funded from general tax revenues. The 1935 Social Security Act is the cornerstone of America's social insurance and public assistance policies.

Europe. The state's concern for the general security of its citizens evolved slowly in Europe after the Industrial Revolution. With dependence upon wages having replaced living off the land, loss of earning power through ill health, old age, or layoff could leave the laborer destitute. Workers polled their resources in mutual benefit societies, paying members unable to work and families of the deceased.

The hazards of industrial life were considerable, given the deplorable working conditions in factories and mines. England began setting working standards in 1802. Not until the 1880s was social insurance against these dangers assumed by a national government, when Germany passed the first sickness insurance law, a workmen's compensation law, and compulsory old-age and disability insurance. For years after, Germany and several central European neighbors were alone in compelling their citizens to be insured against calamity. Many other countries relied on subsidizing voluntary mutual benefit societies. A major shift in emphasis was taken by Great Britain in adopting compulsory health insurance in 1911. In that year Russia passed a sickness insurance law. In the 1920s Great Britain supplemented its old-age assistance law with compulsory contributory old-age and survivors insurance, and France introduced compulsory sickness, maternity, disability, old-age, and survivors insurance.

United States. Private interests and the states were well ahead of the federal government in providing social insurance. Trade unions gave members unemployment insurance, and industries offered private pension plans in the 1800s. The states adopted workmen's compensation laws from 1911, and some states provided general relief to the indigent. A growing public interest in health insurance was buried with entry into World War I, but demand for nationwide social legislation, particularly for the increasing number of elderly, continued to increase. Widespread unemployment following the 1929 stock market crash provided the push necessary to pass the Social Security Act of 1935. The Act and subsequent amendments provide old-age, survivors, and disability insurance; Medicare and Medicaid; unemployment provisions; and a variety of welfare services.

SOCIAL WELFARE: TOPIC GUIDE

Articles on SOCIAL WELFARE may be divided into two groups.

Federal Programs. The most important federal programs are administered by HEALTH AND HUMAN SERVICES, UNITED STATES DEPARTMENT OF. SOCIAL SECURITY, whose taxing provisions were upheld in STEWARD MACHINE COMPANY v. DAVIS, is the most comprehensive social welfare program and embraces MEDICARE and MEDICAID. Eligible military veterans receive benefits from the VETERANS ADMINISTRATION, an independent agency.

Federal legislation has established a POVERTY PROGRAM through such vehicles as the ECONOMIC OPPORTUNITY ACT, HEAD START, and the APPALACHIAN REGIONAL PROGRAM.

General Articles. The course of social welfare is described in WELFARE LEGISLATION. Some of its accomplishments include PUBLIC HOUSING and various types of SOCIAL INSURANCE, such as WORKMEN'S COMPENSATION. Other objectives are the DAY CARE CENTER and a GUARANTEED ANNUAL INCOME.

SOCIALISM, a doctrine advocating collective ownership and control of the means of economic production (that is, land, capital, property) and an equitable distribution of goods among all members of the community. Socialism's theoretical bases are found in the early nineteenth-century writings and activities of F.M.C. Fourier and Saint-Simon in France and Robert Owen in England. It developed as a reaction to the egoism, large accumulations of private property, and the general exploitation of workers that accompanied the development of capitalism in Europe.

Socialists have varied enormously in their views of the means and scope of socialism. Democratic socialism, or the view that socialism can evolve through democratic processes, has always dominated socialist movements in Western Europe. Although most socialists have been materialists, some have been devoutly Christian, insisting that only the common ownership of property and an equitable distribution of goods can produce the brotherhood demanded by Christianity. Karl Marx is undoubtedly the most widely known socialist. Marx and his followers view socialism as an inevitable outcome of historical processes. The transition from capitalism to socialism and finally to communism is to be effected by Communist party leaders who, acting as a dictatorship of the proletariat, are to seize power, overthrow Capitalist states, and lead all people to a community of mankind.

Regardless of differences, the theme of community and a common concern for all men unites socialists. Private property and, especially, capitalist economics are viewed as producing greed and dividing humanity. Socialism is expected to unite people and enable them to live in harmony and peace.   —*Robert F. Smith*

See also Capitalism; Collectivism; Democratic Socialism; Utopia.

SOCIALIST LABOR PARTY, a Marxist-oriented group founded in 1890. Present on every presidential ballot since 1892, the party's aim is to achieve, via the ballot, collective ownership and control of all industries and services. In 1899, a large portion of the membership, in disagreement with their leader, Daniel De Leon, withdrew to join the Socialist party.

See also Political Parties in the United States; Presidential Elections.

SOCIALIST PARTY, founded as the Socialist Democratic Party of America in 1898 by Eugene V. Debs and Victor Berger, was renamed the Socialist party in 1901. Debs, who had been president of the American Railway Union, was the Socialist presidential candidate in nearly every national election from 1900 to 1920, the year in which party influence peaked, with membership reaching 120,000 and Debs received nearly 900,000 votes.

In 1917 a Socialist meeting in St. Louis passed a resolution which called America's entry into the war a criminal act and suggested resistance to conscription and censorship. Debs, after giving an antiwar speech in Canton, Ohio, in 1919, was arrested and sentenced to ten years' imprisonment for violation of the Espionage Act. In 1920 he ran for president while in prison and made the best showing of his career, winning 920,000 votes. He was pardoned the next year by President Harding. After 1928, the party was led by Norman Thomas, who headed the national ticket from 1928 to 1948.

After its more radical members withdrew in 1919 to form the American Communist Party, the Socialists emphasized their role as reformers and called for the abolition of American capitalism by democratic means. Although Socialist programs were intended to attract the urban working classes, the party was strongest in Midwestern agrarian and Western mining regions. Party membership dwindled during the 1930s, and since the 1950s, the Socialists have adopted a policy of endorsing progressive and labor candidates of other parties.

See also Political Parties in the United States; Presidential Elections.

SOCIALIST WORKERS PARTY, a pro-Trotsky faction which was expelled from the American Communist party in 1928 and formally founded as a party in 1938. Marxist in outlook, the party is sympathetic with the "third world" self-liberation movements and with the causes of U.S. blacks and Chicanos. Its programs have called for an end to the Vietnam War, abortion on demand, and the abolition of "right to work" labor laws.

SOCIAL SECURITY. Spurred by the massive unemployment and poverty of the Depression, and confronted with the inability of state and local governments to provide assistance on a significant level, the federal government in the early 1930s began to provide financial assistance in several forms to the states to help them to help the people. As the focal point of public policy in this area shifted from the short-run alleviation of poverty to its long-run prevention, the federal government adopted the idea of broad-based compulsory insurance programs against income interruption from unemployment and old age, together with a public assistance (welfare) program for those remaining in need or not helped by these insurance programs. The major elements of the Social Security Act of 1935 follow.

The Act provides for a system of federal grants to the states to support their own programs of assistance to the needy on condition that the state programs comply with certain requirements spelled out in the Act. The administration of grants-in-aid to the states is supervised by the Social Security Administration (SSA), a division of the Department of Health and Human Services.

Programs. Welfare benefits, in the form of income payments and medical care, are provided for the needy aged, dependent children, the blind, and needy mothers and children.

The insurance programs set up in the Act were for old-age retirement pensions and unemployment compensation. The old-age retirement pension program, popularly but not quite correctly referred to as "Social Security" (it is only one part of the social security program), has been expanded in its benefit provisions to provide more than retirement benefits for the covered recipient. It now provides income benefits for the retiree's dependents, for his/her surviving dependents in the event of his death, benefits for disabled workers, and medical insurance benefits for the aged.

The unemployment compensation benefits are payable to covered eligible recipients through individual state programs. If these state programs meet certain federal standards, federal grants pay administrative expenses. The actual financing of benefits comes through payroll taxes levied by the state, most or all of which can be deducted by the employer from his federal payroll tax liability. In large part, the state unemployment compensation systems are financed by tax money that otherwise would have gone to the federal government.

These three programs, of course, are defined in great detail in the Social Security Act, which spells out the scope, eligibility, disqualification, and many other facets of each, as well as the relevant benefit and tax formulas. The present characteristics of the full social security program, though, largely reflect the numerous and substantial amendments that have been made to the original Act by subsequent legislation.

In recent years, recipients have received an automatic cost-of-living adjustment (COLA) to their benefits. The financial soundness of the old-age retirement pension program has been economically threatened by the dramatic and continuing increase in the number of people aged 65 and over and by COLA's in high inflation periods and politically threatened during periods of high budget deficits. In 1983 reforms were initiated to expand required contributions and to tax benefits of high-income retirees. The changes brought about a dramatic shift to a surplus in the Social Security Trust Fund. However, controversy continues over ever-increasing payroll deductions (7.65 percent in 1990), the regressive nature of the tax, and complaints that the trust fund is being used to meet current government expenses.

It is estimated that by 2020 there may be far more retirees (who are living longer periods after retirement) than workers available to fund the necessary payout to these retirees.

See also Welfare Legislation.

SOCIAL SECURITY CASES. *See* Steward Machine Co. v. Davis.

SOIL BANK, also called land retirement, a federal farm program authorized in 1956 in which farmers are encouraged to take some of their crop land out of production for up to ten years to reduce farm output and to improve the land by tree planting, water storage, and wildlife conservation. In return, the government pays the farmers rental for the retired land. Under the 1956 Soil Bank program, farmers were allowed to retire entire farms; however, farm suppliers protested the resulting loss of business, and Congress ended the retirement of entire farms. By 1960, 28.6 million acres had been retired. Land retirement programs are administered by the Agricultural Stabilization and Conservation Service of the Department of Agriculture.

Under more recent land retirement legislation, such as the Agricultural Act of 1970, which authorized land retirement for 1971-1973, a $10 million annual limit was set for each program. However, by the end of the 1970s the pressures of inflation and the desire to address world food shortages forced major portions of the program to be dropped.

SOIL CONSERVATION SERVICE, established in 1935 in the Department of Agriculture as part of the Depression agricultural programs designed to save farmlands and topsoil from flood, drought, and improper cultivation. SCS offers technical assistance through the 3,000 soil conservation districts. Implementation lies mainly in the hands of local bodies or individual farmers. Along with other agencies, SCS participates in the National Cooperative Soil Survey for planning purposes, as well as river-basin surveys, watershed activities, flood-prevention measures, and programs to assist owners to develop recreational facilities on the land (a major new source of rural income). SCS frequently overlaps functions with the Water and Power Resources Service, the Army Corps of Engineers, or new environmental agencies.

SOLID SOUTH, term used to describe the Democratic bloc voting of the Southern states in local, state, and federal elections. Southern allegiance to the Democratic party dates from the influence of Thomas Jefferson of Virginia, who founded the forerunner of the present party. After the Civil War the Democrats became an all-white party and demonstrated party solidarity from Reconstruction to the Eisenhower era. After court decisions prohibited racial restrictions, enfranchised blacks joined the Democratic party in large numbers, making the South virtually a one-party area.

With the candidacy of Dwight D. Eisenhower, however, Republicans began to make significant inroads. The demise of the Solid South has become more apparent with each succeeding election.

See also Democratic Party.

SOUTER, DAVID HACKETT (1939-   ), associate justice of the Supreme Court (1990-   ). Born in Massachusetts, he graduated from Harvard College and Harvard Law School. After private law practice in New Hampshire, he held several state positions, eventually rising to state supreme court justice in 1983. In 1990, President Bush named him to the U.S. Court of Appeals and then to the Supreme Court, replacing justice William Brennan.

SOUTH CAROLINA v. KATZENBACH, 383 U.S. 301 (1966), concerns voting discrimination in the South. The Voting Rights Act of 1965 abolished literacy tests and poll taxes and enlisted the aid of federal examiners and poll watchers to see that all eligible citizens were permitted to vote in all elections, state as well as federal. South Carolina, which had a literacy test, filed a bill of complaint seeking a declaration that selected provisions of the Voting Rights Act violated the Constitution, and an injunction against enforcement by the attorney general. The Court, in an opinion delivered by Chief Justice Warren, denied South Carolina's request and ruled that Congress, exercising its authority under the Fifteenth Amendment, had validly acted to banish racial discrimination in voting.

See also United States v. Classic.

SOUTHEAST ASIA TREATY ORGANIZATION (SEATO).
Formed in 1955 at the initiative of United States Secretary of State John Foster Dulles, SEATO was designed to fill the vacuum caused by the evacuation of Indochina by the French in 1954. SEATO's members were Australia, France, New Zealand, Pakistan, the Philippines, Thailand, the United Kingdom, and the United States.

By a protocol to the treaty, SEATO extended its protection to Laos, Cambodia, and South Vietnam. The United States also stipulated that it regarded its obligation under the treaty as covering only Communist aggression. Some states in the area, especially India, criticized the pact as bringing the Cold War into a part of the world which ought to remain neutral. Because of a declining effectiveness, the SEATO members voted to dissolve the alliance in 1975.

SOUTHERN CHRISTIAN LEADERSHIP CONFERENCE (SCLC),
founded in Atlanta, Ga., in 1957 by Rev. Martin Luther King, Jr., following the success of the Montgomery, Ala., bus boycott, which he had led. King's goal was the achievement of full civil rights for blacks by direct nonviolent protest and action.

The group initiated a comprehensive campaign of sit-ins, picketing, boycotts, voter registration rallies and marches throughout the South, including the famous confrontations in Birmingham, Ala., in April and May 1963. With the growing militancy of black demands and tactics in the late 1960s and King's assassination, SCLC's national strength was considerably eclipsed, though it continues to exert local influence in Southern areas.

SPEAKER OF THE HOUSE,
the presiding officer of the House of Representatives. The Speaker, always a member of the majority party, is elected by the House at the beginning of each new Congress and is traditionally reelected in succeeding Congresses if the same party is in power. Although a reform of House rules in 1911 removed from the Speaker the authority to appoint the standing committees, the position is potentially one of immense power. As presiding officer, the Speaker is empowered to recognize legislators in floor debate and may choose not to recognize a particular individual or may rule someone out of order. The Speaker's decision on points of order is inevitably final. He may join discussion on a particular measure and may vote. A major power is the referral of bills to committee. He is mandated to appoint select and conference committees and to sign documents on behalf of the House. Upon the death or disability of the president and vice president, the Speaker assumes the presidency until the next election.

In the history of the House, two Speakers have been notable in their control of the deliberations of that body. Joseph Cannon wielded tremendous power from 1903 to 1911, and his dictatorial methods were the impetus for the 1911 reforms. Sam Rayburn held the office longer than any of his predecessors and was instrumental in the policy decisions of the administrations of Franklin Roosevelt, Harry Truman, and John Kennedy.

SPEECH, FREEDOM OF.
See Freedom of Speech and Press.

SPEEDY TRIAL ACT (1974),
legislative enactment designed to reduce the waiting period for trials in federal courts. Despite the Sixth Amendment guarantee of a "speedy trial," overburdened court dockets had resulted in numerous trial delays. Defendants who could not afford bail frequently spent lengthy periods of time in detention while awaiting trial. The complicated Speedy Trial Act provided that by 1980 the period between arrest and trial could not exceed 100 days. Charges must be dismissed if the deadline is not met. However, the law provides for a number of exceptions to the time limit and under certain circumstances (if the charges are dismissed "without prejudice") the charges may even be filed again.

—*Mary L. Carns*

See also Bail System.

SPLIT TICKET,
the practice of voting for candidates of different parties. For example, a voter splits his ticket if he votes for the Democratic presidential candidate and the Republican senatorial candidate. As party loyalties weaken, split-ticket voting becomes more prevalent.

SPOILS SYSTEM.
When President Washington made his initial appointments to the federal service, he followed the principle of choosing the best qualified person for each job, but by the end of his administration most of the appointees were Federalists. The new President Jefferson determined to appoint enough Democratic-Republicans to achieve a balance between the two groups, a goal he achieved about 1803. The problem of national party patronage disappeared for a generation, to be revived by Jackson when he became president in 1829. He dismissed about 10 percent of the 10,000 government employees. His enemies charged him with introducing a "spoils system," although Jackson preferred to call it "rotation in office."

The Pendleton Act of 1883, which established the United States Civil Service Commission, and the OPM and Merit System Protection Board created by the Civil Service Reform Act (1978) are based on the doctrine of party neutrality. Today some 80 percent of all federal employees come under the rules of the Commission.

See also Civil Service, Merit System Protection Board.

SQUATTER   SOVEREIGNTY. *See* Popular Sovereignty.

STANDING *or* STANDING TO SUE, a doctrine of the federal courts to the effect that because the federal judicial power is limited to "cases and controversies" (Constitution, Article 1, Section 2), a complaint of unlawful or unconstitutional government conduct is justiciable only when a substantive right of the plaintiff has been violated. Federal courts will not entertain suits complaining of governmental misfeasance in the abstract.
See also Frothingham v. Mellon; United States v. Butler.

STANDING COMMITTEES, also known as permanent committees, the specialized groups in both Senate and House that do the groundwork on legislative matters for consideration of the parent bodies. The standing committees (16 in the Senate and 22 in the House) screen the thousands of bills and resolutions proposed by members of Congress. In committee a bill can be altered, amended, or disposed of. Often it is assigned to a subcommittee of the standing committee for more detailed work and analysis. The subcommittee reports its findings to the standing committee, which then decides where the bill should go.
The size of a standing committee is determined by its house. The committee's ratio of majority to minority party members depends roughly on the house's ratio. Seniority is well established in the system. Within a party, committeemen advance in rank according to length of continuous service. The top ranking member becomes chairman when his party is in the majority.
See also Committee System of Congress.

STANDING VOTE *or* DIVISION, in the House of Representatives, a method of voting on a particular measure under which the legislators are divided into two groups, one voting for the measure, and one voting against. Each group stands to be counted in a body, those voting for the measure being tallied first. The standing vote is administered by the Speaker of the House following an indecisive voice vote or on demand of one-fifth of the legislators present.

STANLEY v. GEORGIA, 394 U.S. 557 (1969), concerns the private possession of obscene matter. Federal and state agents, while searching Stanley's home for evidence of bookmaking activities, found three reels of film which were found to be obscene. On the basis of the films, Stanley was tried and convicted of knowingly having possession of obscene matter in violation of Georgia law. The Court held that the First and Fourteenth Amendments prohibit making mere private possession of obscene material a crime. The Court also stated that although a state has the broad power to regulate obscenity, the power does not extend to mere possession by the individual in the privacy of his own home.

STAR WARS. *See* Strategic Defense Initiative.

STARE DECISIS (Lat., to adhere to decided cases), the common-law doctrine that once a case has been decided, subsequent cases with similar facts should receive similar decisions. If decided by a higher court of the same jurisdiction, the "precedent" case is binding on the court deciding the subsequent case. The doctrine of *stare decisis* has been fundamental to the development of the common law. However, U.S. courts will occasionally break with precedent by finding that earlier courts were "in error" in their interpretations or judgments. A notable example is the 1954 decision of *Brown v. Board of Education of Topeka,* which rejected the doctrine of "separate but equal" that had been established in the 1896 *Plessy v. Ferguson* decision.
See also Judicial Activism.

START. *See* Disarmament.

STATE, U.S. DEPARTMENT OF, a cabinet department that advises the president on creation and implementation of foreign policy.
History. The department, the oldest in the executive branch, was established during the first administration of George Washington, under the secretaryship of Thomas Jefferson. Its antecedents, however, date from the Continental Congress, which executed the foreign policy of the United States both during the Revolution and under the Articles of Confederation until 1781. A separate Department of Foreign Affairs set up at that time was succeeded by the newly named Department of State in 1789. Although the earlier versions dealt also with certain domestic concerns, including the census, patents, and territorial affairs, the department's current responsibilities are exclusively in foreign policy.
Organization. The department is organized under a Secretary of State appointed by the president with the advice and consent of the Senate. The secretary is assisted by a deputy secretary, who is second in overall command, and an under secretary for political affairs. With the exception of the Arms Control and Disarmament Agency (a separate agency) and the Peace Corps, both of which report directly to the secretary, all other divisions come under the initial purview of the under secretary for political affairs. These departments include economic affairs, protocol, press relations, international scientific and technological affairs, intelligence, educational and cultural affairs,

and the subdivisions for African, European, East Asian, and Inter-American affairs, among others.

Functions. In addition to its advisory and policy-making functions, the State Department acts as the nation's spokesman in the U.N. and some 56 major international organizations and five hundred annual international conferences in which the United States participates. The department negotiates treaties and agreements with foreign countries. It is aided in these tasks by the National Security Council, which advises on matters of national defense.

Although many state departments remain anonymous executors of presidentially inspired policy, some secretaries, like Thomas Jefferson, John Hay, Elihu Root, Cordell Hull, John Foster Dulles, Dean Rusk, and Henry Kissinger, have stamped that policy with their own unique outlook. Nevertheless, although the makeup of the department varies with each changing administration, sudden radical policy changes have been few, and there has been a fairly general policy continuum from the department's beginnings to the present.

STATE OF THE UNION MESSAGE, annual presidential address to Congress, in compliance with the constitutional requirement that the president keep Congress informed about the state of the union. Generally given before the start of a new legislative session, the message may deal with a broad spectrum of problems, but it usually emphasizes the president's forthcoming legislative program. The address' significance lies in underscoring the president's initiative in the arena of legislative action. The leaders of Congress await the president's address in expectation of subsequent specific legislative proposals drawn up by the executive branch. Commonly delivered in person before a joint session of the Senate and the House, the speech gives the chief executive an opportunity to use his personal influence to sway Congress and the nation in favor of his program. The address is another means by which the president can assert his pivotal role in governing the nation.

STATE SOVEREIGNTY. *See* Federalism; States' Rights.

STATES' RIGHTS. As stated in the Tenth Amendment, "powers not delegated to the United States by the Constitution, nor prohibited by it to the States, are reserved to the States respectively, or to the people." In Article 1, Section 8, however, the framers recognized the need for flexibility. This so-called elastic clause granted the national government the power to enact legislation "necessary and proper for carrying into Execution the foregoing Powers." The ensuing battle between what is appropriately a concern of the states alone and what is a proper topic of federal legislation is a key theme of American history.

CHRONOLOGY OF THE STATES

State	Order of Admission to Union	Organized as Territory	Admitted to Union
Delaware	1	....	Dec. 7, 1787
Pennsylvania	2	....	Dec. 12, 1787
New Jersey	3	....	Dec. 18, 1787
Georgia	4	....	Jan. 2, 1788
Connecticut	5	....	Jan. 9, 1788
Massachusetts	6	....	Feb. 6, 1788
Maryland	7	....	April 28, 1788
South Carolina	8	....	May 23, 1788
New Hampshire	9	....	June 21, 1788
Virginia	10	....	June 25, 1788
New York	11	....	July 26, 1788
North Carolina	12	....	Nov. 21, 1789
Rhode Island	13	....	May 29, 1790
Vermont	14	....	March 4, 1791
Kentucky	15	....	June 1, 1792
Tennessee	16	....	June 1, 1796
Ohio	17	....	March 1, 1803
Louisiana	18	March 24, 1804	April 30, 1812
Indiana	19	May 7, 1800	Dec. 11, 1816
Mississippi	20	April 17, 1798	Dec. 10, 1817
Illinois	21	Feb. 3, 1809	Dec. 3, 1818
Alabama	22	March 3, 1817	Dec. 14, 1819
Maine	23	....	March 15, 1820
Missouri	24	June 4, 1812	Aug. 10, 1821
Arkansas	25	March 2, 1819	June 15, 1836
Michigan	26	Jan. 11, 1805	Jan. 26, 1837
Florida	27	March 30, 1822	March 3, 1845
Texas	28	....	Dec. 29, 1845
Iowa	29	June 12, 1838	Dec. 28, 1846
Wisconsin	30	April 20, 1836	May 29, 1848
California	31	....	Sept. 9, 1850
Minnesota	32	March 3, 1849	May 11, 1858
Oregon	33	Aug. 14, 1848	Feb. 14, 1859
Kansas	34	May 30, 1854	Jan. 29, 1861
West Virginia	35	....	June 20, 1863
Nevada	36	March 2, 1861	Oct. 31, 1864
Nebraska	37	May 30, 1854	March 1, 1867
Colorado	38	Feb. 28, 1861	Aug. 1, 1876
North Dakota	39	March 2, 1861	Nov. 2, 1889
South Dakota	40	March 2, 1861	Nov. 2, 1889
Montana	41	May 26, 1864	Nov. 8, 1889
Washington	42	March 2, 1853	Nov. 11, 1889
Idaho	43	March 3, 1863	July 3, 1890
Wyoming	44	July 25, 1868	July 10, 1890
Utah	45	Sept. 9, 1850	Jan. 4, 1896
Oklahoma	46	May 2, 1890	Nov. 16, 1907
New Mexico	47	Sept. 9, 1850	Jan. 6, 1912
Arizona	48	Feb. 24, 1863	Feb. 14, 1912
Alaska	49	Aug. 24, 1912	Jan. 3, 1959
Hawaii	50	June 14, 1900	Aug. 21, 1959

The argument favoring states' rights over federal power has been applied inconsistently, with advocates turning it to their advantage in relation to issues such as slavery, taxation, aid to education, busing, regulation of hours and wages, grants-in-aid, legal counsel, court jurisdiction, and reapportionment. The great centralist theorists were Alexander Hamilton, James Madison, Daniel Webster, and Chief Justice John Marshall, while the leading states' rights theorists included Robert Hayne and John C. Calhoun.

Most key decisions limiting states' rights have been justified by the "due process" clause of the Fourteenth Amendment. Although modern moves toward decentralization ("new federalism") may give new meaning to states' rights, most major legislation of the twentieth century has favored federal power.

See also Federalism; McCulloch v. Maryland; National Supremacy; Nullification.

STATES' RIGHTS PARTY *or* DIXIECRATS, a states' rights party organized by dissident Democrats in 1948. Angered by the passage at the Democratic National Convention of a civil rights plank, the Southerners convened a States' Rights Democratic Convention in Birmingham, Alabama, on July 17. Amidst the waving of Confederate flags and bitter denunciations of Truman, Governor J. Strom Thurmond of South Carolina was nominated for president.

The Dixiecrats soon found themselves at odds with loyal Democratic regulars over the choice of presidential electors in the Southern states. Although the States' Rights supporters hoped to prove that the loss of the South would cost Truman the election, Thurmond carried only four Southern states—South Carolina, Alabama, Mississippi, and Louisiana—for a total of 39 electoral votes, and 1,168,000 popular votes.

In the North, the movement benefited Truman and contributed to the subsequent enactment of his "Fair Deal" program, which included federal anti-lynching laws, the abolition of poll taxes, and the establishment of the Fair Employment Practices Commission.

See also Political Parties in the United States; Presidential Elections.

STATUS OF WOMEN, CITIZEN'S ADVISORY COUNCIL ON THE, a private advisory group empowered by executive order in 1963 to initiate programs to improve the economic and social status of women and to evaluate and report on progress in this area. The council works with the Interdepartmental Committee on the Status of Women to coordinate governmental and private action.

See also Woman Suffrage; Women's Liberation Movement.

STATUTE, a written law passed by a legislature. *See* Bill; Private Bill; Public Bill; Statutes at Large of the United States; Statutory Law; United States Code.

STATUTE OF LIMITATIONS, a term applied to numerous statutes that set a limit on the length of time that may elapse between an event giving rise to a course of action and the commencement of a suit to enforce that course. Such a statute might provide, for example, that an action for damages for breach of contract be instituted within two years of the breach. The purpose is to settle an individual's affairs so that they are not forever subject to doubt.

STATUTES AT LARGE OF THE UNITED STATES, the annual publication containing all acts and resolutions passed during the preceding session of Con-

gress. It is published in two volumes: one contains public acts and joint resolutions; the second contains private acts and joint resolutions, concurrent resolutions, treaties, proposed constitutional amendments, and presidential proclamations. Entries since 1951 have been arranged according to Public Law number.

—*Mary L. Carns*

See also United States Code.

STATUTORY LAW, written law enacted by legislative bodies. It may be contrasted with other forms of law such as common law, which was essentially unwritten, or "judge-made" law based strongly on precedent. The two are closely related in the United States and England, in that statutory law has borrowed heavily from the common law, resulting in what many see as a "mixed" system.

—*Mary L. Carns*

STEERING COMMITTEE, a special, House, party committee primarily concerned with decisions on party strategy. Unlike the Senate's policy committees, steering committees are informal bodies, which have been criticized for not bringing about more accountability in fulfilling pledges in the national party platforms. In organization the House Republican Policy Committee functions as an advisory body to the party leadership; the Democratic body functions as an executive committee of the party caucus.

See also Committee System of Congress.

STEVENS, JOHN PAUL (1920-   ), associate justice of the Supreme Court (1975-   ). Born in Chicago, he received his law degree from Northwestern University Law School in 1947 and served as law clerk (1947-1948) to Supreme Court Justice Wiley Rutledge. A prominent antitrust lawyer, he sat on various federal committees and taught law at Northwestern until he was appointed by President Richard M. Nixon in 1970 to the U.S. Court of Appeals. Nominated by President Gerald Ford for the Supreme Court in 1975, he was a judicial centrist who wrote well-crafted scholarly opinions. He favored the use of capital punishment on a case-by-case basis (*Jurek v. Texas*, 1976) and wrote the majority opinion in (*Roberts v. Louisiana* 1976), which ruled out the death penalty as mandatory for certain classes of crimes. He was against immunity from prosecution for federal officials performing their duties (*Butz v. Economou*, 1978) and the use of federal funds to finance minority business programs (*Fulilove v. Klutznick*, 1980).

STEVENSON, ADLAI (1900-1965), political leader who came to national prominence when he ran as the Democratic presidential candidate in 1952 and 1956. Stevenson came from a politically active family. His grandfather served as vice president under Grover Cleveland (1893-1897), while his father was a promi-

CHIEF JUSTICES AND IMPORTANT SUPREME COURT CASES

Separate articles on important cases will be found in this volume. In addition, the reader will find the cases organized by topic in the table accompanying the article on Constitutional Law.

John Jay (1745–1829)
New York
Appointed by G. Washington
Served 1790–95
Chisholm v. Georgia (1793)

John Rutledge (1739–1800)
South Carolina
Appointed by G. Washington in
    1795; appointment not confirmed
    by Senate.

Oliver Ellsworth (1745–1807)
Connecticut
Appointed by G. Washington
Served 1796–1800

John Marshall (1755–1835)
Virginia
Appointed by J. Adams
Served 1801–35
Barron v. Baltimore (1833)
Cohens v. Virginia (1821)
Dartmouth College v. Woodward
    (1819)
Fletcher v. Peck (1810)
Gibbons v. Ogden (1824)
McCulloch v. Maryland (1819)
Marbury v. Madison (1803)

Roger Brooke Taney (1777–1864)
Maryland
Appointed by A. Jackson
Served 1836–64
Dred Scott v. Sandford (1857)
Genessee Chief, the (1852)
Luther v. Borden (1849)

Salmon Portland Chase (1808–73)
Ohio
Appointed by A. Lincoln
Served 1864–73
Collector v. Day (1871)
Ex parte McCardle (1869)
Ex parte Milligan (1866)
Slaughter House Cases (1873)

Morrison Remick Waite (1816–88)
Ohio

Appointed by U.S. Grant
Served 1874–88
Civil Rights Cases (1883)
Hurtado v. California (1884)

Melville Weston Fuller (1833–1910)
Illinois
Appointed by G. Cleveland
Served 1888–1910
In re Neagle (1890)
Lochner v. New York (1905)
Plessy v. Ferguson (1896)
Pollock v. Farmers' Loan and Trust
    Co. (1895)
U.S. v. E.C. Knight Co. (1895)
U.S. v. Wong Kim Ark (1898)

**Edward Douglass White
(1845–1921)**
Louisiana
Appointed by W.H. Taft
Served 1910–21
Abrams v. U.S. (1919)
Buchanan v. Warley (1917)
Guinn v. U.S. (1915)
Hammer v. Dagenhart (1918)
Missouri v. Holland (1920)
Newberry v. U.S. (1921)
Schenck v. U.S. (1919)
Weeks v. U.S. (1914)

William Howard Taft (1857–1930)
Connecticut
Appointed by W.G. Harding
Served 1921–30
Adkins v. Children's Hospital (1923)
Corrigan v. Buckley (1926)
Frothingham v. Mellon (1923)
Gitlow v. New York (1925)
Griswold v. Connecticut (1965)
Myers v. U.S. (1926)
Nixon v. Herndon (1927)
Olmstead v. U.S. (1928)
U.S. v. Lanza (1922)
Whitney v. California (1927)

Charles Evans Hughes (1862–1948)
New York

Appointed by H. Hoover
Served 1930–41
Ashwander v. T.V.A. (1936)
Herndon v. Lowry (1937)
Horne Building and Loan Association
    v. Blaisdell (1934)
Humphrey's Executor v. U.S. (1935)
Minersville School District v. Gobitis
    (1940)
Nardone v. U.S. (1937 and 1939)
National Labor Relations Board v.
    Jones & Laughlin Steel Corp.
    (1937)
Near v. Minnesota (1931)
Nebbia v. New York (1934)
Nixon v. Condon (1932)
Palko v. Connecticut (1937)
Powell v. Alabama (1932)
Schecter Poultry Corp. v. U.S. (1935)
Steward Machine Co. v. Davis (1937)
Thornhill v. Alabama (1940)
U.S. v. Butler (1936)
U.S. v. Classic (1941)
U.S. v. Curtiss-Wright Corp. (1936)
U.S. v. Darby Lumber Co. (1941)
West Coast Hotel Co. v. Parrish
    (1937)

Harlan Fiske Stone (1872–1946)
New York
Appointed by F.D. Roosevelt
Served 1941–46
Betts v. Brady (1942)
Colegrove v. Green (1946)
Corn Products Co. v. F.T.C. (1945)
Girouard v. U.S. (1946)
Hirabayashi v. U.S. (1943)
Jehovah's Witnesses Cases (1943)
Korematsu v. U.S. (1944)
Screws v. U.S. (1945)
Smith v. Allwright (1944)
Wickard v. Filburn (1942)

Fred Moore Vinson (1890–1953)
Kentucky
Appointed by H.S. Truman
Served 1946–53

(continued on next page)

nent newspaper executive. A graduate of Northwestern University's law school (1926), he began his legal practice in Chicago, but it was often interrupted by periods of public service. During and after World War II he held several government positions.

In 1948 he was elected governor of Illinois, a post in which he distinguished himself with far-reaching legal and administrative reforms. Although reluctant to run

against Republican Dwight D. Eisenhower, Stevenson accepted the Democratic presidential nomination in 1952. He waged a strong and intelligent, although unsuccessful, campaign. In 1956, Stevenson agreed to run again and was soundly defeated a second time. In 1961, when the Democrats returned to power, Stevenson was appointed ambassador to the United Nations, a position he held until his death.

CHIEF JUSTICES AND IMPORTANT SUPREME COURT CASES (Continued)

Dennis v. U.S. (1951)
Everson v. Board of Education (1947)
Feiner v. New York (1951)
Illinois ex rel McCollum v. Board of
Education (1948)
Kunz v. New York (1951)
Shelley v. Kraemer (1948)
Sweatt v. Painter (1950)
Terminiello v. Chicago (1949)
Youngstown Sheet and Tube Co.
v. Sawyer (1952)
Zorach v. Clauson (1952)

Earl Warren (1891–1974)
California
Appointed by D.D. Eisenhower
Served 1953–69
Abington School District v. Schempp
(1963)
Adderly v. Florida (1966)
Afroyim v. Rusk (1967)
Aguilar v. Texas (1964)
Albertson v. Subversive Activities
Control Board (1965)
Aptheker v. Secretary of State (1964)
Arizona v. California (1963)
Baker v. Carr (1962)
Bantam Books, Inc. v. Sullivan (1963)
Barenblatt v. U.S. (1959)
Bartkus v. Illinois (1959)
Bates v. City of Little Rock (1960)
Benton v. Maryland (1969)
Berger v. State of New York (1967)
Board of Education v. Allen (1968)
Bolling v. Sharpe (1954)
Brandenburg v. Ohio (1969)
Brown v. Board of Education of
Topeka (1954)
Brown v. Board of Education (1955)
Communist Party v. Subversive
Activities Control Board (1961)
Edwards v. South Carolina (1963)
Elfbrandt v. Russell (1966)
Elkins v. U.S. (1960)
Engel v. Vitale (1962)
Escobedo v. Illinois (1964)
Federal Trade Commission v. Colgate-
Palmolive Co. (1965)
Flast v. Cohen (1968)
Freedman v. Maryland (1965)
Garrison v. Louisiana (1964)

Gideon v. Wainwright (1963)
Ginsberg v. New York (1968)
Ginsburg v. U.S. (1966)
Gomillion v. Lightfoot: The Tuskegee
Gerrymander Case (1960)
Harper v. Virginia Board of Elections
(1966)
Heart of Atlanta Motel v. U.S. (1964)
In re Gault (1967)
Jones v. Mayer (1968)
Katzenbach v. McClung (1964)
Katzenbach v. Morgan (1966)
Katz v. United States (1967)
Kent v. Dulles (1958)
Keyishian v. Board of Regents (1967)
Kingsley Pictures Corp. v. Regents
(1959)
Klopfer v. North Carolina (1967)
Lamont v. Postmaster General (1965)
McGowan v. Maryland (1961)
Mallory v. Hogan (1964)
Mapp v. Ohio (1961)
Miranda v. Arizona (1966)
Murray v. Curlett (1963)
National Association for the
Advancement of Colored People
v. Alabama (1958)
National Association for the
Advancement of Colored People
v. Button (1963)
Nelson v. Los Angeles (1960)
New York Times v. Sullivan (1964)
Pennsylvania v. Nelson (1956)
Pointer v. Texas (1965)
Radovitch v. National Football
League (1957)
Reitman v. Mulkey (1967)
Reynolds v. Sims (1964)
Robinson v. Florida (1964)
Roth v. U.S. (1957)
Scales v. U.S. (1961)
Schneider v. Rusk (1964)
South Carolina v. Katzenbach (1966)
Stanley v. Georgia (1968)
Sweezy v. New Hampshire (1957)
Tinker v. Des Moines Independent
Community School District (1969)
Torasco v. Watson (1961)
Trop v. Dulles (1958)
Ullman v. U.S. (1956)
U.S. v. Guest (1966)

U.S. v. O'Brien (1968)
U.S. v. Seeger (1965)
Watkins v. U.S. (1957)
Wells v. Rockefeller (1969)
Wesbury v. Sanders (1964)
Whitehill v. Elkins (1967)
Yates v. United States (1957)
Zemel v. Rusk (1965)

Warren Earl Burger (1907–)
Minnesota
Appointed by R.M. Nixon
Served 1969–86
Alexander v. Holmes County Board
of Education (1969)
Buckley v. Valeo (1976)
Federenko v. U.S. (1981)
Furman v. Georgia (1972)
Grove City College v. Bell (1984)
Harris v. McRae (1980)
Harris v. New York (1971)
Immigration and Naturalization
Service v. Chadha (1983)
Miller v. California (1973)
National League of Cities v. Usery
(1976)
Regents of University of California
v. Bakke (1978)
Roe v. Wade (1973)
San Antonio Independent School
District v. Rodriguez (1973)
U.S. v. Nixon (1974)
United Steelworkers of America
v. Weber (1979)
Vance v. Terrazas (1980)

William Rehnquist (1924–)
Appointed by R.W. Reagan
Served 1986–
Arizona v. Youngblood (1988)
City of Richmond v. J.A. Croson
Company (1989)
Edwards v. Aguillard (1987)
Hazelwood School District
v. Kuhlmeier (1988)
Martin v. Wilks (1989)
Skinner v. Railway Executive
Association (1989)
Texas v. Johnson (1989)
Webster v. Reproductive Health
Services (1989)

STEWARD MACHINE CO. v. DAVIS, 301 U.S. 548 (1937), concerns the validity of the tax imposed on employers by the Social Security Act. The company paid a tax of $48.14 in accordance with the statute and sued to recover payment. The Act included tax on employers but provided that if a state had an unemployment scheme acceptable to the federal government and to which the employer contributed, he was entitled to up to 90 percent credit against the federal tax for amounts paid to the state. The company contended that this tax and credit combination was a weapon to coerce the states, destroying and impairing the reserved powers given to them by the Tenth Amendment. The Court, in a 5-to-4 decision delivered by Mr. Justice Cardozo, held that this tax was not a coercion of the state, but a valid exercise of taxing power, as it provided state unemployment compensation and served to aid the general national welfare. The dissenters protested that under the Act money was spent for purposes which lay outside the range of federally delegated power.

See also United States v. Butler.

STONE, HARLAN FISKE (1872-1945), 11th Chief Justice of the Supreme Court, born in Chesterfield, N.H. A teacher at Columbia Law School, he was appointed attorney general in 1924 by President Coolidge. In 1925 he became an associate justice of the Supreme Court. One of his more famous dissents (1935) involved the constitutionality of the first Agricultural Adjustment Act of the New Deal. In 1941 President Roosevelt, ignoring partisan politics and Stone's basically Republican philosophy, selected him to succeed Charles Evans Hughes as chief justice.

See also Supreme Court of the United States.

STOP AND FRISK PROVISION. *See* Search and Seizure.

STRAIGHT TICKET, the practice among some voters of voting for all the candidates of a single party. In the voting booth it is possible on some machines for the voter to vote a straight ticket by pulling a single lever.

STRATEGIC ARMS LIMITATIONS TALKS (SALT), discussions between the United States and the U.S.S.R. to stabilize the nuclear arms competition between the two countries. These discussions were initially proposed in 1964 by President Lyndon Johnson. With the continuation of the buildup of antiballistic missile systems (ABM) and intercontinental ballistic missile systems (ICBM), the United States again approached the U.S.S.R. on discussions to limit ABMs in 1966 and 1967. In 1967 Premier Kosygin agreed to discussions covering offensive and defensive missile systems, and in 1968 he announced that the U.S.S.R. was ready for an "exchange of opinion" on offensive and defensive missile systems.

By this time both countries were engaged in developing a complex and costly new system—multiple independently targeted reentry vehicle (MIRVs)—and appeared anxious for talks to begin. Preliminary talks began in 1969 in Helsinki, Finland, with agreement on the topics of discussion. Negotiations resumed in 1970 and then were held alternately in Vienna and Helsinki. An agreement was signed by both nations during President Nixon's May 1972 visit to Moscow, limiting ABM installations to 200 and freezing the number of offensive missile sites on land and sea; surveillance satellites will provide inspection. The ABM agreement was in treaty form, and the offensive missile accord was an interim agreement.

A second series of talks (SALT II) concluded in 1979 when a new agreement was signed by President Carter and Leonid Brezhnev. However, Senate critics charged the agreement benefited the Soviets, and debate was suspended following the Soviet invasion of Afghanistan (1980). Although SALT II was never ratified, both powers agreed to abide by the arms limits set in the agreement. Discussions were resumed following Reagan's reelection and led to signing of the Intermediate-Range Nuclear Forces Treaty (INF) in 1988. Reforms under Gorbachev made additional arms agreements more likely.

See also Atomic Weapons, Control of; Intermediate-Range Nuclear Forces; Strategic Defense Initiative.

STRATEGIC DEFENSE INITIATIVE (SDI), proposal for a national defense system first announced by President Reagan in March 1983. SDI, more commonly known as Star Wars, was described as a ballistic missile defense (BMD) system to protect the United States from incoming enemy missiles. The term "Star Wars" was adopted because SDI depended on high technology weapons such as lasers, and other still-to-be-developed technology.

Critics of the program were numerous. Some complained that the costs of research would exceed $25 billion and offered no guarantee of success. Still others felt that SDI would only compel the Soviets to develop comparable technology and thus escalate the arms race. Democrats in Congress felt SDI research might violate the 1972 Anti-Ballistic Missile treaty (ABM), which prohibited development and testing of ABM systems.

During the December 1987 Reagan-Gorbachev summit, this issue was the subject of extensive debate, with the Soviet leader warning that SDI could endanger general progress on arms control. However, no decisions on SDI were reached, and the issue continued to divide the superpowers as they proceeded with other arms negotiations. Congress provided $4.1 billion in funding for fiscal 1989 but was considering more modest funding for 1990.

STRICT CONSTRUCTION. *See* Constitutional Construction; Supreme Court of the United States.

STRIKE, an interruption of work, provoked by the employees, to bring about improvements in pay and conditions of work or to protest action by the management. A strike is distinguished from a lockout, which is a suspension of work ordered by the management. Initially, the strike was defense against management; later uses involved noneconomic objectives.

Violence may be a consequence of strikes when the management hires outside workers as strikebreakers or when there is a crossing of the picket line. The outcome of a strike is often a question of endurance; a strike frequently ends by compromise. In the United

States, several laws, like the Wagner and the Taft-Hartley Labor Acts, regulate the right to strike.

See also Labor Movement in the United States.

STUDENT NONVIOLENT COORDINATING COMMITTEE (SNCC), founded in 1960 to promote direct nonviolent action to end segregation. With adherents on many college campuses, the group reached national prominence in 1964 when some 500 volunteers traveled through Mississippi to register black voters and teach in newly established Freedom Schools. By the late 1960s the group's influence began to wane under the leadership of Stokely Carmichael, who discouraged further cooperation with former white supporters and abandoned SNCC's espousal of nonviolence in favor of "black power."

STUDENTS FOR A DEMOCRATIC SOCIETY (SDS), founded (1962) in Port Huron, Mich. Advocating participatory democracy, the radical student group was active in the civil rights movement and, from 1965, was in the vanguard of anti-Vietnam War activities. Later the SDS moved beyond the campus, splitting into three factions in the late 1960s: one seeking to turn students toward working-class movements; another focusing on the campus as the arena for revolutionary action; and the third, the Weatherman faction, working to bring blacks, students, and workers together to foment violent revolution. SDS activities declined after the end of U.S. involvement in the Vietnam War.

SUBMERGED LANDS ACT (1953) resolved long-standing federal-state disputes over undersea lands by establishing boundaries between states and federal offshore lands, some of which had immensely valuable oil deposits. Despite bitter criticism by opponents, who claimed that a few states were being given title to resources that belonged to the entire country, President Eisenhower signed the Act into law. The bill was backed by states' rights advocates, especially representatives of states with large offshore reserves—California, Florida, Louisiana, and Texas.

Under the Act, the federal government gave the states title to mineral resources between low tide and three miles offshore unless the state's historic boundary was farther offshore. The Outer Continental Shelf Act, passed the same year, confirmed federal rights beyond state boundaries and protected certain federal water rights within the areas ceded to the states.

SUBPOENA, under penalty, a document issued by a court to a witness, ordering him to appear to give evidence. There are two types of subpoena. A *subpoena ad testificandum* (under penalty to give testimony) orders testimony. A *subpoena duces tecum* (under penalty you will bring with you) orders the production of documents. Disobedience of a subpoena is punishable as contempt.

See also Summons.

SUBSTANTIVE RIGHTS, guarantees granted to all citizens of the United States under the Constitution. These rights, essential to personal liberty, are listed in the First, Thirteenth, and Fourteenth Amendments and include freedom of speech, press, religion, assembly, and petition. The rights include freedom from involuntary servitude and the right to equal protection under the law. These rights may, however, be limited but only in accordance with due process.

SUBVERSIVE ACTIVITIES CONTROL BOARD, an independent executive agency created by the subversive Activities Control Act (1950) to seek out and arrange for the prosecution of subversives, particularly Communists.

During the 1950s and early 1960s when Congress perceived the internal Communist movement to be a grave threat to national security, the Board investigated thousands of groups and individuals to determine their affiliations and apply penalties. It was instrumental in providing Sen. Joseph McCarthy with information for his investigations into domestic communism. Because of Court decisions that labeling individuals as subversive violates constitutional provisions, the Board's activities were largely restricted to removing from the subversive category organizations now defunct or no longer regarded as security risks. The Board was abolished in 1973.

See also Internal Security Act (1950).

SUFFRAGE. *See* Election; Woman Suffrage.

SUMMONS, the means by which the defendant is notified of civil action, as well as the means by which the court asserts control over the defendant and thereby obtains common-law jurisdiction over the person. Ordinarily, the summons must be personally delivered to the defendant. Some jurisdictions employ summonses in minor criminal cases where arrest is not deemed necessary.

See also Jurisdiction; Subpoena.

SUNSET LEGISLATION, an increasingly popular response to the proliferation of government programs and bureaucracies and to their tendency, once created, to stay in existence even when the initial problem justifying their creation has been resolved or the issue is being addressed by a subsequent program or has become moot. Sunset legislation typically specifies that a government program will automatically expire, along with its administrative bureaucracy, after a certain number of years (often seven). The burden is thus put on the government and on the advocates of the government program to provide for its continuance through repassage of the legislation. In this way, it is thought, outdated laws and programs will be weeded out. Although sunset legislation appears to be an increasingly popular idea, it has not yet become the accepted practice. State governments have taken the lead over the federal government in this field.

SUNSHINE LEGISLATION, a response to government secrecy, especially in the area of processes (especially meetings and hearings) by which many policy decisions are made. In recent years both the state and federal governments have adopted significant legislation requiring that such processes take place "in the sunshine"—that is, publicly—so that democratic control may be more effectively exercised on government at critical points in the policy-making process. Thus, for instance, the government in the Sunshine Act of 1977 requires public meetings (or at least public minutes of those meetings) for about 50 executive agencies, regulatory commissions, advisory committees, and independent offices of the federal government. The Act also bans all unofficial contacts between agencies and persons affected by them. Cabinet departments are exempted from the Act, but Congress has passed rules requiring more "sunshine" in many of its internal deliberations.

SUPERFUND, common term for the Comprehensive Environmental Response, Compensation and Liability Act (1980). This hazardous waste cleanup law created a fund of $1.6 billion and empowered the Environmental Protection Agency to locate and clean up toxic waste dumps. Cleanup costs may be recovered by the government by suing the responsible parties.
—*Mary L. Carns*

SUPPLEMENTAL APPROPRIATION, funds allocated by Congress or other legislative bodies for specific purposes after the regular appropriations bill has been enacted. It provides funds beyond the amounts originally budgeted for either new or existing programs.
—*Mary L. Carns*

SUPREMACY CLAUSE. *See* National Supremacy.

SUPREME COURT OF THE UNITED STATES heads the judicial branch of the American government and is the nation's highest law court. It also performs a political function of tremendous importance as the official interpreter and expounder of the Constitution. Because many of the most important provisions of the Constitution are extremely broad and offer much room for difference of interpretation (for example, "due process of law" or "equal protection of the laws"), the Court's role in the political development of the American republic has been very great, often exceeding that of the president or Congress. The Supreme Court was created by Article III and is

headed by the Chief Justice of the United States. The size of the Court is determined by Congress; since 1869 the Court has been composed of nine justices appointed by the president with the advice and consent of the Senate. They serve during good behavior and are removable only by impeachment.

Jurisdiction. The Supreme Court is primarily an appellate court. It reviews decisions of the lower federal courts by writ of *certiorari,* a discretionary writ granted on the affirmative vote of four of the nine justices. In general the Court grants *certiorari* only in cases presenting novel or significant legal issues. The Court also hears appeals against decisions of state supreme courts that involve a federal question, that is, an interpretation of the federal Constitution, laws, or treaties. The supremacy clause (Article VI) makes the Constitution, laws, and treaties of the United States the "supreme law of the land" and binding on state judges; review by the Supreme Court enforces this obligation. In addition, a few types of cases, principally suits between states, can be filed directly in the original jurisdiction of the Supreme Court without having gone through any other court.

Limitations. As final interpreter of the Constitution, the Supreme Court has the power to invalidate presidential actions or congressional statutes that it regards as unconstitutional. For this reason the American system is sometimes referred to as one of judicial supremacy. However, this nomenclature is misleading, for the Court is, in fact, limited by the countervailing powers of the other two branches. The president can arouse public opinion against Court decisions to which he objects, but his greatest influence is through the appointment of justices to fill vacancies. He must, of course, keep in mind the necessity of securing Senate confirmation; two of President Nixon's nominees were rejected by the Senate, and two of President Reagan's nominees also failed to receive Senate confirmation.

Congress exercises pressure on the Court principally by initiating legislation or constitutional amendments to reverse judicial interpretations. Congress can also threaten impeachment, but no Supreme Court justice has ever been removed in this way. The Constitution provides that the appellate jurisdiction of the Court is subject to "such regulations as the Congress shall make." Court critics in Congress have occasionally threatened to use this authority to punish the Court, but the power has been used only once.

History

1789-1865. From the Court's founding to the Civil War, the major influence was John Marshall, Chief Justice from 1801 to 1835. His strong leadership lifted the Court out of the obscurity of its first decade, and in the great case of *Marbury v. Madison* (1803), he successfully claimed the power to declare acts of Congress unconstitutional. He was a strong nationalist, and his basic strategy was to strengthen the power of the national government by such methods as broad interpretation of the congressional power to regulate commerce (*Gibbons v. Ogden*, 1824) and extension of federal protection to property rights under the contract clause (*Dartmouth College v. Woodward*, 1819).

Marshall's successor as Chief Justice, Roger B. Taney (1836-1864), was a spokesman for states' rights and for agrarian property in land and slaves rather than for the Eastern commercial-creditor class, as Marshall had been. Taney sought to maintain the Court's authoritative position, but his decision in *Dred Scott v. Sandford* (1857), denying the power of Congress to control slavery in the territories and the right of blacks to be citizens, destroyed the standing of the Court for almost a generation and helped bring on the Civil War.

1865-1937. From the Civil War to the New Deal, the Court increased its stature by allying itself with the forces of an emergent capitalism and implementing the nation's industrial development. After some initial reluctance, the Court concluded that the provision in the Fourteenth Amendment (adopted in 1868) protecting property from being taken without due process of law was a directive to the courts to protect business enterprises from legislative regulation. The Court's resistance to governmental interference with free enterprise was demonstrated by decisions invalidating a New York ten-hour law for bakers (*Lochner v. New York*, 1905), holding unconstitutional the federal Child Labor Act (*Hammer v. Dagenhart*, 1918), and voiding the District of Columbia minimum wage law for women (*Adkins v. Children's Hospital*, 1923).

The economic depression of the 1930s brought the Court's conservative views into head-on conflict with the liberalism of Franklin Roosevelt's New Deal. In 1935-1936 the Court declared unconstitutional a number of key statutes in the Roosevelt economic recovery program, in several cases by votes of five to four. Roosevelt sharply attacked the Court's horse-and-buggy thinking and, after his overwhelming re-election in 1936, sought to reform the Court by increasing its size from nine to 15. This effort failed in Congress, but beginning in 1937 vacancies on the Court enabled him to appoint new members who fully accepted the principle of governmental responsibility for the state of economy.

Post-1937. The liberal orientation resulting from Roosevelt's appointments was generally maintained throughout the Truman, Eisenhower, Kennedy, and Johnson administrations. Particularly under the chief justiceship of Earl Warren (1953-1969), the Court took advanced positions in a number of constitutional policy areas. Emphasis was transferred from property rights to civil rights, and the justices gave primary consideration to promoting equality and enforcing the protections of the Bill of Rights.

The Court's major constitutional rulings during this period fall into five areas. First, the Court gave greatly increased protection to the First Amendment rights of speech, press, assembly, and religious freedom. Newspapers were assured against libel prosecutions unless malicious falsehoods were published (*New York Times v. Sullivan*, 1964). Obscenity was defined so broadly as to permit much greater freedom of expression than formerly (*Roth v. United States*, 1957). Peaceful demonstrators were protected form arrest (*Edwards v. South Carolina*, 1963). Individuals or organizations charged with subversion could be punished or denied privileges only for illegal acts, not for mere advocacy, teaching, or membership (*Aptheker v. Secretary of State*, 1964). Civil-rights organizations were protected from official harassment (*NAACP v. Alabama*, 1958). Bible reading and prayers in the public schools were declared unconstitutional as state-imposed exercises amounting to an establishment of religion (*Engel v. Vitale*, 1962).

A second major judicial concern was with the fair-trial rights of individuals accused of crime. The provisions of the Fourth through the Eighth Amendments, which spell out procedures in federal criminal prosecutions, were extended to the states (*Mapp v. Ohio*, 1961). Representation by counsel was made mandatory in all criminal cases (*Gideon v. Wainwright*, 1963) and was extended to the pretrial period (*Escobedo v. Illinois*, 1964). A code of conduct for police in their interrogation of suspects was announced in *Miranda v. Arizona*, (1966). The standards for permissible searches and seizures were tightened (*Katz v. United States*, 1967). Due-process standards were enforced in juvenile court proceedings (*In re Gault*, 1967). In 1972 the Court ruled that capital punishment, as it was then administered, was unconstitutional, but later in the decade the Court upheld capital punishment in several states.

Third, the Court endeavored to make the equal-protection clause of the Constitution a reality. The famous case of *Brown v. Board of Education* (1954) declared racial segregation in the public schools unconstitutional and imposed on the nation's legislatures and school systems the obligation to move toward integrated schools "with all deliberate speed." Subsequent decisions outlawed all racial classifications or discriminatory provisions affecting access to public services. Equal protection was extended to other disadvantaged groups, such as the poor, who were guaranteed against denial of access to the courts because of their poverty (*Griffin v. Illinois*, 1956).

Fourth, the Court undertook to implement the principles of representative government by its decision in *Baker v. Carr* (1962) and subsequent cases requiring that the districts from which legislators are elected be approximately equal in population. Enforcing the principle of "one person, one vote" involved the nation's courts in an unprecedented degree of supervision over the process of legislative apportionment.

Finally, several cases in the 1970s concerned the

rights of women and children. In *Doe v. Bolton* (1973) and *Roe v. Wade* (1973), the Court decided that, under certain conditions, women have the right to abortion. In *Goss v. Lopez* (1975), the Court ruled that a public school system cannot suspend a pupil for any significant length of time without a fair hearing. The Court also ruled in *Ingraham v. Wright* (1977) that spanking of children by school officials did not violate the Constitution.

Outlook

Rulings in all of these fields aroused great opposition, made the Court a major target of political controversy, and stimulated efforts to reverse the decisions or limit the Court's powers. Constitutional amendments to nullify the public school prayer and one-person, one-vote decisions failed in Congress. However, in 1968 Richard Nixon in his campaign for the presidency attacked the Warren Court's decisions, particularly those on criminal trials, and promised that if elected he would change the Court's thinking by appointing "strict constructionists" and judicial conservatives to the Court. To succeed Chief Justice Warren, he appointed Warren Burger, who as a federal appeals court judge had been critical of the Supreme Court's decisions. Burger tended to favor society's rights over individual's rights, but, in a number of civil rights cases, he took a liberal stand.

Burger's unexpected retirement in 1986 led to Justice Rehnquist becoming chief justice. His conservative views, combined with those of other Reagan appointees (Scalia, Kennedy, and O'Connor), have resulted in a new conservative majority. Their decisions have called into question the Court's earlier commitment to abortion rights, affirmative action, and other issues of individual rights.

SURGEON GENERAL, the principal deputy of the Assistant Secretary for Health and Scientific Affairs in the Public Health Service (Department of Health and Human Services). The surgeon general helps manage the main departments of the Public Health Service. His main concerns are advising Americans about health hazards in products and services, developing good health care, and encouraging and reporting advances in medical and scientific research.

SURROGATE'S COURT. *See* Probate Court.

SURVEILLANCE, ELECTRONIC. *See* Wiretapping.

SUSPENSION OF THE RULES, a procedure used in Congress to suspend the regular rules of order in considering bills and amendments. It is a time-saving device used to expedite business and quickly pass noncontroversial measures. The motion will be made "to suspend the rules and pass the bill. . . ."

In the House, a motion for suspension of rules is in order every Monday or Tuesday, at the discretion of the Speaker.

Debate on the motion is limited to twenty minutes on each side, with a two-thirds vote required for passage. If the motion is passed, a representative may introduce any bill for consideration, even if it has not been previously introduced or reported from committee. This method is used for expediting noncontroversial bills; members of a committee whose chairman does not want to report a bill for debate may also use this method to get their bill before the House.

The Senate requires one day's notice in writing for consideration of suspension of rules. Although only a majority vote is required for passage, the motion is subject to debate and filibuster. Suspension of rules is commonly used to change or amend appropriation bills in violation of the Senate's rules on amendment of appropriation bills.

SUTHERLAND, GEORGE (1862-1942), intellectual leader of the "four horsemen," four associate justices of the Supreme Court (Sutherland, McReynolds, Butler, and VanDevanter) who, with Justice Roberts and occasionally Chief Justice Hughes, successfully blocked state and federal regulation of the economy, especially during the early New Deal. Sutherland prevailed because he was thoroughly respected by his colleagues on the Court and was able, by the persuasiveness of his arguments, to forge a majority from a base of only four justices.

By 1937, with the defection of Justice Roberts, Sutherland found himself on the losing side, and soon many of his constitutional views on economic legislation would be overturned. He retired in 1938.

SWEATT v. PAINTER, 339 U.S. 629 (1950), concerns the extent to which the equal protection clause of the Fourteenth Amendment limits the power of a state to distinguish between students of different races in professional and graduate education in a state university. Sweatt, a black, applied for admission to the University of Texas Law School. His application was rejected solely because he was black. The Court held that the equal protection clause requires the state to offer Sweatt the same legal education it offers to students of other races and ordered him admitted to the law school.

SWEEZY v. NEW HAMPSHIRE, 354 U.S. 234 (1957), concerns a state's power to investigate subversion. Sweezy, a university professor, was questioned by the attorney general of New Hampshire concerning his knowledge of the Progressive party and concerning the content of his lectures under legislatively delegated, broad, and undefined power to investigate subversive activities. Sweezy refused to answer the questions and was convicted of contempt. The Court decided the case on the narrow ground that Sweezy had been denied due process of law under the Fourteenth Amendment. Because of the lack of any indication that the New Hampshire legislature wanted the information the attorney general attempted to elicit from Sweezy, the questioning was conducted in the absence of authority. Justices Frankfurter and Harlan, concurring, would have decided the case on the broader constitutional ground that the New Hampshire legislature could not in any instance authorize such an invasion of constitutionally protected academic and political freedoms.

See also Nelson v. County of Los Angeles.

SYNDICALISM, a term for trade unionism in France. The movement, based for the most part on a revolutionary philosophy, was active in the first part of the twentieth century. Its origins in French socialism, syndicalism's exponents, influenced by the works of Georges Sorel, believed that the capitalist system was unfair and exploitive of the worker. Syndicalists also believed that government was a tool of capitalists and that syndicates, or trade unions, should be the center of the revolution and use their power to seize industry and overthrow the government. Their means was the general strike and sabotage.

In France the Confederation Generale du Travail and Federation des Bourses du Travail were syndicalist, as was the International Workers of the World in the United States. When labor unions were able to improve the lot of the worker within the capitalist system after World War I, syndicalism ceased to be influential.

See also Labor Movement in the United States.

TAFT, ROBERT ALPHONSO (1899-1953), American legislator and political leader. He was born in Cincinnati, Ohio, the son of William Howard Taft, 27th President of the United States, graduated from Yale in 1910, and from Harvard Law School in 1913, at the head of his class. He was admitted to the Ohio Bar in 1913 and began practice in Cincinnati. Rejected for military service in World War I because of poor eyesight, he served as assistant counsel in the United States Food Administration (1917-1919) and as counsel to the American Relief Administration in Europe (1919-1921).

Senator. Taft was elected to the Ohio Legislature in 1921 and served as Speaker in 1926. He served in the Ohio Senate (1931-1932), and in 1938 he was elected to the United States Senate. He was reelected in 1944 and 1950. During his years in the Senate, Taft led the conservative wing of the Republican party. He was opposed to the New Deal, resisted American involvement in World War II, and voted against selective service, lend lease, extension of the draft, and revision of the neutrality laws. He was a harsh critic of both Franklin Roosevelt and Harry Truman. Taft was one of the Senate's most influential members and had consid-

erable effect on legislation. He was a sponsor of the Taft-Hartley Labor Act (1947), which replaced the prolabor Wagner Act of 1935. He was a candidate for the Republican nomination for president in 1940, 1948, and 1952. His most successful bid came in 1953 against Dwight Eisenhower. Taft was chairman of the Republican Party Committee (1947-1949) and Senate Majority Leader (1953).

TAFT-HARTLEY ACT (1947) or Labor-Management Relations Act, a law regulating numerous labor activities when interstate commerce is concerned. Passed over President Truman's veto but endorsed by business leaders, the act reflected the antilabor sentiment created by such strikes as John L. Lewis' 1946 coal walkout and by fear of Communist influence in unions.

The act refined the Wagner Act (1935) by defining employers' unfair labor practices; led many states to enact "right to work" laws by limiting the "closed shop"; and ended the "check-off" system, by which employers had collected union dues. The most controversial section required unions to abide by an 80-day "cooling-off" period in strikes involving national emergencies. In addition, union leaders had to swear that they were not Communists. The Landrum-Griffin Act (1959) amended some Taft-Hartley sections.

TAFT, WILLIAM HOWARD (1857-1930), 27th President (1909-1913) of the United States and ninth Chief Justice of the Supreme Court (1921-1930). He was born in Cincinnati on Sept. 15, 1857. His father, Alphonso, was one of the founders of the Republican party in Ohio, and both his son and grandson became U.S. senators. He became a lawyer, was appointed assistant county prosecutor in 1882, and in 1887 became a judge of the Ohio superior court, where his decisions often had an antilabor cast, earning him the lifelong enmity of organized labor.

In 1890 he became solicitor general of the United States, followed by an eight-year stint on the bench of the Sixth Federal Circuit Court. In 1900 he resigned to become governor general of the Philippines, where he remained until Theodore Roosevelt appointed him secretary of war in 1904. He quickly earned Roosevelt's confidence as the Administration's troubleshooter, and when Roosevelt retired in 1908, he engineered the selection of Taft as his successor.

Presidency. Taft evidently had little desire or taste for the presidency, and his administration had one crisis after another, due to the split in his own party. The Insurgents pressed hard for tariff reduction, a federal income tax, and liberalization of the House rules. Taft instituted far more antitrust suits than Roosevelt and backed the income tax and direct election of senators, but he invariably ended up the captive of the conservatives. He reluctantly agreed to the Payne-Aldrich Tariff (1909), vacillated when the Insurgents moved against House Speaker Joseph Cannon, and frustrated the advocates of an immediate income tax by his amendment scheme. He incurred the Insurgents' wrath by proposing to let farm products from Canada be imported without tariff duties.

Taft so alienated the progressive wing of his party that Robert La Follette and Roosevelt were able to beat him in nearly all the primaries. He was able to arrange his renomination in 1912 but ran a poor third nearly everywhere, getting only 25 percent of the vote.

Supreme Court. After his term as president, Taft taught constitutional law at Yale, served as joint chairman of the National War Labor Board, and was appointed chief justice of the Supreme Court in 1921. In the next nine years, the happiest of his life, Taft reorganized the federal court system and wrote a famous dissent upholding a minimum wage law for women. True to his earlier conservative views, however, he wrote opinions that struck down the federal child labor law and held the United Mine Workers liable for damages done during a strike. He died in Washington, D.C., on March 8, 1930, and was buried in Arlington National Cemetery.

See also Presidential Elections; Supreme Court of the United States.

TAMMANY, a political society that for more that a century dominated New York City politics. The Tammany Society, or Columbian Order of New York, founded about 1786, was one of several such societies established in various cities after the American Revolution to engage in social, cultural, and patriotic activities. Only the New York society survived and evolved into a major political force. In the early stages of its political life, Tammany Hall, as it came to be known, agitated for reforms, acting as a spokesman for the inarticulate, powerless mass of citizens under the aegis of the Democratic party. As a result of the personal corruption of several of its leaders, however, notably William Tweed and Richard Croker, the Society became synonymous in the late nineteenth century with political venality.

The scandals of the Tweed Ring were unearthed in the *New York Times* in 1871. The exposé resulted in Tweed's imprisonment, but other guilty parties managed to flee the country with fortunes gained through kickbacks, padded bills, and phony leases.

Under Croker's leadership (1886-1901), Tammany was again entrenched in corruption, but the society's influence waned after its candidates were defeated by a reform movement in 1901. The most telling defeat for Tammany came on the heels of Franklin Roosevelt's New Deal victory in 1932. In the late 1950s the society manifested a resurgence as an outgrowth of the organization Democrats under Carmine De Sapio, but reform Democratic forces under Eleanor Roosevelt and former New York Governor Herbert Lehman engineered a significant victory in 1962. Since that time Tammany has had virtually no influence in city politics.

See also Machine, Political.

TANEY, ROGER B(ROOKE) (1777-1864), fourth Chief Justice of the Supreme Court, born in Calvert City, Md. A prominent Maryland lawyer during the 1820s, Taney allied himself with the Jacksonian Democrats. He gained national recognition when, as Andrew Jackson's attorney general, he persuaded the President to veto a bill to renew the charter of the Bank of the United States.

In 1836, Jackson appointed Taney chief justice, succeeding John Marshall. Although Taney did not believe in slavery, he wrote the opinion of the Court in the Dred Scott decision (1857), which maintained that blacks did not possess rights of citizenship entitling them to sue in federal courts.

With this decision, the prestige of the Court fell to its lowest point, and, with it, the reputation of Taney. Although unpopular at his death, today Taney is considered one of the great justices by conservatives and liberals alike.

See also Dred Scott v. Sandford; Supreme Court of the United States.

TARIFFS, duties or customs fees charged on merchandise entering competition. Tariffs between countries are negotiated and generally formalized with trade treaties. Tariff relations between the United States and other countries are overseen by the Tariff Commission. Records of Tariff rates are maintained by the Bureau of International Commerce of the Department of Commerce. The United States negotiated many of its free-world tariffs through the General Agreement on Tariffs and Trade, in Geneva, Switzerland. This agreement, which went into effect in 1948 and has 72 signatories, was made to promote fair trade in international commerce through a specific code of rules and also to remove trade barriers among the signatories.

Protectionist Tariffs. Until recent years the United States has always had a strong protective tariff that fostered a strong home industry. One of the first acts of the Congress of 1789 was to set tariffs for all imports to stimulate the faltering American economy. Subsequent acts increased these duties under the demand of some United States manufacturers for trade protection, but traders in the South wanted either no duties or low duties to protect the foreign markets for cotton and tobacco. New England shipping interests also favored free trade to protect their business.

New and higher tariffs were approved by Congress with the Tariff Acts (1824, 1828, and 1832). Protest in the South rose to a high pitch, and South Carolina passed an Ordinance of Nullification (1832) prohibiting the collection of tariff duties in the state and raising an army to enforce the ordinance. A new tariff bill with some lower duties was passed (1833) to avert the crisis that almost resulted in civil war, but, again, subsequent acts raised tariffs so that during the Civil War period they averaged 47 percent on imported manufactured goods. American industry continued to grow through the last half of the nineteenth century under this tariff protection.

Expansionist Tariffs. The first significant reduction came with the 1913 Underwood tariff, but then the 1922 Fordney-McCumber and the 1930 Hawley-Smoot tariffs raised taxes on manufactured goods substantially. As a result, European nations could not earn the dollars needed to repay World War I debts to the United States. Financial collapse in Europe and the resulting drop in United States exports contributed to the Depression.

Once again, trade barriers were lowered by the Reciprocal Trade Agreements Act (1934), which gave the president the authority to lower customs duties as much as 50 percent with a nation that agreed to reciprocate. This Act was renewed eleven times until 1962 and reduced tariffs by almost 80 percent to an average of 12 percent on imports.

Post-World War II Developments, such as the emergence of Communist and European economic blocs, the rise of Japanese industry, and the growing deficit in the United States balance of payments resulted in the passage of the Trade Expansion Act (1962). This Act gave the president authority to reduce tariffs by 50 percent on a reciprocal basis and almost entirely eliminated them on goods that were traded by the United States and the Common Market. Under this Act the important Kennedy Round trade negotiations with the European Common Market countries took place in Geneva, Switzerland (1964-1967). The results were tariff reductions averaging 35 percent, substantial reductions on some farm products, and an agreement on an antidumping code. Weaknesses in the U.S. trade position, such as the imbalance in U.S.-Japanese trade, have brought demands for protection. Generally, however, the level of tariff disputes in recent history has been higher than warranted by the relatively small economic significance of tariffs.

See also Balance of Payments; General Agreement on Tariffs and Trade (GATT); Most Favored Nation Status.

TARIFF COMMISSION, UNITED STATES, serves as a fact-finding and advisory body for Congress and the President on tariffs and other aspects of foreign trade. Established by statute in 1916, the commission consists of six members appointed by the president. One particular function is to recommend relief for industries alleged to be adversely affected by trade concessions.

TAXATION. Since the beginning of the twentieth century, the size and importance of government activities have increased dramatically. As this has occurred, the amount of tax revenues and the complexity of the tax structure have also increased.

Kinds. In the 1980s property taxes accounted for approximately 85 percent of the tax receipts of local governments in the United States. Sales taxes and excise taxes (that is, special levies on individual products, such as gasoline and liquor) constituted somewhat less that 10 percent of the total tax collections. Most of the remaining revenues of local governments, not counting those received from higher levels of government, came from the sale of various licenses and permits.

State governments, on the other hand, rely primarily on sales and excise taxes, with income taxes becoming more common recently. Other major sources of state tax revenue include licenses and permits and corporate income taxes. Property, death, and gift taxes provide states with a small proportion of their total tax collections.

The federal government in 1990 received almost $1.06 trillion in tax revenues, 38 percent from the personal income tax, 11 percent from corporation income taxes, 32 percent from social insurance payroll taxes, and the remainder from excise taxes, customs duties, estate and gift taxes, and miscellaneous receipts.

Funding Government. The federal government, if it wished, would not have great difficulty in raising sufficient taxes to meet its payments for government goods and services. In recent years the government has used fiscal policy as a stimulant for the economy.

On the other hand, even though state and local tax receipts have recently risen relative to federal receipts, the lower governments have lately experienced a difficult time raising sufficient revenues to defray their rapidly increasing expenses for highways, education, pollution control, crime control, and social services. As a result, there has been an increasing tendency for higher levels of government to give grants to lower levels. The states now give substantial aid to local governments, and the federal government has given large grants to lower governments. In the past these grants have been given on condition that they be used for specific purposes and that the state and local governments put up a certain amount of their own funds. Economists proposed that federal subsidies be given to states and localities on a no-strings-attached basis, and a federal revenue-sharing proposal of this type has been passed by Congress.

Redistributing Income. Although ostensibly the tax system has attempted to redistribute income from the wealthy to the poor, there is some question as to how effectively this objective has been accomplished. In this connection, taxes may be classified as progressive, proportional, or regressive. A tax is *progressive* if its percentage rate increases as income increases. A *proportional* tax takes the same percentage of each person's income, regardless of how large his income is. A *regressive* tax is one whose percentage rate declines as income increases. Insofar as the tax system is progressive, it places the main burden of tax payment on the higher income groups. The reverse is true if the tax system is regressive. A progressive tax structure, therefore, will generally create a more equal distribution of income after taxes.

Economists have generally agreed that the federal personal income tax is highly progressive, but property and sales taxes are regressive. The value of taxed property constitutes a larger percentage of a poor person's income than of a wealthy person's income. The poor person spends a larger percentage of his income on consumer goods, which are subject to the sales taxes.

Unfortunately, it is not always a simple matter to determine whether some taxes are progressive, proportional, or regressive. This is because the incidence of a tax may be shifted. An excise tax levied against a liquor company, for example, may be paid finally by the purchaser of the liquor because the company raises the price to cover the tax. The incidence of the tax is then said to have been shifted forward from the manufacturer to the consumer. The tax may also be shifted backward from the manufacturer to his suppliers; that is, the manufacturer pays the suppliers less than had there been no tax.

Economists have not been able to determine the exact incidence of most levies on firms, so it is impossible to say for certain whether such taxes are progressive, regressive, or proportional. Intensive studies have, nevertheless, come to the tentative conclusion that when all taxes levied in the United States are taken into consideration, the regressive taxes roughly cancel out the progressive taxes, so that the overall tax structure is approximately proportional. If so, taxes in the United States have no important effect on income distribution.

Controlling the Economy. The majority of economists believe that an alteration of taxes may have a powerful effect on the total demand for goods and thereby affect the level of inflation and unemployment. A decrease of taxes may be expected to raise incomes after taxes and thereby increase the total demand for goods and reduce the level of unemployment. On the other hand, an increase in taxes should decrease incomes after taxes, decreasing the total demand for goods and dampening inflation. In recent years, however, some economists have expressed strong doubts as to the extent of these effects.

Major changes in tax law went into effect in 1986. The intent was to streamline the system by establishing two basic tax rates and by eliminating a number of deductions and loopholes.

See also Tax Reform Act (1986).

TAX COURT, the federal forum in which a taxpayer may contest a tax deficiency asserted by the Internal Revenue Service. The Tax Court hears contests involving deficiencies only. If the taxpayer pays, he must sue the government for a refund in either the Court of Claims or the district court, but not in the Tax Court.

TAX REFORM ACT (1986), sweeping reform act was signed into law by President Reagan on October 22, 1986. The bill underwent numerous revisions in a partisan debate, with special interest groups working actively to protect tax loopholes. Among the key provisions for individuals and businesses were the setting of two basic tax rates on personal income, 15 percent and 28 percent. Income above $17,850 for single taxpayers and $29,750 for married taxpayers filing jointly would be taxed at 28 percent. In addition, the bill set three rates on corporate income, with a maximum of 34 percent. That contrasted with a previous maximum of 46 percent. Despite the reduction, it was estimated that businesses would pay more in taxes because many former deductions and credits were eliminated.

Further, the law, while continuing the deduction for interest on home mortgages, eliminated the deductibility of consumer credit by 1990. It also ended deductions for state sales taxes. There were further income-based restrictions on individual retirement accounts (IRAs). Lawmakers predicted tax reductions for individual taxpayers. It was estimated that some six million low-income earners would have no tax liability.

TAYLOR, ZACHARY (1784-1850), 12th President of the United States (1849-1850), born in Montebello, Va. A frontier Indian fighter and military hero, he was the last Whig elected to the White House. He was victorious over the Florida Seminole Indians (1837) and won major victories in the Mexican War (1846-1847). As President, he found himself in the middle of the growing dispute over the extension of slavery into the territories. Compromise measures attempted by Henry Clay were denounced as concessions by Taylor, who died in the midst of the debates on the subject.

See also Presidential Elections.

TEAMSTERS, INTERNATIONAL BROTHERHOOD OF, a labor union that was organized in 1903. Most of its members are truck drivers. The union experienced rapid growth in size and importance during the 1930s and 1940s. It gained power by threatening to stop deliveries by the rapidly growing long-distance trucking industry. The Teamsters came under fire when charges of corruption were brought against a succession of their presidents. Convictions further tarnished their image, but the union continues to exercise considerable political influence. It makes major contributions to political candidates through its

PAC. The Teamsters were readmitted to the AFL/CIO in 1987.

TELLER VOTE, a method of voting in the House of Representatives whereby members voting yea on a measure file past a point to be counted by tellers, followed by members voting nay. The Legislative Reorganization Act of 1970 provides that one-fifth of the members of the House or of the Committee of the Whole may now demand a recorded teller vote, requiring members to sign and deposit green cards for "yea" or red cards for "nay."

See also Record Vote.

TENNESSEE VALLEY AUTHORITY (TVA), a government-owned corporation formed in 1933. TVA operates the Tennessee River control system, maintains a navigation channel along the river, and operates dams and steam plants that produce inexpensive electric power.

TVA has encouraged development of a seven-state region with rural electrification, strip-mine reclamation, flood control, and conservation education. It has faced hostility throughout its history from advocates of pure free enterprise.

TERMINIELLO v. CHICAGO, 337 U.S. 1 (1949), concerns a breach of peace charge stemming from a speech. Terminiello, who denied he was a fascist, gave a speech filled with racial and religious hatred to a crowd under the sponsorship of the Christian Veterans of America. Outside the auditorium, a milling mob yelled, threw bricks, and could not be contained by the police. Terminiello was tried and convicted of breach of peace which, in Chicago, consisted of stirring the public to anger, inviting dispute, and the like.

The Court, in a 5-to-4 decision, held that a function of free speech under our system of government is to invite dispute, even when it induces a condition of unrest. In his dissent, Justice Jackson said that the local court that tried Terminiello was dealing with a riot and that this situation represented a "clear and present danger" that brought about a substantive evil that the city had a right to punish.

See also Schenck v. United States.

TERRITORIAL COURT, any one of a number of different courts established from time to time by Congress for territories subject to United States jurisdiction. These courts are legislative because their creation is an exercise of the power of Congress to make rules for United States property (Article IV, Section 3).

TERRITORIAL WATERS, the waters under the jurisdiction of a nation or state, including the offshore waters lying between the shore and the high seas (territorial belt or marginal sea); inland lakes and rivers entirely within a state; and boundary rivers, straits, lakes and bays up to the middle point from shore to shore. The jurisdiction of a state extends over territorial waters in matters of fishing rights, navigation, coastal trade, sanitation, and customs duties. Historically, the territorial belt was generally three to six miles, although some nations tried to enforce much wider limits. In December 1988 the United States became the 105th nation to proclaim a 12-mile limit. President Reagan undertook the action, which is authorized under the 1982 United Nations Law of the Sea Convention, to curb Soviet spy ships.

Ships of other nations have the right of innocent passage through the territorial water of any nation as long as the vessels observe the navigation, customs, and sanitation regulations of the countries having jurisdiction over those waters. During war the marginal seas of neutral territory are off limits to battling warships of the nations at war.

See also Law of the Sea Treaty.

TEST-BAN TREATY. *See* Atomic Weapons, International Control of; Disarmament.

TEXAS v. JOHNSON (1989), a bitterly divided Supreme Court opinion in which the Court ruled that burning the American flag as a form of political protest was constitutionally protected free speech under the First Amendment. Justice Brennan, writing for an unusual coalition of liberals and conservatives, argued that government cannot "prohibit expression simply because it does not agree with its message." He ruled that political acts, even when symbolic, cannot be restricted unless there was a clear danger of violence. The decision had the effect of negating numerous state laws and a federal statute that prohibited acts that defaced or defiled the flag.

The ruling was deplored by President Bush and many members of Congress who urged passage of a constitutional amendment to bar flag desecration. After considerable debate, Congress instead passed legislation and rejected an amendment. President Bush allowed the bill to become law (October 1989) without his signature. He remained convinced that an amendment was needed, while others questioned the constitutionality of the new law.

THIRD-PARTY POLITICS. The American political system has not been a monopoly of the Republican and Democratic parties. Frequently, dissatisfied groups from the major parties or the voters have aligned themselves into third parties. They have acted as indicators of political trends, requiring the major parties to recognize the issue; safety-valves, allowing dissident political groups to express their views; and balances of power, forcing one of the major parties to incorporate into its own platform vital elements of the third party's program.

In the 1912 presidential contest the Progressive

party of Theodore Roosevelt was instrumental in producing a significant electoral victory for Woodrow Wilson. In the 1968 presidential election the American Independent party's candidate, George Wallace, received 13.5 percent of the popular vote. The strategy employed by Wallace was to win enough of the vote to deny either Richard Nixon or Hubert Humphrey the necessary majority in the Electoral College.

On the state level third parties have been instrumental in electing governors, members of the state legislature, and the Congress. In New York, for example, the Liberal party has often exercised the balance of power in state politics. —*Samuel Raphalides*

See also Political Parties in the United States; Presidential Elections.

THIRD WORLD. *See* Neutralism.

THORNHILL v. ALABAMA, 310 U.S. 88 (1940), considers the nature of picketing and whether it is economic warfare or an aspect of freedom of speech and press. Thornhill was convicted of violating the "loitering or picketing forbidden" section of the Alabama State Code of 1923. The state contended that the statute was designed to protect the community from violence and breach of peace, which, it asserted, were the concomitants of picketing.

The Court held the statute invalid on its face because the presentation of the facts of a labor dispute in the form of a picket must be regarded as within that area of free discussion that is guaranteed by the Constitution. Today, however, the Court will permit states to ban picketing if (1) it takes place in a violent context, (2) there is no direct economic connection between the pickets and those being picketed, and (3) it is carried on for purposes declared by the state to be unlawful.

THREE-FIFTHS COMPROMISE, at the Constitutional Convention of 1787, an agreement incorporated in the Connecticut Compromise that established the method of determining proportional representation in the lower house of Congress. The earlier Connecticut Compromise held that each state would have one vote in the Senate and be represented in the House according to its population. The ensuing question of whether slaves would be counted was resolved by agreement that representation would be based on the total white population of each state plus three-fifths of its slave population (Article I, Section 2). The Three-Fifths Compromise thus established a powerful voice for the slave states in Congress.

TIDELANDS OIL ACT. *See* Submerged Lands Act of 1953.

TINKER v. DES MOINES INDEPENDENT COMMUNITY SCHOOL DISTRICT, 393 U.S. 503 (1969), concerns students' rights of freedom of expression. The Tinkers, both students in the Des Moines public schools, sued the school district to enjoin enforcement of a regulation prohibiting the wearing of black armbands on school facilities in protest of the Vietnam hostilities.

Speaking for the Court, Justice Fortas stated that in the absence of facts which might reasonably have led the school authorities to forecast substantial disruption of school activities, or any showing that disturbances on school premises had occurred when students wore armbands, the regulation and the resulting suspension of any student who refused to remove the armband were unconstitutional denials of students' rights of expression of opinion. One dissenter felt that the First Amendment rights of children were not coextensive with those of adults.

See also Griswold v. Connecticut.

TITLE IX, part of the Education Amendments of 1972, enacted by Congress and enforced by the U.S. Department of Education's Office for Civil Rights, that prohibits sex discrimination in schools and colleges that receive federal money. Equal access to education for female and male students of all ages is guaranteed. Teachers and other adults involved in education are also protected under Title IX. Practices in schools controlled by religious organizations are exempt from Title IX compliance whenever compliance would be contrary to religious beliefs, as are membership practices of single-sex, tax-exempt "youth service" organizations; university-based social fraternities and sororities; father-son or mother-daughter activities as long as opportunities for "reasonably comparable" activities are offered to students of both sexes; and scholarships or other aids offered by colleges and universities to participants in single-sex pageants that reward the combination of personal appearance, poise, and talent.

As a result of Title IX, admissions policies have been broadened to include more women. Females have been offered more opportunities in sports programs, students have been guaranteed rights to equal treatment both inside and outside the classroom (including protection from sexual harassment and discrimination because of pregnancy and the right to egalitarian guidance counseling), salaries and benefits have been upgraded to provide equal pay for equal work, and more female educators have achieved administrative positions. —*Martin Gruberg*

TOCQUEVILLE, (CHARLES) ALEXIS (HENRI CLÉREL) DE (1805-1859), French political theorist, whose *Democracy in America* remains one of the most penetrating analyses ever written of United States institutions. He was born into a noble Norman family of Verneuil. After studying law, he entered the civil service in 1827.

In 1831 he was sent to the United States to study the prison system. During the year he was in America, he observed closely, traveled widely, particularly in the East, and talked with many prominent people. After his return to France, he coauthored a study of United States prisons, which was followed in 1835 by the first parts of *Democracy in America*.

Democracy in America was an immediate success and led to Tocqueville's election to the French Academy in 1841. In this work he brilliantly explored the effects of popular government and egalitarianism on the social and political system of the only democracy then in existence. He applauded the humanity and greater individual liberty present in a democracy and concluded that it was a successful form of government. But he was wary of the "tyranny of the majority," which he thought the United States had avoided.

In his later years Tocqueville turned more to French affairs. He was elected to the Chamber of Deputies in 1839 and served briefly as foreign minister in 1849. He then wrote his second great work, *The Old Régime and the Revolution* (1856), which pointed out the continuity between the pre-1789 regime and the revolution. He died in Cannes.

TONKIN GULF RESOLUTION, enacted August 7, 1964, by Congress to give President Lyndon Johnson authority to "take all necessary measures" to stop aggression in Southeast Asia. The President asked Congress to enact the resolution after reported attacks on United States destroyers patrolling the Gulf of Tonkin off the coast of North Vietnam. The resolution was passed unanimously by the House and by a vote of 88-2 in the Senate, with Democratic senators Morse and Gruening dissenting.

The President used the resolution to increase military involvement in the area, but many members of Congress considered the resolution vague and believed that the President had gone beyond his constitutional powers in waging war in Vietnam without the consent of Congress. Some critics saw the resolution as Congress's abdication of its power to declare war. Efforts by Congress in the 1970s to restrict presidential war-making powers were seen by many as an attempt to regain the initiative in foreign policy areas. The resolution was repealed in 1970.

See also Pentagon Papers; War Powers Resolution.

TORCASO v. WATKINS, 367 U.S. 488 (1961), concerns the constitutionality of Maryland's religious requirement for persons holding a public office. Torcaso was appointed to the office of notary public by the governor of Maryland but refused a commission to serve because he would not declare his belief in God.

The Court, in an opinion delivered by Justice Black, held that the requirement of declaration of a belief in the existence of God as a test for office invades the freedoms of belief and religion in violation of the First and Fourteenth Amendments.

See also Everson v. Board of Education.

TORT, the breach of a duty to an individual that results in damage to him. Crime, in contrast, may be called the breach of a duty to the public. An act that offends both society and individual receives the classification of the seeker of remedy. Morever, damage need not result for the act to constitute a crime, as in an attempted murder. Note that a tort involves only duties owed to an individual as a matter of law, not duties arising from an agreement (contract) with him. Torts involve violations of civil law other than breach of contract—for example, libel, negligence, or malpractice. The legal remedy is usually a monetary award.

See also Criminal Law.

TOTALITARIANISM, a political system in which total power to define and implement the ends and means of the system is held by one party or group. Actual power is possessed by a few at the top of the party or group, and one person is often designated as the leader. The unlimited, total ends and means of the regime make it a unique twentieth-century phenomenon. Only the physical and psychological power produced by modern science and technology could enable a few men to control as completely the lives of many as was done in Nazi Germany and in the U.S.S.R. The possibilities of the use of this power have produced in totalitarian leaders a grandeur of ambition unlike any experienced before. Moral ideologies have been used as tools of political action to produce in the masses an intense and passionate identification with the policies and aims of totalitarian regimes.

—*Robert F. Smith*

See also Absolutism; Authoritarianism; Facism; National Socialism.

TOWER COMMISSION. *See* Iran-Contra Affair.

TOWN MEETING, a method of self-government in which members of a township meet to make laws and decide town matters. The decisions of the town meeting are carried out by selectmen, who are elected by the people. The town meeting is an example of direct, or pure, democracy, in which the people make their own laws without elected representatives. This method of government is characteristic of New England, where the township is the main unit of local government, superseding the county.

The increase of population in some areas has made the town meeting system impractical, necessitating a limited town meeting of a large body of representatives. Other towns have adopted the town manager system.

See also Local Government.

TOXIC WASTE CLEANUP ACT, the $9 billion, five-year Superfund Toxic Waste Cleanup Bill signed by President Reagan on October 17, 1986. The program targeted the country's most hazardous locations for priority cleanup. Funding was to come from a variety of taxes on producers. If voluntary cooperation could not be secured, the government would undertake the work and sue for reimbursement. The bill also provided stricter compliance standards for companies engaged in the storage and disposal of toxic wastes.

The Superfund, which is administered by the Environmental Protection Agency (EPA), was criticized for its emphasis on containing, rather than destroying, waste sites.

TRANSPORTATION, U.S. DEPARTMENT OF (DOT). Set up in 1966 to develop a national transportation policy and to foster safe, fast, low cost, and efficient transportation systems, DOT combined units from 30 agencies. DOT is headed by a secretary with cabinet status and incorporates the U.S. Coast Guard, the Federal Aviation Administration, the Federal Highway Administration, the Federal Railroad Administration, the Urban Mass Transportation Administration, the Saint Lawrence Seaway Development Corporation, and the National Highway Safety Traffic Administration.

In part, the department was a reaction against the choking of U.S. arteries by excessive automobile traffic and resultant pollution. Since DOT was set up, national emphasis on highway expansion has eased somewhat and new programs for urban mass transportation, airport and airway expansion, and passenger rail service have received new funding. In 1970, the NASA research facility in Cambridge, Mass., became the DOT Transportation Systems Center. DOT is also in charge of national pipeline safety and the time zone laws.

TREASON, levying war against the United States, adhering to its enemies, or giving aid and comfort to the enemy by a citizen of the United States. Treason is cited in Article III, Section 3, of the Constitution. Two witnesses' testimony of the "same overt act" in open court or the accused's confession in open court is sufficient for conviction. A person convicted of treason is given the death penalty or sentenced to at least five years in prison and fined at least $10,000.

The trial of Aaron Burr on charges of treason in 1807 provided an important precedent for future treason trials. Justice John Marshall interpreted the Constitution literally regarding treason, accepting only evidence bearing directly on the act of treason. Because not even one of the two witnesses required by the Constitution had seen Burr in any act of treason, he was acquitted. This precedent has made it difficult to convict a person of treason. Because of this difficulty, Congress has passed its own legislation, such as

the Sedition Act of 1918, the Smith Act of 1940, and the Internal Security Act (McCarran Act) of 1950 to provide some grounds for prosecution.

TREASURY, U.S. DEPARTMENT OF, a cabinet-rank department that advises the president on financial policy and the economy, acts as financial agent for the government, enforces the laws regarding counterfeiting, smuggling, and forging, and guards the president, vice president, and their families. The department was established in 1789 by the First Congress, and the first Secretary of the Treasury was Alexander Hamilton. The Secretary of the Treasury, who heads the department, serves as the chief financial officer of the government and represents the United States in several international financial organizations.

The offices of the department are responsible for its administration. The Under Secretary for Monetary Affairs is concerned with domestic and international financing, balance of payments, and gold and silver policies. The Fiscal Secretary must supervise the financing operations of the treasury and also acts as liaison for the financial operations of other governmental departments. The 4450 national banks are administered by the Comptroller of the Currency.

Probably the best-known bureaus of the Department of Treasury are the Internal Revenue Service (IRS), the United States Secret Service, and the Bureau of Customs. The IRS, created in 1862, determines, assesses, and collects all internal revenue and other taxes. The well-known duties of the Secret Service are to protect the president, the vice president, their families, and candidates for these offices, but the Secret Service also has law-enforcement duties regarding the security of the United States and foreign governments.

Other bureaus include the Bureau of Engraving and Printing, which is responsible for the design and production of currency, treasury bonds, bills, and notes, and postage, revenue, and customs stamps; the Bureau of the Mint, which produces both domestic and foreign coins and medals and also has custody of the country's bullion; the Fiscal Service, which includes the Bureau of Government Financial Operations and the Bureau of the Public Debt. The Office of the Treasurer of the United States receives and pays out public moneys for the government; and the Savings Bond Division, established in 1945, oversees the sale of U.S. Savings Bonds.

TREATY POWER OF THE PRESIDENT, derived from Article II, Section 2, of the Constitution, which states: "[The president] shall have Power, by and with the Advice and Consent of the Senate to make Treaties, provided two thirds of the Senators present concur." The president initiates the formation and negotiation of treaties as an executive function; the actual arrangements are normally drafted by the State Department, under the authority of the chief executive.

See also President of the United States.

TRIAL BY JURY. *See* Jury System.

TROP v. DULLES, 256 U.S. 86 (1958), concerns the relationship between civilian and military authorities and specifically questions the forfeiture of citizenship as a result of a dishonorable discharge from the military. Trop, a native-born American, was denied a passport on the ground that he had lost his citizenship by reason of his conviction of and dishonorable discharge for wartime desertion.

Chief Justice Warren announced the decision of the Court and delivered his own opinion, saying that citizenship is not a license that expires on misconduct and that denationalization as a punishment is barred by the Eighth Amendment. Congress, by taking away citizenship under the Nationality Act of 1940, had exceeded the bounds of the Constitution. The dissenters, Justices Frankfurter, Burton, Clark, and Harlan, argued that expatriation was not punishment and was within the war power of the Congress.

See also Afroyin v. Rusk; Schneider v. Rusk.

TRUE BILL, a bill issued when a grand jury finds that sufficient evidence exists to warrant holding a person for trial in a criminal case; also known as an "indictment." The right to indictment by a grand jury in federal cases is guaranteed by the Fifth Amendment. This provision still has not been incorporated by court interpretation of the Fourteenth Amendment "due process" clause, and states are therefore free to use methods other than indictment to bring charges against a suspect. At present, slightly fewer than one-half of the states use grand jury indictments; other states use an "information." —*Mary L. Carns*

See also Grand Jury; Information; No Bill; Presentment.

TRUMAN, HARRY S. (1884-1972), 33rd President of the United States. The successor of Franklin D. Roosevelt, Truman was president during a period of global crisis and tension. He was born in Lamar, Mo., and moved to Independence as a child. After finishing high school, Truman worked with no notable success at a variety of jobs until World War I, in which he served as an artillery officer.

After the war he was actively involved in Democratic politics, became associated with the Kansas City machine of boss Pendergast, and was elected to local judgeships. Although the machine was noted for corruption, Truman maintained his personal integrity. In 1934 he ran successfully for the Senate as a New Deal

Harry S. Truman, 33rd President, 1945-1953.

advocate. He was reelected in 1940 and gained national prominence heading a committee investigating military costs.

President. In 1944 Roosevelt chose Truman as a compromise running mate. Roosevelt died in 1945, and Truman, with little experience in foreign affairs, pushed the war with Germany to a close in May and made the decision to drop atom bombs on Japan in August.

In the postwar era Truman helped to rebuild a shattered Europe while opposing the spread of communism in Europe and trying to settle the Nationalist-Communist struggles in China. In 1947 the Truman Doctrine and the Marshall Plan, both aimed at aiding Europe, were unveiled. The creation of NATO followed in 1949.

Domestically Truman was hampered by crippling strikes and congressional opposition to his Fair Deal. In 1948, however, he won a stunning upset victory over Republican candidate Thomas E. Dewey after a presidential campaign in which Truman appealed to everyone who had benefited from the New Deal. Soon after the election there were setbacks in Asia, with the Communists winning control of China in 1949 and North Korea invading South Korea in 1950. The Korean situation was complicated by Chinese intervention and by Truman's removal from command of Gen. Douglas MacArthur in 1951. Truman did not stand for reelection in 1952, but he remained a critic of Republican policies after his retirement.

Although often condemned for the spread of communism after World War II, Truman proved a strong leader during a period of unparalleled difficulties. In foreign affairs he oversaw the growth of United States influence. Domestically he tried to fulfill the promise of the New Deal and to win support for the Fair Deal.

TRUMAN DOCTRINE, a principle that if Greece and Turkey fell to the Communists, the entire Middle East might also fall. Enunciated in a 1947 speech before a joint session of Congress by President Harry Truman, the doctrine advocated support of free people resisting takeover by armed minorities or outside pressures. Truman asked Congress to provide $400 million in immediate economic and military aid for Greece and Turkey. The Truman Doctrine was the beginning of a new policy to meet Russian expansion wherever it occurred—the policy of containment. The first major program under the Truman Doctrine was the Marshall Plan, to aid in the postwar recovery of Europe.
See also Containment Policy; Marshall Plan.

TRUSTEESHIP COUNCIL. *See* United Nations.

TRUSTS. *See* Business Regulation in the United States.

TRUTH-IN-LENDING ACT (1968), detailed legislation to protect the consumer by enabling him to compare credit terms realistically. The main provisions regarding installment buying and open-end credit plans call for clear and full disclosure of all credit charges and conditions under which the creditor acquires security from the borrower. The Act prevents the original creditor from hiding violations and fraud behind a collection agency. The Act's straightforward wording prohibits issuing unrequested credit cards and limits the cardholder's liability in the case of unauthorized use to $50. Credit reports are open to review by their subjects, but issuing agencies cannot be prosecuted for false information unless malice is proved.
See also Consumer Protection; Federal Trade Commission.

TRUTH IN PACKAGING LAW (1966) *or* **FAIR PACKAGING AND LABELING ACT.** Designed to help the consumer compare products and be accurately informed, the law provides that all commodity labels must identify the product, give the name and place of business of the manufacturer, packer, or distributor, and list the net quantity of smaller packages. The law prohibits nonfunctional slack fill and regulates "cents-off" promotion labeling as well as size and type of label.

TWO-PARTY SYSTEM. One explanation for the development and persistence of the American two-party system stresses the colonial inheritance of the English system. A second explanation emphasizes the lack of sharp or doctrinaire cleavages in American society, in contrast to those of continental Europe. Another explanation ascribes the persistence of the American two-party system to a unique pattern in the American voting system, particularly the electoral college and the single-member district.

The principle of federalism—the division of powers between national and state governments and the separation of powers among the executive, legislative, and judicial authorities—makes party success in controlling the government difficult to achieve. The loose arrangement of interest groups and the party's ability to cut across interest lines to attract the political interest and support of most independent voters assure a moderating and compromising political environment. As a result, the two parties continue to attract sufficient interests to maintain organization, win elections, exercise power, and preempt the formation of a viable third party.

The flexibility of the major parties accommodates heterogeneous interests and membership in most of the state organizations as well. Many students of the American political system conclude that there are actually 50 Democratic and 50 Republican parties: the state parties act in concert only every four years in order to win a presidential contest. As in the national organizations, the state parties are structurally loose federations dependent upon the municipal and county agencies and interest groups. Because most state governments are patterned on the federal plan, compromise is as essential to the intrastate organizations as between the interests of the several state organizations.   —*Samuel Raphalides*
See also Multiparty System; Political Parties in the United States.

TYLER, JOHN (1790-1862), tenth President of the United States (1841-1845), born in Greenway, Va. A Democrat, he served as U.S. representative (1816-1821), governor of Virginia (1825-1827), and U.S. senator (1827-1836). He was vice president for one month before assuming the presidency upon the death of William Henry Harrison in April 1841. He was primarily important for injecting the carefully avoided slavery issue back into the limelight and, as President, acted on a resolution of Congress (1845) to annex proslavery Texas.
See also Presidential Elections.

ULLMAN v. UNITED STATES, 350 U.S. 422 (1956), concerns the validity of the Immunity Act of 1954, which deprives a witness of the privilege against self-incrimination when national security is at stake and forces him to testify in return for a broad grant of immunity from prosecution. Ullman was convicted for contempt in violation of the immunity statute because he failed to answer questions concerning the membership of the Communist party.

In upholding the conviction, the Court, in an opinion delivered by Mr. Justice Frankfurter, said that the Act explicitly states that the compelled testimony shall not be used against the witness in any proceeding in any court, thus protecting him against state as well as federal prosecution and eliminating the possibility of self-incrimination to the extent of his constitutional immunity.

UN-AMERICAN ACTIVITIES COMMITTEE, HOUSE. *See* Investigative Power of Congress.

UNEMPLOYMENT INSURANCE. *See* Social Security.

UNESCO. *See* United Nations: The Specialized Agencies.

UNFAIR LABOR PRACTICES, acts of employers or labor organizations that are illegal under federal or state statutes. Charges of unfair labor practice are judged by the National Labor Relations Board, and if violations exist, cease and desist orders are issued. These orders are enforceable in the Federal Courts of Appeals.

Of Employers. The five unfair labor practices of employers are: (1) interference with employee rights as stated by the Taft-Hartley Act; (2) domination of unions; (3) discrimination against employees for union activities; (4) retaliation against employees for invoking their rights; and (5) refusing to bargain with a majority representative of the employees.

Of Labor. Unfair labor practices that apply to labor organizations pertain to restraining or forcing employers and employees to take certain actions. The activities include: (1) restraining employees in the exercise of statutory rights; (2) causing an employer to unlawfully discriminate against an employee; (3) refusing to bargain with an employer; (4) attempting to make an employee or self-employed person join a union or forcing anyone to stop doing business with another person; forcing an employer to bargain with a union not certified as bargaining agent; or forcing an employer to give work to a particular union; (5) making employees pay excessive initiation fees; (6) engaging in featherbedding; and (7) taking part in picketing when another union is lawfully recognized as the bargaining agent.

UNICAMERALISM, consisting of one elected house or body. Although Nebraska is generally cited as the first state to develop a single-house legislative body, three states previously experimented with unicameralism: Pennsylvania (1776-1790), Georgia (1777-1789), and Vermont (1777-1836). In each of these states, however, the actions of the unicameral legislature were subject to review by an executive council or its equivalent. Nebraska's unicameral body has 49 members, elected every two years on a nonpartisan basis from districts apportioned according to population. In this century although the voters in Arizona, Oregon, and Oklahoma have rejected proposals for a unicameral legislature, other states in the 1960s and 1970s have seriously considered adopting the structure.

See also Bicameralism.

UNIFORM CODE OF MILITARY JUSTICE. *See* Military Law.

UNION SHOP, a union security provision under which an employer may hire any worker he chooses. The new employee, however, is required to become a member of a union within a certain period, usually 30 days. In a union shop the employee is required to remain a union member or to pay dues for the length of time the collective bargaining agreement is in force.

See also Agency Shop.

UNITED AUTO WORKERS (UAW), an industrial union of workers in the automobile, aircraft, and farm machinery industries. Formed in 1935, the UAW was initially an affiliate of the AFL but changed to CIO. In 1937, it conducted a bitter and prolonged struggle to gain official bargaining recognition from the automobile industry. In 1968, the UAW withdrew from the AFL-CIO but was reaffiliated in 1981. The UAW has over one million members and 1,540 local unions.

UNITED FARM WORKERS (UFW), organization founded in 1962 by César Chavez, and comprising agricultural and migrant workers. The UFW seeks to achieve collective bargaining rights for agricultural workers in the United States. The UFW has over 100,000 members and is affiliated with the AFL-CIO. In the 1960s, the UFW gained national support for its boycott of grapes, wine, and lettuce.

UNITED MINE WORKERS (UMW), union founded in 1890 through the merger of several organizations. It is an independent union with about 280,000 members. The UMW seeks to protect the interests of coal mine workers in the United States. Perhaps its most significant achievement was the attainment of the eight-hour work day in 1898. It is currently concerned with questions of mine safety and worker health.

UNITED NATIONS, an organization aiming at the maintenance of international peace through collective security and at peaceful change and welfare in the world. The U.N. is located in New York City and is modeled after the League of Nations. The United Nations charter was signed on June 16, 1945, by 50

Walter Reuther (R) and George Meany celebrate the unionization of the nation's automobile workers.

nomic and military sanctions to the severance of communications and diplomatic relations. The council is composed of 15 members, of which five are permanent (the United States, the U.S.S.R., the United Kingdom, France, and China) and ten are elected for two-year terms by the General Assembly, taking into account an equitable geographical distribution. The U.N. voted to expel Taiwan in 1981 and seat the People's Republic of China as the representative of China. As a qualified majority of nine, including all the permanent members, is required in important decisions, lack of unanimity by the permanent members can make the council inoperative. This stumbling block is known as the veto power. In less important questions any simple majority is required.

The Economic and Social Council (ECOSOC) is composed of 54 members elected by the General Assembly for three years. Unlike the Security Council, members can be reelected. The voting procedure is always simple majority. ECOSOC meets when necessary, generally twice a year. It has no power to make binding decisions. An important task is to furnish technical and general assistance to the developing countries. ECOSOC's general objectives are higher standards of living and health, international cooperation in educational and scientific endeavors, and fundamental human rights for all. It enters into agreements and maintains contact with the specialized agencies of the organization.

The International Court of Justice, with its seat at The Hague, is the only principal U.N. organ not physically located in New York. The Court is regulated by a statute annexed to the U.N. charter; all members of the U.N. are automatically parties to this statute. The Court consists of 15 judges, elected independently by the General Assembly and the Security Council. No two judges may be of the same nationality; they serve for terms of nine years. The jurisdiction of the Court covers all cases referred to it and all matters provided for in the charter, treaties, or conventions. The Court may be asked for legal opinions; the Security Council may hand it a legal dispute. The Court bases its decisions on international convention and jurisprudence.

The Court has not been effective in resolving international disputes because its authority is limited to cases where states have accepted its jurisdiction. Iran refused to accept a Court decision ordering release of U.S. hostages, and the United States said it would not participate in proceedings to consider Nicaragua's claim of U.S. aggression.

The Secretariat, composed of a staff of international civil servants, is headed by a secretary general, who is appointed by the General Assembly on the recommendation of the Security Council. He is the chief administrative officer of the U.N.; his political functions, not clearly specified, are essentially mediation and conciliation among member states. He can

United Nations headquarters, New York City.

countries; ratification came on October 24, 1945. The membership (159 in 1990) of the organization has expanded considerably since then, mainly as a consequence of the coming to independence of former colonies, which seek membership as a badge of standing in the international community. Any state with peaceful intent and ability to carry out the obligations of the charter can be a member. The principle of sovereign equality of all members is basic in the organization. A member must assist the organization and refrain from the threat or use of force against other states. The U.N. may suspend or expel, but it cannot intervene in the internal affairs of any state. The expenses of the organization are borne by its members, as apportioned by the General Assembly. The assessment of the United States in 1990 was around 25 percent. The official languages are English, French, Russian, Chinese, and Spanish.

The U.N. is composed of six principal organs: the General Assembly, the Security Council, the Economic and Social Council, the Trusteeship Council, the International Court of Justice, and the Secretariat. Subsidiary organs are set up to meet particular needs.

The General Assembly is the center of the organization; each U.N. member country is also a member of the General Assembly. It meets once a year, but special sessions may be called at any time, and it elects a president for each session. Decisions of the assembly may be taken by simple or by two-thirds majority, depending on the importance of the subject under consideration. The General Assembly discusses and recommends. Recommendations may be directed to member nations, to the Security Council, or to both. A resolution of November 3, 1950, empowers the assembly to take over, under certain conditions, some of the powers of the Security Council. The General Assembly, as other U.N. organs, establishes its own rules of procedure.

The Security Council has as its primary responsibility the maintenance of peace and security. The measures taken to terminate aggression go from eco-bring to the attention of the Security Council any matter which, in his opinion, threatens international

peace and security. Among other responsibilities, he coordinates the activities of the U.N.'s worldwide organs. Four persons have occupied the position of secretary general: Trygve Lie of Norway (1946-1953); Dag Hammarskjöld of Sweden (1953-1961), U Thant of Burma (1961-1971), Kurt Waldheim of Austria (1972-1981) and Javier Pérez de Cuéllar of Peru (1982-   ).

The secretary general is assisted by an international staff. During the performance of their duties, they may not seek or receive instructions from any government or from any authority external to the United Nations. Very high standards of performance, competence, and honesty are set for the staff members, who are recruited on the basis of personal merit and geographic distribution. For professional and high-level positions, the number of nationals of any country is proportional to its financial contribution to the organization. Most of the low-level personnel are recruited locally. Certain privileges and immunities are granted to U.N. officials.

United Nations Security Council.

The Specialized Agencies, autonomous although related in various degrees to organization, provide technical assistance to the developing countries. Whereas most of the U.N.'s members are members of the specialized agencies, some non-member states belong to certain of the agencies. The permanent specialized agencies are 13: International Labor Organization (ILO), with headquarters in Geneva; Food and Agricultural Organization (FAO), Rome; United Nations Educational, Scientific, and Cultural Organization (UNESCO), Paris; World Health Organization (WHO), Geneva; International Bank for Reconstruction and Development (IBRD or World Bank), Washington; International Finance Corporation (IFC), Washington; International Development Association (IDA), Washington; International Monetary Fund (IMF), Washington; International Civil Aviation Organization (ICAO), Montreal; Universal Postal Union (UPU), Berne; International Telecommunication Union (ITU), Geneva; World Meteorological Organization (WMO), Geneva; Intergovernmental Maritime Consultative Organization (IMCO), London.

The United States withdrew from the United Nations Educational, Scientific, and Cultural Organization (UNESCO) at the end of 1984, and Great Britain followed in 1985. These actions followed unresolved differences between a number of industrial states and UNESCO over charges of financial mismanagement and anti-Western bias. The United States had paid 25 percent of the organization's annual budget. A commission found that reforms had been made and recommended that the U.S. rejoin UNESCO. In December 1989, the State Department rejected those findings.

Quasi-specialized agencies are the General Agreement on Tariffs and Trade (GATT), Geneva; and the International Atomic Energy Agency (IAEA), Vienna. Other organizations designed to fill special needs are: the U.N. Children's Fund (UNICEF), the U.N. High Commissioner for Refugees (UNHCR), and the U.N. Relief and Works Agency (UNRWA). Regional organizations, such as the Organization of American States (OAS) and the Organization of African Unity (OAU), are permitted by the United Nations, provided that their purpose is consistent with the principles laid down in the charter.

History. In spite of being an organization dedicated to peace, the U.N. has used armed forces to repel aggression. In Korea, 1950-1953, a U.N. command was set up under a U.N. flag, even though the role played by the United States was preponderant. Armed forces were dispatched to Egypt after the war with Israel of 1956. Removal of the United Nations Emergency Force (UNEF) in 1967 was one of the causes of renewed armed conflict between Egypt and Israel. Dispatched to the Congo from 1960 to 1964, ONUC (Operation des Nations Unies au Congo) prevented the disintegration of the newly independent Belgian colony. Present in Cyprus since 1964, the United Nations Force in Cyprus (UNFICYP) attempts to control the explosive situation between Greek majority and Turkish minority. The problem of disarmament has been tackled by the organization with limited success.

Very important is the contribution of the U.N. to the struggle against colonialism. The 1960 declaration against colonialism solemnly proclaimed "the necessity of bringing to a speedy and unconditional end colonialism in all its forms and manifestations." Many other basic documents have been adopted by the U.N., like the Universal Declaration of Human Rights of 1948 and the International Convention on Genocide of 1948.

The organization, emphasizing its concern for developmental problems, proclaimed the decade 1961-1970 U.N. Development Decade. As its objectives were not fully attained, a Second U.N. Development Decade covered the 1970s, attempting to narrow the gap between developed and underdeveloped countries. To this effect, a U.N. Development Program (UNDP) was established in 1965,

UNITED NATIONS
159 Members of General Assembly

Afghanistan	Germany, East	Paraguay
Albania	Germany, West	Peru
Algeria	Ghana	Philippines
Angola	Greece	Poland
Antigua and	Grenada	Portugal
Barbuda	Guatemala	Qatar
Argentina	Guinea	Romania
Australia	Guinea-Bissau	Rwanda
Austria	Guyana	St. Christopher
Bahamas	Haiti	and Nevis
Bahrain	Honduras	St. Lucia
Bangladesh	Hungary	St. Vincent and
Barbados	Iceland	the Grenadines
Belgium	India	
Belize	Indonesia	Samoa (Western)
Benin	Iran	Sao Tome &
Bhutan	Iraq	Principe
Bolivia	Ireland	Saudi Arabia
Botswana	Israel	Senegal
Brazil	Italy	Seychelles
Brunei	Ivory Coast	Sierra Leone
Bulgaria	Jamaica	Singapore
Burkina Faso	Japan	Solomon Islands
(Upper Volta)	Jordan	Somalia
Burma	Kenya	South Africa
Burundi	Kuwait	Spain
Byelorussia	Laos	Sri Lanka
Cambodia	Lebanon	Sudan
(Kampuchea)	Lesotho	Surinam
Cameroon	Liberia	Swaziland
Canada	Libya	Sweden
Cape Verde	Luxembourg	Syria
Central Afr. Rep.	Madagascar	Tanzania
Chad	(Malagasy)	Thailand
Chile	Malawi	Togo
China	Malaysia	Trinidad &
Colombia	Maldives	Tobago
Comoros	Mali	Tunisia
Congo	Malta	Turkey
Costa Rica	Mauritania	Uganda
Cuba	Mauritius	Ukraine
Cyprus	Mexico	Union of Soviet
Czechoslovakia	Mongolia	Soc. Repubs.
Denmark	Morocco	
Djibouti	Mozambique	United Arab
Dominica	Myanmar (Burma)	Emirates
	Nepal	
Dominican Rep.	Netherlands	United Kingdom
Ecuador	New Zealand	United States
Egypt	Nicaragua	Uruguay
El Salvador	Niger	Vanuatu
Equatorial Guinea	Nigeria	Venezuela
	Norway	Vietnam
Ethiopia	Oman	Yemen
Fiji	Pakistan	Yemen (South)
Finland	Panama	
France	Papua	Yugoslavia
Gabon	New Guinea	Zaire
Gambia		Zambia
		Zimbabwe

combining the Expanded Program of Technical Assistance, and the U.N. Special Fund. The U.N. Development Program marked its 40th anniversary year (including its earlier programs) in 1990. In that year, it had funds of $1.3 billion to allocate to 152 developing countries and territories. In 1964 the U.N. Conference on Trade and Development (UNCTAD) had been established as a permanent organ, and the U.N. Industrial Development Organization (UNIDO) was founded in 1966. The U.N. has met with recent success in outer space, seabed, and environmental areas. Important diplomatic contacts take place under the aegis of the U.N.

The changed composition of the U.N. membership has given added importance to the voting blocs. Even before the massive admittance of the newly independent countries to the organization, the Western, the Latin American, and the Communist blocs were clearly discernible. The Afro-Asian bloc, generally demonstrating solidarity in questions concerning colonialism and aid to developing countries, is otherwise divided.

The United Nation's role is circumscribed by the will and behavior of its members. The U.N. does not impose solutions, but it mediates and conciliates; it supplies the machinery if concerned parties desire solutions.   —*Sergio Barzanti*

UNITED NATIONS CHILDREN'S FUND (UNICEF), agency first established in 1946 by the U.N. General Assembly to aid child victims of World War II. Currently, the agency's primary responsibility is to help developing countries care for children, especially when emergencies result from natural disasters such as drought. UNICEF is based in New York but has field offices around the world to coordinate the distribution of food, clothing, and medical supplies. Its executive board consists of representatives from 30 nations elected by the Economic and Social Council. UNICEF funds come primarily from voluntary contributions from U.N. members but also from private sources and the sale of greeting cards. UNICEF's efforts were recognized in 1965 when the agency was awarded the Nobel Peace Prize for its humanitarian work.

UNITED NATIONS RELIEF AND REHABILITATION ADMINISTRATION (UNRRA), created by a Washington, D.C., conference of 44 nations in 1943 to implement relief programs in countries ravaged by war. The conference asked all countries that had not been invaded to contribute one percent of their 1943 national income for international relief. UNRRA supplied personnel and 25 million long tons of material valued at $4 billion. UNRRA was discontinued in 1947, and other U.N. agencies took over the task of global refugee relief.

UNITED STATES AIR FORCE ACADEMY, military

academy located in Colorado Springs, Col. The academy was founded in 1954. It educates and trains men and women for service in the Air Force. Qualified students are admitted by congressional appointment. Graduates receive a Bachelor of Science degree and a commission as second lieutenant.

UNITED STATES CLAIMS COURT, court established in 1982 to replace the Court of Claims and assume all jurisdiction held previously by that court. It serves as the court of original and exclusive jurisdiction over claims brought against the federal government (except tort claims, which are heard by District Court). Prior to the establishment of the Court of Claims in 1855, the United States Government as a sovereign state could not be sued. A claim against the United States could be made only by passage of a private act by Congress granting relief. For the first ten years of the operation of the Court of Claims, its authority was limited to drafting a recommendation for Congress. In 1866 the Court of Claims was granted authority to award damages.

Today, the Claims Court can render money judgments in cases brought concerning the application of the Constitution, acts of Congress, a regulation of an executive department, or upon express or implied contract with the government of the United States.

The court takes testimony and depositions at locations convenient for claimants and witnesses. The court comprises 16 judges, all appointed by the president and confirmed by the Senate. One judge, as designated by the president, serves as chief justice.
                    —*Guy C. Colarulli and Victor F. D'Lugin*
See also Legislative Court.

UNITED STATES CODE, the official compilation of all acts of Congress that are still in force. All applicable statutes were compiled in 1926 into the first edition of the *United States Code,* which was organized into 50 titles classified according to subject matter and published in four volumes. Cumulative supplements are published annually; new editions of the *Code* are published every six years.   —*Mary L. Carns*
See also Statutes at Large of the United States.

UNITED STATES GOVERNMENT ORGANIZATION MANUAL, an official annual government publication describing in detail all of the agencies of the executive, legislative, and judicial branches of the government. The manual outlines the responsibilities of each agency and its principal officers and offers information to those seeking employment or doing business with the federal government. The manual is also helpful to those seeking information about small business opportunities, environmental programs, government publications, and speakers and films available to the public. The manual contains a copy of the Constitution and a list of members of Congress. The publication may be obtained from the Superintendent of Documents, Government Printing Office, Washington, D.C. 20402, or from GPO bookstores in the major cities.

UNITED STATES INFORMATION AGENCY (USIA), formerly the International Communication Agency, a federal agency reestablished by the United States Information Agency Authorization Act of 1978. The USIA is responsible for the dissemination abroad of information and cultural programs about the United States. These include international educational exchange programs, the Voice of America, and the Fulbright Scholarships. It uses a wide variety of media in an effort to strengthen foreign support for, and understanding of, American society and U.S. foreign policy.

A West point graduation tradition: hats off!

UNITED STATES MILITARY ACADEMY (USMA), the historic training institution for U.S. Army officers. It provides cadets with a four-year general education, plus theoretical and practical training as junior officers, that leads to a B.S. degree and a commission as second lieutenant. A few cadets may be commissioned annually in the Air Force or Navy. Cadets receive appointments through a variety of competitive and noncompetitive channels. Opened in 1802 at West Point, N.Y., the academy was for many years the only United States engineering school.

UNITED STATES NAVAL ACADEMY, military academy located in Annapolis, Md. The academy educates and trains men and women for service in the Navy. A four-year program of study results in a Bachelor of Science degree. Graduates are commissioned as second lieutenants in the Marine Corps or as ensigns in the Navy.

U.S. Naval Academy cadets at Annapolis, Md.

UNITED STATES STUDENT ASSOCIATION (USSA), organization formed in 1978 by the merger of the U.S. National Student Association and the National Student Lobby. It is a confederation of approximately 400 college student governments. The USSA is the largest student lobbying group in the country, representing the needs and opinions of college students. In the 1980s it has been active in lobbying for federal programs for college student loans and grants.

UNITED STATES v. BUTLER, 297 U.S. 1 (1936), questions the power of Congress to enforce the Agricultural Adjustment Act of 1933, under which a tax was imposed on processors of farm products, the proceeds of which were to be paid to farmers who reduced their acreage and crops, thus increasing the price of certain products.

The Court held that Congress had exercised its taxing power for an unconstitutional end in attempting to regulate agricultural production without the consent of the state in which it was practiced and hence invaded the reserved rights of the states. Secondly, although Congress does have the power to levy a tax to benefit general national welfare, this tax did not provide such benefit, as its proceeds were earmarked for those farmers complying with prescribed conditions.

See also McCulloch v. Maryland.

UNITED STATES v. CLASSIC, 313 U.S. 299 (1941), concerns the constitutionality of federal regulation of congressional primary elections. Classic, a New Orleans commissioner of elections, was indicted under a federal statute for election fraud in connection with a Louisiana Democratic primary election for congressman.

In the opinion of the Court, the right of voters at a primary to have their votes counted accurately is a right or privilege the federal government is given the right to protect by Article I of the Constitution. Therefore, infringement of that right is a federal offense, punishable under the federal criminal code. Note that the Court rejected a contention that, because no one was elected congressman until the general election, only that election came within the protection of the Constitution.

See also Screws v. United States.

UNITED STATES v. CURTISS-WRIGHT EXPORT CORP., 299 U.S. 304 (1936). Traditional notions of constitutional law hold that the federal government is one of limited powers. This doctrine of specified powers gives meaning to the Tenth Amendment, which says that all powers not specifically delegated to the federal government by the Constitution or prohibited by it to the states are reserved to the states and the people. The corollary of this rule is that the Constitution is the only source of federal power, but there may be an exception in foreign affairs.

In the case of the *United States v. Curtiss-Wright Export Corp.,* the Supreme Court distinguished internal affairs from foreign affairs, rejecting a challenge to a broad delegation of power from Congress to the president that allowed him to prohibit the sale of arms to countries engaged in armed conflict. The Court held that the foreign affairs powers were sovereign powers never held by the states. These powers were transmitted to the federal government as a result of the separation from Great Britain and were not carved from the mass of state powers, as were those delegated to the federal government by the Constitution.
                                    —*Philip J. Hannon*

UNITED STATES v. DARBY, 312 U.S. 100 (1941), questions the validity of the 1938 Fair Labor Standards Act (the Wages and Hours Act), which excluded from interstate commerce all goods produced under conditions which did not conform to specific labor standards.

In the opinion of the Court, the Congress has the constitutional power to prohibit the shipment between states of goods manufactured under conditions not meeting the requirements of the Act. The Court reasoned that the present regulation makes effective the congressional conception of public policy: that interstate commerce should not be made the instrument of competition by the distribution of goods produced under substandard labor conditions, as such competition is injurious to the commerce and to the states involved.

See also Hammer v. Dagenhart.

UNITED STATES v. E.C. KNIGHT CO., 156 U.S. 1 (1895), questions the power of the Congress to con-

trol a monopoly in the manufacture of specific goods. The United States brought suit, under the Sherman Antitrust Act of 1890, against the American Sugar Refining Company and other sugar refining companies to bring about the cancellation of certain agreements in which there was an alleged conspiracy to monopolize the manufacture and sale of refined sugar in the United States.

In the opinion of the Court, the Sherman Act did not apply to combinations in restraint of manufacturing because manufacturing is not interstate commerce. The Court held that the power to control the manufacture of a given item involves in a certain sense the control of its disposition, but that this is a secondary effect and does not constitute control of commerce.

See also NLRB v. Jones & Laughlin Steel Corporation; Radovitch v. NFL.

UNITED STATES v. GUEST, 383 U.S. 745 (1966), concerns the scope of permissible federal protection of individual rights. Guest and five other persons were indicted under a federal statute for conspiracy to deprive blacks of the use of state facilities and of the right to travel in connection with the shotgun murder of Lemuel Penn, a black educator who was traveling through Georgia. The five defendants, private individuals, were alleged to have caused the arrest of blacks by false reports of the commission of criminal acts.

The Court held that such an allegation contained enough possibility of state involvement to permit Congress to enact federal legislation aimed at conspiracies to interfere with the individual rights protected by the Fourteenth Amendment, whether they involved state action or wholly private activities.

UNITED STATES v. LANZA, 260 U.S. 377 (1922), concerns the protection against double jeopardy, as guaranteed by the Fifth Amendment. Lanza, convicted by the State of Washington for violating the state's prohibition act, was then indicted in a federal court for violation of the National Prohibition Act.

In a controversial decision which was overruled in 1969 by *Benton v. Maryland,* the Court held that the Fifth Amendment applies only to proceedings by the federal government. The defendants committed two different offenses by the same act, a violation of a state law and a violation of the National Prohibition Act. The Court believed that the two prosecutions were for different crimes and therefore did not constitute double jeopardy. The Attorney General of the United States has since ordered that no federal case can be brought to trial when there has already been a state prosecution for substantially the same act.

See also Benton v. Maryland.

UNITED STATES v. NIXON, 418 U.S. (1974), case in which a unanimous Supreme Court ordered President Richard Nixon to comply with a subpoena for tapes of certain White House conversations, sought by a special prosecutor for use as evidence against White House aides charged with obstruction of justice in the investigation of the break-in at the Democratic National Headquarters (the "Watergate Scandal").

While not rejecting entirely the legitimacy of "executive privilege," the Court held that neither the separation of powers nor the need to preserve the confidentiality of presidential communications could justify an absolute privilege to resist judicial demands for evidence to be used in a criminal trial.

UNITED STATES v. O'BRIEN, 391 U.S. 367 (1968), concerns the burning of selective service registration certificates, or "draft cards," in violation of the Universal Military Training and Service Act. O'Brien and three companions burned their draft cards on the steps of the South Boston Courthouse in protest of the Vietnam hostilities. O'Brien argued that prohibiting the knowing destruction or mutilation of these certificates was unconstitutional because it abridged the protected right of "symbolic" speech guaranteed by the First Amendment.

In the opinion of the Court, delivered by Chief Justice Warren, the multiple functions of the draft cards give Congress a legitimate and substantial interest in preventing their wanton and unrestrained destruction. The Court also stated that when speech and nonspeech elements are combined in the same act, a sufficiently important governmental interest in regulating the nonspeech element can justify incidental limitation on speech elements protected by the First Amendment.

UNITED STATES v. SEEGER, 380 U.S. 163 (1965), considers the validity of Seeger's conviction for refusing to submit to induction into the armed forces after he was denied conscientious objector status. The Selective Service Act provided that a "Supreme Being" is of central importance to a claim of conscientious objection. Seeger maintained that although he did not believe in a Supreme Being, he was conscientiously opposed to participation in war in any form by reason of his religious beliefs.

The Court overturned the conviction, holding that any sincere and meaningful belief which occupies in an individual's life a place parallel to belief in a "Supreme Being" qualifies for the exemption. Subsequently, a conviction of a nonreligious objector to the Vietnam conflict was reversed on the ground that the Act, as amended following the Seeger decision, still amounted to an establishment of religion, violating the establishment clause of the First Amendment.

UNITED STATES v. WONG KIM ARK, 169 U.S. 649 (1898), concerns the scope of the citizenship provision of the Fourteenth Amendment, which reads, "All persons born or naturalized in the United States,

and subject to the jurisdiction thereof, are citizens of the United States and of the state wherein they reside." Wong Kim Ark had been born in San Francisco in 1873 of parents who were subjects of the emperor of China but who were permanently domiciled in the United States. In 1894 he went to China, and on his return to the United States in 1895, the customs officer refused him admission on the ground that he was not a citizen.

The Court held that Wong was a citizen, saying that the Fourteenth Amendment affirms the ancient and fundamental rule of citizenship by birth within a territory in the allegiance and under the protection of the country, regardless of the nationality of the parents.

See also Dred Scott v. Sandford; Slaughterhouse Cases.

UNITED STEELWORKERS OF AMERICA v. WEBER, 433 U.S. 193 (1979), (also known as *U.S. v. Weber* and *Kaiser Aluminum v. Weber*), a case in which the Supreme Court held that Title VII of the Civil Rights Act does not prevent employers from voluntarily adopting a temporary affirmative action program of promotion designed to alleviate traditional racial imbalances in advanced job categories. Relying heavily on the legislative intent and "historical context" to overcome the apparent meaning of the literal language of Title VII, the Court concluded that the "purposes of the plan in question mirror those of the statute. Both were designed to break down old patterns of racial segregation and hierarchy . . . to open employment opportunities" for blacks "in occupations which have been traditionally closed to them."

UNIT RULE, the practice among some state delegations to the national convention of voting in a bloc, regardless of individual preference, for a single presidential candidate. The Democratic convention permits this practice, which was most frequently used by southern delegations to increase their influence at the convention. The unit rule can be instituted by the majority of a state's delegates, providing that no rule exists against its use; or it may be ordained by a state party convention. The Republican party forbids the unit rule at its national convention.

UNIVERSAL SUFFRAGE. *See* Election; Woman Suffrage.

URBAN LEAGUE, NATIONAL. *See* National Urban League.

URBAN MASS TRANSPORTATION ADMINISTRATION (UMTA). Set up in 1964 and switched from the Housing and Urban Development Department to the Department of Transportation in 1968, UMTA's goals are to relieve the dependence of America on the automobile and to develop area-wide transit systems integrating existing bus, rail, and road systems with new streamlined hardware, modern terminals, and high-speed systems. Concerned with low-cost facilities, UMTA has a special Office of Civil Rights and Service Development. Most of UMTA's efforts are through capital assistance (up to two-thirds financing). The administration also supports technical studies and personnel training.

URBAN PLANNING, the process of guiding the development and change of towns and cities in a manner that will improve the quality of life for their inhabitants. As a process, planning includes the formulation of goals and objectives, the collection and analysis of information relative to achieving these goals, the development of plans designed to achieve the desired results, and their implementation. Such a process can only be meaningful as it strives to promote a harmonious relationship between people and their urban environment. By the very nature of its subject, urban planning is a dynamic endeavor. Cities are complex, manmade organisms composed of many interrelated elements; economic, social, physical, demographic, natural, and political. The various elements of cities are in constant transition. Urban planning must therefore deal not only with these specific elements, but with the phenomenon of continuous change among them as well.

History. Men have planned cities for thousands of years. However, contemporary urban planning is essentially a product of the twentieth century, growing out of the reform era of the 1890s when planners were architects and engineers concerned primarily with the physical appearance of cities. The mounting problems of urbanization during the early 1900s demanded a shift in emphasis from urban form to urban function and efficiency. Planners became concerned with controlling land uses and regulating building heights. New York City adopted the nation's first comprehensive zoning ordinance in 1916. Municipal administration and slum housing were also important issues during these early years. The first graduate program in city and regional planning was offered by Harvard University in 1929, acknowledging the arrival of a distinct profession in its own right.

Public housing and public works became important planning concerns during the 1930s. Limited interest was also generated in new towns. A major impetus to urban planning at the local level was the 1949 Housing Act, which, among other thing, made federal funds available for the preparation o comprehensive land-use plans in cities and towns across the country. Urban renewal, a federally assisted program to rid the central cities of slums and blighted areas, was also a product of this Act. Taking a variety of forms over the years, urban renewal has achieved some of its stated goals. However, it never really attacked the social problems that created slums, and many of the urban poor found themselves little better off for it.

As the automobile has become the dominant mode of urban transportation, tremendous resources have been allocated by all levels of government to transportation planning and highway construction. The 41,000-mile interstate highway system begun in 1956 stands out as the single most aggressive effort in this area. Today, increasing attention is being paid to mass rapid transportation, yet it has never received an emphasis similar to that given the automobile in this country.

Over 100 new towns or communities had been built in the United States by 1970, most of them by private developers. After receiving limited attention for several decades, interest in new towns was revived during the 1960s, spurred on by the results of Columbia, Md., and Reston, Va. Recent federal legislation authorizes the U.S. Department of Housing and Urban Development to financially guarantee numerous new town developments in the years ahead. Usually sited within relative proximity to major metropolitan centers, new towns are being designed to accommodate future populations in excess of 100,000 people each. Such developments are not a panacea for the ills of decaying cities, but the new cities provide planners with the opportunity to utilize a growing body of knowledge to avoid previous mistakes.

A Broader Approach. Urban planning has traditionally been a function of local government. National urban growth or planning policies have yet to be developed by the federal government, in spite of the growing amount of attention this subject has received. However, as the problems of cities have spilled over jurisdictional boundaries, the needs for coordinative economic and developmental planning on a regional scale have become widely recognized. The 1929 *Regional Plan of New York and Its Environs* was a pioneering regional planning effort. More recently, the 1965 Housing Act has encouraged the formation of hundreds of metropolitan and regional planning agencies, many located within councils of government. Such agencies have been concerned with a variety of urban problems, including economic development, water and sewer systems, open-space networks, and criminal-justice planning.

The nature of urban planning today has been greatly shaped by two major phenomena. First, cities have become increasingly complex and besieged with a host of problems, ranging from crime and air pollution to urban sprawl and municipal bankruptcy. The categorization of America's urban crisis fills literally volumes of writings. Second, only in recent years have planners shown evidence of their increasing awareness of the interrelated nature of the city's elements. The social, economic, health, and environmental effects of physical developments are being considered with greater frequency than ever before. Although an integrated approach may still be more the exception than the rule, requirements such as submitting environmental-impact statements for certain federally assisted developments evidence this important trend.

As planners have gained a better understanding of the complexity of urban problems and the interrelationships among the elements of the city, the scope of urban planning has been substantially broadened. Out of the general land-use planning orientation of the 1950s have grown such specialities as health, environmental, criminal-justice, recreational, and social planning. Along with the application of computer technology to urban planning has come an increasingly sophisticated array of new tools and techniques, including simulation models, network analysis, computer graphics, and planning-programming-budgeting-systems. This maturation process that urban planning has been experiencing has made one point increasingly clear, however: the solution to most of America's urban problems will require the coordinated application of the skills of many related fields of knowledge rather than those of any single discipline.
—David R. Mosena

UTOPIA, a term derived from the Greek *ou topos,* "no place." It was coined by Sir Thomas More in his book *Utopia* (1516). By a play on the word *eu,* meaning "best," More suggested that utopia was a nonexistent best place. It most commonly refers to an ideal, harmonious, or best society. The term is also used pejoratively toward ideas and behavior that are overly idealistic.

Utopias have been developed in a variety of literary forms and for many purposes. The first utopia, Plato's *Republic,* was a paradigmatic description of the just city. More's *Utopia* depicts an island where all men were equal, prosperous, educated, and wise. Utopias are often satirical. Thus Swift's *Gulliver's Travels* sought to show the ludicrous qualities of English social and political life. Aldous Huxley's contemporary *Brave New World* is meant as a warning against the dangerous combination of modern science and utilitarian politics.

VAN BUREN, MARTIN (1782-1862), eighth President of the United States (1837-1841), born in Kinderhook, N.Y. A leader in the New York State Democratic party, he served in the U.S. Senate (1820-1828), served briefly as New York governor, and became secretary of state (1829-1831) and vice president (1833-1837) under President Andrew Jackson. The years of his presidency coincided with a major depression, which undermined his popularity, and he was defeated for the presidency in 1840 and again in 1848 when he ran as the Free-Soil party candidate.
See also Presidential Elections.

VANCE v. TERRAZAS, 444 U.S. 252 (1980), Supreme Court decision concerning the question of the standard of proof to be used in determining loss of citizenship. Laurence Terrazas acquired dual American/Mexican citizenship at birth. At the age of 22, he applied for a certificate of Mexican nationality in which he "expressly renounced loyalty to the United States." The U.S. government, via Secretary of State Cyrus Vance, issued a certificate of loss of American nationality, and Terrazas appealed. He argued the government must prove his expatriating act was accompanied by an intent to renounce his American citizenship. The Supreme Court agreed and also upheld the statutory requirement that the government must prove intent "by a preponderance of the evidence." The case was remanded to the Court of Appeals.
See also Citizenship.

VENUE refers to the locality in which a suit may be tried. Venue is different from jurisdiction, the power of a court to hear a case. For example, any federal court has jurisdiction in a federal question, but a Vermont plaintiff is not entitled to sue a Maine defendant in federal court in California. The Maine defendant could waive objections to the suit in that court, however, and the suit could proceed. By contrast, a lack of jurisdiction can never be waived, and the court itself will dismiss a suit if jurisdiction is lacking.

The Sixth Amendment requires that criminal prosecutions shall be conducted in the "State and district wherein the crime shall have been committed." A "change of venue" is occasionally granted, usually on the basis of excessive pre-trial publicity and the likelihood that a fair and impartial jury could not be selected from that locality.
See also Change of Venue.

VETERANS AFFAIRS, DEPARTMENT OF, cabinet-level department of the federal government. It was established as the Veterans Administration in 1930 to provide benefits for veterans and their dependents. Included were pensions, compensation benefits for disabilities or death, education, rehabilitation, home loan guarantees, and a medical program that involves a comprehensive system of clinics, nursing homes, and hospitals.

President Reagan signed legislation elevating the Veterans Administration to cabinet-level status. The law took effect in March 1989, making the VA the 14th cabinet-level department. Critics of the change from agency to cabinet status expressed concern that the department and its programs might become politicized. President Bush nominated Edward Derwinski, a Republican congressman from Illinois, as the first Secretary of Veterans Affairs.

VETERANS OF FOREIGN WARS (VFW), group whose members have served overseas during foreign wars of the United States. It was organized in 1913 through the merger of various veterans' groups. The VFW looks after the interests of veterans through lobbying, charitable activities, and community and legal services. There are 10,000 local chapters, which serve the VFW's nearly two million members. In addition to lobbying and providing direct health services to veterans, the VFW is a strong voice for the promotion of national defense and calls for patriotism.

VETO (Lat., I forbid). When the president rejects a bill sent to him by both houses he writes "veto" across it. Then the bill returns to the house of its origin. Both houses must pass the rejected bill by a two-thirds majority if it is to become law. The president can also refrain from either signing or vetoing a bill (pocket veto). In this case, the bill automatically becomes law after ten congressional working days unless Congress adjourns before the ten-day period had elapsed. If Congress adjourns, the pocket veto stands and the bill is dead. The president is obligated to give a reason for vetoing a bill. The pocket veto carries no such obligation. The president often uses the pocket veto at the end of a legislative session, when Congress is likely to adjourn itself before the ten-day period has ended.

It is relatively rare for Congress to override a presidential veto, owing to the difficulty of procuring a two-thirds majority. State governors also possess veto power, although the majority needed in the state legislatures to override varies from state to state. In addition to the ordinary veto, some states allow their governors to reject part of an appropriations bill rather than the whole (item veto).

VICE PRESIDENT OF THE UNITED STATES, the second highest official of the United States federal government, first in line to succeed the president in case of his death, resignation, removal, or incapacitation. The vice president is elected on the same ticket as the president, although in the early years of the republic each was elected separately. The vice president is also the president of the Senate, but as presiding officer he is not allowed to vote except to break a tie. He has no other specific constitutional functions; he is not a member of the Senate, does not participate in debates or committee work, and has little actual power beyond his own personal influence and the prestige of his office. He is totally dependent on the president for extraconstitutional responsibilities.

Historically, the vice president was chosen to balance a ticket or heal a split in the party and not for any conspicuous talent. As a result, the office was considered insignificant and a dead end for an ambitious politician. The office has been upgraded recently, largely because energetic men have filled it. The vice presidents Richard M. Nixon, Lyndon B. Johnson, Hubert Humphrey, and Spiro Agnew were major national figures. They attended cabinet meetings, trav-

Vice President	Term	President
1. John Adams	1789-97	Washington
2. Thomas Jefferson	1797-1801	J. Adams
3. Aaron Burr	1801-05	Jefferson
4. George Clinton	1805-09	Jefferson
George Clinton[A]	1809-12	Madison
5. Elbridge Gerry[B]	1813-14	Madison
6. Daniel D. Tompkins	1817-25	Monroe
7. John C. Calhoun	1825-29	J.Q. Adams
John C. Calhoun[C]	1829-32	Jackson
8. Martin Van Buren	1833-37	Jackson
9. Richard M. Johnson	1837-41	Van Buren
10. John Tyler[D]	1841	W.H. Harrison
11. George M. Dallas	1845-49	Polk
12. Millard Fillmore[E]	1849-50	Taylor
13. William R.D. King[F]	1853	Pierce
14. John C. Breckinridge	1857-61	Buchanan
15. Hannibal Hamlin	1861-65	Lincoln
16. Andrew Johnson[G]	1865	Lincoln
17. Schuyler Colfax	1869-73	Grant
18. Henry Wilson[H]	1873-75	Grant
19. William A. Wheeler	1877-81	Hayes
20. Chester A. Arthur[I]	1881	Garfield
21. Thomas A. Hendricks[J]	1885	Cleveland
22. Levi P. Morton	1889-93	B. Harrison
23. Adlai E. Stevenson	1893-97	Cleveland
24. Garret A. Hobart[K]	1897-99	McKinley
25. Theodore Roosevelt[L]	1901	McKinley
26. Charles W. Fairbanks	1905-09	T. Roosevelt
27. James S. Sherman[M]	1909-12	Taft
28. Thomas R. Marshall	1913-21	Wilson
29. Calvin Coolidge[N]	1921-23	Harding
30. Charles G. Dawes	1925-29	Coolidge
31. Charles Curtis	1929-33	Hoover
32. John N. Garner	1933-41	F. Roosevelt
33. Henry A. Wallace	1941-45	F. Roosevelt
34. Harry S. Truman[O]	1945	F. Roosevelt
35. Alben W. Barkley	1949-53	Truman
36. Richard M. Nixon	1953-61	Eisenhower
37. Lyndon B. Johnson[P]	1961-63	Kennedy
38. Hubert H. Humphrey	1965-69	Johnson
39. Spiro T. Agnew[Q]	1969-73	Nixon
40. Gerald R. Ford[R]	1973-74	Nixon
41. Nelson A. Rockefeller	1974-77	Ford
42. Walter F. Mondale	1977-81	Carter
43. George Bush	1981-89	Reagan
44. Dan Quayle	1989-	Bush

(A)   Died April 20, 1812.
(B)   Died Nov. 23, 1814.
(C)   Resigned Dec. 28, 1832, to become United Stats Senator.
(D)   Succeeded to presidency April 6, 1841, following the death of William Henry Harrison.
(E)   Succeeded to presidency July 10, 1850, following death of Zachary Taylor.
(F)   Died April 18, 1853.
(G)   Succeeded to presidency April 15, 1865, following the assassination of Abraham Lincoln.
(H)   Died Nov. 22, 1875.
(I)   Succeeded to presidency Sept. 20, 1881, following the assassination of James A. Garfield.
(J)   Died Nov. 25, 1885.
(K)   Died Nov. 21, 1899.
(L)   Succeeded to presidency Sept. 14, 1901, following the assassination of William McKinley.
(M)   Died Oct. 30, 1912.
(N)   Succeeded to presidency Aug. 3, 1923, following the death of Warren G. Harding.
(O)   Succeeded to presidency April 12, 1945, following the death of Franklin D. Roosevelt.
(P)   Succeeded to presidency Nov. 22, 1963, following the assassination of John F. Kennedy.
(Q)   Resigned Oct. 10, 1973.
(R)   Succeeded to presidency Aug. 9, 1974, following the resignation of Richard M. Nixon.

eled abroad, and conveyed the president's wishes to Congress. Both Nixon and Johnson ascended to the presidency, and Hubert Humphrey became the presidential candidate of his party. George Bush also used his experience as vice president to his advantage when he ran successfully for president in 1988. The Twenty-Fifth Amendment (1967) allows the president, with the consent of Congress, to choose another vice president when the office becomes vacant.

VIETNAMIZATION, a U.S. policy during the Vietnam War consisting of turning over the responsibility for fighting in Vietnam to the South Vietnamese troops, while United States would limit its activities mainly to air support and to supplying equipment until the Army of the Republic of Vietnam (ARVN) would be able to stand alone, at some undetermined date. The North Vietnamese would then hopefully agree to a peace acceptable to the United States. Such policy was revealed to the American public by President Richard Nixon in 1969 and immediately became controversial, one of the main criticisms being that it would indefinitely prolong United States involvement in Vietnam.

The Nixon administration relied heavily on the new policy, and in 1971 Nixon reported that it had succeeded. However, in the spring of 1972 when the doctrine was tested against the reality of a sudden, well-planned attack of the North Vietnamese, the result did not justify such optimistic statements. The fundamental shortcomings of the ARVN were corrupt, inept commanders and lack of motivation. The massive use of United States air and sea power and the interdiction of supplies from overseas, following the mining of the port of Haipong, were effective, but they were outside the program of Vietnamization. In the summer of 1972 it was clear that from a military standpoint the policy was not the success claimed by the administration, but by reducing the U.S. presence and casualties, the policy calmed public opinion and the campuses sufficiently to postpone the end of United States involvement in Vietnam.

VINSON, FREDERICK M(OORE) (1890-1953), 12th Chief Justice of the Supreme Court, born in Louisa, Ky. He was noted for his support of the broad interpretation of the powers of the federal government. From 1923 until 1938, except for one two-year term, he served in the House of Representatives. He became an influential congressman, supporting Franklin Roosevelt's New Deal.

He was appointed in 1946 to the Supreme Court. As chief justice, Vinson's judicial philosophy often led him to reject claims of individual rights asserted in opposition to the exercise of governmental authority. Vinson's failure to unite a faction-ridden court and make it a major force in American life led critics to consider him one of the less successful justices. He

did, however, help to improve the rights of members of racial minorities under the equal protection clause of the Fourteenth Amendment (*Shelley v. Kraemer*, 1948).

See also Supreme Court of the United States.

VIRGINIA PLAN. At the very outset the delegates to the Constitutional Convention of 1787 were confronted with strong differences of opinion as to the purpose of their meeting. Some delegates were authorized and content to revise the existing Articles of Confederation, while other delegates believed in the construction of a new national government under an entirely new constitution. The advocates of a new constitution, among them James Madison, James Wilson, and Edmund Randolph, presented the Virginia, or large-state, Plan (sometimes referred to as the Randolph Plan).

The plan provided for a strong national government with a single national executive elected by the legislature, a judiciary with judges appointed for life by the Senate, and a two-house legislature with a House and Senate apportioned according to population. This plan would have given a majority in the proposed legislature to the large states of Virginia, Massachusetts, and Pennsylvania. The Virginia Plan called for an oath of office, a negative exercised by a Council of Revision that included the executive, and a "convenient number of the judiciary" to examine every act of the national legislature and all state laws contravening the Constitution.

Besides placing the small states in a distinct position of inequality, the plan was criticized at the convention for implying that the new government derived its consent directly from the people, thus circumventing the states. After two weeks of debate William Paterson offered the New Jersey, or small-state, plan to countervail the inequalities of the Virginia Plan.

—Samuel Raphalides

See also Connecticut Compromise; Constitutional Convention of 1787; New Jersey Plan.

VISA. *See* Passports and Visas.

VOICE OF AMERICA, the broadcasting arm of the International Communication Agency (USICA), which operates at USICA posts abroad to publicize and advance U.S. foreign policies.

VOICE VOTE, method of voting in which members are asked to vote by responding "yea" or "nay." Victory is determined by volume of sound. In the Committee of the Whole, members may challenge the chair's decision and demand a standing vote.

—Mary L. Carns

VOLUNTEERS IN SERVICE TO AMERICA (VISTA), formerly under the auspices of the Office of

PARTICIPATION IN ELECTIONS FOR PRESIDENT

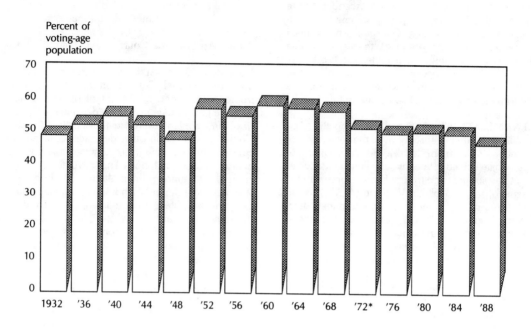

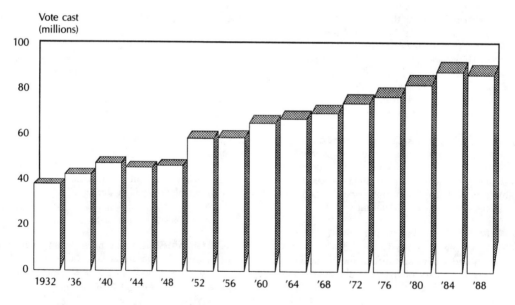

*Reflects expansion of eligibility with enfranchisement of 18-21 year olds.

Economic Opportunity, is now under the direction of ACTION, an agency created in 1971 to bring all federal voluntary action programs together. VISTA works in domestic poverty areas throughout the United States and its territories, the volunteers fighting poverty, disease, and ignorance by living among the people, teaching them new skills, and providing them with medical and technical assistance.

VOTER PARTICIPATION. For most citizens voting is the only positive political activity performed. Other activities, such as working for political parties or candidates, contributing money, or belonging to political organizations, are engaged in by less than 15 percent of the population.

The percentage of the eligible voting population has declined over the years to the point where it barely exceeds 50 percent. At the state and local levels and in primary elections, participation is lower. For example, the vote in elections in nonpresidential years for U.S. Representative is less than half the voting-age population. It is not unusual for local elections to register turnouts of a third or less. During the latter part of the nineteenth century, participation was higher, ranging from 70-80 percent of the male adults.

In strictly statistical terms, an individual vote can be shown to have only a miniscule effect on political decisions, yet there are strong cultural pressures toward voting participation in the United States. The idea that each citizen has not only the right but the duty to vote is traditional even in a society in which most people do not take a direct interest in politics. Voting has a ritual aspect in a democracy, since it brings the population together in a common activity designed to produce a binding decision about the leadership in the society. This gives the individual vote a symbolic importance beyond its cumulative arithmetical weight.

Participation Rates. There are tendencies for groups in the population to participate in voting at different rates. Education and socioeconomic variables are especially strong in their effect. For example, in a national survey, 80 percent of college-educated persons report voting, while for those with a high school education, the figure is 58 percent, and 40 percent for grade school. Other variations reflect these socioeconomic and other social roles: whites are more likely to vote than blacks, Republicans more than Democrats, and older people more than younger.

In addition, people are more likely to vote depending on the visibility of the office for which the election is being held, the perceived importance of the issues involved, and the clarity of the alternatives presented by the candidates. Those who are most committed to ideologies or political parties tend to be more active participants.

The history of voter participation in the United States can be traced in the expansion of the franchise. First to fall were restrictions based on property and taxpaying, then race, then sex. The role of political parties is central to voting participation. As the parties became mobilizers of popular support, one of their key functions became the organization of voters at the local level. Participation is higher in those areas in which there is more party competition. There has been a growing tendency for voters to act independently of political parties, however, by registering as independents, by voting for third parties, or by splitting tickets to vote for candidates of different parties at the

same election. These may be indications of a realignment of the voting groups in the population.

—*Earl M. Baker*

VOTER REGISTRATION is the entry of a person's name on the list of eligible voters for elections. In the U.S. federal system, election administration, including registration, is the responsibility of individual states, subject to the Constitution and federal law concerning election of federal officers.

Process. In the typical registration process, the person wishing to be enrolled goes to the local registration office, swears that he meets legal requirements such as age and length of residence, and states a political party affiliation. His name is placed on a list, which is merged with the existing list prior to every election. This list is available for inspection by candidates, party officials, and local election officials, who may use it to check the identity and qualifications of voters or for campaign purposes. As a person appears at the polls, he is checked on the list, and challenges may be made. In a primary election, the voter normally may vote to select nominees for a subsequent general election only in his stated party (except in the few "crossover" states).

Administration. Registration is generally administered by a county or city board of election and (or) registration. While almost every state now has permanent registration, in which the voter does not have to register for each election, many states periodically remove names from the roll if the person does not vote during a certain period of time, for example, two years. This is intended to eliminate those who move or are deceased. Registration books are open during stated periods, closing a month or more before the election. About half of the states allow registration in local election districts (precincts) or with some form of traveling register.

Until the latter part of the nineteenth century, there was no widespread mandated registration in the United States, although lists of voters were sometimes kept in towns in New England and elsewhere. Voting was a simple process, with residents known personally to election authorities, but with the growth of urban areas and the influx of immigrants, the absence of an authorized listing procedure increased the possibility of election fraud. This stimulated detailed registration statutes by reformist legislatures. In the South, the trend in the late 1800s toward the one-party system was enhanced by registration requirements that could be used to limit participation.

Some of the voting requirements enforced by registration in the United States are or have been:

1. Residence: typically one year in the state, three months in the locality, although the Supreme Court in 1972 sharply curtailed lengthy residence requirements.

2. Age: except in four states, 21 years of age until the ratification of the Twenty-sixth Amendment in

1971, which established 18 as a minimum voting age.

3. Literacy: because this requirement was often used to restrict voting in the 20 states with literacy tests, Congress in the Voting Rights Act of 1970 prohibited such tests on the basis of racial discrimination.

4. Poll Tax: usually a nominal fee, it had been applied by five states when outlawed at the federal level by the Twenty-fourth Amendment. Later Congress eliminated this discriminatory tax at the local level.

5. Sex: while individual states allowed women to vote beginning in 1890, voting was not a general right until the Nineteenth Amendment in 1920.

6. Property or Payment of Taxes: all but four states had eliminated property or taxes as criteria by the Civil War.

7. Civil Status: residents of mental or correctional institutions and convicted felons are ineligible in all states.

Effect. About 60 percent of the population of voting age votes in presidential elections and less in local and state elections. Approximately 75 percent of those eligible to register nationwide are registered. Registration is considered one of the reasons for the low turnout, from the perspective of the entire population, compared with the last century or with foreign nations. Simply requiring advance action prior to an election will exclude the least knowledgeable and least motivated portion of the citizenry. The more additional requirements, the higher the "cost" in time and effort, with an equivalent decrease in the size of the effective electorate. The residency requirement by itself in a nation with a mobility rate of 20 percent in any year has had a disenfranchising effect. In addition, in 15 states it is difficult to get an absentee ballot for those who are routinely be away from their place of residence. A recent study shows that states with the strictest registration system also have the lowest voting participation rates.   —*Earl M. Baker*

See also Election; Voter Participation.

VOTING. *See* Ballot; Election; Voter Participation; Voter Registration.

VOTING, LEGISLATIVE. *See* Electronic Voting; Standing Vote; Teller Vote; Voice Vote.

VOTING RIGHTS ACT (1965). From 1870 to 1960 the supremacy of states' rights retarded federal legislation supporting the Fifteenth Amendment. Although making ample reference to voting rights, the civil rights acts of 1957, 1960, and 1964 relied upon slow-moving court procedures.

Dissatisfaction with the speed of desegregation and the 1964 electoral procedures stirred support for President Lyndon Johnson's bill to put state electoral machinery under direct federal supervision. One ma-

jor provision outlawed discriminatory voter-registration tests—in particular, literacy tests—thereby opening registration to thousands of Spanish and other ethnic minorities. The second major section authorized federal registration and voting procedures in any state or political subdivision evidencing electoral discrimination or unduly low registration or participation after November 1, 1964. In addition, the Act stated that the state poll tax was, in Congress' opinion, unconstitutional.

The effects of the Act were immediate: within one week 45 federal examiners had been dispatched to the South; the challenge to the poll tax was initiated in August 1965 and upheld by the Supreme Court the next year; and a massive voter-registration drive spread through the country.

The Act was renewed in 1970, 1975, and 1982. Provisions were extended to include a number of additional states and specified election changes such as bilingual ballots and reduction in state residency requirements for voting in presidential elections (maximum 30 days). The 1982 Act extended the provisions to include Spanish-speaking Americans, Native Americans, Asian-Americans, and other minority groups.

WAGES AND HOURS ACT. *See* Fair Labor Standards Act.

WAGNER ACT. *See* National Labor Relations Board (NLRB).

WAITE, MORRISON R. (1816-1888), Chief Justice of the Supreme Court (1874-1888). Born in Connecticut and educated at Yale, he moved to Ohio, where he soon became successful as a lawyer for banks and railroads. He ran unsuccessfully for Congress but remained an active member of the new Republican party. Waite supported Lincoln and emancipation but was not enthusiastic about other measures aiding blacks.

President Grant appointed Waite as the seventh chief justice of the Supreme Court in 1874. Although Waite had been a Unionist, once on the Court he vigorously supported the states' ability to legislate economic regulation and civil rights. In 1877, Waite wrote the opinion in *Munn v. Illinois*, in which he found the interest of the state superior to that of business "affected with a public interest." His opinions in this area, however, were based not on the absolute right of a state to regulate for the public welfare, but on the reasonableness of the regulation. Later Courts used the reasonableness doctrine to limit state regulation.

Waite's Court continued to emasculate the enforcement clauses of the Fourteenth and Fifteenth Amendments. In the *Civil Rights Cases* (1883), the Court ruled the Fourteenth Amendment did not prohibit racial discrimination by private individuals and corporations. Waite believed the states had primary authority in regulating social relations among their citizens. That view prevailed well into the twentieth century.

WALLACE, GEORGE C(ORLEY) (1919-),
American political leader and presidential candidate, graduated from the University of Alabama Law School in 1942 and entered private law practice after serving in World War II. In 1958 he made an unsuccessful bid for the governorship but was elected to that office in 1962. As governor he had nationwide publicity for his opposition to federal civil rights legislation, and in 1964 he had considerable support in Democratic state primaries as a presidential candidate.

During the 1968 presidential campaign, Wallace ran as the candidate of his American Independent party. An outspoken supporter of states' rights, his platform advocated "law and order" and condemned urban riots and protest demonstrations. He received about 13 percent of the vote and won five states.

On May 15, 1972, while making another bid for the presidency, Wallace was the victim of an unsuccessful assassination attempt. He was paralyzed from the waist down and was forced to withdraw from the race. He was reelected governor in 1974 and in 1976 campaigned unsuccessfully for the Democratic presidential nomination. Campaigning as a populist in 1982, he successfully attracted black voters and again was elected governor.

WALLACE, HENRY AGARD (1889-1965), agriculturalist and radical politician. Wallace was the son of a secretary of agriculture and the grandson of the founder of an Iowa farm journal. Raised a Republican, Wallace, a farmer and plant geneticist in his own right, supported Al Smith in 1928 and Franklin D. Roosevelt in 1932. As Roosevelt's secretary of agriculture, he was a principal author of the Agricultural Adjustment Act.

Wallace was considered by Roosevelt to be the most consistent and loyal of the New Dealers and was chosen as his running mate in 1940. By 1944 Wallace's latent humanitarianism had carried him considerably to the Left, and he was found unacceptable by conservatives in the Democratic party. When a compromise vice-presidential candidate, Harry S. Truman, was chosen, Wallace dutifully served as secretary of commerce.

After the war he continued to move to the Left, urging thoroughgoing economic reform and friendly relations with the Soviet Union. He became the leader of a third party, the Progressives, in 1947 and campaigned for the presidency, supported by New Dealers and by Communists and other leftists. After the campaign he retired to conduct experiments to increase agricultural production in underdeveloped countries.
—Allen F. Kifer
See also New Deal Legislation; Progressive Party.

WAR CRIMES are major violations of the laws of war, the perpetrators of which are liable to punishment. In the United States, persons under U.S. military law who commit war crimes are prosecuted under the Uniform Code of Military Justice. Besides the observance, from ancient times, of customary laws of war, several conventions in modern times purported to regulate the violence of war. The guiding principle is stated in the Hague Convention of 1907: "The right of belligerents to adopt means of injuring the enemy is not unlimited."

History. The first attempt in modern times to prosecute individuals for war crimes is registered in the post-World War I Treaty of Versailles, where provisions were made for the trial of the German Kaiser and members of his armed forces. An international tribunal had to be constituted, but due to a number of practical reasons, it never materialized. However, the principle had been established that individuals who had violated the laws of war could be held responsible. The principle was enacted after the end of World War II in the Nuremberg and Tokyo trials of Nazi and Japanese war criminals. As later stated by the International Law Commission of the United Nations: "The crimes hereinafter set out are punishable as crimes under international law: (a) Crimes against peace: Planning, preparation, initiation or waging of a war of aggression or a war in violation of international treaties, agreements or assurances; . . . (b) War crimes: Violations of the laws or customs of war which include, but are not limited to, murder, ill-treatment or deportation to slave-labour or for any other purpose of civilian population of or in occupied territory, murder or ill-treatment of prisoners of war or persons on the seas, killing of hostages, plunder of public or private property, wanton destruction of cities, towns, or villages, or devastation not justified by military necessity; (c) Crimes against humanity: Murder, extermination, enslavement, deportation and other inhuman acts done against any civilian population, or persecutions on political, racial or religious grounds . . . "

The United States, which had played a leading role in establishing these principles, incorporated them together with those of The Hague and Geneva conventions in the Field Manual of the United States Army, FM 27-10. The manual specifically states that: "The fact that the law of war has been violated pursuant to an order of a superior authority, whether military or civil, does not deprive the act in question of its character of a war crime . . . The fact that a person who committed an act which constitutes a war crime acted as the head of a State or as a responsible government official does not relieve him from responsibility for his act."

However, the Nuremberg trials did establish the concept of "mitigating circumstances." Defendants who were not considered policy makers were given consideration for the claim that they were following superior orders.

Recent Developments. War crimes can be committed in an international or in a civil war; it is immaterial whether the war is just or not, defensive or not. Technological changes are reflected in the evolution of war laws. For instance, in spite of explicit prohibition in conventional law, there is a tendency to accept the bombardment of population centers. The commission of war crimes is more difficult to ascertain in a guerrilla situation than in a conventional war; many war crimes were perpetrated by both sides in Vietnam. Political, more than legal, considerations seem to determine whether war crimes go unpunished or not.

—*Sergio Barzanti*

WAR DEMOCRATS, a coalition of those who favored the Civil War as the only means of restoring the Union. Led by Senator Stephen A. Douglas of Illinois and by Andrew Jackson, the group supported Lincoln's war policies and stood opposed to the pro-Confederate "Peace" Democrats.

WAR ON POVERTY. *See* Poverty Program.

WAR POWERS OF THE PRESIDENT. The war power of the president is shared with the Congress. In the words of Article II, Section 2, of the Constitution, the president is "Commander in Chief of the Army and Navy, and of the militia of the several States when called into the actual service of the United States." However, only Congress has the power to "declare war" (Article 1, Section 8). Moreover, the courts have held that emergencies do not endow the president with new or unlimited powers: rather, authority is extended to the executive through statutory and treaty authorization.

Nevertheless, dramatic events in history have witnessed the president's use of war powers without a formal declaration of war or congressional approval. In most cases this circumvention has occurred in sending United States forces abroad.

Historically, presidents have justified the exercise of war powers for the protection of American lives and property, preservation of the Union, defense of treaty obligations and executive agreements, upholding international law, national honor, and national interest. Tradition has as much to do with the president's war power as does the Constitution. The Korean and Vietnam conflicts are examples of the susceptibility of statutory, congressional, and constitutional provisions to conflicting interpretations of the president's war power. In wartime situations, however, the powers of the president are greatly expanded by congressional authorization. During World War II, for example, only one presidential request was denied.

See also Emergency Powers of the President.

WAR POWERS RESOLUTION, resolution passed by Congress in 1973 over the veto of President Nixon, who argued that his authority as commander in chief was being unconstitutionally restricted. The resolution was a reaction to the feeling that Congress had not sufficiently participated in the decisions that led to U.S. involvement in Vietnam.

The resolution states the president may commit U.S. armed forces when: (1) Congress has declared war, (2) specific statutory authority is provided, or (3) an armed attack on U.S. forces occurs. Under the third condition, the president must inform Congress within 48 hours of sending troops abroad. If Congress does not approve the action, the troops must be removed within 60 days unless the president requests and is granted a 30-day extension. Since its passage, the resolution has been weakened by a succession of events in which it was ignored (Grenada), its provisions modified by negotiations between Congress and the President (Lebanon), and its constitutionality questioned by a decision of the Supreme Court.

WARREN, EARL (1891-1974). Not since John Marshall has a chief justice of the Supreme Court been credited with engendering as many social and political changes as Earl Warren. Appointed by President Eisenhower in 1953, Warren came to the Court as a successful politician imbued more with social values than with a judicial code of behavior. Born in Los Angeles, he graduated from the University of California Law School at Berkeley. From 1920 Earl Warren spent his entire career in appointive and elective offices: deputy district attorney, district attorney, attorney general, and governor of California. He was also the Republican candidate for vice president in 1948.

President Eisenhower, hoping Warren would be a moderate, unifying force on the Court, was very surprised at the subsequent behavior of his chief justice, although Warren's background indicated future judicial activism rather than restraint. "The Warren Revolution" began almost immediately in 1954, when Warren argued that state-imposed segregation of public schools was unconstitutional, because it engendered feelings of inferiority (*Brown v. Board of Education*).

By the 1960s—with a secure majority behind him—Warren led the Court to establish a strict one-man, one-vote standard in the apportionment of legisltive districts (*Reynolds v. Sims,* 1964). The Warren Court also expanded First Amendment freedoms and the requirements for counsel for defendants (*Gideon v. Wainwright,* 1963), and ruled on the necessity of informing defendants of particular rights (*Miranda v. Arizona,* 1966), the invalidation of illegally seized evidence at trial (*Mapp v. Ohio,* 1961), and the outlawing of prayers in public schools (*Engel v. Vitale,* 1962).

Although he always concerned himself with the

Chief Justice Earl Warren.

immediate social issue before him, Warren's opinions were more often filled with justifications for a certain policy than with legal precedents. He rarely referred back to one of his own opinions, preferring to approach each case as a new problem in need of a practical rather than a legalistic solution. Warren became the personal symbol of the Court's expanded role and was the object of both the highest praise and deepest criticism. He retired in 1969.   —*David Forte*

WARREN COMMISSION, the commission assigned to report on the assassination of President John F. Kennedy, headed by Chief Justice Warren.

The commission was established by executive order in Nov. 1963 to study and report on the Kennedy shooting and subsequent shooting of Lee Harvey Oswald, the man arrested in connection with the assassination. The commission's report, submitted to Kennedy's successor, Lyndon Johnson, in Sept. 1964, rejected the possibility of an assassination conspiracy,

finding that Oswald acted alone. The commission further determined that Jack Ruby, the man convicted of killing Oswald, also acted alone.

WASHINGTON, GEORGE (1732-1799), American soldier, statesman, and first President of the United States. Washington was born at Bridges Creek, Westmoreland County, Va., on February 22, 1732. He was the fifth child of Augustine Washington, a third-generation American and well-to-do planter, who died when his son was 12. As a result, Washington was educated in Virginia, not in England as his brothers had been. His formal education ended at age 16, when he went to work for Lord Fairfax, under whom Washington learned woodcraft, surveying, and military tactics. In 1752 he became a major in the Virginia militia and received his early military training there. He then served with General Braddock and his English troops against the French until 1758 and the fall of Quebec.

During the early quarrels between England and her American colonies, Washington supported the rights of the colonies and served as a delegate to the First Continental Congress in 1774 and to the Second Continental Congress in 1775. In an effort to ally the Southern colonies with those of the North, Washington was chosen commander in chief of the Continental Army.

He acquired much military experience in the early days of the Revolution. After winning Boston but losing New York, he went on to cross the Delaware and take Trenton and Princeton. In spite of the other reversals and the cold winter of 1777 at Valley Forge, Washington arrived at Yorktown to help Lafayette

General Washington as commander of the Continental Army in the Revolutionary War.

An aerial view of the Capitol and surrounding government buildings in Washington, D.C.

defeat Cornwallis and finally defeat the English in 1781.

Washington was elected president of the Convention held in Philadelphia in May 1787 and was then elected first President of the United States. He took office in April 1789 and served two terms. During his presidency Washington chose strong men to serve with him, and with the help of Hamilton, Knox, and Jefferson, he forged a strong conservative, central government. He died at Mt. Vernon, Va., on December 4, 1799.

WASHINGTON, D.C. In the late twentieth century, Washington, D.C., has become some, if not all, of the things envisioned by its wise and gifted planners in the late eighteenth century.

The Planners. The first and third presidents, George Washington and Thomas Jefferson, were the principal planners with technical assistance from an ill-educated but talented Frenchman Pierre L'Enfant, who drew the first plan. They envisioned what the city has become: a truly federal capital, a centralizing authority that knits the diverse regions of a sprawling nation.

Some other needs and developments remained unknown at the time, such as the immensity that would be entailed by 50 states, the quality of civilization that would result from industrialization, the worldwide power that would accrue to these states, and, finally, the automobile. Jefferson, as the Leonardo-type multi-talented man, might have been expected to foresee the impact of individually owned combustion-fueled vehicles on his carefully conceived new city and his growing nation. His failure of imagination is forgivable, considering how little hint was contained in the science and society of 1800, when a fledgling government moved from Philadelphia to a raw, contrived town carved out of farmlands and woodlots belonging to prosperous Marylanders.

He foresaw and deplored that his beloved agrarian republic would soon fall into the hands of mercantile types, forerunners of the industrialists who were in full control of both Washington and the nation after the Civil War. It was one of their major products, the automobile, that reshaped, revised, and reordered the capital and the other cities of the United States. What is remarkable about Washington, however, is how much of the original planning survived the onslaught of the automobile, congressional neglect, and time's attrition.

The Present. Washington with its suburbs numbers about three million inhabitants. The center of concentration is the monumental federal section of the city, which still bears a striking resemblance to the first design L'Enfant submitted to President Washington.

The Capitol dominates the city from Jenkins' Hill, looking down across the classical Mall to the Washington and Lincoln monuments, to the White House on the right and the Jefferson Memorial on the left. Pennsylvania Avenue, the route of inaugural parades and national funerals, stretches west and a little north, connecting with the circles, diagonals, and grids that L'Enfant was confident would be ample to support a great city of the future.

Some of his streets have been widened, some circles tunneled, and some avenues extended. Still, they have somehow been able to support the mounting traffic as Washington grew from the muddy provincialism of Civil War times, through the 1874 modernization of Boss Shepherd, and into the swelling, crowding, struggling expansion caused by two world wars, which thrust the capital into a role, at least temporarily, of world dominion.

Washington is virtually unique among contemporary American cities, having preserved its horizontality, a concept first expounded by Jefferson and later implemented by stringent building height limits, about ten stories, so that no structure competes with either the high-domed Capitol or the soaring abstract monument to the First President. Thousands of trees, many a blessing left behind by Boss Shepherd, intersperse low classical buildings that house the Supreme Court, Labor, Agriculture, and all the myriad functions of a forever-growing federal establishment.

The effect is of greenness and whiteness, restful optically, unified conceptually, a touch monotonous but harmonious withal. The dominant architectural style is Greco-Roman with now and then a pleasant, more up-to-date intrusion—a Housing and Urban Development Building by Marcel Breuer, a downtown public library by Mies van der Rohe, the dark red, brick restoration of Lafayette Square.

Nowhere does the city forget its reason for being— Congress, Court, and President are everywhere. In session or out, Congress holds the ultimate power, even though presidents often seem more actively potent. Pentagon authority, penetrating far parts of the world, comes back for replenishment from Congress. So does NASA, back even from the far side of the moon.

The president, manipulating Congress, Pentagon, and press as much as he can, sets the tone of Washington, a subtle emanation that ripples out around the country and the world and, if he is a strong man, profoundly colors the times. For his term or two, the city is the president's, although a certain vitality beats

Washington Monument rises behind the White House in the nation's capital.

without his seeming participation. There is a Washington not purely federal. Of business in the Pittsburgh or Chicago sense, there is little. Instead, we find only an intellectual life has grown up to provide some balance to the congressional-military-governmental life, which is all-encompassing. The Smithsonian Institution, itself as parthenogenetic as the Pentagon, is perhaps the city's greatest agglomeration of intellectual projects, and the Library of Congress, the Bureau of Standards, the National Institutes of Health, and the Brookings Institute—to name a few—comprise a formidable constellation of organizations dedicated to learning, both the collection and the dissemination thereof. The arts, scantly noticed in the city's first century, now are nourished by the National Gallery, the Phillips and Dumbarton Oaks Collections, the Kennedy Center for the Performing Arts, and a host of smaller cultural groups whose existence and vigor would both please and surprise the early planners.

Local Government. Only in the matter of local government does the glowing image blur. Such a vast federal establishment has one suffocating negative effect—city government is swamped. Irony of ironies, the capital of the democratic republic does not enjoy real self-government.

A few stumbling steps have been made recently in that direction—only a few. Since the mid-nineteenth century the District of Columbia was ruled by three presidentially appointed commissioners whose authority was nominal, while committees of Congress held the purse strings and made the rules. By 1964 a constitutional amendment permitted district residents to vote for president and vice president, but that was all, no representation in the Senate and only a nonvoting delegate in the House of Representatives.

Finally, President Johnson issued a series of executive orders abolishing the commission form of government and substituting a mayor and city council, all still appointive. In 1975 the city inaugurated its first elected mayor and council. The White House staff that supervised city affairs was abolished, but Congress retained authority over the city's budget as well as the power to repeal legislation passed by the city council.

—*William Walton*

WATCHDOG COMMITTEE, congressional special committee or a subcommittee of a standing committee, charged with oversight investigation, in contrast with the standing committees' routine consideration of bills. Watchdog committees are usually authorized by each house independently, although on occasion both houses have acted concurrently in setting up a joint watchdog committee. The committees have inquired into lobbying activities, corrupt practices and campaign expenditures, and government stockpiling of strategic materials.

See also Committee System of Congress; Oversight, Legislative.

WATER AND POWER RESOURCES SERVICE, established as the Bureau of Reclamation and renamed in 1979. An agency within the Department of the Interior, the service administers programs to help develop the water and related land resources throughout the Western states and Hawaii. The service's functions include municipal and industrial water supply, hydroelectric power generation, flood control, river regulation, outdoor recreation, fish and wildlife enhancement, water quality improvement, and wind and solar power research.

Methods. To achieve its goals, the service develops plans for the regulation and conservation of water resources and builds dams, reservoirs, canals, and power plants. It conducts extensive research into new sources of water supply and new methods of developing existing water supplies. A significant feature of the service's programs is that to a large extent the beneficiaries of a service project pay for it. Nearly 85 percent of the construction costs of the projects is repayable to the Treasury, many with interest, and project beneficiaries also pay operational and maintenance costs.

Projects. Among the service's outstanding structures are Colorado's Hoover Dam, which is the largest concrete dam in the United States; Grand Coulee Dam on the Columbia River, largest concrete edifice in the world; Glen Canyon Dam on the Colorado River, and its reservoir Lake Powell; thin-arch, concrete Morrow Point Dam on the Gunnison River in Colorado, with a free-fall spillway twice as high as Niagara Falls; and the Alva B. Adams and Charles B. Boustead Tunnels, which burrow beneath the Continental Divide to convey water from the western to the eastern slope of the Rocky Mountains.

See also Interior, U.S. Department of the.

WATERGATE, political scandal of the Nixon administration. In June 1972, a group of men burglarized the offices of the Democratic National Committee in the Watergate building in Washington, D.C., in an attempt to find documents that would embarrass presidential candidate George McGovern. They were hired and paid by the Republicans' Committee to Reelect the President (CREEP). Shortly afterwards, President Nixon and top aides formulated a plan to obstruct the criminal investigation of this burglary. They might have been successful if it had not been for the investigative reporting of two *Washington Post* reporters and the actions of a federal district court judge (Judge John J. Sirica), which ultimately led to the 1973 Senate hearings and the appointment of special prosecutors. In late July 1974, as a result of the initial cover-up and the continued actions of the President and his appointees (both in government and on his reelection committee), the Judiciary Committee of the House of Representatives voted three articles of impeachment of President Nixon, one of which was a charge of obstruction of justice.

On Aug. 9, 1974, Richard M. Nixon became the first president to resign and to do so in disgrace. His resignation made unnecessary the impeachment by the full House and a likely trial in the Senate.

—*Guy C. Colarulli and Victor F. D'Lugin*

WATER POLLUTION CONTROL ACT OF 1948. *See* Business Regulation in the United States.

WATER QUALITY IMPROVEMENT ACT (1970), Title I of a broad environmental act, administered by the Environmental Protection Agency. The Act required the president to issue regulations for spill prevention and constitute a National Contingency Plan for clean-up. The law expanded research and training facilities to combat pollution and, more controversially, stiffened penalties for oil-spill violations to the larger of $100 per gross ton or $14 million for ship owners and operators and up to $8 million for owners of onshore and offshore facilities.

Other provisions mandate federal jurisdiction and standards in vessel sewage control, acid and mine water pollution, and pollution in the Great Lakes. Anyone knowingly discharging "harmful" amounts of spill or anyone not immediately notifying authorities of a discharge is liable to a fine of $10,000 and/or one year in prison. Shipowners using United States ports and rivers must file evidence of financial responsibility equal to the maximum fine, and all activities that might lead to oil discharge must be licensed by some government agency, with a federal veto over licenses.

WATKINS v. UNITED STATES, 354 U.S. 178 (1957), questions the principles of congressional investigative committees and their authority to pass judgment on individuals. Watkins, a union officer, testified before the House Committee on Un-American Activities. When he refused to answer questions which he believed were not relevant to the work of the committee, he was cited for contempt of Congress.

The Court, in an opinion delivered by Chief Justice Warren, held that when the definition of jurisdiction is as uncertain and wavering as it is in the case of the Un-American Activities Committee, it becomes extremely difficult for the committee to limit its inquiry to that which is pertinent. Thus, the committee, unable to define clearly the meaning of "un-American," was illegally undertaking exposure for the sole purpose of exposure. The Court stated that Congress is responsible for seeing that the committee's power is used only in furtherance of a legislative purpose.

See also Sweezy v. New Hampshire.

WAYS AND MEANS COMMITTEE, a powerful standing committee of the U.S. House of Representatives with jurisdiction over revenue bills, Social Security, and debt and tax legislation, as well as having major responsibilities over the federal budget. It is one of the traditional "money committees" of Congress.
—*Mary L. Carns*

WEAPONS CONTROL. *See* Atomic Weapons, International Control of; Disarmament.

WEBB-POMERENE EXPORT TRADE ACT (1918) permitted exporters to organize associations, without liability under antitrust laws, to enhance their ability to compete in foreign markets. The Act was introduced after a 1915 probe into the effect of antitrust laws on the international trade of the United States and was designed to allow firms to compete on an equal basis with the great foreign cartels. The exemption from the Sherman Antitrust Act permitted United States companies to combine to act as a unit in international trade. Companies that wished to acquire part or whole ownership in these foreign trading associations were exempted from the Clayton Antitrust Act. Webb-Pomerene forbids corporations from restraining competition or from extending their cooperation to domestic markets.

WEBSTER, DANIEL (1782-1852), New England poli-

Daniel Webster, famed orator and one of the most powerful senators before the Civil War.

tician and orator. A native of New Hampshire, Webster was elected to Congress in 1812. He resigned in 1816 to practice law, arguing several significant cases before the Marshall court. Returning to the House from a new political base in Boston in 1823, Webster moved to the Senate in 1827, where he served until 1850, with an interlude as secretary of state (1841-1842, 1850-1851).

In *Dartmouth College v. Woodward* (1819), Webster argued successfully against public control of an institution established under charter; in *McCulloch v. Maryland* (1819), his eloquence in support of the Bank provided Marshall material for his famous opinion; in *Gibbons v. Ogden* (1824), Webster contributed to Marshall's nationalist definition of congressional power under the commerce clause.

During the War of 1812, Webster had faithfully represented the sentiments of his section in his stand against the war with England and against the imposition of protective tariffs. In 1827 in response to changing attitudes of influential men of wealth in Boston, he guided the "Tariff of Abominations" through the House. He consistently took a moderate stand on the slavery issue. His Senate debate with Hayne in 1830 States lagged behind for a variety of reasons. American devotion to the ideal of individual responsibility made it difficult to persuade people that society bore any responsibility for these conditions. The abundance of free land, the relative shortage of labor, and the constant expansion of industry during the nineteenth century prevented conditions from becoming as serious as they were in Europe. Prior to 1900 the care of the unfortunate was left to private charities, churches, machine politicians, fraternal organizations, or to poorhouses and poor farms, which threw together the unfortunate with the insane and the retarded.

First Efforts. The Progressive Era brought increased demands for relief from the lower classes and new theories of social responsibility from economists and social scientists. For the most part the problems were attacked at the state level. Illinois enacted a mother's pension law in 1911, and other states followed suit; Alabama and Massachusetts pioneered in the field of old age pensions for state employees; comprehensive pension systems were common by 1933. Conditions of labor, especially for women and children, were closely regulated by nearly every state, and 21 states created industrial commissions to oversee work conditions. New York produced the nation's first comprehensive workmen's compensation law in 1910, and all but four states had adopted some form of it by 1935. The maximum number of working hours was slowly whittled down, particularly for women and children, with Massachusetts achieving a 48-hour week by 1920. Several states experimented with minimum wage laws during the Progressive Era. Railroad workers were limited to an eight-hour day, and merchant seamen were guaranteed better conditions of labor. The U.S. Employment Service and the Department of Labor were established, and bills were introduced for minimum wage legislation and old age pensions. The biggest struggle, however, came over attempts to bar the products of child labor from interstate commerce. The first Keating-Owen Act (1916) was declared unconstitutional (1918), and a second (1919) lasted only until 1922 before the Supreme Court struck it down. A federal child labor amendment was then submitted to the states but was not ratified.

The New Deal Programs. Although many states expanded their programs during the 1920s, the Great Depression demonstrated the need for much greater federal involvement. For the first time direct relief to the unemployed was provided through public works projects and the efforts of the Federal Emergency Relief Agency, the Work Projects Administration, and the Civilian Conservation Corps. Most significantly, the Social Security Act of 1935 provided for federal old age pensions and a joint federal-state system of unemployment compensation.

Modern Legislation. Since 1940 attempts to expand the federal welfare state have produced only spotty results. The minimum wage has been raised several times and its coverage extended to many formerly excluded occupations. Social Security benefits and coverage have expanded and been augmented: survivor's benefits (1939), disability insurance (1954), and medical care for the aged (1965). Other efforts have been much less fruitful. Although the Full

Employment Act of 1946 theoretically committed the federal government to providing jobs for all who were able to work, it was riddled with exemptions and shorn of enforcement machinery.

The Department of Housing and Urban Development was created in the 1960s but has been rarely funded sufficiently to provide for the nation's housing demonstrated his devotion to the Union rather than to the anti-slavery cause. He supported the Compromise of 1850.

When the Whigs came to power, Webster headed the State Department. He alone of Harrison's appointees stayed on in the hostile Tyler administration to negotiate the Webster-Ashburton treaty, a landmark in British-American relations, and to oversee efforts to open the China trade. Both accomplishments were in the interests of New England. One of the best-known public men of his day, Webster was ambitious for the presidency, but he was always too sectionally oriented to be considered by the national Whigs.

—Allen F. Kifer

WEBSTER v. REPRODUCTIVE HEALTH SERVICES (1989), a 5-to-4 Supreme Court decision holding that provisions of a Missouri statute regulating abortions were not unconstitutional. The statute prohibited public employees from performing abortions or using public facilities unless the life of the mother was at risk. In addition, physicians were required to test all 20-plus-week fetuses to determine viability before performing an abortion.

Chief Justice Rehnquist, joined by Justices White, O'Connor, Scalia, and Kennedy, found these provisions of the Missouri law "placed no governmental obstacle in the path of a woman who chose to terminate her pregnancy." The testing provisions were also seen as constitutional because they "permissibly furthered Missouri's interest in protecting human life."

The ruling did not overturn the 1973 abortion precedent set in *Roe v. Wade.* It did, however, further narrow *Roe*'s application and set the stage for other state legislatures to enact comparable statutes. In addition to the resulting political controversy that led to national demonstrations, the Court scheduled several new abortion cases for its calendar.

See also Roe v. Wade.

WEEKS v. UNITED STATES, 232 U.S. 383 (1914), concerns illegal seizure of property and use of such as evidence. Weeks was arrested at his place of business. His house was searched, first by a police officer and then by a United States marshal, who took letters and other documents away from the premises. No warrants had been obtained for either the arrest or the search.

The Court concluded that the letters in question were taken from the house of the accused by an official of the United States, acting under color of his